Issues in Race and Ethnicity

Issues in Race and Ethnicity

SIXTH EDITION

Los Angeles | London | New Delhi
Singapore | Washington DC

SELECTIONS FROM **CQ RESEARCHER**

Los Angeles | London | New Delhi
Singapore | Washington DC

FOR INFORMATION:

CQ Press
An Imprint of SAGE Publications, Inc.
2455 Teller Road
Thousand Oaks, California 91320
E-mail: order@sagepub.com

SAGE Publications Ltd.
1 Oliver's Yard
55 City Road
London EC1Y 1SP
United Kingdom

SAGE Publications India Pvt. Ltd.
B 1/I 1 Mohan Cooperative Industrial Area
Mathura Road, New Delhi 110 044
India

SAGE Publications Asia-Pacific Pte. Ltd.
3 Church Street
#10-04 Samsung Hub
Singapore 049483

Acquisitions Editor: Elise Fraser
Production Editor: Laura Stewart
Typesetter: C&M Digitals (P) Ltd.
Cover Designer: Candice Harman
Marketing Manager: Jonathan Mason

Copyright © 2013 by CQ Press, an Imprint of SAGE Publications, Inc. CQ Press is a registered trademark of Congressional Quarterly Inc.

All rights reserved. No part of this book may be reproduced or utilized in any form or by any means, electronic or mechanical, including photocopying, recording, or by any information storage and retrieval system, without permission in writing from the publisher.

Printed in the United States of America

Library of Congress Control Number: 2012945757

ISBN 978-1-4522-2781-8

This book is printed on acid-free paper.

12 13 14 15 16 10 9 8 7 6 5 4 3 2 1

Contents

ANNOTATED CONTENTS ix
PREFACE xiii
CONTRIBUTORS xvii

CHANGING DEMOGRAPHICS

1. Redistricting Debates   1
    Should partisan gerrymandering
        be restricted? 5
    Should district lines be drawn to help
        minorities get elected to office? 6
    Should redistricting be done by independent
        commissions instead of state legislatures? 8
    Background 9
        Political Thickets 9
        Legal Puzzlers 11
        Crosscurrents 14
    Current Situation 16
        Advantage: Republicans 16
        Forecast: Cloudy 18
    Outlook: Not a Pretty Picture? 19
    Notes 21
    Bibliography 22

2. Changing U.S. Electorate   25
    Are whites losing political clout? 29
    Are suburbs shifting to the Democrats? 31
    Are young voters more liberal? 32
    Background 33
        After the New Deal 33
        Reagan Democrats 38
        Clinton and Bush 40
    Current Situation 42
        "The Big Sort" 42
        Lack of Competition 43
        Picking Out Raisins 43
    Outlook: Creating a New Map 44
    Update 45
        Hispanic Power 45
        Government's Role 45
        Tea Party Influence 46
        Mid-Term Pressure 47
    Notes 47
    Bibliography 49

3. Census Controversy   51
    Will the census be accurate? 54
    Should the census include
        undocumented immigrants? 55
    Should the census long form be replaced
        by the American Community Survey? 57
    Background 59
        The First Census 59
        Rural-Urban Fight 60
        Litigation Over Sampling 62
        Political Debate 64

CONTENTS

Current Situation	66
Redistricting	66
Counting Prisoners	68
Doling Out Funds	68
Outlook: Changing Times	69
Notes	70
Bibliography	73

ETHNICITY AND IMMIGRATION

4. Immigration Conflict — 75
- Is illegal immigration an urgent national problem? — 79
- Should state and local police enforce immigration laws? — 81
- Should Congress make it easier for illegal immigrants to become citizens? — 82
- Background — 84
  - Constant Ambivalence — 84
  - Cracking Down? — 87
  - Getting Tough — 88
- Current Situation — 89
  - Obama's Approach — 89
  - Supreme Court Action — 92
- Outlook: A Broken System — 93
- Notes — 94
- Bibliography — 97

5. American Indians — 99
- Is the federal government neglecting Native Americans? — 102
- Have casinos benefited Indians? — 104
- Would money alone solve American Indians' problems? — 105
- Background — 105
  - Conquered Homelands — 105
  - Forced Assimilation — 107
  - Termination — 107
  - Activism — 110
  - Self-Determination — 112
- Current Situation — 113
  - Self-Government — 113
  - Limits on Gambling — 114
  - Trust Settlement — 117
  - Supreme Court Ruling — 117
- Outlook: Who Is an Indian? — 118
- Update — 119
  - Critics of Gambling — 120
  - Supreme Court Ruling — 120
  - Government Action — 121
  - Crimes Against Women — 121
  - Education Issues — 121
- Notes — 122
- Bibliography — 125

LEGAL ISSUES AND LAW ENFORCEMENT

6. Affirmative Action — 127
- Has affirmative action outlived its usefulness? — 130
- Does race-based affirmative action still face powerful public opposition? — 132
- Has affirmative action diverted attention from the poor quality of K-12 education in low-income communities? — 134
- Background — 135
  - Righting Wrongs — 135
  - Reversing Course — 139
  - Mending It — 140
- Current Situation — 141
  - "Formal Equality" — 141
  - Over Their Heads? — 145
- Outlook: End of the Line? — 146
- 2010 Update — 147
  - Poll Results Differ — 147
  - Obama Criticized — 148
  - Research Claims Challenged — 148
- 2012 Update — 149
  - College Admissions — 149
  - Public Schools — 150
  - Employment, Contracting — 151
- Notes — 151
- Bibliography — 154

7. Hate Groups — 157
- Could the election of a black president and the nation's economic crisis spark a resurgence of far-right political activity or violence? — 161
- Are immigrants in danger from extremist violence? — 162
- Is right-wing and extremist speech encouraging hate crimes? — 164
- Background — 165
  - Building Movements — 165

Fighting and Killing	166		Notes	232
Explosion and Aftermath	170		Bibliography	233

Current Situation 171
    Hate in April 171
    Free Speech, Hate Speech 174
    Recruiting Veterans 175
Outlook: Guns in Holsters 177
Notes 178
Bibliography 182

EDUCATION

10. Racial Diversity in Public Schools 235
    Should school systems promote racial diversity in individual schools? 238
    Should school systems seek to promote socioeconomic integration in individual schools? 241
    Is the focus on diversity interfering with efforts to improve education in all schools? 242
    Background 243
        The "Common School" 243
        "Elusive" Equality 247
        "Diversity" Challenged 250
    Current Situation 251
        "Resegregation" Seen 251
        Legal Options Eyed 253
    Outlook: "Minimal Impact"? 254
    Update 255
    Notes 257
    Bibliography 259

8. Police Misconduct 185
    Should police do more to control excessive force? 189
    Should police do more to prevent racial and ethnic profiling? 191
    Should police adopt stronger disciplinary measures for misconduct? 192
    Background 193
        Police Problems 193
        Police Accountability 196
        Changing Priorities 197
    Current Situation 200
        Investigations Urged 200
        Reforms Outlined 202
    Outlook: Police Under Pressure 203
    Notes 204
    Bibliography 207

11. Bilingual Education vs. English Immersion 261
    Is bilingual education effective for English-language learners? 266
    Is "English immersion" effective for English learners? 267
    Should funding for English-language learning be increased? 268
    Background 269
        American Languages 269
        Language Debates 271
        Language Tests 274
    Current Situation 276
        Lagging Indications 276
        Fighting in Court 278
    Outlook: Getting Results? 279
    Notes 280
    Bibliography 282

9. Hate Speech 209
    Have ethnic jokes and insults become too pervasive in society? 212
    Should the government do more to restrain hate speech? 214
    Should Don Imus have been fired? 216
    Background 219
        Historical Stereotypes 219
        Shock Value 223
        Stereotypes Spreading? 225
    Current Situation 226
        New Crackdown 226
        Fairness Revisited? 228
    Outlook: Business as Usual? 229
    Update 230
        Use of N-word Criticized 230
        New Breed 231
        Banned in England 231
        Fairness Doctrine 231

12. Fixing Urban Schools 285
    Has the No Child Left Behind law helped urban students? 288

Should governments make schools more racially and economically diverse?	290	Outlook: Agreeing to Disagree	305
		2010 Update	305
Are teachers prepared to teach successfully in urban classrooms?	292	Lagging in Math	306
		Paying for Success	307
		A Call for Flexibility	307
Background	293	2012 Update	308
Educating the Poor	293	Funding Cuts	308
Two Tracks	299	Alternatives Sought	309
Minority Schools	300	Cheating Scandals	310
Poor in School	301	Adding Values	311
Current Situation	303	Test Results	311
Congress Divided	303	Notes	312
Retooling NCLB?	304	Bibliography	316

Annotated Contents

CHANGING DEMOGRAPHICS
Redistricting Debates
The once-every-decade process of redrawing legislative and congressional districts is getting under way in state capitals around the country. To start, Sun Belt states will gain and Rust Belt states will lose seats in the U.S. House of Representatives. But win or lose, states have to redraw lines to make sure that legislative and congressional districts have equal populations and give fair opportunities to minority groups. The process is intensely political, with parties maneuvering for advantage and incumbents seeking to hold on to friendly territory. Republicans are in a good position after gaining control of legislatures in a majority of states last November. But demographic trends, especially the growth of Latino populations in some states, may limit the GOP's opportunities. In addition, California and Florida will be operating under new rules pushed by good-government groups that seek to limit "gerrymandering," line-drawing for purely partisan reasons. After redistricting plans are completed, many will be challenged in court, where outcomes are difficult to predict.

Changing U.S. Electorate
Demographics played nearly as large a role in the 2008 presidential race as health care, war and the economy. The Democratic field came down to an African-American man dominating voting among blacks, the young and highly educated voters and a white woman winning older voters, Hispanics and the white working class.

Census Controversy

The 2010 census sparked bitter partisanship. Some conservative Republicans, for example, criticized the census as an unconstitutional intrusion on privacy; others warned that census participation is important for maintaining GOP power, since the count is used to apportion congressional seats and allocate federal money to cities and states. Liberal Democrats were more supportive of census procedures, which for the first time counted same-sex couples. To raise response rates, the Census Bureau sent every household the same brief 10-question form and dropped use of the "long form" — a lengthy questionnaire seeking data on housing, transportation, education and income. The long form was replaced by a separate, ongoing monthly survey that provided timelier data, but from a smaller sample of households. Researchers generally hailed the change but say it would cause some problems, at least initially.

ETHNICITY AND IMMIGRATION
Immigration Conflict

Americans are very concerned about illegal immigration but ambivalent about what to do about it — especially the 11 million aliens currently in the United States illegally. Frustrated with the federal government's failure to secure the borders, several states passed laws allowing state and local police to check the immigration status of suspected unlawful aliens. Civil rights organizations warn the laws will result in ethnic profiling of Latinos. The Obama administration sued to block several of the laws for infringing on federal prerogatives. Advocates of tougher enforcement say undocumented workers are taking jobs from U.S. citizens, but many business and agricultural groups say migrant workers are needed to fill jobs unattractive to U.S. workers. In 2010, the U.S. Supreme Court upheld an Arizona law providing stiff penalties for employers that knowingly hire illegal aliens. In 2012, the justices heard arguments on the controversial, new Arizona law that inspired other states to crack down on illegal immigration.

American Indians

Winds of change are blowing through Indian Country, improving prospects for many of the nation's 4.4 million Native Americans. The number of tribes managing their own affairs has increased dramatically, and an urban Indian middle class is quietly taking root. The booming revenues of many Indian-owned casinos seem the ultimate proof that Indians are overcoming a history of mistreatment, poverty and exclusion. Yet most of the gambling houses don't rake in stratospheric revenues. And despite statistical upticks in socioeconomic indicators, American Indians are still poorer, more illness-prone and less likely to be employed than their fellow citizens. Meanwhile, tribal governments remain largely dependent on direct federal funding of basic services — funding that Indian leaders and congressional supporters decry as inadequate. But government officials say they are still providing essential services despite budget cuts.

LEGAL ISSUES AND LAW ENFORCEMENT
Affirmative Action

Since the 1970s, affirmative action has played a key role in helping minorities get ahead. But many Americans say school and job candidates should be chosen on merit, not race. In November 2008, ballot initiatives in Colorado and Nebraska would have eliminated race as a selection criterion for job or school candidates but would have allowed preferences for those trying to struggle out of poverty, regardless of their race. It's an approach endorsed by foes of racial affirmative action. Big states, meanwhile, including California and Texas, are still struggling to reconcile restrictions on the use of race in college admissions designed to promote diversity. Progress toward that goal has been slowed by a major obstacle: Affirmative action hasn't lessened the stunning racial disparities in academic performance plaguing elementary and high school education. Still, the once open hostility to affirmative action of decades ago has faded. Even some race-preference critics don't want to eliminate it entirely but seek ways to keep diversity without eroding admission and hiring standards. In the fall of 2012, the Supreme Court will revisit the issue of affirmative action and will hear arguments in the Texas case, *Fisher v. University of Texas*.

Hate Groups

National crises create opportunities for extremists. Today the global economic crisis now wreaking havoc on millions of American households is hitting while the first black president is in the White House and the national debate over illegal immigration remains unresolved. Already, some far-right extremists are proclaiming that their moment is arriving. Indeed, an annual tally by the Southern Poverty Law Center shows 926 hate groups operating in 2008, a 50 percent increase over the number in 2000. And the Department of Homeland Security concludes that conditions may favor far-right recruitment. But a mix of conservatives and liberal free-speech activists warn that despite concerns about extremism, the administration of Barack Obama should not be intruding on constitutionally protected political debate. Some extremism-monitoring groups say Obama's election showed far-right power is waning, not strengthening. But that equation may change if the economic crisis deepens, the experts caution.

Police Misconduct
The U.S. Department of Justice is stepping up its oversight of local police departments, pressuring them to limit the use of force in civilian encounters and eliminate racial profiling during traffic stops and other enforcemen, the Justice Department's civil rights division has criticized long-troubled police agencies in such places as New Orleans, Seattle and Maricopa County, Ariz., which includes Phoenix. The department's power stems from a 1994 law allowing the federal government to identify a "pattern or practice" of constitutional violations and threaten court action to force police agencies to adopt changes. Seattle officials have proposed a detailed plan to answer the government's criticisms, but negotiations are stalled in New Orleans and Maricopa County, where Sheriff Joe Arpaio is balking at the government's demand for court supervision of policy changes. Meanwhile, the racially charged shooting death of a Florida teenager by a neighborhood watch volunteer focused attention on police handling of the case.

Hate Speech
When Don Imus labeled the Rutgers University women's basketball team "nappy-headed hos" in April 2007, it first looked to be just one more insult hurled in his long career. Imus was penalized initially with a two-week suspension. But when the incident appeared on the Internet site youtube.com, organizations ranging from the National Association of Black Journalists to the liberal media watchdog group Media Matters for America urged a tougher stance against racial stereotyping on public airwaves. Advertisers began pulling their sponsorship from Imus' show, and both networks that carried it — CBS Radio and MSNBC TV — fired him. The outcome was hailed by some as a long-needed response to an increasingly uncivil culture in which shock jocks, comedians, rappers and other media figures traffic in name-calling, racism and misogyny. However, other analysts say silencing Imus was unfair.

EDUCATION
Racial Diversity in Public Schools
Fifty years after the Supreme Court outlawed racial segregation in public schools,ew 2007 rulias raised doubts about how far local school boards can go to integrate classrooms. The court's 5-4 ruling in cases from Seattle and Louisville bars school districts from using race as a factor in individual pupil assignments. Like many other school districts, the two school systems used racial classifications to promote diversity in the face of segregated housing patterns. But parents argued the plans improperly denied their children their school of choice because of race. Dissenting justices said the ruling was a setback for racial equality. In a pivotal concurrence, however, Justice Anthony M. Kennedy said schools still have some leeway to pursue racial diversity. Meanwhile, some experts argue that socioeconomic integration — bringing low-income and middle-class students together — is a more effective way to pursue educational equity.

Fixing Urban Schools
African-American and Hispanic students — largely in urban schools — lag far behind white students, who mostly attend middle-class suburban schools. Critics argue that when Congress reauthorizes the 2002 No Child Left Behind Act (NCLB), it must retarget the legislation to help urban schools tackle tough problems, such as encouraging the best teachers to enter and remain in high-poverty schools, rather than focusing on tests and sanctions. Some advocates propose busing students across district lines to create more socioeconomically diverse student bodies. But conservative analysts argue that busing wastes students' time and that permitting charter schools to compete with public schools will drive improvement.

Meanwhile, liberal analysts point out that successful charter programs are too costly for most schools to emulate, and that no one has yet figured out how to spread success beyond a handful of schools, public or private.

Bilingual Education vs. English Immersion

More than 5 million public school students have limited English proficiency, and the number is growing. Most English learners enter school behind fluent English speakers, and many never catch up either in language or other academic areas. In the 1960s and '70s, the federal government supported bilingual education: teaching English learners in both their native language and in English. A backlash developed in the 1980s and '90s among critics who attacked bilingual education as academically ineffective and politically divisive. They favored instead some form of "English immersion." Educators and policy makers continue to wage bitter debates on the issue, with each of the opposing camps claiming that research studies support its position. Some experts say the debate should focus instead on providing more resources, including more and better-trained teachers.

Preface

As minority populations continue to grow apace, and concerns about U.S. border security and immigration intensify, issues in race and ethnicity resonate ever more profoundly with Americans. These topics confound even well-informed citizens and often lead to cultural and political conflicts, because they raise the most formidable public policy questions: Should police do more to prevent racial and ethnic profiling? Should states crack down on unlawful aliens? Should district lines be drawn to help minorities get elected to office? To promote change and hopefully reach viable resolution, scholars, students, and policymakers must strive to understand the context and content of each of these issues, as well as how these debates play out in the public sphere.

With the view that only an objective examination that synthesizes all competing viewpoints can lead to sound analysis, this sixth edition of *Issues in Race and Ethnicity* provides comprehensive and unbiased coverage of today's most pressing policy problems. It enables instructors to fairly and comprehensively uncover opposing sides of each issue, and illustrate just how significantly they impact citizens and the government they elect. This book is a compilation of twelve recent reports from *CQ Researcher*, a weekly policy backgrounder that brings into focus key issues on the public agenda. *CQ Researcher* fully explains complex concepts in plain English. Each article chronicles and analyzes past legislative and judicial action as well as current and possible future maneuvering. Each report addresses how issues affect all levels of government, whether at the local, state, or federal level, and also the lives and futures of all citizens. *Issues in Race and Ethnicity* is designed to promote in-depth discussion, facilitate further research, and help readers think critically and formulate their own positions on these crucial issues.

This collection is organized into four sections: Changing Demographics," "Ethnicity and Immigration," "Legal Issues and Law Enforcement," and "Education." Each section spans a range of important public policy concerns. These pieces were chosen to expose students to a wide range of issues, from affirmative action to illegal immigration. We are gratified to know that *Issues in Race and Ethnicity* has found a following in a wide range of departments in political science and sociology.

CQ RESEARCHER

CQ Researcher was founded in 1923 as *Editorial Research Reports* and was sold primarily to newspapers as a research tool. The magazine was renamed and redesigned in 1991 as *CQ Researcher*. Today, students are its primary audience. While still used by hundreds of journalists and newspapers, many of which reprint portions of the reports, *Researcher*'s main subscribers are now high school, college and public libraries. In 2002, *Researcher* won the American Bar Association's coveted Silver Gavel Award for magazine excellence for a series of nine reports on civil liberties and other legal issues.

Researcher staff writers — all highly experienced journalists — sometimes compare the experience of writing a *Researcher* report to drafting a college term paper. Indeed, there are many similarities. Each report is as long as many term papers — about 11,000 words — and is written by one person without any significant outside help. One of the key differences is that the writers interview leading experts, scholars and government officials for each issue.

Like students, staff writers begin the creative process by choosing a topic. Working with *Researcher*'s editors, the writer identifies a controversial subject that has important public policy implications. After a topic is selected, the writer embarks on one to two weeks of intense research. Newspaper and magazine articles are clipped or downloaded, books are ordered and information is gathered from a wide variety of sources, including interest groups, universities and the government. Once the writers are well informed, they develop a detailed outline and begin the interview process. Each report requires a minimum of ten to fifteen interviews with academics, officials, lobbyists and people working in the field. Only after all interviews are completed does the writing begin.

CHAPTER FORMAT

Each issue of *CQ Researcher,* and therefore each selection in this book, is structured in the same way. A selection begins with an introductory overview, which is briefly explored in greater detail in the rest of the report.

The second section chronicles the most important and current debates in the field. It is structured around a number of key issues questions, such as "Are immigrants in danger from extremist violence?" and "Is the focus on diversity interfering with efforts to improve education in all schools? This section is the core of each selection. The questions raised are often highly controversial and usually the object of much argument among scholars and practitioners. Hence, the answers provided are never conclusive, but rather detail the range of opinion within the field.

Following those issue questions is the "Background" section, which provides a history of the issue being examined. This retrospective includes important legislative and executive actions and court decisions to inform readers on how current policy evolved.

Next, the "Current Situation" section examines important contemporary policy issues, legislation under consideration and action being taken. Each selection ends with an "Outlook" section that gives a sense of what new regulations, court rulings and possible policy initiatives might be put into place in the next five to ten years.

Each report contains features that augment the main text: sidebars that examine issues related to the topic, a pro/con debate by two outside experts, a chronology of key dates and events and an annotated bibliography that details the major sources used by the writer.

CUSTOM OPTIONS

Interested in building your ideal CQ Press Issues book, customized to your personal teaching needs and interests? Browse by course or date, or search for specific topics or issues from our online catalog of over 500 *CQ Researcher* issues at http://custom.cqpress.com.

ACKNOWLEDGMENTS

We wish to thank many people for helping to make this collection a reality. Thomas J. Billitteri, managing editor of *CQ Researcher,* gave us his enthusiastic support and cooperation as we developed this edition. He and his talented staff of editors and writers have amassed a first-class collection of *Researcher* articles, and we are fortunate to have access to this rich cache. We also thankfully acknowledge the advice and feedback from current readers and are gratified by their satisfaction with the book.

Some readers may be learning about *CQ Researcher* for the first time. We expect that many readers will want regular access to this excellent weekly research tool. For subscription information or a no-obligation free trial of *Researcher,* please contact CQ Press at www.cqpress.com or toll-free at 1-866-4CQ-PRESS (1-866-427-7737).

We hope that you will be pleased by the sixth edition of *Issues in Race and Ethnicity.* We welcome your feedback and suggestions for future editions. Please direct comments to Charisse Kiino, Publisher, College Publishing Group, CQ Press, 2300 N St, NW, Suite 800, Washington, DC 20037; or send e-mail to *ckiino@cqpress.com.*

—*The Editors of CQ Press*

Contributors

Thomas J. Billitteri is managing editor of the *CQ Researcher*. He has more than 30 years' experience covering business, nonprofit institutions and public policy for newspapers and other publications. He holds a BA in English and an MA in journalism from Indiana University.

Charles S. Clark is a veteran Washington freelancer who writes for The Washington Post, National Journal and other publications. He previously served as a staff writer at the *CQ Researcher* and writer-researcher at Time-Life Books. He graduated in political science from McGill University.

Staff writer **Marcia Clemmitt** is a veteran social-policy reporter who previously served as editor in chief of *Medicine & Health* and staff writer for *The Scientist*. She has also been a high school math and physics teacher. She holds a liberal arts and sciences degree from St. John's College, Annapolis, and a master's degree in English from Georgetown University. Her recent reports include "Genes and Health" and "Animal Intelligence."

Alan Greenblatt covers foreign affairs for National Public Radio. He was previously a staff writer at *Governing* magazine and *CQ Weekly*, where he won the National Press Club's Sandy Hume Award for political journalism. He graduated from San Francisco State University in 1986 and received a master's degree in English literature from the University of Virginia in 1988. For the *CQ Researcher*, his reports include "Confronting Warming," "Future of the GOP" and "Immigration Debate." His most recent *CQ Global Researcher* reports were "Attacking Piracy" and "Rewriting History."

Associate Editor **Kenneth Jost** graduated from Harvard College and Georgetown University Law Center. He is the author of the *Supreme Court Yearbook* and editor of *The Supreme Court from A to Z* (both *CQ Press*). He was a member of the *CQ Researcher* team that won the American Bar Association's 2002 Silver Gavel Award. His previous reports include "States and Federalism" and "Bilingual Education vs. English Immersion." He is also author of the blog *Jost on Justice* (http://jostonjustice.blogspot.com).

Peter Katel is a *CQ Researcher* staff writer who previously reported on Haiti and Latin America for *Time* and *Newsweek* and covered the Southwest for newspapers in New Mexico. He has received several journalism awards, including the Bartolomé Mitre Award for coverage of drug trafficking, from the Inter-American Press Association. He holds an A.B. in university studies from the University of New Mexico. His recent reports include "Prisoner Reentry" and "Downsizing Prisons."

Patrick Marshall is a freelance writer in Seattle, Wash., who writes about public policy and technology issues. He is a computer columnist for *The Seattle Times* and holds a BA in anthropology from the University of California at Santa Cruz and a master's in international studies from the Fletcher School of Law & Diplomacy at Tufts University.

1
Redistricting Debates

Kenneth Jost

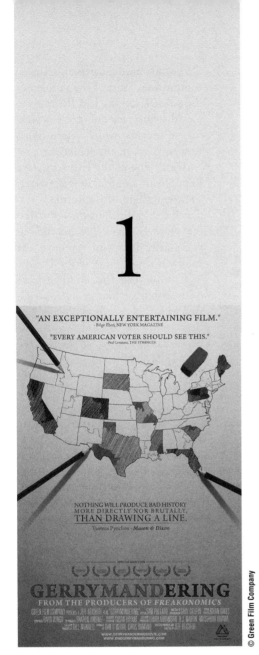

A poster promotes Gerrymandering, a documentary released last fall that sharply criticizes the controversial practice of drawing congressional districts to help political friends and hurt foes. Jeff Reichert, a self-described liberal who made the film, says he wants "more people involved in the redistricting process."

From *CQ Researcher*, February 25, 2011.

Meet Cynthia Dai: high-tech management consultant in San Francisco, Asian-American, outdoor adventurer, out lesbian, registered Democrat.

Meet Michael Ward: chiro-practor in Anaheim, Calif., disabled veteran, former polygraph examiner, Native American, registered Republican.

Dai has been interested in politics since 1984, when she helped register voters before reaching voting age herself. Ward has worked with college Republican groups since his undergraduate days.

Despite their interests, neither Dai nor Ward had ever held or sought public office until last year. For the next year, however, they and 12 other Californians, most with limited if any political experience, will be up to their necks in politics as members of the state's newly established Citizens Redistricting Commission.[1]

Along with the rest of the states, California must redraw its legislative and congressional maps in 2011 to make districts equal in population according to the latest U.S. Census Bureau figures. The every-10-year process is required to comply with the Supreme Court's famous "one person, one vote" rule, which requires districts to be divided according to population so each person is equally represented in government. The intricate line-drawing invites political maneuvering of all sorts, including the practice known as "gerrymandering" — irregularly shaping district maps specifically to help or hurt a political party or individual officeholder or candidate.

With the redistricting cycle just getting under way, California's citizens commission provides a high-profile test of the latest idea

GOP Has Grip on Redistricting Authority

Republicans control 23 of the state legislatures that draw either state or congressional districts or both, including Nebraska's nominally nonpartisan legislature; Democrats control only 12. Legislatures in seven states with redistricting authority are split, with each of the major parties having a majority in one of the chambers. Eight states use commissions to draw both legislative and congressional lines; five others use commissions just for congressional redistricting.

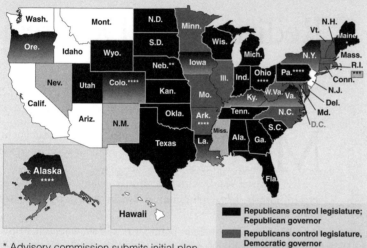

Congressional Redistricting Authority by State

- Republicans control legislature; Republican governor
- Republicans control legislature, Democratic governor
- Split legislature.
- Democrats control legislature; Democratic governor
- Democrats control legislature; Republican governor
- Commission or board

* Advisory commission submits initial plan. Legislature must pass plan or an alternative by 2/3 vote.

** Legislature technically nonpartisan, but Republican.

*** Governor is independent, but served in the U.S. Senate as a Republican.

**** Use commissions for state legislative redistricting authority but not congressional.

Sources: National Conference on State Legislatures; U.S. Department of Justice Civil Right Division; U.S. House of Representatives

Democrats on the partisan-balanced commission. "Part of the problem is the politicians have had the right to pick the voters instead of voters picking politicians, which seems like a very big myth in our democracy."

Ward, one of the five registered Republican commissioners, agrees. "The condition of California is evidence that politicians draw districts that serve their own interests and not necessarily first and foremost the communities that they serve," he says.

Completing the commission's membership are four people unaffiliated with either of the two major parties. The maps to be drawn by the commission, due to be completed by Aug. 15, must meet a series of criteria, including "to the extent practicable" compactness. But the commission is specifically prohibited from "favoring or discriminating against" any incumbent, candidate or political party. The final maps must be approved by a bipartisan supermajority of the commission, with votes from at least three Democrats, three Republicans and three independents.

No one knows how the experiment will work. "It's fair to say that the mechanism that we came up with is not simple, but we're hopeful that it will work out," says Derek Cressman, Western regional director for the public interest group Common Cause. Along with the state's former Republican governor, Arnold Schwarzenegger, California's Common Cause chapter was the driving force behind Proposition 11, which in 2008 created the new commission to redraw state legislative districts.

With approval of the measure, California became the second state, after Arizona, to establish a citizens redistricting commission. Arizona's commission, created through a ballot initiative approved in 2000, has responsibility for legislative and congressional districts.

for reforming the often-discredited process. By taking the job away from the state legislature through ballot measures approved in 2008 and 2010, California voters sought to cut out the bizarre maps and unsavory deal-making that good-government groups say prevent the public from ousting incumbents or holding them accountable for their performance in office.

"There's a fair amount of cynicism about how California is being run now," says Dai, one of five

California voters in 2010 approved a second measure, Proposition 20, that gave the commission power over congressional districts too.*

Redistricting is an arcane process that stirs more interest among political junkies than the general public. But experts say the decennial line-drawing helps shape voters' relationships with their elected officials and can affect the balance of power between rival political parties. "This is one of the most important events in our democracy," says Kristen Clarke, co-director of the political participation group for the NAACP Legal Defense and Educational Fund, a major advocacy group for African-American interests.[2]

The redistricting cycle flows out of the Constitution's requirement that seats in the U.S. House of Representatives be "apportioned" among the states according to an "enumeration" of the population — the census — to be conducted every 10 years (Article I, Section 2). Under the figures released by the U.S. Census Bureau in December, eight states will gain and 10 will lose House seats to be filled in the 2012 election.

The new apportionment has the potential to strengthen the Republican majority that the GOP gained in November 2010. States gaining seats are mostly in the Republican-leaning Sun Belt in the South and West, while states losing seats are mostly in the Democratic-leaning Rust Belt in the Northeast and Midwest.

Thanks to gains in state elections in November, Republicans are positioned to take control of the micro-level line-drawing of congressional and state legislative districts in a near majority of the states. Among states where legislatures draw either congressional or legislative maps or both, Republicans have undivided control

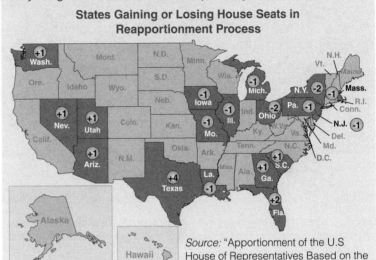

Twelve Seats Shift in Reapportionment Process

Ten states will lose a total of 12 seats in the U.S. House of Representatives during reapportionment. Those seats will be reallocated among eight other states, with Texas and Florida the big winners. They will gain four and two seats, respectively.

States Gaining or Losing House Seats in Reapportionment Process

Source: "Apportionment of the U.S House of Representatives Based on the 2010 Census," U.S. Census Bureau

in 19, including Nebraska's nominally nonpartisan unicameral legislature; Democrats in only eight. "Republicans are in the best position ever in the modern era of redistricting," says Tim Storey, a veteran redistricting expert with the National Conference of State Legislatures.

Democrats are disadvantaged not only because they lost ground at the polls in November but also because some states with Democratic-controlled legislatures — most notably, California — assign redistricting to non-legislative boards or commissions. "Democrats are going to have less influence [in California] than they had in the past," says Charles Bullock, a professor of political science at the University of Georgia in Athens.

In fact, California's post-2000 redistricting is Exhibit No. 1 in the reformers' case against the prevailing practice of allowing state lawmakers to draw their own districts as well as those of members of Congress. In the reformers' view, Democrats and Republicans in the state legislature agreed on district lines aimed at protecting incumbents of both parties — a so-called bipartisan gerrymander.

---

*The commission is also charged with drawing the four districts for the state's Board of Equalization, which administers the state's tax laws.

CHANGING DEMOGRAPHICS

Over the next year, 14 Californians, all with post-graduate degrees but most with limited if any political experience, will redraw the state's legislative and congressional maps as members of the state's newly established Citizens Redistricting Commission. Here they pose for an official photograph midway through a three-day public meeting Feb. 10-12. Michael Ward, a chiropractor, presided as rotating chair; Connie Galambos Malloy, a community organizer, is to his right. Others standing, left to right, are Jodie Filkins Webber (attorney), Gabino Aguirre (city councilman; retired high school principal), Vincent Barabba (online-commerce consultant), Michelle DiGuilo (stay-at-home mom), Maria Blanco (foundation executive), Peter Yao (ex-city council member; retired engineer), Cynthia Dai (management consultant), Libert "Gil" Ontai (architect), Jeanne Raya (insurance agent), Angelo Ancheta (law professor), Stanley Forbes (bookstore owner) and M. Andre Parvenu (urban planner). The panel includes four Asian-Americans, three Hispanic-Americans, one African-American, one Native American and five whites.

Supporters of the new citizens commission say the legislative plan worked as the lawmakers intended. In the five elections from 2002 through 2010, only one of the state's 53 congressional seats changed hands. The districts "represent the legislators' interest, not the voters,'" says Cressman of Common Cause.

Some redistricting experts, however, discount the reformers' complaints about self-interested line-drawing. "The effect of redistricting in the incumbency advantage is unclear," says Nathan Persily, director of the Center for Law and Politics at Columbia University Law School in New York City. "Incumbents win not only because they draw the district lines, but for all kinds of reasons."

Political calculations in redistricting are also limited by legal requirements dating from the Supreme Court's so-called reapportionment revolution in the 1960s. In a series of decisions, the justices first opened federal courts to suits to require periodic redistricting by state legislatures and then mandated congressional and legislative districts to be equal in population within each state.

The Voting Rights Act, passed in 1965, has also played a major role in redistricting. In particular, the act's Section 5 requires that election law changes in nine states and local jurisdictions in seven others be "pre-cleared" with the Justice Department or a federal court in Washington, D.C. Beginning with the post-1990 redistricting cycle, the Justice Department used its leverage to pressure states into drawing "majority-minority" districts to protect African-Americans' and Latinos' voting rights, with some of the districts very irregularly shaped. The Supreme Court limited the practice somewhat, however, with rulings in the 1990s that bar the use of race or ethnicity as the "predominant" factor in a district's boundaries.[3]

African-American and, in particular, Latino groups are looking for more "minority opportunity" districts in the current redistricting cycle. "I hope we will have an increase in the number of districts where Latinos can elect candidates of their choice," says Arturo Vargas, executive director of the National Association of Latino Elected and Appointed Officials (NALEO). Among the states being closely watched is Texas, which will gain four House seats in large part because of the state's growing Hispanic population.

The Supreme Court decisions limiting racial line-drawing came in suits filed by white voters and backed by groups opposed to racial preferences, including the Washington-based Project on Fair Representation. Edward Blum, the group's president, says it will bring similar legal challenges if it sees "evidence of unconstitutional racial gerrymandering" in the current redistricting.

As Blum acknowledges, however, the Voting Rights Act requires some consideration of race, nationwide, to prevent what is termed "retrogression" — new districts that reduce the ability of minority groups to elect their preferred candidate. "Race must be one factor among many that line drawers use," says Clarke with the Legal Defense Fund. It has joined with the Mexican American Legal Defense and Educational Fund (MALDEF) and the Asian American Justice Center in publishing a 78-page booklet aimed at educating and mobilizing minority communities on redistricting issues.

Increased public participation is also the goal of good-government groups, including Common Cause and the League of Women Voters. "There are a lot of opportunities for greater public participation and better maps," says Nancy Tate, the league's executive director.

In addition, two reform-minded academics — George Mason University political scientist Michael McDonald and Harvard University quantitative social scientist Micah Altman — have formed the straightforwardly named Public Mapping Project to put mapping data and software into the hands of interest groups, community organizations and even students to propose redistricting plans. The goal, McDonald says, "is to allow redistricting to be done out of people's homes."

Despite the reformers' hopes, one longtime redistricting expert doubts that public or media pressure will carry much weight as state legislatures go about their work. "I don't see state legislatures buckling much to that," says Peter Galderisi, a lecturer in political science at the University of California-San Diego. "In most situations, they don't have the direct ability to influence this at all."

As state legislatures and redistricting commissions get down to work, here are some of the major questions being debated:

Should partisan gerrymandering be restricted?

Texas Republicans chafed for more than a decade under the post-1990 congressional redistricting, a Democratic-drawn plan that helped Democrats hold a majority of the House seats through the decade. When Republicans gained control of both houses of the state legislature and the governorship in 2002, it was payback time.

Despite an attempted boycott by outnumbered Democrats, the GOP majorities approved an artful plan aimed at giving Republicans an edge wherever possible. In the first election under the new map, the GOP in 2004 gained 21-11 control of the state's congressional delegation. Democrats cried foul and argued all the way to the U.S. Supreme Court that the plan was a partisan gerrymander that violated Democratic voters' constitutional rights. The justices could not agree on a legal rule to govern gerrymandering, however, and left the map intact except to require redrawing a majority Latino district in the Rio Grande Valley.

The ruling in the Texas case marked the third time that the Supreme Court had entertained a constitutional claim against gerrymandering — and the third time that the justices failed to give any guidance on when, if ever, federal courts could strike down a partisan power-grab as going too far.[4]

Legal experts say the judicial impasse is likely to continue. Justice Anthony M. Kennedy straddles the divide between four conservatives uncomfortable with or opposed to gerrymandering challenges altogether and four liberals unable to agree on a standard to police the practice. "Four-and-a-half justices have demonstrated that they don't want to deal with this, and the other four-and-a-half cannot agree on how to deal with it," says Justin Levitt, an associate professor at Loyola Law School in Los Angeles who formerly worked on redistricting issues at the Brennan Center for Justice at New York University School of Law.

For many political scientists, the effort to control gerrymandering through the courts is simply at war with U.S. political traditions dating back to the 19th century.

"We've gotten used to the fact that when one party controls, you get partisan gerrymanders," says Galderisi at UC-San Diego.

With courts on the sidelines, the critics of partisan gerrymandering are looking to two approaches in the current redistricting cycle to control the practice. The California citizens commission — and the citizens commission created in Arizona for the post-2000 cycle — take the job away from legislators and establish guidelines, including geographically compact districts. In Florida, reform groups, allied with major Democratic interest groups, won adoption of constitutional amendments in November that prohibit the legislature from drawing districts "with the intent to favor or disfavor a political party or an incumbent."

Bullock, the University of Georgia professor, says the commission approach has the potential to create more competitive districts, one of the main goals of the gerrymandering critics. (Competitiveness is one of the criteria in Arizona, though not in California.) But longtime political expert Thomas Mann, a senior fellow in governance studies at the Brookings Institution in Washington, says geographically compact districting schemes do not necessarily increase competitiveness because like-minded voters often live in the same neighborhood. "In some states, you've got to do real gerrymandering to create more competitive districts," Mann says.

In Florida, even supporters of the anti-gerrymandering amendment acknowledge doubts about how faithfully the Republican-controlled legislature will comply with the provision. "Your guess is as good as mine," says Ellen Freidin, a Miami attorney-activist who headed the Fair Districts Florida campaign for the amendments. Meanwhile, some political scientists see the command not to favor or disfavor an incumbent in drawing district lines as a logical impossibility. "Either it's going to favor them or disfavor them," says Thomas Brunell, a professor of political science at the University of Texas at Dallas. "It's got to be one of those things."

Brunell, in fact, takes the contrarian position of opposing the maximization of competitive districts. In his book *Redistricting and Representation*, Brunell argues that competitive elections are not essential for good government and in fact increase voter discontent. "The more competitive the district, the more upset voters you have," he says.[5]

For incumbents, partisan gerrymandering may actually have a downside, according to UC-San Diego's Galderisi, if likely party voters in one district are spread around to enhance the party's chances of winning in others. "Incumbents don't feel well off unless they have a comfortable margin of victory," he says.

In fact, cutting political margins too thin in a particular district can result in a party's loss of a once-safe seat — a process that redistricting expert Bernard Grofman at the University of California-Irvine calls "a dummymander." In the current cycle, Galderisi thinks Republicans may take that lesson to heart and concentrate on protecting the gains they made in November. "A lot of efforts are going to be to shore up new incumbents rather than engage in traditional partisan gerrymanders," he says.

McDonald, the George Mason University political scientist in the Public Mapping Project, says that with so much political volatility in the last few elections, Democrats and Republicans alike will be more interested in political security than partisan advantage. "Incumbents are going to want safer districts," he says.

Should district lines be drawn to help minorities get elected to office?

Rep. Luis Gutierrez, a Chicago Democrat, has represented since 1993 a congressional district that only a redistricting junkie could love. Dubbed the "ear muff" district, Illinois-4 includes predominantly Latino neighborhoods from close-in suburbs along the city's southern border and other Latino neighborhoods in Chicago itself that are connected only by a stretch of the Tri-State Tollway.

The district was drawn that way in 1991 not to help or hurt an individual officeholder or candidate but to comply with the federal Voting Rights Act. In a city with a history of racially polarized voting and a state with no previous Hispanic member of Congress, Latinos were entitled to a majority Latino district, a federal court ruled. But the new map had to avoid carving up the majority African-American districts that lay between Latino neighborhoods. "This is not gerrymandering," the Mexican American Legal Defense and Educational Fund explains, "but rather protecting voting rights."[6]

Latino and African-American groups will be working again in the current redistricting cycle to try to protect minority incumbents and increase opportunities for minority candidates. "We know that Latinos have increased significantly in population," says Nina Perales, MALDEF's litigation director. "We hope to see a redistricting that fairly reflects that growth."

With the African-American population growing less rapidly, Clarke says the NAACP Legal Defense Fund will first be "looking to ensure that existing opportunities are not taken away." In particular, Clarke says LDF wants to guard against the possibility that the Supreme Court's most recent decision on racial redistricting is not "misinterpreted" to call for dismantling so-called crossover or influence districts — districts where a racial or ethnic minority comprises less than a majority of the population but can form coalitions with white voters to elect a candidate.

For their part, critics of racial redistricting would like to see less attention to race and ethnicity in map-drawing. Blum, with the Project on Fair Representation, says district maps should be drawn without access to racial and ethnic data and checked only at the end to see whether redistricters had "inadvertently" reduced minority voting rights.

The Supreme Court has played the lead role in shaping the current law on racial redistricting. In a trio of decisions in the 1990s, the court struck down oddly shaped, majority-minority congressional districts in Georgia, North Carolina and Texas on the grounds that race or ethnicity was the predominant factor in drawing them. But the court in 1998 upheld the Illinois redistricting with the majority-Latino "earmuff" district. And in 2001 the court ruled in effect that redistricters may draw a majority-minority district if done for a partisan purpose — in the specific case, to make the district Democratic.[7]

The post-2000 redistricting generated fewer major decisions on racial redistricting, but the court's 2009 ruling on a North Carolina legislative map troubles minority groups. The decision, *Bartlett v. Strickland*, required the redrawing of a once majority-black legislative district that had been reconfigured in a way to prevent the African-American population from falling below the threshold needed to form a "crossover" district. In a splintered 5-4 decision, the Supreme Court said a racial or ethnic minority could not challenge a redistricting map as impermissible "vote dilution" under the Voting Rights Act unless it comprised a majority of the district's population.[8]

The ruling "is not an invitation to dismantle existing influence districts," says Clarke. "Majority-minority districts along with influence and crossover districts continue to represent some of the most diverse constituencies in our country."

Minority groups bristle at the criticism of racial line-drawing as gerrymandering. They argue that oddly shaped districts are often the only way to bring together

---

Rules of the Road for California Redistricting

Ballot measures creating the California Citizens Redistricting Commission to redraw the state's legislative and congressional maps set out mandatory criteria and prohibited districts aimed at helping or hurting an incumbent, candidate or political party.

Districts must:

- Have "reasonably equal population," except where "deviation" is required to comply with the federal Voting Rights Act.
- Comply with the Voting Rights Act. The law prohibits race- or ethnicity-based interference with voting rights
- Be "geographically contiguous."
- Respect the "geographic integrity" of any county, city, neighborhood or "community of interest" to the extent possible. "Communities of interest" do not include "relationships with political parties, incumbents or political candidates."
- Be "drawn to encourage geographical compactness" to the extent practicable.
- Be drawn, to the extent practicable, so that each state Senate district encompasses precisely two Assembly districts.
- The commission is prohibited from considering an incumbent's or candidate's residence in drawing district lines. Districts "shall not be drawn for the purpose of favoring or discriminating against an incumbent, political candidate, or political party."

Source: California Citizens Redistricting Commission, http://wedrawthelines.ca.gov/downloads/voters_first_act.pdf

"communities of interest." "People don't live in squares, circles and triangles," says Vargas, with the Latino officeholders' group. "So it's hard to draw districts that have nice geometric shapes."

Blum counters that the dispersal of ethnic and racial minorities from central cities into suburbs forces redistricters to ignore geographic communities in order to create majority-minority districts. "What you have to do is draw a district that basically harvests African-Americans block by block, neighborhood by neighborhood, all across the county or across multiple counties," Blum says. "That breaks up communities of interest that are far more powerful in America today than cobbling together these racially apartheid homelands."

As in Chicago, some of the line-drawing may come in areas with Latino, African-American or Asian-American neighborhoods in close, sometimes overlapping, proximity. Both Clarke and Perales acknowledge the potential for cross-racial tensions but say their groups aim to work cooperatively.

In any event, redistricting experts say minority groups have a huge stake in the maps to be drawn. "Racial and ethnic minorities have historically been disadvantaged by deliberate efforts to mute their voices in redistricting cycles," says Costas Panagopoulos, an assistant professor of political science at Fordham University in New York City and executive editor of the magazine *Campaigns and Elections*. "Minority groups want to be sure that that does not happen this time."

Should redistricting be done by independent commissions instead of state legislatures?

As head of Arizona's first citizens' redistricting commission, Steve Lynn spent thousands of hours over the past decade redrawing legislative and congressional districts in Arizona and defending the new maps in federal and state courts. Lynn, a utility company executive in Tucson who says he is both a former Democrat and former Republican, counts the commission's work a success: no judicial map-drawing, more opportunities for minorities and — in his view at least — more competitive districts.

Surprisingly, however, Lynn voted against Proposition 106 when it was on the Arizona ballot in 2000. Back then, he had no quarrel with the state legislature doing the job. Today, Lynn endorses independent commissions, but somewhat equivocally. "It's one way to do it," Lynn told a redistricting conference sponsored by the National Conference of State Legislatures in late January. "It's not the only way to do it. Either way can work."[9]

Thirteen states now have redistricting commissions or boards with primary responsibility for drawing legislative districts; seven of those also have responsibility for drawing congressional districts.* Apart from the Arizona and California citizen commissions, the other bodies consist of specifically designated officeholders or members chosen in various ways by political officeholders with an eye to partisan balance. Five other states have backup commissions that take over redistricting in the event of a legislative impasse; two others have advisory commissions.

Two of the non-legislative bodies are long-standing: Ohio's, created in 1850; and the Texas backup commission, established in 1947. McDonald, the George Mason professor with the Public Mapping Project, says those commissions and others created in the 1960s and since were designed to make sure that redistricting was completed on time, not to divorce the process from politics. Indeed, McDonald says, there is "no evidence" that the commissions, despite their description as "bipartisan," have reduced the kind of self-interested or partisan line-drawing that gives redistricting a bad name.

By contrast, the Arizona and California commissions consist of citizens who apply for the positions in screening processes somewhat akin to college admissions. Candidates must specify that they have not served within a specified time period in any party position or federal or state office.

In Arizona, applicants for the five-member commission are screened by the appellate court nominating commission, which approves a pool of 25 candidates: 10 Republicans, 10 Democrats and five independents. From that pool, the majority and minority leaders of the state House of Representatives and Senate each pick one member; those four then pick one of the independents to serve as chair.

California's process is even more complex. The state auditor's office screens candidates, forming a pool of 60,

---

*The number includes Montana, which currently has one House member, elected at large; Montana lost its second House seat after the 1990 census.

equally divided among Republicans, Democrats and independents. Those lists are provided to legislative leaders, who can strike a total of 24 applicants. The auditor's office then chooses the first eight commissioners by randomly pulling names from a spinning basket: three from each of the major parties and two independents. Those eight then pick six more: two Democrats, two Republicans and two independents.

Cressman, with Common Cause, acknowledges the complexity of the process. "It is challenging to come up with a system that gives you a combination of expertise and diversity and screens out conflict of interest and self-interest," he says.

Opponents of California's Proposition 11 cited the complexity in campaigning against the ballot measure in 2008. They also argued the commission would be both costly and politically unaccountable. In 2010, opponents qualified an initiative to abolish the commission, which appeared on the same ballot with the measure to expand the commission's role to congressional redistricting. The repealer, Proposition 27, failed by a 40 percent to 60 percent margin.

Political veterans in California continue to complain about the commission — in private. But longtime redistricting expert Bruce Cain, a professor of political science at the University of California-Berkeley and now executive director of the university's Washington, D.C., program, publicly challenged the commission approach in a presentation to the state legislators' group in January.

Cain told the legislators that commissions result in added costs because of the need to train commission members, hire additional staff and consultants and hold extra rounds of public hearings. In any event, Cain said that reformers "oversell" the likely benefits of commissions. Commissions "cannot avoid making political judgments" and are as likely as legislatures to run afoul of legal requirements, he says.

"It doesn't matter whether you have a pure heart," Cain concludes. "If you wind up with a plan that's unfair to one group or another, you're going to have trouble."

Cressman is optimistic about the California commission, which heard from a series of experts in training sessions in January and held its first public hearing in February. "They have a lot of expertise," Cressman says. "They strongly reflect the diversity of California. And they are quite ready to attack their job quite seriously."

Still, experts across the board profess uncertainty about whether the California commission will deliver on the supporters' promise of a fairer redistricting plan. "It's a very open question whether those hopes will be realized," says Douglas Johnson, president of the National Demographics Corporation, which consults on redistricting issues for governments and public interest groups. Johnson himself helped draft the initiative.

BACKGROUND
Political Thickets

The modern era of redistricting began in the 1960s when the Supreme Court intervened to force an end to state legislatures' decades-long neglect of the obligation to redraw legislative and congressional districts to reflect population changes. In a series of decisions, the court first opened the federal courts to redistricting suits and then laid down the famous "one person, one vote" requirement of mathematical equality — strict for congressional districts, slightly relaxed for legislative lines. The rulings redressed the underrepresentation of urban and suburban voters, but they also forced legislatures and the courts into the political thicket of redistricting every 10 years.[10]

The political uses of redistricting date back more than two centuries. Patrick Henry engineered district lines in an unsuccessful effort to prevent the election of his adversary James Madison to the House of Representatives in the nation's first congressional vote in 1788. The salamander-shaped district that Gov. Elbridge Gerry crafted for an 1812 legislative election in Massachusetts gave birth to the pejorative term "gerrymander" for politically motivated line-drawing.*

Through the 19th century, Congress passed laws requiring representatives to be elected in contiguous, single-member districts. A 1901 act — re-enacted in 1911 — specified that districts also be compact and contain "as nearly as practicable an equal number of inhabitants." The provisions went unenforced, however. Most notably, the House failed to act on a committee's recommendation

---

*Gerry pronounced his name with a hard "g," but "gerrymander" came to be pronounced with a soft "g."

CHRONOLOGY

Before 1960, *Congress, courts take hands-off approach to reapportionment, redistricting lapses.*

1908 House of Representatives refuses to enforce equal-population requirement, allows seating of member chosen from malapportioned district in Virginia.

1932 Supreme Court rejects voters' suit challenging malapportioned Mississippi congressional districts.

1946 Supreme Court rejects voters' suit challenging malapportioned Illinois congressional districts.

1960s-1970s *Supreme Court's "one-person, one-vote" revolution forces states to redraw legislative and congressional districts.*

1962-1964 Supreme Court says federal courts can entertain suits to challenge state legislature's failure to reapportion (1962). . . . Adopts "one-person, one-vote" requirement for state legislative districts (1963). . . . Applies equal-population requirement to House seats, both chambers of state legislatures (1964).

1965 Voting Rights Act prohibits interference with right to vote based on race (Section 2); imposes "preclearance" requirements for election law changes on nine states, local jurisdiction in seven others (Section 5).

1969-1973 Supreme Court strikes down congressional districting plan because of 3 percent population variation (1969), but later allows nearly 10 percent variation for state legislative districts (1973).

1980s-1990s *Supreme Court allows suits to challenge partisan gerrymanders, racial line-drawing.*

1980-1982 Supreme Court says Section 2 of Voting Rights Act prohibits only intentional discrimination; two years later, Congress adds "effects" test to prohibit any election law changes that abridge right to vote because of race.

1983 Supreme Court strikes down congressional map with 1 percent variation between districts.

1986 Supreme Court, in Indiana case, says federal courts can entertain suits to challenge legislative districting as partisan gerrymander; on remand, Republican-drawn plan is upheld against Democratic challenge.

1993-1996 Supreme Court allows white voters' suit to challenge majority African-American congressional district in North Carolina (1993). . . . Later rulings strike down majority-minority districts in Georgia (1995), North Carolina (1996), Texas (1996).

2000s *Redistricting reform proposals advance.*

2000 Arizona voters approve creation of independent citizens' redistricting commission (Prop. 106).

2001 Supreme Court upholds creation of majority African-American district in North Carolina; motivation was partisan, not racial, court finds.

2001-2004 Republican-controlled Pennsylvania legislature redraws congressional districts to GOP's benefit (2001); Republicans gain 12-7 majority in state delegation (2002); Supreme Court rejects Democrats' challenge to plan; in splintered ruling, Justice Kennedy leaves door open to gerrymandering suits (2004).

2003-2006 Republican-controlled Texas legislature reopens congressional districts, draws new map to GOP's benefit (2003); Republicans gain 21-11 majority in state delegation (2004); Democrats' challenge rejected by Supreme Court (2006).

2008-2010 California voters approve citizens' commission to redraw state legislative districts (Prop. 11); two years later, add congressional redistricting to commission's responsibility (Prop. 20).

2009 Supreme Court says states may reduce minority voters' influence if they constitute less than majority of voters in district.

2010 Florida voters approve anti-gerrymandering constitutional amendments (Nov. 2). . . . House seats shift from Northeast, Midwest to South, West (Dec. 21).

2011 States begin work on redistricting. . . . Louisiana, Mississippi, New Jersey, Virginia to hold legislative elections in November.

to bar a representative elected in 1908 from a malapportioned Virginia district redrawn earlier in the year to his benefit.[11]

Twice in the first half of the 20th century, the Supreme Court also balked at enforcing reapportionment requirements. In 1932, the court rejected a suit by Mississippi voters challenging the congressional district map drawn by the state legislature on the ground that it violated the 1911 act's requirements. The majority opinion held that the 1911 law had lapsed; four justices went further and said the federal courts should not have entertained the suit. The high court adopted that latter position in 1946 in turning aside a suit by Illinois voters challenging a congressional map as violating a state law requiring equal-population districts. Writing for a three-justice plurality in *Colegrove v. Green*, Justice Felix Frankfurter sternly warned against judicial review. "Courts ought not to enter this political thicket," Frankfurter wrote. A fourth justice joined in a narrower opinion, while three justices said in dissent they would have allowed the suit to go forward.[12]

The Supreme Court reversed direction in its landmark ruling in a Tennessee case, *Baker v. Carr*, in 1962. With Frankfurter in dissent, the court detailed Tennessee's failure to reapportion state legislative districts since 1901 and found urban voters entitled to use the Equal Protection Clause to challenge the malapportionment in federal court. The ruling went only so far as to send the case back to a lower court for a full trial, but in short order the Supreme Court went further. In 1963, it struck down Georgia's county-unit system for apportioning state legislative seats on the grounds that it disadvantaged large urban counties. "The concept of political equality," Justice William O. Douglas wrote in the 8-1 ruling, "can mean only one thing — one person, one vote." A year later, the court applied the equal-population requirement to congressional districts and to both chambers of bicameral state legislatures.[13]

The Supreme Court's rulings opened the door to a flood of reapportionment and redistricting lawsuits in the states. By one count, more than 40 states faced legal challenges by the time of the 1964 decisions. State legislatures across the country became more representative of the growing urban and suburban populations. In Tennessee, for example, both the House of Representatives and the Senate elected urban members as speakers at the turn of the decade. The rulings also affected membership in the U.S. House of Representatives, if somewhat less dramatically. After the 1970 reapportionment, one study found that the number of members from rural districts had dropped from 59 to 51 while the number from urban and suburban districts rose from 147 to 161.[14]

In further cases, the court confronted how close to equal districts had to be to meet the one-person, one-vote test. For Congress, the court required strict and later stricter equality. In 1969, the justices rejected a Missouri redistricting plan because it resulted in as much as a 3.1 percent variation from perfectly equal population districts. Years later, the court in 1983 rejected, on a 5-4 vote, a New Jersey plan with less than 1 percent variation in population because the state had offered no justification for the discrepancies. States were given somewhat more leeway. In a pair of decisions in 1973, the court upheld Connecticut and Texas plans with variances, respectively, of 7.8 percent and 9.9 percent. And in 1983, on the same day as the ruling in the New Jersey case, the court upheld a Wyoming plan that gave each county at least one member in the state House of Representatives despite the large variation in district population that resulted.[15]

Legal Puzzlers

The Supreme Court in the 1980s and '90s confronted but gave only puzzling answers to two second-generation redistricting issues: whether to open federal courts to challenges to partisan or political gerrymandering or to racially or ethnically based line-drawing. On the first issue, the court ostensibly recognized a constitutional claim against partisan gerrymandering, but gave such little guidance that no suits had succeeded in federal courts by the turn of the 21st century — or, indeed, have since. On the second issue, the court in a series of decisions in the 1990s allowed white voters to challenge racially or ethnically based districting plans and eventually barred using race or ethnicity as the "predominant" motive in redrawing districts.

The political gerrymandering issue reached the Supreme Court in a challenge by Indiana Democrats to a state legislative redistricting plan drawn by Republicans after the 1980 census that helped fortify GOP majorities in the 1982 elections. A federal district court agreed with the Democrats that the plan violated the Equal Protection Clause because it was intentionally designed to preserve Republicans' dominance. The Supreme Court ruled, 6-3,

'Underrepresented' Voters Get No Help in Court

"It's pretty clear that this is not equal and it's not as equal as practicable."

The Constitution created the House of Representatives with 65 members, each representing no more than 30,000 people. Today, the House has 435 members, and their districts average about 710,000 constituents, according to the 2010 census.

That average conceals a wide variation from one state to another. Delaware's only congressman, freshman Democrat John Carney, represents about 900,000 people. In Wyoming, the state's only member of Congress, two-term Republican Cynthia Lummis, represents about 563,000 people.[1]

"One person, one vote" requires congressional districts to be equal in population within each state so that each person is equally represented in government. But the constitutional provision allotting one seat to each state combines with the need to round some fractions up and others down to make mathematical equality impossible from state to state.

Plaintiffs from five of the states disadvantaged in House seats under the 2000 census — Delaware, Mississippi, Montana, South Dakota and Utah — filed suit in federal court in Mississippi to challenge the disparities as a violation of their rights to equal representation in Congress. At the time, Montana had more than 900,000 people, just below the threshold then needed for a second House seat.

"We believe that it's pretty clear that this is not equal and it's not as equal as practicable," says Michael Farris, a constitutional lawyer in Northern Virginia and well-known conservative activist. Farris, a home-schooling advocate, recruited the plaintiffs for the case after being approached by another home-schooling father in the area.

In defending the suit, the government argued that complete elimination of the interstate disparities would require "an astronomical increase" in the size of the House. The number of House seats has been fixed since 1911 except for temporary increases to accommodate new states: Arizona and New Mexico in 1912, Alaska and Hawaii in the late 1950s.

Farris countered that an increase of as few as 10 seats would have reduced state disparities by half. And he noted that the British House of Commons has more than 500 members for a country with 62 million residents — one-fifth of the U.S. population of 308 million.

---

in *Davis v. Bandemer* (1986) that the suit presented a "justiciable" claim — that is, one that federal courts could hear. Only two of the six justices, however, agreed that the Indiana Democrats had proved their case. As a result, the case was sent back to the lower court, with no guidelines and for an eventual ruling against the Democrats. Challengers in gerrymandering cases over the next two decades were similarly unsuccessful.[16]

The Supreme Court first encountered a racial gerrymander in the late 1950s in a case brought by African-American voters who, in effect, had been carved out of the city of Tuskegee, Ala., by new, irregular municipal boundaries. The court in 1960 ruled unanimously that district lines drawn only to disenfranchise black voters violated the 15th Amendment.[17] The Voting Rights Act, passed and signed into law five years later, went further by specifically prohibiting interference with the right to vote (Section 2) and forcing states and counties with a history of discrimination against minorities to preclear any election or voting changes with the Justice Department or a federal court in Washington (Section 5).

The Supreme Court upheld the act, but in 1980 held that Section 2 barred election law changes only if shown to be intentionally discriminatory. Two years later, Congress amended Section 2 by adding a "results" or "effects" test that prohibits any voting or election law change, nationwide, that denies or abridges anyone's right to vote on account of race or color. In applying the law to a North Carolina legislative redistricting case, the court crafted a three-part test for a so-called vote dilution claim. Under

The government also contended that the suit raised a "political question" that, in effect, was none of the federal courts' business. Ruling last summer, the three-judge district court hearing the case held that the plaintiffs had no right to equal representation in the House. "We see no reason to believe that the Constitution as originally understood or long applied imposes the requirements of close equality among districts in different States that the Plaintiffs seek here," the court wrote in the July 8 ruling.[2]

On appeal, the Supreme Court rejected the suit even more firmly by setting aside the district court's ruling with instructions to dismiss the case altogether. The court gave no explanation, but Farris says he assumed the justices decided the case on political-question grounds.

Farris is not the only advocate for increasing the size of the House. In an op-ed essay in *The New York Times*, two professors argued that a significantly larger House would allow representatives to be closer to their constituents, reduce the cost of campaigns and limit the influence of lobbyists and special interests. "It's been far too long since the House expanded to keep up with population growth," New York University sociologist Dalton Conley and Northwestern University political scientist Jacqueline Stevens wrote. As a result, Conley and Stevens contended, the House "has lost touch with the public and been overtaken by special interests."[3]

Farris also believes a larger House would be politically more responsive — and, in his view, more conservative. "Bigger districts create more liberal legislators," he says. "The more it costs to campaign, the more beholden you are to people who want something from government."

Farris also warns that the disparities in the size of districts will increase over time. But he acknowledges that another court challenge may meet the same fate as his and that House members are unlikely to vote, in effect, to reduce their power by increasing the body's size. "The foxes have been given complete control of the henhouse," he says.

In the meantime, however, one of the states with the greatest underrepresentation under the 2000 apportionment — Utah — will be picking up a seat in the 2012 election. Under the new apportionment, Utah's four representatives will have about 692,000 constituents each, slightly below the national average. Delaware, Montana and South Dakota each remains well above the average district size, while Mississippi's four districts have about 744,000 people each, only slightly above the national average.

— Kenneth Jost

---

[1] For an interactive map showing average size of House districts state by state, see the Census Bureau's website: http://2010.census.gov/2010census/data/.

[2] *Clemons v. Department of Commerce*, No. 3:09-cv-00104 (U.S.D.C. — N.D. Miss.), July 8, 2010, www.apportionment.us/DistrictCourtOpinion.pdf. For coverage, see Jack Elliott Jr., "Judges reject lawsuit to increase size of House," The Associated Press, July 9, 2010.

[3] Dalton Conley and Jacqueline Stevens, "Build a Bigger House," *The New York Times*, Jan. 24, 2011, p. A27.

---

the so-called *Gingles* test, a plaintiff must show a concentrated minority voting bloc, a history of racially polarized voting and a change that diminishes the minority voters' effective opportunity to elect a candidate of their choice.[18]

Under President George H. W. Bush, the Justice Department interpreted the act in advance of the 1990 redistricting cycle to require states in some circumstances to draw majority-minority districts. Along with other factors, including incumbent protection and partisan balance, the requirement resulted in some very irregularly shaped districts. White voters challenged the district plans in several states, including North Carolina, Georgia and Texas, and won favorable rulings from the Supreme Court in each. The 1993 ruling in *Shaw v. Reno* reinstated a challenge to a majority-black district created by stitching together African-American neighborhoods in three North Carolina cities. Subsequent rulings threw out majority-black districts in Georgia in 1995 and in Texas in 1996. In the Georgia case, the court declared that a district map could be invalidated if race was shown to be "the predominant factor motivating the legislature's decision to place a significant number of voters within or without a particular district."[19]

With a new decade beginning, however, the court recognized an escape hatch of sorts for states drawing majority-minority districts. In *Hunt v. Cromartie*, the court in 2001 upheld North Carolina's redrawing of the disputed majority-black 12th Congressional District in the center of the state. A lower federal court had found the district lines still to be "facially race driven," but the

Supreme Court instead said the state's motivation was "political rather than racial" — aimed at putting "reliably Democratic," African-American voters in the district. The message of the ruling, as *New York Times* reporter Linda Greenhouse wrote at the time, "was that race is not an illegitimate consideration in redistricting as long as it is not the 'dominant and controlling' one."[20]

The racial line-drawing combined with demographics to increase minority representatives in Congress. The number of African-Americans in the House of Representatives increased from 26 in 1991 to 37 in 2001, and the number of Hispanics from 11 to 19.[21] Minority groups hoped to continue to make gains in the new cycle.

Meanwhile, states braced for more litigation as the new redistricting cycle got under way. In the 1990s, 39 states were forced into court to defend redistricting plans on substantive grounds.[22] Most were upheld, but some legislatures were forced to redraw lines. And courts took over the process altogether in a few states, most notably California. There, a Democratic-controlled legislature and a Republican governor deadlocked at the start of the decade, forcing the California Supreme Court to appoint a team of special masters to draw the legislative and congressional maps.

Crosscurrents

The post-2000 redistricting cycle brought a new round of political fights and legal challenges along with the nation's first experience in Arizona with an independent citizens redistricting commission. As in the previous decade, state or federal courts in many states forced legislatures to redraw redistricting plans or drew redistricting plans themselves after legislative impasses. Arizona's independent commission itself faced protracted litigation over its plans but ended with its maps left largely intact. The Supreme Court, meanwhile, retreated somewhat from its activist posture of the 1990s. The court declined twice to crack down on partisan gerrymandering, while its rulings on racial line-drawing gave legislatures somewhat more discretion to avoid drawing favorable districts for minorities.[23]

Arizona's Proposition 106 grew out of discontent with a Republican-drawn redistricting plan in 1992 that solidified GOP control of the legislature while giving little help to the state's growing Hispanic population. The ballot measure gained approval on Nov. 7, 2000, with 56 percent of the vote after a campaign waged by good-government groups, including Common Cause and the League of Women Voters, and bankrolled by a wealthy Democratic activist. The congressional and legislative plans drawn by the five-member commission were challenged in court by Democrats and minority groups for failing to create enough competitive districts. In state court, the congressional map was upheld, while the legislative map was initially ordered redrawn. In a second ruling, however, the state court in 2008 found the commission had given sufficient consideration to competitiveness along with the other five criteria listed in the measure.

In other states, redistricting was still being played as classic political hardball. In Pennsylvania, a GOP-controlled legislature and Republican governor combined in 2001 to redraw a congressional map after the loss of two House seats that helped the GOP win a 12-7 edge in the state's delegation in the 2002 election. The Democratic challenge to the Pennsylvania plan went to the Supreme Court, where the justices blinked at the evident partisan motivation. Justice Kennedy's refusal to join four other conservatives in barring partisan gerrymandering suits left the issue for another day. But the four liberals' failure to agree on a single standard for judging such cases gave little help to potential challengers in future cases.[24]

Two years later, the Texas redistricting case produced a similarly disappointing decision for critics of partisan gerrymandering. Preliminarily, the court found no bar to Texas's mid-decade redistricting. On the gerrymandering claim, Kennedy wrote for three justices in finding that the new map better corresponded to the state's political alignment than the previous districts; two others — Antonin Scalia and Clarence Thomas — repeated their call for barring gerrymandering challenges altogether. Kennedy also led a conservative majority in upholding the breaking up of African-American voters in Dallas and Houston, but he joined with the liberal bloc to find the dispersal of Latino voters in the Rio Grande Valley a Voting Rights Act violation.[25]

In other Voting Rights Act cases, the Supreme Court and lower federal courts generally moved toward giving state legislators more leeway on how to draw racial and ethnic lines. In 2003, the high court upheld a Democratic-drawn plan in Georgia that moved African-American voters out of majority-black legislative districts to create adjoining "influence" districts where they could form majorities with like-minded voters. In the North Carolina

Bringing Redistricting to the Big Screen

"I would like to see more people involved in the redistricting process."

Jeff Reichert, a self-described left-wing political junkie, remembers being both fascinated and outraged at the political shenanigans that Texas Republicans carried out to redraw congressional districts to their benefit in 2003. Reichert, who was working with a film-distribution company at the time, began to think of going behind the camera himself to bring the somewhat arcane subject of redistricting to the big screen.

"I just couldn't shake it," Reichert says today of his urge to make *Gerrymandering*, an 81-minute documentary released to theaters in fall 2010. "I thought there was a way of making a movie out of this."

True to its origins, the film takes a hard and mostly critical look at legislators' time-dishonored practice of drawing district lines to help one's friends and hurt one's foes.[1] Presidents of both parties — Democrats John F. Kennedy and Barack Obama and Republicans Ronald Reagan and George H. W. Bush — denounce the practice in the film's opening. The Texas story is told at length, with semicomic efforts by outvoted Democrats to decamp to Oklahoma to deny Republicans a quorum needed to complete their legislative coup.

The film gains more structure and immediacy from the successful effort in 2008 to pass California's Proposition 11, a ballot initiative to create an independent citizens redistricting commission charged with drawing state legislative boundaries. Gov. Arnold Schwarzenegger, the face of the initiative, and state Common Cause Executive Director Kathay Feng, the organizational mastermind, are presented as crusaders for the public good. "Pass Proposition 11," placards read, "to hold politicians accountable."

Documentary filmmaker Jeff Reichert defends *Gerrymandering's* one-sided examination of redistricting practices. "A lot of people feel that redistricting isn't working," he says.

The film cost "mid-six figures" to produce, Reichert says, with much of that money coming from "folks in California who had worked on the reform effort." The reformers made good use of the investment. In 2010, supporters of the 2008 ballot initiative put their weight behind a new effort — Proposition 20 — to give the citizens' commission responsibility for congressional redistricting as well. The supporters bought 660,000 copies of Reichert's DVD to send to California voters before the November midterm elections. Proposition 20 passed, with a better margin than its predecessor two years earlier.

The film drew some attention when shown in festivals in spring and summer 2010. The reviews on *Rotten Tomatoes*, a popular movie-fan website, are mixed. "Sincere but slick," one commenter writes. *New York Times* film critic Stephen Holden faulted the Proposition 11 story as "sloppily told" and took Reichert to task for failing to show anyone in defense of redistricting practices.[2]

Reichert makes no apologies for the film's one-sided critique of gerrymandering. "Documentary filmmakers aren't journalists," he says. "I have a perspective. I would like to see more people involved in the redistricting process."

Still, Reichert takes a time-will-tell attitude toward California's experiment with citizen-drawn district lines and reform efforts in other states. Some will succeed, he says, and some won't. For now, however, "a lot of people feel that redistricting isn't working."

— Kenneth Jost

---

[1] For background, see the film's website: www.gerrymanderingmovie.com.

[2] Stephen Holden, "The Dark Art of Drawing Political Lines," *The New York Times*, Oct. 15, 2010, p. C18.

case six years later, however, the court made plain that legislators were also free to decide not to create such "crossover" or "influence" districts. In that case, a lower state court had interpreted the Voting Rights Act to require concentrating minority voters even if they did not constitute a majority in the district.[26]

As the decade neared an end, new attention was focused on reform proposals. In California, Gov. Schwarzenegger had made redistricting reform a major issue since taking office in 2003. In 2005, voters rejected by a 3-2 margin his ballot measure, Proposition 77, to give redistricting authority to a panel of retired judges. Three years later, Schwarzenegger worked closely with Common Cause and the League of Women Voters to push the more complex citizens' commission proposal, Proposition 11. In a crucial decision, supporters sought to neutralize potential opposition from members of Congress by leaving congressional redistricting in the legislature's hands. The plan won approval by fewer than 200,000 votes out of 12 million cast (51 percent to 49 percent). Two years later, with House Democrats focused on midterm elections, the measure to add congressional redistricting to the commission's authority, Proposition 20, passed easily.

In Florida, reformers suffered a setback mid-decade when the state supreme court barred a redistricting proposal in 2005 as violating the state's "single-subject rule" for initiatives. The redrawn proposals, on the ballot in November 2010 as Amendments 5 and 6, set out parallel criteria for the legislature to follow in redrawing legislative and congressional districts: contiguous, compact where possible, "not drawn to favor or disfavor an incumbent or political party" and "not drawn to deny racial or language minorities the equal opportunity to participate in the political process and elect representatives of their choice." Fair Districts Florida received major contributions from teachers' unions; the opposition group, Protect Our Vote, got the bulk of its money from the state's Republican Party. The measure passed with 62.6 percent of the vote.

CURRENT SITUATION

Advantage: Republicans

Republican control of congressional redistricting machinery in major states adding or losing House seats puts the GOP in a favorable position to gain or hold ground in the 2012 elections. But Democrats will try to minimize partisan line-drawing and lay the groundwork for court challenges later.

The November 2010 elections gave Republicans undivided control of 25 state legislatures plus Nebraska's nominally nonpartisan unicameral body. Democrats control 16, while eight other states have divided party control between two chambers. "Republicans control more legislatures," says Columbia law professor Persily. "They are in the driver's seat when it comes to drawing lines."

But Jeffrey Wice, a Democratic redistricting attorney in Washington, says pressure by good-government groups for greater transparency and public participation adds a new element that may reduce partisan gerrymandering. "We're too early in the game to predict winners and losers," Wice says. "There's no simplicity in this process."

Out of eight states picking up House seats in the current reapportionment, Republicans control both houses of the state legislature and the governor's offices in five, including the two biggest gainers: Texas, with four new seats, and Florida, with two. The GOP also has undivided control in Georgia, South Carolina and Utah, each picking up one seat. All five states currently have majority-Republican delegations.

Republicans also have undivided control in three states to lose seats: Ohio, giving up two seats, as well as Michigan and Pennsylvania. In those states, Republican lawmakers are likely to draw maps to try to avoid losing House seats in the currently majority-GOP delegations.

Democrats start the congressional redistricting process with significantly less leverage. They have undivided control of redistricting machinery in none of the three other states to gain seats. Arizona and Washington both use bipartisan commissions to redraw congressional districts. In Nevada, Democrats have majorities in both legislative chambers, but Republican Gov. Brian Sandoval could veto a redistricting plan approved by the legislature.

Among states losing seats, Democrats have undivided control only in Illinois, where Republicans currently have an 11-8 majority in the House delegation, and Massachusetts, where Democrats hold all nine current House seats. In New York, which loses two seats, Democrats control the Assembly and Republicans the Senate — setting the stage for a likely deal in which each party yields one House district.

AT ISSUE

Should redistricting be done by independent commissions?

YES
Derek Cressman
Western regional director, Common Cause

Written for *CQ Researcher*, February 2011

Throughout 2011, states will redraw their political districts in a process usually controlled either directly or indirectly by state legislators, the very people with the most to gain or lose from the outcome. The process will almost always cater to incumbent or partisan self-interests. Too often, it also will divide communities, dilute the political strength of ethnic voters and virtually guarantee re-election for the vast majority of incumbents. Unable to hold politicians accountable, too many voters will be left feeling powerless, and citizen participation in politics will suffer.

Reforming this dysfunctional process is fundamental to restoring both a truly representative government and one that can solve societal problems. When voters are disengaged and stay home on election day, legislators have little incentive to act, whatever the issue.

Gerrymandering — manipulating district lines in a way that essentially predetermines election results — has been with us since the early days of our republic. Today, it's more sophisticated, and more sinister, than ever.

Using powerful computer-mapping software, legislators and their political consultants can draw boundaries that remove a potential opponent from a district, add or subtract voters of a certain ethnicity, bring in big donors or concentrate members of an opposing party in a single district to reduce their overall representation. Elections in the ensuing decade are so predetermined that there is little left for voters to choose.

This is a mess best addressed by turning over redistricting to independent, citizen commissions whose members have no stake in where the lines are drawn. California recently made this move, creating a citizens commission of five Democrats, five Republicans and four independent or minor-party voters. The new law requires the panel to make compliance with the federal Voting Rights Act a priority and avoid splitting communities. The commission is prohibited from drawing districts to aid any incumbent legislator off-the-record. Most important, the commission has to conduct all hearings in public, with no off-record conversations about maps allowed.

Other states have created similar panels, though none go as far as California to wring partisanship and self-interest from the redistricting process. And while no commission can be expected to produce maps that please everyone, any effort that shifts the focus of redistricting toward the voters' interest in accountable, effective government and away from the politicians' interest in self-preservation and partisan advantage is a step in the right direction.

NO
Bruce E. Cain
Heller Professor of Political Science, University of California, Berkeley, and Executive Director, UC Washington Center

Written for *CQ Researcher*, February 2011

Replacing legislative redistricting with independent commissions is high on the reform agenda, but is it really so obviously irrational or shameful for a state to resist this trend?

Even the most independent commissions, such as those in Arizona and California, have peculiar issues. Most basically, there is the composition problem. Legislatures are imperfectly reflective of state populations, but they are at least democratically elected and relatively large. Commissions are both appointed (in California's case by an odd, convoluted mix of jury selection and college application-style procedures) and small (making it harder to reflect population diversity). If there is controversy over the lines, as there usually is, these composition disputes can figure prominently in the ensuing litigation.

For good and bad reasons, commissions tend to be more expensive. There are high costs associated with being more open and independent. Greater transparency means more hearings and outreach efforts, which are costly and time consuming to set up, and the yield in terms of broad public participation as opposed to the usual interested groups will likely be low. And given that any association with political parties or elected officials is grounds for exclusion by virtue of excessive political interest, commissions cannot borrow from legislative and political staff. They must hire consultants instead.

Commissions are also no less likely to end up in lawsuits or political controversies. Redistricting is inherently political, involving choices and trade-offs related to race, communities of interest, the integrity of city and county boundaries, the number of competitive seats and so on. However one chooses, someone is going to feel aggrieved. Commissioners cannot be sequestered like jury members or insulated from political influences. Doing without political or incumbency data only means making controversial decisions blindly, not avoiding them. The losers in redistricting disputes will derive little consolation from the commission's efforts at impartiality by empirical blindness, which is why commissions to date have been no more successful in avoiding legal challenges.

On the other side, the sins of legislative redistricting have been grossly exaggerated. Partisan redistricting is rare, and in states with term limits, redistricting is less important than it used to be. Studies show that effects of redistricting on competition and party polarization are marginal at best, casting doubt on the hyperventilated assertions of commission advocates.

So adopt a commission if you must, but expect no miracles. Just be prepared to pay the consultants' bills.

CHANGING DEMOGRAPHICS

Ed Cook, legal counsel for the Iowa Legislative Services Agency, displays a map Feb. 9 that is being used to help draw new congressional district lines in the state. Iowa is losing a seat in the U.S. House of Representatives during reapportionment. Unique among the states, Iowa essentially assigns legislative and congressional redistricting to professional staff, subject to legislative enactment and gubernatorial approval.

Louisiana's legislature is also divided, with Republicans in control in the House and the two parties tied with one vacancy in the Senate. Democrats hold only one of the state's current seven House seats. In Missouri, a Republican-controlled legislature will draw congressional districts, but Democratic Gov. Jay Nixon has to sign or veto any plan approved by lawmakers.

New Jersey, the one other state losing a House seat, uses a bipartisan commission. Democrats have a 7-6 majority in the state's current congressional delegation, but the state is losing population in the predominantly Democratic north and gaining population in Republican areas to the west and south.

California poses the biggest question mark for the 2012 congressional districts. The state's current congressional map favors Democrats, who hold 35 of the 53 House seats. Democrats also hold a nearly 2-to-1 majority in both legislative chambers.

A chart presented to the Citizens Redistricting Commission in an early training session shows that congressional districts in predominantly Democratic Los Angeles and San Francisco are now underpopulated, while districts in some Republican areas — such as the so-called Inland Empire to the east of Los Angeles — are overpopulated.[27] As a result, Los Angeles and San Francisco could lose seats or at least shed voters to adjoining districts.

The commission has pointedly avoided deciding so far whether — or to what extent — to use the existing legislative and congressional districts as a starting point for the new maps. But commission members Ward and Dai both stressed that the ballot measures creating the commission specifically prohibit any consideration of protecting incumbents. "The idea of creating competitive districts," Ward adds, "seems to be unanimous among the commissioners."

In some Republican-controlled states, demographics may limit the GOP's opportunity to gain ground. In particular, Latino advocacy groups believe that Texas will be required to make two of the four new congressional districts majority Latino. That would benefit Democrats since Latinos in Texas and elsewhere have been voting predominantly Democratic in recent elections.

In Virginia, a different demographic change — the growth of the Northern Virginia suburbs surrounding Washington, D.C. — is seen as a possible benefit for Democrats in redrawing the existing 11 House seats despite the GOP's control of the redistricting machinery. Northern Virginia is seen as more liberal than rural counties in the state's south and west, some of which are losing population, according to the Census Bureau.

Forecast: Cloudy

California's new Citizens Redistricting Commission is just getting organized even as a midsummer deadline looms for the 14 map-drawing neophytes to complete the nation's largest legislative and congressional redistricting.

The commission spent two-and-a-half days in mid-February working on housekeeping matters without touching on any of the politically sensitive issues members will face in redrawing lines for 53 congressional districts, 40 state Senate districts and 80 state Assembly districts in the nation's most populous state

"We do believe we're behind schedule," says Ward, the Anaheim chiropractor who held the rotating position of chair for the commission's Feb. 10-12 sessions. "Given the compressed time line, I don't believe you can ever be on schedule."

As in California, redistricting is still in initial stages in most states, but is moving faster in the four that must redraw legislative lines quickly because of general elections scheduled this fall and primary elections beginning this summer. Besides New Jersey, the others are Louisiana, Mississippi and Virginia — Southern states with divided legislatures and significant African-American populations. Under the Voting Rights Act, all three must have redistricting maps precleared by either the Justice Department or a federal court in Washington.

The California commission is working on an ambitious series of four public sessions in each of nine regions in the state, with informational or educational workshops to explain the redistricting process hoped to begin in March. Plans then call for more formal public-input meetings to be held before maps are drawn, as they are being drawn and again after the maps are completed.

Proposition 20, the 2010 ballot measure, established an Aug. 15 deadline for the maps to be certified to the state's secretary of state. But commission member Dai explains that to allow time for public notice and for preclearance — five of the state's counties are subject to the Voting Rights Act's Section 5 — the commission's target date for completion is July 25.

The four states with legislative elections this year are all moving to get redistricting maps up for decisions in March or April.

In New Jersey, the 10-member legislative redistricting commission — with five members appointed by each of the Democratic and Republican state chairs — is holding a series of public hearings aimed at submitting a map by an early April deadline. "The two delegations have been working on tentative maps," says Alan Rosenthal, a professor of political science at Rutgers University in Newark, who is a likely candidate to be named by the state's chief justice as a tie-breaker if the commission reaches an impasse. The separate commission to redraw New Jersey's congressional districts — to be reduced from 13 to 12 — has not been appointed yet.

In Louisiana, the legislature's governmental affairs committees were due to complete eight public hearings around the state by March 1; the legislature was then to convene on March 20 in special session to redraw legislative and congressional districts. Mississippi's Standing Joint Committee on Reapportionment also held public hearings in February, with an announced plan to bring redistricting proposals to the floor of each chamber in early March.

In Virginia the General Assembly's Joint Reapportionment Committee set up an Internet site in December for public comment on redistricting proposals and then laid plans for a special session to begin April 6. Meanwhile, Republican Gov. Bob McDonnell fulfilled a campaign pledge on Jan. 9 by appointing a bipartisan, 11-member advisory commission on redistricting. The commission plans to propose legislative and congressional redistricting plans by April 1, but the legislature will not be bound to follow the recommendations.

Meanwhile, political skirmishes are breaking out in other states. Litigation is already under way in Florida over the newly passed anti-gerrymandering ballot measures. Two minority-group members of Congress filed a federal court suit immediately after the election challenging Amendment 6 on congressional redistricting as a violation of the Constitution and the Voting Rights Act. Reps. Mario Diaz-Balart, a Hispanic Republican, and Corrine Brown, an African-American Democrat, argue standards for congressional district-drawing are up to Congress, not the states; in addition, they say the Voting Rights Act requires protection for already-elected minority legislators. Separately, supporters of the amendment have filed suit against Republican Gov. Rick Scott for failing to submit Amendment 6 to the Justice Department for preclearance.[28]

In other states, Democratic legislators in New York are pressing the GOP-controlled state Senate to stick to pre-election campaign pledges by Republican members and candidates to support an independent commission to redraw lines. In Michigan, a coalition of reform groups is urging the GOP-controlled legislature to allow more public input by posting any redistricting maps on the Internet at least 30 days before taking action. And in Illinois, Democratic Gov. Pat Quinn is weighing whether to sign a bill approved by the Democratic-controlled legislature to require four public hearings on any redistricting proposal and, significantly, to require creation of minority group-protective "crossover" and "influence" districts where feasible.

OUTLOOK

Not a Pretty Picture?

The 20 "most gerrymandered" congressional districts in the United States selected by the online magazine *Slate* present an ugly picture of the redistricting process. The boundaries of the districts — 16 of them represented by

Democrats as of 2009 — zig and zag, twist and turn and jut in and out with no apparent logic.[29]

To redistricting expert Storey, however, many of the districts amount to marvels of political-representation engineering. As one example, Storey points to Arizona-2, which stretches from the Phoenix suburbs to the state's northwestern border and then connects only by means of the Colorado River to a chunk of territory halfway across the state to the east.

As Storey explains, the safely Republican district was drawn in the post-2000 cycle to include a Hopi reservation while placing the surrounding reservation of the rival Navajo nation in an adjoining district. And the districting scheme was crafted not by a politically motivated legislature but by the then brand-new independent citizens redistricting commission.

Among *Slate*'s list of worst districts are others drawn to connect minority communities, such as Illinois-4 (majority Hispanic) and several majority African-American districts in the South (Alabama-7, Florida-23, North Carolina-12). "Lines that look funny may represent real communities without any partisan motivation," says Loyola law professor Levitt.

"There are reasons why districts aren't pretty," adds Cynthia Canary, director of the Illinois Campaign for Political Reform. "But people want pretty."

The people who "want pretty" may well be disappointed again with the post-2010 redistricting cycle despite the concerted efforts of reform-minded groups and experts to improve the process. "This is going to be hardball politics," Sherri Greenberg, a professor at the University of Texas Lyndon B. Johnson School of Public Affairs in Austin and a former Texas legislator, says of the state's redistricting process just now under way. "This is a process that creates enemies, not friends."

In California, however, members of the Citizens Redistricting Commission are professing optimism that they can reach a bipartisan agreement on maps that are both fairer and more competitive than the existing legislative and congressional districts. "There really has been no evidence of partisanship among the commissioners," says Dai, one of the Democratic members. Asked whether a bipartisan agreement is "doable," Republican commissioner Ward replies simply: "Undoubtedly, yes, it is doable."

Reformers are similarly hopeful about the likely outcome of the anti-gerrymandering measures in Florida. "It's going to stop the most egregious gerrymanders," says MacDonald, the professor who co-founded the Public Mapping Group. But John Ryder, the Tennessean who heads the Republican National Committee's redistricting committee, says the Florida measures — with the stated prohibition against helping or hurting a political party or candidate — defy logic. "It's simply an unenforceable standard," he says.

Latino advocacy groups have high hopes — and expectations — for the current round of redistricting. MALDEF president Thomas Saenz predicts nine new majority-Hispanic districts, including two in Texas. Perales, the group's litigation director, makes clear that MALDEF is prepared to go to court to defend plans that increase Latinos' political influence and challenge any that do not.

For her part, the NAACP Legal Defense Fund's Clarke declines to predict whether the redistricting cycle will help elect more African-Americans to the next Congress. "We don't have quotas," Clarke says. But she stresses that the Legal Defense Fund is closely monitoring developments in states to try to prevent dismantling existing influence districts as well as those with majority black population.

Politically, experts are predicting Republican gains in the 2012 congressional elections, thanks to geographic shifts as well as political control of redistricting machinery in close to half the states. Galdaresi, the UC-Irvine professor, expects the GOP to pick up seven to 15 House seats.

Political pros profess uncertainty. "I think it takes a pretty good crystal ball to predict what the net effect of redistricting is," the RNC's Ryder says. Democratic attorney Wice thinks public pressure may reduce Republicans' ability to engineer favorable plans. "It's not over by any means to give the Republicans the final word," he says.

Whatever happens in the first round, many, perhaps most, of the redistricting plans will be headed for a second round in the courts. "It's hard not to predict litigation in redistricting," says Perales. "Somebody's always unhappy after the plan is done."

Increased public participation may influence the process not only in legislatures and commissions but also in the courts, according to Norman Ornstein, a longtime Congress watcher now at the conservative American Enterprise Institute think tank. "Courts will have more information to use in evaluating or drawing maps," he says.

But the calls for more public participation will be a challenge to citizen groups. "This is an incredibly complex topic," says Canary. "Nobody out in the public knows why it is so complicated."

NOTES

1. Dai's and Ward's background taken in part from their application for the positions, posted on the California Citizens Redistricting Commission's website: http://wedrawthelines.ca.gov//.

2. For previous *CQ Researcher* coverage, see Kenneth Jost, "Redistricting Disputes," March 12, 2004, pp. 221-248; Jennifer Gavin, "Redistricting," Feb. 16, 2001, pp. 113-128; Ronald D. Elving, "Redistricting: Drawing Power With a Map," Feb. 15, 1991, pp. 98-113.

3. For background, see Nadine Cohodas, "Electing Minorities," *CQ Researcher*, Aug. 12, 1994; pp. 697-720.

4. The Texas case is *League of United Latin American Citizens (LULAC) v. Perry*, 548 U.S. 399 (2006). The previous cases are *Vieth v. Jubelirer*, 541 U.S. 267 (2004); and *Davis v. Bandemer*, 478 U.S. 109 (1986).

5. Thomas Brunell, *Redistricting and Representation: Why Competitive Elections Are Bad for America* (2008).

6. The quote is from a power-point presentation, "Redistricting 101," by the Brennan Center for Justice and MALDEF, dated Feb. 23, 2010, www.midwestredistricting.org/. The court case is *Hastert v. State Board of Elections*, 777 F.Supp. 634 (N.D. Ill. 1991). For coverage, see Thomas Hardy, "GOP in clover as federal judges approve congressional remap," *Chicago Tribune*, Nov. 7, 1991, p. 2.

7. The first three decisions are *Miller v. Johnson*, 515 U.S. 900 (1995) (Georgia); *Shaw v. Hunt*, 517 U.S. 889 (1996) (North Carolina); and *Bush v. Vera*, 517 U.S. 952 (1996) (Texas). The Supreme Court summarily upheld the Illinois plan in *King v. Illinois Board of Elections*, 522 U.S. 1087 (1998). The final ruling is *Hunt v. Cromartie*, 532 U.S. 234 (2001). For a summary compilation, see "Redistricting Disputes," *op. cit.*, p. 228.

8. The citation is 556 U.S. 1 (2009).

9. The Arizona Independent Redistricting Commission's website is at www.azredistricting.org/?page=.

10. For a comprehensive overview, see "Reapportionment and Redistricting" in *Guide to Congress* (6th ed., 2008), pp. 1039-1072. See also "The Right to an Equal Vote" in David G. Savage, *Guide to the U.S. Supreme Court* (5th ed., 2010), Vol. 1, pp. 640-653.

11. Edward W. Saunders was elected from Virginia's 5th congressional district in 1908 after Floyd County was transferred to the adjoining 6th district. The transfer left the 5th district with significantly less population than the 6th. Saunders' opponent, who would have won the election in the district as previously drawn, challenged Saunders' seating on the ground of the 1901 apportionment act; a committee recommended the challenger be seated, but the House did not act on the recommendation. See "Reapportionment and Redistricting," *op. cit.*, p. 1049.

12. The Mississippi case is *Wood v. Broom*, 287 U.S. 1 (1932). The citation for *Colegrove v. Green* is 327 U.S. 549 (1946). The dissenting justices were Hugo L. Black, William O. Douglas and Francis Murphy.

13. See *Baker v. Carr*, 369 U.S. 186 (1962); *Gray v. Sanders*, 372 U.S. 368 (1963); *Wesberry v. Sanders*, 376 U.S. 1 (1964); *Reynolds v. Sims*, 377 U.S. 533 (1964).

14. Jack L. Noragon, "Congressional Redistricting and Population Composition, 1964-1970," *Midwest Journal of Political Science*, Vol. 16, No. 2 (May 1972), pp. 295-302, www.jstor.org/pss/2110063.

15. The cases are detailed in Savage, *op. cit.*, pp. 646-650.

16. The citation is 478 U.S. 109 (1986).

17. The case is *Gomillon v. Lightfoot*, 364 U.S. 339 (1960).

18. The decision is *Thornburg v. Gingles*, 478 U.S. 30 (1986); the earlier ruling is *Mobile v. Bolden*, 446 U.S. 55 (1980).

19. For a summary compilation, with citations, see "Redistricting Disputes," *op. cit.*, p. 228.

20. See Linda Greenhouse, "Justices Permit Race as a Factor in Redistricting," *The New York Times*, April 19, 2001, p. A1.

21. "Redistricting Disputes," *op. cit.*, p. 233.
22. *Outline of Redistricting Litigation: The 1990s*, National Conference of State Legislatures, www.senate.mn/departments/scr/redist/redout.htm.
23. Coverage drawn in part from *Outline of Redistricting Litigation: The 2000s, National Conference of State Legislatures*, www.senate.mn/departments/scr/redist/redsum2000/redsum2000.htm.
24. The case is *Vieth v. Jubelirer, op. cit.* For a comprehensive account, see Kenneth Jost, *Supreme Court Yearbook 2003-2004*.
25. The case is *LULAC v. Perry, op. cit.* For a comprehensive account, see Kenneth Jost, *Supreme Court Yearbook 2005-2006*. See also Steve Bickerstaff, *Lines in the Sand: Congressional Redistricting in Texas and the Downfall of Tom DeLay* (2007).
26. The decisions are *Georgia v. Ashcroft*, 539 U.S. 461 (2003); *Bartlett v. Strickland, op. cit.*
27. Karin MacDonald and Nicole Boyle, "Redistricting California: An Overview of Data, Processes and GIS," Statewide Database_Berkeley Law, p. 53, http://wedrawthelines.ca.gov/downloads/crc_public_meeting_20101130_training_karin_mac_donald_nicole_boyle.pdf.
28. See Marc Caputo and Lee Logan, "Redistricting Amendment Challenged," *St. Petersburg Times*, Nov. 4, 2010, p. 4B; Steve Bousquet, "Scott's Action May Stall Ban on Gerrymandering," *ibid.*, Jan. 26, 2011, p. 1B.
29. See "The 20 Most Gerrymandered Districts," *Slate*, www.slate.com/id/2274411/slideshow/2208554/fs/0//entry/2208555/. The unsigned, undated slide show was apparently posted in 2009.

BIBLIOGRAPHY

Books

Brunell, Thomas, *Redistricting and Representation: Why Competitive Elections Are Bad for America,* **Routledge, 2008.**
A professor at the University of Texas at Dallas argues that competitive elections are not vital for effective representation, but in fact increase the number of people who "are left unrepresented in Congress." Includes notes, references.

Bullock, Charles S. III, *Redistricting: The Most Political Activity in America,* **Rowman & Littlefield, 2010.**
A professor at the University of Georgia summarizes background information on congressional and legislative redistricting and examines the strategies and tactics of a process that he says is inevitably political if in control of elected officials. Includes notes.

Cox, Gary W., and Jonathan N. Katz, *Elbridge Gerry's Salamander: The Electoral Consequences of the Reapportionment Revolution,* **Cambridge University Press, 2002.**
The authors argue that, contrary to conventional wisdom, the reapportionment revolution of the 1960s onward was not without political consequence but had two lasting effects: strengthening the Democratic advantage in the U.S. House of Representatives and the advantage of incumbents over challengers. Cox is a professor emeritus at the University of California-San Diego, Katz a professor at the California Institute of Technology. Includes notes, references

Galderisi, Peter F. (ed.), *Redistricting in the New Millennium,* **Lexington Books, 2005.**
The 14 essays by 18 contributors include overviews of events through the turn of the 21st century, detailed examination of race and redistricting and case studies of redistricting in several states. Editor Galderisi is a lecturer at the University of California-San Diego. Includes notes, 12-page bibliography.

Winburn, Jonathan, *The Realities of Redistricting: Following the Rules and Limiting Gerrymandering in State Legislative Redistricting,* **Lexington Books, 2008.**
A professor at the University of Mississippi examines the "realities" of redistricting as seen in four institutional settings: unified partisan control of the state legislature; divided partisan control; partisan commission; and bipartisan commission. Includes selected bibliography.

Yarbrough, Tinsley, *Race and Redistricting: The Shaw-Cromartie Cases,* **University Press of Kansas, 2002.**
A professor at East Carolina University chronicles the decadelong fight over congressional redistricting in

North Carolina that first recognized constitutional objections to racially drawn district lines but ended with upholding a plan with district lines drawn to take race into account to some degree. Includes chronology, short bibliographical essay.

Articles

"Reapportionment and Redistricting," in *Guide to Congress* (6th ed.), CQ Press, 2007, pp. 1039-1072, http://library.cqpress.com/congressguide/toc.php?mode=guides-toc&level=3&values=Part+VII%3A+Congress+and+the+Electorate~Ch.+33++Reapportionment+and+Redistricting (purchase required).

The chapter provides a comprehensive overview of developments in regard to congressional reapportionment and redistricting from the Constitutional Convention through the mid-2000's. Includes select bibliography.

Reports and Studies

"The Impact of Redistricting in YOUR Community: A Guide to Redistricting," NAACP Legal Defense and Educational Fund/Asian American Justice Center/Mexican American Legal Defense and Educational Fund, 2010.

The 78-page guide covers redistricting practices and policies as they affect racial and ethnic minorities. Includes state-by-state listing of contact information for redistricting authorities.

Levitt, Justin, "A Citizen's Guide to Redistricting," Brennan Center for Justice at New York University School of Law, 2010, http://brennan.3cdn.net/7182a7e7624ed5265d_6im622teh.pdf.

The 127-page guide published by the nonpartisan public policy and law institute covers from an often critical perspective the basics of current redistricting practices and outlines current reform proposals. Includes additional resources, notes, other appendix materials. Levitt is now an associate professor at Loyola Law School in Los Angeles.

"Redistricting Law 2010," National Conference of State Legislatures, 2009.

The 228-page guide covers current redistricting practices, step by step and subject by subject. Includes notes, extensive appendix materials.

On the Web

GovTrack, www.govtrack.us/congress/findyourreps.xpd.

This private, unofficial website includes well-organized, state-by-state information and maps on congressional districts and current members of Congress.

Note: For earlier works, see "Bibliography" in Kenneth Jost, "Redistricting Debates," CQ Researcher, March 12, 2004, p. 243.

For More Information

Asian America Justice Center, 1140 Connecticut Ave., N.W., #1200, Washington, DC 20036; (202) 296-2300; www.advancingequality.org. Organization founded in 1991 to advance human and civil rights of Asian Americans.

Brennan Center for Justice, New York University Law School, 161 Sixth Ave., 12th Floor, New York, NY 10013; (646) 292-8310; www.brennancenter.org. Nonpartisan public policy and law institute founded in 1995 that focuses in part on voting rights and campaign and election reform.

Common Cause, 1250 Connecticut Ave., N.W., #600, Washington, DC 20036; (202) 833-1200; www.commoncause.org. Nonpartisan public-interest advocacy organization founded in 1970.

League of United Latin American Citizens, 2000 L St., N.W., Suite 610, Washington, DC 20036; (202) 833-6130; www.lulac.org. Organization founded in 1929 to advance the economic condition, educational attainment, political influence, housing, health and civil rights of the U.S. Hispanic population.

League of Women Voters, 1730 M St., N.W., Suite 1000, Washington, DC 20036-4508; (202) 429-1965; www.lwv.org. Nonpartisan organization founded in 1920 to promote government reform through education and advocacy.

Mexican American Legal Defense and Educational Fund, 634 S. Spring St., Los Angeles, CA; (213) 629-2512; www.maldef.org. Leading Latino civil rights advocacy organization, founded in 1968.

NAACP Legal Defense and Educational Fund, 99 Hudson St., 6th Floor, New York, NY 10013-6289; (212) 965-2200; http://naacpldf.org. Nonprofit civil rights law firm founded in 1940.

National Association of Latino Elected and Appointed Officials, 600 Pennsylvania Ave., S.E., Suite 230, Washington, DC 20003; (202) 546-2536; www.naleo.org. Organization founded in 1976 as a national forum for Latino officials.

National Conference of State Legislatures, 7700 E. First Place, Denver, CO 80230; (303) 364-7700; www.ncsl.org. Bipartisan organization that provides research, technical assistance and other support for legislators and legislative staff in the states, commonwealths and territories.

Project on Fair Representation, 1150 17th St., N.W., #910, Washington, DC 20036; (703) 505-1922; www.projectonfairrepresentation.org. Legal defense fund founded in 2005 to support litigation that challenges racial and ethnic classifications and preferences in state and federal courts.

Public Mapping Project, Prof. Michael MacDonald, George Mason University, Department of Public and International Affairs, 4400 University Drive — 3F4, Fairfax, VA 22030-4444; www.publicmappingproject. A project founded for the post-2010 redistricting cycle to make census data and redistricting software available to general public.

The two major political parties' national committees:

Democratic National Committee, 430 South Capitol St., S.E., Washington, DC 20003; (202) 863-8000; www.dnc.org.

Republican National Committee, 310 1st St., S.E., Washington, DC 20003; (202) 863-8500; www.rnc.org.

2
Changing U.S. Electorate

Alan Greenblatt and Patrick Marshall

White, working-class Americans like this Ford worker in Wayne, Mich., have helped New York Sen. Hillary Clinton beat Barack Obama in California, Pennsylvania and other large states. Since the Great Depression, workingclass whites had been loyal Democrats, but many of them defected in the 1970s and '80s due to liberal Democratic policies. Sen. John McCain, the presumptive Republican presidential nominee, may appeal to working-class voters, who sometimes support GOP candidates because of their conservative social stances.

From *CQ Researcher*,
May 30, 2008 (updated August 9, 2010).

Given the historic nature of the Democratic presidential primary contest — with the nomination coming down to a battle between a white woman and an African-American man — perhaps it's not surprising that there have been splits among voters along racial, geographic, age, income and educational divides.[1]

"I don't think there's any way this election could have been anything but demographically focused, given the candidates left standing," says Scott Keeter, associate director of the Pew Research Center for People & the Press.

The Democrats' internal splits have them nervous about repairing the breaches in order to get all party supporters on board for the fall contest against Arizona Sen. John McCain, the presumptive Republican nominee. McCain might well appeal to white, working-class voters, including the so-called Reagan Democrats, who have sometimes supported GOP candidates because of their relatively conservative stances on social issues.

New York Sen. Hillary Rodham Clinton has repeatedly pointed out that, thanks to working-class support, she has beaten Illinois Sen. Barack Obama in the largest states — California, New York, Ohio, among others — which a Democrat would need to carry in order to win in November against McCain.

In an interview with *USA Today* conducted the day after the May 6 Indiana and North Carolina primaries, Clinton cited an Associated Press report "that found how Sen. Obama's support among working, hard-working Americans, white Americans, is weakening again, and how whites in both states who had not completed college were supporting me."[2]

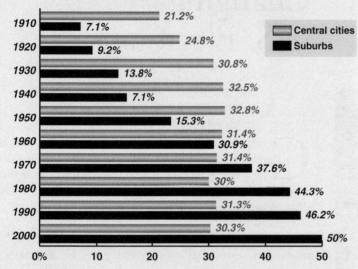

More Americans Moving to the Suburbs

Half of all Americans lived in suburbs in 2000, a sevenfold increase from 90 years earlier. The Democratic Party has been making significant inroads into the traditional GOP turf in the suburbs. Meanwhile, the percentage of Americans in central cities has remained at around 30 percent since 1930, also favoring Democrats.

Percentage of Total Population Living in Central Cities and Suburbs, 1910-2000

Year	Central cities	Suburbs
1910	21.2%	7.1%
1920	24.8%	9.2%
1930	30.8%	13.8%
1940	32.5%	7.1%
1950	32.8%	15.3%
1960	31.4%	30.9%
1970	31.4%	37.6%
1980	30%	44.3%
1990	31.3%	46.2%
2000	30.3%	50%

Source: Ruy Teixeira, "The Future of Red, Blue and Purple America," Brookings Institution, January 2008

In exit polls conducted during the April 22 Pennsylvania Democratic primary, 16 percent of white voters said that race had influenced their decision, with almost half of these saying they would not support Obama in the fall. Only 60 percent of Catholics said they would vote for him in November.

"Mr. Obama was supposed to be a transformational figure, with an almost magical ability to transcend partisan difference," writes Paul Krugman, a *New York Times* columnist who has been supporting Clinton. "Well, now he has an overwhelming money advantage and the support of much of the Democratic establishment — yet he still can't seem to win over large blocs of Democratic voters, especially among the white working class. As a result, he keeps losing big states."[3]

Obama supporters, meanwhile, are concerned that his supporters — particularly young people and African-Americans — will feel disenfranchised if Clinton wins the nomination through a coronation by party officials, because it seems certain she will trail Obama in delegates and overall popular vote support after all the primaries are concluded on June 3.

"We keep talking as if it doesn't matter, it doesn't matter that Obama gets 92 percent of the black vote, [that] because he only got 35 percent of the white vote he's in trouble," House Majority Whip James E. Clyburn, D-S.C., the highest-ranking African-American in Congress, told *The Washington Post* following the Pennsylvania primary.

"Well, Hillary Clinton only got 8 percent of the black vote. . . . It's almost saying black people don't matter. The only thing that matters is how white people respond."[4]

Whatever the outcome, Obama's candidacy has already highlighted many of the ways in which the American electorate is starting to shift — as well as the ways that it hasn't changed quite yet.

"The biggest trend is that the U.S. is no longer going to be a majority-white country," says Scott Page, a University of Michigan political scientist. Given the growth of the Asian and, particularly, the Hispanic share of the population, most demographers predict that whites will no longer comprise a majority by 2050.

"Within 40 years, no single racial group will be a majority," Page says. "Second, interracial marriage is increasing, and many of these marriages are in the upper-income groups, which means that many of our future leaders will be multiracial," like Obama.

In leading the battle for Democratic delegates and total votes, Obama has forged a coalition unlike any seen before in his party. It's typical for one candidate to appeal to educated elites, as Obama does, while a rival appeals to "beer track" blue-collar voters, as Clinton does.

What Obama has done differently is wed African-Americans, who typically vote along with lower-income whites in Democratic primaries, to his base among elites. "This is the first time African-Americans have sided with the educated class," says David Bositis, an elections analyst at the Joint Center for Political and Economic Studies.

Referring to the leading contenders of the 1984 Democratic primary race, Bositis continues, "Obama is Gary Hart, but with the black vote. Hillary Clinton is Walter Mondale but without any black support. Obama's going to be the first nominee who represents the more educated and higher-income Democrats."

Assuming he does ultimately win the nomination, an Obama victory will be the result not only of this historic shift in black voting but also the fact that educated and upper-income voters are both growing in number and becoming more Democratic. He has also benefited from unusually high levels of support among young voters of all races.

But the white working-class vote, while shrinking as a share of the total electorate, is still a predominant factor in American politics. Many Democrats — as well as Republicans — believe that Obama's inability to appeal to this group will prove an Achilles' heel.

"Hillary supporters are going to be very unhappy," says Herbert I. London, president of the conservative Hudson Institute. London predicts that McCain will do very well in the fall among the older Democrats who have supported Clinton — and could make inroads into other Democratic constituencies as well.

"This age gap [between Clinton and Obama] is so persistent that I would be concerned about it," says Robert David Sullivan, managing editor of *CommonWealth* magazine, "especially because McCain might have a particular appeal to older independents."

"Older whites are really going to stick with McCain," echoes Dowell Myers, a University of Southern California demographer. "They're going to think that he speaks to their interests."

William H. Frey, a demographer at the Brookings Institution, suggests that Obama's candidacy does represent a possible future for American politics. His candidacy has been "post-ethnic" in terms of his appeal to upper-income whites, as well as other white voters in states such as Wisconsin and Virginia. It's also "post-boomer," with Obama appealing to millions of "millennial" voters (referring to the generation born since 1982) and seeking, not entirely successfully, to move politics beyond the culture clashes that have marked American politics since the 1960s.

"Obama got a lot of initial support from people who liked his post-boomer sensibility — a way to get beyond moralistic politics," says Pew's Keeter. But as for a post-boomer period, he adds, "I don't think we're there yet."

Frey also cautions that Obama's candidacy may represent the shape of a political future that hasn't yet fully arrived. The trends that have benefited Obama — the rise of the youth vote, the increasing size of the upscale Democratic electorate — will continue, but may not yet be sufficiently in place to overcome the type of traditional, white working-class voters who have long dominated American politics and have fueled Clinton's campaign.

"Maybe 20 years down the road there will be more of the Obama group overall, but for now everything is split," Frey says. "It's not 2030 yet."

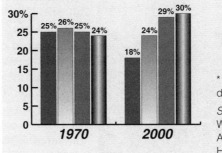

Whites Moving to More Republican Areas

The percentage of whites living in what are considered Republican counties has steadily increased since 1970. Thirty and 29 percent lived in what are considered "Republican landslide" and "Republican competitive" counties, respectively, in 2000, compared to 24 and 25 percent three decades earlier. By contrast, the number of whites living in what are considered "Democratic landslide" counties has decreased by 7 percentage points during the 30-year span.

Percentage of Population That Is White, 1970-2000*
(by county type)

Political Leaning of County
- Democratic landslide
- Democratic competitive
- Republican competitive
- Republican landslide

1970: 25%, 26%, 25%, 24%
2000: 18%, 24%, 29%, 30%

* Percentages may not add to 100 due to rounding

Source: Bill Bishop, "The Big Sort: Why the Clustering of Like-Minded America Is Tearing Us Apart," Houghton Mifflin, May 2008

The Candidates

Sens. Hillary Rodham Clinton, D-N.Y., and Barack Obama, D-Ill., have carved out distinct groups of voters as they battle for the Democratic presidential nomination. Sen. John McCain, R-Ariz., the presumptive Republican nominee, is seeking to appeal to conservatives, blue-collar workers and religious fundamentalists.

Many demographic trends appear to be moving more generally in the Democrats' favor, including support from voters in their 20s, the increasing number of unmarried adults and secular-minded voters, the party's inroads into traditional GOP turf in the suburbs and the support of a majority of Hispanics — the nation's largest and fastest-growing minority group, who have been put off by the hard line many Republicans have taken on illegal immigration.

In seven states that held primaries in March and April alone, 1 million new voters registered as Democrats, while Republican numbers mostly "ebbed or stagnated." In Indiana and North Carolina, which held their Democratic primaries on May 6, the rate of new registrants tripled from 2004.[5]

Ruy Teixeira, another Brookings scholar and coauthor of the 2002 book *The Emerging Democratic Majority*, not surprisingly suggests that all these trends should help his party. But he concedes that Republicans still have some potent arrows in their quiver.

"The good news for the Republicans is that despite some of these various demographic factors that are moving against them, they have held the loyalties of lower-income white voters pretty well," he says.

Other structural advantages that Republicans have enjoyed in recent years — dominance of the South and the interior West, the rock-solid support of regular churchgoers, large margins of victory in the nation's fastest-growing communities — also remain in place.

And McCain's candidacy may dash Democratic hopes of running up a bigger margin among Hispanics that could help them prevail in states President Bush has carried, such as Nevada, New Mexico and Colorado. McCain has famously taken a more conciliatory stance toward immigrants than much of his party. "McCain takes Democrats out of their Western strategy entirely," says John Morgan, a Republican demographer.

With Democrats not quite settled on a candidate, it's premature to guess how the persistent demographic differences that have played out in the primaries will manifest themselves in the fall. Bositis suggests that Clinton's performance has been an indication of support for her among white women, in particular — not of white antipathy toward Obama. White working-class Democrats will mainly "come home" to support Obama in the fall, he suggests.

McCain's candidacy also has engendered some concerns on the Republican side that evangelicals — the conservative Christians who have been the party's most loyal supporters of late — will not support him with any enthusiasm. McCain consistently trailed among evangelical white Protestants during his primary race against former Govs. Mike Huckabee of Arkansas and Mitt Romney of Massachusetts.

How all these crosscurrents of support — or lack thereof — will play out in the fall remains to be seen, of course. What this year's election season has indicated more than anything, however, is that the nature and shape of the American electorate is in a state of flux just now, with the allegiances of various groups shifting between and within the two major parties — and with new constituencies making their presence very much felt.

"We're seeing more people registering now than we've ever seen before," says Kimball Brace, a Democratic consultant. "How that is going to change the demographics and nature of voting is one of the larger questions coming into play."

As the election season wears on, here are some of the other questions being asked about America's changing electorate:

Are whites losing political clout?

After the release of the 2000 census figures, some Republican strategists recognized that their party faced a serious long-term demographic challenge. Rich Bond, a former Republican National Committee chairman, told *The Washington Post*, "We've taken white guys about as far as that group can go. We are in need of diversity, women, Latino, African-American, Asian . . . That is where the future of the Republican Party is."[6]

Republicans count on a disproportionate share of the white vote. Even in 2006, as Democrats regained control of Congress, white males supported GOP candidates by an eight-percentage-point margin.[7] The overall white vote that year favored Republicans by 4 percentage points — although that was down from a 15 percent margin in 2004. Whites were, in effect, outvoted by

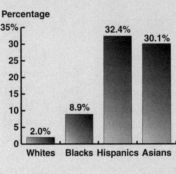

Hispanic Population Grew Rapidly

The number of Hispanics in the United States has grown by nearly a third since 2000. By contrast, blacks and whites have only grown by 9 and 2 percent, respectively. Democrats are favored by a majority of Hispanics — the nation's largest and fastest-growing minority group — who have been put off by the hard line many Republicans have taken on illegal immigration.

Growth in U.S. Population by Ethnicity, 2000-2008

Whites: 2.0%
Blacks: 8.9%
Hispanics: 32.4%
Asians: 30.1%

Source: William H. Frey, analysis of U.S. Census estimates

Hispanics, blacks and Asians, who gave massive margins to Democratic candidates (favoring Democrats by 39-, 79- and 25-point margins, respectively).[8]

Obama, the leading Democratic candidate, appears to be prevailing despite his inability to win a majority among white voters. He's doing well among young and well-educated whites and has carried 9 out of 10 black voters. But Clinton has carried the overall white vote in many states. In an analysis of the primary vote through the end of April, former *Los Angeles Times* editor Bill Boyarsky concluded that Obama's share of the white vote was "short [of] a majority, but still substantial."[9]

So if Democrats can nominate a candidate who fails to receive a majority of the white vote, and if whites' share of the total vote is shrinking, does that mean that white voters are losing influence?

Ronald Walters, a University of Maryland political scientist, believes that white influence will decline, given the growth in both immigration and naturalization. "I would think in the future you're going to have substantial demographic shifts bringing in more Hispanics and African-Americans," he says. "What it will mean in terms of whites is that they will have to adjust to the loss of political power."

Walters estimates that 13 states — comprising 43 percent of the Electoral College — have combined black and Hispanic populations topping 25 percent of their total. "You really have to have those votes in order to win," he says.

During the 1950s, whites made up more than 90 percent of the electorate (95 percent in 1952).[10] During the decades since then, blacks have secured their place in the voting booth through passage of voting-rights laws, and the Latino share of the population has skyrocketed. White males alone made up nearly half of the

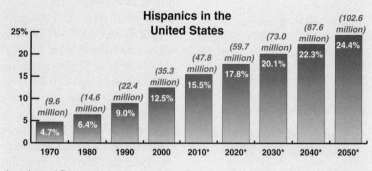

Hispanics' Share of U.S. Electorate Increasing

The number of Hispanics living in the United States is expected to total about 48 million in 2010, or about 16 percent of the total U.S. population. This represents a fivefold increase compared to 1970. By 2050, a quarter of the electorate is projected to be Hispanic, numbering just over 100 million people.

Hispanics in the United States

Year	Population	Percent
1970	9.6 million	4.7%
1980	14.6 million	6.4%
1990	22.4 million	9.0%
2000	35.3 million	12.5%
2010*	47.8 million	15.5%
2020*	59.7 million	17.8%
2030*	73.0 million	20.1%
2040*	87.6 million	22.3%
2050*	102.6 million	24.4%

* projected figures

Source: Ethnicity and Ancestry Branch, Population Division, U.S. Census Bureau

electorate in 1952, according to Emory University political scientist Alan Abramowitz. Their share had dropped to 33.1 percent by 2004.

"Thanks to the recent growth in the Latino population . . . the white male share is now dropping about a percentage point a year, accelerating a decline that began with the increased enfranchisement of African-Americans in the civil rights era," Thomas F. Schaller wrote in *Salon* last September. "In [this] year's election, white males may account for fewer than one out of three voters. Bubba is no longer a kingmaker."[11]

But not everyone is convinced that whites are in any danger of losing their sway over elections. Karlyn Bowman, a senior fellow at the American Enterprise Institute (AEI), points out that "the black share of the electorate doesn't appear to be growing. That could change if Obama's the nominee, but at least at this point it doesn't appear to be growing. Asians are growing, but they are still a small percentage."

Despite the rapid growth and spread of Hispanics, their political power does not yet mirror their numbers, which, after all, includes millions of non-citizens. And the median age of Hispanics in the U.S. is just 27 compared to 39 for Anglos, meaning that a much higher percentage of Hispanics don't vote simply because they're too young.[12]

"White people are going to have less power," says Teixeira at the Brookings Institution, "but it's not going to be as fast as you think because of the lack of eligible voters" among Latinos.

Fernando Guerra, a political scientist at Loyola Marymount University in Los Angeles, also disputes the notion that growing minority populations will translate either into monolithic voting patterns or influence exceeding that of Anglos.

"Whites continue to be the majority or plurality everywhere, with the exception of some cities and counties," Guerra says. "There are states where African-Americans and Latinos make up more than 30 percent of the population, but none are above 50 percent."

It's become conventional wisdom in the South, where the black share of the vote tops 35 percent in some states — and is a share that votes heavily Democratic — that Republicans have to take at least 60 percent of the white vote in order to prevail in statewide elections. But they've had no apparent problem doing so.

Guerra notes that whites represent a majority of the electorate even in states with exceptionally large minority populations, such as California, New Mexico and Hawaii. Myers, the USC demographer, has reached a similar conclusion about his own state.

"In California, whites are already down to 45 percent of the population, but they're about 70 percent of the voters," Myers says. "Whites will remain a majority [of the state electorate] until 2031. Despite their shrinking numbers, they're older, and older people tend to vote. Also, they're all citizens."

Nationwide, whites still make up a large and disproportionate share of the electorate. According to Brookings demographer Frey, whites' share of the population is down to 66 percent, but they still make up 74 percent of eligible voters and 78 percent of actual voters.

"The role of whites is diminishing," says Clark Bensen, a Republican demographer and consultant.

"Whether it actually reaches a critical mass where it doesn't matter is another story."

Are suburbs shifting to the Democrats?

The vote in most states splits along predictable geographic lines. Big cities are primarily Democratic, while rural areas are reliably Republican. The suburbs have become the most important battlegrounds, the biggest trove of votes nationwide, with enough numbers to sway most statewide elections.

Because of their success in fast-growing counties — President Bush carried 97 of the nation's 100 fastest-growing counties in 2004 — Republicans have been hopeful that their appeal to suburban voters on issues such as tax rates and national security would be enough to assure victory in most presidential contests for the foreseeable future.[13]

"Suburban and exurban areas . . . were central to Republican political guru Karl Rove's grand scheme for cementing GOP dominance for decades in the wake of President Bush's 2004 re-election victory," writes political journalist David Mark.[14]

Voters in exurban areas — counties on the fringe of metropolitan areas — seem naturally receptive to the GOP's overarching message about the need to limit government spending. They tend to be highly sensitive to tax increases and have sought out areas where the private sector, rather than local governments, provides services — from privately owned cars for transportation to homeowners' associations for parks and gated communities for maintenance of streetscapes.

Joel Kotkin, an expert on development and living patterns at Chapman University in Anaheim, Calif., told Minnesota Public Radio in February that for the past 40 years cities have lost middle-class white people with children who moved to suburbs seeking better schools,

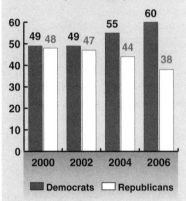

Young Voters Trending Democratic

Three out of every five voters ages 18 to 29 voted Democratic in 2006, an 11-percentage-point increase from 2000. Republican votership declined by a similar amount during the same period.

Congressional Voting by Voters Ages 18-29
(2000-2006)

Year	Democrats	Republicans
2000	49	48
2002	49	47
2004	55	44
2006	60	38

Source: Ruy Teixeira, "The Future of Red, Blue and Purple America," Brookings Institution, January 2008

more space and increased security. That left cities with what Kotkin calls an array of demographic "niches."

"And that niche tends to be either minorities, poor people, young people or people without children — all of whom tend to be much more liberal."

Democratic author and researcher Teixeira agrees "there's a density gradient for Democratic voting. The question is, where does it tip?" Teixeira argues that, despite the long-standing notion that suburban voters are more conservative than city folks, voters in older, more established "inner-ring" suburbs are increasingly favoring Democrats.

Democrats carried nearly 60 percent of the 2006 U.S. House vote in the inner-ring suburbs of the nation's 50 largest metropolitan areas — up from 53 percent in 2002 — according to an analysis by the Metropolitan Institute at Virginia Tech. They won nearly 55 percent of the next ring of "mature" suburbs, up from 50 percent four years earlier.[15]

In Virginia, Republicans pinned their hopes for retaining control of the state Senate last fall on campaigns that stressed a hard line against illegal immigration. They lost the chamber and lost state House seats by ceding Northern Virginia suburbs that had once been firm GOP territory.

In Minnesota in 2006, Republicans lost 19 state House seats, and control of that chamber, largely in suburban districts around the Twin Cities, where voters were skeptical of the GOP's emphasis on social issues. And, in a particularly painful symbolic loss in March, Democrat Bill Foster picked up the suburban Chicago House seat formerly occupied by Republican Speaker Dennis Hastert.

"I doubt the Karl Roves of the world would disagree with the fact that the Democrats have been able to push

Nascar fans stand during the prayer before a race at the California Speedway in Fontana. Nascar fans tend to be blue-collar, patriotic, and Republican. In recent elections, candidates of all stripes have sought to "microtarget" voters — tailoring messages to appeal to particular demographic niches, such as "Nascar dads," "soccer moms" and "angry white males."

out more into the suburbs, and Republicans have to push them back," says AEI's Bowman.

Demographer Robert Lang of Virginia Tech says that population growth rates are highest in Republican-leaning emerging suburbs — about 17 percent, he says, compared with just 4 percent growth in the inner-ring and mature suburbs. But the existing population in the latter category is so much greater that their growth in absolute numbers is about the same as the outer suburbs.

"The outer suburbs are not gaining everything," he says. "The rural and exurban growth cannot offset urbanizing suburbs much longer."

Republican demographer Morgan agrees that the older suburbs are filling up with people coming out from cities — including immigrants increasingly drawn to suburbs. But he says Republicans are moving to outer suburbs and exurban areas.

"The main county [in a metropolitan area] is no longer Republican, or it breaks about even," he says. "But what we have is hundreds of counties becoming exurban Republican. Around Atlanta, all of North Georgia is exurban and all Republican."

What's happening is that some inner-ring suburbs are coming to resemble center cities in their population density and makeup. Morgan says, "The older suburbs aren't genuinely suburbs, so many people are coming out from the cities."

Michael Barone, an AEI resident fellow and senior writer for *U.S. News & World Report*, notes that Arlington, Va., just outside Washington, was once "family territory, with young families and was Republican. In Arlington now, most people live in apartments, it's full of singles and it's become very heavily Democratic." Barone notes that similar changes have happened in other metropolitan areas as well.

The key to suburban control, as Teixeira suggests, is determining how far the line of Democratic dominance extends out from the core city. Republicans concede they are losing the inner suburbs, while Teixeira notes that "the exurbs are likely to remain solidly Republican.

"The question," he says, "is will the emerging suburbs" — the areas growing in population but closer to the city than the exurbs on the fringe — "remain competitive, as they were in 2006, or will they be solidly Republican? If the GOP can't keep the emerging suburbs solidly Republican, the math suggests they'll lose the suburbs overall."

Others are not willing to concede the suburbs to the Democrats quite yet. "This trend of the close-in suburbs becoming more Democratic seems to have started in the North, but there's still some question of whether it will happen in the South," says Robert David Sullivan, managing editor of *CommonWealth* magazine.

"If the suburbs of Atlanta act in the same way as the suburbs of Boston and Chicago, that is good news for the Democrats, but it hasn't started happening yet. That's a question for this fall."

Are young voters more liberal?

In April, the Pew Research Center for the People & the Press released survey data that suggested voters in their 20s strongly identified with the Democratic Party. More than half — 58 percent — identified with the Democrats, compared with 33 percent who affiliated with the GOP.[16] "This makes Generation Next the least Republican generation," according to the center.[17]

The findings received a good deal of attention, with some observers speculating that the unpopular presidency of George W. Bush and the war in Iraq might cost the Republicans a generation's support. The overwhelming preference for Obama among young voters in this year's Democratic primaries and caucuses also spoke to the party's hopes for winning over this fresh cohort of voters.

Voters ages 18 to 29 gave 60 percent of their support to Democrats in 2006, giving the party a 22-point margin, compared with a closer 55-to-44 percent split in 2004.[18]

"Clearly, George Bush does not appeal to them positively," says Barone, the political commentator and AEI fellow. "Unlike Presidents Reagan and Clinton, he has not attracted young voters to his party.

"Certainly, they did not go through the experiences of the 1970s — stagflation, the overregulation of the economy — that left a lot of Americans skeptical about big-government policies," Barone continues. "That's been a help to Republicans in preceding years. It's not now."

Morley Winogrand and Michael D. Hais, the Democratic authors of the new book *Millennial Makeover: MySpace, YouTube and the Future of American Politics*, go so far as to suggest that the party capturing the White House this year has "a historic opportunity to become the majority party for at least four more decades."[19]

But even though many conservatives such as Barone — and even some Republican political consultants — are willing to concede an advantage for Democrats among young voters today, they argue that such an advantage could prove fleeting. Today's young may be sour on the Republican "brand," but that doesn't mean they'll be lifelong liberals who will remain loyal to the Democrats.

"This is a generation that's up for grabs," says Bowman, Barone's AEI colleague. She concedes that "they're leaning very heavily Democratic today" but argues that their attitudes toward both big government and big business could "tip them Republican as they start their careers."

"Democrats may have the young for a couple of elections," Republican demographer Morgan says.

Bowman also argues that, although today's young people tend to be more tolerant toward gays than their forebears, "attitudes on abortion and drugs have not become more liberal over time. They're not so much liberal or conservative," she says. "They're just different."

James Gimpel, a political scientist and expert on demographics at the University of Maryland, says that young voters are skewing more liberal on social and cultural issues, but he suggests that the Democrats' current success among them has as much to do with the party's active recruitment and appeal to these voters as ideology.

"The Democrats and progressive forces have been much more aggressive," he says. "Republicans have been very slow at recruiting younger people. The Republicans are maybe hanging back and hoping when people get into their 30s, they'll switch."

Gimpel suggests that the potential for intergenerational warfare — with younger voters resentful about having to pay high payroll taxes to support Social Security and health benefits for aging boomers — could redound to the GOP's benefit. "The opportunity is there for Republican candidates who offer lower taxes and smaller government," he says.

But not everyone believes that waiting for changing conditions will prove a winning strategy for the GOP. Myers, the USC demographer, says that each younger generation tends to exaggerate the political climate of the time in which they came to maturity. He argues that despite the fact people's voting habits change to some extent due to their place in the "life cycle" — people with children tend to become more conservative, for instance — "these cohorts tend to hold their orientations for the rest of their lives."

Mark Grebner, a Democratic consultant based in Michigan, agrees. He says that people who came of age under Reagan were heavily Republican and have remained so. "The people born around 1962, 1964, they're about as Republican as any age cohort that we've seen in a long time," he says.

But the people who are coming up under the Bush presidency, Grebner argues, are strongly Democratic. "People who are now 18 to 28 are much more Democratic — dramatically," he says.

A poll of 18-to-24-year-olds conducted in March and April for Harvard University's Institute of Politics found that they favor Obama over McCain, 53 percent to 32 percent, while giving Clinton a much smaller margin over McCain (44 to 39 percent).[20]

"Certainly the Bush presidency has not been a big plus for the Republican Party," Grebner says.

BACKGROUND

After the New Deal

American politics in recent decades has been a massive square dance, with regions and demographic groups switching parties. The Northeast, for example, was the most solidly Republican part of the country into the

CHRONOLOGY

1950s-1960s *Democratic dominance of American politics starts to ebb.*

1952 Dwight D. Eisenhower is elected president — the only Republican president from 1933 to 1969.

1954 Supreme Court's *Brown v. Board of Education* ruling overturns "separate but equal" segregation policies in schools, leading to "white flight" from cities. . . . Democrats gain House and Senate majorities that endure for decades.

1965 President Lyndon B. Johnson signs Voting Rights Act, guaranteeing suffrage for black Americans. . . . Johnson also signs an immigration law that moves away from quotas favoring Western Europeans, signaling the beginning of enormous Latino immigration.

1966 In response to Johnson's Great Society programs, Republicans gain 47 House seats, three Senate seats and eight governorships.

1968 Assassination of Rev. Martin Luther King Jr. sparks riots in more than 100 cities. . . . Richard M. Nixon wins the presidency by pursuing a "Southern strategy" that addresses whites' concerns about law and order and changing social mores. His is the first of five Republican wins out of six elections.

1970s-1980s *Republicans dominate voting for the White House, but Democratic majorities in Congress mostly endure.*

1970 For the first time, suburban residents outnumber city dwellers.

1973 Supreme Court's *Roe v. Wade* decision legalizing abortion spurs evangelicals to greater political involvement.

1974 President Nixon resigns amidst the Watergate scandal; 75 new Democrats, "known as Watergate babies," are elected to the House, compared to just 17 Republicans.

1980 Ronald Reagan addresses 20,000 evangelicals at a gathering later called "the wedding ceremony of evangelicals and the Republican Party"; in his first election, Reagan moves millions of white working-class voters and much of the South into the GOP's column.

1990s-2000s *Political parity and increasing polarization lead to close competition between the two parties.*

1992 Democrat Bill Clinton wins the White House by appealing on economic issues to working-class voters who "play by the rules."

1994 Republicans win House for first time in 40 years, along with the Senate, through the support of "angry white males."

2000 Church attendance becomes a predictor of Republican voting; George W. Bush carries 74 percent of evangelical vote.

2004 Record 40 percent of Latinos vote for President Bush. . . . Nearly 50 percent of Americans live in "landslide counties" where one of the presidential candidates won by 20 percent or more; the figure in 1976 was 27 percent.

2005 Republican Party Chairman Ken Mehlman apologizes to African-American voters for seeking "to benefit politically from racial polarization." . . . House Republicans pass an immigration bill that would reclassify illegal immigrants as felons, angering Hispanics. . . . Twenty-eight percent of adults hold college degrees, compared with 5 percent in 1940.

2006 Democrats regain control of Congress; whites give marginal support to Republicans but are outvoted by heavy Democratic voting among blacks, Hispanics and Asians.

2008 Christian leader James Dobson says he would not vote for Sen. John McCain, R-Ariz., "under any circumstances" (Jan. 13). . . . Sen. Hillary Clinton, D-N.Y., carries 67 percent of the Hispanic vote in Texas (March 4). . . . Answering criticism about the Rev. Jeremiah Wright, his former pastor, Sen. Barack Obama gives widely praised speech on race in America (March 18). . . . Obama tells San Francisco fundraiser that working-class voters are "bitter" and "cling to guns or religion" for solace (April 4). . . . Bush's disapproval rating hits 69 percent (April 22). . . . Voters in Montana, South Dakota close out Democratic primary season (June 3).

November — Barack Obama becomes first African-American to be elected president. . . . Since 2004, the share of blacks voting Democratic rises 7 percent, youths 13 percent and Hispanics 14 percent, with the latter the largest shift toward the left by any group in history.

2009

Republican Scott Brown of Massachusetts is elected to the U.S. Senate, the first time the seat is held by a Republican in 38 years. . . . National Popular Vote, a California-based group, advocates presidential elections based on the popular vote rather than the Electoral College system. . . . The House passes a popular-vote bill and sends it to the Senate.

2010

February — The National Tea Party Convention is held in Nashville, Tenn.

April — Tea Party supporters protest tax day and hold rallies nationwide to spread their message.

May — Tea Party candidate Rand Paul wins the Republican Senate nomination in Kentucky.

1960s but now is the Democrats' strongest base. Conversely, the "solid South" is no longer wholly Democratic but mostly Republican.

Roman Catholics, once predominantly Democratic in their voting habits, now divide their votes evenly between the parties. African-Americans in the North, for whose allegiance both parties competed effectively up until about 1960, are now the most loyal voting bloc for Democrats. The list of groups shifting loyalties between the parties goes on and on and will remain a crucial factor this year, as Democrats struggle to hold onto a sizable share of the white working-class vote, which will likely prove decisive.

White working-class voters for decades comprised the majority of the Democratic vote as the largest bloc within the New Deal coalition, which dominated U.S. politics from 1932, with the election of Franklin D. Roosevelt as president, until 1968.

Republicans had enjoyed near-permanent occupancy of the White House since the Civil War, winning 14 of the 18 presidential elections since 1860. But in 1932, in response to the federal government's weak response to the Great Depression, Roosevelt not only won big but put together an enduring political coalition that included members of labor unions, big-city political machines in the North, farm groups, intellectuals, minority groups including Jews and the South.

The New Deal coalition propelled Democrats to victory in all but two of the nine presidential elections from 1932 to 1964. "The Republicans were the party of the Northeast, of business, of the middle classes and of white Protestants, while the Democrats enjoyed a clear majority among the working classes, organized labor, Catholics and the South" at all political levels, wrote pollster Everett Carll Ladd Jr.[21]

Even during the Democrats' years in the wilderness — the two-term presidency of Dwight D. Eisenhower — New Deal-style politics and programs continued to dominate the national agenda, with the expansion of government social-welfare programs continuing unabated. Eisenhower, for instance, oversaw the creation of the Department of Health, Education and Welfare.[22] In addition, during Eisenhower's second year in office, Democrats won majorities in the House and Senate that would endure for 40 and 26 years, respectively.

The high-water mark for Democrats came with the election of 1964, when Lyndon B. Johnson won the largest share of the popular presidential vote in modern times, and the party took two-thirds of the House and Senate seats. Their landslide led to the passage of a slew of domestic legislation known as the Great Society, including the creation of Medicare, the Voting Rights Act of 1965 and a rewrite of the nation's immigration law, abolishing a system of quotas that had limited immigration mainly to newcomers from Western Europe.

The price tag and policy directions of many of these bills prompted a backlash in 1966, when Republicans gained 47 House seats, three Senate seats and eight governorships, including the election of Ronald Reagan in

The Gap Between Blacks and Hispanics

Will racial politics affect the Democratic nomination?

One of the most notable racial divides in voting this year has been the gap between African-Americans and Hispanics during the Democratic primary campaign. Blacks have been supporting Illinois Sen. Barack Obama by margins as great as 9-to-1, while Hispanics have given New York Sen. Hillary Clinton a 2-to-1 advantage in multiple states.

Is this just a fluke, or does it speak to some underlying enmity between the nation's two largest minority groups? There does appear to be evidence of tension between blacks and Hispanics in some areas, based on economic and political competition. But many observers say that claims of a deep divide are overblown.

A widely cited comment by Sergio Bendixen, Clinton's Hispanic pollster, set the template for debate about this issue on the presidential campaign trail. "The Hispanic voter — and I want to say this very carefully — has not shown a lot of willingness or affinity to support black candidates," Bendixen told *The New Yorker* in January. [1]

There have been some schisms between the two groups. Traditionally black areas such as South Los Angeles and Compton have become majority Latino, and Hispanics have also made strong inroads in Southern states such as North Carolina and Georgia, "bringing change to communities where blacks had gained economic and political power after years of struggle against Jim Crow laws," writes Stephan Malanga, a senior fellow at the Manhattan Institute. [2]

Studies of Southern cities conducted by Duke University political scientist Paula D. McClain have found that blacks believe Latinos have robbed them of jobs, while Hispanics regard blacks as "slothful and untrustworthy." [3]

"There is considerable anger among African-Americans about the immigrant labor force that has taken over whole sections of the economy and excluded African-Americans from those jobs," says Ronald Walters, director of the University of Maryland's African American Leadership Center. Walters notes that Hispanics sometimes complain in turn that black mayors or members of Congress don't do much for them in areas where black and brown residents live together.

In local elections, there have been examples both of coalitions built between the two groups, and of one constituency's refusal to vote for candidates drawn from the other. In Democratic primary campaigns over the years in New York and Texas, Hispanics have tended to vote for whites over blacks, and blacks have returned the favor when it comes to contests between Anglos and Hispanics. [4] On the other hand, Hispanics have lent overwhelming support to several black big-city mayors, while at least eight African-American congressmen currently represent areas that are heavily Latino. [5]

In Los Angeles, Latinos now represent 46.5 percent of the population — up from just 18.5 percent 30 years ago. The black share of the population, in the meantime, has shrunk from 17 percent to 11.2 percent, fueling some animosity from both sides as blacks continue to enjoy disproportionate sway. [6] Antonio Villaraigosa, a Latino politician, carried just 20 percent of the black vote in his first race for mayor of Los Angeles against James Hahn, who is Anglo.

California. Notably, the election represented a breakthrough for the GOP in the South, which had given virtually all of its support to Democrats since the Civil War. Several Southern states were among the few to support Arizona Sen. Barry M. Goldwater over Johnson in 1964. Further breaking with tradition, about a third of the South's House districts elected Republicans in 1966.

The South began to turn mainly for one reason — the passage of federal civil rights laws granting equal opportunity and voting privileges to African-Americans. The share of Southern blacks registered to vote rose from 29 percent in 1960 to 62 percent in 1970, but their presence on the voter rolls was not enough to offset the conservative and increasingly Republican voting patterns of white Southerners.[23]

Other demographic patterns began to work in the GOP's favor, including the explosive growth during the post-World War II era of the suburbs, triggered by a combination of factors that included the nationwide construction of new highways and the postwar "baby boom." The suburbs also gained population due to "white flight," with white parents taking their children out of urban school districts that were undergoing integration by race.

But Villaraigosa carried blacks during his successful rematch against Hahn in 2005. "When people say to me, African-Americans didn't vote for you in your first race, I say, well, they didn't know me," Villaraigosa told the *Chicago Tribune*. "In my second race, they did, and they voted for me overwhelmingly." [7]

Hahn's family had enjoyed a long history of support from L.A.'s black community. Such personal ties, as opposed to racial preferences, may go a long way toward explaining Clinton's performance among Hispanics this year.

Hispanics were big supporters of Bill Clinton and have proven to be a key constituency for Hillary Clinton as well. According to exit polling, she took 64 percent of the Latino vote in the Nevada caucuses, to Obama's 26 percent. Her share of the Hispanic vote in California was 67 percent, while in Texas it was 64 percent.

"If you look at the demographics of Latinos — working class, lower educational attainment — it's very similar to the demographics of whites who are supporting Hillary," says Loyola Marymount University political scientist Fernando Guerra.

Guerra adds that, "African-Americans would be supporting Hillary overwhelmingly, if everything about Obama's background and platform were the same, but he was white."

Los Angeles Mayor Antonio Villaraigosa.

David Bositis, an expert on black voting behavior at the Joint Center for Political and Economic Studies, says that Hispanics are choosing to support Clinton, as opposed to voting against Obama. Taken as a group, Hispanics did well economically during her husband's time in the White House.

Although that is also true about African-Americans, the latter group has been motivated by Obama's historic candidacy but put off by the Clinton campaign's occasional injection of his race as an issue. "If Hillary hadn't blown it with them, she would have been receiving at least a third of the black vote, instead of none," Bositis says.

---

[1] Ryan Lizza, "Minority Reports," *The New Yorker*, Jan. 21, 2008.

[2] Stephen Malanga, "The Rainbow Coalition Evaporates," *City Journal*, winter 2008, p. 35.

[3] Arian Campo-Flores, "Everything to Everyone," *Newsweek*, Feb. 4, 2008, p. 33.

[4] James Traub, "The Emerging Minority," *The New York Times Magazine*, March 2, 2008, p. 15.

[5] Clarence Page, "Clinton's Hispanic Edge Over Obama," *Chicago Tribune*, Jan. 30, 2008, p. 21.

[6] Susan Anderson, "The Clout That Counts," *Los Angeles Times*, Nov. 11, 2007, p. M4.

[7] Clarence Page, "When the Melting Pot Boils Over," *Chicago Tribune*, Feb. 6, 2008, p. 25.

During this era, the Supreme Court issued numerous rulings that did not sit well with conservatives, including requirements that white families send their children by bus to schools dominated by blacks; a ban on prayer in public schools; the lifting of restrictions on contraception; and increased protections for criminal defendants. The Republican Party platform began to complain about "moral decline and drift."

Cultural ferment extended well beyond the reach of the court, with peaceful civil rights marches giving way to riots in hundreds of cities in 1967 and 1968. Republican Richard M. Nixon played to the fears of the "silent majority," promising in 1968 to restore law and order — a message that had particularly strong partisan resonance after rioting took place at that year's Democratic National Convention in Chicago.

Nixon also devised a "Southern strategy" of appealing to the fears of whites in response to the growing political power and demands of African-Americans. Nixon strategist Kevin Phillips popularized the phrase, explaining that Republicans would never get more than 20 percent of "the Negro vote" but nevertheless would enforce the Voting

Diversity Blamed for "Social Isolation"

Do Obama's problems in mixed states prove the point?

One of the many striking features of this year's Democratic presidential primary contest has been the difference in the kinds of states Illinois Sen. Barack Obama has won and lost. He easily carried states with large African-American populations such as Mississippi and South Carolina, as well as nearly all-white states such as Maine, Vermont and Idaho, yet he lost nearly all the states with a broader demographic mix, including Pennsylvania, California, Ohio and New York.

"As some bloggers have shrewdly pointed out, Obama does best in areas that have either a large concentration of African-American voters or hardly any at all, but he struggles in places where the population is decidedly mixed," writes political reporter Matt Bai in *The New York Times Magazine*. "What this suggests, perhaps, is that living in close proximity to other races — sharing industries and schools and sports arenas — actually makes Americans less sanguine about racial harmony rather than more so." [1]

If that is indeed the case, the Obama campaign may serve as an important illustration of a point made last year by Robert D. Putnam, a Harvard University political scientist. In a study that attracted widespread attention and engendered a good deal of controversy despite its appearance in a journal called *Scandinavian Political Studies*, Putnam posited that diversity — despite its near-universal approbation as one of America's major strengths — actually causes significant social harm, at least in the near-term.

Putnam and his team conducted detailed telephone interviews with 30,000 Americans — a far larger sample than usual in such surveys — and dug more deeply into 41 communities across the country. Even controlling for factors such as income disparities and local crime rates, Putnam found that residents of diverse communities are less likely to trust their neighbors — even those of their own race — than people who live in more homogenous areas.

"Diversity seems to trigger . . . social isolation," Putnam writes in the study. "In colloquial language, people living in ethnically diverse settings appear to 'hunker down' — that is, to pull in like a turtle. . . ."

"Inhabitants of diverse communities tend to withdraw from collective life, to distrust their neighbors, regardless of the color of their skin, to withdraw even from close friends, to expect the worst from their community and its leaders, to volunteer less, give less to charity and work on community projects less often, to register to vote less, to agitate for social reform more, but have less faith that they can actually make a difference and to huddle unhappily in front of the television." [2]

Other social scientists have reached similar conclusions. A pair of Harvard economists found that about half the difference in social-welfare spending between Europe and the U.S. could be attributed to greater ethnic diversity in America. Two other economists reviewed 15 recent studies and concluded that ethnic diversity was linked to lower school funding and trust, as well as declines in other measures of "social capital" (a phrase Putnam helped popularize with his 2000 best-seller *Bowling Alone*). [3]

Putnam's work on diversity was soon seized upon by conservatives who saw it as a necessary corrective to the "Politically Correct Police" who had championed diversity

---

Rights Act. "The more Negroes who register as Democrats in the South, the sooner the Negrophobe whites will quit the Democrats and become Republicans," he explained to *The New York Times*.[24]

The Democratic share of the presidential vote plummeted from a record 61 percent in 1964 to just 43 percent in 1968, with third-party candidate George Wallace appealing even more directly to voter anxiety than Nixon. In his 1969 book *The Emerging Republican Majority*, Phillips wrote, "This repudiation visited upon the Democratic Party for its ambitious social programming, and inability to handle the urban and Negro revolutions, was comparable to that given conservative Republicanism in 1932 for its failures to cope with the economic crisis of the Depression."[25]

Reagan Democrats

Republicans would go on to win all but one of the next six presidential elections. (The one exception came in 1976, when the party was punished for the Watergate

as an unquestionable virtue — and as a warning against the effects of immigration, both legal and illegal. "I'm not at all surprised by what Mr. Putnam has found in his study," says Herbert I. London, president of the Hudson Institute. "[Diversity's] going to breed resentment and, to some extent, hostility."

The Orange County Register ran an editorial called "Greater Diversity Equals More Misery," while Putnam's work was favorably cited on the Web site of former Ku Klux Klan leader David Duke.[4] This sort of response clearly left Putnam uncomfortable. "It certainly is not pleasant when David Duke's Web site hails me as the guy who found out racism is good," the liberal Putnam said.[5]

More important than his discomfort, though, was Putnam's frustration that the second half of his argument was often left out of the commentary — that both immigration and diversity, over the long term, would prove to be pluses. We forget, he suggested in an interview, that there were similar levels of discomfort among communities receiving European immigrants a century or more ago.

He maintains that the current waves of immigrants can be successfully assimilated over time if social divisions are subsumed within the sort of shared identity that has always unified Americans. The areas that are attracting immigrants today are among the nation's most economically vibrant, Putnam points out.

"Immigration policies may at first seem tangential to productivity, but they are not," says Scott Page, a University of Michigan political scientist and author of a 2007 book about diversity called *The Difference*. "Diversity is crucial to the development of a nation, especially economically. Diverse people bring diverse skills, which prove invaluable for innovation and growth."

"Chief diversity officers" have become a staple of *Fortune* 500 companies, not to please the P.C. Police but to keep abreast of demographic trends that are changing the makeup of the skilled workforce. "If you define the global talent pipeline as all those individuals around the world who have at least a college degree, only 17 percent of this pipeline comprises white males," says Sylvia Ann Hewlett, an economist at the New York-based Center for Work-Life Policy. "Increasingly, talent management is diversity management."

As Putnam himself argues, diversity may be uncomfortable, but it's beneficial — and inevitable — over the long haul. "The most certain prediction that we can make about almost any modern society is that it will be more diverse a generation from now than it is today," he writes in his study.

In the short term, however, one of the most important political questions of the year is whether Obama, assuming he's the Democratic nominee, will be able to win over the white working-class voters who have largely supported New York Sen. Hillary Clinton in the more mixed states that she has won.

"Rather than serving to heal America's racial wounds," writes conservative columnist Jonah Goldberg, "maybe Obama's campaign is more like a dye marker that helps us better diagnose the complexity of the problem."[6]

---

[1] Matt Bai, "What's the Real Racial Divide?," *The New York Times Magazine*, March 16, 2008, p. 15.

[2] Robert D. Putnam, "E Pluribus Unum: Diversity and Community in the Twenty-First Century," *Scandinavian Political Studies*, June 2007, p. 137.

[3] Michael Jonas, "The Downside of Diversity," *The Boston Globe*, Aug. 5, 2007, p. D1.

[4] Ilana Mercer, "Greater Diversity Equals More Misery," *The Orange County Register*, July 22, 2007; available at www.ocregister.com/opinion/putnam-diversity-social-1781099-racial-greater.

[5] Jonas, *op. cit.*

[6] Jonah Goldberg, "Obama: Winning White Votes in White States," *The Kansas City Star*, Feb. 14, 2008, p. B9.

---

scandal that ended the Nixon presidency.) The GOP appeared to have a lock on the Electoral College, with victory virtually assured throughout the South, the Rocky Mountain West and the Plains states. The Sun Belt, which had about as many electoral votes as Snow Belt states in the 1970s, continues to pick up votes with each census.[26]

Underlying Republican success, however, was the fracturing of the New Deal coalition and the GOP's ability to tap into white working-class votes that had long been denied its candidates. Reagan's presidential campaigns of 1980 and 1984 moved the South further into the GOP corner. Despite his antagonism toward unions, Reagan's hard line on foreign policy appealed to working-class voters, as did his economic optimism — which was borne out by a lengthy period of economic expansion on his watch.

The white working class had been loyal to Democrats in previous decades largely because of economic policies the party pursued that redistributed income toward lower-income voters. But many of them were put off by Democratic platforms during the 1970s and '80s that seemed to emphasize liberal stances on social and cultural issues. Blue-collar voters had been 12 percent more Democratic than the electorate as a whole in 1948, but by 1972 they were 4 percent less. (There was a similar drop in Democratic support among urban Catholics).[27]

In 1972, when the National Election Survey asked who composed the Democratic Party, respondents still made it sound like it was still the party of the New Deal — the poor, working class, blacks, Catholics and unions. By 1984, responses to the same survey painted a different picture, saying the party was made up of black militants, feminists, civil rights leaders, people on welfare, gays and unions.[28]

Even as Democrats were losing some of their traditional supporters, Republicans were benefiting from the re-emergence of an important force — white evangelical Protestants. They had largely retreated from politics following the battles during the 1920s and '30s over Prohibition and evolution. As late as 1965, the Rev. Jerry Falwell said that pastors should win souls, not concern themselves with fighting communism and political reform.

The liberal decisions of the Supreme Court, particularly in the 1973 *Roe v. Wade* case that legalized abortion, angered evangelicals, however. In May 1979, secular conservative leaders met with Falwell and urged him to form an organization that would mobilize fundamentalists. He did so a month later, founding the Moral Majority.

The following year, Reagan appealed for their support directly, addressing a gathering of 20,000 evangelicals, praising their efforts and questioning evolution. Ralph Reed, later the executive director of the Christian Coalition, which would supersede the Moral Majority as the leading force among Christian-right groups during the 1990s, called the meeting "the wedding ceremony of evangelicals and the Republican Party."[29] Evangelicals in recent election cycles have generally been estimated to represent 40 percent of the GOP primary vote.

Clinton and Bush

Bill Clinton in 1992 would become the only Democratic presidential candidate of the post-Reagan era to carry any Southern states. He won back a larger share of the

> With the rapid growth of Hispanics and other minority groups, some GOP strategists were concerned that their party's dependence on white male voters, in particular, was too limiting. In 2000, Bush sought to portray himself as an inclusive candidate, featuring many black and Hispanic speakers at his nominating convention.

white working-class vote by emphasizing economic issue (his campaign's unofficial slogan was "it's the economy, stupid") and signaled a shift away from "identity politics" by promising to "end welfare as we know it."

But Clinton's success did not translate into victories for his party. Democrats relinquished their 40-year hold on the House in 1994 and lost the Senate as well, as white male voters turned against the party, particularly in the South. By 2004, Clinton's home state of Arkansas was unique among Southern states in sending more Democrats than Republicans to Congress. There were 16 Republican senators from the region that year, compared with just four Democrats.[30]

Although he lost the popular vote in 2000, George W. Bush benefited from the demographic trends that had been moving voters into the Republican column. He carried every Southern state, as well as 74 percent of the evangelical vote.[31] The most certain predictor of support for Bush in both his elections was regular church attendance.

With the rapid growth of Hispanics and other minority groups, some GOP strategists were concerned that their party's dependence on white male voters, in particular, was too limiting. In 2000, Bush sought to portray himself as an inclusive candidate, featuring many black and Hispanic speakers at his nominating convention. He was

AT ISSUE

Do demographic trends favor Democrats?

YES Ruy Teixeira
Visiting fellow, The Brookings Institution

From "The Future of Red, Blue and Purple America," The Brookings Institution, January 2008

A new wave of demographic and geographic change is currently washing over the United States and is sure to have profound effects on our future politics, just as earlier changes helped give birth to the politics we know today. Here is a quick outline of several of the political and demographic trends that are leading to a Democratic and center-left majority in the United States:

- **Immigration and minorities.** Immigration and differential fertility have driven minority voters from about 15 percent of voters in 1990 to 21 percent today, and will produce a voting electorate that is about one-quarter minority by the middle of the next decade. Presently, with some exceptions — such as President Bush's 40 percent support among Hispanics in the 2004 election — these rising constituencies tend to give the Democrats wide margins (69-30 percent among Hispanics and 62-37 percent among Asians in the 2006 congressional elections).
- **Family changes.** Changes in household structure and differences in fertility are reshaping American families. Consider these dramatic trends: Married couples with children now occupy fewer than one in four households. Single women have recently become a majority of all adult women. These trends intersect in increasingly important ways with political behavior. Married voters are far more likely to vote Republican than are unmarried voters, eclipsing the effects of the celebrated gender gap. In the 2006 congressional election, married voters slightly favored Republicans (50-48 percent), while unmarried voters favored Democrats (64-34 percent).
- **Suburbs.** Much will ride on how the changing mix of residents votes in the different parts of suburbia. In 2006, Democratic House pickups in areas like suburban Denver, suburban Philadelphia, Connecticut and southern Florida were powered by coalitions where professionals and minorities took a leading role. Jim Webb's Senate victory in Virginia was largely due to his margin in Northern Virginia's high-tech suburbs.
- **Young voters.** According to one standard definition, 80 million Americans today are Millennials (birth years 1978-1996). By 2008, the number of citizen-eligible Millennial voters will be nearing 50 million. Now they seem to be leaning Democratic. In the 2006 congressional election, the first election in which almost all 18-to-29-year-olds were Millennials, they supported Democrats by a 60-38 percent margin.

NO Michael J. New
Assistant Professor, University of Alabama

Written for CQ Researcher, May 2008

In recent years, many observers have argued that the rising Hispanic population in America will do serious damage to the electoral prospects of the Republican Party. However, these analysts overlook a number of other trends that bode favorably for Republicans. For instance, investors are a reliable Republican constituency. In 1980 only 20 percent of American households owned stock. Today that number is up to 50 percent, and rising. Other groups that consistently vote for Republicans, including gun owners and home-schoolers, are growing rapidly as well. Better yet, many policies that have been advanced by the Republican Party, including concealed carry laws and expanded IRAs, have successfully expanded these Republican constituencies.

Furthermore, the membership trends of various religions should give serious pause to those who think that demographic trends favor Democrats. Indeed, many religious groups whose members are likely to support Republicans, including Evangelical Protestants, Mormons and Orthodox Jews, are seeing their memberships grow. Conversely, religious groups whose memberships are mostly Democrats, including mainline Protestants and Reform Jews, are actually getting smaller. It should also be noted that other important Democratic constituencies, including labor unions, are seeing their memberships shrink in absolute terms as well.

These demographic trends will strengthen a number of political trends that already favor Republicans. For instance, in close presidential elections in 2000 and 2004, President Bush won 30 and 31 states, respectively. Since Republican Senate candidates should be at an advantage in these states, Republicans should eventually accumulate over 60 Senate seats — good for a filibuster-proof majority. The rise of the Internet and talk radio has given conservatives greater ability to promote their ideas, free of interference from the mainstream media.

Finally, there is evidence to suggest that Hispanics may not be a lost cause for the Republican Party. First, Hispanics who are evangelical Protestants and those from Cuba are already likely to support Republican candidates. Furthermore, Republicans have been successful in capturing a large percentage of the Hispanic vote in states like Florida and Texas, which have pro-immigrant governors and less generous welfare benefits.

The best strategy might be to follow the lead of these governors and implement policies that will create and expand Republican constituencies among Hispanic voters. One way this can be done is to continue to pursue policies that will make Hispanics more sensitive toward taxes and less supportive of government programs.

A poll worker in New Orleans signs up a voter last February. Barack Obama has added African-Americans, who typically vote along with lower-income whites in Democratic primaries, to his base among elites. If Obama wins the nomination, it will reflect this historic shift in black voting and also the fact that educated and upper-income voters are growing in number and becoming more Democratic.

also careful not to take as hard a line against immigrants as some members of his party.

But many suburban and highly educated voters began to turn against the GOP, concerned about the party's stances on social issues, such as opposition to stem-cell research, skepticism about evolution and political interference with the decision about keeping alive Terri Schiavo, a brain-dead Florida woman.

Bush's attempts to reach beyond his political base proved futile during his second term, as when the Republican-controlled House in 2006 refused to vote on a moderate Senate-passed immigration bill that had been negotiated with his administration. But what drove down Bush's approval ratings and cost his party control of Congress in 2006 was, primarily, the war in Iraq.

Bush's widely criticized handling of the devastation in New Orleans wrought by Hurricane Katrina erased any small gains his party had made among African-Americans, while a tougher immigration bill passed by the House drove down GOP support among Hispanics from 40 percent in 2004 to 30 percent or less in 2006.[32]

Brother political scientists Earl Black and Merle Black wrote last year, "In modern American politics, a Republican Party dominated by white Protestants faces a Democratic Party in which minorities plus non-Christian whites far outnumber white Protestants."[33]

CURRENT SITUATION
"The Big Sort"

Despite the close balance between the parties in recent years — neither party has enjoyed a large majority in either congressional chamber for years, and no presidential candidate received a majority of the popular vote from 1992 until 2004 — comparatively few geographical areas remain in close contention.

Nationwide, the parties might be nearly tied, but candidates on either side can count on blowouts one way or the other within most counties. Compare the results of the presidential elections of 1976 and 2004, both of which were extremely close. In 1976, fewer than 25 percent of Americans lived in "landslide counties" that one candidate or the other carried by a margin of 20 points or greater. By 2004, nearly half the country — 48.3 percent — lived in a landslide county.[34]

Today, suggests journalist Bill Bishop in his new book *The Big Sort*, "Zip codes have political meaning. . . . As Americans have moved over the past three decades, they have clustered in communities of sameness, among people with similar ways of life, beliefs and, in the end, politics."[35]

It's not that liberals or conservatives ask their real-estate agents for printouts of precinct voting data when they're shopping for houses, but they do make lifestyle choices that place them among people who tend to live — and vote — much the way they do.

"There are lifestyle differences between liberals and conservatives that there weren't 30 years ago," says Notre Dame political scientist David Campbell. "The parties are well sorted ideologically, and we live in an era when it's easy to signal where you stand on these things by the type of car you drive and whether you shop at the farmer's market or Sam's Club. It's a way of constructing an identity, and those identities are playing out in politics."

Political analyst Charles Cook sometimes jokes that Democratic candidates have trouble carrying any district that doesn't include a Starbucks.[36] Rural areas are strongly Republican, cities are Democratic and the two parties fight their major turf wars in the suburbs, with fast-growing outer suburbs favoring the GOP and inner-ring suburbs becoming denser and more Democratic.

Such generalizations have long carried an element of truth, but some experts think the truth grows more compelling with each passing election year. "Even if you drop below the broad regional level, you find that neighborhoods and communities are looking more homogeneous than they ever have before," says Gimpel at the University of Maryland. "You have Republicans settling in around Republicans and Democrats settling around Democrats."

Lack of Competition

Although it's something of a myth that there are Republican "red" or Democratic "blue" states — plenty of states vote one way for president and the opposite for senator or governor — increasingly there are red and blue counties. That's why there are so few competitive House or state legislative seats.

Redistricting has been widely blamed for the fact that few legislative seats — perhaps less than 10 percent — are competitive at either the congressional or state level. It's become normal for a major state such as California to pass through an entire election cycle with none of its legislative seats — U.S. House, state Assembly or state Senate — changing partisan hands.

It's true that partisan redistricting, in which lines are generally drawn by state legislators for both Congress and their own seats, lumps together as many Republicans or Democrats together into districts that heavily favor one party or another. But most political scientists seem to believe that such partisan mapmaking simply exaggerates the natural ideological or partisan sorting that people are already doing by settling within like-minded communities.

In 2004, a third of U.S. voters lived in counties that had voted for the same party in each presidential election dating back all the way to 1968; just under half hadn't switched allegiances since 1980; and 73 percent lived in counties that had voted the same way in every election since 1992 — four in a row.[37]

Along with the geographical sorting, there is also an ideological sorting in terms of media choices, with citizens turning to media that gibe with their established worldview. Conservatives watch Fox News Channel and read blogs such as Instapundit, while liberals tune into National Public Radio and leave comments at DailyKos.com.

Journalist Bishop argues in his book that all this self-sorting amplifies people's natural preferences — that progressives grow more liberal in the exclusive company of left-leaning neighbors and media outlets, with the same "echo chamber" effect pushing conservatives further to the right. He contends it's one of the major reasons for today's heated partisan bickering and lack of interparty cooperation.

"Like-minded, homogeneous groups squelch dissent, grow more extreme in their thinking and ignore evidence that their positions are wrong," Bishop writes. "As a result, we now live in a giant feedback loop."[38]

Picking Out Raisins

Candidates and consultants are well aware of the way counties or districts are likely to favor one party or another. In recent election years, they have sought to "microtarget" voters — tailoring messages to appeal to particular groups of voters within a community, rather than the community as a whole.

Every recent election cycle seems to bring about talk of new niche demographic groups who are being courted by candidates and consultants, such as "angry white males," "soccer moms" and "Nascar dads." Microtargeting represents an effort to appeal to dozens of different demographic groups, generally defined by their lifestyle and consumer choices.

Only a few years ago, party databases still targeted voters solely by precinct. Now they crack open each subdivision and make a good guess about which residents are socially liberal and which ones are anti-tax conservatives. Sophisticated campaigns are trying to become more precise with their messages, as well. Rather than sending out six or seven pieces of mail districtwide, they may send 20 different mailings to five different groups, such as veterans, seniors or gun owners.

How do they know which voter should get which piece of mail — and, more important, which swing voters should have the candidate show up personally on their doorsteps? Consultants such as Mark Grebner, an Ingham County commissioner in Michigan, look at every piece of information they can find about each voter — their ethnicity; whether they live in a precinct that turns out for hot Democratic primaries but not Republican ones; which magazines they subscribe to; and whether they ever have signed a petition to put an initiative or a candidate on a ballot. (To learn more about voters for his clients in Wisconsin, where he has less data, Grebner pays a fellow in Bangladesh to read every letter to the editor in state papers via the Web and code them according to likely party preference.)

Grebner takes all this information, runs a bunch of statistical analyses and assigns a percentage to each voter's likelihood of voting Democratic. Further narrowing the universe of potentially receptive voters is what winning close campaigns is all about. "If you don't want raisins in your cereal," Grebner says, "buy cereal that doesn't have raisins — don't pick them out one at a time."

OUTLOOK
Creating a New Map

In Bishop's analysis, it's Republicans who "were the winners in the big sort." From 1980 to 2006, Republican counties outgrew Democratic ones, on average, by more than 1 million people a year. Nearly all of that was due to people moving in, not natural population growth. "From 1990 to 2006 alone, 13 million people moved from Democratic to Republican counties."[39]

Republicans have taken advantage of the fact that much recent domestic migration has been toward the South and West, lending them added advantages in the Electoral College. Brookings demographer Frey predicts that the states that voted for Bush in 2004 will gain an additional 17 electoral votes (and House seats) by 2030.[40]

"In 2012, we gain a 15-electoral-vote advantage over the Democrats, on top of the earlier advantage," says GOP consultant Morgan. "That leaves the Dems really scrambling, like 270 [electoral votes] would be out of reach for them."

That is based on two assumptions. The first is that recent state population trends will continue through the rest of the decade, which is not necessarily the case. "The increase we've had in population growth in a lot of areas has just evaporated, except for Arizona and Texas," says Clark Bensen, another Republican consultant.

The other assumption is that states will continue to vote the way they have in the past. That has seemed like a good bet through the early part of this decade, with only three small states — New Hampshire, Iowa and New Mexico — switching their votes between 2000 and 2004. But nothing in politics is static.

Although Brookings scholar and author Teixeira is optimistic that demographic trends favor Democrats, including increasing support from Hispanics and "millennials" now in their 20s, the fact that parts of the electorate are changing can cause an opposite reaction in other parts. Republicans benefited from the rise of the Christian Right and their gains in the South, but these gains cost them support among moderate voters in the Northeast and suburbs in general.

"The very fact that the Democrats are benefiting from demographic trends, such as the rise of single women, could drive other voters into the arms of Republicans," he says. "They might not like Democrats as the party of single people."

Teixeira and other Democrats believe that this year's election represents a chance for their party not only to consolidate the demographic trends that have been breaking their way but also to capitalize on the unpopularity of President Bush, the war in Iraq and uncertainty about the economy.

"Even though McCain was probably the best person Republicans could nominate, I think the Democrats win no matter who ends up being the nominee, Clinton or Obama," says Guerra, the Loyola Marymount political scientist. "It's not only the changing demographics that is going to reward Democrats. We get tired of a certain party, and we're going to punish Republicans for their policies, even if McCain was not always on their side."

But as they wrap up the primary season, even Democrats are debating whether they might blow an election in which they appear to have many advantages. A lot of that debate comes down to the question of demographics. If Clinton is the nominee, African-Americans and the young will not be as motivated as they would be by an Obama candidacy. But Obama has yet to prove he can carry white working-class voters in the preponderance of swing states.

Head-to-head polls have shown as many as 14 states breaking different ways, depending on the Democratic nominee. Political analyst Rhodes Cook suggests that Clinton would likely carry 18 to 22 states — roughly the same group that Al Gore carried in 2000 and John Kerry won in 2004. Cook predicts that Obama, however, might win as many as 30 states — or as few as 10.

Although Obama lost the Pennsylvania primary, he carried the state's 300,000 newly registered Democrats by about 20 points. Republican registrations in the state were down by 70,000. Obama has launched a voter-registration effort that seeks to replicate such new-minted support in all 50 states.

"Hillary goes deeper and stronger in the Democratic base than Obama, but her challenge is that she doesn't go as wide," said Peter Hart, a Democratic pollster. "Obama goes much further reaching into the independent and Republican vote, and has a greater chance of creating a new electoral map for the Democrats."[41]

UPDATE

Voting patterns in the election of Barack Obama to the presidency in November 2008 reflected several major changes in the U.S. electorate, according to experts and exit polls.

The presence of a black candidate, not surprisingly, generated expectations for a huge turnout of black voters. But according to exit polls, while more blacks voted than in recent years, their share of the voting electorate did not increase significantly. Indeed, while black voters accounted for 11 percent of the votes in 2004 they accounted for 13 percent in 2008, an increase of only 2 percentage points.[42]

And while some analysts expected Obama to bring out the youth vote in unprecedented numbers, the share of the votes cast by those ages 18-29 rose only a single percentage point between 2004 and 2008, from 17 percent to 18 percent.

Although Obama didn't bring out significantly greater numbers of black and young voters, however, he did attract more of those voters to the Democratic Party. From 2004 to 2008, the Democrats' share of the black vote rose seven points, while the party's share of the youth vote jumped 13 points.[43]

The biggest shift took place among Latino voters. Latinos moved to Obama from the Republican Party in large numbers, ensuring an Obama victory in the battleground states of Colorado, New Mexico and Nevada. Obama also attracted a majority of the Latino vote in Florida, the first time a Democrat has done that since 1988.

Hispanic Power

Indeed, Obama's support among Hispanic voters increased by 14 points compared with support for the Democratic nominee, Sen. John Kerry of Massachusetts, in 2004 — the biggest shift toward the Democrats by any voter group. Nationwide, Hispanics favored Obama over the Republican candidate, Sen. John McCain of Arizona, 61 percent to 38 percent.[44]

"They really delivered," says Efrain Escobedo, director of civic engagement at the National Association of Latino Elected Officials, a bipartisan group that ran voter-registration drives across the country. "This is an electorate that now understands the importance of voting, and they made a significant shift in the political landscape."[45]

Obama also did well with white voters. McCain attracted a majority in only one category of voters: those over age 60. Although whites made up just under three-quarters of the voters, it was their smallest share ever in a presidential election.[46]

Obama attracted significant support from voters, particularly in the Midwest, who generally align with conservative candidates but who voted for the Democratic candidate primarily out of frustration with the Bush administration. But some commentators believe voting patterns in the 2008 race reflect more far-reaching changes than short-term misgivings about the prior administration.

"Even though Obama's victory was nowhere near as numerically lopsided as Franklin D. Roosevelt's in 1932, his margins among decisive and growing constituencies make clear that this was a genuinely realigning election," wrote *Washington Post* columnist Harold Meyerson.[47]

Government's Role

In addition to the growing Latino vote, Meyerson pointed to Obama's strong support among the growing ranks of well-educated professionals. "The final element of this realignment is the shift in public sentiment toward governmental activism — a shift in good measure occasioned by our long-term economic decline and short-term economic collapse," wrote Meyerson, noting exit polls that showed that 51 percent of Americans believed government "should do more" than it is doing — a reversal of the Reagan-era majorities that believed government should do less.

While Obama's campaign may have realigned the electorate, there already has been a strong counter-reaction from the right in the form of a loosely knit political movement known as the Tea Party.

Even before the 2008 election, apparently unorganized conservatives evoked the rebelliousness of the

Republican presidential candidate John McCain and his running mate, then-Alaska Gov. Sarah Palin, attend a campaign event at Van Dyke Park in Fairfax, Va., on Sept. 10, 2008.

Boston Tea Party and used "tea party" symbols and labels at political rallies protesting policy positions of Obama and Sen. Hillary Rodham Clinton, his primary competitor for the Democratic presidential nomination. This year, one analyst described the Tea Party as being comprised of "hundreds of local groups, three loose national networks with Tea Party in their titles and allied conservative groups."[48]

"Members of the professional political class in Washington are uncertain whether they're observing a loud-mouthed flash in the pan or the birth of an important and lasting national movement," wrote Joseph J. Schatz in *CQ Weekly*. "Either way, the tea partiers' vituperative and vocal activism has accumulated into the strongest new force on the electoral landscape for this year and for both parties."[49]

Indeed, the Tea Party movement was credited with the biggest political upset since 2008, the election of Republican Scott P. Brown to the Senate seat left empty by the death of Sen. Edward M. Kennedy in August 2009. Brown's victory marked the first time in 38 years the seat had been held by a Republican.

Although members of the Tea Party movement generally favor Republican candidates, they tend to support policies even more conservative than many Republicans, and they are not disposed to compromise. For that reason, the Tea Party has proved problematic for the GOP.

"Urged on by prominent conservative commentators such as Glenn Beck and courted by Sarah Palin and other national Republican figures, tea party-affiliated groups have the mainstream GOP looking over its collective shoulder, more concerned than ever about the price of dealing with Democrats," wrote Schatz.[50]

Tea Party Influence

While Tea Party supporters tend to have more politically conservative views than the general public, they are demographically very much in the mainstream. According to the Gallup Poll News Service, "compared with average Americans, supporters are slightly more likely to be male and less likely to be lower-income. In several other respects, however — their age, educational background, employment status, and race — Tea Partiers are quite representative of the public at large."[51]

Despite the Tea Party movement's growing numbers and influence, some analysts say that diffuse nature may prevent it from having a lasting impact.

"It's like an amoeba. Its strength is there isn't a structure to collapse. Their strength is that they're coming at you in all different directions and different ways, and if there's a crack they're going to work their way into it and try to get what they want done," said Charles Zelden, a professor of history and legal studies at Nova Southeastern University in South Florida. "The weakness is they don't have a structure. Amoebas don't stand up very well. Without a skeleton, a structure, they just sort of sit there."[52]

Indeed, as those supported by the Tea Party have experienced political success and have had to endure media scrutiny and take specific positions on issues, they have generated controversy both within the movement and in broader Republican circles.

When Rand Paul, a Tea Party candidate, won the Republican senate nomination in Kentucky in May 2010, his suggestion that the Civil Rights Act of 1964 shouldn't apply to private businesses generated controversy within his own party. "The case of Mr. Paul . . . shows the risks that have emerged as new figures move to the forefront of conservative politics, as candidates with little experience and sometimes unorthodox policy positions face the kind of scrutiny and pressure that could trip up even the most experienced politicians," wrote Adam Nagourney and Carl Hulse of *The New York Times*.[53]

Similarly, when Sen. Brown joined four other Republicans in voting to remove procedural hurdles blocking a $15 billion job-creation package being pushed by Democrats, he was called "Benedict Brown" by some in the movement. "Brown, whose prospects for winning a full term in two years will almost surely require him to toe a moderate line, tried to play down his apparent apostasy, urging his critics to 'read the bill' and learn that it wouldn't raise taxes," wrote Schatz.[54]

Mid-Term Pressure

As the Democratic and Republican parties approach the mid-term election in November 2010, they face an electorate that is to an unusual degree feeling pressed by multiple issues.

"The generation-high jobless rate, coupled with the erosion of the financial safety net over some years, is elevating middle-class voter anxiety and raising doubts with the public about Washington's ability to help," wrote Clea Benson of *CQ Weekly*. "Between now and Election Day on Nov. 2, jobs and the economy will be the defining issue for voters, but it isn't evident there is much lawmakers and government officials can do to change things anytime soon."[55]

Analysts also expect that, as is common with mid-term elections, local issues will have more impact on the voting electorate than national issues.

"For a voter sitting out there, there is not just one focal point to this election. There are lots of things that are making people angry right now," Democratic pollster Geoff Garin said. "It's clear that there are lots of moving parts to this election that have and will affect individual races. It's not a neat, simple story line."[56]

One trend, however, is expected to continue: Despite significant shifts in the electorate since the election of 2008, poor and minority groups will remain underrepresented at the polls.

"The unregistered and non-voting populations remain disproportionately composed of low-income and minority Americans," concluded a recent report of Project Vote, a nonprofit voter advocacy group.[57] And that's especially true for mid-term elections, which don't attract the same level of media attention as presidential elections, says the report.

NOTES

1. Alan Greenblatt, "The Partisan Divide," *CQ Researcher*, April 30, 2004, pp. 373-396.
2. Kathy Kiely and Jill Lawrence, "Clinton Makes Case for Staying In," *USA Today*, May 8, 2008, p. 1A.
3. Paul Krugman, "Self-Inflicted Confusion," *The New York Times*, April 25, 2008, p. A27.
4. Jonathan Weisman and Matthew Mosk, "Party Fears Racial Divide," *The Washington Post*, April 26, 2008, p. A1.
5. Eli Saslow, "Democrats Registering in Record Numbers," *The Washington Post*, April 28, 2008, p. A1.
6. Thomas B. Edsall, "Census a Clarion Call for Democrats, GOP," *The Washington Post*, July 8, 2001, p. A5.
7. Susan Page, "GOP Coalition Fractured by Opposition to War," *USA Today*, Nov. 8, 2006, p. 1A.
8. Larry J. Sabato, *The Sixth-Year Itch* (2008), p. 22. For background, see the following *CQ Researcher* reports: David Masci, "Latinos' Future," Oct. 17, 2003, pp. 869-892; Alan Greenblatt, "Race in America," July 11, 2003, pp. 593-624, and Nadine Cohodas, "Electing Minorities," Aug. 12, 1994, pp. 697-720.
9. Bill Boyarsky, "Courting the White Vote," *Truthdig*, April 24, 2008, www.truthdig.com/report/item/20080425_courting_the_white_vote/.
10. Earl Black and Merle Black, *Divided America* (2007), p. 10.
11. Thomas F. Shaller, "So Long, White Boy," *Salon*, Sept. 17, 2007, www.salon.com/opinion/feature/2007/09/17/white_man/.
12. Alan Greenblatt, "Slow March to the Polls," *Governing*, June 2006, p. 17.
13. Ronald Brownstein and Richard Rainey, "GOP Plants Flag on New Voting Frontier," *Los Angeles Times*, Nov. 22, 2004, p. A1.
14. David Mark, "The Battle Over Suburban, Exurban Vote," *Politico*, Dec. 4, 2007. Mary H. Cooper, "Smart Growth," *CQ Researcher*, May 28, 2004, pp. 469-492.

15. Jill Lawrence, "Democratic Gains in Suburbs Spell Trouble for GOP," *USA Today*, Nov. 26, 2006, p. 6A.
16. Scott Keeter *et al*, "Gen Dems: The Party's Advantage Among Young Voters Widens," Pew Research Center for the People & the Press, April 28, 2008.
17. "A Portrait of 'Generation Next': How Young People View Their Lives, Futures and Politics," Pew Research Center for the People & the Press, Jan. 9, 2007; available at http://people-press.org/reports/pdf/300.pdf.
18. Sabato, *op. cit.*, p. 22.
19. Michiko Kakutani, "Why Are These Democrats Smiling? It's Cyclical," *The New York Times*, April 22, 2008, p. E7.
20. "Obama Dominating Highly-Charged Youth Vote in Presidential Race, Harvard Poll Finds," Harvard Institute of Politics, news release April 24, 2008.
21. Everett Carll Ladd Jr., "The Shifting Party Coalitions, 1932 to 1976," in Seymour Martin Lipset, ed., *Emerging Coalitions in American Politics* (1978), p. 83.
22. Kenneth S. Baer, *Reinventing Democrats* (2000), p. 14.
23. Barbara Sinclair, *Party Wars* (2006), p. 17.
24. James Boyd, "Nixon's Southern Strategy," *The New York Times*, May 17, 1970, p. 215.
25. Kevin Phillips, *The Emerging Republican Majority* (1969), p. 25.
26. Kenneth Jost and Greg Giroux, "Electoral College," *CQ Researcher*, Dec. 8, 2000, pp. 977-1008.
27. Ladd, *op. cit.*, p. 94.
28. Baer, *op. cit.*, p. 35.
29. Sinclair, *op. cit.*, p. 49.
30. *Ibid.*, p. 14.
31. *Ibid.*, p. 51.
32. "Latinos and the 2006 Midterm Election," Pew Hispanic Center, Nov. 27, 2006.
33. Black and Black, *op. cit.*, p. 29.
34. Bill Bishop, *The Big Sort* (2008), p. 6.
35. *Ibid.*, p. 5.
36. Alan Greenblatt, "Whatever Happened to Competitive Elections?", *Governing*, October 2004, p. 22.
37. Bishop, *op. cit.*, p. 45.
38. *Ibid.*, p. 39.
39. *Ibid.*, p. 56.
40. William H. Frey, "The Electoral College Moves to the Sun Belt," The Brookings Institution, May 2005, p. 4.
41. Patrick Healy, "For Democrats, Questions Over Race and Electability," *The New York Times*, April 24, 2008, p. A1.
42. Chris Cillizza, "Myths About One Mythic Election," *The Washington Post*, Nov. 16, 2008, p. B3.
43. *Ibid.*
44. Julia Preston, "What Got Obama Elected," *The New York Times*, Nov. 7, 2008, p. A24.
45. *Ibid.*
46. Marjorie Connelly, "Dissecting the Changing Electorate," *The New York Times*, Nov. 9, 2008, WK5.
47. Harold Meyerson, "A Real Realignment," *The Washington Post*, Nov. 7, 2008, p. A19.
48. Joseph J. Schatz, "Reading the Tea Leaves at the Capitol," *CQ Weekly*, Feb. 28, 2010.
49. *Ibid.*
50. *Ibid.*
51. Lydia Saad, "Tea Partiers Are Fairly Mainstream in Their Demographics; Skew right politically, but have typical profile by age, education, and employment," Gallup Poll News Service, April 5, 2010, www.gallup.com/poll/ 127181/Tea-Partiers-Fairly-Mainstream-Demo graphics.aspx?utm_source=alert&utm_medium= email&utm_campaign=syndication&utm_con tent=morelink&utm_term= All+Gallup+Head lines+-+Politics#1.
52. Anthony Man, "November or Beyond? Tea Party Faces Choices; As Grassroots Movement Grows, So Do Questions About Direction," *Fort Lauderdale Sun-Sentinel*, July 4, 2010, p. 1B.
53. Adam Nagourney and Carl Hulse, "Tea Party Pick Causes Uproar on Civil Rights," *The New York Times*, May 21, 2010, p. A1.
54. Schatz, *op. cit.*
55. Clea Benson, "The Price of Perception," *CQ Weekly*, Jan. 17, 2010.

56. Dan Balz, " 'Angry electorate' could be unpredictable at polls this fall," *The Washington Post*, June 13, 2010, p. A2.

57. Douglas R. Hess and Jody Herman, "Representational Bias in the 2008 Electorate," Project Vote, November 2009, http://projectvote.org/ reports-on-the-electorate-/440.html.

BIBLIOGRAPHY

Books

Bishop, Bill, with Robert G. Cushing, *The Big Sort: Why the Clustering of Like-Minded America is Tearing Us Apart*, **Houghton Mifflin, 2008.**
A journalist shows how many more Republicans and Democrats are moving into communities that are partisan enclaves, contributing to the polarization of U.S. politics.

Bowman, Karlyn, and Ruy Teixeira, eds., *Red Blue and Purple America; The Future of Election Demographics*, **Brooking Institution Press (forthcoming).**
In a book coming this fall, a group of political scientists and demographers examine how trends in religion, geography, immigration and income and class are affecting voting habits.

Fisher, Claude S., and Michael Hout, *Century of Difference: How America Changed in the Last Hundred Years*, **Russell Sage Foundation, 2006.**
University of California, Berkeley sociologists draw on census data and polling surveys to present a comprehensive description of demographic, economic and cultural changes since 1900.

Singer, Audrey, Susan W. Hardwick and Caroline B. Brettell, eds., *Twenty-First Century Gateways: Immigrant Immigration in Suburban America*, **Brookings Institution Press, 2008.**
Academic authors examine the impact of immigrants no longer settling in urban cores so much as the suburbs.

Articles

Brownstein, Ron, "The Warrior and the Priest," *Los Angeles Times*, **March 25, 2007, p. M1.**
An influential column argues Barack Obama would appeal to upscale voters while Hillary Clinton would assume the role of "warrior" defending the interests of blue-collar voters.

Curry, Tom, "How Reagan Hobbled the Democrats," MSNBC.com, June 7, 2004, www.msnbc.msn.com/id/5151912/.
Curry examines how the Republican president captured lower- and middle-income whites and the South through clear economic and foreign policies.

Frum, David, "Why the GOP Lost the Youth Vote," *USA Today*, **April 9, 2008, p. 12A.**
A former speechwriter for President George W. Bush says Republicans must pay more attention to payroll taxes and environmental and social issues to woo young voters.

Healy, Patrick, "For Democrats, Questions Over Race and Electability," *The New York Times*, **April 24, 2008, p. A1.**
The split among Democratic primary voters has party leaders debating who has the best chance to prevail in the fall.

Malanga, Steven, "The Rainbow Coalition Evaporates," *City Journal*, **Winter 2008.**
A conservative author examines tensions between African-Americans and immigrants in urban neighborhoods.

Mark, David, "The Battle Over Suburban, Exurban Vote," *Politico*, **Dec. 4, 2007.**
A political journalist looks at how emerging suburbs have become a contested battleground.

Schaller, Thomas F., "So Long, White Boy," *Salon*, **Sept. 17, 2007.**
White males have abandoned the Democrats, so party candidates should learn to win without their support.

Reports and Studies

Frey, William H., "The Electoral College Moves to the Sun Belt," The Brookings Institution Research Brief, May 2005.
Sun Belt states, which had a nearly equal amount of electoral votes as the Northeast and Midwest in 1972, will have 146 more by 2030.

Keeter, Scott, Juliana Horowitz and Alex Tyson, "Gen Dems: The Party's Advantage Among Young Voters Widens," Pew Research Center for the People & the

Press, April 28, 2008, http://pewresearch.org/pubs/813/gen-dems.
Fifty-eight percent of voters under 30 are leaning toward the Democrats, fueling party growth much as young voters drove GOP growth during the 1990s.

Marcelo, Karlo Barrios, *et al.*, "Young Voter Registration and Turnout Trends," Rock the Vote and the Center for Information & Research on Civic Learning and Engagement, February 2008.
The turnout of young voters — typically low since 18-year-olds got the vote in 1972 — rose in both the 2004 and 2006 elections and is likely to increase again this year.

McKee, Seth C. and Daron S. Shaw, "Suburban Voting in Presidential Elections," *Presidential Studies Quarterly*, March 2003.
The decisive suburban vote edged away from Republican candidates during the 1990s in the North, but not in the South.

Putnam, Robert D., "E Pluribus Unum: Diversity and Community in the Twenty-First Century," *Scandinavian Political Studies*, June 2007, p. 137.
Based on a nationwide survey, the Harvard political scientist finds decreased levels of trust and social participation in communities that are more diverse.

For More Information

American Enterprise Institute, 1150 17th St., N.W., Washington, DC 20036; (202) 862-5800; www.aei.org. A conservative public policy think tank that conducts research and education on politics, economics and social welfare.

Atlas of U.S. Elections; uselectionatlas.org. A Web site providing comprehensive mapping of election results by state, city and county.

Brookings Institution, 1775 Massachusetts Ave., N.W., Washington, DC 20036; (202) 797-6000; www.brookings.edu. A centrist think tank that issues regular reports on politics, immigration and demographics through its Metropolitan Policy and Governance Studies programs.

Joint Center for Political and Economics Studies, 1090 Vermont Ave., N.W., Suite 1100, Washington, DC 20005; (202) 789-3500; (202) 789-3500; www.jointcenter.org. Studies issues of importance to African-Americans.

Patchwork Nation Project, *The Christian Science Monitor*, 210 Massachusetts Ave., Boston, MA 02115; (617) 450-2300; www.csmonitor.com/patchworknation. Tracks political demographic information and hosts blogs by residents of 11 representative types of communities.

Pew Research Center for The People & The Press, 1615 L St., N.W., Suite 700, Washington, DC 20036; (202) 419-4350; people-press.org. Conducts public opinion polls and research on media and political issues.

UCLA Higher Education Research Institute, 3005 Moore Hall/Box 951521, Los Angeles, CA 90095; (310) 825-1925; www.gseis.ucla.edu/heri/. Has conducted nationwide surveys of college freshmen for more than 40 years.

U.S. Census Bureau, 4600 Silver Hill Rd., Suitland, MD 20746; (202) 501-5400; www.census.gov. The primary source for information about the U.S. population.

William C. Velásquez Institute, 206 Lombard St., First Floor, San Antonio, TX 78226; (210) 992-3118; www.wcvi.org. Conducts research as part of its mission of improving the level of political participation among Latinos.

3

Census Controversy

Thomas J. Billitteri

Census workers kick off the 2010 census at a rally in New York City's Times Square on Jan. 4. Censuses have been controversial since the first one in 1790, and this year's is no exception. Partisans on the right and left raised questions about a range of issues, including accuracy, invasion of privacy, counting of same-sex couples and U.S. immigration policy.

From *CQ Researcher*,
May 14, 2010.

First, the good news: When the Pew Research Center asked Americans in March for their views about the 2010 U.S. census, most respondents said they were ready to participate in the once-every-decade portrait of the national population.[1]

Now the not-so-good news: The positive public response masked an angry debate over this year's census, including concerns about its accuracy. "This is probably the most polarized, political census I've seen," says Jacqueline Byers, director of research and outreach at the National Association of Counties and a veteran of four censuses.

As the census moved into full swing this spring, the decennial ritual became a lens through which partisans on both the right and left filtered their views on a range of policy issues. Ultraconservative Republicans, for example, criticized the census as an unconstitutional intrusion on privacy. Evangelical Latino pastors urged undocumented immigrants to boycott the count to protest congressional inaction on immigration reform. Liberals hailed a new census policy allowing same-sex couples to be counted as married; some conservatives called it political pandering.[2] Even the census form's question on racial background has sparked debate.

In fact, every census — going back to the first one in 1790 — has been controversial. That's no surprise, given the political power and money at stake: Census counts are used to apportion congressional seats, redraw congressional, state and local legislative districts, and, according to a new study, allocate $447 billion in federal assistance to states and localities.[3]

The 2010 census is the most expensive ever at an estimated cost of $14.5 billion, but its impact on government outlays will be vast. "The outsized influence of census statistics on federal funding indicates the enormous return on taxpayer investment in federal statistics," Brooking Institution fellow Andrew Reamer wrote. "One way to think about this is that the $14 billion life-cycle cost of the 2010 census will enable the fair allocation of nearly $5 trillion in funds over the coming decade (not adjusting for inflation or other changes)."[4]

Yet the census has faced myriad logistical and ideological challenges.

Last year a government report said "uncertainties" surrounded the Census Bureau's readiness for the 2010 census.[5] One problem concerned a planned technical innovation: the use of special hand-held computers to verify addresses and conduct follow-up interviews with non-responding households. The devices didn't work as hoped, however, and are being used only for address verification, forcing the bureau to do pencil-and-paper follow-up interviews. And congressional squabbling over the Obama administration's appointment of a new secretary at the Commerce Department, which oversees the Census Bureau, and confirmation of a new bureau director disrupted planning.

Still, census officials are optimistic about the 2010 count and in late April were citing an encouraging sign: 72 percent of census forms had been returned by households that received them, matching the rate in the 2000 census.[6]

"Response rates in surveys have declined each year throughout the Western world," bureau director Robert M. Groves wrote in his blog. "I fully expected the census to achieve lower participation rates this decade than it did in 2000. It basically didn't happen." Even so, he added, "there is much hard work ahead to follow up on the approximately 48 million households that did not mail back a form," or didn't receive one, "and risks remain."[7]

The bureau made several significant changes this year, in part to encourage a stronger response. For example, after employing a paid advertising campaign for the first time in the 2000 census, the bureau increased its advertising and promotion efforts for the 2010 count to a total of $340 million — inviting criticism from budget hawks. As of May, a census official said the bureau spent $171 million for TV, radio, digital, print and outdoor advertising in 28 languages — including television ads before and during the Super Bowl. The bureau also sponsored a NASCAR race car and a 13-vehicle nationwide promotional road tour. The bureau also has used the Internet to boost response rates, offering, among other things, an interactive map that tracks community participation rates.[8] Certain areas of the country are receiving questionnaires in both English and Spanish.[9]

But perhaps the most far-reaching change has to do with the questionnaire itself. In another effort to encourage response, the bureau eliminated the traditional detailed "long form" survey on demographic, housing and economic factors sent to about a sixth of households since 1960. Instead, a brief 10-question form is being sent to every household. To replace the data collected by the old long form, the Census Bureau is using a separate questionnaire, the American Community Survey (ACS), which is sent to about 250,000 households each month, providing researchers with a steady flow of "rolling" socio-economic data throughout the decade rather than a once-per-decade snapshot.

For demographers, statisticians and scholars, the change is huge — and not without some anxiety. In the short term, researchers say the switch will force them to learn how to use the rolling data and reconcile it with decennial statistics gathered by the old long form. Some worry the new ACS survey sample size may curtail the amount of useful data. But ultimately, many say, the change will be beneficial. The switch will be "extremely positive, even transforming," because it will provide more timely data, asserts Kenneth Prewitt, Census Bureau director in the Clinton administration and now a professor of public affairs at Columbia University.

Against the backdrop of operational challenges and technical change, the 2010 census has sparked bitter partisanship, raising concern that some Americans might not participate in the count even though federal law makes it mandatory to do so.

Non-cooperation costs the taxpayers heavily. The government saves $85 million for each percentage-point increase in the mail-back response rate for this year's census, Groves noted. When households don't complete a form in a timely way, the bureau must send out paid "enumerators" — some 635,000 temporary workers this year — to knock on doors and collect the information firsthand. On average, it costs 42 cents when people mail back their form, but $57 for a census taker's visit.[10]

Heightening public wariness of the census has been a tide of conservative rhetoric raising the specter of unwarranted government intrusion. U.S. Rep. Michele Bachman, R-Minn., vowed not to provide any information except the number of people in her household, claiming last year that census questions had become "very intricate, very personal."[11] Rep. Ron Paul, R-Texas, the only House member to oppose a resolution urging census participation, opined that the census "was never intended to serve as a vehicle for gathering personal information on citizens."[12] And Republican blogger Erick Erickson, founder of the conservative website RedState.com, said he would pull out a shotgun to scare away a census worker who showed up at his house. "We are becoming enslaved by the government," he declared.[13]

But Rep. Patrick McHenry, R-N.C., warned against such anti-census rhetoric. Boycotting the census "offends me as an American patriot," he said, warning of potential negative consequences for the GOP. Writing on RedState.com, he said he worried about "blatant misinformation coming from otherwise well-meaning conservatives" who "are helping big-government liberals by discouraging fellow conservatives from filling out their census forms." Not responding to the census would "reduce conservatives' power in elections, allow Democrats to draw more favorable congressional boundaries and help put more tax-hiking politicians in office," he wrote.[14]

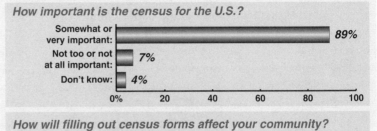

Most Americans Support 2010 Census

Most people think the census will benefit their communities and are willing to fill out their forms. Nearly 90 percent of Americans consider the census important.

How important is the census for the U.S.?
- Somewhat or very important: 89%
- Not too or not at all important: 7%
- Don't know: 4%

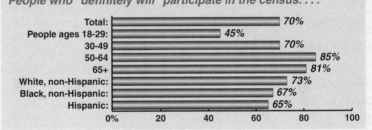

How will filling out census forms affect your community?
- Benefit community: 62%
- Harm community: 3%
- Neither benefit nor harm: 29%
- Don't know/other: 6%

People who "definitely will" participate in the census....
- Total: 70%
- People ages 18-29: 45%
- 30-49: 70%
- 50-64: 85%
- 65+: 81%
- White, non-Hispanic: 73%
- Black, non-Hispanic: 67%
- Hispanic: 65%

Source: "With Growing Awareness of Census, Most Ready to Fill Out Forms," Pew Research Center for the People & the Press, March 2010

Of course, Americans of every political persuasion sometimes balk at filling out census forms. Steven Jost, associate director of communications for the Census Bureau, said the challenges in conducting the census "go across the whole demography of our country."

In researching public attitudes toward the census, he found that "about 19 percent of the people we interviewed . . . are just cynical about government. And when we looked at the makeup of that cynical fifth, it was identical to the makeup of the population as a whole — age, race, gender, education, income levels. We're in a tough environment in our country now with mistrust of government, and we happen to be the face of the government right now."[15]

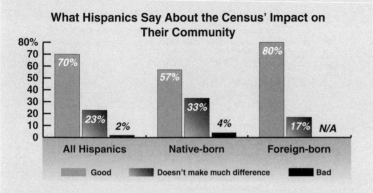

Hispanics' Support for Census Varies

Four-fifths of foreign-born Hispanics in the United States think the census is good for their communities, compared with less than 60 percent of native-born Hispanics.

What Hispanics Say About the Census' Impact on Their Community

All Hispanics: Good 70%, Doesn't make much difference 23%, Bad 2%
Native-born: Good 57%, Doesn't make much difference 33%, Bad 4%
Foreign-born: Good 80%, Doesn't make much difference 17%, Bad N/A

Source: "Latinos and the 2010 Census: The Foreign Born Are More Positive," Pew Hispanic Center, April 1, 2010

As this year's census controversy heats up, here are some of the questions being asked:

Will the census be accurate?

A key goal of this year's census marketing blitz has been to persuade as many people as possible to participate. But getting an accurate count isn't easy. Undercounting is a recurring challenge for the Census Bureau, especially among minorities, low-income households, renters and immigrants.[16] The political implications of that are high, because people in those categories tend to vote Democratic. Double-counting people can be a problem, too.

The 1990 census produced a net undercount — the difference between incorrect omissions and incorrect inclusions — of about 4 million people, or 1.6 percent of the population, but the rate was far higher for blacks (4.6 percent), Hispanics (5.0 percent) and children (3.2 percent). The rate for whites was 0.7 percent.[17]

The 2000 census did a better job, with the undercount rate for blacks falling to 1.8 percent and for Hispanics to 0.7 percent.[18] But for the first time in history, the census had a net overcount. It double-counted nearly 5.8 million people, helping create a net overcount of 1.3 million.[19] Overcounts can happen when, for instance, a college student is tallied at a dorm and counted again by parents back home. This year's form warns households not to count college students, soldiers or others who are living separately but may come home later.

Many census experts are optimistic about this year's count. "I think it will be very accurate," says Brown University demographer John Logan, who directs a program on the 2010 census for the Russell Sage Foundation, a New York research center. "They've done a very professional job and are rolling with the punches," he says of the Census Bureau.

Still, the bureau faces several challenges in arriving at a reliable count. One is the nation's growing immigrant population — legal and illegal — both of which the census tallies.

To be sure, many immigrants are highly supportive of the census — foreign-born immigrants all the more so. The Pew Hispanic Center found in a March poll that 85 percent of Hispanics said they had already sent in their census form or definitely would do so. The return rate for foreign-born Hispanics was 91 percent and for native-born Hispanics 78 percent. What's more, 69 percent of foreign-born Hispanics correctly said the census can't be used to determine legal status, compared with 57 percent of native-born Hispanics.[20]

Even so, experts are concerned that many immigrants may be wary of participating. "There's a huge fear factor," says Prewitt, the former Census Bureau director. Contributing to that fear, he says, are such actions as Arizona's passage last month of a strict new law aimed at identifying and deporting illegal immigrants.[21]

"You can say over and over that the census is confidential, but in parts of the country that message is very hard to communicate," says Prewitt. He expects it to be "much, much harder to count the undocumented" this year "because of a serious change in the environment" surrounding immigration.

Angelo Falcón, president of the National Institute for Latino Policy, a New York City-based think tank, says he is sure "there will be an undercount of Latinos" — due both to the fear factor and the difficulty of counting some demographic groups. "People are trying to get the word out locally" about the census, Falcón says. "We're hoping there aren't any further problems in terms of an anti-immigrant sentiment or the Department of Homeland Security doesn't have any major high-profile raids" during the census count. "Those types of things can affect whether people want to cooperate or not." And as the Census Bureau sends workers to neighborhoods to contact non-responding households, Falcón says, "it will be a test to see if the bureau did a good job in hiring people from those same neighborhoods" so residents will be willing to let the census workers into their homes.

Another roadblock to census accuracy is the difficulty of locating people in certain locales. For example, in hurricane-ravaged New Orleans, "determining how many people live [there] will not be an easy task, given the thousands who are still homeless or living with relatives as they await permanent housing," *The New York Times* noted. The newspaper added that the Census Bureau was "allowing some unconventional counting practices," such as distributing forms to people who are not at verified addresses.[22]

The fragile national economy also can upset population counts in several ways. With unemployment in the 10 percent range, some people have left home in search of work and are hard to pin down. Others may be homeless or living in temporary group quarters.

What's more, many states and localities have been short on funds for census outreach. In California, which is facing a $20 billion budget shortfall, money for census outreach was slashed to $2 million, compared with nearly $25 million in 2000. The state could lose nearly $3,000 a year in federal assistance for each resident not counted. "We need to make a push to make sure we at least stay even," said Louis Stewart, deputy director of California's census outreach. "There is a lot riding on this count."[23]

Charities and community-based groups have taken up some of the slack left by depleted state budgets. The philanthropic community poured some $15 million into census-promotion efforts, much of it directed to difficult-to-count areas and community groups serving them, according to Terri Ann Lowenthal, a census consultant and former staff director of the House census oversight subcommittee. She said the collaboration has helped

Actress Rosario Dawson announces in Los Angeles on March 10 a multimedia plan by the Mexican American Legal Defense and Educational Fund (MALDEF) and Voto Latino to encourage young California Latinos to fill out their census forms. At right is Nancy Agosto, national census director for MALDEF.

push response rates above the national average in some hard-to-count areas.[24]

Deep-seated mistrust of government also can influence how people respond to the census. A new Pew Research Center survey found that only 22 percent of respondents said they could trust the government in Washington almost always or most of the time, the lowest by far since at least the Kennedy administration.[25]

Asked why he thought Republican opposition existed toward this year's census, Reamer, the Brookings Institution fellow, said "some people are using the census as a symbol of big, intrusive government, seeking to stoke fear and paranoia about government in general and the Democrats in particular." In addition, he said, "straight-up political reality is that Republicans benefit from an undercount of non-whites, who tend to vote Democratic. Democrats are the beneficiaries of a low undercount."[26]

Should the census include undocumented immigrants?

Last fall, Republican Sens. Bob Bennett of Utah and David Vitter of Louisiana proposed an amendment requiring that the census include a question on citizenship, a move aimed at removing undocumented immigrants from the count. The Senate rejected their amendment, but Bennett vowed to keep pushing for it in future censuses "so we can fairly determine congressional representation and ensure that legal residents are equally represented."[27]*

But many say such a move runs counter to the historical roots of the census. The 1790 Census Act said the decennial census "should count everyone living in the country where they usually reside," bureau director Groves told a press briefing last fall. "That applied to every census since 1790."[28]

Groves said he had "no idea how people would react" to a census question asking if a person is in the country legally or not, saying it was "really hard" to say. But experts say asking people whether they're citizens would lead many immigrants not to participate for fear of harassment or deportation. "I just want to know how you get somebody to respond to say they're citizens or not," says Byers of the National Association of Counties.

Beyond that practical consideration, many argue that given the census' key uses — to apportion congressional seats and allocate federal money — a count of all inhabitants is crucial.

"Everyone is protected by the law, so everyone should be counted in determining how many seats a state gets to write those laws," wrote Robert J. Shapiro, a former Commerce Department official who oversaw the 2000 census. "And whether or not someone has citizenship or residency papers, they still put claims on public services, which the funding for those services should reflect."

Shapiro said the implications of using the census to identify undocumented immigrants are "enormous." California "may have as many as 4 or 5 million undocumented inhabitants," he wrote. "Exclude them and the state could lose perhaps a half-dozen seats in Congress and tens of billions of dollars in federal funds. Texas and other states with large Hispanic populations would lose seats and funding as well."[29]

The controversy over citizenship goes beyond the census and flows into the country's fractious debate over immigration reform. The Rev. Miguel Rivera, leader of the National Coalition of Latino Clergy and Christian Leaders, which represents 20,000 churches in 34 states, has urged undocumented immigrants to boycott the census to protest Congress' failure to overhaul immigration laws.

As explained by National Public Radio last year, Rivera realized members of Congress have a big stake in the census because their seats and federal funding for their districts depend on the count. "So if they don't want lacking of funding for their constituents, [and] maybe losing seats at the congressional level, then what they have to do is roll [up] their sleeves and move forward with comprehensive immigration reform," Rivera said.[30]

But other Hispanic leaders who back immigration reform see it differently. "It's sad. It's unfortunate. Ultimately, it means more political power for the people who don't like immigrants," said the Rev. Luis Cortes, president of Esperanza, a faith-based network that claims more than 12,000 Hispanic congregations and other organizations.[31]

In this year's Pew Hispanic Center poll, 70 percent of Hispanics said the census is good for the Hispanic

Midwest Returned Most Census Forms

The 10 areas with the best records for returning 2010 census forms are in the Midwest; Livonia, Mich., held the record, at 87 percent. Nationwide, 72 percent of American households returned forms before the May 1 deadline.

Top 10 areas to return census forms

1.	Livonia, Mich.	87%
2.	Green Township, Ohio	86%
3.	Maple Grove, Minn.	86%
4.	Appleton, Wis.	85%
5.	Carmel, Ind.	85%
6.	Clay Township, Ind.	85%
7.	Eau Claire, Wis.	85%
8.	Frankfort Township, Ill.	85%
9.	Lakeville, Minn.	85%
10.	Macomb Township, Mich.	85%

Top five states to return census forms

1.	Wisconsin	81%
2.	Minnesota	80%
3.	Indiana	78%
4.	Iowa	78%
5.	Michigan	77%

Source: "Take 10 Map: 2010 Census Participation Rates," U.S. Census Bureau, April 27, 2010

---

* Bennett, a three-term, 76-year-old Senate veteran, was denied his party's nomination for a fourth term on May 8 by the Utah GOP convention, making him one of the first congressional victims of the growing power of the conservative Tea Party movement.

States Receive Most Census-Based Federal Funds

State governments received most of the federal funds distributed on the basis of census data (top). Four major program areas — health, housing, transportation and education — received more than 90 percent of census-based funds (bottom).

Geographic Distribution of Federal Funds Based on Census Data, FY 2008

Geographic Level	Programs	Expenditures (in $ billions)	% of Total*
State	116	$386.0	86.4%
Local area	75	$78.4	17.6%
County	49	$50.3	11.3%
Metropolitan Statistical Area	45	$49.4	11.1%
School district	7	$10.3	2.3%
Census tract	7	$76.2	0.0%

Census-Guided Programs by Budget Function, FY 2008

Budget Function	Programs	Expenditures (in $ billions)	% of Total
Health	24	$272.2	60.9%
Section 8 Housing Subsidies	31	$55.3	12.4%
Transportation	11	$48.3	10.8%
Education, Training, Employment and Social Services	54	$40.0	9.0%
Community and Regional Development	34	$10.5	2.4%
Commerce and Housing Credit	13	$9.8	2.2%
Energy	4	$2.3	0.5%
Other	44	$8.0	1.8%

* Totals add to more than 100 percent because one program can use data for more than one geographic level.

Source: "Counting for Dollars: The Role of the Decennial Census in the Distribution of Federal Funds," Brookings Institution, March 9, 2010

community. What's more, foreign-born Hispanics were more positive and knowledgeable about this year's census than were native-born Hispanics, Pew found.[32]

"We should be counting everybody," says Falcón of the National Institute for Latino Policy. "That's what the Constitution said. . . . It's a question of people who live here, who use the services here, who contribute here. Whether they're here legally or not, legally at a certain point becomes irrelevant. Even for reapportionment you can make the argument that these are people who require the political system to be responsive to them. They do contribute, and they are part of the body politic. Maybe they can't vote, but they might be able to contribute money or participate in campaigns. . . . I'm part of that group that would like to get a lot of these people legalized and become part of American society. By counting them you basically include them in the process."

But Mark Krikorian, executive director of the Center for Immigration Studies, a conservative think tank in Washington, is "ambivalent" on whether undocumented immigrants should be counted. He would "much rather enforce the immigration laws so it is a less salient issue in the first place," he says. A "second-best" approach would be to count everybody and use that number for dispensing federal funds, but use only a count of U.S. citizens for determining House and state legislative seats.

But that would require asking about citizenship status — a step that many say would make the census count unreliable.

Should the census long form be replaced by the American Community Survey?

For decades, while most Americans filled out a regular census form, about one in six households received a more in-depth "long-form" questionnaire that asked about everything from education levels and commuting patterns to home-heating fuel and family income. The data served many purposes. Government officials used it, for example, to plan new roads, measure poverty and allocate federal funds. Demographers used it to spot social trends. Businesses used it to decide where to build everything from stores to power plants.

The Census Bureau is still asking such questions, but starting this year it is using the ongoing American Community Survey (ACS) to do so in place of the old decennial census long form. Each month the ACS is mailed to about 250,000 households — 3 million a year — and, as with the census, recipients are legally bound to fill it out.

The ACS has both pluses and minuses compared to the old long form, demographers, researchers and census scholars say. On the plus side, the flow of data will be continual and far timelier than information gleaned from the once-a-decade long form.

"With the [ACS], it's no longer necessary to rely on a single snapshot of an area that becomes increasingly dated throughout the decade," the Census Bureau says. "Instead, the survey provides a moving picture of community characteristics — a more efficient use of taxpayer dollars."[33]

Five-year data will be published on areas with fewer than 20,000 residents. Three- and five-year data will be available on areas with populations between 20,000 and 65,000. And annual data, plus three- and five-year data, will be published on areas with 65,000 or more people.

The Census Bureau began developing the ACS in the early 2000s and rolled it out in 2005. Three-year data are out now, and later this year the bureau will produce its first set of five-year ACS data, covering 2005 through 2009.

On the downside, say census experts, the ACS samples fewer households than the old long form did, though the Obama administration is seeking additional funding to increase the sample size. What's more, data on small communities won't be available as quickly as for larger cities and regions. And while multiyear data are often more useful than a 10-year snapshot, they can blur sharp economic ups and downs, presenting an unreliable picture of prevailing conditions.

"There are lots of rationales for what the Census Bureau is doing," says Byers of the National Association of Counties. Areas with 65,000 or more residents make up 82 percent of the U.S. population, she notes. But "they don't do as frequent an update of the smaller counties. And we're a nation of smaller counties."

CQ Weekly noted in December that the ACS "has been surveying a smaller and smaller portion of the population every year because its budget has remained essentially flat." In fiscal 2009, about $200 million was spent on the survey, which paid for interviews of about 3 million households, roughly the same number as in prior years, the magazine said. "That used to amount to about 2.5 percent of all the households in the United States," it said, but with population growth the same survey reaches just over 2 percent of households. Some experts say the sampling of small geographic areas or population groups, such as teen mothers or people older than 85, "is becoming too small to be statistically reliable," noted the *Weekly*.[34]

Cynthia Taeuber, a retired Census Bureau statistician who runs a consulting firm on census issues, said "this is a very big loss to businesses and to state, local and federal governments. It means that federal programs are distributing funds — say, for poverty within cities or population within rural areas — on shaky data."[35]

Reamer, the Brookings Institution scholar, says while the ACS data will be more timely, "the tradeoff is that it's not an estimate of a point in time like the traditional long-form data." That can matter in periods when the economy is in flux, such as the one the nation has been experiencing, Reamer says. "Late in 2010, we'll get 2005-2009 data" for areas under 20,000 population, "which was the end of a boom period and the beginning and middle of recession. We're going to get somewhat of a muddled picture of economic conditions" at the neighborhood level.

For transportation planners, among the heaviest users of census data, the switch to the ACS is especially challenging. Alan Pisarski, author of a series of reports on commuting patterns published by the National Academy of Sciences, warned that the number of households surveyed in any given year will be too small to provide the kind of granular data needed to plan bus routes, traffic intersections and other needs. The old long form "gave you not only county-level detail but census tract detail — it even gave you block-group-level data," he says. With the ACS's "very small" sample, Pisarski says, "it's enough to give you good national stuff, but nowhere near as close as blocks. That means that a lot of the stuff [won't] be useful."

The ACS is "a very big change," one with "a short-term cost," says Logan, the Brown University demographer. Noting its smaller sample size, he says, "When we get Census 2010 data, we're not going to know as much, with as much accuracy and detail, about the population in neighborhoods of big cities or about small towns or smaller counties, even areas of 40,000 or 50,000 people. We're going to be dependent on the ACS, which is not a substitute for that one-time, very detailed and pretty accurate picture."

Still, Logan says, researchers will get used to the ACS. "It will be a very big contribution to see trends as they are appearing. It's something we could not do" with the 10-year snapshot provided by the long form.

Indeed, many say the switch to the ACS will be a plus in the long run. Census scholar Margo J. Anderson, a professor of history and urban studies at the University of Wisconsin-Milwaukee, points out that the long form had been spurring "increasing questions about privacy and its onerous length," dragging down response rates.

Because the ACS will provide a steady flow of timely data on local population characteristics, Anderson says it "will be very nice for local-government planning, allocation of federal money and so forth." On the downside, she notes, it'll be a different kind of data. "Users are going to have to get used to it. But in the long term it's an improvement."

Joseph Salvo, New York City's chief demographer, says the advantages of the switch outweigh the disadvantages, which include educating data users to learn to work with multiyear averages rather than data based on a fixed point in time.

But overall, the switch is clearly "positive," Salvo says. "If you go back to 2000 and look at data from the long form, a lot of it is bad," he says. "For example, the economic data in the Bronx was compromised because a whole bunch of people did not respond." The degree to which the Census Bureau had to substitute values for the missing data was "very high in a whole bunch of items in a whole bunch of communities."

Salvo also expects response rates on the ACS to be better because professional interviewers are following up with non-responders.

"The major plus is that we get data more than once a decade," Salvo says. "We get data — new estimates — every year."

BACKGROUND

The First Census

This spring, a first edition of the first U.S. census, signed in 1791 by then-Secretary of State Thomas Jefferson, sold at auction for more than $122,000.[36] Jefferson's signature helped make the 56-page document a historical prize, but that first census is notable for another reason, too: Like every U.S. census that followed, the 1790 count spurred discord and doubt.

The first census, which broke out the 1790 population into free people and slaves, concluded that the new nation contained 3.9 million people. Jefferson and President George Washington both expected the count to be higher — at least 4 million if not, in Jefferson's mind, 4 to 5 million.[37]

"Washington had expected a population about 5 percent higher and blamed the 'inaccuracy' on avoidance by some residents as well as on negligence by those responsible for taking the census," former Census Bureau director Prewitt wrote. "This was not an idle irritation on Washington's part," Prewitt added. Washington "worried that a small population would tempt America's European enemies to military action."[38]

That first census was controversial for another reason, too: politics. Washington exercised the first of his two presidential vetoes on a bill to apportion House seats. Opposing sides had formed around two competing formulas, one proposed by Alexander Hamilton of New York and the other supported by Jefferson of Virginia. Washington's veto led Congress to adopt Jefferson's method.[39]

"This battle between North and South, between political parties, between geographic areas with large populations and those with small populations, or between urban and rural areas, is central to nearly all controversy over apportionment and districting from 1790 to the present," wrote census expert David McMillen.[40]

In the 1800s, the North-South battle was fought not only with Civil War cannons but also with census counts, and the slavery issue was at the heart of it.

Under an infamous compromise made during the Constitutional Convention in 1787, only three-fifths of the slave population was to be counted when apportioning seats in the House. The result was growing political power among Republican-dominated Northern states compared with the Democrat-controlled South, where most slaves lived. But in 1865, slavery was abolished through the 13th Amendment, effectively ending the three-fifths compromise. On paper, at least, that shifted more political power to the South. Even so, slavery's legacy and its relationship to the census remained an issue and became a factor in the push for civil rights in the post-Civil War South.

"Northern Republicans realized that the census and reapportionment would work to their political *dis*advantage after the Civil War and Reconstruction," wrote Anderson, the University of Wisconsin historian. With the demise of the three-fifths compromise, "the Southern states would gain a windfall of increased representation in Congress. However, since few policymakers expected the freed slaves to be able to vote initially, they realized that a disfranchised free black population would strengthen the white-led Southern states and permit the Democrats to come dangerously close to gaining control of the presidency as early as 1868. The logic of population counting and apportionment, therefore, was one of the major forces driving Congress to extend further political and civil rights to the freedmen."[41]

Rural-Urban Fight

Just as the census and reapportionment factored in Civil War-era racial tensions, they also formed a backdrop for another major battle — this one between cities and rural regions.

As a result of the 1920 census, the government announced that most Americans now lived in urban areas, a monumental shift that, as Anderson wrote, "threatened to undermine the rural states' domination of national politics and the rural towns' domination of state politics."[42] Rural legislators challenged the 1920 census count and refused to give up power, and for the only time in U.S. history Congress did not pass a reapportionment bill after a census.

The rural-urban squabble had lasting effects. As part of a reapportionment bill based on the 1930 census, Congress set aside a requirement that congressional districts be roughly equal in size. "In short, Congress redistributed political power among the states but quietly permitted malapportioned districts within states in order to preserve rural and small-town dominance of Congress," Anderson wrote. She added that malapportionment remained the norm until the 1960s.[43]

In 1962, in the landmark ruling *Baker v. Carr*, the Supreme Court held that voters could bring a constitutional challenge to a state's legislative apportionment. The decision opened the door to a series of rulings that local and state legislative bodies as well as congressional districts must be apportioned according to what became known as the "one-person, one-vote rule" — in other words, districts had to contain a roughly equal number of people as tallied in the decennial census. "Other methods of drawing legislative districts, which might use political or geographic boundaries, were invalid if those districts were not equal in population," Anderson noted.[44]

Meanwhile, the growing focus on antidiscrimination laws was helping to spotlight the issue of census accuracy and the problem of undercounting minorities. Undercounting had been a concern ever since the first census in 1790, but for 150 years demographers and census officials had little in the way of hard proof that undercounting — particularly of African-Americans — existed to any significant degree. That changed in 1940 at the advent of World War II.

As noted by the Census Bureau, demographic analysis showed that 3 percent more draft-age men, including 13 percent more blacks, registered for the World War II draft pool than were counted in the 1940 census, proving that censuses were missing part of the population.[45]

Concerns about undercounting — especially of minorities — led to major changes in modern census methods. Over the past six decades those changes have led to controversies and charges of politicization of the census — charges that persisted through the planning for Census 2010.

At the heart of the controversy has been the practice of sampling — using data on part of the population to make broader conclusions about the whole.

The 1950 census produced a net undercount of 4.4 percent of the population, but the undercount rate for blacks was 9.6 percent.[46] In 1957 Congress passed a new Census Act, which allowed sampling to be used in the 1960 census "in such form and content as" the secretary of Commerce "may determine," but the law said sampling could not be used for reapportioning House seats.[47]

By 1970, the stakes in census accuracy had grown significantly, in large part because of the passage of civil rights legislation that demanded reliable counts to monitor the application of antidiscrimination laws. In addition, big U.S. cities were under increasing financial pressure, raising the importance of census counts in the allocation of federal assistance. Judicial rulings requiring legislative districts to be equal in population also demanded accurate census counts.

CHRONOLOGY

1790-1800s *Constitution's mandate for a decennial census sparks political conflict over how the American population is counted.*

1790 First census puts population at 3.9 million, lower than the figure President George Washington and then-Secretary of State Thomas Jefferson hoped for; slaves counted as three-fifths of a person; Washington vetoes apportionment bill he saw as unfair.

1865 Thirteenth Amendment abolishes slavery, ending three-fifths count for African-Americans and effectively shifting more political power to the South.

1900-1950s *Farm-to-city population shifts and undercounting of minorities cast new attention on census data.*

1902 Congress creates Census Office.

1920 Census finds that most Americans live in cities; rural legislators challenge census count, and Congress fails to pass a reapportionment bill.

1940 First hard evidence of undercounting emerges as demographic analysis shows that 3 percent more draft-age men, including 13 percent more blacks, registered for the draft pool than were counted in the 1940 census.

1951 Newly invented Univac computer used in final stages of 1950 census.

1957 Census Act allows sampling to be used in the 1960 census.

1960s-1980s *Concern about undercounting grows among civil rights groups, cities and states.*

1969 *Ebony* magazine pushes for "accurate Black count," telling readers that census counts are important to government and industry for apportionment, program planning and analysis.

1976 In effort to address undercount, Congress amends the Census Act to require the Commerce secretary to use sampling "if he considers it feasible."

1980 Undercount reduced again, but some cities and states seek to force Census Bureau to adjust figures.

1990-Present *Conflict arises over use of statistical adjustment of census data to reduce undercounting.*

1990 For first time since 1940 Census Bureau fails to reduce undercount; population reaches 249 million.

1991 Commerce Secretary Robert A. Mosbacher declines Census Bureau recommendation to adjust the 1990 census to deal with undercount; critics say the decision is politically driven, and several states and cities sue to force adjustment.

1996 U.S. Supreme Court, in *Wisconsin v. City of New York*, rejects cities' effort to force adjustment of 1990 census. . . . Census Bureau announces "re-engineered census" plan aimed at reducing undercount and avoiding lawsuits; congressional Republicans say the plan violates the Constitution.

1999 Supreme Court rules that the Census Act bars use of statistical sampling for reapportionment but leaves door open for using it to allocate federal funds and draw state legislative districts.

2000 Census Bureau buys ads for the first time to encourage responses.

2009 Robert M. Groves chosen to head Census Bureau, says won't use sampling to adjust the 2010 count. . . . Census Bureau cuts ties with Association of Community Organizations for Reform Now (ACORN) after employees of the antipoverty group are filmed appearing to give advice encouraging tax fraud and prostitution.

2010 Census Bureau replaces long-form questionnaire with American Community Survey while sending all households a short 10-question form. . . . Total cost of 2010 census estimated at $14.5 billion, including $340 million promotional campaign that includes $171 million in advertising; conservative Republicans criticize census as intrusive, and some Latino advocates try to boycott it to protest lack of immigration reform; mail-back response rate of 72 percent matches 2000 rate; bureau begins effort to contact non-responders.

Gay Couples to Be Counted for First Time

But census won't provide complete count of gays in America.

With eight states and Washington, D.C., recognizing same-sex marriages, the U.S. Census for the first time this year will include data about same-sex marriages nationwide, regardless of whether they are legal.

In previous censuses, the Census Bureau considered same-sex couples who checked the "married" box as "unmarried partners."[1] But since the last census in 2000, five states and the district have legalized same-sex marriages, and three more recognize out-of-state same-sex marriages.

The Census Bureau is even encouraging same-sex couples who aren't legally married but identify themselves as such to check the "married" box. And since the census is confidential, there will be no legal repercussions for same-sex married couples who live in states in which same-sex marriages aren't legal.

"The census is a portrait of America," Che Ruddell-Tabisola, the manager of the lesbian, gay, bisexual and transgender program at the Census Bureau, told *The Kansas City Star*. "Our job is to get an accurate count. . . . One of the most important things is for same-sex couples to know that it is 100 percent safe to participate in the census."[2]

The decision to count same-sex married couples is hailed by some gay rights advocates as an important first step in getting a complete count of the lesbian, gay, bisexual and transgender (LGBT) community in the United States. "Even in the absence of federal recognition of our relationships, we have an opportunity to say on an official form that, 'Yes, we are married,' 'Yes, our relationships are every bit as equal to everyone else's,' " said Josh Friedes, executive director of the LGBT advocacy group Equal Rights Washington.[3]

Some gay rights advocates, however, say more needs to be done to recognize the U.S. LGBT community in terms of data and gathering more statistics. "[At] the moment, it's not that easy for us to answer a simple question, like 'How many LGBT people are there,' " Gary Gates, a member of Our Families Count, a census campaign to count the LGBT community, told National Public Radio's "Tell Me More" program. In data-gathering, "When a group is essentially invisible, it's hard to make an argument that they have needs or that they are treated differently."[4]

Because the census will count only same-sex couples who live together, many say a large proportion of the community will not be counted, and the only remedy for this is to include a question on the census about sexual orientation. But the only way to add questions to the census is to get approval by Congress, so that does not appear likely anytime soon.

Some conservative same-sex-marriage opponents worry that these new statistics will aid gay rights advocates in the fight for legal same-sex marriage in more states. Some have even said that counting same-sex couples violates the federal Defense of Marriage Act (DOMA), which defines marriage as a legal union between a man and a woman.

In January 1969 an *Ebony* magazine editorial pushed "for an accurate Black count" and told readers that census counts were important to government and industry for apportionment, program planning and analysis. "And," the magazine claimed, "the figures they use are a lie" because about 10 percent of "non-Whites (primarily Blacks)" were "missed." The magazine noted that most census workers were white, and it advocated for black interviewers to take the census to "ghetto areas."[48]

The following year the Urban League organized a Coalition for a Black Count to monitor the 1970 census and urge participation "to assure a full and accurate minority count."[49]

Undercounts persisted, though. The 1970 census produced a net undercount of 2.9 percent of the population, but 8 percent of blacks.[50]

In 1957 Congress amended the Census Act to allow sampling, but not for apportionment. In 1976 the law was strengthened to allow the Commerce secretary to use sampling "if he considers it feasible," though again not for apportionment. The change was technical in nature and not aimed at improving the undercount.[51]

Litigation Over Sampling

But over the next quarter-century, the idea of using sampling to statistically adjust for the undercount arose

"Marriage is only for a man and woman. That's the law they need to follow. Somebody needs to sue the federal government to enforce the Defense of Marriage Act," said Randy Thomasson, president of SaveCalifornia.com, a pro-family advocacy group. The Family Research Council (FRC), which promotes family, marriage and human life in national policy, agrees the Census Bureau's actions may violate DOMA.

"For the Census Bureau to actually encourage same-sex couples to mark themselves as married is a clear violation of the Defense of Marriage Act," says Peter Sprigg, a senior fellow for policy studies at FRC. Sprigg says the data being collected could have been interesting because some states that have legalized same-sex marriages don't record data on how many marriages are performed. But, because the census will count *all* same-sex couples who consider themselves married — legally or not — "the data really isn't very useful."

Because Congress mandated that a marriage can be only between a man and a woman, the FRC believes the idea of same-sex marriage is an oxymoron, according to Sprigg.

And while it might be one thing for the census to simply count same-sex married couples, he said it's another thing for the Census Bureau to distribute messages encouraging same-sex couples to check the "married" box.

To promote its new way of counting same-sex couples, the Census Bureau sent a task force to reach out to the LGBT community and encourage it to be honest on its survey responses. The bureau also broadcast public service ads on the gay-oriented channel Logo about counting same-sex marriages and posted them on the Census Bureau Web site.

"We have to reach out and engage this part of the population," a Census Bureau official said. "Anything less than that is a failure."[5]

— *Julia Russell*

This year's census will include data about same-sex marriages for the first time. Rocky Galloway and Reggie Stanley, above, celebrate after applying for their marriage license in Washington, D.C., last March.

[1] "Census Form Question Stirs Controversy, U.S. Census Bureau to Acknowledge Couples Differently," KCRA (Sacramento), April 1, 2010, www.kcra.com/news/23024784/detail.html.

[2] Eric Adler, "Bureau wants same-sex couples to check the 'married' box on census form," *The Kansas City Star* (Missouri), April 6, 2010, www.kansascity.com/2010/04/06/1861880/census-bureau-seeking-count-of.html.

[3] Lornet Turnbull, "Census will count gay couples who check 'husband or wife,'" *The Seattle Times*, March 30, 2010, http://seattletimes.nwsource.com/html/localnews/2011483128_lgbtcensus31m.html.

[4] "2010 Census Will Count Same-Sex Couples," "Tell Me More," National Public Radio, Nov. 25, 2009, www.npr.org/templates/story/story.php?storyId=120816467.

[5] "Census Bureau urges same-sex couples to be counted," *USA Today*, April 6, 2010, www.usatoday.com/news/nation/census/2010-04-05-census-gays_N.htm.

---

repeatedly, resulting in court fights, a landmark Supreme Court ruling and charges of politicizing the census to gain a partisan edge in the apportionment of congressional seats, drawing of legislative districts and allocation of federal money to the states.

After the 1980 census, the Census Bureau stepped up its research on methods for statistically adjusting the 1990 census to correct for undercounting, but the Commerce Department subsequently decided against the idea. That led to litigation. In late 1988 New York City and a coalition of other state and local entities, joined by the NAACP and other advocacy groups, sued the Census Bureau in an effort to stop "chronic under-counting" of urban blacks and Latinos.[52]

"From a civil rights point of view, it has to do with equal voting rights," Neil Corwin, New York City's assistant corporation counsel, explained at the time. "From the federal-funding point, there are a number of programs based on population figures. If New York has more people than the Census Bureau gives it credit for, they are going to suffer in the amount of federal funds they get."[53]

In 1990 the Census Bureau failed to reduce the undercount for the first time since 1940. The overall rate was 1.6 percent, but 4.6 percent for blacks and 5 percent for Hispanics. Renters were undercounted by 4.5 percent, and many children were missed.[54]

The bureau recommended that the 1990 results be adjusted, but Commerce Secretary Robert Mosbacher, a Republican serving in the George H. W. Bush administration, declined. While conceding that minorities and some jurisdictions had been undercounted, he argued that the proposed adjustment methods, employing sampling, weren't accurate enough to improve the overall census results.[55] Critics promptly tagged his decision as without merit and politically driven. New York City Mayor David Dinkins called it "nothing less than statistical grand larceny."[56]

More litigation followed. New York City and others challenged Mosbacher's decision, but a federal district court judge ruled that it was constitutional and did not violate the Census Act. A federal appellate court overturned that decision, ruling "that because a disproportionate undercount of minorities raised concerns about equal representation, the government was required to prove that its refusal to adjust the census figures 'was necessary to achieve some legitimate goal.'"[57]

But in 1996, the Supreme Court upheld Mosbacher's decision not to adjust the 1990 count.

Using statistical means to deal with undercounting wasn't dead, however. After the string of lawsuits over the 1990 count, the Census Bureau came up with a new plan for a "reengineered census" in 2000 that it thought would correct the miscounting and avoid litigation. It was "the culmination of a four-year process of discussion and review of census plans by a broad spectrum of experts, advisors and stakeholders," according to the bureau.[58]

The plan, which became public in early 1996, called again for the use of statistical sampling. As described by *The New York Times*, the technique "was loosely similar to that of public opinion polls in that it would extrapolate information about the population from partial data. But the bureau's plans are more sophisticated. They involve using traditional methods to count everyone in 90 percent of the households in a census tract — a neighborhood of about 1,700 dwellings. Data from the 90 percent would be used to determine the number and characteristics of the remaining 10 percent, and the population would be further adjusted on the basis of a survey of 750,000 households."[59]

Congressional Republicans, who had gained control of both houses of Congress in the 1994 midterm elections, objected, saying the technique violated federal law and the Constitution. As *The Times* noted, "with House Republicans holding a razor-thin majority, both parties [were] acutely conscious of any question that might give one side an advantage."[60]

In 1998 a federal court ruled against the sampling plan, and the ruling was appealed to the Supreme Court. In 1999, in a landmark 5-4 decision, the justices barred the use of statistical sampling to arrive at population totals for the purpose of reapportionment. But the court left the door open to using sampling for other purposes, such as allocating federal funds and state districting.[61]

Political Debate

New controversies arose as the 2010 census approached. One involved last year's White House nomination of Sen. Judd Gregg, a Republican from New Hampshire, to head the Commerce Department.

"Obama's pick . . . raised alarm among some minority advocates, who noted that Gregg had opposed increases to census funding and could not be trusted to do everything necessary to reduce undercounts," *Boston Globe* correspondent James Burnett wrote. "To mollify those critics, White House spokesman Ben LaBolt indicated that for 2010 the census director would now 'work closely with White House senior management.' To some census observers — especially those observing from GOP congressional seats — this looked like a power grab."[62]

Gregg withdrew, citing the census as key among "irresolvable conflicts" with the Obama administration.[63] In picking a replacement — Washington Gov. Gary Locke, a Democrat — the White House sought to reassure critics that the census wouldn't be politicized.

But yet another controversy erupted after the Association of Community Organizations for Reform Now — a grassroots antipoverty group commonly known as ACORN — signed on as an unpaid census-promotion partner for the 2010 census. Long a target of conservative critics, ACORN had been accused by Republicans of voter-registration fraud during the 2008 presidential campaign, and its involvement in the census touched off strong GOP objections.[64]

"It's a concern, especially when you look at all the different charges of voter fraud," Rep. Lynn A. Westmoreland, R-Ga., vice ranking member of the House Oversight Subcommittee on Information Policy, Census and National Archives, told FoxNews.com.

Census Leads to Power Shift in Congress

Population migration transfers House seats to Sun Belt states.

When William Howard Taft occupied the White House in 1911, Congress set the number of seats in the U.S. House of Representatives at 435, the same as today. But every 10 years, when the census is conducted, an element of suspense surrounds that set-in-stone figure.

House seats are distributed among the states based on population figures gathered in the census, with apportionment occurring the year following the census. With every new census, some states gain seats (and the political power that goes with them) and others lose seats. Following the 2000 census, for instance, 12 seats shifted; after the 1990 count, 19 seats transferred.[1]

Political analysts often can reliably forecast winners and losers ahead of time, but some states are cliff-hangers until the Census Bureau releases its official post-census results. This year that will happen by Dec. 31.

For years, House seats and political power have been shifting toward the Sun Belt — the Southern and Western states — and away from the Midwest and Northeast, a trend expected to continue in next year's reapportionment. That trend began in earnest after World War II, spurred by the baby boom and air conditioning, says Kimball W. Brace, president of Election Data Services (EDS), a Manassas, Va., consulting firm specializing in redistricting, election administration and census analysis.

Returning veterans started families, the U.S. population grew and people moved seeking jobs — not just to the suburbs but also to warm-weather states, such as California, Texas and Florida. "With the advent of air conditioning, they ended up not feeling bad going to hot places," Brace notes.

The migratory trend continues, but with some recent twists that could have a strong impact on reapportionment, he says. "If you look at the Census Bureau's yearly studies of movement . . . since World War II, you generally find that about 17 or 18 percent of the population moves every year" whether across town or cross-country. But in the last two years, that 17 percent has dropped to 11 percent, mainly because of the housing crisis and economic upheaval, he says.

With migration slow, some states may not gain as many House seats as expected before the recent recession. According to estimates by EDS, seven states — Arizona, Florida, Georgia, Nevada, South Carolina, Utah and Washington — would each gain a seat, and Texas would gain three, based on 2009 Census Bureau population estimates, the latest available until the 2010 census is counted.[2]

Before the economy soured, Brace says, Florida was on track to gain two seats but will now be "lucky to gain one."

Texas, on the other hand, has held steady, and in fact could gain a fourth seat, depending on the 2010 census, Brace says. The migration of people to Texas from Louisiana in the wake of Hurricane Katrina in 2005 may have boosted Texas' population enough to give the state another seat, Brace says. "The issue is, have any of those people gone back? We're not sure yet."

A separate study by Polidata, a Virginia group that analyzes political data, projected that Texas could gain four seats, though the strength of that projection has decreased, it said late last year.[3]

The EDS study noted that Arizona and Nevada have both seen their population growth decline over the past decade. "Arizona's lower growth rate has impacted whether it will gain a second seat" in 2010, it said. "Nevada, on the other hand, has enough population to keep its additional seat."

Eight states — Illinois, Iowa, Louisiana, Massachusetts, Michigan, New Jersey, New York and Pennsylvania — will probably each lose a seat, according to EDS estimates, and Ohio stands to lose two.

Minnesota is an uncertainty. Based on the 2009 population data, it would not lose a seat, but if 2009 population trends continue into 2010, it will, according to EDS.

California is also a cliff-hanger — and perhaps the most consequential because of its size. Depending on the 2010 census, the state could lose a congressional seat for the first time since it achieved statehood in 1850, EDS said.

That marks a dramatic turn of events for California. Brace says when 2005 Census Bureau data were projected out to 2010, California looked to be in line to gain a seat. But then came the recession, which hit California earlier than the rest of the country, and the state's population growth rate fell behind that of some other states, he says.

If the census counted only U.S. citizens and did not include undocumented immigrants — an idea embraced by some conservatives — California could wind up losing five congressional seats, Brace says. "Immigration does have an impact."

— *Thomas J. Billitteri*

---

[1] Greg Giroux, "Before Redistricting, That Other 'R' Word," *CQ Weekly*, Nov. 20, 2009, p. 2768.

[2] "New Population Estimates Show Additional Changes for 2009 Congressional Apportionment, With Many States Sitting Close to the Edge for 2010," Election Data Services, Dec. 23, 2009, www.electiondataservices.com/images/ File/NR_Appor09wTables.pdf.

[3] "Congressional Apportionment: 2010 Projections Based Upon State Estimates as of July 1, 2009," Polidata, Dec. 23, 2009, www.polidata.org/news.htm#20091223.

To encourage Americans to return their census questionnaires, the Census Bureau this year sponsored a NASCAR race car, above, a 13-vehicle nationwide promotional road tour and television ads before and during the Super Bowl.

"We want an enumeration. We don't want to have any false numbers."[65]

What came next all but sealed ACORN's fate. After conservative activists secretly filmed ACORN employees appearing to offer advice encouraging tax fraud to activists posing as a prostitute and her pimp, the Census Bureau cut ties with the group. "It is clear," wrote bureau director Groves, "that ACORN's affiliation with the 2010 census promotion has caused sufficient concern in the general public, has indeed become a distraction from our mission, and may even become a discouragement to public cooperation, negatively impacting 2010 census efforts."[66]

Groves himself had also stirred partisan controversy when he was nominated to the post a little over five months before the ACORN flap exploded. As a Census Bureau official in the early 1990s, he had advocated statistical adjustment to the 1990 census to deal with the undercount. After Obama nominated him to run the Census Bureau, Republicans expressed alarm.

"Conducting the census is a vital constitutional obligation," House minority leader Rep. John A. Boehner, R-Ohio, said after Groves' nomination. "It should be as solid, reliable and accurate as possible in every respect. That is why I am concerned about the White House decision to select" Groves. Rep. Darrell Issa, R-Calif., the ranking Republican on the House Committee on Oversight and Government Reform, said Groves' selection was "incredibly troubling" and "contradicts the administration's assurances that the census process would not be used to advance an ulterior political agenda."[67]

But at his confirmation hearing in May, Groves told a Senate panel he wouldn't use sampling to adjust the 2010 census. And, he said, "there are no plans to do that for 2020."[68]

CURRENT SITUATION

Redistricting

In late April the Census Bureau announced that 72 percent of 2010 census forms had been mailed back by households that received them. On his Census Web site blog, Groves expressed satisfaction with the response, calling it a "remarkable display of civic participation."[69]

But census experts cautioned that the so-called participation rate doesn't tell the full story. "[T]he measure is limited to the universe of homes to which the Census Bureau mailed . . . or hand-delivered . . . questionnaires and asked residents to mail them back," wrote Lowenthal, the census consultant and former House staffer.

"Not in the equation," she noted, are people counted separately — everyone from American Indians living on reservations and college students living in dorms to people living in migrant farm-worker camps and RV (recreational vehicle) parks. And those "additional counting operations are just part of the partial story," she said. Concluded Lowenthal, "We don't really know how many Americans have joined our decennial national portrait so far. But one conclusion is beyond doubt: The hardest part is yet to come."[70]

In fact, in various ways, Census 2010 is only at the midpoint.

From May through July census takers will be knocking on roughly 48 million doors of households that didn't mail back their census form or didn't receive one. From August through December the bureau will conduct a separate "Coverage Measurement Survey" to evaluate the accuracy of the census count.

December 31 is the deadline for the bureau to provide the White House and Congress with the official population count by state. The individual states then use the data to apportion House seats to various congressional districts.

In March 2011 the bureau will begin providing redistricting data to the states.[71] And in 2012 the results of the Coverage Measurement Survey will become available.

AT ISSUE
Should the census ask questions about race?

YES
Melissa Nobles
Associate Professor of Political Science, Massachusetts Institute of Technology

Written for *CQ Researcher*, May 2010

For nearly 170 years, the Census Bureau's mission in asking about race was clear: define and then distinguish who was "white" from who was "non-white, and especially from who was "black."

Today, the dismantling of formal racial segregation, the enforcement of civil rights legislation and significant increases in immigration to the United States have all introduced new purposes for racial categorization in census taking. Asking people to categorize themselves by race provides important data about our country's growing diversity and serves to support the nation's civil rights laws — especially the Voting Rights Act. Indeed, census data on race are used in a range of public policies, many of which are designed to counteract entrenched material disadvantage among minorities.

In my view, these are purposes worthy of the continued inclusion of the race question in U.S. census taking. The issue has been contentious mostly because it is impossible to disassociate the history of racial thought and politics that have fundamentally shaped census-taking from the start. For most of its history, census-taking supported a politics of racial segregation and subordination.

For example, the 1840 and 1850 censuses were directly intertwined with debates about slavery. Data from the largely discredited 1840 census purportedly disclosed higher rates of insanity among free blacks, thereby "proving" that freedom drove free black people crazy. The 1850 census first introduced the category "mulatto," at the behest of a Southern physician, in order to gather data about the presumed deleterious effects of "racial mixture." Post-Civil War censuses continued to include the "mulatto" category, reflecting the enduring preoccupation with "racial mixing."

Twentieth-century racial and ethnic census categorization remained intertwined with the century's core political and social issues: racial segregation and immigration.

In regard to segregation, categories and instructions for the censuses from 1930 to 1950 largely mirrored the racial status quo in politics and law. Southern laws defined persons with any trace of "Negro blood" as legally "Negro" and subject to all of the political, economic and social disabilities such designation conferred. Southern law treated other "non-white" persons similarly. Census categories and definitions followed suit, essentially bringing the logic of racial segregation into national census taking itself.

Thus, for most of American history the census wasn't used for edifying reasons. But today it supports the political and social policies that seek to guarantee civil rights and equality.

NO
Hans A. Von Spakovsky
Senior Legal Fellow, The Heritage Foundation; former counsel to the assistant attorney general for civil rights, U.S. Justice Department

Written for *CQ Researcher*, May 2010

Americans are uncomfortable with the Census Bureau demand that everyone identify their "race" on the 2010 Census. Despite the bureau's insidious commercials urging Americans to return the form so their communities can get their "fair share" of government largesse (earmarks writ large), the constitutional reason for the census is to reapportion congressional representation. The race question invades our privacy and is part of a continuing effort to divide Americans by race and enable official discrimination.

Some justify this because the census has historically asked for racial information. That information was required prior to the Civil War because black Americans who were slaves were counted as only three-fifths of a person in reapportionment. So why must we check the race box in this day and age? Two reasons: 1) to facilitate racially gerrymandered congressional districts, a pernicious practice that segregates voters by race; and 2) to discriminate in the provision of government benefits based on race.

For Americans who chafed at the race question and either left it blank or wrote in "American," a census worker may visit their homes to get them to change their answer. If they don't, the census will impute the person's race based on what he looks like or where he lives — an offensive example of stereotyping and racial profiling in a society where so many of us are of mixed race and ancestry. Small wonder the U.S. Commission on Civil Rights recommended that this question be made voluntary — a recommendation the Census Bureau ignored.

The options given for answering the race question also reflect political correctness and half-baked, liberal social-policy theories that have nothing to do with biology and genetics. Although the question asks for your race, it gives you choices like "Japanese" that are nationalities, not racial categories. "Race" is a very imprecise term that scientists disagree about. Moreover, many people have no idea what their apparent racial background is for more than a few generations.

Classifying and subdividing Americans on the basis of race is repugnant. *E pluribus unum* — "out of many, one" — is both our motto and our objective. It is one we should strive for every day, and the census' continued preoccupation with race is detrimental to the great progress we've made as a nation toward achieving that goal.

Census experts say that if it shows significant undercounts, states could wind up suing to press the bureau to adjust the figures because of the importance of census results to federal funding allocations and the drawing of legislative boundaries.

Counting Prisoners

As the 2010 census moves forward, advocacy groups are continuing to spotlight how certain population groups are counted, especially prison inmates.

Currently, the Census Bureau counts prison inmates where they are incarcerated. Critics argue that areas where prisons are located benefit in the allotment of political representation to the detriment of prisoners' home communities.

"Most people in prison in America are urban and African-American or Latino," Rep. William Lacy Clay, D-Mo., chairman of the House census subcommittee, wrote to the Census Bureau. But, he added, the 2010 census "will again be counting incarcerated people as residents of the rural, predominantly white communities that contain prisons."[72]

Some change on the issue is coming. In May 2011, a few months earlier than in the past and in time for redistricting in most states, the Census Bureau will identify the location and population counts of prisons and other group quarters, according to Aleks Kajstura, legal director at Prison Policy Initiative, a Massachusetts-based group pushing for change in the way prisoners are counted. States can choose whether they want to collect the home addresses of prisoners and adjust the census counts before redistricting, she says.

Ultimately, advocates want the Census Bureau to change the way prisoners are counted in time for the 2020 census. But some states are acting on their own. In April, Maryland became the first state to pass legislation requiring inmates to be counted in the jurisdiction of their last permanent address rather than where they are incarcerated.[73] Similar legislation is pending or under consideration in eight other states, including New York, Florida, Illinois and Pennsylvania, Kajstura said.

"In a lot of states the trend has been to build new prisons at locations far removed from the home community of incarcerated persons, which means a shift in political and representation power and representation away from these home communities to generally more rural areas where prisons are located," says Brenda Wright, director of the Democracy Program at Dēmos, a liberal research and advocacy group in New York that also is pushing for a change in how prisoners are counted. "At the same time, we emphasize it's not just a rural versus urban problem at heart, because the issue of how prisoners are counted affects local county and city redistricting as well."[74]

How the Census Bureau counts prisoners also "inflates the weight of the vote of any district where a prison happens to be located at the expense of all other districts that do not have a prison," Wright says.

Doling Out Funds

Prisoner counts are just one part of the larger census picture, of course, and the stakes for states and localities in the ability of the Census Bureau to produce an accurate count are huge — not only for legislative districting and congressional seats but also for allocations of federal money.

A new study by the Brookings Institution's Reamer found that in fiscal 2008, 215 federal domestic-assistance programs used census-related data to guide $447 billion in distributions to the states, local governments and other recipients, mostly for Medicaid and other aid for low-income households and highway programs.[75]

Census accuracy is especially important to low-income recipients of federal help, the study notes. Based on 2000 census data, it said, "each additional person included in [that census] resulted in an annual additional Medicaid reimbursement to most states of between several hundred and several thousand dollars."

In an interview, Reamer notes the census' widespread importance — to apportionment and redistricting, enforcement of antidiscrimination laws, distribution of federal funds and the information needs of business, for example. "To the extent the census is inaccurate, we have a less efficient economy if businesses are making decisions based on faulty data," he says.

His study notes that the decennial census is the basis for 10 other data sets that help shape federal-assistance funding, including a Bureau of Economic Analysis series on per capita income.

The effectiveness of the decennial census depends, of course, in no small part on how seamlessly it is planned and executed. In Congress a bipartisan group of legislators want to see that future censuses run more smoothly than many past ones have, including the 2010 census.

A bill called the Census Oversight, Efficiency and Management Reform Act would, among other things, make the Census Bureau directorship a five-year appointment so census planning isn't disrupted by a presidential election.[76] The 10-year decennial cycle would be split into two five-year phases — the first for planning and the second for operations, fostering consistency across administrations. Under the current system, every president appoints a new director.

In addition, the bill would give bureau directors more independence by having them report directly to the Commerce secretary and letting them give recommendations or testimony to Congress that represents their views and not necessarily those of the administration. It also would keep directors from having to testify on census issues they didn't agree with.[77]

Seven former Census Bureau directors endorsed the bill in March, stating that "the time has come for the Census Bureau to be much more independent and transparent."[78]

They said that after 30 years in "which the press and Congress frequently discussed the Decennial Census in explicitly partisan terms, it is vitally important that the American public have confidence that the census results have been produced by a nonpartisan, apolitical and scientific Census Bureau."

In addition, they said the importance of the Census Bureau "waxes and wanes, peaking as the decennial approaches but then drifting down the [Commerce] Department's priority list," but that the bureau "needs to more efficiently focus on [its] continuous responsibilities," which include not only the decennial census but other measurement projects.

And third, the former directors noted, "each of us experienced times when we could have made much more timely and thorough responses to congressional requests and oversight if we had dealt directly with the Congress."

OUTLOOK
Changing Times

As census experts look beyond the completion of the 2010 count, they see prospects for important changes in the way the government creates its every-10-year national portrait. Social and cultural shifts are likely to make census taking more challenging in 2020 and beyond, yet technology could also make it cheaper, easier and more effective.

In 1970, 78 percent of households receiving a census form mailed it back. That rate fell to 65 percent in 1990, rose modestly in 2000 — thanks in part to heavy spending on advertising — and remained largely flat in 2010. Some of the long-term decline in response no doubt reflects growing concerns about privacy and a wariness of how information collected by the census might be used, experts say. That wariness may grow, particularly in the nation's expanding immigrant communities — especially if Congress fails to pass comprehensive immigration reform before the next census.

Lifestyle changes also have made it more challenging — and costly — for the Census Bureau to do its work. The growth of same-sex unions and inter-racial marriages, increases in joint custody of children, the expansion of second-home purchases among the nation's aging baby-boom population and other trends may make it more difficult for the Census Bureau to get a firm fix on population and demographic trends.

But other developments may work in the Census Bureau's favor. One is the growth of communications technology, which could make census taking cheaper for the government and more convenient for households.

An online data-collection option is a probable evolution in 2020. The bureau said an Internet option was deemed feasible from a technical standpoint. But "without time to fully test the entire system, security concerns led the Census Bureau to decide to not offer the 2010 census questionnaire online," it said. The bureau said it plans to introduce an Internet option in the next census.[79]

One thing seems likely: Criticism of the census will be around in future decades much as it has been in the past.

After the bureau announced the 72 percent mail response to this year's census, Rep. Jason Chaffetz, R-Utah, phoned *The Washington Post* to point out that while this year's mail-back rate matched the 2000 figure, the cost of the 2010 count was more than double that of the 2000 census. And, he criticized the amount the bureau spent on advertising, saying "they're getting poor results in the places we know we have problems."

However, Jost, the bureau communications official, told *The Post* the 2010 advertising budget was the same as for 2000 on an inflation-adjusted basis. "We spent just 5 percent more in equivalent dollars this year on a population that was 10 percent bigger."[80]

NOTES

1. "With Growing Awareness of Census, Most Ready to Fill Out Forms," Pew Research Center, March 16, 2010, http://people-press.org/report/596/census-forms.

2. See Michelle Malkin, "True Confessions from America's Census Workers," April 7, 2010, http://news.yahoo.com/s/uc/20100407/cm_uc_crm max/op_1913518.

3. Andrew D. Reamer, "Counting for Dollars: The Role of the Decennial Census in the Geographic Distribution of Federal Funds," Brookings Institution, March 2010, www.brookings.edu/reports/ 2010/0309_Census_dollars.aspx.

4. Andrew Reamer, "Census Brings Money Home," April 6, 2010, www.brookings.edu/opinions/2010/0315_census_reamer.aspx?p=1.

5. "2010 Census: Fundamental Building Block of a Successful Enumeration Faces Challenges," U.S. Government Accountability Office (GAO), March 5, 2009, www.gao.gov/new.items/d094 30t.pdf.

6. Rate achieved by April 27.

7. Robert M. Groves, "A Surprise Reaction," The Director's Blog, U.S. Bureau of the Census, April 23, 2010, http://blogs.census.gov/2010 census/.

8. "Take 10 Map," http://2010.census.gov/2010census/take10map/.

9. See "How the 2010 Census is Different," Population Reference Bureau, www.prb.org/Articles/2009/changesin2010.aspx.

10. Robert M. Groves, The Director's Blog, U.S. Bureau of the Census, entries for April 14, 15 and 16, 2010, http://blogs.census.gov/2010 census/.

11. Stephen Dinan, "Exclusive: Minn. Lawmaker vows not to complete Census," *The Washington Times*, June 17, 2009.

12. Naftali Bendavid, "Republicans Fear Undercounting in Census," *The Wall Street Journal*, April 5, 2010, p. 4A. Paul's comment appeared in a weekly column in April 2010.

13. Andy Barr, "Erickson's census 'shotgun' threat," *Politico*, April 2, 2010, www.politico.com/news/stories/0410/35338.html.

14. Patrick McHenry, "Returning the Census is Our Constitutional Duty," *RedState.com*, April 1, 2010, www.redstate.com/rep_patrick_mchenry/2010/04/01/returning-the-census-is-our-constitutional-duty/.

15. Transcript, "The 2010 Census," "The Diane Rehm Show," National Public Radio, March 3, 2010.

16. For background, see the following *CQ Researcher* reports: David Masci, "Latinos' Future," Oct. 7, 2003, pp. 869-892; Kenneth Jost, "Census 2000," May 1, 1998, pp. 385-408, and R. K. Landers, "1990 Census: Undercounting Minorities," *Editorial Research Reports*, March 10, 1989, pp. 117-132.

17. "What is the 1990 Undercount?" U.S. Census Bureau, www.census.gov/dmd/www/techdoc1.html.

18. "Technical Assessment of A.C.E. Revision II," U.S. Census Bureau, March 12, 2003, www.cen sus.gov/dmd/www/pdf/ACETechAssess.pdf.

19. *Ibid.*

20. Mark Hugo Lopez and Paul Taylor, "Latinos and the 2010 Census: The Foreign Born Are More Positive," Pew Hispanic Center, April 1, 2010, http://pewhispanic.org/files/reports/121.pdf.

21. Randal C. Archibold, "Arizona Enacts Stringent Law on Immigration," *The New York Times*, April 23, 2010, www.nytimes.com/2010/04/24/us/politics/24immig.html?scp=5&sq=arizona%20and%20immigrants&st=cse.

22. Campbell Robertson, "Suspense Builds Over Census for New Orleans," *The New York Times*, April 7, 2010, www.nytimes.com/2010/04/08/us/08orleans.html?ref=us.

23. The Associated Press, "State, local government budgets hamper census outreach," *The Washington Post*, April 12, 2010, www. washingtonpost.com/wp-dyn/content/article/2010/04/11/AR2010041103832.html.

24. *Ibid.*
25. "Distrust, Discontent, Anger and Partisan Rancor," Pew Research Center, April 18, 2010, http://pewresearch.org/pubs/1569/trust-in-government-distrust-discontent-anger-partisan-rancor.
26. Reamer, "The Scouting Report Web Chat: 2010 Census," *op. cit.*
27. Matt Canham, "Bennett's census-immigration amendment rejected," *Salt Lake Tribune*, Nov. 5, 2009, www.sltrib.com/news/ci_13721132.
28. "2010 Census Operational Briefing Transcript," U.S. Census Bureau, Sept. 23, 2009, www.census.gov/Press-Release/www/releases/pdf/2010 Census Briefing_Transcript.pdf.
29. Rob Shapiro, "The Latest Attack on the Census is an Attack on All of Us," New Policy Institute, Oct. 1, 2009, www.newpolicyinstitute. org/2009/10/the-latest-attack-on-the-census-is-an-attack-on-all-of-us/.
30. Jennifer Ludden, "Hispanics Divided Over Census Boycott," National Public Radio, July 13, 2009, www.npr.org/templates/story/story.php?storyId=106555313.
31. *Ibid.*
32. Lopez and Taylor, *op. cit.*
33. "An Introduction to the American Community Survey," U.S. Census Bureau, summer 2009, www.census.gov/Press-Release/www/2009/pdf/ 09ACS_intro.pdf.
34. Clea Benson, "The Data Catch: Not Enough Information," *CQ Weekly*, Dec. 7, 2009, p. 2810.
35. Quoted in *ibid.*
36. The Associated Press, "Thomas Jefferson Signed Census Sells for $122,500," *The Huffington Post*, April 15, 2010, www.huffingtonpost.com/2010/04/15/thomas-jefferson-signed-c_n_ 538634.html.
37. "A Century of Population Growth: From the First Census of the United States to the Twelfth, 1790-1900," 1909, Bureau of the Census, Department of Commerce and Labor, p. 48, www.archive.org/details/centuryofpopulat00unit. On Jan. 23, 1791, Jefferson wrote: "The census has made considerable progress, but will not be completed till midsummer. It is judged at present that our numbers will be between four and five millions."
38. Kenneth Prewitt, "The American People: Politics and Science in Census Taking," Russell Sage Foundation and Population Reference Bureau, 2003, p. 6, accessed at www.thecensus project.org/factsheets/PrewittSAGE-PRBCensus 2000Report.pdf.
39. David McMillen, "Apportionment and districting," in Margo J. Anderson, ed., *Encyclopedia of the U.S. Census* (2000), pp. 34-35.
40. *Ibid.*, p. 34.
41. *Ibid.*, p. xiii.
42. *Ibid.*
43. *Ibid.*, p. xiv.
44. *Ibid.* The case is *Baker v. Carr*, 369 U.S. 186 (1962).
45. "United States Census 2000: Press Briefing Background Documents," U.S. Census Bureau, June 14, 2000, p. 6, www.census.gov/Press-Release/www/background.pdf.
46. Margo J. Anderson and Stephen E. Fienberg, *Who Counts? The Politics of Census-Taking in Contemporary America* (1999), p. 60. Figures are estimated net census undercounts as measured by a technique called Demographic Analysis, in which the best estimate of the previous census count is updated with various kinds of administrative statistics on births, deaths and net immigration, along with Medicare data, to produce an estimate of the population separately from the current census count. The authors cite Robert E. Fay, *et al.*, *The Coverage of the Population in the 1980 Census*, Bureau of the Census, 1988.
47. "United States Census 2000," U.S. Census Bureau, *op. cit.*
48. Anderson and Fienberg, *op. cit.*, p. 38.
49. *Ibid.*, p. 39.
50. *Ibid.*, p. 60. Figures are estimated net census undercounts as measured by demographic analysis.
51. "United States Census 2000," U.S. Census Bureau, *op cit.*
52. Sam Burchell, "Big Cities Sue for Changes in '90 Census," United Press International, Nov. 3, 1988,

53. Quoted in Burchell, *op. cit.*
54. "United States Census 2000," U.S. Census Bureau, *op. cit.*
55. Anderson, "Litigation and the census," in Anderson, ed., *Encyclopedia of the Census, op. cit.*, p. 270.
56. Anderson and Fienberg, *op. cit.*, p. 128. The authors attribute the Dinkins quote to *The New York Times*, July 16, 1991.
57. Linda Greenhouse, "High Court Hears Arguments For Census Alteration by Race," *The New York Times*, Jan. 11, 1996, www.nytimes.com/1996/01/11/us/high-court-hears-arguments-for-census-alteration-by-race.html?pagewanted=1.
58. "2000 Overview," U.S. Census Bureau, www.census.gov/history/www/through_the_decades/overview/2000.html.
59. Steven A. Holmes, "Court Voids Plan to Use Sampling for 2000 Census," *The New York Times*, Aug. 25, 1998, www.nytimes.com/1998/08/25/us/court-voids-plan-to-use-sampling-for-2000-census.html?scp=1&sq=2000%20census%20and%20sampling&st=cse.
60. *Ibid.*
61. Linda Greenhouse, "Jarring Democrats, Court Rules Census Must Be by Actual Count," *The New York Times*, Jan. 26, 1999, www.nytimes.com/1999/01/26/us/jarring-democrats-court-rules-census-must-be-by-actual-count.html?scp=1&sq=census%20and%20sampling%20and%20supreme%20court&st=cse.
62. James Burnett, "Night of the census taker," *The Boston Globe*, Oct. 18, 2009, www.boston.com/bostonglobe/ideas/articles/2009/10/18/look_out_obama_is_sending_his_minions_to_your_house_the_deep_history_of_a_conspiracy_theory/.
63. Joseph Curl and Kara Rowland, "Census battle intensifies; GOP leader threatens lawsuit," *The Washington Times*, Feb. 13, 2009, www.washingtontimes.com/news/2009/feb/13/gregg-withdrawal-foreshadows-census-debate/.
64. "Times Topics: Acorn," *The New York Times*, http://topics.nytimes.com/top/reference/times topics/organizations/a/acorn/index.html.
65. Cristina Corbin, "ACORN to Play Role in 2010 Census," FOXNews.com, March 18, 2009, www.foxnews.com/politics/2009/03/18/acorn-play-role-census/.
66. The Associated Press, "Census Bureau Drops Acorn from 2010 Effort," *The New York Times*, Sept. 12, 2009, www.nytimes.com/2009/09/12/us/politics/12acorn.html.
67. Quoted in David Stout, "Obama's Census Choice Unsettles Republicans," *The New York Times*, April 3, 2009, www.nytimes.com/2009/04/03/washington/03census.html?scp=6&sq=gary%20locke%20and%20judd%20gregg%20and%20census&st=cse.
68. Timothy J. Alberta, "Census Nominee Rules Out Statistical Sampling in 2010," *The Wall Street Journal*, May 15, 2009, http://online.wsj.com/article/SB124241977657124963.html.
69. "A Surprise Reaction," *op. cit.*
70. Terri Ann Lowenthal, "Taking Stock: A Mid-Census Reality Check," The Census Project Blog, April 20, 2010, http://censusprojectblog.org/.
71. For background see Jennifer Gavin, "Redistricting," *CQ Researcher*, Feb. 16, 2001, pp. 113-128.
72. Sam Roberts, "New Option for the States on Inmates in the Census," *The New York Times*, Feb. 11, 2010, www.nytimes.com/2010/02/11/us/politics/11census.html.
73. Erica L. Green, "Baltimore will gain residents in prison count shift," *The Baltimore Sun*, April 24, 2010, http://articles.baltimoresun.com/2010-04-24/news/bs-md-inmate-census-20100425_1_prison-towns-state-and-federal-inmates-census-bureau.
74. See also Dēmos, "A Dilution of Democracy: Prison-Based Gerrymandering," www.demos.org/pubs/prison_gerrymand_factsheet.pdf.
75. Reamer, "Counting for Dollars," *op. cit.*

76. "Count Us in Favor," *The New York Times*, March 29, 2010, www.nytimes.com/2010/03/ 29/opinion/29mon2.html?scp=1&sq=count%20us%20in%20favor&st=cse. The bill is HR 4945 and S3167.
77. "Statement in Support of The Census Oversight, Efficiency and Management Reform Act," The Census Project, March 25, 2010, www.the census-project.org/letters/cp-fmrdirs-bill-25march 2010.pdf.
78. *Ibid.*
79. "Census on Campus: Students' Frequently Asked Questions," U.S. Bureau of the Census, http://2010.census.gov/campus/pdf/FAQ_Census OnCampus.pdf.
80. Ed O'Keefe, "Was 2010 Census a Success?" Federal Eye blog, *The Washington Post*, April 26, 2010, http://voices.washingtonpost.com/federal-eye/2010/04/was_2010_census_a_success.html.

BIBLIOGRAPHY

Books

Anderson, Margo J., ed., *Encyclopedia of the U.S. Census*, CQ Press, 2000.
An expert on the census who is a professor of history and urban studies at the University of Wisconsin, Milwaukee, offers dozens of articles on topics ranging from redistricting to government use of census data, plus an appendix with historical data.

Anderson, Margo J., and Stephen E. Fienberg, *Who Counts? The Politics of Census-Taking in Contemporary America*, Russell Sage Foundation, 1999.
Census expert Anderson and a professor of statistics and social science at Carnegie Mellon University examine how well the census counts the U.S. population.

Nobles, Melissa, *Shades of Citizenship: Race and the Census in Modern Politics*, Stanford University Press, 2000.
An MIT political scientist examines issues surrounding race during U.S. and Brazilian censuses and argues that "census-taking is one of the institutional mechanisms by which racial boundaries are set."

Articles

Farley, Rob, "Census takers contend with suspicion and spin over the 2010 count," *St. Petersburg Times*, April 11, 2010, www.tampabay.com/incoming/census-takers-contend-with-suspicion-and-spin-over-the-2010-count/1086739.
The newspaper examines three assertions about the census designed to quell Republican fears that the census is intrusive and cumbersome.

Roberts, Sam, "New Option for the States on Inmates in the Census," *The New York Times*, Feb. 11, 2010, www.ny times.com/2010/02/11/us/politics/11census.html?scp=1&sq=new%20option%20for%20the%20states%20on%20inmates%20in%20the%20census&st=cse.
In time for congressional and legislative reapportionment, the Census Bureau in May 2011 will give states more flexibility on how to count prison inmates.

Robertson, Campbell, "Suspense Builds Over Census for New Orleans," *The New York Times*, April 7, 2010, www.nytimes.com/2010/04/08/us/08orleans.html?scp=1&sq=suspense%20builds%20over%20census%20for%20new%20orleans&st=cse.
The final census count for hurricane-battered New Orleans "will go far in determining how [the city] thinks about itself, whether it is continuing to mount a steady comeback or whether it has sputtered and stalled," says *The Times*.

Santos, Fernanda, "Door to Door, City Volunteers Try to Break Down Resistance to the Census," *The New York Times*, March 31, 2010, www.nytimes.com/2010/04/01/us/01count.html?scp=1&sq=Door%20to%20Door,%20city%20volunteers%20try%20to%20break%20down&st=cse.
The work of volunteers in helping to encourage participation is crucial, as demonstrated by their efforts in New York City, a reporter finds.

Williams, Juan, "Marketing the 2010 census with a conservative-friendly face," *The Washington Post*, March 1, 2010, www.washingtonpost.com/wp-dyn/content/article/ 2010/02/28/AR2010022803364.html.
The Census Bureau has responded to challenges from conservatives with "unprecedented outreach," including putting the bureau's name on a NASCAR auto.

Reports and Studies

"Preparing for the 2010 Census: How Philadelphia and Other Cities Are Struggling and Why It Matters," Pew Charitable Trusts, Oct. 12, 2009, www.pewtrusts.org/uploaded Files/wwwpewtrustsorg/Reports/Philadelphia-area_grantmaking/Census%20Report%20101209_FINAL.pdf?n=8566.
Most of the 11 cities studied had less money and smaller staffs for local census preparation than they did a decade ago, raising concerns about undercounting in urban areas.

Prewitt, Kenneth, "The American People, Census 2000: Politics and Science in Census Taking," **Russell Sage Foundation and Population Reference Bureau, 2003,** www.thecensusproject.org/factsheets/PrewittSAGE-PRBCensus2000Report.pdf.
A former Census Bureau director writes in this lengthy and useful analysis that while the census may sound "dull and technical," it "is a drama at the very center of our political life."

Williams, Jennifer D., "The 2010 Decennial Census: Background and Issues," Congressional Research Service, April 27, 2009, http://assets.opencrs.com/rpts/R40551_20090427.pdf.
"Far from being simple . . . , the attempt to find and correctly enumerate 100 percent of U.S. residents is increasingly complicated and expensive," declares this overview.

On the Web

The Census Bureau (www.census.gov) offers extensive data and other information on the U.S. population, households, business, congressional districts and more. A separate Web site for Census 2010 (www.2010.census.gov) includes details, in multiple languages, about this year's decennial census, plus a blog by Census Bureau Director Robert M. Groves.

For More Information

Brookings Institution, 1775 Massachusetts Ave., N.W., Washington, DC 20036; (202) 797-6000; www.brookings.edu. Centrist think tank that studies a wide range of policy issues.

Center for Immigration Studies, 1522 K St., N.W., Suite 820, Washington, DC 20005-1202; (202) 466-8185; www.cis.org. Conservative nonprofit research organization that provides information on immigration.

Dēmos, 220 5th Ave., 5th Floor, New York, NY 10001; (212) 633-1405; www.demos.org. Liberal research and advocacy group that follows economic, voter-participation and other policy issues.

Election Data Services, 6171 Emerywood Ct., Manassas, VA 20112; (202) 789-2004; www.electiondataservices.com. Political consulting firm specializing in redistricting, election administration and analysis and presentation of census and political data.

Heritage Foundation, 214 Massachusetts Ave., N.E., Washington, DC 20002-4999; (202) 546-4400; www.heritage.org. Conservative think tank that studies wide range of policy issues, including the census.

National Association of Counties, 25 Massachusetts Ave., N.W., Suite 500, Washington, DC 20001; (202) 393-6226; www.naco.org. National organization representing county governments.

National Institute for Latino Policy, 101 Avenue of the Americas, Suite 313, New York, NY 10013; (800) 590-2516; www.latinopolicy.org. Nonprofit think tank that focuses on policies affecting the Latino community.

Pew Research Center, 1615 L St., N.W., Suite 700, Washington, DC 20036; (202) 419-4300; www.pewresearch.org. Nonpartisan group that provides information on issues, attitudes and trends shaping the United States and world.

Prison Policy Initiative, P.O. Box 127, Northampton, MA 01061; www.prisonpolicy.org. Nonprofit group that researches impact of Census Bureau policy that counts people where they are incarcerated rather than in their home communities.

Russell Sage Foundation, 112 East 64th St., New York, NY 10065; (212) 750-6000; www.russellsage.org. A research center on the social sciences that performs scholarly analysis of census results.

U.S. Census Bureau, 4600 Silver Hill Rd., Washington, DC 20233; (301) 763-4636; www.census.gov. Federal agency that conducts the decennial census.

4 Immigration Conflict

Kenneth Jost

Arizona residents rally in Phoenix on July 31, 2010, in support of the state's hard-hitting immigration law, which gives police new responsibilities to look for immigration law violators. Five states last year followed Arizona's lead. The U.S. Supreme Court will hear arguments on the disputed Arizona measure on April 25.

From *CQ Researcher*, March 9, 2012.

Micky Hammon minced no words when he urged his fellow Alabama legislators to enact what would become the toughest of a batch of new state laws cracking down on illegal immigrants. "This bill is designed to make it difficult for them to live here so they will deport themselves," Hammon, leader of the Alabama House of Representatives' Republican majority, said during the April 5, 2011, debate on the bill.[1]

Immigrant-rights groups say the law, which took effect Sept. 28 after partly surviving a court challenge, is as tough as Hammon hoped — and more. "It's been pretty devastating," says Mary Bauer, legal director of the Southern Poverty Law Center in Montgomery, Alabama's capital. "Tens of thousands of people have left, and the people who remain are completely terrorized by this law."

Among other provisions, Alabama's law requires state and local law enforcement officers to determine the immigration status of anyone arrested, detained or stopped if there is a "reasonable suspicion" that the person is an alien "unlawfully present" in the United States. Failure to carry alien-registration papers is made a state crime, punishable by up to 30 days in jail for a first offense.

Alabama, with an estimated 120,000 unlawful aliens living within its borders as of 2010, was one of five states that last year followed Arizona's lead a year earlier in giving police new responsibilities to look for immigration law violators.* Republican-controlled legislatures in each of the states said they were forced to

---

* The others were Utah, Indiana, Georgia and South Carolina.

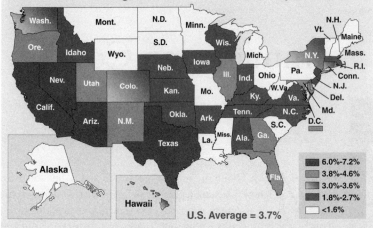

West Has Highest Share of Unlawful Aliens

Undocumented immigrants comprise at least 6 percent of the population of Arizona, California, Nevada and Texas and at least 3.8 percent of the population of New Mexico, Oregon and Utah. Unlawful immigrants also make up sizable percentages of several other states' populations, including New Jersey and Florida. The nationwide average is 3.7 percent.

Unauthorized Immigrants as a Share of State Population, 2010

Source: Jeffrey Passel and D'Vera Cohn, "Unauthorized Immigrant Population: National and State Trends, 2010," Pew Research Center, February 2011, p. 29, www.pewhispanic.org/files/reports/133.pdf

act because the federal government was not doing enough to control illegal immigration at the border or in U.S. workplaces. Opponents warned the laws risked profiling Latinos, including U.S. citizens and aliens with legal status.

All six of the laws are being challenged in federal court, with the "stop and check" provisions blocked except in Alabama's case. In the most important case, the Arizona measure is scheduled to be argued before the U.S. Supreme Court on April 25 after a federal appeals court struck some of the law enforcement provisions as interfering with federal immigration policy.[2]

Alabama's law includes a unique provision that prohibits unlawful aliens from entering into any "business transaction" with state or local governments. Some public utilities in the state interpreted the provision to require proof of immigration status for water or electricity service. Until a federal judge's injunction on Nov. 23, some counties were applying the law to prevent unlawful immigrants from renewing permits for mobile homes.[3]

Once the law went into effect, school attendance by Latino youngsters dropped measurably in response to a provision — later blocked — requiring school officials to ascertain families' immigration status. The fear of deportation also led many immigrants in Alabama to seek help in preparing power-of-attorney documents to make sure their children would be taken care of in case the parents were deported, according to Isabel Rubio, executive director of the Hispanic Interest Coalition of Alabama. "You have to understand the sheer terror that people fear," Rubio says.

The law is having a palpable effect on the state's economy as well, according to agriculture and business groups. With fewer migrant workers, "some farmers have planted not as much or not planted at all," says Jeff Helms, spokesman for the Alabama Farmers Federation. Jay Reed, president of Associated Builders and Contractors of Alabama, says it has been harder to find construction workers as well.

Reed, co-chair of the multi-industry coalition Alabama Employers for Immigration Reform, wants to soften provisions that threaten employers with severe penalties, including the loss of operating licenses, for hiring undocumented workers. He and other business leaders also worry about the perception of the law outside the state's borders. "Some of our board members have expressed concern about our state's image and the effect on economic-development legislation," Reed says.

Reed says the state's Republican governor, Robert Bentley, and leaders in the GOP-controlled legislature are open to some changes in the law. But the two chief sponsors, Hammon and state Sen. Scott Beason, are both batting down any suggestions that the law will be repealed or its law enforcement measures softened.

"We are not going to weaken the law," Hammon told reporters on Feb. 14 as hundreds of opponents of the measure demonstrated outside the State House in Montgomery. "We are not going to repeal any section of the law."[4]

On the surface, Alabama seems an improbable state to take a leading role in the newest outbreak of nativist concern about immigration and immigrants. Alabama's unauthorized immigrant population has increased nearly fivefold since 2000, but the state still ranks relatively low in the proportion of unauthorized immigrants in the population and in the state's workforce.

Alabama's estimated 120,000 unauthorized immigrants comprise about 2.5 percent of the state's total population. Nationwide, the estimated 11.8 million unauthorized immigrants represent about 3.7 percent of the population. Alabama's estimated 95,000 unauthorized immigrants with jobs represent about 4.2 percent of the workforce. Nationwide, 8 million undocumented workers account for about 5.2 percent of the national workforce.[5]

Nationwide, the spike in anti-immigrant sentiment is also somewhat out of synch with current conditions. Experts and advocates on both sides of the immigration issues agree that the total unauthorized immigrant population has fallen somewhat from its peak in 2007, mainly because the struggling U.S. economy offers fewer jobs to lure incoming migrant workers.

"The inflow of illegals has slowed somewhat," says Mark Krikorian, executive director of the Center for Immigration Studies (CIS) in Washington. The center describes its stance as "low-immigration, pro-immigrant."[6]

Jobs were a major focus of the debate that led to Alabama's passage of the new law. "This is a jobs bill," Beason said as the measure, known as HB 56, reached final passage in June. "We have a problem with an illegal workforce that displaces Alabama workers. We need to put those people back to work."[7]

Today, Beason, running against an incumbent congressman for the U.S. House seat in the Birmingham area, credits the law with helping Alabama lower its

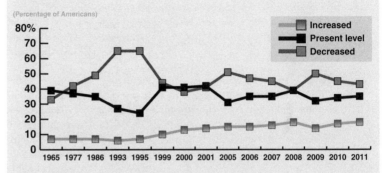

Americans Want Less Immigration

More than 40 percent of Americans say they favor a lower level of immigration, reflecting a view that has prevailed over most of the past half-century. About one in six want immigration to increase, while about one-third favor the current level.

Should immigration be kept at its present level, increased or decreased?

Sources: Jeffrey M. Jones, "Americans' Views on Immigration Holding Steady," Gallup, June 2011, www.gallup.com/poll/148154/americans-views-immigration-holding-steady.aspx; Roger Daniels, Guarding the Golden Door, Hill and Wang Press, December 2004, p. 233

unemployment rate from 9.8 percent in September to 8.1 percent in December. "I promised that the anti-illegal immigration law would open up thousands of jobs for Alabamians, and it has done that," Beason said in a Jan. 26 statement.

A University of Alabama economist, however, doubts the law's claimed effect on unemployment. Samuel Addy, director of the university's Center for Business and Economic Research in Tuscaloosa, notes that unemployment actually has increased, rather than declined, in the four sectors in the state viewed as most dependent on immigrant labor: agriculture, construction, accommodation and food and drinking places.[8]

In a nine-page study released in January, Addy contends instead that the immigration law is likely to hurt the state's economy overall. After assuming that 40,000 to 80,000 workers leave the state, Addy calculated that the law could reduce the state's gross domestic product by $2.3 billion to $10.8 billion. State income and sales taxes could take a $56.7 million to $265.4 million hit, Addy projected, while local sales tax revenue could decline by $20.0 million to $93.1 million. Hammon dismissed the report as "baloney."[9]

Immigration Law Basics

Even experts find it confusing.

Immigrating legally to the United States is difficult at best for those who fit into categories defined in mind-numbing detail by federal law and impossible for those who do not. Here is a primer on a body of law that is complex and confusing even to immigration experts, and all the more so for would-be Americans.

The Immigration and Nationality Act — sets an overall limit of 675,000 permanent immigrants each year. The limit does not apply to spouses, unmarried minor children or parents of U.S. citizens, but the sponsoring U.S. citizen must have an income above the U.S. poverty level and promise to support family members brought to the United States.

Who gets visas — Out of the 675,000 quota, 480,000 visas are made available under family-preference rules, and up to 140,000 are allocated for employment-related preferences. Unused employment-related visas may be reallocated to the family-preference system.

The family-sponsored visas are allocated according to a preference system with numerical limits for each category. Unmarried adult children of U.S. citizens are in the first category, followed, in this order, by spouses and minor children of lawful permanent residents; unmarried adult children of lawful permanent residents; married adult children of U.S. citizens; and brothers and sisters of U.S. citizens. No other relatives qualify for a family preference. Again, the sponsor must meet financial and support requirements.

Visa categories —The employment-based preference system also sets up ranked, capped categories for would-be immigrants. The highest preference is given to "persons of extraordinary ability" in the arts, science, education, business or athletics; professors and researchers; and some multinational executives. Other categories follow in this order: persons with professional degrees or "exceptional" abilities in arts, science or business; workers with skills that are in short supply and some "unskilled" workers for jobs not temporary or seasonal; certain "special immigrants," including religious workers; and, finally, persons who will invest at least $500,000 in a job-creating enterprise that employs at least 10 full-time workers.

In addition to the numerical limits, the law sets a cap of 7 percent of the quota for immigrants from any single country. The limit in effect prevents any immigrant group from dominating immigration patterns.

Refugees — Separately, Congress and the president each year set an annual limit for the number of refugees who can be admitted based on an inability to return to their home country because of a fear of persecution. Currently, the overall ceiling is 76,000. The law also allows an unlimited number of persons already in the United States, or at a port of entry, to apply for asylum if they were persecuted or fear persecution in their home country. A total of 21,113 persons were granted asylum in fiscal 2010. Refugees and asylees are eligible to become lawful permanent residents after one year.

Debate over the rules — An immigrant who gets through this maze and gains the coveted "green card" for lawful permanent residents is eligible to apply for U.S. citizenship after five years (three years for the spouse of a U.S. citizen). An applicant must be age 18 or over and meet other requirements, including passing English and U.S. history and civics exams. About 675,000 new citizens were naturalized in 2010, down from the peak of slightly more than 1 million in the pre-recession year of 2008.

Applying for citizenship — Immigration advocates say the quotas are too low, the rules too restrictive and the waiting periods for qualified applicants too long. Low-immigration groups say the record level of legal and illegal immigration over the past decade shows the need to lower the quotas and limit the family-reunification rules.

— Kenneth Jost

Five months after it took effect, however, the law's impact may be ebbing. Police appear not to have enforced the law vigorously, perhaps stung by the nationwide embarrassment when a visiting Mercedes-Benz executive from Germany carrying only a German identification card was held after a traffic stop until he could retrieve his passport. With police enforcement lagging, some of the immigrants who left appear to be coming back. "Some people have returned," Rubio says.[10]

Meanwhile, attorneys for the Obama administration and the state were preparing for arguments on March 1 before the federal appeals court in Atlanta in the government's suit challenging the state law on grounds of federal pre-emption, the doctrine used to nullify state laws that conflict with U.S. laws and policies. The Hispanic Interest Coalition had challenged the law on broader grounds in an earlier suit, represented by the American Civil Liberties Union and other national groups.

In a massive, 115-page ruling, U.S. District Court Judge Sharon Blackburn upheld major parts of the law on Sept. 28 and then allowed the upheld parts to go into effect even as the government and civil rights groups appealed. Blackburn blocked half a dozen provisions on pre-emption grounds but found no congressional intent to prevent states from checking the immigration status of suspected unlawful aliens.[11]

With the legal challenges continuing, the political debates over immigration are intensifying. Republican presidential candidates generally agree on criticizing the Obama administration for failing to control illegal immigration even though the administration has increased the number of immigrants deported to their home countries. The Republican hopefuls disagree among themselves on the steps to deal with the problem.

For his part, Obama concedes that Congress will not approve a broad immigration overhaul in this election year. But he used his State of the Union speech to call for passage of a bill — the so-called DREAM Act — to allow legal status for some immigrants who have served in the U.S. military or completed college.

As the immigration debates continue, here are some of the major questions being considered:

Major State Immigration Laws in Court

Five states have followed Arizona's lead in giving state and local police a role in enforcing federal immigration law. With some variations, the laws authorize or require police after an arrest, detention or stop to determine the person's immigration status if he or she is reasonably suspected of being unlawfully in the United States. In legal challenges, federal courts have blocked major parts of five of the laws; the Supreme Court is set to hear arguments on April 25 in Arizona's effort to reinstate the blocked portions of its law.

State	Bill, date signed	Legal challenge
Arizona	S.B. 1070: April 23, 2010	*United States v. Arizona* Major parts enjoined; pending at Supreme Court
Utah	H.B. 497: March 15, 2011	*Utah Coalition of La Raza v. Herbert* Major parts blocked; suit on hold pending Supreme Court ruling in Arizona case
Indiana	SB 590: May 10, 2011	*Buquer v. City of Indianapolis* Major parts blocked; suit on hold pending Supreme Court ruling in Arizona case
Georgia	HB 87: May 13, 2011	*Georgia Latino Alliance v. Deal* Major parts blocked; on hold at 11th Circuit
Alabama	HB 56: June 9, 2011	*United States v. Alabama* Major parts upheld; on hold at 11th Circuit
South Carolina	S20: June 27, 2011	*United States v. South Carolina* Major parts blocked; suit on hold pending Supreme Court ruling in Arizona case

Sources: National Conference of State Legislatures, http://www.ncsl.org/issues-research/immig/omnibus-immigration-legislation.aspx; American Civil Liberties Union; news coverage.

Is illegal immigration an urgent national problem?

As the anti-illegal immigration bill HB 56 was being signed into law, Alabama's Republican Party chairman depicted the measure as needed to protect the state's taxpayers and the state's treasury. "Illegal immigrants have become a drain on our state resources and a strain on our taxpaying, law-abiding citizens," Bill Armistead declared as Republican governor Bentley signed it into law on June 9, 2011.[12]

Today, Republican officials continue to defend the law in economic terms. "Unemployment was sky high, especially in areas where there's high concentration of these undocumented workers," says Shana Kluck, the party's spokeswoman. Kluck also points to the cost on

Unlawful Immigration High Despite Dip

Despite a dip beginning in 2007, an estimated 11.2 million unauthorized immigrants live in the United States, one-third more than a decade ago (top graph). An estimated 8 million are in the civilian labor force, a 45 percent increase since 2000 (bottom graph).

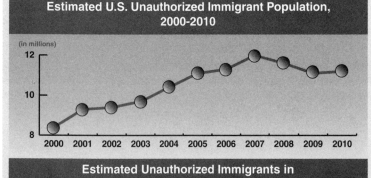

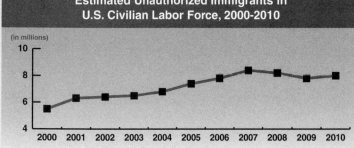

Source: Jeffrey Passel and D'Vera Cohn, "Unauthorized Immigrant Population: National and State Trends, 2010," Pew Research Center, February 2011, pp. 1, 17, www.pewhispanic.org/files/reports/133.pdf

public treasuries. "The public-assistance budgets were bursting at the seams," she says. "That's why HB 56 was necessary."

Nationally, groups favoring tighter immigration controls make similar arguments about immigrants' economic impact, especially on jobs and wages for citizen workers. "We need to slow down immigration," says Dan Stein, president of the Federation for American Immigration Reform (FAIR), pointing to the current high levels of unemployment and underemployment.

"Immigration helps to decimate the bargaining leverage of the American worker," Stein continues. "If you use a form of labor recruitment that bids down the cost of labor, that leads you to a society where a small number are very, very rich, there's nobody in the middle, and everyone is left scrambling for crumbs at the bottom."

"The longer this economic doldrum continues, the more likely you are to see some real pushback on immigration levels as such, not just illegal immigration," says Krikorian with the low-immigration group Center for Immigration Studies. The group's research director, Steven Camarota, said if illegal immigrants are forced to go back to their home countries, there is "an ample supply of idle workers" to take the jobs freed up.[13]

Pro-immigration groups say their opponents exaggerate the costs and all but ignore the benefits of immigrant labor. "They never take into account the contributions that undocumented immigrants make," says Mary Giovagnoli, director of the American Immigration Council's Immigration Policy Center.

"We've had an economy that depends on immigration," says Ali Noorani, executive director of the National Immigration Forum. "It would be an economic and social disaster for 11 million people to pick up and leave."

Madeleine Sumption, a senior labor market analyst with the pro-immigration Migration Policy Institute in Washington, acknowledges that immigration may have what she calls a "relatively small" impact on employment and wages for citizen workers. But the costs are more than offset, she says, by the benefits to employers, consumers and the overall economy.

The benefits can be seen particularly in sectors that employ large numbers of immigrants, according to Sumption. "The United States has a large agriculture industry," she says. "Without immigration labor, it would almost certainly not be possible to produce the same volume of food in the country." The health care industry also employs a high number of immigrants, especially in low-end jobs, such as home-health aides and hospital orderlies. "These are jobs for which there is a growing demand and an expectation of an even more rapidly growing demand in the future," Sumption says.

In Alabama, Rubio with the Hispanic coalition and the leaders of the agriculture and construction groups all discount Camarota's contention that citizen workers are available to take the jobs currently being filled by immigrants. "We did not have a tomato crop [last] summer because the immigrants who pick that crop weren't there," Rubio says. "This is hard work, and many people don't want to do it."

Reed, president of the state's builders and contractors' organization, says construction companies similarly cannot find enough workers among the citizen labor force. "Traditionally, in our recruitment efforts we have unfortunately not found those that are unemployed are ready and willing to perform these kinds of jobs that require hard labor in extreme weather conditions," Helms says.

The claimed costs and benefits from immigration for public treasuries represent similarly contentious issues. Low- or anti-immigration groups emphasize the costs in government services, especially education and medical care. Pro-immigration groups point to the taxes that even unlawful aliens pay and the limits on some government benefits under federal and state laws. In an independent evaluation of the issue, the nonpartisan Congressional Budget Office in 2007 found a net cost to state and local governments but called the impact "most likely modest."[14]

The cost-benefit debates are more volatile in stressed economic times, according to David Gerber, a professor of history at the University of Buffalo and author of a primer on immigration. "People get angry when they feel that immigrants are competing for jobs of people in the United States or when they feel that immigrants are getting access to social benefits that the majority is paying for," Gerber says. "In harder times, it makes people angrier than in times of prosperity."[15]

Even so, David Coates, a professor at Wake Forest University in Winston-Salem, N.C., and co-editor of a book on immigration issues, notes that fewer undocumented workers are entering the United States now than in the peak year of 2007, and the Obama administration has been deporting unlawful aliens in significantly greater numbers than previous administrations. Asked whether illegal immigration should be less of an issue for

Republican Alabama Gov. Robert Bentley addresses lawmakers at the state capitol on June 9, 2011, before signing the state's new immigration law. Republican cosponsors of the law, Sen. Scott Beason (left), and state Rep. Micky Hammon (right), both oppose softening or repealing the law. But state business interests want to ease provisions that threaten employers with severe penalties for hiring undocumented workers. They also worry about the perception of the law outside the state.

state legislators and national politicians, Coates replies simply: "Yes, in terms of the numbers."

Should state and local police enforce immigration laws?

Alabama's HB 56 was stuffed with more provisions for state and local governments to crack down on illegal immigrants than the Arizona law that inspired it or any of the copy-cat laws passed in four other states. Along with the stop-and-check section, the law includes provisions making it a state crime for an unauthorized alien to apply for work and barring unauthorized aliens from court enforcement of any contracts. Another provision made it illegal to conceal, harbor or rent to an illegal immigrant or even to stop in a roadway to hire workers.

Opponents harshly criticized the enforcement provisions as they were signed into law. "It turns Alabama into a police state where anyone could be required to show their citizenship papers," said Cecillia Wang, director of the ACLU's Immigrant Rights Project. Noorani, with the National Immigration Forum, called the law "a radical departure from the concepts of fairness and equal treatment under the law," adding, "It makes it a crime, quite literally, to give immigrants a ride without checking their legal status."[16]

Today, even with the harboring provision and several others blocked from taking effect, opponents say the law is having the terrorizing effect that they had predicted on immigrants both legal and illegal as well as U.S. citizens of Hispanic background. "We've heard numerous accounts of people who have been stopped under very suspicious circumstances, while driving or even while walking on the street," says Justin Cox, an ACLU staff attorney in Atlanta working on the case challenging the law.

The law "has had the effect that it was intended to have," Cox says, "which was to make immigration status a pervasive issue in [immigrants'] everyday lives."

Supporters of the law are defending it, but without responding to specific criticisms. "We've seen an awful lot of illegal immigrants self-deport," House Majority Leader Hammon said as opponents rallied in Montgomery on Feb. 14. "We're also seeing Americans and legal immigrants taking these jobs."[17]

When questioned by a Montgomery television station about critical documentaries prepared for the progressive group Center for American Progress, Hammon declined to look at the films but attacked the filmmaker. "We don't need an activist director from California to come in here and tell us whether this law is good or not," Hammon said. "The people in Alabama can see it for themselves."[18]

Nationally, immigration hawks view the new state laws as unexceptionable. "They're helping the feds to enforce immigration laws," says Center for Immigration Studies executive director Krikorian. "The question is [whether] local police use immigration laws as one of the tools in their tool kit to help defend public safety."

"Every town is a border town, every state is a border state," Krikorian continues. "Immigration law has to be part of your approach, part of your strategy in dealing with some kind of a significant problem."

FAIR president Stein strongly objects to the Obama administration's legal challenges to the state laws. "It should be a massive, industrial-strength issue that the Obama administration" has attacked the laws on grounds of federal pre-emption. But Giovagnoli with the pro-immigration American Immigration Council says the state laws should be struck down. "Congress has established that immigration enforcement is a federal matter," she says. "The more states get into the mix, the more you create a real patchwork of laws that don't make sense together."

As Krikorian notes, federal law already provides for cooperative agreements between the federal government and state or local law enforcement agencies to enforce immigration laws. U.S. Immigration and Customs Enforcement (ICE), the successor agency to the Immigration and Naturalization Service, touts the so-called 287(g) program on its website as one of the agency's "top partnership initiatives." The program, authorized by an immigration law overhaul in 1996, permits the federal agency to delegate enforcement power to state or local law enforcement after officers have received training on federal immigration law.[19]

Pro-immigration groups say the training requirement distinguishes 287(g) programs from the broader roles being given state and local police by the new state laws. "State and local law enforcement officers are not trained to do this kind of work," says Cox. "Inevitably, they're going to rely on pernicious stereotypes about what an undocumented immigrant looks like." The result, Cox continues, "is a breakdown of trust between the immigrant community and law enforcement, which ultimately affects all of us. It undermines public safety."

Alabama Republicans, however, insist that the state law fulfills a 2010 campaign pledge that helped the GOP gain control of both houses of the state legislature and that it remains popular despite the criticisms and legal challenges. "We've definitely been criticized," party spokeswoman Kluck acknowledges, but she blames the criticisms on "misinformation." As for possible changes in the law, Hammon and other legislative leaders are guarding details until a bill with proposed revisions can be completed by late March.

Should Congress make it easier for illegal immigrants to become citizens?

With many Republican primary and caucus voters viewing illegal immigration as a major issue, presidential candidate and former Massachusetts Gov. Mitt Romney says he has a simple solution: Get undocumented immigrants to "self-deport" to their home countries and then get in the legal waiting line for U.S. citizenship. But one of his rivals for the Republican nomination, former House speaker Newt Gingrich, pushing stronger enforcement at the border, mocks Romney's belief that 11 million unlawful aliens will go back home voluntarily. Speaking to a Spanish-language television network in late January on the eve of the Florida presidential primary, Gingrich called Romney's plan "an Obama-level fantasy."[20]

Pro-immigration groups agree that Romney's stance is unrealistic. "It's a fantasy to think that people are going to self-deport," says the National Immigration Forum's Noorani. Unlike border-control advocates, however, Noorani and other pro-immigration advocates and experts say the solution is "a path to legal citizenship" for the undocumented.

"We need a functioning legal immigration system, a system that has the necessary legal channels for a person to immigrate here whether for a job or his family," Noorani says. "That doesn't exist here." Without "a solution," Noorani says, "the only ones who are winning are the crooked employer who is more than happy to exploit the undocumented, poor third-country worker."

Immigration hawks quickly denounce any broad legalization proposal as an "amnesty" that they say is neither workable nor deserved. "All amnesties attract future immigration," says the CIS's Krikorian. "All amnesties reward lawbreakers." As evidence, immigration critics point to the broad amnesty granted under the 1986 immigration act to some 3 million immigrants — and its evident failure within a matter of years to stem the flow of illegal immigrants from across the country's Southern borders.

As an alternative to broader proposals, pro-immigration groups are pushing narrower legislation that in its current form would grant conditional legal status to immigrants who came to the United States before age 16 and have lived in the United States for at least five years. The so-called DREAM Act — an acronym for the Development, Relief and Education for Alien Minors Act — had majority support in both chambers of the Democratic-controlled Congress in 2010 but failed to get a Senate floor vote in the face of Republican opposition.

The DREAM Act starts with the assumption that immigrants who came to the United States as children have grown up as Americans and are innocent of any intentional immigration violations. They would be eligible for a conditional permanent residency and could then earn a five-year period of temporary residency by completing two years in the U.S. military or two years in a four-year college or university.

"The intent of the DREAM Act is to provide legal status for individuals who are enlisting in our armed services or pursuing higher education," says Noorani. "Whether they came here at age 5 or 15, I think we only stand to benefit."

"It's a good way to show that if you provide legal status to folks like this, the world is not going to fall apart," says Giovagnoli with the American Immigration Council. "In fact, the country would be better off if these people were in the system."

Similar proposals have been introduced in Congress since 2001. Immigration hawks acknowledge the proposals' appeal and argue over details. "The concept that people who have been here from childhood, that it might be prudent to legalize people in that position, is a plausible one," says Krikorian. But, he adds, "As it exists, it is not a good piece of legislation."

As one change, Krikorian says the eligibility age should be lowered, perhaps to age 10 or below. "The reason they pick 16 is it legalizes more," he says. Paradoxically, Krikorian also says the bill is too narrow by allowing temporary residency only by joining the military or going to college. "What if you're not college material?" he asks.

Krikorian also dismisses the idea of absolving those who arrived as youngsters of any responsibility for immigration violations. "The parents . . . did know what they were doing," he says. The bill needs to be changed, he says, "to ensure that no parent would ever be able to benefit" under family-reunification rules.

Gingrich and some GOP lawmakers favor a narrower version of the DREAM Act that would extend legal status for serving in the military but not for going to college. Supporters oppose the narrower version. "If you read the bill carefully, it would actually allow a fewer number of immigrants to enlist in the military than the original," Noorani says. Krikorian also dismisses the alternative. He calls it "phony," adding that it would help "only a few thousand people a year."

The White House pushed hard for the bill in the Democratic-controlled Congress's lame-duck session in December 2010 but fell short in the Senate. Obama continues to speak out for the bill, most prominently in his State of the Union address. "[I]f election-year politics keeps Congress from acting on a comprehensive plan, let's at least agree to stop expelling responsible young people who want to staff our labs, start new businesses, defend this country," Obama said near the end of the Jan. 24 speech. "Send me a law that gives them the chance to earn their citizenship. I will sign it right away."[21]

BACKGROUND
Constant Ambivalence

The United States is a nation of immigrants that has been ambivalent toward immigration through most of its history. Immigrants are alternately celebrated as the source of diversity and criticized as agents of disunity. Immigrants were recruited to till the soil, build the cities and labor in the factories, but often criticized for taking jobs from and lowering wages for the citizen workforce. The federal government reflected popular sentiment in restricting immigration in the late 19th and early 20th century, only to draw later criticism for exclusionary policies. Today, the government is drawing criticism for liberalized policies adopted in the 1960s and for ineffective border enforcement from the 1980s on.[22]

African slaves were the first source of immigrant labor in America, but Congress banned importation of slaves in 1808. Otherwise, the United States maintained an open-door policy on immigration until the late 19th century. Europe's mid-century agricultural crisis drove waves of German and Irish peasants to the United States in the 1840s and '50s. Many were met by ethnic and anti-Catholic hostility, embodied in the first nativist political movement: the American or so-called Know-Nothing Party. The party carried one state in the 1856 presidential election and then faded from history.

Significant Chinese immigration began with the California Gold Rush of 1849 and increased with the post-Civil War push to complete the transcontinental railroad. Stark warnings of the "Yellow Peril" led to a series of restrictions at the federal level — most notably, the Chinese Exclusion Act of 1882, which suspended immigration of Chinese laborers and barred citizenship for those already in the United States. Significantly for present-day debates, efforts to deport those in the country or to seal the borders against new Chinese immigrants were no more than partly successful.[23]

Congress laid the basis for present-day immigration law and policy in a series of increasingly restrictive enactments from the 1890s through the early 1920s that coincided with the great waves of immigration from Europe, including regions previously unrepresented in the American polity. The Immigration Act of 1891 established the Bureau of Immigration, then under the Treasury Department, and provided for border inspections and deportation of unlawful aliens. Additional laws prescribed admission procedures, created categories of inadmissible immigrants and tightened the exclusion of immigrants from Asia.

The restrictive policies drew support from nativists worried about assimilation, pro-labor groups concerned about the impact on jobs and wages and progressive leaders fearful of the impact on the urban environment. The restrictions culminated in the passage of the first and second Quota Acts in 1921 and 1924, which established the first quantitative limitation on immigration (350,000, lowered to 150,000) and a national-origins system that favored immigrants from Northern and Western Europe. In reporting the bill in 1924, a House committee stated: "If the principle of liberty . . . is to endure, the basic strain of our population must be preserved."[24]

The Quota Acts' exception for Western Hemisphere immigrants combined with the unrest associated with the Mexican Revolution (1910-1929) to produce what Stanford historian Albert Camarillo calls "a tsunami" in immigration across the United States' Southern border. Camarillo says 1.5 million Mexicans — one-tenth of the country's population — relocated to the United States by the end of the 1930s.[25] The influx fueled ethnic prejudice embodied in the derogatory term "wetback" to refer to the Mexican immigrants, most of whom actually entered by crossing arid regions rather than fording the Rio Grande River.

During the Great Depression of the 1930s, the federal and state governments — concerned about the impact on jobs for Anglo workers — sent tens of thousands of Mexicans back to their home country, sometimes with force and little regard for due process. During World War II, however, the government worked with Mexico to establish the so-called bracero program to use temporary immigrant labor for agricultural work. The "temporary" program continued into the 1960s.

CHRONOLOGY

Before 1960 *Congress establishes immigration quotas.*

1920s Quota Act (1921), Johnson-Reed Act (1924) establish national-origins quota system, favoring Northern European immigrants over those from Southern Europe, elsewhere.

1952 McCarran-Walter Act retains national-origins system but adds small quotas for some Asian countries.

1960s *Congress opens door to immigration from outside Europe.*

1965 Immigration and Nationality Act of 1965 abolishes national-origins quota system dating from 1920s; allows dramatic increase in immigration from Central and South America, Asia.

1980s-1990s *Illegal immigration increases, becomes major public issue.*

1986 Immigration Reform and Control Act allows amnesty for many unlawful aliens, prohibits employers from employing undocumented workers; enforcement proves elusive.

1996 Illegal Immigration Reform and Immigrant Responsibility Act seeks to strengthen border security, streamline deportation proceedings; creates optional E-Verify system for employers to electronically check immigration status of workers and job applicants.

2000-Present *Illegal immigration increases; immigration reform falters in Congress; state laws to crack down on illegal immigration challenged in court.*

2001 Al Qaeda 9/11 attacks on U.S. soil underscore national security threat from failure to track potential terrorists entering United States (Sept. 11); USA Patriot Act gives immigration authorities more power to exclude suspected terrorists (Oct. 26).

2005-2006 Immigration reform measures fail in GOP-controlled Congress despite support from Republican President George W. Bush; Congress approves Secure Fence Act, to require double-layer fence on U.S.-Mexico border.

2007 Immigration reform measure dies in Senate; three motions to cut off debate fail (June 7). . . . Arizona legislature passes employer-sanctions law; companies threatened with loss of operating license for knowingly hiring undocumented aliens, required to use federal E-Verify system; signed into law by Democratic Gov. Janet Napolitano (July 2). . . . Unauthorized immigrant population in United States peaks near 12 million.

2008 Democrat Barack Obama elected president after campaign with little attention to immigration issues (Nov. 4); Obama carries Hispanic vote by 2-1 margin.

2009 Obama endorses immigration reform, but without specifics; issue takes back seat to economic recovery, health care.

2010 Arizona enacts law (S.B. 1070) to crack down on illegal immigrants; measure requires police to check immigration status if suspect or detainee is reasonably believed to be unlawful alien; makes it a crime to fail to carry alien registration papers; signed by Republican Gov. Jan Brewer (April 23); federal judge blocks parts of law (July 28). . . . DREAM Act to allow legal status for unlawful aliens who entered U.S. as minors approved by House of Representatives (Dec. 8) but fails in Senate: 55-41 vote is short of supermajority needed for passage (Dec. 18).

2011 Utah, Indiana, Georgia follow Arizona's lead in giving state, local police immigration-enforcement powers (March, May). . . . Federal appeals court upholds injunction against parts of Arizona's S.B. 1070 (April 11). . . . Supreme Court upholds Arizona's employer-sanctions law 5-3 (May 21). . . . Alabama enacts nation's toughest state law on illegal immigrants, HB 56 (June 9). . . . Federal judge blocks some parts of HB 56, allows others to take effect (Sept. 28).

2012 Immigration is flashpoint for Republican presidential candidates. . . . Obama urges passage of DREAM Act (Jan. 24). . . . Alabama, Georgia laws argued before U.S. appeals court (March 1). . . . Supreme Court to hear arguments on Arizona's S.B. 1070 (April 25); ruling due by end of June.

Journalist Reveals His Immigration Secret

"There's nothing worse than being in limbo."

When journalist-turned-immigration rights activist Jose Antonio Vargas traveled to Alabama with a documentary filmmaker, he found a Birmingham restaurant patron who strongly supported the state law cracking down on undocumented aliens. "Get your papers or get out," the patron said.

"What if I told you I didn't [have papers]?" Vargas is heard asking off camera. "Then you need you get your ass home then," the patron rejoined.[1]

Vargas says he is home — in America, where he has lived since his Filipina mother sent him, at age 12, to live in California with his grandparents in 1993. "I'm an American without papers," says Vargas, who came out as an undocumented immigrant in dramatic fashion in a 4,300-word memoir in *The New York Times Magazine* in June 2011.[2]

In the story, Vargas recounts how he learned at age 16 that he was carrying a fake green card when he applied for a driver's license. The DMV clerk let him go. Back home, Vargas confronted his grandfather, who acknowledged the forgery and told Vargas not to tell anyone else.

For the next 14 years, Vargas kept his non-status secret from all but a handful of enablers as he completed high school and college and advanced rapidly from entry-level newspaper jobs to national-impact journalism at *The Washington Post*, *Huffington Post* and glossy magazines. His one attempt at legal status ended in crushing disappointment in 2002 when an immigration lawyer told him he would have to return to the Philippines and wait for 10 years to apply to come back.

Vargas was inspired to write about his life by the example of four undocumented students who walked from Miami to Washington, D.C., in 2010 to lobby for the DREAM Act, the status-legalizing proposal for immigrants who came to the United States as minors. Vargas's story, published by *The Times* after *The Washington Post* decided not to, quickly went viral in old and new media alike.

In the eight months since, Vargas has founded and become the public face for a Web-based campaign, Define American (www.defineamerican.org). "Define American brings new voices into the immigration conversation, shining a light on a growing 21st century Underground Railroad: American citizens who are forced to fill in where our broken immigration system fails," the mission statement reads. "Together, we are going to fix a broken system."

The DREAM Act fell just short of passage in Congress in December 2010 and has gotten little traction since. Broader proposals to give legal status to some of the 11 million unlawful

Journalist Jose Antonio Vargas disclosed in *The New York Times* in June 2011 that he was an undocumented immigrant.

aliens are far off the political radar screen. Vargas is critical of Alabama's law cracking down on illegal immigration but acknowledges the states' frustration with federal policies. "At the end of the day, the federal government hasn't done anything on this issue," he says.

In the meantime, Vargas waits. "There's nothing worse than being in limbo," he says. In the story, he cited some of the hardships for the undocumented. As one example, he cannot risk traveling to the Philippines, so he has yet to meet his 14-year-old brother. But Vargas says he has no plan to "self-deport." "I love this country," he says.

— *Kenneth Jost*

---

[1] "The Two Faces of Alabama," http://isthisalabama.org/. The films by director Chris Weitz were prepared under the auspices of the Center for American Progress. Some comments from Vargas are from a Feb. 15, 2012, screening of the videos at the center.

[2] Jose Antonio Vargas, "Outlaw," *The New York Times Magazine*, June 26, 2011, p. 22. Disclosure: the author is a professional acquaintance and Facebook friend of Vargas.

Congress liberalized immigration law with a 1952 statute that included restrictionist elements as well and then, dramatically, with a 1965 law that scrapped the Eurocentric national-origins system and opened the gate to increased immigration from Latin America and Asia.

The 1952 law preserved the national-origins system but replaced the Chinese Exclusion Act with very small quotas for countries in the so-called Asia-Pacific Triangle. The act also eliminated discrimination between sexes. Over the next decade, immigration from European countries declined, seemingly weakening the rationale for the national-origins system. Against the backdrop of the civil rights revolution, the national-origins system seemed to many also to be antithetical to American values. The result was the Immigration Act of 1965, which replaced the national-origins system with a system of preferences favoring family reunification or to lesser extents admissions of professionals or skilled or unskilled workers needed in the U.S. workforce.

Quickly, the demographics of immigration shifted — and dramatically. Immigration increased overall under the new law, and the new immigrants came mostly from Latin America and Asia. By 1978, the peak year of the decade, 44 percent of legal immigration came from the Americas, 42 percent from Asia and only 12 percent from Europe.[26]

Cracking Down?

Immigration to the United States increased overall in the last decades of the 20th century, and illegal immigration in particular exploded to levels that fueled a public and political backlash. Congress and the executive branch tried to stem the flow of undocumented aliens first in 1986 by combining employer sanctions with an amnesty for those in the country for several years and then a decade later by increasing enforcement and deportations.

Then, in the wake of the Sept. 11, 2001, terrorist attacks on the United States, Congress and President George W. Bush joined in further efforts to tighten admission procedures and crack down on foreigners in the country without authorization.

Estimates of the number of immigrants in the United States illegally are inherently imprecise, but the general upward trend from the 1980s until a plateau in the 2000s is undisputed. As Congress took up immigration bills in the mid-1980s, the Census Bureau estimated the number of those undocumented at 3 million to 5 million; many politicians used higher figures. The former Immigration and Naturalization Service put the number at 3.5 million in 1990 and 7.0 million a decade later. Whatever the precise number, public opinion polls registered increasing concern about the overall level of immigration. By the mid-1990s, Gallup polls found roughly two-thirds of respondents in favor of decreasing the level of immigration, one-fourth in favor of maintaining the then-present level and fewer than 10 percent for an increase.[27]

The congressional proposals leading to the Immigration Reform and Control Act in 1986 sought to stem illegal immigration while recognizing the reality of millions of undocumented immigrants and the continuing need for immigrant labor, especially in U.S. agriculture. The law allowed legal status for immigrants in the country continuously since 1982 but aimed to deter unauthorized immigration in the future by forcing employers to verify the status of prospective hires and penalizing them for hiring anyone without legal status. Agricultural interests, however, won approval of a new guest worker program. Some 3 million people gained legal status under the two provisions, but illegal immigration continued to increase even as civil rights groups warned that the employer sanctions would result in discrimination against Latino citizens.

The backlash against illegal immigration produced a new strategy for reducing the inflows: state and federal laws cutting off benefits for aliens in the country without authorization. California, home to an estimated 1.3 million undocumented aliens at the time, blazed the path in 1994 with passage of a ballot measure, Proposition 187, that barred any government benefits to illegal aliens, including health care and public schooling. The education provision was flatly unconstitutional under a 1982 ruling by the U.S. Supreme Court that guaranteed K-12 education for school-age alien children.[28]

The measure mobilized Latino voters in the state. They contributed to the election of a Democratic governor in 1998, Gray Davis, who dropped the state's defense of the measure in court in his first year in office. In the meantime, however, Congress in 1996 had approved provisions — reluctantly signed into law by President Bill Clinton — to deny unauthorized aliens most federal benefits, including food stamps, family assistance and Social Security. The law allows states to deny state-provided benefits

A Maricopa County deputy arrests a woman following a sweep for illegal immigrants in Phoenix on July 29, 2010. The police operation came after protesters against Arizona's tough immigration law clashed with police hours after the law went into effect. Although the most controversial parts of the law have been blocked, five other states — Utah, Indiana, Georgia, Alabama and South Carolina — last year enacted similar laws.

as well; today, at least a dozen states have enacted such further restrictions.

The centerpieces of the 1996 immigration law, however, were measures to beef up enforcement and toughen deportation policy. The Illegal Immigration Reform and Immigrant Responsibility Act authorized more money for the Border Patrol and INS, approved more funding for a 14-mile border fence already under construction and increased penalties for document fraud and alien smuggling. It sought to streamline deportation proceedings, limit appeals and bar re-entry of any deportee for at least five years. And it established an Internet-based employer verification system (E-Verify) aimed at making it easier and more reliable for employers to check legal status of prospective hires. The law proved to be tougher on paper, however, than in practice. The border fence remains incomplete, deportation proceedings backlogged and E-Verify optional and — according to critics — unreliable. And illegal immigration continued to increase.

The 9/11 attacks added homeland security to the concerns raised by the nation's porous immigration system. In post-mortems by immigration hawks, the Al Qaeda hijackers were seen as having gained entry into the United States with minimal scrutiny of their visa applications and in many cases having overstayed because of inadequate follow-up.[29] The so-called USA Patriot Act, enacted in October 2001 just 45 days after the attacks, gave the INS — later renamed the U.S. Citizenship and Immigration Service and transferred to the new Department of Homeland Security — greater authority to exclude or detain foreigners suspected of ties to terrorist organizations. The act also mandated information-sharing by the FBI to identify aliens with criminal records. Along with other counterterrorism measures, the act is viewed by supporters today as having helped prevent any successful attacks on U.S. soil since 2001. Illegal immigration, however, continued to increase — peaking at roughly 12 million in 2007.

Getting Tough

Congress and the White House moved from post-9/11 security issues to broader questions of immigration policy during Bush's second term, but bipartisan efforts to allow legal status for unlawful aliens fell victim to Republican opposition in the Senate. As a presidential candidate, Democrat Obama carried the Hispanic vote by a 2-1 margin over Republican John McCain after a campaign with limited attention to immigration issues. In the White House, Obama stepped up enforcement in some respects even as he urged Congress to back broad reform measures. The reform proposals failed with Democrats in control of both the House and the Senate and hardly got started after Republicans regained control of the House in the 2010 elections.

Bush lent support to bipartisan reform efforts in the Republican-controlled Congress in 2005 and 2006 and again in the Democratic-controlled Congress in his final two years in office. Congress in 2006 could agree only on authorizing a 700-mile border fence after reaching an impasse over a House-passed enforcement measure and a Senate-approved path-to-citizenship bill. Bush redoubled efforts in 2007 by backing a massive, bipartisan bill that would have allowed "earned citizenship" for aliens who had lived in the United States for at least eight years and met other requirements. As in the previous Congress, many Republicans rejected the proposal as an unacceptable amnesty. The bill died on June 7 after the Senate rejected three cloture motions to cut off debate.[30]

Immigration played only a minor role in the 2008 presidential campaign between Obama and McCain,

Senate colleagues who had both supported reform proposals. Both campaigns responded to growing public anger over illegal immigration by emphasizing enforcement when discussing the issue, but the subject went unmentioned in the candidates' three televised debates. McCain, once popular with Hispanics in his home state of Arizona, appeared to have paid at the polls for the GOP's hard line on immigration. Exit polls indicated that Obama won 67 percent of a record-size Hispanic vote; McCain got 31 percent — a significant drop from Bush's 39 percent share of the vote in 2004.[31]

With Obama in office, Congress remained gridlocked even as the president tried to smooth the way for reform measures by stepping up enforcement. The congressional gridlock had already invited state lawmakers to step into the vacuum. State legislatures passed more than 200 immigration-related laws in 2007 and 2008, according to a compilation by the National Conference on State Legislatures; the number soared to more than 300 annually for the next three years.[32]

The numbers included some resolutions praising the country's multi-ethnic heritage, but most of the new state laws sought to tighten enforcement against undocumented aliens or to limit benefits to them. Among the earliest of the new laws was an Arizona measure — enacted in June 2007, two weeks after the Senate impasse in Washington — that provided for lifting the business licenses of companies that knowingly hired illegal aliens and mandated use of the federal E-Verify program to ascertain status of prospective hires. Business and labor groups, supported by the Obama administration, challenged the law on federal preemption grounds. The Supreme Court's 5-3 decision in May 2011 to uphold the law prompted several states to enact similar mandatory E-Verify provisions.[33]

The interplay on immigration policy between Washington and state capitals is continuing. In Obama's first three years in office, the total number of removals increased to what ICE calls on its website "record levels." Even so, Arizona lawmakers and officials criticized federal enforcement as inadequate in the legislative debate leading to SB 1070's enactment in April 2010. Legal challenges followed quickly — first from a Latino organization; then from a broad coalition of civil rights and civil liberties groups; and then, on July 6, from the Justice Department. The most controversial parts of the law have been blocked, first by U.S. District Court Judge Susan Bolton's injunction later that month and then by the Ninth Circuit's decision affirming her decision in April 2011. The legal challenges did not stop five other states — Utah, Indiana, Georgia, Alabama and South Carolina — from enacting similar laws in spring and early summer 2011. Civil rights groups and the Justice Department followed with similar suits challenging the new state enactments.

As the 2012 presidential campaign got under way, immigration emerged as an issue between Republican candidates vying for the party's nomination. The issue posed difficulties for the GOP hopefuls as they sought to appeal to rank-and-file GOP voters upset about illegal immigration without forfeiting Latino votes in the primary season and in the general election. Presumed frontrunner Mitt Romney took a hard stance against illegal immigration in early contests but softened his message in advance of winning the pivotal Jan. 31 primary in Florida with its substantial Hispanic vote.

Despite differences in details and in rhetoric, the three leading GOP candidates — Romney, Newt Gingrich and Rick Santorum — all said they opposed the DREAM Act in its present form even as Obama called for Congress to pass the bill in his State of the Union speech.

CURRENT SITUATION

Obama's Approach

The Obama administration is claiming success in increasing border enforcement and removing unlawful aliens while injecting more prosecutorial discretion into deportation cases. But the mix of firm and flexible policies is resulting in criticism from both sides of the issue.

U.S. Immigration and Customs Enforcement (ICE) counted a record 396,906 "removals" during fiscal 2011, including court-ordered deportations as well as administrative or voluntary removals or returns. The number includes a record 216,698 aliens with criminal convictions.[34]

Meanwhile, Homeland Security Secretary Janet Napolitano says illegal border-crossing attempts have decreased by more than half in the last three years. In a Jan. 30 speech to the National Press Club in Washington, Napolitano linked the decline to an increase in the number of Border Patrol agents to 21,000, which she said was more than double the number in 2004.

"The Obama administration has undertaken the most serious and sustained actions to secure our borders in our nation's history," Napolitano told journalists. "And it is clear from every measure we currently have that this approach is working."[35]

Immigration hawk Krikorian with the Center for Immigration Studies gives the administration some, but only some, credit for the removal statistics. "They're not making up the numbers," Krikorian says. But he notes that immigration removals increased during the Bush administration and that the rate of increase has slowed under Obama.

In addition, Krikorian notes that new figures compiled by a government information tracking service indicate the pace of new immigration cases and of court-processed deportations slowed in the first quarter of fiscal 2012 (October, November and December 2011). A report in early February by Syracuse University's Transactional Records Access Clearinghouse (TRAC) shows 34,362 court-ordered removals or "voluntary departures" in the period, compared to 35,771 in the previous three months — about a 4 percent drop.

A separate TRAC report later in the month showed what the service called a "sharp decline" in new ICE filings. ICE initiated 39,331 new deportation proceedings in the nation's 50 immigration courts during the first quarter of fiscal 2012, according to the report, a 33 percent decline from the 58,639 new filings in the previous quarter.[36]

"The people in this administration would like to pull the plug on enforcement altogether," Krikorian complains. "They refuse to ask for more money for detention beds and then plead poverty that they can't do more."

From the opposite perspective, some Latino officials and organizations have been critical of the pace of deportations. When Obama delivered a speech in favor of immigration reform in El Paso, Texas, in May 2011, the president of the National Council of La Raza tempered praise for the president's position with criticism of the deportation policy.

"As record levels of detention and deportation continue to soar, families are torn apart, innocent youth are being deported and children are left behind without the protection of their parents," Janet Murguía said in a May 10 press release. "Such policies do not reflect American values and do little to solve the problem. We can do better."[37]

Latinos disapprove of the Obama administration's handling of deportations by roughly a 2-1 margin, according to a poll by the Pew Hispanic Center in December 2011. Overall, the poll found 59 percent of those surveyed opposed the administration's policy while 27 percent approved. Disapproval was higher among foreign-born Latinos (70 percent) than those born in the United States (46 percent).[38]

Napolitano and ICE Director John Morton are both claiming credit for focusing the agency's enforcement on the most serious cases, including criminal aliens, repeat violators and recent border crossers. Morton announced the new "prosecutorial discretion" policy in an agency-wide directive in June 2011.[39]

TRAC, however, questions the claimed emphasis on criminal aliens. The 39,331 new deportation filings in the first quarter of fiscal 2012 included only 1,300 against aliens with convictions for "aggravated felonies," as defined in immigration law. "Even this small share was down from previous quarters," the Feb. 21 report states. Aliens with aggravated felony convictions accounted for 3.3 percent of deportations in the period, compared to 3.8 percent in the previous quarter.[40]

The administration is also being questioned on its claim — in Obama's El Paso speech and elsewhere — to have virtually completed the border fence that Congress ordered constructed in the Secure Fence Act of 2006.[41] The act called for the 652-mile barrier to be constructed of two layers of reinforced fencing but was amended the next year — with Bush still in office — to give the administration more discretion in what type of barriers to use.

As of May 2011, the barrier included only 36 miles of double-layer fencing, according to PolitiFact, the fact-checking service of the *Tampa Bay Times*. The rest is single-layer fencing or vehicle barriers that critic Krikorian says are so low that a pedestrian can step over them. PolitiFact calls Obama's claim "mostly false."[42]

Meanwhile, the administration is preparing to extend nationwide its controversial "Secure Communities" program, which tries to spot immigration law violators by matching fingerprints of local arrestees with the database of the Department of Homeland Security (DHS). A match allows U.S. Immigration and Customs Enforcement (ICE)

AT ISSUE

Should Congress pass the DREAM Act?

YES
Walter A. Ewing
Senior Researcher, Immigration Policy Center American Immigration Council

Written for *CQ Researcher*, March 2012

The Development, Relief and Education for Alien Minors Act is rooted in common sense. To begin with, it would benefit a group of unauthorized young people who, in most cases, did not come to this country of their own accord. Rather, they were brought here by their parents. The DREAM Act would also enable its beneficiaries to achieve higher levels of education and obtain better, higher-paying jobs, which would increase their contributions to the U.S. economy and American society. In short, the DREAM Act represents basic fairness and enlightened self-interest.

More than 2 million young people would benefit from the DREAM Act, and their numbers grow by roughly 65,000 per year. They came to the United States before age 18, many as young children. They tend to be culturally American and fluent in English. Their primary ties are to this country, not the countries of their birth. And the majority had no say in the decision to come to this country without authorization — that decision was made by the adult members of their families. Punishing these young people for the actions of their parents runs counter to American social values and legal norms. Yet, without the DREAM Act, these young people will be forced to live on the margins of U.S. society or will be deported to countries they may not even know.

Assuming they aren't deported, the young people who would benefit from the DREAM Act face enormous barriers to higher education and professional jobs because of their unauthorized status. They are ineligible for most forms of college financial aid and cannot work legally in this country. The DREAM Act would remove these barriers, which would benefit the U.S. economy.

The College Board estimates that over the course of a working lifetime, a college graduate earns 60 percent more than a high school graduate. This higher income translates into extra tax revenue flowing to federal, state and local governments.

The DREAM Act is in the best interest of the United States both socially and economically. It would resolve the legal status of millions of unauthorized young people in a way that is consistent with core American values. And it would empower these young people to become better-educated, higher-earning workers and taxpayers. Every day that goes by without passage of the DREAM Act is another day of wasted talent and potential.

NO
Mark Krikorian
Executive Director, Center for Immigration Studies

Written for *CQ Researcher*, March 2012

The appeal of the DREAM Act is obvious. People brought here illegally at a very young age and who have grown up in the United States are the most sympathetic group of illegal immigrants. Much of the public is open to the idea of amnesty for them.

But the actual DREAM Act before Congress is a deeply flawed measure in at least four ways:

• Rather than limiting amnesty to those brought here as infants and toddlers, it applies to illegal immigrants who arrived before their 16th birthday. But if the argument is that their very identity was formed here, age 7 would be a more sensible cutoff. That is recognized as a turning point in a child's psychological development (called the "age of reason" by the Catholic Church, hence the traditional age for First Communion). Such a lower-age cutoff, combined with a requirement of at least 10 years' residence here, would make a hypothetical DREAM Act 2.0 much more defensible.

• All amnesties are vulnerable to fraud, even more than other immigration benefits. About one-fourth of the beneficiaries of the amnesty granted by Congress in 1986 were liars, including one of the leaders of the 1993 World Trade Center bombing. But the DREAM Act specifically prohibits the prosecution of anyone who lies on an amnesty application. So you can make any false claim you like about your arrival or schooling in America without fear of punishment. A DREAM Act 2.0 would make clear that any lies, no matter how trivial, will result in arrest and imprisonment.

• All amnesties send a signal to prospective illegal immigrants that, if you get in and keep your head down, you might benefit from the next amnesty. But the bill contains no enforcement provisions to limit the need for another DREAM Act a decade from now. That's why a serious proposal would include measures such as electronic verification of the legal status of all new hires, plus explicit authorization for state and local enforcement of immigration law.

• Finally, all amnesties reward illegal immigrants — in this case including the adults who brought their children here illegally. A credible DREAM Act 2.0 would bar the adult relatives of the beneficiaries from ever receiving any immigration status or even a right to visit the United States. If those who came as children are not responsible, then those who are responsible must pay the price for their lawbreaking.

to issue a so-called detainer against violators, sending their cases into the immigration enforcement system. The administration touts the program as "a simple and common sense" enforcement tool. Critics note, however, that it has resulted in wrongful detention of U.S. citizens in a considerable but unknown number of cases. One reason for the mistakes: The DHS database includes all immigration transactions, not just violations, and thus could show a match for an immigrant with legal status.[43]

Supreme Court Action

All eyes are on the Supreme Court as the justices prepare for arguments on April 25 in Arizona's effort to reinstate major parts of its trend-setting law cracking down on illegal immigrants.

The Arizona case is the furthest advanced of suits challenging the six recently enacted state laws that give state and local police responsibility for enforcing federal immigration laws. After winning an injunction blocking major parts of the Arizona law, the Obama administration filed similar suits against Alabama's HB 56 as well as the Georgia and South Carolina measures.

The ACLU's Immigrants Rights Project, along with Hispanic and other civil rights groups, has filed separate challenges on broader grounds against all six laws. Federal district courts have blocked parts of all the laws, though some contentious parts of Alabama's law were allowed to take effect.

District court judges in the Indiana, South Carolina and Utah cases put the litigation on hold pending the Supreme Court's decision in the Arizona case. Alabama and Georgia asked the Eleventh U.S. Circuit Court of Appeals to postpone the scheduled March 1 arguments in their cases, but the court declined.

Judge Charles R. Wilson opened the Atlanta-based court's March 1 session, however, by announcing that the three-judge panel had decided to withhold its opinion until after the Supreme Court decides the Arizona case. "Hopefully, that information will help you in framing your arguments today," Wilson told the assembled lawyers.[44]

Wilson and fellow Democratic-appointed Circuit Judge Beverly B. Martin dominated the questioning during the three hours of arguments in the cases. Both judges pressed lawyers defending Alabama and Georgia on the effects of their laws on the education of children, the ability of illegal aliens to carry on with their lives while immigration courts decided their cases and what would happen if every state adopted their approach to dealing with immigration violations. The third member of the panel, Richard Voorhees, a Republican-appointed federal district court judge, asked only three questions on technical issues.

Opening the government's argument in the Alabama case, Deputy Assistant U.S. Attorney General Beth Brinkmann said the state's law attempts to usurp exclusive federal authority over immigration. "The regulation of immigration is a matter vested exclusively in the national government," Brinkman said. "Alabama's state-specific regulation scheme violates that authority. It attacks every aspect of an alien's life and makes it impossible for the alien to live."

Alabama Solicitor General John C. Neiman Jr. drew sharp challenges from Wilson and Martin even before he began his argument. Wilson focused on the law's Section 10, which makes it a criminal misdemeanor for an alien unlawfully present in the United States to fail to carry alien registration papers.

"You could be convicted and sent to jail in Alabama even though the Department of Homeland Security says, 'You're an illegal alien, but we've decided you're going to remain here in the United States?' " Wilson asked.

Neiman conceded the point. "If the deportation hearing occurred after the violation of Section 10, then yes," Neiman said. "Someone could be held to be in violation of Section 10 and then later be held not removable."

Wilson also pressed Neiman on the potential effects on the federal government's ability to control immigration policy if states enacted laws with different levels of severity. "These laws could certainly have the effect of making certain states places where illegal aliens would be likely to go," the state's attorney acknowledged.

Representing the ACLU in the separate challenge, Immigrants Rights Project director Wang sharply attacked the motive behind the Alabama law. The law, she said, was written to carry out the legislature's stated objective "to attack every aspect of an illegal immigrant's life so that they will deport themselves."*

---

*The appeals court on March 8 issued a temporary injunction blocking enforcement of two provisions, those prohibiting unlawful aliens from enforcing contracts in court or entering into business transactions with state or local government agencies.

In Washington, lawyers for Arizona filed their brief with the Supreme Court defending its law, SB 1070, in early February. Among 20 *amicus* briefs filed in support of Arizona's case is one drafted by the Michigan attorney general's office on behalf of 16 states similarly defending the states' right to help enforce federal immigration law. A similar brief was filed by nine states in the Eleventh Circuit in support of the Alabama law.

The government's brief in the Arizona case is due March 19. Following the April 25 arguments, the Supreme Court is expected to decide the case before the current term ends in late June.

Meanwhile, legal challenges to other parts of the state's law are continuing in federal court in Arizona. In a Feb. 29 ruling, Bolton blocked on First Amendment grounds a provision prohibiting people from blocking traffic when they offer day labor services on the street.[45]

OUTLOOK
A Broken System

The immigration system is broken. On that much, the pro- and low-immigration groups agree. But they disagree sharply on how to fix it. And the divide defeats any attempts to fix it even if it can be fixed.

Pro-immigration groups like to talk about the "three-legged stool" of immigration reform: legal channels for family- and job-based immigration; a path to citizenship for unlawful aliens already in the United States; and better border security. Low-immigration groups agree on the need for better border controls but want to make it harder, not easier, for would-be immigrants and generally oppose legal status for the near-record number of unlawful aliens.

Public opinion is ambivalent and conflicted on immigration issues even as immigration, legal and illegal, has reached record levels. The nearly 14 million new immigrants, legal and illegal, who came to the United States from 2000 to 2010 made that decade the highest ever in U.S. history, according to the low-immigration Center for Immigration Studies. The foreign-born population reached 40 million, the center says, also a record.[46]

Some public opinion polls find support for legal status for illegal immigrants, especially if the survey questions specify conditions to meet: 66 percent supported it, for example, in a Fox News poll in early December 2011. Three weeks earlier, however, a CNN poll found majority support (55 percent) for concentrating on "stopping the flow of illegal immigrants and deporting those already here" instead of developing a plan for legal residency (42 percent).[47]

Other polls appear consistently to find support for the laws in Arizona and other states to crack down on illegal immigrants — most recently by a 2-1 margin in a poll by Quinnipiac University in Connecticut.[48] "Popular sentiment is always against immigration," says Muzaffar Chishti, director of the Migration Policy Institute's office at New York University School of Law and himself a naturalized U.S. citizen who emigrated from his native India in 1974.

Pro-immigration groups say the public is ahead of the politicians in Washington and state capitals who are pushing for stricter laws. State legislators "have chosen to scapegoat immigration instead of solving tough economic challenges," says Noorani with the National Immigration Forum. "There are politicians who would rather treat this as a political hot potato," he adds, instead of offering "practical solutions."

From the opposite side, the Federation for American Immigration Reform's Stein says he is "pessimistic, disappointed and puzzled" by what he calls "the short-sighted views" of political leaders. Earlier, Stein says, "politicians all over the country were touting the virtues of engagement in immigration policy." But now he complains that even Republicans are talking about "amnesty and the DREAM Act," instead of criticizing what he calls the Obama administration's "elimination of any immigration enforcement."

Enforcement, however, is one component of the system that, if not broken, is at least completely overwhelmed. In explaining the new prosecutorial discretion policy, ICE director Morton frankly acknowledged the agency "has limited resources to remove those illegally in the United States."[49] The nation's immigrant courts have a current backlog of 300,225 cases, according to a TRAC compilation, double the number in 2001.[50]

Employers' groups say the system's rules for hiring immigrants are problematic at best. In Alabama, Reed with the contractors' group says employers do their best to comply with the status-verification requirements but find the procedures and paperwork difficult. The farm federation's Helms says the same for the rules for temporary guest workers. "We're working at the national level to have a more effective way to hire legal migrant workers to do those jobs that it's hard to find local workers to do," he says.

The rulings by the Supreme Court on the Arizona law will clarify the lines between federal and state enforcement responsibilities, but the Center for Immigration Studies' Krikorian says the decision is likely to increase the politicization of the issue. A ruling to uphold the law will encourage other states to follow Arizona's lead, he says, but would also "energize the anti-enforcement groups." A ruling to find the state laws pre-empted, on the other hand, will mobilize pro-enforcement groups, he says.

The political and legal debates will be conducted against the backdrop of the nation's rapidly growing Hispanic population, attributable more to birth rates than to immigration.[51] "Whoever the next president is, whoever the next Congress is, will have to address this issue," says Giovagnoli with the American Immigration Council. "The demographics are not going to allow people to ignore this issue.

"I do believe we're going to reform the immigration system," Giovagnoli adds "It's going to be a lot of work. Even under the best of circumstances, it's a lot of work."

NOTES

1. Quoted in Kim Chandler, "Alabama House passes Arizona-style immigration bill," *The Birmingham News*, April 6, 2011, p. 1A.

2. The case is *Arizona v. United States*, 11-182. Background and legal filings compiled on SCOTUSblog, www.scotusblog.com/case-files/cases/arizona-v-united-states/?wpmp_switcher=desktop.-

3. See Human Rights Watch, "No Way to Live: Alabama's Immigration Law," December 2011, www.hrw.org/news/2011/12/13/usalabama-no-way-live-under-immigrant-law.

4. Quoted in David White, "Hundreds rally at State House seeking immigration law repeal," *The Birmingham News*, Feb. 15, 2012, p. 1A.

5. See "Unauthorized Immigrant Population: State and National Trends, 2010," Pew Hispanic Center, Feb. 1, 2011, pp. 23, 24, www.pewhispanic.org/files/reports/133.pdf. The U.S. Department of Homeland Security estimates differ slightly; for 2010, it estimates nationwide unauthorized immigrant population at 10.8 million.

6. For previous *CQ Researcher* coverage, see: Alan Greenblatt, "Immigration Debate," pp. 97-120, updated Dec. 10, 2011; Reed Karaim, "America's Border Fence," Sept. 19, 2008, pp. 745-768; Peter Katel, "Illegal Immigration," May 6, 2005, pp. 393-420; David Masci, "Debate Over Immigration," July 14, 2000, pp. 569-592; Kenneth Jost, "Cracking Down on Immigration," Feb. 3, 1995.

7. Quoted in David White, "Illegal immigration bill passes," *The Birmingham News*, June 3, 2011, p. 1A.

8. See Dana Beyerle, "Study says immigration law has economic costs," *Tuscaloosa News*, Jan. 31, 2012, www.tuscaloosanews.com/article/20120131/news/120139966. For Beason's statement, see http://scottbeason.com/2012/01/26/beason-statement-on-the-impact-of-hb-56-on-alabama-unemployment-rate/.

9. Samuel Addy, "A Cost-Benefit Analysis of the New Alabama Immigration Law," Center for Business and Economic Research, Culverhouse College of Commerce and Business Administration, University of Alabama, January 2012, http://cber.cba.ua.edu/New%20AL%20Immigration%20Law%20-%20Costs%20and%20Benefits.pdf; Hammon quoted in Brian Lyman, "Studies, surveys examine immigration law's impact," *The Montgomery Advertiser*, Feb. 1, 2012.

10. See Alan Gomez, "Immigrants return to Alabama," *USA Today*, Feb. 22, 2012, p. 3A; Jay Reeves, "Immigrants trickling back to Ala despite crackdown," The Associated Press, Feb. 19, 2012.

11. The decision in *United States v. Alabama*, 2:11-CV-2746-SLB, U.S.D.C.-N.D.Ala. (Sept. 28, 2011), is available via *The New York Times*: http://graphics8.nytimes.com/packages/pdf/national/112746memopnentered.pdf. For coverage, see Brian Lyman, "Judge allows key part of immigration

law to go into effect," *The Montgomery Advertiser*, Sept. 29, 2011; Brian Lawson, "Judge halts part of immigration law," *The Birmingham News*, Sept. 29, 2011, p. 1A. The Alabama Office of the Attorney General has a chronology of the legal proceedings: www.ago.state.al.us/Page-Immigration-Litigation-Federal.

12. Quoted in Eric Velasco, "Immigration law draws praise, scorn," *The Birmingham News*, June 10, 2011, p. 1A.

13. Steven A. Camarota, "A Need for More Immigrant Workers?," Center for Immigration Studies, June 2011, http://cis.org/no-need-for-more-immigrant-workers-q1-2011.

14. "The Impact of Unauthorized Immigrants on the Budgets of State and Local Governments," Congressional Budget Office, Dec. 6, 2007, p. 3, / www.cbo.gov/sites/default/files/cbofiles/ftp docs/87xx/doc8711/12-6-immigration.pdf.

15. David Gerber, *American Immigration: A Very Short Introduction* (2011).

16. Quoted in Velasco, *op. cit.*

17. Quoted in White, *op. cit.* Hammon's office did not respond to several *CQ Researcher* requests for an interview.

18. "Alabama's Illegal Immigration Law Gets Hollywood's Attention," WAKA/CBS8, Montgomery, Feb. 21, 2012, www.waka.com/home/top-stories/Alabamas-Illegal-Immigration-Law-Gets-Attention-From-Hollywood-139937153.html. The four separate videos by Chris Weitz, collectively titled "Is This Alabama?" are on an eponymous website: http://isthisalabama.org/.

19. See "Delegation of Immigration Authority 287(g) Immigration and Nationality Act," www.ice.gov/287g/ (visited February 2012).

20. See Sandhya Somashekhar and Amy Gardner, "Immigration is flash point in Fla. Primary," *The Washington Post*, Jan. 26, 2012, p. A6.

21. Text available on the White House website: www.whitehouse.gov/the-press-office/2012/01/24/remarks-president-state-union-address.

22. General background drawn from Gerber, *op. cit.*; Otis L. Graham Jr., *Unguarded Gates: A History of America's Immigration Crisis* (2004). Some country-by-country background drawn from Mary C. Waters and Reed Ueda (eds.), *The New Americans: A Guide to Immigration Since 1965* (2007).

23. Roger Daniels, *Guarding the Golden Door: American Immigration Policy and Immigrants Since 1882* (2004), pp. 19-22.

24. Quoted in Graham, *op. cit.*, p. 51.

25. Albert M. Camarillo, "Mexico," in Waters and Ueda, *op. cit.*, p. 506.

26. Figures from *INS Statistical Yearbook*, 1978, cited in Daniels, *op. cit.*, p 138.

27. Polls cited in Daniels, *op. cit.*, p. 233.

28. See *Plyler v. Doe*, 452 U.S. 202 (1982).

29. See Graham, *op. cit.*, Chap. 17, and sources cited therein.

30. "Immigration Rewrite Dies in Senate," *CQ Almanac 2007*, pp. 15-9 — 15-11, http://library.cqpress.com/cqalmanac/cqal07-1006-44907-2047763.

31. See Julia Preston, "Immigration Cools as Campaign Issue," *The New York Times*, Oct. 29, 2008, p. A20, www.nytimes.com/2008/10/29/us/politics/29immig.html; Mark Hugo Lopez, "How Hispanics Voted in the 2008 Election," Pew Hispanic Research Center, Nov. 5, 2008, updated Nov. 7, 2008, http://pewresearch.org/pubs/1024/exit-poll-analysis-hispanics.

32. "Immigration Policy Report: 2011 Immigration-Related Laws and Resolutions in the States (Jan. 1- Dec. 7, 2011)," National Conference of State Legislatures, www.ncsl.org/issues-research/immigration/state-immigration-legislation-report-dec-2011.aspx.

33. The decision is *Chamber of Commerce v. Whiting*, 563 U.S. — (2011). For coverage, see Kenneth Jost, *Supreme Court Yearbook 2010-2011*, http://library.cqpress.com/scyb/document.php?id=scyb10-1270-72832-2397001&type=hitlist&num=0.

34. See "ICE Removals, Fiscal Years 2007-2011," in Mark Hugo Lopez, *et al.*, "As Deportations Rise to Record Levels, Most Latinos Oppose Obama's Policy," Pew Hispanic Center, Dec. 28, 2011, p. 33, http://pewresearch.org/pubs/2158/

latinos-hispanics-immigration-policy-deportations-george-bush-barack-obama-administration-democrats-republicans. The report notes that ICE's statistics differ somewhat from those released by DHS, its parent department.

35. "Secretary of Homeland Security Janet Napolitano's 2nd Annual Address on the State of America's Homeland Security: Homeland Security and Economic Security," Jan. 30, 2012, www.dhs.gov/ynews/speeches/napolitano-state-of-america-homeland-security.shtm.

36. "Share of Immigration Cases Ending in Deportation Orders Hits Record Low," *TRAC Reports*, Feb. 7, 2012, http://trac.syr.edu/immigration/reports/272/; "Sharp Decline in ICE Deportation Filings," Feb. 21, 2012, http://trac.syr.edu/immigration/reports/274/. For coverage, see Paloma Esquivel, "Number of deportation cases down by a third," *Los Angeles Times*, Feb. 24, 2012, p. AA2, http://articles.latimes.com/2012/feb/24/local/la-me-deportation-drop-20120224.

37. Text of La Raza statement, www.nclr.org/index.php/about_us/news/news_releases/janet_murgua_president_and_ceo_of_nclr_responds_to_president_obamas_speech_in_el_paso_texas/. For coverage of the president's speech, see Milan Simonich, "In El Paso, President Obama renews national immigration debate, argues humane policy would aid national economy," *El Paso Times*, May 11, 2011.

38. Lopez, *op. cit.*, p. 16.

39. U.S. Immigration and Customs Enforcement: Memorandum, June 17, 2011, www.ice.gov/doclib/secure-communities/pdf/prosecutorial-discretion-memo.pdf. For coverage, see Susan Carroll, "ICE memo urges more discretion in immigration changes," *Houston Chronicle*, June 21, 2011, p. A3.

40. "Sharp Decline," *op. cit.*

41. For background, see Reed Karaim, "America's Border Fence," *CQ Researcher*, Sept. 19, 2008, pp. 745-768.

42. "Obama says the border fence is 'now basically complete,'" PolitiFact, www.politifact.com/truth-o-meter/statements/2011/may/16/barack-obama/obama-says-border-fence-now-basically-complete/. The original rating of "partly true" was changed to "mostly false" on July 27, 2011.

43. See "Secure Communities," on the ICE website: www.ice.gov/secure_communities/; Julia Preston, "Immigration Crackdown Snares Americans," *The New York Times*, Dec. 14, 2011, p. A20, www.nytimes.com/2011/12/14/us/measures-to-capture-illegal-aliens-nab-citizens.html?pagewanted=all.

44. Coverage of the hearing by contributing writer Don Plummer. For additional coverage, see Brian Lawson, "11th Circuit won't rule on Alabama/Georgia laws until after Supreme Court rules on Arizona," *The Huntsville Times*, March 2, 2012; Jeremy Redmon, "Court to rule later on Georgia, Alabama anti-illegal immigrant laws," *The Atlanta Journal-Constitution*, March 2, 2012.

45. See Jacques Billeaud, "Judge blocks day labor rules in AZ immigration law," The Associated Press, March 1, 2012.

46. Steven A. Camarota, "A Record-Setting Decade of Immigration, 2000-2010," Center for Immigration Studies, October 2011, www.cis.org/articles/2011/record-setting-decade.pdf.

47. Fox News poll, Dec. 5-7, 2011, and CNN/ORC International poll, Nov. 18-20, 2011, cited at www.PollingReport.com/immigration.htm.

48. Quinnipiac University poll, Feb. 14-20, 2011, cited *ibid*.

49. ICE memo, *op. cit.*

50. "Immigration Court Backlog Tool," Transactional Records Access Clearinghouse, http://trac.syr.edu/phptools/immigration/court_backlog/ (visited March 2012).

51. "The Mexican-American Boom: Births Overtake Immigration," Pew Hispanic Center, July 24, 2011, www.pewhispanic.org/files/reports/144.pdf. The report depicts the phenomenon as "especially evident" among Mexican-Americans; it notes that Mexican-Americans are on average younger than other racial or ethnic groups and that Mexican-American women have more children than their counterparts in other groups. For background, see David Masci, "Latinos' Future," *CQ Researcher*, Oct. 17, 2003, pp. 869-892.

BIBLIOGRAPHY

Books

Coates, David, and Peter M. Siavelis (eds.), *Getting Immigration Right: What Every American Needs to Know,* **Potomac, 2009.**
Essays by 15 contributors representing a range of backgrounds and views examine, among other issues, the economic impact of immigration and proposed reforms to address illegal immigration. Includes notes, two-page list of further readings. Coates holds a professorship in Anglo-American studies at Wake Forest University; Siavelis is an associate professor of political science there.

Daniels, Roger, *Guarding the Golden Door: American Immigration Policy and Immigrants Since 1882,* **Hill and Wang, 2004.**
A professor of history emeritus at the University of Cincinnati gives a generally well-balanced account of developments and trends in U.S. immigration policies from the Chinese Exclusion Act of 1882 through the immediate post-9/11 period. Includes detailed notes, 16-page bibliography.

Gerber, David, *American Immigration: A Very Short Introduction,* **Oxford University Press, 2011.**
A professor of history at the University of Buffalo gives a compact, generally positive overview of the history of immigration from colonial America to the present. Includes two-page list of further readings.

Graham, Otis L. Jr., *Unguarded Gates: A History of America's Immigration Crisis,* **Rowman & Littlefield, 2004.**
A professor emeritus at the University of California-Santa Barbara provides a critical account of the United States' transition from an open-border policy with relatively small-scale immigration to a system of managed immigration that he views today as overwhelmed by both legal and illegal immigration. Includes notes.

Reimers, David M., *Other Immigrants: The Global Origins of the American People,* **New York University Press, 2005.**
A New York University professor of history emeritus brings together new information and research about the non-European immigration to the United States, emphasizing the emergence of "a new multicultural society" since 1940. Individual chapters cover Central and South America, East and South Asia, the Middle East, "new black" immigrants and refugees and asylees. Includes extensive notes, six-page list of suggested readings.

Waters, Mary C., and Reed Ueda (eds.), *The New Americans: A Guide to Immigration Since 1965,* **Harvard University Press, 2007.**
The book includes essays by more than 50 contributors, some covering broad immigration-related topics and others providing individual portraits of immigrant populations by country or region of origin. Includes detailed notes for each essay, comprehensive listing of immigration and naturalization legislation from 1790 through 2002. Waters is a professor of sociology at Harvard University, Ueda a professor of history at Tufts University.

Articles

"Reap What You Sow," *This American Life,* **Jan. 27, 2012, www.thisamericanlife.org/radio-archives/episode/456/reap-what-you-sow.**
The segment by reporter Jack Hitt on the popular public radio program found that Alabama's law to encourage undocumented immigrants to self-deport was having unintended consequences.

Kemper, Bob, "Immigration Reform: Is It Feasible?," *Washington Lawyer,* **October 2011, p. 22, www.dcbar.org/for_lawyers/resources/publications/washington_lawyer/october_2011/immigration_reform.cfm.**
The article gives a good overview of recent and current immigration debates, concluding with the prediction that any "permanent resolution" will likely prove to be "elusive."

Reports and Studies

"No Way to Live: Alabama's Immigrant Law," Human Rights Watch, December 2011, www.hrw.org/reports/2011/12/14/no-way-live-0.
The highly critical report finds that Alabama's law cracking down on illegal immigrants has "severely affected" the state's unlawful aliens and their children, many of them U.S. citizens, as well as "the broader community linked to this population."

Baxter, Tom, "Alabama's Immigration Disaster: The Harshest Law in the Land Harms the State's Economy

and Society," Center for American Progress, February 2012, www.americanprogress.org/issues/2012/02/pdf/alabama_immigration_disaster.pdf.
The critical account by journalist Baxter under the auspices of the progressive Center for American Progress finds that Alabama's anti-illegal immigration law has had "particularly harsh" social and economic costs and effects.

Passel, Jeffrey S., and D'Vera Cohn, "Unauthorized Immigrant Population: National and State Trends, 2010," Pew Hispanic Center, Feb. 1, 2011, www.pewhispanic.org/files/reports/133.pdf.
The 32-page report by the Washington-based center provides national and state-by-state estimates of the unauthorized immigrant population and the number of unauthorized immigrants in the workforce.

For More Information

American Civil Liberties Union, Immigrant Rights Project, 125 Broad St., 18th floor, New York, NY 10004; 212-549-2500; www.aclu.org/immigrants-rights. Seeks to expand and enforce civil liberties and civil rights of immigrants.

American Immigration Council, 1331 G St., N.W., 2nd floor, Washington, DC 20005; 202-507-7500; www.americanimmigrationcouncil.org. Supports sensible and humane immigration policies.

America's Voice, 1050 17th St., N.W., Suite 490, Washington, DC 20036; 202-463-8602; http://americasvoiceonline.org/. Supports "real, comprehensive immigration reform," including reform of immigration enforcement practices.

Center for Immigration Studies, 1522 K St., N.W., Suite 820, Washington, DC 20005-1202; 202-466-8185; www.cis.org. An independent, nonpartisan research organization that supports what it calls low-immigration, pro-immigrant policies.

Define American, www.defineamerican.com/. Founded by journalist and undocumented immigrant Jose Antonio Vargas, the web-based organization seeks to fix what it calls a "broken" immigration system.

Federation for American Immigration Reform, 25 Massachusetts Ave., N.W., Suite 330, Washington, DC 20001; 202-328-7004; www.fairus.org. Seeks "significantly lower" immigration levels.

Migration Policy Institute, 1400 16th St., N.W., Suite 300, Washington, DC 20036; 202-266-1940; www.migrationpolicy.org. A nonpartisan, nonprofit think tank dedicated to analysis of the movement of people worldwide.

National Council of La Raza, 1126 16th St., N.W., Suite 600, Washington, DC 20036-4845; 202-785-1670; www.nclr.org. The country's largest national Hispanic advocacy and civil rights organization.

National Immigration Forum, 50 F St., N.W., Suite 300, Washington, DC 20001; 202-347-0040; www.immigrationforum.org. Advocates for the values of immigration and immigrants to the nation.

Pew Hispanic Center, 1615 L St., N.W., Suite 700, Washington, DC 20036; 202-419-4300; www.pewhispanic.org/. Seeks to improve understanding of the U.S. Hispanic population and to chronicle Latinos' growing impact on the nation.

5 American Indians

Peter Katel and Charles S. Clark

Jerolyn Fink lives in grand style in the housing center built by Connecticut's Mohegan Tribe using profits from its successful Mohegan Sun casino. Thanks in part to booming casinos, many tribes are making progress, but American Indians still face daunting health and economic problems, and tribal leaders say federal aid remains inadequate.

From *CQ Researcher*,
April 28, 2006 (updated August 5, 2010).

It's not a fancy gambling palace, like some Indian casinos, but the modest operation run by the Winnebago Tribe of Nebraska may just help the 2,300-member tribe hit the economic jackpot.

Using seed money from the casino, it has launched 12 businesses, including a construction company and an Internet news service. Projected 2006 revenues: $150 million.

"It would be absolutely dumb for us to think that gaming is the future," says tribe member Lance Morgan, the 37-year-old Harvard Law School graduate who runs the holding company for the dozen businesses. "Gaming is just a means to an end — and it's done wonders for our tribal economy."

Indian casinos have revived a myth dating back to the early-20th-century Oklahoma oil boom — that Indians are rolling in dough.[1] While some of the 55 tribes that operate big casinos indeed are raking in big profits, the 331 federally recognized tribes in the lower 48 states, on the whole, endure soul-quenching poverty and despair.

Arizona's 1.8-million-acre San Carlos Apache Reservation is among the poorest. The rural, isolated community of about 13,000 people not only faces devastating unemployment but also a deadly methamphetamine epidemic, tribal Chairwoman Kathleen W. Kitcheyan, told the Senate Indian Affairs Committee in April.

"We suffer from a poverty level of 69 percent, which must be unimaginable to many people in this country, who would equate a situation such as this to one found only in Third World countries," she said. Then, speaking of the drug-related death of one of her own grandsons, she had to choke back sobs.

Conditions on Reservations Improved

Socioeconomic conditions improved more on reservations with gambling than on those without gaming during the 1990s, although non-gaming reservations also improved substantially, especially compared to the U.S. population. Some experts attribute the progress among non-gaming tribes to an increase in self-governance on many reservations.

Socioeconomic Changes on Reservations, 1990-2000*
(shown as a percentage or percentage points)

	Non-Gaming	Gaming	U.S.
Real per-capita income	+21.0%	+36.0%	+11.0%
Median household income	+14.0%	+35.0%	+4.0%
Family poverty	-6.9	-11.8	-0.8
Child poverty	-8.1	-11.6	-1.7
Deep poverty	-1.4	-3.4	-0.4
Public assistance	+0.7	-1.6	+0.3
Unemployment	-1.8	-4.8	-0.5
Labor force participation	-1.6	+1.6	-1.3
Overcrowded homes	-1.3	-0.1	+1.1
Homes lacking complete plumbing	-4.6	-3.3	-0.1
Homes lacking complete kitchen	+1.3	-0.6	+0.2
College graduates	+1.7	+2.6	+4.2
High school or equivalency only	-0.3	+1.8	-1.4
Less than 9th-grade education	-5.5	-6.3	-2.8

* The reservation population of the Navajo Nation, which did not have gambling in the 1990s, was not included because it is so large (175,000 in 2000) that it tends to pull down Indian averages when it is included.

Source: Jonathan B. Taylor and Joseph P. Kalt, "Cabazon, The Indian Gaming Regulatory Act, and the Socioeconomic Consequences of American Indian Governmental Gaming: A Ten-Year Review, American Indians on Reservations: A Databook of Socioeconomic Change Between the 1990 and 2000 Censuses," Harvard Project on American Indian Economic Development, January 2005

"Our statistics are horrific," says Lionel R. Bordeaux, president of Sinte Gleska University, on the Rosebud Sioux Reservation in South Dakota. "We're at the bottom rung of the ladder in all areas, whether it's education levels, economic achievement or political status."[2]

National statistics aren't much better:

- Indian unemployment on reservations nationwide is 49 percent — 10 times the national rate.[3]
- The on-reservation family poverty rate in 2000 was 37 percent—four times the national figure of 9 percent.[4]
- Nearly one in five Indians age 25 or older in tribes without gambling operations had less than a ninth-grade education. But even members of tribes with gambling had a college graduation rate of only 16 percent, about half the national percentage.[5]
- Death rates from alcoholism and tuberculosis among Native Americans are at least 650 percent higher than overall U.S. rates.[6]
- Indian youths commit suicide at nearly triple the rate of young people in general.[7]
- Indians on reservations, especially in the resource-poor Upper Plains and West, are the nation's third-largest group of methamphetamine users.[8]

The immediate prognosis for the nation's 4.4 million Native Americans is bleak, according to the Harvard Project on American Indian Economic Development. "If U.S. and on-reservation Indian per-capita income were to continue to grow at their 1990s' rates," it said, "it would take half a century for the tribes to catch up."[9]

Nonetheless, there has been forward movement in Indian Country, though it is measured in modest steps. Among the marks of recent progress:

- Per-capita income rose 20 percent on reservations, to $7,942, (and 36 percent in tribes with casinos, to $9,771), in contrast to an 11 percent overall U.S. growth rate.[10]
- Unemployment has dropped by up to 5 percent on reservations and in other predominantly Indian areas.[11]
- Child poverty in non-gaming tribes dropped from 55 percent of the child population to 44 percent (but the Indian rate is still more than double the 17 percent average nationwide).[12]

More than two centuries of court decisions, treaties and laws have created a complicated system of coexistence between tribes and the rest of the country. On one level, tribes are sovereign entities that enjoy a government-to-government relationship with Washington. But the sovereignty is qualified. In the words of an 1831 Supreme Court decision that is a bedrock of Indian law, tribes are "domestic dependent nations."[13]

The blend of autonomy and dependence grows out of the Indians' reliance on Washington for sheer survival, says Robert A. Williams Jr., a law professor at the University of Arizona and a member of North Carolina's Lumbee Tribe. "Indians insisted in their treaties that the Great White Father protect us from these racial maniacs in the states — where racial discrimination was most developed — and guarantee us a right to education, a right to water, a territorial base, a homeland," he says. "Tribes sold an awful lot of land in return for a trust relationship to keep the tribes going."

Today, the practical meaning of the relationship with Washington is that American Indians on reservations, and to some extent those elsewhere, depend entirely or partly on federal funding for health, education and other needs. Tribes with casinos and other businesses lessen their reliance on federal dollars.

Unlike other local governments, tribes don't have a tax base whose revenues they share with state governments. Federal spending on Indian programs of all kinds nationwide currently amounts to about $11 billion, James Cason, associate deputy secretary of the Interior, told the Senate Indian Affairs Committee in February.

But the abysmal conditions under which many American Indians live make it all too clear that isn't enough, Indians say. "This is always a discussion at our tribal leaders' meetings," says Cecilia Fire Thunder, president of the Oglala Sioux Tribe in Pine Ridge, S.D. "The biggest job that tribal leaders have is to see that the government lives up to its responsibilities to our people. It's a battle that never ends."

Indeed, a decades-old class-action suit alleges systematic mismanagement of billions of dollars in Indian-owned assets by the Interior Department — a case that has prompted withering criticism of the department by the judge.

Government officials insist that, despite orders to cut spending, they've been able to keep providing essential services. Charles Grim, director of the Indian Health

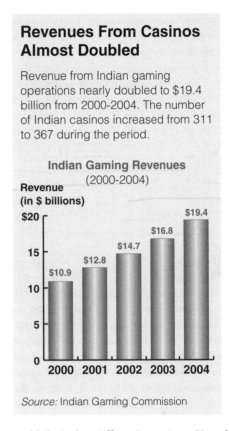

Revenues From Casinos Almost Doubled

Revenue from Indian gaming operations nearly doubled to $19.4 billion from 2000-2004. The number of Indian casinos increased from 311 to 367 during the period.

Indian Gaming Revenues (2000-2004)

Year	Revenue (in $ billions)
2000	$10.9
2001	$12.8
2002	$14.7
2003	$16.8
2004	$19.4

Source: Indian Gaming Commission

Service, told the Indian Affairs Committee, "In a deficit-reduction year, it's a very strong budget and one that does keep pace with inflationary and population-growth increases."

In any event, from the tribes' point of view, they lack the political muscle to force major increases. "The big problem is the Indians are about 1 percent of the national population," says Joseph Kalt, co-director of the Harvard Project. "The voice is so tiny."

Faced with that grim political reality, Indians are trying to make better use of scarce federal dollars through a federally sponsored "self-governance" movement. Leaders of the movement say tribes can deliver higher-quality services more efficiently when they control their own budgets. Traditionally, federal agencies operate programs on reservations, such as law enforcement or medical services.

But since the 1990s, dozens of tribes have stepped up control of their own affairs both by building their own businesses and by signing self-governance "compacts" with the federal government. Compacts provide tribes with large chunks of money, or block grants, rather than individual grants for each service. Then, with minimal federal oversight, the tribes develop their own budgets and run all or most services.

The self-governance trend gathered steam during the same time that Indian-owned casinos began booming. For many tribes, the gambling business provided a revenue stream that didn't flow from Washington.

According to economist Alan Meister, 228 tribes in 30 states operated 367 high-stakes bingo halls or casinos in 2004, earning an estimated $19.6 billion.[14]

The gambling houses operate under the 1988 Indian Gaming Regulatory Act (IGRA), which was made possible by a U.S. Supreme Court ruling upholding tribes' rights to govern their own activities.[15] A handful of tribes are doing so well that $80 million from six tribes in 2000-2003 helped fuel the scandal surrounding one-time Washington super-lobbyist Jack Abramoff, whose clients were among the most successful casino tribes.[16]

If the Abramoff scandal contributed to the notion of widespread Indian wealth, one reason may be the misimpression that tribes don't pay taxes on their gambling earnings. In fact, under the IGRA, federal, state and local governments took in $6.3 billion in gambling-generated tax revenues in 2004, with 67 percent going to the federal government. In addition, tribes paid out some $889 million in 2004 to state and local governments in order to get gambling operations approved.[17]

The spread of casinos has prompted some cities and counties, along with citizens' groups and even some casino-operating tribes, to resist casino-expansion plans.

The opposition to expansion is another reason tribal entrepreneur Morgan doesn't think gaming is a good long-range bet for Indians' future. His vision involves full tribal control of the Indians' main asset — their land. He argues for ending the "trust status" under which tribes can't buy or sell reservation property — a relic of 19th-century protection against rapacious state governments.

Indian Country needs a better business climate, Morgan says, and the availability of land as collateral for investments would be a big step in that direction. "America has a wonderful economic system, probably the best in the world, but the reservation tends to be an economic black hole."

As Indians seek to improve their lives, here are some of the issues being debated:

Is the federal government neglecting Native Americans?

There is wide agreement that the federal government bears overwhelming responsibility for Indians' welfare, but U.S. and tribal officials disagree over the adequacy of the aid Indians receive. Sen. John McCain, R-Ariz., chairman of the Senate Indian Affairs Committee, and Vice Chairman Byron L. Dorgan, D-N.D., have been leading the fight for more aid to Indians. "We have a full-blown crisis . . . particularly dealing with children and elderly, with respect to housing, education and health care," Dorgan told the committee on Feb. 14. He characterized administration proposals as nothing more than "nibbling around the edges on these issues . . . making a few adjustments here or there.' "

Administration officials respond that given the severe federal deficit, they are focusing on protecting vital programs. "As we went through and prioritized our budget, we basically looked at all of the programs that were secondary and tertiary programs, and they were the first ones on the block to give tradeoffs for our core programs in maintaining the integrity of those," Interior's Cason told the committee.

For Indians on isolated reservations, says Bordeaux of the Rosebud Sioux, there's little alternative to federal money. He compares tribes' present circumstances to those after the buffalo had been killed off, and an Army general told the Indians to eat beef, which made them sick. "The general told them, 'Either that, or you eat the grass on which you stand.' "

But David B. Vickers, president of Upstate Citizens for Equality, in Union Springs, N.Y., which opposes Indian land claims and casino applications, argues that accusations of federal neglect are inaccurate and skirt the real problem. The central issue is that the constitutional system is based on individual rights, not tribal rights, he says. "Indians are major recipients of welfare now. They're eligible. They don't need a tribe or leader; all they have to do is apply like anybody else."

Pat Ragsdale, director of the Bureau of Indian Affairs (BIA), acknowledges that Dorgan's and McCain's criticisms echo a 2003 U.S. Commission on Civil Rights report, which also called underfunding of Indian aid a crisis. "The government is failing to live up to its trust responsibility to Native peoples," the commission concluded. "Efforts to bring Native

Americans up to the standards of other Americans have failed in part because of a lack of sustained funding. The failure manifests itself in massive and escalating unmet needs."[18]

"Nobody in this government disputes the report, in general," says Ragsdale, a Cherokee. "Some of our tribal communities are in real critical shape, and others are prospering."

The commission found, for example, that in 2003 the Indian Health Service appropriation amounted to $2,533 per capita — below even the $3,803 per capita appropriated for federal prisoners.

Concern over funding for Indian programs in 2007 centers largely on health and education. Although 90 percent of Indian students attend state-operated public schools, their schools get federal aid because tribes don't pay property taxes, which typically fund public schools. The remaining 10 percent of Indian students attend schools operated by the BIA or by tribes themselves under BIA contracts.

"There is not a congressman or senator who would send his own children or grandchildren to our schools," said Ryan Wilson, president of the National Indian Education Association, citing "crumbling buildings and outdated structures with lead in the pipes and mold on the walls."[19]

Cason told the Indian Affairs Committee the administration is proposing a $49 million cut, from $157.4 million to $108.1 million, in school construction and repair in 2007. He also said that only 10 of 37 dilapidated schools funded for replacement by 2006 have been completed, with another 19 scheduled to finish in 2007. Likewise, he said the department is also behind on 45 school improvement projects.

McCain questioned whether BIA schools and public schools with large Indian enrollments would be able to meet the requirements set by the national No Child Left Behind Law.[20] Yes, replied Darla Marburger, deputy assistant secretary of Education for policy. "For the first time, we'll be providing money to . . . take a look at how students are achieving in ways that they can tailor their programs to better meet the needs of students." Overall, the Department of Education would spend about $1 billion on Indian education under the administration's proposed budget for 2007, or $6 million less than in 2006.

Controversial Whiteclay, Neb., sells millions of cans of beer annually to residents of the nearby Pine Ridge Reservation in South Dakota. Alcohol abuse and unemployment continue to plague the American Indian community.

McCain and Dorgan are also among those concerned about administration plans to eliminate the Indian Health Service's $32.7 million urban program, which this year made medical and counseling services available to some 430,000 off-reservation Indians at 41 medical facilities in cities around the nation. The administration argues that the services were available through other programs, but McCain and Dorgan noted that "no evaluation or evidence has been provided to support this contention."[21]

Indian Health Service spokesman Thomas Sweeney, a member of the Citizen Potawatomi Nation of Oklahoma, says only 72,703 Indians used urban health centers in 2004 and that expansion of another federal program would pick up the slack.[22]

In Seattle, elimination of the urban program would cut $4 million from the city's Indian Health Board budget, says Executive Director Ralph Forquera. "Why pick on a $33 million appropriation?" he asks. In his skeptical view, the proposal reflects another "unspoken" termination program. You take a sub-population — urban Indians — and eliminate funding, then [you target] tribes under 1,000 members, and there are a lot of them. Little by little, you pick apart the system."

The IHS's Grim told the Senate committee on Feb. 14 the cuts were designed to protect funding that "can be used most effectively to improve the health status of American Indian and Alaskan Native people."

Have casinos benefited Indians?

Over the past two decades, Indian casinos have become powerful economic engines for many tribal economies. But the enthusiasm for casinos is not unanimous.

"If you're looking at casinos in terms of how they've actually raised the status of Indian people, they've been an abysmal failure," says Ted Jojola, a professor of planning at the University of New Mexico and a member of Isleta Pueblo, near Albuquerque. "But in terms of augmenting the original federal trust-responsibility areas — education, health, tribal government — they've been a spectacular success. Successful gaming tribes have ploughed the money either into diversifying their economies or they've augmented funds that would have come to them anyway."

Tribes with casinos near big population centers are flourishing. The Coushatta Tribe's casino near Lake Charles, La., generates $300 million a year, enough to provide about $40,000 to every member.[23] And the fabled Foxwoods Resort Casino south of Norwich, Conn., operated by the Mashantucket Pequot Tribe, together with Connecticut's other big casino, the Mohegan Tribe's Mohegan Sun, grossed $2.2 billion just from gambling in 2004.[24]

There are only about 830 Coushattas, so their benefits also include free health care, education and favorable terms on home purchases.[25] The once poverty-stricken Mashantuckets have created Connecticut's most extensive welfare-to-work program, open to both tribe members and non-members. In 1997-2000, the program helped 150 welfare recipients find jobs.[26]

Most tribes don't enjoy success on that scale. Among the nation's 367 Indian gambling operations, only 15 grossed $250 million or more in 2004 (another 40 earned $100 million to $250 million); 94 earned less than $3 million and 57 earned $3 million to $10 million.[27]

"We have a small casino that provides close to $3 million to the tribal nation as a whole," says Bordeaux, on the Rosebud Sioux Reservation. The revenue has been channeled into the tribe's Head Start program, an emergency home-repair fund and other projects. W. Ron Allen, chairman of the Jamestown S'Klallam Tribe in Sequim, Wash., says his tribe's small casino has raised living standards so much that some two-dozen students a year go to college, instead of one or two.

Efforts to open additional casinos are creating conflicts between tribes that operate competing casinos, as well as with some of their non-Indian neighbors. Convicted lobbyist Abramoff, for example, was paid millions of dollars by tribes seeking to block other tribal casinos.[28]

Some non-Indian communities also oppose casino expansion. "We firmly believe a large, generally unregulated casino will fundamentally change the character of our community forever," said Liz Thomas, a member of Tax Payers of Michigan Against Casinos, which opposes a casino planned by the Pokagon Band of Potawotami Indians Tribe in the Lake Michigan town of New Buffalo, where Taylor and her husband operate a small resort.

"People are OK with Donald Trump making millions of dollars individually," says Joseph Podlasek, executive director of the American Indian Center of Chicago, "but if a race of people is trying to become self-sufficient, now that's not respectable."

Nevertheless, some American Indians have mixed feelings about the casino route to economic development. "I don't think anyone would have picked casinos" for that purpose, says the University of Arizona's Williams. "Am I ambivalent about it? Absolutely. But I'm not ambivalent about a new fire station, or Kevlar vests for tribal police fighting meth gangs."

"There's no question that some of the money has been used for worthwhile purposes," concedes Guy Clark, a Corrales, N.M., dentist who chairs the National Coalition Against Legalized Gambling. But, he adds, "If you do a cost-benefit analysis, the cost is much greater than the benefit." Restaurants and other businesses, for example, lose customers who often gamble away their extra money.

Even some Indian leaders whose tribes profit from casinos raise caution flags, especially about per-capita payments. For Nebraska's Winnebagos, payments amount to just a few hundred dollars, says CEO Morgan. What bothers him are dividends "that are just big enough that you don't have to work or get educated — say, $20,000 to $40,000."

But there's no denying the impact casinos can have. At a January public hearing on the Oneida Indian Nation's attempt to put 17,000 acres of upstate New York land into tax-free "trust" status, hundreds of the 4,500 employees of the tribe's Turning Stone Resort and Casino, near Utica, showed up in support. "When I was a kid, people worked for General Motors, General Electric, Carrier and Oneida Ltd.," said casino Human

Resources Director Mark Mancini. "Today, people work for the Oneida Indian Nation and their enterprises."[29]

For tribes that can't build independent economies any other way, casinos are appealing. The 225,000-member Navajo Nation, the biggest U.S. tribe, twice rejected gaming before finally approving it in 2004.[30] "We need that infusion of jobs and revenue, and people realize that," said Duane Yazzie, president of the Navajos' Shiprock, N.M., chapter.[31]

But the Navajos face stiff competition from dozens of casinos already in operation near the vast Navajo reservation, which spreads across parts of Arizona, New Mexico and Utah and is larger than the state of West Virginia.

Would money alone solve American Indians' problems?

No one in Indian Country (or on Capitol Hill) denies the importance of federal funding to American Indians' future, but some Indians say it isn't the only answer.

"We are largely on our own because of limited financial assistance from the federal government," said Joseph A. Garcia, president of the National Congress of American Indians, in his recent "State of Indian Nations" speech.[32]

Fifty-two tribal officials and Indian program directors expressed similar sentiments in March before the House Appropriations Subcommittee on the Interior. Pleading their case before lawmakers who routinely consider billion-dollar weapons systems and other big projects, the tribal leaders sounded like small-town county commissioners as they urged lawmakers to increase or restore small but vital grants for basic health, education and welfare services.

"In our ICWA [Indian Child Welfare Act] program, currently we have a budget of $79,000 a year," said Harold Frazier, chairman of the Cheyenne River Sioux, in South Dakota. "We receive over 1,300 requests for assistance annually from 11 states and eight counties in South Dakota. We cannot give the type of attention to these requests that they deserve. Therefore, we are requesting $558,000."

To university President Bordeaux, federal funding is vital because his desolate reservation has few other options for economic survival. "What's missing is money," he says.

Money is crucial to improving Indians' health, says Dr. Joycelyn Dorscher, director of the Center of American Indian and Minority Health at the University of Minnesota-Duluth. Especially costly are programs to combat diabetes and other chronic diseases, says Dorscher, a Chippewa. While health programs have to be carefully designed to fit Indian cultural patterns, she says, "Everything comes down to time or money in the grand scheme of things."

But with funding from Washington never certain from year to year, says the Harvard Project's Kalt, "The key to economic development has not been federal funding" but rather "tribes' ability to run their own affairs."

For tribes without self-government compacts, growing demands for services and shrinking funding from Washington make keeping the dollars flowing the highest priority. "We're always afraid of more cutbacks," says Oglala Sioux President Fire Thunder.

But an Indian education leader with decades of federal budgetary negotiations acknowledges that problems go beyond funding shortfalls. "If you ask students why they dropped out, they say, 'I don't see a future for myself,' " says David Beaulieu, director of Arizona State University's Center for Indian Education. "Educators need to tie the purposes of schooling to the broad-based purposes of society. We're more successful when we tie education to the meaning of life."

The University of Arizona's Williams says a tribe's success and failure may be tied more to the way its government is organized than to how much funding it gets.

Williams says the first priority of tribes still using old-style constitutions should be reorganization, because they feature a weak executive elected by a tribal council. "That's what the BIA was used to," he explains. "It could play off factions and families, and the economic system would be based on patronage and taking care of your own family." Under such a system, he adds, "there's not going to be any long-term strategic planning going on."[33]

Yet other needs exist as well, says the American Indian Center's Podlasek. "It's so difficult for us to find a place to do a traditional ceremony," he says. "We had a traditional healer in town last month, and he wanted to build a sweat lodge. We actually had to go to Indiana. Doing it in the city wasn't even an option."

BACKGROUND

Conquered Homelands

Relations between Indian and non-Indian civilizations in the Americas began with the Spanish Conquistadors'

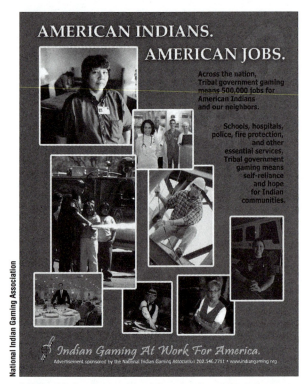

A National Indian Gaming Association advertisement touts the benefits of tribal gaming operations to American Indian communities. Some 228 tribes in 30 states operated 367 high-stakes bingo halls or casinos in 2004.

explorations of the 1500s, followed by the French and British. By turns the three powers alternated policies of enslavement, peaceful coexistence and all-out warfare against the Indians.[34]

By 1830, with the Europeans largely gone, white settlers moved westward into Georgia, Mississippi and Alabama. Unwilling to share the rich frontier land, they pushed the Indians out. President Andrew Jackson backed the strategy, and Congress enacted it into the Indian Removal Act of 1830, which called for moving the region's five big tribes into the Oklahoma Territory.

If the law didn't make clear where Indians stood with the government, the treatment of Mississippi's Choctaws provided chilling evidence. Under a separate treaty, Choctaws who refused to head for Oklahoma could remain at home, become citizens and receive land. In practice, none of that was allowed, and Indians who stayed in Mississippi lived marginal existences.

Georgia simplified the claiming of Cherokee lands by effectively ending Cherokee self-rule. The so-called "Georgia Guard" reinforced the point by beating and jailing Indians. Jackson encouraged Georgia's actions, and when Indians protested, he said he couldn't interfere. The lawsuit filed by the Cherokees eventually reached the Supreme Court.

Chief Justice John Marshall's 1831 majority opinion, *Cherokee Nation v. Georgia*, would cast a long shadow over Indians' rights, along with two other decisions, issued in 1823 and 1832. "Almost all Indian policy is the progeny of the conflicting views of Jackson and Marshall," wrote W. Dale Mason, a political scientist at the University of New Mexico.[35]

In concluding that the court couldn't stop Georgia's actions, Marshall defined the relationship between Indians and the U.S. government. While Marshall wrote that Indians didn't constitute a foreign state, he noted that they owned the land they occupied until they made a "voluntary cession." Marshall concluded the various tribes were "domestic dependent nations." In practical terms, "Their relations to the United States resembles that of a ward to his guardian."[36]

Having rejected the Cherokees' argument, the University of Arizona's Williams writes, the court "provided no effective judicial remedy for Indian tribes to protect their basic human rights to property, self-government, and cultural survival under U.S. law."[37]

Along with the *Cherokee* case, the other two opinions that make up the so-called Marshall Trilogy are *Johnson v. M'Intosh* (also known as *Johnson v. McIntosh*), and *Worcester v. State of Georgia*.[38]

In *Johnson*, Marshall wrote that the European empires that "discovered" America became its owners and had "an exclusive right to extinguish the Indian title of occupancy, either by purchase or by conquest. The tribes of Indians inhabiting this country were fierce savages. . . . To leave them in possession of their country was to leave the country a wilderness."[39]

However, Marshall used the 1832 *Worcester* opinion to define the limits of state authority over Indian tribes, holding that the newcomers couldn't simply eject Indians.

"The Cherokee nation... is a distinct community occupying its own territory... in which the laws of Georgia can have no force," Marshall wrote. Georgia's conviction and sentencing of a missionary for not swearing allegiance to the state "interferes forcibly with the relations established between the United States and the Cherokee nation."[40] That is, the federal government — not states — held the reins of power over tribes.

According to legend, Jackson remarked: "John Marshall has made his decision — now let him enforce it." Between Jackson's disregard of the Supreme Court and white settlers' later manipulation of the legal system to vacate Indian lands, the end result was the dispossession of Indian lands.

Forced Assimilation

The expulsions of the Native Americans continued in the Western territories — especially after the Civil War. "I instructed Captain Barry, if possible to exterminate the whole village," Lt. Col. George Green wrote of his participation in an 1869 campaign against the White Mountain Apaches in Arizona and New Mexico. "There seems to be no settled policy, but a general policy to kill them wherever found."[41]

Some military men and civilians didn't go along. But whether by brute force or by persuasion, Indians were pushed off lands that non-Indians wanted. One strategy was to settle the Indians on reservations guarded by military posts. The strategy grew into a general policy for segregating Indians on these remote tracts.

Even after the Indians were herded onto lands that no one else wanted, the government didn't respect reservation boundaries. They were reconfigured as soon as non-Indians saw something valuable, such as mineral wealth.

The strategy of elastic reservation boundaries led to the belief — or rationalization — that reservations served no useful purposes for Indians themselves. That doctrine led to a policy enshrined in an 1887 law to convert reservations to individual landholdings. Well-meaning advocates of the plan saw it as a way to inculcate notions of private property and Euro-American culture in general.

All tribal land was to be divided into 160-acre allotments, one for each Indian household. The parcels wouldn't become individual property, though, for 25 years.

Indian consent wasn't required. In some cases, government agents tried persuading Indians to join in; in others, the divvying-up proceeded even with many Indians opposed. In Arizona, however, the government backed off from breaking up the lands of the long-settled Hopis, who resisted attempts to break up their territory. The vast Navajo Nation in Arizona, Utah and New Mexico was also left intact.

While widely reviled, the "forced assimilation" policy left a benign legacy for the affected Indians: the grant of citizenship. Beyond that, the era's Indians were restricted to unproductive lands, and with little means of support many fell prey to alcoholism and disease.

The bleak period ended with President Franklin D. Roosevelt. In his first term he appointed a defender of Indian culture, John Collier, as commissioner of Indian affairs. Collier pushed for the Indian Reorganization Act of 1934, which ended the allotment program, financed purchases of new Indian lands and authorized the organization of tribal governments that enjoyed control over revenues.

Termination

After World War II, a new, anti-Indian mood swept Washington, partly in response to pressure from states where non-Indians eyed Indian land.

Collier resigned in 1945 after years of conflict over what critics called his antagonism to missionaries proselytizing among the Indians and his sympathies toward the tribes. The 1950 appointment of Dillon S. Myer — fresh from supervising the wartime internment of Japanese-Americans — clearly reflected the new attitude. Myer showed little interest in what Indians themselves thought of the new policy of shrinking tribal land holdings. "I realize that it will not be possible always to obtain Indian cooperation.... We must proceed, even though [this] may be lacking."[42]

Congress hadn't authorized a sweeping repeal of earlier policy. But the introduction of dozens of bills in the late 1940s to sell Indian land or liquidate some reservation holdings entirely showed which way the winds were blowing. And in 1953, a House Concurrent Resolution declared Congress' policy to be ending Indians' "status as wards of the United States, and to grant them all of the rights and privileges pertaining to American citizenship." A separate law granted state jurisdiction over Indian reservations in

CHRONOLOGY

1800s *United States expands westward, pushing Indians off most of their original lands, sometimes creating new reservations for them.*

1830 President Andrew Jackson signs the Indian Removal Act, forcing the Cherokees to move from Georgia to Oklahoma.

1832 Supreme Court issues the last of three decisions defining Indians' legal status as wards of the government.

1871 Congress makes its treaties with tribes easier to alter, enabling non-Indians to take Indian lands when natural resources are discovered.

Dec. 29, 1890 U.S. soldiers massacre at least 150 Plains Indians, mostly women and children, at Wounded Knee, S.D.

1900-1950s *Congress and the executive branch undertake major shifts in Indian policy, first strengthening tribal governments then trying to force cultural assimilation.*

1924 Indians are granted U.S. citizenship.

1934 Indian Reorganization Act authorizes expansion of reservations and strengthening of tribal governments.

1953 Congress endorses full assimilation of Indians into American society, including "relocation" from reservations to cities.

1960s-1980s *In the radical spirit of the era, Native Americans demand respect for their traditions and an end to discrimination; federal government concedes more power to tribal governments, allows gambling on tribal lands.*

1969 American Indian Movement (AIM) seizes Alcatraz Island in San Francisco Bay to dramatize claims of injustice.

July 7, 1970 President Richard M. Nixon vows support for Indian self-government.

Feb. 27, 1973 AIM members occupy the town of Wounded Knee on the Pine Ridge, S.D., Sioux Reservation, for two months; two Indians die and an FBI agent is wounded.

1988 Indian Gaming Regulatory Act allows tribes to operate casinos under agreements with states.

1990s *Indian-owned casinos boom; tribal governments push to expand self-rule and reduce Bureau of Indian Affairs (BIA) supervision.*

1994 President Bill Clinton signs law making experimental self-governance compacts permanent.

March 27, 1996 U.S. Supreme Court rules states can't be forced to negotiate casino compacts, thus encouraging tribes to make revenue-sharing deals with states as the price of approval.

June 10, 1996 Elouise Cobell, a member of the Blackfeet Tribe in Montana, charges Interior Department mismanagement of Indian trust funds cheated Indians out of billions of dollars. The case is still pending.

Nov. 3, 1998 California voters uphold tribes' rights to run casinos; state Supreme Court later invalidates the provision, but it is revived by a 1999 compact between the tribes and the state.

2000s *Indian advocates decry low funding levels, and sovereignty battles continue; lobbying scandal spotlights Indian gambling profits.*

2000 Tribal Self-Governance Demonstration Project becomes permanent.

2003 U.S. Commission on Civil Rights calls underfunding for Indians a crisis, saying federal government spends less for Indian health care than for any other group, including prison inmates.

Feb. 22, 2004 *Washington Post* reports on Washington lobbyist Jack Abramoff's deals with casino tribes.

March 29, 2005 U.S. Supreme Court blocks tax exemptions for Oneida Nation of New York on newly purchased land simply because it once owned the property.

April 5, 2006 Tribal and BIA officials testify in Congress that methamphetamine addiction is ravaging reservations.

2006 Congress passes Indian Gaming Regulatory Act Amendments to protect Indian casino operators from Indian tribes operating gaming facilities outside reservations. . . . American Indian Probate Reform Act (AIPRA) overhauls federal probate process for Indian trust property and helps to consolidate Indian land ownership across the nation.

2007 Cherokee Nation Principal Chief Chad Smith urges state lawmakers to quash proposed "English only" legislation that would make English Oklahoma's official language. . . . Department of Health and Human Services urges Senate to reauthorize Indian Health Care Improvement Act.

2008 Revenues from Indian casinos in 30 states increase from $19.6 billion in 2004 to $26.7 billion in 2008. . . . Native American Housing Assistance and Self-Determination Reauthorization Act reauthorizes affordable housing programs for Native Americans and creates a promised loan program for economic development and community activities for Indian tribes. . . . President George W. Bush says he would veto the Indian Health Care Improvement Act of 2007 because of "cost and Medicaid documentation concerns," after Sen. Byron Dorgan, D-N.D., sponsors the bill for new funding for the Indian Health Service. . . . President Bush signs Emergency Economic Stabilization Act of 2008, allowing qualified Indian reservation property placed in service by Jan. 1, 2008, to be depreciated over shorter time periods.

2009 Obama administration's economic stimulus package provides Indian Health Service with $500 million, including $227 million for construction of health facilities and $100 million for maintenance and improvements. . . . Supreme Court rules 7-2 against an Interior Department move to obtain 31 acres in Charlestown, R.I., for the Narragansett tribe that was to be used for a gambling facility. . . . Navajo Nation reports 225 youth gangs, many involving drug-trafficking, operate within its population of 250,000.

2010

March — Obama's health care reform legislation reauthorizes 1976 Indian Health Care Improvement Act.

May — National Indian Education Association requests $500 million for a deferred-maintenance backlog at almost 4,500 Indian schools and also seeks improved youth-violence prevention programs.

June — After the Mashpee Wampanoag tribe in Cape Cod, Mass., applies for a casino license to the Bureau of Indian Affairs, Interior Secretary Ken Salazar offers to give the tribe an exemption under the 1988 Federal Indian Gaming Regulatory Act, reviving the issue in the Massachusetts legislature and providing a licensing preference to Indian tribes. . . . At Sovereignty Symposium in Oklahoma City, National Indian Gaming Association Chairman Ernie Stevens Jr. praises local tribes for their improvements in education, transportation and health care and success at providing jobs.

June 17 — Cherokee Nation Principal Chief Smith calls for more diverse curriculum in No Child Left Behind law, including emphasis on native culture and language, to help Indian students better face adversity and adaptation challenges.

July — Sen. Dorgan hosts summit meeting on suicide prevention among Native Americans, reports that the youth suicide rate on Indian lands is 70 percent higher than that of the general population. . . . On July 29 President Obama signs Tribal Law and Order Act giving tribal courts tougher sentencing powers, setting stricter rules to gather and collect more data on crimes and appointing special U.S. prosecutors to tackle what advocates of the law describe as an epidemic of violence on reservations.

Budget Cuts Target Health Clinics

When Lita Pepion, a health consultant and a member of the Blackfeet Nation, learned that her 22-year-old-niece had been struggling with heroin abuse, she urged her to seek treatment at the local Urban Indian Clinic in Billings, Mont.

But the young woman had so much trouble getting an appointment that she gave up. Only recently, says Pepion, did she overcome her addiction on her own.

The clinic is one of 34 federally funded, Indian-controlled clinics that contract with the Indian Health Service (IHS) to serve urban Indians. But President Bush's 2007 budget would kill the $33-million program, eliminating most of the clinics' funding.

Indians in cities will still be able to get health care through several providers, including the federal Health Centers program, says Office of Management and Budget spokesman Richard Walker. The proposed budget would increase funding for the centers by nearly $2 billion, IHS Director Charles W. Grim told the Senate Indian Affairs Committee on Feb. 14, 2006.[1]

But Joycelyn Dorscher, president of the Association of American Indian Physicians, says the IHS clinics do a great job and that, "It's very important that people from diverse backgrounds have physicians like themselves."

Others, however, including Pepion, say the clinics are poorly managed and lack direction. Ralph Forquera, director of the Seattle-based Urban Indian Health Institute, says that while the clinics "have made great strides medically, a lack of resources has resulted in services from unqualified professionals." In addition, he says, "we have not been as successful in dealing with lifestyle changes and mental health problems."

Many Indian health experts oppose the cuts because Indians in both urban areas and on reservations have more health problems than the general population, including 126 percent more chronic liver disease and cirrhosis, 54 percent more diabetes and 178 percent more alcohol-related deaths.[2]

Indian health specialists blame the Indians' higher disease rates on history, lifestyle and genetics — not just on poverty. "You don't see exactly the same things happening to other poor minority groups," says Dorscher, a North Dakota Chippewa, so "there's something different" going on among Indians.

In the view of Donna Keeler, executive director of the South Dakota Urban Indian Health program and an Eastern Shoshone, historical trauma affects the physical wellness of patients in her state's three urban Indian clinics.

Susette Schwartz, CEO of the Hunter Urban Indian Clinic in Wichita, Kan., agrees. She attributes Indians' high rates of mental health and alcohol/substance abuse to their long history of government maltreatment. Many Indian children in the 19th and early 20th centuries, she points out, were taken from their parents and sent to government boarding schools where speaking native

---

five Midwestern and Western states and extended the same authority to other states that wanted to claim it.[43]

The following year, Congress "terminated" formal recognition and territorial sovereignty of six tribes. Four years later, after public opposition began building (spurred in part by religious organizations), Congress abandoned termination. In the meantime, however, Indians had lost 1.6 million acres.

At the same time, though, the federal government maintained an associated policy — relocation. The BIA persuaded Indians to move to cities — Chicago, Denver and Los Angeles were the main destinations — and opened job-placement and housing-aid programs. The BIA placed Indians far from their reservations to keep them from returning. By 1970, the BIA estimated that 40 percent of all Indians lived in cities, of which one-third had been relocated by the bureau; the rest moved on their own.[44]

Activism

Starting in the late 1960s, the winds of change blowing through American society were felt as deeply in Indian Country as anywhere. Two books played a crucial role. In 1969, Vine Deloria Jr., member of a renowned family of Indian intellectuals from Oklahoma, published his landmark history, *Custer Died For Your Sins,* which portrayed American history from the Indians' viewpoint. The

languages was prohibited. "Taking away the culture and language years ago," says Schwartz, as well as the government's role in "taking their children and sterilizing their women" in the 1970s, all contributed to Indians' behavioral health issues.

Keeler also believes Indians' low incomes cause their unhealthy lifestyles. Many eat high-fat, high-starch foods because they are cheaper, Pepion says. Growing up on a reservation, she recalls, "We didn't eat a lot of vegetables because we couldn't afford them."

Opponents of the funding cuts for urban Indian health centers also cite a recent letter to President Bush from Daniel R. Hawkins Jr., vice president for federal, state and local government for the National Association of Community Health Centers. He said the urban Indian clinics and community health centers are complementary, not duplicative.

While Pepion does not believe funding should be cut entirely, she concedes that alternative health-care services are often "better equipped than the urban Indian clinics." And if American Indians want to assimilate into the larger society, they can't have everything culturally separate, she adds. "The only way that I was able to assimilate into an urban society was to make myself do those things that were uncomfortable for me," she says.

But Schwartz believes a great benefit of the urban clinics are their Indian employees, "who are culturally competent and sensitive and incorporate Native American-specific cultural ideas." Because of their history of cultural abuse, it takes a long time for Native Americans to trust non-Indian health providers, says Schwartz. "They're not just going to go to a health center down the road."

Native Americans in downtown Salt Lake City, Utah, demonstrate on April 21, 2006, against the elimination of funding for Urban Indian Health Clinics.

Dorscher and Schwartz also say the budget cuts could lead to more urban Indians ending up in costly emergency rooms because of their reluctance to trust the community health centers. "Ultimately, it would become more expensive to cut the prevention and primary care programs than it would be to maintain them," Dorscher says.

—*Melissa J. Hipolit*

---

[1] Prepared testimony of Director of Indian Health Service Dr. Charles W. Grim before the Senate Committee on Indian Affairs, Feb. 14, 2006.

[2] Urban Indian Health Institute, "The Health Status of Urban American Indians and Alaska Natives," March 16, 2004, p. v.

---

following year, Dee Brown's *Bury My Heart at Wounded Knee* described the settling of the West also from an Indian point of view. The books astonished many non-Indians. Among young Indians, the volumes reflected and spurred on a growing political activism.

It was in this climate that the newly formed American Indian Movement (AIM) took over Alcatraz Island, the former federal prison site in San Francisco Bay (where rebellious Indians had been held during the Indian Wars), to publicize demands to honor treaties and respect Native Americans' dignity. The takeover lasted from Nov. 20, 1969, to June 11, 1971, when U.S. marshals removed the occupiers.[45]

A second AIM-government confrontation took the form of a one-week takeover of BIA headquarters in Washington in November 1972 by some 500 AIM members protesting what they called broken treaty obligations. Protesters charged that government services to Indians were inadequate in general, with urban Indians neglected virtually completely.

Another protest occurred on Feb. 27, 1973, when 200 AIM members occupied the village of Wounded Knee on the Oglala Sioux's Pine Ridge Reservation in South Dakota. U.S. soldiers had massacred at least 150 Indians at Wounded Knee in 1890. AIM was protesting what it called the corrupt tribal government. And a weak,

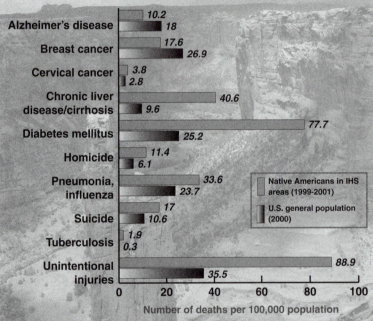

Death Toll Higher Among Indians

American Indians served by the Indian Health Service (IHS) — mainly low-income or uninsured — die at substantially higher rates than the general population from liver disease, diabetes, tuberculosis, pneumonia and influenza as well as from homicide, suicide and injuries. However, Indians' death rates from Alzheimer's disease or breast cancer are lower.

Health Status of American Indians* Compared to General Population
(deaths per 100,000 population)

Cause	Native Americans in IHS areas (1999-2001)	U.S. general population (2000)
Alzheimer's disease	10.2	18
Breast cancer	17.6	26.9
Cervical cancer	3.8	2.8
Chronic liver disease/cirrhosis	40.6	9.6
Diabetes mellitus	77.7	25.2
Homicide	11.4	6.1
Pneumonia, influenza	33.6	23.7
Suicide	17	10.6
Tuberculosis	1.9	0.3
Unintentional injuries	88.9	35.5

*Living in areas served by the IHS

Source: "Indian Health Service: Health Care Services Are Not Always Available to Native Americans," Government Accountability Office, August 2005

Background image: Canyon de Chelly, Navajo Nation, Arizona (Navajo Tourism)

wounded. The occupation ended on May 8, 1973.

Self-Determination

Amid the surging Indian activism, the federal government was trying to make up for the past by encouraging tribal self-determination.[46]

In 1975, Congress passed the Indian Self-Determination and Education Assistance Act, which channeled federal contracts and grants directly to tribes, reducing the BIA role and effectively putting Indian communities in direct charge of schools, health, housing and other programs.

And to assure Indians that the era of sudden reversals in federal policy had ended, the House in 1988 passed a resolution reaffirming the "constitutionally recognized government-to-government relationship with Indian tribes." Separate legislation set up a "self-governance demonstration project" in which eligible tribes would sign "compacts" to run their own governments with block grants from the federal government.[47]

By 1993, 28 tribes had negotiated compacts with the Interior Department. And in 1994, President Bill Clinton signed legislation that made self-governance a permanent option.

For the general public, the meaning of newly strengthened Indian sovereignty could be summed up with one word: casinos. In 1988, Congress enacted legislation regulating tribal gaming operations. That move followed a Supreme Court ruling (*California v. Cabazon*) that authorized tribes to run gambling operations. But tribes could not offer a form of gambling specifically barred by the state.

The law set up three categories of gambling operations: Class I, traditional Indian games, controlled exclusively by tribes; Class II, including bingo, lotto, pull tabs and

involuntary manslaughter charge against a non-Indian who had allegedly killed an Indian near the reservation had renewed Indian anger at discriminatory treatment by police and judges.

The occupation soon turned into a full-blown siege, with the reservation surrounded by troops and federal law-enforcement officers. During several firefights two AIM members were killed, and an FBI agent was

some card games, which are allowed on tribal lands in states that allow the games elsewhere; and Class III, which takes in casino games such as slot machines, roulette and blackjack, which can be offered only under agreements with state governments that set out the size and types of the proposed casinos.

Limits that the Indian Gaming Regulatory Act put on Indian sovereignty were tightened further by a 1996 Supreme Court decision that the Seminole Tribe couldn't sue Florida to force negotiation of a casino compact. The decision essentially forced tribes nationwide to make revenue-sharing deals with states in return for approval of casinos.[48]

Meanwhile, particularly on reservations from Minnesota to the Pacific Northwest, a plague of methamphetamine addiction and manufacturing is leaving a trail of death and shattered lives. By 2002, Darrell Hillaire, chairman of the Lummi Nation, near Bellingham, Wash., said that members convicted of dealing meth would be expelled from the tribe.[49]

But the Lummis couldn't stop the spread of the scourge on other reservations. National Congress of American Indians President Garcia said early in 2006: "Methamphetamine is a poison taking Indian lives, destroying Indian families, and razing entire communities."[50]

CURRENT SITUATION
Self-Government

Some Indian leaders are advocating more power for tribal governments as the best way to improve the quality of life on reservations.

Under the Tribal Self-Governance Demonstration Project, made permanent in 1994, tribes can replace program-by-program grants by entering into "compacts" with the federal government, under which they receive a single grant for a variety of services. Some 231 tribes and Alaskan Native villages have compacts to administer a total of about $341 million in programs. Of the Indian communities now living under compacts, 72 are in the lower 48 states.[51]

Under a set of separate compacts, the Indian Health Service has turned over clinics, hospitals and health programs to some 300 tribes and Alaskan villages, 70 of them non-Alaskan tribes.

Native American children and adults in the Chicago area keep in touch with their cultural roots at the American Indian Center. About two-thirds of the nation's Indians live in urban areas.

The self-governance model has proved especially appropriate in Alaska, where the majority of the native population of 120,000 is concentrated in 229 villages, many of them remote, and compact in size, hence well-suited to managing their own affairs, experts say.

Another advantage of Alaska villages is the experience they acquired through the 1971 Alaska Native Claims Settlement Act, which granted a total of $962 million to Alaska natives born on or before Dec. 18, 1971, in exchange for giving up their claims to millions of acres of land. Villages formed regional corporations to manage the assets. In addition, all Alaska residents receive an annual dividend ($946 in 2005) from natural-resource royalty income.[52]

"The emergence of tribal authority is unprecedented in Indian Country's history," says Allen, of the Jamestown S'Klallam Tribe, one of the originators of the self-governance model. "Why not take the resources you have available and use them as efficiently as you can — more efficiently than currently being administered?"[53]

But the poorer and more populous tribes of the Great Plains and the Southwest have turned down the self-governance model. "They can't afford to do it," says Michael LaPointe, chief of staff to President Rodney Bordeaux of the Rosebud Sioux Tribe. "When you have a lot of poverty and not a lot of economic activity to generate tribal resources to supplement the unfunded mandates, it becomes impossible."

In contrast with the Jameston S'Klallam's tiny membership of 585 people, there are some 24,000 people on the Rosebud Sioux' million-acre reservation. The tribe does operate law enforcement, ambulances and other services under contracts with the government. But it can't afford to do any more, LaPointe says.

A combined effect of the gambling boom and the growing adoption of the self-governance model is that much of the tension has gone out of the traditionally strained relationship between the BIA and tribes. "BIA people are getting pushed out as decision-makers," Kalt says. Some strains remain, to be sure. Allen says he senses a growing reluctance by the BIA to let go of tribes. "They use the argument that that the BIA doesn't have the money [for block grants]," he says.

BIA Director Ragsdale acknowledges that tougher financial-accounting requirements sparked by a lawsuit over Interior Department handling of Indian trust funds are slowing the compact-approval process. But, he adds, "We're not trying to hinder self-governance."

Limits on Gambling

Several legislative efforts to limit Indian gaming are pending. Separate bills by Sen. McCain and House Resources Committee Chairman Richard Pombo, R-Calif., would restrict tribes' ability to acquire new land for casinos in more favorable locations.

More proposals are in the pipeline. Jemez Pueblo of New Mexico wants to build a casino near the town of Anthony, though the pueblo is 300 miles away.[54]

In eastern Oregon, the Warm Springs Tribe is proposing an off-reservation casino at the Columbia River Gorge. And in Washington state, the Cowlitz and Mohegan tribes are planning an off-reservation casino near Portland.[55] The process has been dubbed "reservation shopping."

Under the Indian Gaming Regulatory Act of 1988, a tribe can acquire off-reservation land for casinos when it is:

- granted as part of a land claim settlement;
- granted to a newly recognized tribe as its reservation;
- restored to a tribe whose tribal recognition is also restored; or
- granted to a recognized tribe that had no reservation when the act took effect.

The most hotly debated exemption allows the secretary of the Interior to grant an off-reservation acquisition that benefits the tribe without harming the community near the proposed casino location. Both Pombo and McCain would repeal the loophole created by this so-called "two-part test." Under Pombo's bill, tribes acquiring land under the other exemptions would have to have solid historic and recent ties to the property. Communities, state governors and state legislatures would have to approve the establishment of new casinos, and tribes would reimburse communities for the effects of casinos on transportation, law enforcement and other public services.

McCain's bill would impose fewer restrictions than Pombo's. But McCain would give the National Indian Gaming Commission final say over all contracts with outside suppliers of goods and services.

The bill would also ensure the commission's control over big-time gambling — a concern that arose from a 2005 decision by the U.S. Court of Appeals for the District of Columbia that limited the agency's jurisdiction over a Colorado tribe. The commission has been worrying that applying that decision nationwide would eliminate federal supervision of casinos.

McCain told a March 8 Senate Indian Affairs Committee hearing that the two-part test "is fostering opposition to all Indian gaming."[56]

If the senator had been aiming to soften tribal opposition to his bill, he didn't make much headway. "We believe that it grows out of anecdotal, anti-Indian press reports on Indian gaming, the overblown issue of off-reservation gaming, and a 'pin-the-blame-on-the-victim' reaction to the Abramoff scandal," Ron His Horse Is Thunder, chairman of the Standing Rock Sioux Tribe of North Dakota and South Dakota, told the committee. He argued that the bill would amount to unconstitutional meddling with Indian sovereignty.

But the idea of restricting "reservation-shopping" appeals to tribes facing competition from other tribes. Cheryle A. Kennedy, chairwoman of the Confederated Tribes of the Grand Ronde Community of Oregon, said

Urban Indians: Invisible and Unheard

Two-thirds of the nation's 4.4 million American Indians live in towns and cities, but they're hard to find.[1] "Indians who move into metropolitan areas are scattered; they're not in a centralized geographical area," says New Mexico Secretary of Labor Conroy Chino. "You don't have that cohesive community where there's a sense of culture and language, as in Chinatown or Koreatown in Los Angeles."

Chino's interest is professional as well as personal. In his former career as a television journalist in Albuquerque, Chino, a member of the Acoma Pueblo, wrote an independent documentary about urban Indians. His subjects range from a city-loving San Franciscan who vacations in Hawaii to city-dwellers who return to their reservations every vacation they get. Their lives diverge sharply from what University of Arizona anthropologist Susan Lobo calls a "presumption that everything Indian is rural and long, long ago."[2]

Indian society began urbanizing in 1951, when the Bureau of Indian Affairs (BIA) started urging reservation dwellers to move to cities where — it was hoped — they would blend into the American "melting pot" and find more economic opportunity and a better standard of living.[3]

But many found the urban environment oppressive and the government assistance less generous than promised. About 100,000 Indians were relocated between 1951 and 1973, when the program wound down; unable to fit in, many fell into alcoholism and despair.[4]

Still, a small, urban Indian middle class has developed over time, partly because the BIA began systematically hiring Indians in its offices. Indians keep such a low profile, however, that the Census Bureau has a hard time finding them. Lobo, who consulted for the bureau in 1990, recalls that the agency's policy at the time was to register any household where no one answered the door as being in the same ethnic group as the neighbors. That strategy worked with urban ethnic groups who tended to cluster together, Lobo says, but not with Native Americans because theirs was a "dispersed population."

By the 2000 census that problem was resolved, but another one cropped up. "American Indians are ingenious at keeping expenses down — by couch-surfing, for instance," Lobo says. "There's a floating population that doesn't get counted because they weren't living in a standard residence."

But other urban Indians live conventional, middle-class lives, sometimes even while technically living on Indian land. "I am highly educated, a professor in the university, and my gainful employment is in the city of Albuquerque," says Ted Jojola, a professor of planning at the University of New Mexico (and a member of the Census Bureau's advisory committee on Indian population). "My community [Isleta Pueblo] is seven minutes south of Albuquerque. The reservation has become an urban amenity to me."

Some might see a home on Indian land near the city as a refuge from discrimination. "There have been years where you couldn't reveal you were native if you wanted to get a job," says Joseph Podlasek, executive director of the American Indian Center of Chicago.

Joycelyn Dorscher, president of the Association of American Indian Physicians, recalls a painful experience several years ago when she rushed her 6-year-old daughter to a hospital emergency room in Minneapolis-St. Paul, suspecting appendicitis. The young intern assigned to the case saw an Indian single mother with a sick child and apparently assumed that the daughter was suffering from neglect. "She told me if I didn't sit down and shut up, my daughter would go into the [child-protective] system," recalls Dorscher, who at the time was a third-year medical student.

Even Chino, whose mainstream credentials include an M.A. from Princeton, feels alienated at times from non-Indian city dwellers. He notes that Albuquerque officials ignored Indians' objections to a statue honoring Juan de Oñate, the 16th-century conqueror who established Spanish rule in what is now New Mexico. "Though native people protested and tried to show why this is not a good idea," Chino says, "the city went ahead and funded it."[5]

In the long run, Chino hopes a growing presence of Indian professionals — "we're not all silversmiths, or weavers" — will create more acceptance of urban Indians and more aid to combat high Indian dropout rates and other problems. "While people like having Indians in New Mexico and like visitors to get a feel for the last bastion of native culture," he says, "they're not doing that much for the urban Indian community, though we're paying taxes, too."

---

[1] Urban Indians were 64 percent of the population in 2000, according to the U.S. Census Bureau. For background, see, "We the People: American Indians and Alaska Natives in the United States," U.S. Census Bureau, 2000, p. 14, www.census.gov/prod/2006pubs/censr-28.pdf.

[2] "Looking Toward Home," *Native American Public Telecommunications*, 2003, www.visionmaker.org.

[3] Donald L. Fixico, *The Urban Indian Experience in America* (2000), pp. 9-11.

[4] *Ibid.*, pp. 22-25.

[5] Oñate is especially disliked at Acoma, Chino's birthplace, where the conqueror had the feet of some two-dozen Acoma men cut off in 1599 after Spanish soldiers were killed there. For background, see Wren Propp, "A Giant of Ambivalence," *Albuquerque Journal*, Jan. 25, 2004, p. A1; Brenda Norrell, "Pueblos Decry War Criminal," *Indian Country Today*, June 25, 2004.

AT ISSUE

Should tribes open casinos on newly acquired land?

YES
Ernest L. Stevens Jr.
Chairman, National Indian Gaming Association

From statement before U.S. House Committee on Resources, Nov. 9, 2005

Indian gaming is the Native American success story. Where there were no jobs, now there are 553,000 jobs. Where our people had only an eighth-grade education on average, tribal governments are building schools and funding college scholarships. Where the United States and boarding schools sought to suppress our languages, tribal schools are now teaching their native language. Where our people suffer epidemic diabetes, heart disease and premature death, our tribes are building hospitals, health clinics and wellness centers.

Historically, the United States signed treaties guaranteeing Indian lands as permanent homes, and then a few years later, went to war to take our lands. This left our people to live in poverty, often on desolate lands, while others mined for gold or pumped oil from the lands that were taken from us.

Indian gaming is an exercise of our inherent right to self-government. Today, for over 60 percent of Indian tribes in the lower 48 states, Indian gaming offers new hope and a chance for a better life for our children.

Too many lands were taken from Indian tribes, leaving some tribes landless or with no useful lands. To take account of historical mistreatment, the Indian Gaming Regulatory Act (IGRA), provided several exceptions to the rule that Indian tribes should conduct Indian gaming on lands held on Oct. 17, 1988.

Accordingly, land is restored to an Indian tribe in trust status when the tribe is restored to federal recognition. For federally recognized tribes that did not have reservation land on the date IGRA was enacted, land is put into trust. Or, a tribe may apply to the secretary of the Interior. The secretary consults with state and local officials and nearby Indian tribes to determine whether an acquisition of land in trust for gaming would be in the tribe's "best interest" and "not detrimental to the surrounding community."

Now, legislation would require "newly recognized, restored, or landless tribes" to apply to have land taken in trust through a five-part process. Subjecting tribes to this new and cumbersome process discounts the fact that the United States mistreated these tribes by ignoring and neglecting them, taking all of their lands or allowing their lands to be stolen by others.

We believe that Congress should restore these tribes to a portion of their historical lands and that these lands should be held on the same basis as other Indian lands.

NO
State Rep. Fulton Sheen, R-Plainwell
Michigan House of Representatives

From statement to U.S. House Committee on Resources, April 5, 2006

The rampant proliferation of tribal gaming is running roughshod over states' rights and local control and is jeopardizing everything from my own neighborhood to — as the Jack Abramoff scandal has demonstrated — the very integrity of our federal political system.

In 1988, Congress passed the Indian Gaming Regulatory Act (IGRA) in an effort to control the development of Native American casinos and, in particular, to make sure that the states had a meaningful role in the development of any casinos within their borders. At that time, Native American gambling accounted for less than 1 percent of the nation's gambling industry, grossing approximately $100 million in revenue.

Since that time, the Native American casino business has exploded into an $18.5 billion industry that controls 25 percent of gaming industry revenue. Despite this unbridled growth, IGRA and the land-in-trust process remain basically unchanged.

When Congress originally enacted IGRA, the general rule was that casino gambling would not take place on newly acquired trust land. I believe Congress passed this general rule to prevent precisely what we see happening: a mad and largely unregulated land rush pushed by casino developers eager to cash in on a profitable revenue stream that is not burdened by the same tax rates or regulations that other businesses have to incur. "Reservation shopping" is an activity that must be stopped. And that is just one component of the full legislative overhaul that is needed.

IGRA and its associated land-in-trust process is broken, open to manipulation by special interests and in desperate need of immediate reform. It has unfairly and inappropriately fostered an industry that creates enormous wealth for a few select individuals and Las Vegas interests at the expense of taxpaying families, small businesses, manufacturing jobs and local governments.

Our research shows that while local and state governments receive some revenue-sharing percentages from tribal gaming, the dollars pale in comparison to the overall new costs to government and social-service agencies from increased infrastructure demands, traffic, bankruptcies, crime, divorce and general gambling-related ills.

I do not think this is what Congress had in mind. Somewhere along the way, the good intentions of Congress have been hijacked, and it is time for this body to reassert control over this process. It is imperative that Congress take swift and decisive steps today to get its arms around this issue before more jobs are lost and more families are put at risk.

her tribe's Spirit Mountain Casino could be hurt by the Warm Springs Tribes' proposed project or by the Cowlitz and Mohegan project.[57]

Pombo's bill would require the approval of new casinos by tribes that already have gambling houses up and running within 75 miles of a proposed new one.

The House Resources Committee heard another view from Indian Country at an April 5 hearing. Jacquie Davis-Van Huss, tribal secretary of the North Fork Rancheria of the Mono Indians of California, said Pombo's approval clause would doom her tribe's plans. "This provision is anti-competitive," she testified. "It effectively provides the power to veto another tribe's gaming project simply to protect market share."

Trust Settlement

McCain's committee is also grappling with efforts to settle a decade-old lawsuit that has exposed longstanding federal mismanagement of trust funds. In 1999, U.S. District Judge Royce Lamberth said evidence showed "fiscal and governmental irresponsibility in its purest form."[58]

The alternative to settlement, McCain and Dorgan told the Budget Committee, is for the case to drag on through the courts. Congressional resolution of the conflict could also spare the Interior Department further grief from Lamberth. In a February ruling, he said Interior's refusal to make payments owed to Indians was "an obscenity that harkens back to the darkest days of United States-Indian relations."[59]

Five months later, Lamberth suggested that Congress, not the courts, may be the proper setting for the conflict. "Interior's unremitting neglect and mismanagement of the Indian trust has left it in such a shambles that recovery may prove impossible."[60]

The court case has its roots in the 1887 policy of allotting land to Indians in an effort to break up reservations. Since then, the Interior Department has been responsible for managing payments made to landholders, which later included tribes, for mining and other natural-resource extraction on Indian-owned land.

But for decades, Indians weren't receiving what they were owed. On June 10, 1996, Elouise Cobell, an organizer of the Blackfeet National Bank, the first Indian-owned national bank on a reservation, sued the Interior Department charging that she and all other trust fee recipients had been cheated for decades out of money that Interior was responsible for managing. "Lands and resources — in many cases the only source of income for some of our nation's poorest and most vulnerable citizens — have been grossly mismanaged," Cobell told the Indian Affairs Committee on March 1.

The mismanagement is beyond dispute, said John Bickerman, who was appointed to broker a settlement. Essentially, Bickerman told the Senate Indian Affairs Committee on March 28, "Money was not collected; money was not properly deposited; and money was not properly disbursed."

As of 2005, Interior is responsible for trust payments involving 126,079 tracts of land owned by 223,245 individuals — or, 2.3 million "ownership interests" on some 12 million acres, Cason and Ross Swimmer, a special trustee, told the committee.

Bickerman said a settlement amount of $27.5 billion proposed by the Indian plaintiffs was "without foundation." But the Interior Department proposed a settlement of $500 million based on "arbitrary and false assumptions," he added. Both sides agree that some $13 billion should have been paid to individual Indians over the life of the trust, but they disagree over how much was actually paid.

Supreme Court Ruling

Powerful repercussions are expected from the Supreme Court's latest decision in a centuries-long string of rulings involving competing claims to land by Indians and non-Indians.

In 2005, the high court said the Oneida Indian Nation of New York could not quit paying taxes on 10 parcels of land it owns north of Utica.[61]

After buying the parcels in 1997 and 1998, the tribe refused to pay property taxes, arguing that the land was former tribal property now restored to tribal ownership, and thereby tax-exempt.[62]

The court, in an opinion written by Ruth Bader Ginsburg, concluded that though the tribe used to own the land, the property right was too old to revive. "Rekindling the embers of sovereignty that long ago grew cold" is out of the question, Ginsburg wrote. She invoked the legal doctrine of "laches," in which a party who waits too long to assert his rights loses them.[63]

Lawyers on both sides of Indian law cases expect the case to affect lower-court rulings throughout the country.

"The court has opened the cookie jar," Williams of the University of Arizona argues. "Does laches only apply to claims of sovereignty over reacquired land? If a decision favoring Indians is going to inconvenience too many white people, then laches applies — I swear that's what it says." Tribes litigating fishing rights, water rights and other assets are likely to suffer in court as a result, he argues.

In fact, only three months after the high court decision, the 2nd U.S. Circuit Court of Appeals in New York invoked laches in rejecting a claim by the Cayuga Tribe. Vickers of Upstate Citizens for Equality says that if the 2nd Circuit "thinks that laches forbids the Cayugas from making a claim because the Supreme Court said so, you're going to find other courts saying so."

In Washington, Alexandra Page, an attorney with the Indian Law Resource Center, agrees. "There are tribes in the West who have boundary disputes on their reservations; there are water-law cases where you've got people looking back at what happened years ago, so the Supreme Court decision could have significant practical impact. The danger is that those with an interest in limiting Indian rights will do everything they can to expand the decision and use it in other circumstances."

OUTLOOK

Who Is an Indian?

If advocates of Indian self-governance are correct, the number of tribes running their own affairs with minimal federal supervision will keep on growing. "The requests for workshops are coming in steadily," says Cyndi Holmes, self-governance coordinator of the Jamestown S'Klallam Tribe.

Others say that growth, now at a rate of about three tribes a year, may be nearing its upper limit. "When you look at the options for tribes to do self-governance, economics really drives whether they can," says LaPointe of the Rosebud Sioux, whose tribal government doesn't expect to adopt the model in the foreseeable future.

But the longstanding problems of rural and isolated reservations are not the only dimension of Indian life. People stereotypically viewed as tied to the land have become increasingly urban over the past several decades, and the view from Indian Country is that the trend will continue.

That doesn't mean reservations will empty out or lose their cultural importance. "Urban Indian is not a lifelong label," says Susan Lobo, an anthropologist at the University of Arizona. "Indian people, like everyone else, can move around. They're still American Indians."

For Indians, as for all other peoples, moving around leads to intermarriage. Matthew Snipp, a Stanford University sociologist who is half Cherokee and half Oklahoma Choctaw, notes that Indians have long married within and outside Indian society. But the consequences of intermarriage are different for Indians than for, say, Jews or Italians.

The Indian place in American society grows out of the government-to-government relationship between Washington and tribes. And most tribes define their members by what's known as the "blood quantum" — their degree of tribal ancestry.

"I look at it as you're kind of USDA-approved," says Podlasek of the American Indian Center. "Why is no other race measured that way?"

Podlasek is especially sensitive to the issue. His father was Polish-American, and his mother was Ojibway. His own wife is Indian, but from another tribe. "My kids can be on the tribal rolls, but their kids won't be able to enroll, unless they went back to my tribe or to their mother's tribe to marry — depending on what their partners' blood quantum is. In generations, you could say that, by government standards, there are no more native people."

Snipp traces the blood-quantum policy to a 1932 decision by the Indian Affairs Commission, which voted to make one-quarter descent the minimum standard. The commissioners were concerned, Snipp says, reading from the commission's report, that thousands of people "more white than Indian" were receiving "shares in tribal estates and other benefits." Tribes are no longer bound by that decision, but the requirement — originally inserted at BIA insistence — remains in many tribal constitutions.

On the Indian side, concern over collective survival is historically well-founded. Historian Elizabeth Shoemaker of the University of Connecticut at Storrs calculated that the Indian population of what is now the continental United States plummeted from a top estimate of 5.5 million in 1492 to a mere 237,000 in 1900. Indian life expectancy didn't begin to rise significantly until after 1940.[64]

Now, Indians are worrying about the survival of Indian civilization at a time when Indians' physical survival has never been more assured.

Even as these existential worries trouble some Indian leaders, the living conditions that most Indians endure also pose long-term concerns.

Conroy Chino, New Mexico's Labor secretary and a member of Acoma Pueblo, says continuation of the educational disaster in Indian Country is dooming young people to live on the margins. "I'm out there attracting companies to come to New Mexico, and these kids aren't going to qualify for those good jobs."

Nevertheless, below most non-Indians' radar screen, the Indian professional class is growing. "When I got my Ph.D. in 1973, I think I was the 15th in the country," says Beaulieu of Arizona State University's Center for Indian Education. "Now we have all kinds of Ph.D.s, teachers with certification, lawyers." And Beaulieu says he has seen the difference that Indian professionals make in his home state of Minnesota. "You're beginning to see an educated middle class in the reservation community, and realizing that they're volunteering to perform lots of services."

In Albuquerque, the University of New Mexico's Jojola commutes to campus from Isleta Pueblo. Chairman of an advisory committee on Indians to the U.S. Census Bureau, Jojola shares concerns about use of "blood quantum" as the sole determinant of Indian identity. "A lot of people are saying that language, culture and residence should also be considered," he says.

That standard would implicitly recognize what many Indians call the single biggest reason that American Indians have outlasted the efforts of those who wanted to exterminate or to assimilate them. "In our spirituality we remain strong," says Bordeaux of the Rosebud Sioux. "That's our godsend and our lifeline."

UPDATE

American Indians have continued their reliance on casinos as an engine of tribal economic growth. Moreover, despite moral objections from anti-gambling organizations, Indians have emerged as major political donors in Washington, where they have lobbied successfully to maintain federal spending on Indian health and education.

Revenues from the 442 so-called Indian "gaming" facilities in 30 states rose from $19.6 billion in 2004 to

Harvard Law School graduate Lance Morgan, a member of Nebraska's Winnebago Tribe, used seed money from his tribe's small casino to create several thriving businesses. He urges other tribes to use their casino profits to diversify. "Gaming is just a means to an end," he says.

$26.7 billion in 2008, though they declined by 1 percent in 2009, according to the National Indian Gaming Commission.

In recent years casinos in California and Oklahoma have been the most successful, and in June National Indian Gaming Association Chairman Ernie Stevens Jr. attended the annual Sovereignty Symposium in Oklahoma City to praise local tribes for their work in providing jobs and making money to pay for improvements in education, health care and transportation.[65] "Oklahoma is No. 2 in Indian gaming," said Stevens. "I think that is tremendous. Is it an accident? Is it because of luck? I don't think so. This comes from hard work. This comes from a lot of dialogue and information sharing."

"Gaming has been transformative for tribes," says Washington, D.C., attorney Alan R. Fedman, former director of enforcement for the gaming commission.

President Barack Obama, surrounded by members of the administration and Native American leaders, signs the Tribal Law and Order Act during a ceremony in the East Room at the White House on July 29, 2010.

"The experience of tribal councils successfully running their own businesses has given them the confidence to diversify into other means of economic growth," such as medical-records processing and government contracting. Only about half of the 564 federally recognized tribes are involved in gaming, Fedman adds, and the ones that are not are doing about the same economically as they were 20 years ago.

Critics of Gambling

But the reliance on gambling is not healthy in the long term, according to Les Bernal, executive director of Stop Predatory Gambling (formerly the National Coalition Against Legalized Gambling). "The political momentum is definitely against Indian tribes relying on casinos for economic growth because gambling is the most predatory business in America," he says. Decrying "casino capitalism" that "milks existing wealth instead of creating new wealth," the anti-gambling group laments the way tribal casinos, "funded by millionaire casino investors," continue to "force their way into communities across the nation."[66]

Bernal objects to political giving by tribes, noting that six of the top 11 donors to candidates in federal and state elections are Native American interests, according to a study of the 2007-08 election cycle by the Washington-based Center for Responsive Politics.[67]

But many tribes believe that playing the Washington "pay to play" game is a political imperative. "Native American interests have already been largely ignored in Washington," said Heather Dawn Thompson, past president of the National Native Bar Association and a partner at the D.C. law firm Sonnenschein Nath & Rosenthal. "It has been an uphill battle for tribes, with corporate and union interests active in political contributing, often against tribal interests.

Supreme Court Ruling

Indian casino expansion hit a roadblock in February 2009, when the Supreme Court ruled against an Interior Department move to acquire 31 acres in Charlestown, R.I., for the Narragansett tribe, which envisioned using the land for a gambling facility. The court ruled 7-2 in *Carcieri v. Salazar* that because the tribe had not been federally recognized before enactment of the 1934 Indian Reorganization Act, the federal government could not take the land into trust and thus exempt it from many state gambling laws and taxes.[68]

The decision affected the Mashpee Wampanoag tribe on Cape Cod. Its application to the Bureau of Indian Affairs for a casino license drew backing in a June 2010 memo from Interior Secretary Ken Salazar, who offered to give the tribe an exemption allowed under the 1988 Federal Indian Gaming Regulatory Act. The act is the chief law governing tribal casinos. It often pits revenue-hungry states against tribes seeking federal trust status in hopes of opening gambling facilities free from state taxation.[69] Salazar's memo revived the issue in the Massachusetts legislature, which is considering a gambling bill that would give a licensing preference to Indian tribes.

Nationally, Salazar and many Indian tribes are working to persuade Congress to enact legislation to overturn the *Carcieri* ruling and permit more recently recognized tribes to take land into trust. On July 13, 2010, Indian advocates representing 17 tribal organizations came to Washington and met with Sen. Byron Dorgan, D-N.D., chair of the Senate Indian Affairs Committee, which had reported out related legislation in December 2009.[70] Dorgan at the time warned that the Supreme Court's interpretation "would have the effect of creating two classes of Indian tribes — those who were recognized as of 1934, for whom land may be taken into trust, and those recognized after 1934 that would be unable to have land taken into trust." He called that an "unacceptable" decision that flew in the face of prior acts of Congress and said it would harm Indians' employment and development projects, such as the building of homes and community centers.[71]

Government Action

On July 26, the House Interior Appropriations Subcommittee voted to add a "*Carcieri* fix" to a spending bill, but prospects for enactment this Congress appeared uncertain.

American Indians have seen new infusions of federal funds and other aid under the Obama administration. Under the economic stimulus package — the American Recovery and Reinvestment Act of 2009 — which President Barack Obama signed during his second month in office, the Indian Health Service received $500 million, including $227 million for health facilities construction and $100 million for maintenance and improvements.[72]

The landmark health care reform law signed by Obama in March 2010 included permanent reauthorization of the 1976 Indian Health Care Improvement Act. "Our responsibility to provide health services to American Indians and Alaska Natives derives from the nation-to-nation relationship between the federal and tribal governments," he said. "With this bill, we have taken a critical step in fulfilling that responsibility by modernizing the Indian health care system and improving access to health care for American Indians and Alaska Natives."

The president noted that the new law, among other effects, will allow urban Indian health programs to provide employee health benefits under the Federal Employees Health Benefits Program; exempt urban Indian health providers from licensing and registration fees; make federal medical-supply sources available to Indian clinics; and require the Indian Health Service and the Health and Human Services Department to confer with tribes before putting new policies into place.

In another sign of Native American clout in Washington, Obama on July 29 signed an anti-crime bill that will require more reporting of rapes and assaults on Indian reservations while adding federal prosecutors and toughening sentences for violators.

Crimes Against Women

American Indian and Alaska Native women are nearly three times as likely to experience a rape or sexual assault compared to white, African-American or Asian-American women, according to a 2008 federally funded study.[73]

The signing of the act is "a significant and historic moment for tribal nations and federal law enforcement officials across the country," said Jefferson Keel, president of the National Congress of American Indians. "This legislation will empower tribal nations to begin to address crime rates that have risen in our communities as a result of jurisdictional and resource limitations," he said.

Dorgan said the next big step for Native Americans would be to secure more funding to boost law enforcement on the reservations. The Bureau of Indian Affairs says that only about 3,000 police officers patrol 56 million acres of Indian land, about 48 percent below the national average.[74]

Perhaps the most pressing issue still unfolding for American Indians is the coming reauthorization of the Elementary and Secondary Education Act, commonly known as No Child Left Behind.

Education Issues

At a June 17, 2010, hearing before the Senate Indian Affairs Committee, Chad Smith, principal chief of the Cherokee Nation, acknowledged the eight-year-old law has improved accountability measures intended to boost performance by both students and teachers. But "the Nation would specifically like to see less emphasis on testing and more flexibility in establishing our own measurables," he said. "We feel that a more diverse curriculum will better fit the needs of our students by including increased focus on native culture and language. Culturally relevant education is successful with Indian students because [our cultural strengths] have helped us to face adversity, adapt, survive, prosper and excel for generations. Our younger children, immersion students included, are also forced to take tests in English while many students in rural areas are English-language learners, meaning they arrive at school knowing little or no English, which causes them to test poorly."[75]

School safety is also an ongoing concern to American Indians. According to May 2010 testimony by Quinton Roman Nose, a board member of the National Indian Education Association, "appalling disparities exist in the levels of safety, both structural and personal, in Bureau of Indian Education-funded schools, creating educational environments that are a threat to the emotional and physical well-being of native students." He said the association is seeking funds for a deferred-maintenance backlog estimated at $500 million at nearly 4,500 Indian school buildings.

The group also called for improved youth-violence prevention programs, arguing that "tribal communities are in the best position to advise and help develop culturally relevant and appropriate methods for addressing issues like bullying prevention, substance abuse prevention, anti-gang programming and suicide prevention."[76]

Such social problems continue to drive much of the Native American agenda. The Navajo Nation in 2009 reported that the number of youth gangs among its widespread population of 250,000 in recent years has grown to 225, many of them involved in drug trafficking.[77]

Christopher Grant, former chief of detectives in Rapid City, S.D., who is now a national Native American gang specialist, said gangs and drug traffickers often take advantage of meager tribal law enforcement resources and confusion over whether federal, state, local or tribal officers have jurisdiction.[78]

Meanwhile, suicide remains a serious concern. The youth suicide rate on Indian lands is now 70 percent higher than that of the general population, according to the office of Sen. Dorgan, who on July 26 hosted a summit meeting in Washington on suicide prevention among Native Americans. Calling the situation an "urgent and pressing crisis," Dorgan said that "building partnerships between Indian Country, [the] federal government and the private sector is critical to developing better strategies and programs for reaching at-risk Native American teens."[79]

NOTES

1. For background, see "The Administration of Indian Affairs," *Editorial Research Reports 1929* (Vol. II), at *CQ Researcher Plus Archive*, CQ Electronic Library, http://library.cqpress.com.

2. For background see Phil Two Eagle, "Rosebud Sioux Tribe, Demographics," March 25, 2003, www.rosebudsiouxtribe-nsn.gov/demographics.

3. "American Indian Population and Labor Force Report 2003," p. ii, Bureau of Indian Affairs, cited in John McCain, chairman, Senate Indian Affairs Committee, Byron L. Dorgan, vice chairman, letter to Senate Budget Committee, March 2, 2006, http://indian.senate.gov/public/_files/Budget5.pdf.

4. Jonathan B. Taylor and Joseph P. Kalt, "American Indians on Reservations: A Databook of Socioeconomic Change Between the 1990 and 2000 Censuses," Harvard Project on American Indian Economic Development, January 2005, pp. 8-13; www.ksg.harvard.edu/hpaied/pubs/pub_151.htm. These data exclude the Navajo Tribe, whose on-reservation population of about 175,000 is 12 times that of the next-largest tribe, thus distorting comparisons, Taylor and Kalt write.

5. *Ibid.*, p. 41.

6. McCain and Dorgan, *op. cit.*

7. "Injury Mortality Among American Indian and Alaska Native Youth, United States, 1989-1998," *Morbidity and Mortality Weekly Report*, Centers for Disease Control and Prevention, Aug. 1, 2003, www.cdc.gov/mmwr/preview/mmwrhtml/mm5230a2.htm#top.

8. Robert McSwain, deputy director, Indian Health Service, testimony before Senate Indian Affairs Committee, April 5, 2006.

9. *Ibid.*, p. xii.

10. Taylor and Kalt, *op. cit.*

11. *Ibid.*, pp. 28-30.

12. *Ibid.*, pp. 22-24.

13. The decision is *Cherokee Nation v. Georgia*, 30 U.S. 1 (1831), http://supreme.justia.com/us/30/1/case.html.

14. Alan Meister, "Indian Gaming industry Report," Analysis Group, 2006, p. 2. Publicly available data can be obtained at, "Indian Gaming Facts," www.indiangaming.org/library/indian-gaming-facts; "Gaming Revenues, 2000-2004," National Indian Gaming Commission, www.nigc.gov/TribalData/GamingRevenues20042000/tabid/549/Default.aspx.

15. The ruling is *California v. Cabazon Band of Mission Indians*, 480 U.S. 202 (1987), http://supreme.justia.com/us/480/202/case.html.

16. For background, see Susan Schmidt and James V. Grimaldi, "The Rise and Steep Fall of Jack Abramoff," *The Washington Post*, Dec. 29, 2005, p. A1. On March 29, Abramoff was sentenced in Miami to 70 months in prison after pleading to fraud, tax evasion and conspiracy to bribe public officials in charges growing out of a Florida business deal. He is cooperating with the Justice Department in its Washington-based political-corruption investigation. For background see Peter Katel, "Lobbying Boom," *CQ Researcher*, July 22, 2005, pp. 613-636.

17. Meister, *op. cit.*, pp. 27-28. For additional background, see John Cochran, "A Piece of the Action," *CQ Weekly*, May 9, 2005, p. 1208.

18. For background, see, "A Quiet Crisis: Federal Funding and Unmet Needs in Indian Country," U.S. Commission on Civil Rights, July, 2003, pp. 32, 113. www.usccr.gov/pubs/na0703/na0731.pdf.

19. Ryan Wilson, "State of Indian Education Address," Feb. 13, 2006, www.niea.org/history/SOIEAddress06.pdf.

20. For background see, Barbara Mantel, "No Child Left Behind," *CQ Researcher*, May 27, 2005, pp. 469-492.

21. McCain and Dorgan, *op. cit.*, pp. 14-15.

22. According to the Health and Human Services Department's budget proposal, recommended funding of $2 billion for the health centers would allow them to serve 150,000 Indian patients, among a total of 8.8 million patients. For background, see "Budget in Brief, Fiscal Year 2007," Department of Health and Human Services, p. 26, www.hhs.gov/budget/07budget/2007BudgetInBrief.pdf.

23. Peter Whoriskey, "A Tribe Takes a Grim Satisfaction in Abramoff's Fall," *The Washington Post*, Jan. 7, 2006, p. A1.

24. Meister, *op. cit.*, p. 15.

25. Whoriskey, *op. cit.*

26. For background see Fred Carstensen, *et al.*, "The Economic Impact of the Mashantucket Pequot Tribal National Operations on Connecticut," Connecticut Center for Economic Analysis, University of Connecticut, Nov. 28, 2000, pp. 1-3.

27. "Gambling Revenues 2004-2000," National Indian Gaming Commission, www.nigc.gov/TribalData/GamingRevenues20042000/tabid/549/Default.aspx.

28. Schmidt and Grimaldi, *op. cit.*

29. Alaina Potrikus, "2nd Land Hearing Packed," *The Post-Standard* (Syracuse, N.Y.), Jan. 12, 2006, p. B1.

30. For background see "Profile of the Navajo Nation," Navajo Nation Council, www.navajonationcouncil.org/profile.

31. Leslie Linthicum, "Navajos Cautious About Opening Casinos," *Albuquerque Journal*, Dec. 12, 2004, p. B1.

32. For background, see "Fourth Annual State of Indian Nations," Feb. 2, 2006, www.ncai.org/News_Archive.18.0.

33. For background see Theodore H. Haas, *The Indian and the Law* (1949), p. 2; thorpe.ou.edu/cohen/tribalgovtpam2pt1&2.htm#Tribal%20Power%20Today.

34. Except where otherwise noted, material in this section is drawn from Angie Debo, *A History of the Indians of the United States* (1970); see also, Mary H. Cooper, "Native Americans' Future," *CQ Researcher*, July 12, 1996, pp. 603-621.

35. W. Dale Mason, "Indian Gaming: Tribal Sovereignty and American Politics," 2000, p. 13.

36. *Cherokee Nation v. Georgia, op. cit.*, 30 U.S.1, http://supct.law.cornell.edu/supct/html/historics/USSC_CR_0030_0001_ZO.html.

37. Robert A. Williams Jr., *Like a Loaded Weapon: the Rehnquist Court, Indians Rights, and the Legal History of Racism in America* (2005), p. 63.

38. *Johnson v. M'Intosh*, 21 U.S. 543 (1823), www.Justia.us/us21543/case.html; *Worcester v. State of Ga.*, 31 U.S. 515 (1832), www.justia.us/us/31/515/case.html.

39. *Johnson v. M'Intosh, op. cit.*

40. *Worcester v. State of Ga., op. cit.*

41. Quoted in Debo, *op. cit.*, pp. 219-220.

42. Quoted in *ibid.*, p. 303.

43. The specified states were Wisconsin, Minnesota (except Red Lake), Nebraska, California and Oregon

(except the land of several tribes at Warm Springs). For background, see Debo, *op. cit.*, pp. 304-311.

44. Cited in Debo, *op. cit.*, p. 344.
45. For background see Troy R. Johnson, *The Occupation of Alcatraz Island: Indian Self-Determination and the Rise of Indian Activism* (1996).
46. For background, see Mary H. Cooper, "Native Americans' Future," *CQ Researcher*, July 12, 1996, pp. 603-621.
47. For background see "History of the Tribal Self-Governance Initiative," Self-Governance Tribal Consortium, www.tribalselfgov.org/Red%20Book/SG_New_Partnership.asp.
48. Cochran, *op. cit.*
49. For background see Paul Shukovsky, "Lummi Leader's Had It With Drugs, Sick of Substance Abuse Ravaging the Tribe," *Seattle Post-Intelligencer*, March 16, 2002, p. A1.
50. "Fourth Annual State of Indian Nations," *op. cit.*
51. Many Alaskan villages have joined collective compacts, so the total number of these agreements is 91.
52. For background see Alexandra J. McClanahan, "Alaska Native Claims Settlement Act (ANCSA)," Cook Inlet Region Inc., http://litsite.alaska.edu/aktraditions/ancsa.html; "The Permanent Fund Dividend," Alaska Permanent Fund Corporation, 2005, www.apfc.org/alaska/dividendprgrm.cfm?s=4.
53. For background see Eric Henson and Jonathan B. Taylor, "Native America at the New Millennium," Harvard Project on American Indian Development, Native Nations Institute, First Nations Development Institute, 2002, pp. 14-16, www.ksg.harvard.edu/hpaied/pubs/pub_004.htm.
54. Michael Coleman, "Jemez Casino Proposal At Risk," *Albuquerque Journal*, March 10, 2006, p. A1; Jeff Jones, "AG Warns Against Off-Reservation Casino," *Albuquerque Journal*, June 18, 2005, p. A1.
55. For background see testimony, "Off-Reservation Indian Gaming," House Resources Committee, Nov. 9, 2005, http://resourcescommittee.house.gov/archives/109/full/110905.htm.
56. Jerry Reynolds, "Gaming regulatory act to lose its 'two-part test,' " *Indian Country Today*, March 8, 2006.
57. Testimony before House Resources Committee, Nov. 9, 2005.
58. Matt Kelley, "Government asks for secrecy on its lawyers' role in concealing document shredding," The Associated Press, Nov. 2, 2000.
59. "Memorandum and Order," Civil Action No. 96-1285 (RCL), Feb. 7, 2005, www.indiantrust.com/index.cfm?FuseAction=PDFTypes.Home&PDFType_id=1&IsRecent=1.
60. "Memorandum Opinion," Civil Action 96-1285 (RCL), July 12, 2005, www.indiantrust.com/index.cfm?FuseAction=PDFTypes.Home&PDFType_id=1&IsRecent=1.
61. Glenn Coin, "Supreme Court: Oneidas Too Late; Sherrill Declares Victory, Wants Taxes," *The Post-Standard* (Syracuse), March 30, 2005, p. A1.
62. *Ibid.*
63. *City of Sherrill, New York, v. Oneida Indian Nation of New York*, Supreme Court of the United States, 544 U.S._(2005), pp. 1-2, 6, 14, 21.
64. Elizabeth Shoemaker, *American Indian Population Recovery in the Twentieth Century* (1999), pp. 1-13.
65. "Indian Gaming Update," National Indian Gaming Association, June 2010, www.indian gaming.org/info/newsletter/2010/NIGA_NEWSLETTER_06-10.pdf.
66. Stop Predatory Gambling, blog, www.stop predatorygambling.org, June 15, 2010.
67. For the study, see www.opensecrets.org/ orgs/list_stfed.php?order=A. For related commentary, see "Guess who is among the top lobbying spenders in D.C.-Indian gaming," *San Jose Mercury News*, editorial, Feb. 11, 2010.
68. Matthew L. M. Fletcher, "Decision's in. 'Now' begins work to fix Carcieri," guest editorial, *Indian Country Today*, Feb. 25, 2009; Casey Ross, "A Crapshoot for Mass.," *The Boston Globe*, May 26, 2010, www.boston.com/business/articles/2010/05/26/indian_gaming_debate_has_mass_in_limbo?mode=PF.
69. George Brennan, "Tribe's Casino Odds Improve," *Cape Cod Times*, June 30, 2010.
70. John E. Mulligan, "Tribal-Rights Advocates Seek Fix in Washington," *Providence Journal-Bulletin*, July 14, 2010.
71. Gale Courey Toensing, "Most Negative Impact," *Indian Country Today*, Dec. 30, 2009, www.indiancountrytoday.com/home/content/ 40290987.html.

72. Indian Health Service, www.ihs.gov/ recovery/.
73. Ronet Bachman, *et al.*, "Violence Against American Indian and Alaska Native Women and the Criminal Justice Response: What is Known," National Criminal Justice Reference Service, August 2008, www.ncjrs.gov/pdffiles1/ nij/grants/223691.pdf, p. 33.
74. Michael W. Savage, "Obama to sign bill targeting violent crime on Indian reservations," *The Washington Post*, July 29, 2010, p. A21.
75. Chad Smith, testimony before Senate Committee on Indian Affairs oversight hearing on Indian education, June 17, 2010.
76. Quinton Roman Nose, testimony before Senate Indian Affairs Committee oversight hearing on Indian school safety, May 13, 2010.
77. "Gang Violence on the Rise on Indian Reservations," "Tell Me More," NPR, Aug. 25, 2009.
78. *Ibid.*
79. *Red Lake Net News*, July 27, 2010, www.rlnn.us/ Art012010DorganHostsSummitPartnerAid Indian YouthSuicidePrevEfforts.html.

BIBLIOGRAPHY

Books

Alexie, Sherman, *The Toughest Indian in the World*, **Grove Press, 2000.**
In a short-story collection, an author and screenwriter draws on his own background as a Spokane/Coeur d'Alene Indian to describe reservation and urban Indian life in loving but unsentimental detail.

Debo, Angie, *A History of the Indians of the United States*, **University of Oklahoma Press, 1970.**
A pioneering historian and champion of Indian rights provides one of the leading narrative histories of the first five centuries of Indian and non-Indian coexistence and conflict.

Deloria, Vine Jr., *Custer Died For Your Sins: An Indian Manifesto*, **University of Oklahoma Press, 1988.**
First published in 1969, this angry book gave many non-Indians a look at how the United States appeared through Indians' eyes and spurred many young Native Americans into political activism.

Mason, W. Dale, *Indian Gaming: Tribal Sovereignty and American Politics*, **University of Oklahoma Press, 2000.**
A University of New Mexico political scientist provides the essential background on the birth and early explosive growth of Indian-owned gambling operations.

Williams, Robert A., *Like a Loaded Weapon: The Rehnquist Court, Indians Rights, and the Legal History of Racism in America*, **University of Minnesota Press, 2005.**
A professor of law and American Indian Studies at the University of Arizona and tribal appeals court judge delivers a detailed and angry analysis of the history of U.S. court decisions affecting Indians.

Articles

Bartlett, Donald L., and James B. Steele, "Playing the Political Slots; How Indian Casino Interests Have Learned the Art of Buying Influence in Washington," *Time*, **Dec. 23, 2002, p. 52.**
In a prescient article that preceded the Jack Abramoff lobbying scandal, veteran investigative journalists examine the political effects of some tribes' newfound wealth.

Harden, Blaine, "Walking the Land with Pride Again; A Revolution in Indian Country Spawns Wealth and Optimism," *The Washington Post*, **Sept. 19, 2004, p. A1.**
Improved conditions in many sectors of Indian America have spawned a change in outlook, despite remaining hardships.

Morgan, Lance, "Ending the Curse of Trust Land," *Indian Country Today*, **March 18, 2005, www.indiancountry.com/content.cfm?id=1096410559.**
A lawyer and pioneering tribal entrepreneur lays out his vision of a revamped legal-political system in which Indians would own their tribal land outright, with federal supervision ended.

Robbins, Ted, "Tribal cultures, nutrition clash on fry bread," "All Things Considered," National Public Radio, Oct. 26, 2005, transcript available at www.npr.org/templates/story/story.php?storyId=4975889.
Indian health educators have tried to lower Native Americans' consumption of a beloved but medically disastrous treat.

Thompson, Ginger, "As a Sculpture Takes Shape in New Mexico, Opposition Takes Shape in the U.S.," *The New York Times*, Jan. 17, 2002, p. A12.
Indian outrage has clashed with Latino pride over a statue celebrating the ruthless Spanish conqueror of present-day New Mexico.

Wagner, Dennis, "Tribes Across Country Confront Horrors of Meth," *The Arizona Republic*, March 31, 2006, p. A1.
Methamphetamine use and manufacturing have become the scourge of Indian Country.

Reports and Studies

"Indian Health Service: Health Care Services Are Not Always Available to Native Americans," Government Accountability Office, August 2005.
Congress' investigative arm concludes that financial shortfalls combined with dismal reservation conditions, including scarce transportation, are stunting medical care for many American Indians.

"Strengthening the Circle: Interior Indian Affairs Highlights, 2001-2004," Department of the Interior (undated).
The Bush administration sums up its first term's accomplishments in Indian Country.

Cornell, Stephen, *et al.*, "Seizing the Future: Why Some Native Nations Do and Others Don't," Native Nations Institute, Udall Center for Studies in Public Policy, University of Arizona, Harvard Project on American Indian Economic Development, John F. Kennedy School of Government, Harvard University, 2005.
The authors argue that the key to development lies in a tribe's redefinition of itself from object of government attention to independent power.

For More Information

Committee on Indian Affairs, U.S. Senate, 838 Hart Office Building, Washington, DC 20510; (202) 224-2251; http://indian.senate.gov/public. A valuable source of information on developments affecting Indian Country.

Harvard Project on American Indian Economic Development, John F. Kennedy School of Government, 79 John F. Kennedy St., Cambridge, MA 02138; (617) 495-1480; www.ksg.harvard.edu/hpaied. Explores strategies for Indian advancement.

Indian Health Service, The Reyes Building, 801 Thompson Ave., Suite 400, Rockville, MD 20852; (301) 443-1083; www.ihs.gov. One of the most important federal agencies in Indian Country; provides a wide variety of medical and administrative information.

National Coalition Against Legalized Gambling, 100 Maryland Ave., N.E., Room 311, Washington, DC 20002; (800) 664-2680; www.ncalg.org. Provides anti-gambling material that touches on tribe-owned operations.

National Indian Education Association, 110 Maryland Ave., N.E., Suite 104, Washington, DC 20002; (202) 544-7290; www.niea.org/welcome. Primary organization and lobbying voice for Indian educators.

National Indian Gaming Association, 224 Second St., S.E., Washington, DC 20003; (202) 546-7711; www.indiangaming.org. Trade association and lobbying arm of the tribal casino industry.

Self-Governance Communication and Education Tribal Consortium 1768 Iowa Business Center, Bellingham, WA 98229; (360) 752-2270, www.tribalselfgov.org. Organizational hub of Indian self-governance movement; provides a wide variety of news and data.

Upstate Citizens for Equality, P.O. Box 24, Union Springs, NY 13160; http://upstate-citizens.org. Opposes tribal land-claim litigation.

6
Affirmative Action

Peter Katel, Charles S. Clark, and Kenneth Jost

Law student Jessica Peck Corry, executive director of the Colorado Civil Rights Initiative, supports Constitutional Amendment 46, which would prohibit all government entities in Colorado from discriminating for or against anyone because of race, ethnicity or gender. Attorney Melissa Hart counters that the amendment would end programs designed to reach minority groups.

From *CQ Researcher*, October 17, 2008 (updated August 5, 2010 and June 19, 2012).

No white politician could have gotten the question George Stephanopoulos of ABC News asked Sen. Barack Obama. "You said . . . that affluent African-Americans, like your daughters, should probably be treated as pretty advantaged when they apply to college," he began. "How specifically would you recommend changing affirmative action policies so that affluent African-Americans are not given advantages and poor, less affluent whites are?"[1]

The Democratic presidential nominee, speaking during a primary election debate in April, said his daughters' advantages should weigh more than their skin color. "You know, Malia and Sasha, they've had a pretty good deal."[2]

But a white applicant who has overcome big odds to pursue an education should have those circumstances taken into account, Obama said. "I still believe in affirmative action as a means of overcoming both historic and potentially current discrimination," Obama said, "but I think that it can't be a quota system and it can't be something that is simply applied without looking at the whole person, whether that person is black, or white or Hispanic, male or female."[3]

Supporting affirmative action on the one hand, objecting to quotas on the other — Obama seemed to know he was threading his way through a minefield. Decades after it began, affirmative action is seen by many whites as nothing but a fancy term for racial quotas designed to give minorities an unfair break. Majority black opinion remains strongly pro-affirmative action, on the grounds that the legacy of racial discrimination lives on. Whites and blacks are 30 percentage points apart on the issue, according to a 2007 national survey by the nonpartisan Pew Research Center.[4]

Americans Support Boost for Disadvantaged

A majority of Americans believe that individuals born into poverty can overcome their disadvantages and that society should be giving them special help (top poll). Fewer, however, endorse race-based affirmative action as the way to help (bottom).

	Agree	Disagree
We should help people who are working hard to overcome disadvantages and succeed in life.	93%	6
People who start out with little and work their way up are the real success stories.	91	7
Some people are born poor, and there's nothing we can do about that.	26	72
We shouldn't give special help at all, even to those who started out with more disadvantages than most.	16	81

If there is only one seat available, which student would you admit to college, the high-income student or the low-income student?

	Percentage selecting:	
	Low-income student	High-income student
If both students get the same admissions test score?	63%	3%
If low-income student gets a slightly lower test score?	33	54
If the low-income student is also black, and the high-income student is white?	36	39
If the low-income student is also Hispanic, and the high-income student is not Hispanic?	33	45

Source: Anthony P. Carnevale and Stephen J. Rose, "Socioeconomic Status, Race/Ethnicity, and Selective College Admissions," The Century Foundation, March 2003

admissions to top-tier state schools, such as the University of California at Los Angeles (UCLA) based on race, gender or ethnic background. Graduating from such schools is seen as an affordable ticket to the good life, but there aren't enough places at these schools for all applicants, so many qualified applicants are rejected.

Resentment over the notion that some applicants got an advantage because of their ancestry led California voters in 1996 to ban affirmative action in college admissions. Four years later, the Florida legislature, at the urging of then-Gov. Jeb Bush, effectively eliminated using race as an admission standard for colleges and universities. And initiatives similar to the California referendum were later passed in Washington state and then in Michigan, in 2006.

Race is central to the affirmative action debate because the doctrine grew out of the civil rights movement and the Civil Rights Act of 1964, which outlawed discrimination based on race, ethnicity or gender. The loosely defined term generally is used as a synonym for advantages — "preferences" — that employers and schools extend to members of a particular race, national origin or gender.

"The time has come to pull the plug on race-based decision-making," says Ward Connerly, a Sacramento, Calif.-based businessman who is the lead organizer of the Colorado and Nebraska ballot initiative campaigns, as well as earlier ones elsewhere. "The Civil Rights Act of 1964 talks about treating people equally without regard to race, color or national origin. When you talk about civil rights, they don't just belong to black people."

Connerly, who is black, supports extending preferences of some kind to low-income applicants for jobs — as long as the beneficiaries aren't classified by race or gender.

But affirmative action supporters say that approach ignores reality. "If there are any preferences in operation in our society, they're preferences given to people with white skin and who are men and who have financial and other advantages that come with that," says Nicole Kief,

Now, with the candidacy of Columbia University and Harvard Law School graduate Obama turning up the volume on the debate, voters in two states will be deciding in November whether preferences should remain in effect in state government hiring and state college admissions.

Originally, conflict over affirmative action focused on hiring. But during the past two decades, the debate has shifted to whether preference should be given in

New York-based state strategist for the American Civil Liberties Union's racial justice program, which is opposing the Connerly-organized ballot initiative campaigns.

Yet, of the 38 million Americans classified as poor, whites make up the biggest share: 17 million people. Blacks account for slightly more than 9 million and Hispanics slightly less. Some 576,000 Native Americans are considered poor. Looking beyond the simple numbers, however, reveals that far greater percentages of African-Americans and Hispanics are likely to be poor: 25 percent of African-Americans and 20 percent of Hispanics live below the poverty line, but only 10 percent of whites are poor.[5]

In 2000, according to statistics compiled by *Chronicle of Higher Education* Deputy Editor Peter Schmidt, the average white elementary school student attended a school that was 78 percent white, 9 percent black, 8 percent Hispanic, 3 percent Asian and 30 percent poor. Black or Hispanic children attended a school in which 57 percent of the student body shared their race or ethnicity and about two-thirds of the students were poor.[6]

These conditions directly affect college admissions, according to The Century Foundation. The liberal think tank reported in 2003 that white students account for 77 percent of the students at high schools in which the greatest majority of students go on to college. Black students account for only 11 percent of the population at these schools, and Hispanics 7 percent.[7]

A comprehensive 2004 study by the Urban Institute, a nonpartisan think tank, found that only about half of black and Hispanic high school students graduate, compared to 75 and 77 percent, respectively, of whites and Asians.[8]

Politically conservative affirmative action critics cite these statistics to argue that focusing on college admissions and hiring practices rather than school reform was a big mistake. The critics get some support from liberals who want to keep affirmative action — as long as it's based on socioeconomic status instead of race. "Affirmative action based on race was always kind of a cheap and quick fix that bypassed the hard work of trying to develop the talents of low-income minority students generally," says Richard D. Kahlenberg, a senior fellow at The Century Foundation.

Basing affirmative action on class instead of race wouldn't exclude racial and ethnic minorities, Kahlenberg argues, because race and class are so closely intertwined.

President Lyndon B. Johnson noted that connection in a major speech that laid the philosophical foundations for affirmative action programs. These weren't set up for another five years, a reflection of how big a change they represented in traditional hiring and promotion practices, where affirmative action began. "You do not take a person who, for years, has been hobbled by chains and liberate him, bring him up to the starting line of a race and then say, 'You are free to compete with all the others,' and still justly believe that you have been completely fair," Johnson said in "To Fulfill These Rights," his 1965 commencement speech at Howard University in Washington, D.C., one of the country's top historically black institutions.[9]

Elite Schools Graduate Fewest Minorities

Among college-bound blacks and Hispanics, larger percentages graduated from "less advantaged" high schools than from the "most advantaged" schools.

Percentage of High School Seniors Going to Four-year Colleges, by Race

Attended More-Advantaged Schools:
- 6% / 11% / 7% / 77%
- 7% / 17% / 9% / 76%
- 4% / 13% / 14% / 68%
- 9% / 13% / 13% / 65%

Attended Less-Advantaged Schools

Legend: Asian, Black, Hispanic, White

Source: Anthony P. Carnevale and Stephen J. Rose, "Socioeconomic Status, Race/Ethnicity, and Selective College Admissions," Century Foundation, March 2003

Asian-American enrollment at the University of California at Berkeley rose dramatically after California voters in 1996 approved Proposition 209, a ballot initiative that banned affirmative action at all state institutions. Enrollment of African-American, Hispanic and Native American students, however, plunged.

By the late 1970s, a long string of U.S. Supreme Court decisions began setting boundaries on affirmative action, partly in response to white job and school applicants who sued over "reverse discrimination." The court's bottom line: Schools and employers could take race into account, but not as a sole criterion. Setting quotas based on race, ethnicity or gender was prohibited. (The prohibition of gender discrimination effectively ended the chances for passage of the proposed Equal Rights Amendment [ERA], which feminist organizations had been promoting since 1923. The Civil Rights Act, along with other legislation and court decisions, made many supporters of women's rights "lukewarm" about the proposed amendment, Roberta W. Francis, then chair of the National Council of Women's Organizations' ERA task force, wrote in 2001).[10]

The high court's support for affirmative action has been weakening through the years. Since 1991 the court has included Justice Clarence Thomas, the lone black member and a bitter foe of affirmative action. In his 2007 autobiography, Thomas wrote that his Yale Law School degree set him up for rejection by major law firm interviewers. "Many asked pointed questions unsubtly suggesting that they doubted I was as smart as my grades indicated," he wrote. "Now I knew what a law degree from Yale was worth when it bore the taint of racial preference."[11]

Some of Thomas' black classmates dispute his view of a Yale diploma's worth. "Had he not gone to a school like Yale, he would not be sitting on the Supreme Court," said William Coleman III, a Philadelphia attorney who was general counsel to the U.S. Army in the Clinton administration.[12]

But that argument does not seem to impress Thomas, who was in a 5-4 minority in the high court's most recent affirmative action ruling, in which the justices upheld the use of race in law-school admissions at the University of Michigan. But even Justice Sandra Day O'Connor, who wrote the majority opinion, signaled unease with her position. In 25 years, she wrote, affirmative action would "no longer be necessary."[13]

Paradoxically, an Obama victory on Nov. 4 might be the most effective anti-affirmative action event of all.

"The primary rationale for affirmative action is that America is institutionally racist and institutionally sexist," Connerly, an Obama foe, told The Associated Press. "That rationale is undercut in a major way when you look at the success of Sen. [Hillary Rodham] Clinton and Sen. Obama."

Asked to respond to Connerly's remarks, Obama appeared to draw some limits of his own on affirmative action. "Affirmative action is not going to be the long-term solution to the problems of race in America," he told a July convention of minority journalists, "because, frankly, if you've got 50 percent of African-American or Latino kids dropping out of high school, it doesn't really matter what you do in terms of affirmative action; those kids are not getting into college."[14]

As critics and supporters discuss the future of affirmative action, here are some of the questions being debated:

Has affirmative action outlived its usefulness?

In the United States of the late 1960s and '70s, even some outright opponents of race-based affirmative action conceded that it represented an attempt to deal with the consequences of longstanding, systematic racial discrimination, which had legally ended only shortly before.

But ever since opposition to affirmative action began growing in the 1980s, its opponents themselves have invoked the very principles that the civil rights movement had embraced in its fight to end discrimination. Taking a job or school applicant's race or ethnicity into account is immoral, opponents argue, even for supposedly benign purposes. And a policy of racial/ethnic preferences, by definition, cannot lead to equality.

In today's United States, critics say, minority applicants don't face any danger that their skin color or ethnic heritage will hold them back. Instead, affirmative-action beneficiaries face continuing skepticism from others — and even from themselves, that they somehow were given an advantage that their academic work didn't entitle them to receive.

Meanwhile, opponents and supporters readily acknowledge that a disproportionate share of black and Latino students receive substandard educations, starting in and lasting through high school. Affirmative action hasn't eliminated the link between race/ethnicity and poverty and academic deprivation, they agree.

Critics of race preferences, however, say they haven't narrowed the divide that helped to trigger affirmative action in the first place. Affirmative action advocates favor significantly reforming K-12 education while simultaneously giving a leg up to minorities who managed to overcome their odds at inadequate public schools.

And some supporters say affirmative action is important for other reasons, which transcend America's racial history. Affirmative action helps to ensure continuation of a democratic political culture, says James E. Coleman Jr., a professor at Duke University Law School.

"It's not just about discrimination or past discrimination," says Coleman, who attended all-black schools when growing up and then graduated from Harvard College and Columbia Law School in the early 1970s, during the early days of affirmative action. "It's in our self-interest. We want leaders of all different backgrounds, all different races; we ought to educate them together."

But Connerly, the California businessman behind anti-affirmative action ballot initiatives, says that race and gender preferences are the wrong tool with which to promote diversity, because they effectively erode

Few Poor Students Attend Top Schools

Nearly three-quarters of students entering tier 1 colleges and universities come from the wealthiest families, but only 3 percent of students from the bottom quartile enter top schools. Far more students from poorer backgrounds enroll in less prestigious schools, and even more in community colleges.

Socioeconomic Status of Entering College Classes

School prestige level	First quartile (lowest)	Second quartile	Third quartile	Fourth quartile (highest)
Tier 1	3%	6%	17%	74%
Tier 2	7	18	29	46
Tier 3	10	19	36	35
Tier 4	16	21	28	35
Community Colleges	21	30	27	22

Source: Anthony P. Carnevale and Stephen J. Rose, "Socioeconomic Status, Race/Ethnicity, and Selective College Admissions," The Century Foundation, March 2003

academic standards. "Excellence can be achieved by any group of people," says Connerly, a former member of the University of California Board of Regents. "So we will keep the standards where they ought to be, and we will expect people to meet those standards."

But legislators interested in a "quick fix" have found it simpler to mandate diversity than to devise ways to improve schools. "There are times when someone has to say, 'This isn't right. We're going to do something about it,' " Connerly says. "But in the legislative process, I can find no evidence of leadership anywhere."

Like others, Connerly also cites the extraordinary academic achievements of Asian-American students — who haven't benefited from affirmative action. Affirmative action supporters don't try to dispute that point. "At the University of California at Berkeley, 40 percent of the students are Asian," says Terry H. Anderson, a history professor at Texas A&M University in College Station. "What does that say about family structure? It makes a big statement. Family structure is so important, and it's something that affirmative action can't help at all."

But if encouraging minority-group enrollment at universities doesn't serve as a social and educational cure-all, says Anderson, who has written a history of affirmative

Few Poor Students Score High on SAT

Two-thirds of students who scored at least 1300 on the SAT came from families ranking in the highest quartile of socioeconomic status, compared with only 3 percent of students from the lowest-income group. Moreover, more than one-fifth of those scoring under 1000 — and 37 percent of non-test-takers — come from the poorest families.

SAT Scores by Family Socioeconomic Status*

Score	First Quartile (lowest)	Second Quartile	Third Quartile	Fourth Quartile (highest)
>1300	3%	10%	22%	66%
1200–1300	4	14	23	58
1100–1200	6	17	29	47
1000–1100	8	24	32	36
<1000	21	25	30	24
Non-taker	37	30	22	10

* The maximum score is 1600

Note: Percentages do not add to 100 due to rounding.

Source: Anthony P. Carnevale and Stephen J. Rose, "Socioeconomic Status, Race/ Ethnicity, and Selective College Admissions," The Century Foundation, March 2003

Does race-based affirmative action still face powerful public opposition?

At the state and federal level, affirmative action has generated enormous conflict over the decades, played out in a long chain of lawsuits and Supreme Court decisions, as well as the hard-fought ballot initiatives this year in Arizona, Missouri and Oklahoma — all three of which ended in defeat for race, ethnic and gender preferences.

But today's political agenda — dominated by the global financial crisis, the continuing downward slide of real estate prices, the continuing conflict in Iraq and escalated combat in Afghanistan — would seem to leave little space for a reignited affirmative action conflict.

Nevertheless, supporters and opponents of affirmative action fought hard in five states over proposed ballot initiatives, two of which will go before voters in November.

Nationally, the nonpartisan Pew Research Center reported last year that black and white Americans are divided by a considerable margin on whether minority group members should get preferential treatment. Among blacks, 57 answered yes, but only 27 percent of whites agreed. That gap was somewhat bigger in 1991, when 68 percent of blacks and only 17 percent of whites favored preferences.[15]

Obama's statement to ABC News' Stephanopoulos that his daughters shouldn't benefit from affirmative action reflected awareness of majority sentiment against race preference.[16]

Still, the exchange led to some predictions that it would resurface. "The issue of affirmative action is likely to dog Sen. Obama on the campaign trail as he seeks to win over white, blue-collar voters in battleground states like Michigan," *The Wall Street Journal* predicted in June.[17]

Just two and a half weeks before the election, that forecast hadn't come to pass. However, earlier in the year

action, the policy still serves a valuable purpose. "It's become part of our culture. On this campus, it's been 'out' to be racist for years and years. I'm looking at kids born in 1990; they just don't feel self-conscious about race or gender, they just expect to be treated equally."

Standing between the supporters and the enemies of affirmative action's racial/ethnic preferences are the affirmative action reformers. "I don't think it's time to completely abolish all forms of affirmative action," says the Century Foundation's Kahlenberg. "But it's clear there are strong legal, moral and political problems with relying solely on race."

And at the practical level, race isn't the only gauge of hardship that some students must overcome, even to be capable of competing for admission to a top-tier school. "There are students from low-income backgrounds," Kahlenberg says, "who aren't given the same opportunities as wealthier students are given, and they deserve a leg up in admissions. Someone's test scores and grades are a reflection not only of how hard they work and how talented they are, but what sorts of opportunities they've had."

interest remained strong enough that campaigners for state ballot initiatives were able to gather 136,589 signatures in Nebraska and about 130,000 in Colorado to require that the issue be put before voters in those states.

Meanwhile, the initiative efforts in Arizona, Missouri and Oklahoma were doomed after the validity of petition signatures was challenged in those states. Connerly, the chief organizer of the initiatives, blames opponents' tactics and, in Oklahoma, an unusually short, 90-day window during which signatures must be collected. But once initiatives get on ballots, he says, voters approve them. "There is something about the principle of fairness that most people understand."

Without congressional legislation prohibiting preferences, Connerly says, the initiatives are designed to force state governments "to abide by the moral principle that racial discrimination — whether against a white or black or Latino or Native American — is just wrong."

But reality can present immoral circumstances as well, affirmative action defenders argue. "Racial discrimination and gender discrimination continue to present obstacles to people of color and women," says the American Civil Liberties Union's (ACLU) Kief. "Affirmative action is a way to chip away at some of these obstacles."

Kief says the fact that Connerly has played a central role in all of the initiatives indicates that true grassroots opposition to affirmative action is weak in states where initiatives have passed or are about to be voted on.

However, The Century Foundation's Kahlenberg points out that pro-affirmative action forces work hard to block ballot initiatives, because when such initiatives have gone before voters they have been approved. And the most recent successful ballot initiative, in Michigan in 2006, passed by a slightly bigger margin — 57 percent to 43 percent — than its California counterpart in 1996, which was approved by 54-46.[18]

Further evidence that anti-affirmative action initiatives are hard to fight surfaced this year in Colorado, where the group Coloradans for Equal Opportunity failed to round up enough signatures to put a pro-affirmative action initiative on the ballot.

Kahlenberg acknowledges that affirmative action politics can be tricky. Despite abiding public opposition to preferences, support among blacks is so strong that Republican presidential campaigns tend to downplay affirmative action, for fear of triggering a huge turnout among black

Democratic presidential candidate Sen. Barack Obama, speaking in Philadelphia on Oct. 11, 2008, represents the new face of affirmative action in the demographically changing United States: His father was Kenyan and a half-sister is half-Indonesian.

voters, who vote overwhelmingly Democratic. In 1999, then-Florida Gov. Jeb Bush kept a Connerly-sponsored initiative out of that state largely in order to lessen the chances of a major black Democratic mobilization in the 2000 presidential election, in which his brother would be running.[19]

"When you have an initiative on the ballot," Kahlenberg says, "some Republicans think that it increases minority turnout, so they're not sure whether these initiatives play to their party or not." Republican opposition to affirmative action goes back to the Reagan administration. Reagan, however, passed up a chance to ban affirmative action programs throughout the federal government, displaying a degree of GOP ambivalence. However, Connerly is an outspoken Republican.[20]

Nevertheless, an all-out Republican push against affirmative action during the past decade failed to catch on at the national level. In 1996, former Republican Senate Majority Leader Bob Dole of Kansas was running for president, and the affirmative action initiative was on the same ballot in California. "The initiative passed, but there was no trickle-down help for Bob Dole," says Daniel A. Smith, a political scientist at the University of Florida who has written on affirmative action politics.

This year, to be sure, anxieties growing out of the financial crisis and economic slowdown could rekindle passions over preferences. But Smith argues the economic environment makes finger-pointing at minorities less likely. "Whites are not losing jobs to African-Americans," he says. "Whites and African-Americans are losing jobs to the Asian subcontinent — they're going to Bangalore. The global economy makes it more difficult to have a convenient domestic scapegoat for lost jobs."

Has affirmative action diverted attention from the poor quality of K-12 education in low-income communities?

If there's one point on which everyone involved in the affirmative action debate agrees, it's that public schools attended by most low-income students are worsening.

"The educational achievement gap between racial groups began growing again in the 1990s," Gary Orfield, a professor of education and social policy at Harvard University, wrote. "Our public schools are becoming increasingly segregated by race and income, and the segregated schools are, on average, strikingly inferior in many important ways, including the quality and experience of teachers and the level of competition from other students. . . . It is clear that students of different races do not receive an equal chance for college."[21]

The decline in education quality has occurred at the same time various race-preference policies have governed admission to the nation's best colleges and universities. The policies were designed to provide an incentive for schools and students alike to do their best, by ensuring that a college education remains a possibility for all students who perform well academically.

But the results have not been encouraging. In California alone, only 36 percent of all high school students in 2001 had taken all the courses required for admission to the state university system, according to a study by the Civil Rights Project at Harvard University. Among black students, only 26 percent had taken the prerequisites, and only 24 percent of Hispanics. Meanwhile, 41 percent of white students and 54 percent of Asians had taken the necessary courses.[22]

In large part as a result of deficient K-12 education, decades of race-preference affirmative action at top-tier colleges and universities have yielded only small percentages of black and Hispanic students. In 1995, according to an exhaustive 2003 study by The Century Foundation, these students accounted for 6 percent of admissions to the 146 top-tier institutions.[23]

Socioeconomically, the picture is even less diverse. Seventy-four percent of students came from families in the wealthiest quarter of the socioeconomic scale; 3 percent came from families in the bottom quarter.[24]

For race-preference opponents, the picture demonstrates that efforts at ensuring racial and ethnic diversity in higher education would have been better aimed at improving K-12 schools across the country.

"If you've tried to use race for 40-some years, and you still have this profound gap," Connerly says, "yet cling to the notion that you have given some affirmative action to black and Latino and American Indian students — though Asians, without it, are outstripping everybody — maybe the way we've been doing it wasn't the right way to do it."

Meanwhile, he says, making a point that echoes through black, conservative circles, "Historically black colleges and universities (HBCUs) — if you look at doctors and pharmacists across our nation, you'll find them coming from schools that are 90 percent black. These schools are not very diverse, but they put a premium on quality."

But not all HBCUs are in that class, affirmative action supporters point out. "A lot of people who come out with a degree in computer science from minority-serving institutions know absolutely no mathematics," says Richard Tapia, a mathematics professor at Rice University and director of the university's Center for Equity and Excellence in Education. "I once went to a historically black university and had lunch with a top student who was going to do graduate work at Purdue, but when I talked to her I realized that her knowledge of math was on a par with that of a Rice freshman. The gap is huge."

Tapia, who advocates better mentoring for promising minority students at top-flight institutions, argues that the effect of relegating minority students to a certain defined group of colleges and universities, including historically black institutions, limits their chances of advancement in society at large. "From the elite schools you're going to get leadership."

Still, a question remains as to whether focusing on preferential admissions has helped perpetuate the very conditions that give rise to preferences in the first place.

"At the K-12 level you could argue that affirmative action has led to stagnation," says Richard Sander, a professor of law at UCLA Law School. "There's very little forward movement, very little closing of the black-white gap of the past 20 to 30 years."

Coleman of Duke University agrees that public education for most low-income students needs help. But that issue has nothing to do with admissions to top-drawer universities and professional schools, he says. "Look at minority students who get into places like that," he says. "For the most part, they haven't gone to the weakest high schools; they've often gone to the best."

Yet the affirmative action conflict focuses on black students, who are assumed to be academically under-qualified, Coleman says, while white students' place at the best schools isn't questioned. The classroom reality differs, he says. "We have a whole range of students with different abilities. All of the weak students are not minority students; all of the strong students are not white students."

BACKGROUND

Righting Wrongs

The civil rights revolution of the 1950s and '60s forced a new look at the policies that had locked one set of Americans out of most higher-education institutions and higher-paying jobs.

As early as 1962, the Congress of Racial Equality (CORE), one of the most active civil-rights organizations, advocated hiring practices that would make up for discrimination against black applicants. "We are approaching employers with the proposition that they have effectively excluded Negroes from their work force a long time, and they now have a responsibility and obligation to make up for their past sins," the organization said in a statement from its New York headquarters.[25]

Facing CORE-organized boycotts, a handful of companies in New York, Denver, Detroit, Seattle and Baltimore changed their hiring procedures to favor black applicants.

In July 1964, President Lyndon B. Johnson pushed Congress to pass the landmark Civil Rights Act, which had been championed by President John F. Kennedy since his 1960 presidential election campaign.

The law's Title VII, which prohibits racial, religious or sexual discrimination in hiring, said judges enforcing the law could order "such affirmative action as may be appropriate" to correct violations.[26]

Title VII didn't specify what kind of affirmative action could be decreed. But racial preferences were openly discussed in the political arena as a tool to equalize opportunities. Official working definitions of affirmative action didn't emerge until the end of the 1960s, under President Richard M. Nixon.

In 1969, the administration approved the "Philadelphia Plan," which set numerical goals for black and other minority employment on federally financed construction jobs. One year later, the plan was expanded to cover all businesses with 50 or more employees and federal contracts of at least $50,000. The contracts were to set hiring goals and timetables designed to match up a firm's minority representation with the workforce demographics in its area. The specified minorities were: "Negro, Oriental, American Indian and Spanish Surnamed Americans."[27]

The sudden change in the workplace environment prompted a wave of lawsuits. In the lead, a legal challenge by 13 black electric utility workers in North Carolina led to one of the most influential U.S. Supreme Court decisions on affirmative action, the 1971 *Griggs v. Duke Power Co.* case.[28]

In a unanimous decision, the high court concluded that an aptitude test that was a condition of promotion for the workers violated the Civil Rights Act. Duke Power may not have intended the test to weed out black applicants, Chief Justice Warren E. Burger wrote in the decision. But, he added, "Congress directed the thrust of the Act to the consequences of employment practices, not simply the motivation."[29]

If the point of the Civil Rights Act was to ensure that the consequences of institutions' decisions yielded balanced workforces, then goals and timetables to lead to that outcome were consistent with the law as well. In other words, eliminating racial discrimination could mean paying attention to race in hiring and promotions.

That effort would produce a term that captured the frustration and anger among white males who were competing with minority-group members for jobs, promotions or school admissions: "reverse discrimination."

The issue went national with a challenge by Allan Bakke, a white, medical school applicant, to the University of California. He'd been rejected two years in a row while minority-group members — for whom 16 slots in the 100-member class had been set aside — were admitted with lower qualifying scores.

After the case reached the Supreme Court, the justices in a 5-4 decision in 1978 ordered Bakke admitted and prohibited the use of racial quotas. But they allowed race to be considered along with other criteria. Representing the University of California was former Solicitor General

CHRONOLOGY

1960s *Enactment of civil rights law opens national debate on discrimination.*

1964 Civil Rights Act of 1964 bars discrimination in employment and at federally funded colleges.

1965 President Lyndon B. Johnson calls for a massive national effort to create social and economic equality.

1969 Nixon administration approves "Philadelphia Plan" setting numerical goals for minority employment on all federally financed building projects.

1970s-1980s *Affirmative action expands throughout the country, prompting legal challenges and growing voter discontent, leading to new federal policy.*

1971 The U.S. Supreme Court's landmark *Griggs v. Duke Power Co.* decision, growing out of a challenge by 13 black electric utility workers in North Carolina, is seen as authorizing companies and institutions to set out goals and timetables for minority hiring.

1978 Supreme Court's decision in *University of California Regents v. Bakke,* arising from a medical-school admission case, rules out racial quotas but allows race to be considered with other factors.

1980 Ronald W. Reagan is elected president with strong support from white males who see affirmative action as a threat.

1981-1983 Reagan administration reduces affirmative action enforcement.

1985 Attorney General Edwin Meese III drafts executive order outlawing affirmative action in federal government; Reagan never signs it.

1987 Supreme Court upholds job promotion of a woman whose advancement was challenged by a male colleague claiming higher qualifications.

1990s *Ballot initiatives banning race and gender preferences prompt President Bill Clinton to acknowledge faults in affirmative action.*

1994 White voter discontent energizes the "Republican revolution" that topples Democrats from control of Congress.

1995 Supreme Court rules in *Adarand Constructors v. Peña* that affirmative action programs must be "narrowly tailored" for cases of extreme discrimination. . . . Clinton concedes that affirmative action foes have some valid points but concludes, "Mend it, but don't end it." . . . Senate votes down anti-affirmative action bill.

1996 California voters pass nation's first ballot initiative outlawing racial, ethnic and gender preferences. . . . 5th U.S. Circuit Court of Appeals rules that universities can't take race into account in evaluating applicants.

1998 Washington state voters pass ballot initiative identical to California's.

2000s *Affirmative action in university admissions stays on national agenda, leading to major Supreme Court ruling; Sen. Barack Obama's presidential candidacy focuses more attention on the issue.*

2003 Supreme Court's *Gratz v. Bollinger* ruling rejects University of Michigan undergraduate admission system for awarding extra points to minority applicants, but simultaneous *Grutter v. Bollinger* decision upholds UM law school admissions policy, which includes race as one factor among many. . . . Justice Sandra Day O'Connor writes in 5-4 majority opinion in *Grutter* that affirmative action won't be necessary in 25 years. . . . Century Foundation study finds strong linkage between socioeconomic status, race and chances of going to college.

2006 Michigan passes nation's third ballot initiative outlawing racial, ethnic and gender preferences.

2008 Opponents of affirmative action in Arizona, Missouri and Oklahoma fail to place anti-affirmative action initiatives on ballot, but similar campaigns succeed in Colorado and Nebraska. . . . U.S. Civil Rights Commission opens study of minority students majoring in science and math. . . . Saying his daughters are affluent and shouldn't benefit from race preferences, Obama endorses affirmative action for struggling, white college applicants.

2008 Colorado voters reject ballot initiative to enact state bans on race-conscious selection methods in employment and college admissions.

2009

June — Arizona legislature approves putting a proposed plan to outlaw affirmative action on the November 2010 ballot.... On June 29, Supreme Court rules 5-4 in favor of white firefighters from New Haven, Conn., in Ricci v. DeStefano. The firefighters had challenged the city's decision to discard a competency test for determining promotions after black firefighters taking the test had underperformed. A Quinnipiac University poll shows American voters favor abolishing affirmative action, 55-36 percent.

2010

Education Secretary Arne Duncan announces in Selma, Ala., that his department is launching new desegregation compliance investigations around the country. Obama administration's departments of Education and Justice together file a friend-of-the-court brief on behalf of the University of Texas at Austin, which is defending its use of race as part of its process of achieving diversity.... Russlynn H. Ali, Assistant Education Secretary for Civil Rights, says she anticipates more civil rights activity in her office.... Study finds drop in percentage of black and Mexican-American law students.

2008

Nov. 4 — Colorado voters reject ballot initiative to enact state bans on race-conscious selection methods in employment and college admissions.

2009

June 29 — Supreme Court favors white firefighters in New Haven, Conn., reverse-discrimination case; 5-4 ruling limits government employers' ability to favor minorities in hiring, promotion to avoid discrimination claims.

2010

March 8 — Education Secretary Arne Duncan announces in Selma, Ala., that his department is launching new desegregation compliance investigations around the country.

Nov. 2 — Arizona voters approve measure to ban affirmative action in public education, public employment, government contracting.

2011

Jan. 18 — University of Texas admissions policy upheld by federal appeals court; rehearing denied (June 17).

July 1 — Michigan ban on affirmative action struck down by federal appeals court.

July 28 — White firefighters in New Haven, Conn., agree to accept $2 million in damages in reverse-discrimination suit after Supreme Court victory.

Sept. 30 — Jefferson County (Louisville), Ky., pupil assignment plan struck down by state court; school district appeals to state high court; arguments heard April 18, 2012.

Dec. 2 — Obama administration lists steps for colleges, universities to increase diversity.

2012

Feb. 21 — Supreme Court agrees to hear University of Texas case; arguments in fall 2012, decision by June 2013.

April 2 — California ban on affirmative action upheld by federal court.

June 11 — Supreme Court allows black New Haven firefighter to pursue discrimination claim against city over scoring of promotion test.

Nov. 6 — Oklahoma to vote on affirmative action ban.

"Percent Plans" Offer Alternative to Race-Based Preferences

But critics say approach fails to level playing field.

In recent years, voters and judges have blocked race and ethnicity preferences in university admissions in three big states with booming minority populations — California, Florida and Texas. Nonetheless, lawmakers devised a way to ensure that public universities remain open to black and Latino students.

The so-called "percent plans" promise guaranteed admission based on a student's high school class standing, not on skin tone. That, at least is the principle.

But the man who helped end racial affirmative action preferences in two of the states involved argues affirmative action is alive and well, simply under another name. Moreover, says Ward Connerly, a black businessman in Sacramento, Calif., who has been a leader in organizing anti-affirmative action referendums, the real issue — the decline in urban K-12 schools — is being ignored.

"Legislatures and college administrators lack the spine to say, 'Let's find the problem at its core,'" says Connerly, a former member of the University of California Board of Regents. "Instead, they go for a quick fix they believe will yield the same number of blacks and Latinos as before."

Even Connerly's opponents agree "percent plans" alone don't put high schools in inner cities and prosperous suburbs on an equal footing. "In some school districts in Texas, 50 percent of the graduates could make it here easily," says Terry H. Anderson, a history professor at Texas A&M University in College Station. "Some school districts are so awful that not one kid could graduate here, I don't care what race you're talking about."

All the plans — except at selective schools — ignore SAT or ACT scores (though students do have to present their scores). The policy troubles Richard D. Kahlenberg, a senior fellow at The Century Foundation, who champions "class-based" affirmation action. "The grade of A in one high school is very different from the grade of A in another," he says.

Texas lawmakers originated the percent plan concept after a 5th U.S. Circuit Court of Appeals decision in 1996 (*Hopwood v. Texas*) prohibited consideration of race in college admissions. Legislators proposed guaranteeing state university admissions to the top 10 percent of graduates of the state's public and private high schools. Then-Gov. George W. Bush signed the bill, which includes automatic admission to the flagship campuses, the University of Texas at Austin and Texas A&M.[1]

In California, the impetus was the 1996 voter approval of Proposition 209, which prohibited racial and ethnic preferences by all state entities. Borrowing the Texas idea, California lawmakers devised a system in which California high school students in the top 4 percent of their classes are eligible for the California system, but not necessarily to attend the two star institutions, UC Berkeley and UCLA. (Students in the top 4 percent-12.5 percent range are admitted to community colleges and can transfer to four-year institutions if they maintain 2.4 grade-point averages.)[2]

Connerly was active in the Proposition 209 campaign and was the key player — but involuntarily — in Florida's adoption of a percent plan. In 1999, Connerly was preparing to mount an anti-affirmative action initiative in Florida. Then-Gov. Jeb Bush worried it could hurt his party's standing with black voters — with possible repercussions on his brother

Archibald Cox, the Watergate special prosecutor who was fired on orders of President Nixon in 1973. Cox's granddaughter, Melissa Hart, helps lead the opposition to an anti-affirmative action ballot initiative in Colorado.[30]

In 1979 and 1980, the court upheld worker training and public contracting policies that included so-called set-asides for minority-group employees or minority-owned companies. But in the latter case, the deciding opinion specified that only companies that actually had suffered discrimination would be eligible for those contracts.[31]

Divisions within the Supreme Court reflected growing tensions in the country as a whole. A number of white people saw affirmative action as injuring the educational

George's presidential campaign. Instead Gov. Bush launched "One Florida," a percent plan approved by the legislature.

In Florida, the top 20 percent of high school graduates are guaranteed admission to the state system. To attend the flagship University of Florida at Gainesville they must meet tougher standards. All three states also require students to have completed a set of required courses.

Percent plan states also have helped shape admissions policies by experimenting with ways to simultaneously keep academic standards high, while ensuring at least the possibility that promising students of all socioeconomic circumstances have a shot at college.

In Florida, the consequences of maintaining high admissions standards at UF were softened by another program, "Bright Futures," which offers tuition reductions of 75 percent — or completely free tuition — depending on completion of AP courses and on SAT or ACT scores.

The effect, says University of Florida political scientist Daniel A. Smith, is to ensure a plentiful supply of top students of all races and ethnicities. "We have really talented minorities — blacks, Latinos, Asian-Americans — because 'One Florida' in combination with 'Bright Futures' has kept a lot of our talented students in the state. We have students who turned down [partial] scholarships to Duke and Harvard because here they're going for free."

At UCLA, which also has maintained rigorous admission criteria, recruiters spread out to high schools in low-income areas in an effort to ensure that the school doesn't become an oasis of privilege. The realities of race and class

"The time has come to pull the plug on race-based decision-making," says Ward Connerly, a Sacramento, Calif., businessman who spearheaded anti-affirmative action ballot initiatives in Colorado, Nebraska and other states.

mean that some of that recruiting work takes place in mostly black or Latino high schools.

"It's the fallacy of [Proposition] 209 that you can immediately move to a system that doesn't take account of race and that treats everybody fairly," said Tom Lifka, a UCLA assistant vice chancellor in charge of admissions. He said the new system meets legal standards.[3]

Consciously or not, Lifka was echoing the conclusion of the most thorough analysis of the plans' operations in the three states. The 2003 study, sponsored by Harvard University's Civil Rights Project, concluded that the states had largely succeeded in maintaining racial and ethnic diversity on their campuses.

But the report added that aggressive recruitment, academic aid to high schools in low-income areas and similar measures played a major role.

"Without such support," wrote Catherine L. Horn, an education professor at the University of Houston, and Stella M. Flores, professor of public policy and higher education at Vanderbilt, "the plans are more like empty shells, appearing to promise eligibility, admission and enrollment for previously excluded groups but actually doing very little."[4]

---

[1] Catherine L. Horn and Stella M. Flores, "Percent Plans in College Admissions: A Comparative Analysis of Three States' Experiences," Civil Rights Project, Harvard University, 2003, pp. 20-23, www.civilrightsproject.ucla.edu/research/affirmativeaction/tristate.pdf.

[2] Ibid.

[3] Quoted in David Leonhardt, "The New Affirmative Action," *The New York Times Magazine*, Sept. 30, 2007, p. 76.

[4] Horn and Flores, *op. cit.*, pp. 59-60.

---

and career advancement of people who hadn't themselves caused the historical crimes that gave rise to affirmative action.

Reversing Course

President Ronald W. Reagan took office in 1981 with strong support from so-called "Reagan Democrats" — white, blue-collar workers who had turned against their former party on issues including affirmative action.[32]

Initially, Reagan seemed poised to fulfill the hopes of those who wanted him to ban all preferences based on race, ethnicity and gender. The latter category followed an upsurge of women fighting to abolish limits on their education and career possibilities.

Supporters of affirmative action in Lansing, Mich., rally against a proposed statewide anti-affirmative action ballot initiative in September 2006; voters approved the proposal that November. The initiative followed a 2003 U.S. Supreme Court ruling upholding the use of race in law-school admissions at the University of Michigan. Justice Sandra Day O'Connor, who wrote the majority 5-4 opinion, predicted, however, that in 25 years affirmative action would "no longer be necessary."

Yet Reagan's appointees were divided on the issue, and the president himself never formalized his rejection of quotas and related measures. Because no law required the setting of goals and timetables, Reagan could have banned them by executive order. During Reagan's second term, Attorney General Edwin Meese III drafted such an order. But Reagan never signed it.

Nevertheless, the Reagan administration did systematically weaken enforcement of affirmative action. In Reagan's first term he cut the budgets of the Equal Employment Opportunity Commission and the Office of Federal Contract Compliance — the two front-line agencies on the issue — by 12 and 34 percent, respectively, between 1981 and 1983. As a result, the compliance office blocked only two contractors during Reagan's two terms, compared with 13 that were barred during President Jimmy Carter's term.

The Justice Department also began opposing some affirmative action plans. In 1983, Justice won a partial court reversal of an affirmative action plan for the New Orleans Police Department. In a police force nearly devoid of black supervisors, the plan was designed to expand the number — a move considered vital in a city whose population was nearly one-half black.

Affirmative action cases kept moving through the Supreme Court. In 1984-1986, the court overturned plans that would have required companies doing layoffs to disregard the customary "first hired, last fired" rule, because that custom endangered most black employees, given their typically short times on the job.

And in 1987, a 5-4 Supreme Court decision upheld an Alabama state police plan requiring that 50 percent of promotions go to black officers. The same year, the court upheld 6-3 the promotion of a woman employee of Santa Clara County, Calif., who got promoted over a male candidate who had scored slightly higher on an assessment. The decision marked the first court endorsement of affirmative action for women.

In the executive branch, divided views persisted in the administration of Reagan's Republican successor, George H. W. Bush. In 1990 Bush vetoed a pro-affirmative action bill designed to reverse recent Supreme Court rulings, one of which effectively eased the way for white men to sue for reverse discrimination.

The legislation would have required "quotas," Bush said, explaining his veto. But the following year, he signed a compromise, the Civil Rights Act of 1991.[33] Supported by the civil rights lobby, the bill wrote into law the *Griggs v. Duke Power* requirement that an employer prove that a job practice — a test, say — is required for the work in question. A practice that failed that test could be shown to result in discrimination, even if that hadn't been the intention.

Bush also reversed a directive by his White House counsel that would have outlawed all quotas, set-asides and related measures. The administration's ambivalence reflected divided views in American society. Local government and corporate officials had grown appreciative of affirmative action for calming racial tensions. In 1985, the white Republican mayor of Indianapolis refused a Justice Department request to end affirmative action in the police department. Mayor William Hudnut said that the "white majority has accepted the fact that we're making a special effort for minorities and women."[34]

Yet among white males, affirmative action remained a very hot-button issue. "When we hold focus groups," a Democratic pollster said in 1990, "if the issue of affirmative action comes up, you can forget the rest of the session. That's all . . . that's talked about."[35]

Mending It

From the early 1990s to 2003 race-based affirmative action suffered damage in the political arena and the courts.

In 1994, white male outrage at preferences for minority groups and women was a key factor in congressional elections that toppled Democrats from control of both houses. As soon as the Congress changed hands, its new leaders targeted affirmative action. "Sometimes the best-qualified person does not get the job because he or she may be one color," Majority Leader Dole said in a television interview. "That may not be the way it should be in America."[36]

The following year, the U.S. Supreme Court imposed limits on the use of preferences, ruling on a white, male contractor's challenge to a federal program that encouraged general contractors to favor minority subcontractors. Justice O'Connor wrote in the 5-4 majority opinion in *Adarand Constructors v. Peña* that any racial or ethnic preferences had to be "narrowly tailored" to apply only to "pervasive, systematic and obstinate discriminatory conduct."[37]

Some justices had wanted all preferences overturned. Though that position failed to win a majority, the clear unease that O'Connor expressed added to the pressure on politicians who supported affirmative action.

In that climate, President Bill Clinton gave a 1995 speech at the National Archives in Washington in which he acknowledged that critics had a point. He said he didn't favor "the unjustified preference of the unqualified over the qualified of any race or gender." But affirmative action was still needed because discrimination persisted, Clinton added. His bottom line: "Mend it, but don't end it."[38]

The slogan seemed to match national politicians' mood. One day after Clinton's speech, the Senate voted down a bill to abolish all preferences, with 19 Republicans siding with Democrats in a 61-36 vote.

But in California, one of the country's major affirmative action laboratories, the "end it" argument proved more popular. Racial/ethnic preferences had become a major issue in a state whose minority population was booming. California's higher-education system also included two of the nation's top public institutions: the University of California at Berkeley (UCB) and UCLA.

Among many white, Anglo Californians, affirmative action had come to be seen as a system under which black and Latino applicants were getting into those two schools at the expense of whites or Asians with higher grades and SAT scores.

By 1996, the statewide university system's majority-Republican Board of Regents voted to end all race, ethnic and gender preferences in admissions. The board did allow universities to take applicants' socioeconomic circumstances into account.

And in the same year, California voters approved Proposition 209, which outlawed all race, ethnicity and gender preferences by all state entities. Connerly helped organize that referendum and followed up with successful campaigns in Washington state in 1998 and in Michigan in 2003.

Meanwhile, the "reverse discrimination" issue that had been decided in the *Bakke* case flared up in Texas, where Cheryl Hopwood and two other white applicants to the University of Texas law school challenged their rejections, pointing to the admissions of minority students with lower grades and test scores. In 1996, the 5th U.S. Circuit Court of Appeals decided for the plaintiffs, ruling that universities couldn't take race into account when assessing applicants.

The appeals judges had overruled the *Bakke* decision, at least in their jurisdiction of Texas, Mississippi and Louisiana, yet the Supreme Court refused to consider the case.

But in 2003, the justices ruled on two separate cases, both centering on admissions to another top-ranked public higher education system: the University of Michigan. One case arose from admissions procedures for the undergraduate college, the other from the system for evaluating applicants to the university's law school.[39]

The Supreme Court decided against the undergraduate admissions policy because it automatically awarded 20 extra points on the university's 150-point evaluation scale to blacks, Latinos and American Indians. By contrast, the law school took race into account in what Justice O'Connor, in the majority opinion in the 5-4 decision, called a "highly individualized, holistic review" of each candidate aimed at producing a diverse student population.[40]

CURRENT SITUATION
"Formal Equality"

In the midst of war and the Wall Street meltdown, affirmative action may not generate as many headlines as it used to. But the issue still packs enough punch to have put anti-affirmative action legislation up for popular vote in Colorado and Nebraska this year.

The Preference Program Nobody Talks About

How "legacies" get breaks at top colleges.

Many critics say race-based affirmative action gives minority college applicants an unfair advantage. But reporter Peter Schmidt found an even more favored population — rich, white kids who apply to top-tier schools.

"These institutions feel very dependent on these preferences," Schmidt writes in his 2007 book, *Color and Money: How Rich White Kids Are Winning the War Over College Affirmative Action*. "They throw up their hands and say, 'There's no other way we can raise the money we need.'"

Colleges admit these students — "legacies," in college-admission lingo — because their parents are donation-making graduates. Offspring of professors, administrators or (in the case of top state universities) politically influential figures get open-door treatment as well.

"Several public college lobbyists, working in both state capitals and with the federal government in and around Washington, have told me that they spend a significant portion of their time lobbying their own colleges' admissions offices to accept certain applicants at the behest of public officials," Schmidt writes.[1]

Especially in regard to legacies and the families' donations, Schmidt says, "There is a utilitarian argument that the money enables colleges to serve students in need. But there isn't a correlation between how much money they're bringing in and helping low-income students."

As deputy editor of the *Chronicle of Higher Education*, Schmidt has been covering affirmative action conflicts since his days as an Associated Press reporter writing about protests over racial tensions at the University of Michigan in the mid-1990s.

His book doesn't deal exclusively with applicants from privileged families — who, by the nature of American society, are almost all white and academically well-prepared. But Schmidt's examination of privileged applicants frames his reporting on the more familiar issues of preferences based on race, ethnicity and gender.

According to Schmidt, Harvard as of 2004 accepted about 40 percent of the legacies who applied, compared to about 11 percent of applicants overall. In the Ivy League in general, children of graduates made up 10-15 percent of the undergraduates.

Though the issue is sensitive for college administrators, Schmidt found some members of the higher-education establishment happy to see it aired.

"Admissions officers are the ones who are finding the promising kids — diamonds in the rough — and getting emotionally invested in getting them admitted, then sitting down with the development officer or the coach and finding that these kids are knocked out of the running," he says.

Some education experts dispute that conclusion. Abigail Thernstrom, a senior fellow at the conservative Manhattan Institute and vice-chair of the U.S. Commission on Civil Rights, opposes "class-based" affirmative action (as well as racial/ethnic preferences), calling it unnecessary. She says that when top-tier schools look at an applicant from a disadvantaged background "who is getting a poor education — a diamond in the rough but showing real academic progress — and compare that student to someone from Exeter born with a silver spoon in his mouth, there's no question that these schools are going to take that diamond in the rough, if they think he or she will be able to keep up."

But some of Schmidt's findings echo what affirmative action supporters have observed. James E. Coleman Jr., a law professor at Duke University, argues against the tendency to focus all affirmative action attention on blacks and Latinos. "The idea is that any white student who gets here deserves to be here. They're not questioned. This has always been true."

At the same time, Coleman, who is black, agrees with Schmidt that those who start out near the top of the socioeconomic ladder have access to first-class educations before they even get to college. Coleman himself, who graduated from Harvard and from Columbia Law School, says he never had a single white classmate in his Charlotte, N.C., schools until he got accepted to a post-high school preparatory program at Exeter, one of the nation's most prestigious prep schools. "I could tell that my educational background and preparation were woefully inadequate compared to students who had been there since ninth grade," he recalls. "I had to run faster."

Schmidt says the politics of affirmative action can give rise to tactical agreements between groups whose interests might seem to conflict. In one dispute, he says, "Civil rights groups and higher-education groups had a kind of uneasy alliance: The civil rights groups would not challenge the admissions process and go after legacies as long as affirmative action remained intact."

But, he adds, "There are people not at the table when a deal like that is struck. If you're not a beneficiary of one or the other side of preferences, you don't gain from that agreement."

---

[1] Peter Schmidt, *Color and Money: How Rich White Kids Are Winning the War Over College Affirmative Action* (2007), p. 32.

AT ISSUE

Would many black and Latino science and math majors be better off at lesser-ranked universities?

YES
Rogers Elliott
Professor Emeritus, Department of Psychology and Brain Sciences, Dartmouth College

From testimony before U.S. Civil Rights Commission, Sept. 12, 2008

Race preferences in admissions in the service of affirmative action are harming the aspirations, particularly, of blacks seeking to be scientists.

The most elite universities have very high levels in their admission standards, levels which minorities — especially blacks — don't come close to meeting.

[Thus], affirmative action in elite schools, which they pursue vigorously and successfully, leaves a huge gap, probably bigger than it would be for affirmative action at an average school. That is what constitutes the problem.

At elite schools, 90 percent of science majors [got] 650 or above on the SAT math score. About 80 percent of the white/Asian group are 650 or above, but only 25 percent of the black group have that score or better. The gaps that are illustrated in these data have not gotten any better. They have, in fact, gotten a little bit worse: The gap in the SAT scores between blacks and whites, which got to its smallest extent in about 1991 — 194 points — is back to 209.

The higher the standard at the institution, the more science they tend to do. But the [lower-ranking schools] still do science, and your chances of becoming a scientist are better. Now, obviously, there are differences. The higher institutions have eliteness going for them. They have prestige going for them, and maybe getting a degree from Dartmouth when you want to be a doctor will leave you better off in this world even though you're not doing the thing you started with as your aspiration.

Seventeen of the top 20 PhD-granting institutions for blacks in this country, are HBCUs [historically black colleges and universities].

Elite institutions are very performance-oriented. They deliberately take people at a very high level to begin with — with a few exceptions — and then they make them perform, and they do a pretty good job of it. If you're not ready for the first science course, you might as well forget it. Some of these minority students had mostly A's . . . enough to get to Dartmouth or Brown or Cornell or Yale. They take their first course, let's say, in chemistry; at least 90 percent of the students in that course are bright, motivated, often pre-med, highly competitive whites and Asians. And these [minority] kids aren't as well-prepared. They may get their first C- or D in a course like that because the grading standards are rigorous, and you have to start getting it from day one.

NO
Prof. Richard A. Tapia
Director, Center on Excellence and Equity, Rice University

From testimony before U.S. Civil Rights Commission, Sept. 12, 2008

The nation selects leaders from graduates and faculty of U.S. universities with world-class science, technology, engineering and math (STEM) research programs. If we, the underrepresented minorities, are to be an effective component in STEM leadership, then we must have an equitable presence as students and faculty at the very top-level research universities.

Pedigree, unfortunately, is an incredible issue. Top research universities choose faculty from PhDs produced at top research universities. PhDs produced at minority-serving schools or less-prestigious schools will not become faculty at top research universities. Indeed, it's unlikely they'll become faculty at minority-serving institutions. A student from a research school with a lesser transcript is stronger than a student from a minority-serving institution with all A's.

So are the students who come from these minority-serving institutions incompetent? No. There's a level of them that are incredibly good and will succeed wherever they go. And usually Stanford and Berkeley and Cornell will get those. Then there's a level below that you can work with. I produced many PhDs who came from minority-serving institutions. Is there a gap in training? Absolutely.

We do not know how to measure what we really value: Creativity. Underrepresented minorities can be quite creative. For example, the Carl Hayden High School Robotic Team — five Mexican-American students from West Phoenix — beat MIT in the final in underwater robotics. They were not star students, but they were incredibly creative.

Treating everyone the same is not good enough. Sink or swim has not worked and will not work. It pays heed to privilege, not to talent. Isolation, not academics, is often the problem. We must promote success and retention with support programs. We must combat isolation through community-building and mentoring.

Ten percent of the students in public education in Texas are accepted into the University of Texas, automatically — the top 10 percent. They could have said look, these students are not prepared well. They're dumped at our doorstep, let's leave them. They didn't. The Math Department at the University of Texas at Austin built support programs where minorities are retained and succeed. It took a realization that here they are, let's do something with them.

Race and ethnicity should not dictate educational destiny. Our current path will lead to a permanent underclass that follows racial and ethnic lines.

"This is a progressive approach," said Jessica Peck Corry, executive director of the Colorado Civil Rights Initiative, which is campaigning for proposed Constitutional Amendment 46. The amendment would prohibit all state government entities from discriminating for or against anyone because of race, ethnicity or gender. "America is too diverse to put into stagnant race boxes," she says.

Melissa Hart, a co-chair of "No On 46," counters that the amendment would require "formal equality" that shouldn't be confused with the real thing. She likens the proposal to "a law that says both the beggar and the king may sleep under a bridge." In the real world, she says, only one of them will spend his nights in a bedroom.

Unlike California, Michigan and Washington — the states where voters have approved initiatives of this type over the past 12 years — the Colorado campaign doesn't follow a major controversy over competition for university admissions.

To be sure, Corry — a libertarian Republican law student, blogger and past failed candidate for state Senate — has publicly opposed affirmative action for several years.[41] But Corry, who is also a policy analyst at the Denver-based Independence Institute, a libertarian think tank, acknowledges that the referendum campaign in Colorado owes its start to Connerly. He began taking the ballot initiative route in the 1990s, after concluding that neither state legislatures nor Congress would ever touch the subject.

"They just seem to lack the stomach to do what I and the majority of Americans believe should be done," Connerly says. "Clearly, there's a disconnect between elected officials and the people themselves."

Connerly's confidence grows out of his success with the three previous initiatives. But this year, his attempts to get his proposal before voters in Arizona, Missouri and Oklahoma all failed because his campaign workers didn't gather enough valid signatures to get the initiatives on the ballot.

Connerly blames what he calls an overly restrictive initiative process in Oklahoma, as well as organized opposition by what he calls "blockers," who shadowed signature-gatherers and disputed their explanations of the amendments.

Opponents had a different name for themselves. "Our voter educators were simply that — voter educators," said Brandon Davis, political director of the Service Employees International Union in Missouri. "Ward Connerly should accept what Missourians said, and he should stop with the sore-loser talk."[42]

The opposition began deploying street activists to counter what they call the deliberately misleading wording of the proposed initiatives. In Colorado, Proposition 46 is officially described as a "prohibition against discrimination by the state" and goes on to ban "preferential treatment to any individual or group on the basis of race, sex, color, ethnicity or national origin."[43]

"We want an acknowledgement that disadvantage cannot be specifically determined based on looking at some race data or gender data," Corry says. But tutoring, counseling and other activities should be extended to all who need help because of their socioeconomic circumstances, she contends.

Likewise, a project to interest girls in science and math, for instance, would have to admit boys. "In a time when America is losing its scientific advantage by the second, why are you excluding potential Nobel prize winners because they're born with the wrong biology?" she asks rhetorically.

Hart says that many tutoring and similar programs tailored to low-income students in Colorado already welcome all comers, regardless of race or ethnicity. But she questions why a math and science program tailored for girls should have to change its orientation. Likewise, Denver's specialized public schools for American Indian students would have to change their orientation entirely. "Class-based equal opportunity programs are not substitutes for outreach, training and mentoring on the basis of race and gender," she says.

The issue of class comes up in personal terms as well. Corry portrays herself as the product of a troubled home who had to work her way through college and graduate school. Though her father was a lawyer, her mother abandoned the family and wound up living on the streets. And Corry depicts Hart as a member of the privileged class, a granddaughter of former Solicitor General Cox and a graduate of Harvard University and Harvard Law School. "People like Melissa, I believe, are well-intentioned but misguided," Corry says. "The worst thing you can do to someone without connections is to suggest that they can't make it without preferences."

Hart, rapping Corry for bringing up personal history rather than debating ideas, adds that her father and his part of the family are potato farmers from Idaho.

"I am proudly the granddaughter of Archibald Cox, proud of the fact that he argued the *Bakke* case for the

University of California, and proud to be continuing a tradition of standing up for opportunity in this country," she says.

The Nebraska campaign, taking place in a smaller state with little history of racial or ethnic tension and a university where competition for admission isn't an issue, has generated somewhat less heat. But as in Colorado, college-preparation and other programs of various kinds that target young women and American Indians would be threatened by the amendment, says Laurel Marsh, executive director of the Nebraska ACLU.

Over Their Heads?

The U.S. Civil Rights Commission is examining one of the most explosive issues in the affirmative action debate: whether students admitted to top universities due to racial preferences are up to the academic demands they face at those institutions.

Math and the hard sciences present the most obvious case, affirmative action critics — and some supporters — say. Those fields are at the center of the commission's inquiry because students from high schools in low-income areas — typically minority students — tend to do poorly in science and math, in part because they require considerable math preparation in elementary and high school.

Sander of UCLA, who has been studying the topic, testified to the commission that for students of all races who had scored under 660 on the math SAT, only 5 percent of blacks and 3.5 percent of whites obtained science degrees. But of students who scored 820 or above on the SAT, 44 percent of blacks graduated with science or engineering degrees. Among whites, 35 percent graduated with those degrees — illustrating Sander's point that that issue is one of academic preparation, not race.

Abigail Thernstrom, the commission's vice-chair, says that most graduates of run-of-the-mill urban schools labor under a major handicap in pursuing math or science degrees. "By the time they get to college they're in bad shape in a discipline like math, where all knowledge is cumulative," she says. "The colleges are inheriting a problem that, in effect, we sweep under the rug."

Thernstrom, a longtime affirmative action critic, bases her views both on her 11 years of service on the Massachusetts state Board of Education and on data assembled by academics, including Sander. "Test scores do predict a lot, high school grades predict a lot," Sander says in an interview, disputing critics of his work

TV cameramen in Lincoln, Neb., shoot boxes of signed voter petitions that qualified a proposed initiative to be put on the ballot in Nebraska this coming November calling for a ban on most types of affirmative action.

who say students from deficient high schools can make up in college what they missed earlier.

Testifying to the commission on Sept. 12, Sander presented data showing that black and Hispanic high school graduates tend to be more interested than their white counterparts in pursuing science and math careers, but less successful in holding on to majors in those fields in college. Lower high school grades and test scores seem to account for as much as 75 percent of the tendency to drop out of those fields, he says.

Sander added that a student's possibilities can't be predicted from skin color and that the key factor associated with inadequate academic preparation is socioeconomic status. "We ought to view that as good news, because that means there's no intrinsic or genetic gap," he testified.

Rogers Elliott, an emeritus psychology and brain sciences professor at Dartmouth College, told the commission that the best option for many black and Hispanic students who want to pursue science or math careers is to attend lower-rated universities. Among institutions that grant the most PhDs to blacks, 17 of the top 20 are HBCUs, Elliott said, "and none of them is a prestige university."

Richard Tapia, a Rice University mathematician, countered that consigning minority-group students who aren't stars to lower-ranking universities would be disastrous. Only top-tier universities, he argued, provide their graduates with the credibility that allows them to assert leadership. "Research universities must be responsible for providing programs that promote success," he said, "rather than be let off the hook by saying that minority students should go to minority-serving institutions or less prestigious schools."

Tapia directs such a program — one of a handful around the country — that he says has helped Rice students overcome their inadequate earlier schooling. But he accepts Sander's and Elliott's data and says students with combined SAT scores below 800 would not be capable of pursuing math or science majors at Rice.

Tapia, the son of Mexican immigrants who didn't attend college, worked at a muffler factory after graduating from a low-achieving Los Angeles high school. Pushed by a co-worker to continue his education, he enrolled in community college and went on to UCLA, where he earned a doctorate. He attributes his success to a big dose of self-confidence — something that many people from his background might not have but that mentors can nurture.

A commission member sounded another practical note. Ashley L. Taylor Jr., a Republican lawyer from Richmond, Va., who is black, argued that colleges have a moral obligation to tell applicants if their SAT scores fall within the range of students who have a shot of completing their studies. "If I'm outside that range, no additional support is going to help me," he said.

Sander agrees. "African-American students and any other minority ought to know going into college the ultimate outcomes for students at that college who have their profile."

Tapia agreed as well. "I had a student that I was recruiting in San Antonio who had a 940 SAT and was going to Princeton. I said, 'Do you know what the average at Princeton is?'" He said, "Well, my teachers told me it was about 950.' I said, 'Well, I think you'd better check it out.'"

In fact, the average combined math and verbal SAT score of students admitted to Princeton is 1442.[44]

OUTLOOK

End of the Line?

Social programs don't come with an immortality guarantee. Some supporters as well as critics of affirmative action sense that affirmative action, as the term is generally understood, may be nearing the end of the line.

"I expect affirmative action to die," says Tapia. "People are tired of it. And if we had to depend on affirmative action forever, then there was something wrong. If you need a jump-start on your battery, and you get it jumped, fine. If you start needing it everywhere you go, you'd better get another battery."

Tapia's tone is not triumphant. He says the decline in public school quality is evidence that "it didn't work, and we didn't do a good job." But he adds that the disparities between the schooling for low-income and well-off students is what makes affirmative action necessary. "Sure, in an ideal world, you wouldn't have to do these things, but that's not the world we live in."

UCLA's Sander, who favors reorienting affirmative action — in part by determining an academic threshold below which students admitted by preference likely will fail — sees major change on the horizon. For one thing, he says, quantities of data are now accessible concerning admission standards, grades and other quantifiable effects of affirmative action programs.

In addition, he says, today's reconfigured Supreme Court likely would rule differently than it did on the 2003 University of Michigan cases that represent its most recent affirmative action rulings.

Justice O'Connor, who wrote the majority decision in the 5-4 ruling that upheld the use of race in law-school admissions, has retired, replaced by conservative Justice Samuel A. Alito. "The Supreme Court as it stands now has a majority that's probably ready to overrule" that decision, Sander says. A decision that turned on the newly available data "could lead to a major Supreme Court decision that could send shockwaves through the system."

For now, says Kahlenberg of The Century Foundation, affirmative action has already changed form in states that have restricted use of racial and ethnic preferences. "It's not as if universities and colleges have simply thrown up their hands," he says. "They now look more aggressively at economic disadvantages that students face. The bigger picture is that the American public likes the idea of diversity but doesn't want to use racial preferences to get there."

Anderson of Texas A&M agrees that a vocabulary development marks the shift. "We've been changing affirmative action and quotas to diversity," he says. "Diversity is seen as good, and has become part of our mainstream culture."

In effect, diversity has come to mean hiring and admissions policies that focus on bringing people of different races and cultures on board — people like Obama, for example. "Obama's talking about merit, and keeping the doors open for all Americans, and strengthening the middle class," Anderson says.

Obama, whose father was Kenyan and whose half-sister is half-Indonesian, also represents another facet of the changing face of affirmative action. "Our society is becoming a lot more demographically complicated," says Schmidt, of *The Chronicle of Higher Education* and author of a recent book on affirmative action in college admissions. "All of these racial groups that benefit from affirmative action as a result of immigration — they're not groups that have experienced oppression and discrimination in the United States. And people are marrying people of other races and ethnicities. How do you sort that out? Which parent counts the most?"

All in all, Schmidt says, the prospects for affirmative action look dim. "In the long term, the political trends are against it," he says. "I don't see a force out there that's going to force the pendulum to swing the other way."

At the same time, many intended beneficiaries — African-Americans whose history set affirmative action in motion — remain untouched by it because of the deficient schools they attend.

The catastrophic state of public schools in low-income America remains — and seems likely to remain — a point on which all sides agree. Whether anything will be done about it is another story.

Top schools will continue to seek diverse student bodies, says Coleman of Duke law school. But the public schools continue to deteriorate. "I haven't seen any effort by people who oppose affirmative action, or people who support it, to do anything to improve the public school system. We ought to improve the quality of education because it's in the national interest to do that."

2010 UPDATE

The Supreme Court's June 29, 2009, ruling in favor of white firefighters in New Haven, Conn., was perhaps the key event in affirmative action over the past two years. The firefighters had challenged the city's decision to discard a competency test for determining promotions after black firefighters taking the test had underperformed. The 5-4 decision in *Ricci, et al. v. DeStefano, et al.* prompted Fordham University law professor Sheila Foster to declare that it "will change the landscape of civil rights law."[45]

The court majority ruled against New Haven's action to discard the performance results. It did, however, say an employer can invoke fear of litigation — suits that might be brought by either the white or the black firefighters citing disparate impact — as a defense against the white firefighters' charge that discarding the competency test was unlawful discrimination. But the lead opinion, written by Justice Anthony Kennedy, said such a defense is available only where the employer has "strong . . . evidence" that it would be held liable, which the New Haven Fire Department did not have.[46]

In a dissent, Justice Ruth Bader Ginsburg wrote that the white firefighters "understandably attract this court's sympathy. But they had no vested right to promotion. Nor have other persons received promotion in preference to them."[47]

Notably, the ruling overturned an earlier appeals court ruling signed by then-federal Judge Sonia Sotomayor in the midst of the confirmation process for her elevation to the U.S. Supreme Court. Opinion polls just before the ruling showed some public skepticism toward affirmative action. American voters, by 55-36 percent, said that affirmative action should be abolished, and 71 percent disagreed with Sotomayor's ruling in the New Haven firefighters' case, according to a June 2009 Quinnipiac University poll.

Poll Results Differ

But The Associated Press, using different phrasing in poll questions, got a different result: 56 percent of Americans favor affirmative action, it reported, with 36 percent opposed. An NBC News-*Wall Street Journal* poll showed 63 percent agreeing that "affirmative action programs are still needed to counteract the effects of discrimination against minorities, and are a good idea as long as there are no rigid quotas."

The election of the first African-American president focused additional attention on Americans' attitudes about using affirmative action as a tool to ease racial disparities. President Barack Obama displayed his approach to such change in his Supreme Court appointments of Sotomayor and Elena Kagan, in the naming of an assertive chief of civil rights at the Education Department, and his administration's switch away from Bush-era litigation priorities in the area of race-conscious legal remedies.

Congratulating Obama for his 2008 victory, ReNee Dunman, president of the Washington-based American Association for Affirmative Action, said, "Where there is inequality and exclusion, affirmative action remains essential in promoting equal opportunity in the workplace, higher education and contracting." She went on to blast what she called the "scorched-earth campaign to end equal opportunity in America" waged in several states by longtime affirmative action critic Ward Connerly.[48]

Connerly's Sacramento-based American Civil Rights Institute continued its efforts to enact state bans on race-conscious selection methods in employment and college admissions. In November 2008, voters in Colorado narrowly rejected a ballot initiative to that effect, and proposed bans were kept off the ballots by opponents in Arizona, Missouri and Oklahoma. That left Connerly's group with one victory, in Nebraska, to add to existing bans in California, Michigan and Washington State.

Obama Criticized

"Obama is hostile to my effort to end race-based preferences," Connerly said in a recent interview, recalling that Obama as a presidential candidate "mentioned me by name and called my efforts 'divisive.' That is what you say if you can't disagree on the merits of an issue." Connerly said Obama will rely on the "disparate-impact theory to argue ipso facto that if minorities" are shown to be in fewer numbers in universities and public employment, "then that is the same as discrimination, forgetting that the level of preparation is not where it needs to be."

A key player in Obama's handling of affirmative action is Education Secretary Arne Duncan. In March 2010 he journeyed to Selma, Ala., site of an historic civil rights march in 1965, and announced that his department was launching new desegregation-compliance investigations around the country. He also said the Education Department's Office for Civil Rights "has not been as vigilant as it should have been" in confronting discrimination over the past 10 years.[49]

On April 15, 2010, the Duncan-appointed assistant Education secretary for civil rights, Russlynn H. Ali, told *The Chronicle of Higher Education* she saw a more active civil rights office in the future. When she first arrived on the job, she said, "what we found [were] some tireless civil-rights pioneers that are hungry and eager, in their words, 'to do civil rights again.'"[50]

The government's muscular approach to litigation reflects a new emphasis on civil rights. On March 12, 2010, the Obama administration's departments of Education and Justice together filed a friend-of-the-court brief on behalf of the University of Texas at Austin, which is defending its race-conscious methods "to achieve the educational benefits of diversity."[51]

By contrast, George W. Bush administration policy sided with the Supreme Court's 2003 decision in *Gratz v. Bollinger* striking down a University of Michigan law school affirmative action plan as too mechanistic. The current Texas litigation was brought by white students Abigail Noel Fisher and Rachel Multer Michalewicz, who said the denial of their applications for admission as undergraduates violated the 14th Amendment's Equal Protection Clause.

The university permits the use of race as one factor in an index in applying efforts to use "top 10 percent" admission plans based on a 1996 Texas law that guarantees admission to state universities to all high-school seniors in the top 10 percent of their class. After that law was implemented, minority representation at the University of Texas dropped sharply. The case is pending in the Fifth U.S. Circuit Court of Appeals.

Universities and think tanks, meanwhile, published new studies on the impact of race-conscious methods and efforts at diversity in the workplace and on campus. According to a study by Columbia Law School Professor Conrad Johnson, from 1993 to 2008 the percentage of black and Mexican-American law students nationwide fell, despite the opening of 3,000 new places and clear improvements in the aggregate Law School Admission Test scores of the two groups.[52]

Research Claims Challenged

The study's results were challenged by scholars organized at the UCLA Law School under the banner of Project SEAPHE (Scale and Effects of Admissions Preferences in

Higher Education). In a Feb. 16, 2010, critique, it said the claims by the researchers were not borne out by the data. "Using the same reference period as the article, (1993 to 2008), accurate statistics show that absolute numbers of black matriculants are up, and Hispanic matriculants are way up," SEAPHE wrote. "Meanwhile, improvements in the average credentials of minority law school applicants have been trivial or non-existent over this same period."[53]

In preparation for elections in fall 2010, friends and foes of affirmative action studied lessons from the 2008 victory for the affirmative action ban in Nebraska and the defeat of the one in Colorado. Some 58 percent of largely white Nebraska voters backed the ban, even though the University of Nebraska Board of Regents had opposed it. Roger Clegg, president of the Center for Equal Opportunity, which opposes consideration of race in admissions, said that part of the legal defense of considering race involves public colleges saying that they have no alternative ways to promote diversity. As more states eliminate the consideration of race — and many of them find ways to still have diverse classes — how plausible is it to make that claim? he asked.[54]

In Colorado, opinion polls showed voters initially appeared to favor the proposal to amend the state constitution to ban preferential treatment to individuals based on race, color, sex, ethnicity or national origin. But a door-to-door campaign against it helped turn the tide (final tally 51 percent to 49 percent), and opponents, such as Democratic Gov. Bill Ritter, called the measure deceptive, saying it would jeopardize outreach programs for minority children.[55]

The chief organizer of Colorado's proposed ban, Jessica Corry, said voters were confused by too many items on the ballot and that the ban would have passed any other year.

Those seeking to outlaw affirmative action were cheered when the Arizona legislature in June 2009 approved a plan to put a proposed ban on the November 2010 ballot. It was the first time a state legislature had enacted a ballot referendum as opposed to citizens' groups gathering signatures, noted Connerly. His group has hopes for Utah taking up a ban next year.

Over the long term, Connerly says, he is working to get rid of race-based classifications as legal categories, such as those on the 2010 census forms, by encouraging Americans to decline to fill out such information.

2012 UPDATE

The Supreme Court is set to re-examine the contentious issue of whether colleges and universities can consider an applicant's race in a selective admission process.

The justices will hear arguments in fall 2012 in a challenge to admissions policies at the University of Texas' flagship campus in Austin brought by an unsuccessful white applicant. Nancy Fisher contends that the school's use of race as a factor in the admissions process violated her constitutional rights by disadvantaging her in comparison to minority applicants.

The case, Fisher v. University of Texas, will mark the first time the court under Chief Justice John G. Roberts Jr. revisits the issue since the 2003 decision in Grutter v. University of Michigan allowed universities to make limited use of racial preferences in admissions.[56]

The Roberts court's other race-related rulings on K-12 pupil-assignment systems and government hiring and promotion policies cheered critics of racial preferences and dismayed traditional civil rights groups. Roberts and Justice Samuel A. Alito Jr., both appointed by President George W. Bush, cast pivotal votes in the 5-4 rulings. Advocates and experts on both sides of the affirmative action debate expect the Texas case also to be closely divided, with Justice Anthony M. Kennedy viewed as likely to hold the decisive vote.

Under President Obama, the administration has cheered traditional civil rights groups by endorsing steps to promote racial diversity in K-12 and higher education and challenging use of standardized tests and other employment practices that may limit hiring of minorities. But critics of race-based policies say their views are advancing in lower-court rulings, local school board decisions and two new statewide bans on affirmative action in public education, public employment and government contracting.

College Admissions

The Texas case involves a challenge to changes adopted by the University of Texas Board of Regents after Grutter for the entering class of 2005 that allowed race to be considered as one factor in an applicant's Personal

Achievement Index (PAI). Other factors include an applicant's essays, leadership experience and extracurricular activities. Applicants continued to be qualified for automatic admission to the flagship Austin campus if they graduated in the top 10 percent of their high school class.

Fisher, who failed to qualify under the top-10 percent rule, was denied admission to the Austin campus for the entering class of 2008. She contended that the rejection violated her right to equal protection because she had academic credentials superior to those of minority applicants who were admitted. The university countered that its admissions process conformed to the limited use of race allowed under Grutter and had resulted in a marked increase in African-American students needed for racial diversity.

A three-judge panel of the Fifth U.S. Circuit Court of Appeals upheld the admissions policies in a lengthy opinion on Jan. 18, 2011. "UT undoubtedly has a compelling interest in obtaining the educational benefits of diversity," Judge Patrick E. Higginbotham wrote for the court, "and its reasons for implementing race-conscious admissions . . . mirror those approved by the Supreme Court in Grutter." Five months later, the full court voted 7-5 against rehearing the case, but four of the dissenters joined an opinion by Judge Edith Jones that said the ruling went beyond Grutter and called on the Supreme Court to review the decision.[57]

The high court agreed to review the decision on Feb. 21, setting the stage for arguments likely in October or November. Fisher, who went on to graduate from Louisiana State University in June 2012, said in a statement that she hoped the court would decide that future applicants "will be allowed to compete for admission without their race or ethnicity being a factor." UT-Austin President William Powers countered that the university needs "to weigh a multitude of factors when making admissions decisions about the balance of students who will make up each entering class."[58]

Meanwhile, two federal appeals courts have differed on the validity of statewide ballot measures banning racial preferences in university admissions as well as employment and government contracting. A Michigan measure approved by voters in 2006 was struck down by the Sixth U.S. Circuit Court of Appeals in July 2011.[59] In April 2012, however, the Ninth U.S. Circuit Court of Appeals reaffirmed an earlier decision upholding California's similar measure adopted by voters in 1996.[60] In related developments, similar measures were approved by Arizona voters in November 2010 and by the New Hampshire legislature in 2011.[61] Oklahoma voters will decide on a similar ballot measure on Nov. 6.

For its part, the Obama administration issued companion policy memos in December 2011 setting out steps that public schools, colleges and universities can take to promote racial diversity. The memos, issued jointly by the Education and Justice departments, differed from Bush administration directives that cautioned against race-conscious pupil assignment or admissions policies.[62]

The Texas case will be heard by only eight justices. Justice Elena Kagan recused herself; she was U.S. solicitor general when the government filed a brief supporting the university before the Fifth Circuit. A 4-4 vote would affirm the Fifth Circuit's decision, thus leaving the university's policy in place.

Public Schools

Local school systems are also evaluating pupil enrollment policies in light of the Roberts court's 2007 decision that generally prohibits the use of race as a determinative factor in assigning individual students to schools. The 5-4 ruling in Parents Involved in Community Schools v. Seattle School District No. 1 struck down pupil-assignment policies in Seattle and Jefferson County, Ky., which includes Louisville.[63]

In the main opinion, Roberts appeared to condemn any use of race in pupil assignments or in other government policies. "The way to stop discrimination on the basis of race," Roberts wrote, "is to stop discriminating on the basis of race." In a pivotal concurring opinion, however, Kennedy called diversity a "compelling interest" for school systems and listed permissible "race-conscious mechanisms," including redrawing attendance zones and "strategic" site selection, to further the goal.

The Seattle school board had already suspended the use of its so-called racial tie breaker for pupil assignments during the litigation. Today, school spokeswoman Teresa Wippel says the system uses a neighborhood assignment system. "We don't base it on race at all anymore," Wippel says.

In Louisville, the school system is now in court defending the pupil-assignment system adopted after the court ruling. An intermediate state court of appeal ruled in October 2011 that the plan violated a state law allowing parents to enroll their children in the school closest to their home. In arguments in April on the school system's appeal, however, justices of the Kentucky Court of Appeal, the state's highest court, were reported to appear inclined toward upholding the policy.[64]

The Supreme Court's decision appears to have moved school systems away from explicit use of race in pupil assignments. Controversies continue to flare, however. The Wake County, N.C., school system, which includes the state capital of Raleigh, had an income-based plan for promoting diversity in place for several years until it was scrapped by a newly elected, majority Republican school board in 2010; civil rights groups protested the decision.[65] A suit currently under way in Nashville, Tenn., challenges a 2009 redistricting plan that African-American families allege zoned black children away from higher-achieving schools in predominantly white neighborhoods; the suit also seeks to bar the startup of new charter schools that are racially isolated.[66]

Employment, Contracting

The court's ruling in the New Haven firefighters case is creating problems for government personnel administrators and lawyers in determining what steps if any can be taken to avoid charges of discriminating against minorities without risking reverse-discrimination claims by white employees or applicants. "It's damned if you do and damned if you don't," says Roger Clegg, president of the Center for Equal Opportunity, a Washington area-based advocacy group that opposes racial preferences.

The subsequent developments in the New Haven case illustrate the problem. The city agreed in July 2011 to pay $2 million in damages to the plaintiffs — all of them white, including one Hispanic — who had been denied promotions. The city also was to pay $3 million in attorneys' fees and court costs.[67]

Meanwhile, however, some black firefighters were continuing to challenge the test-scoring system used in determining promotion as racially biased against minorities. A federal district court judge threw out the suit, but the Second U.S. Circuit Court of Appeals ruled in August 2011 that one of the plaintiffs could proceed with his suit. The appeals court said the high court's decision did not prevent Michael Briscoe from trying to prove that the city's decision to give greater weight to the written instead of the oral portion of the promotion exam had a "disparate impact" on minority applicants in violation of federal civil rights law.[68]

The Obama administration has been "aggressive," according to Clegg, in using disparate-impact theories in civil rights litigation in employment, housing and lending. As one example, the Justice Department filed a suit on April 23, 2012, against the Jacksonville, Fla., Fire and Rescue Department challenging the use of a written promotion exam for supervisory positions as discriminatory against minority firefighters.[69]

Minority preferences in government contracting also appear to be drawing more critical scrutiny from courts, both federal and state. In one important case, the U.S. Court of Appeals for the Federal Circuit in 2008 struck down a Defense Department program that gave preferences to minority-owned contractors. The court said the program was unconstitutional without any evidence that it was needed to remedy past discrimination by the Pentagon.[70]

NOTES

1. See "Transcript: Obama and Clinton Debate," ABC News, April 16, 2008, http://abcnews.go.com/Politics/DemocraticDebate/story?id=4670271&page=1.

2. *Ibid.*

3. *Ibid.*

4. See "Trends in Political Values and Core Attitudes: 1987-2007," Pew Research Center for People and the Press, March 22, 2007, pp. 40-41, http://people-press.org/reports/pdf/312.pdf.

5. See Alemayehu Bishaw and Jessica Semega, "Income, Earnings, and Poverty Data from the 2007 American Community Survey," U.S. Census Bureau, August 2008, p. 20, www.census.gov/prod/2008pubs/acs-09.pdf.

6. See Peter Schmidt, *Color and Money: How Rich White Kids Are Winning the War Over College Affirmative Action* (2007), p. 47.

7. See Anthony P. Carnevale and Stephen J. Rose, "Socioeconomic Status, Race/Ethnicity, and Selective College Admissions," The Century

Foundation, March 2003, pp. 26, 79, www.tcf.org/Publications/Education/carnevale_rose.pdf.

8. See Christopher B. Swanson, "Who Graduates? Who Doesn't? A Statistical Portrait of High School Graduation, Class of 2001," The Urban Institute, 2004, pp. v-vi, www.urban.org/UploadedPDF/410934_WhoGraduates.pdf.

9. Quoted in Ira Katznelson, *When Affirmative Action Was White: An Untold History of Racial Inequality in Twentieth-Century America* (2005), p. 175.

10. See Roberta W. Francis, "Reconstituting the Equal Rights Amendment: Policy Implications for Sex Discrimination," 2001, www.equalrightsamendment.org/APSA2001.pdf.

11. See Clarence Thomas, *My Grandfather's Son: A Memoir* (2007), p. 126.

12. Quoted in "Justice Thomas Mocks Value of Yale Law Degree," The Associated Press, Oct. 22, 2007, www.foxnews.com/story/0,2933,303825,00.html. See also, Coleman profile in Berger&Montague, P.C., law firm Web site, www.bergermontague.com/attorneys.cfm?type=1.

13. See Linda Greenhouse, "Justices Back Affirmative Action by 5 to 4, But Wider Vote Bans a Racial Point System," *The New York Times*, June 24, 2003, p. A1.

14. "Barack Obama, July 27, 2008, Unity 08, High Def, Part II," www.youtube.com/watch?v=XIoRzNVTyH4&eurl= http://video.google.com/videosearch?q=obama%20UNITY&ie=UTF-8&oe=utf-8&rls=org.mozilla:enUS:official&c.UNITY is a coalition of the Asian-American Journalists Association, the National Association of Black Journalists, the National Association of Hispanic Journalists and the Native American Journalists Association, www.unityjournalists.org.

15. See "Trends in Political Values . . .," *op. cit.*, pp. 40-41.

16. See http://abcnews.go.com/Politics/DemocraticDebate/story?id=4670271.

17. See Jonathan Kaufman, "Fair Enough?" *The Wall Street Journal*, June 14, 2008.

18. See Christine MacDonald, "Ban lost in college counties," *Detroit News*, Nov. 9, 2006, p. A16; and "1996 General Election Returns for Proposition 209," California Secretary of State, Dec. 18, 1996, http://vote96.sos.ca.gov/Vote96/html/vote/prop/prop-209.961218083528.html.

19. See Sue Anne Pressley, "Florida Plan Aims to End Race-Based Preferences," *The Washington Post*, Nov. 11, 1999, p. A15.

20. See Walter Alarkon, "Affirmative action emerges as wedge issue in election," *The Hill*, March 11, 2008, http://thehill.com/campaign-2008/affirmative-action-emerges-as-wedge-issue-in-election-2008-03-11.html.

21. *Ibid.*, p. viii.

22. Catherine L. Horn and Stella M. Flores, "Percent Plans in College Admissions: A Comparative Analysis of Three States' Experiences," The Civil Rights Project, Harvard University, February 2003, pp. 30-31, http://eric.ed.gov/ERICDocs/data/ericdocs2sql/content_storage_01/0000019b/80/1a/b7/9f.pdf.

23. See Carnevale and Rose, *op. cit.*, pp. 10-11.

24. *Ibid.*

25. Quoted in Terry H. Anderson, *The Pursuit of Fairness: A History of Affirmative Action* (2004), p. 76. Unless otherwise indicated, material in this subsection is drawn from this book.

26. For background, see the following *Editorial Research Reports*: Richard L. Worsnop, "Racism in America," May 13, 1964; Sandra Stencel, "Reverse Discrimination," Aug. 6, 1976; K. P. Maize and Sandra Stencel, "Affirmative Action Under Attack," March 30, 1979; and Marc Leepson, "Affirmative Action Reconsidered," July 31, 1981, all available in *CQ Researcher Plus Archive*.

27. Quoted in Anderson, *op. cit.*, p. 125. For more background, see Richard L. Worsnop, "Racial Discrimination in Craft Unions," *Editorial Research Reports*, Nov. 26, 1969, available in *CQ Researcher Plus Archive*.

28. *Griggs v. Duke Power*, 401 U.S. 424 (1971), http://caselaw.lp.findlaw.com/scripts/getcase.pl?court=US&vol=401&invol=424. For background, see Mary H. Cooper, "Racial Quotas," *CQ Researcher*, May 17, 1991, pp. 277-200; and Kenneth Jost, "Rethinking Affirmative Action," *CQ Researcher*, April 28, 1995, pp. 269-392.

29. Ibid.
30. See *University of California Regents v. Bakke*, 438 U.S. 265 (1978), http://caselaw.lp.findlaw.com/scripts/getcase.pl?court=US&vol=438&invol=265.
31. See *United Steelworkers of America, AFL-CIO-CLC v. Weber, et al.*, 443 U.S. 193 (1979), http://caselaw.lp.findlaw.com/scripts/getcase.pl?court=US&vol=443&invol=193; and *Fullilove v. Klutznick*, 448 U.S. 448 (1980), www.law.cornell.edu/supct/html/historics/USSC_CR_0448_0448_ZS.html.
32. Unless otherwise indicated, this subsection is drawn from Anderson, *op. cit;* and Jost, *op. cit.*
33. For background, see Cooper, *op. cit.*
34. Anderson, *op. cit.*, p. 186.
35. *Ibid.*, p. 206.
36. Quoted in *ibid.*, p. 233. Unless otherwise indicated this subsection is drawn from Anderson, *op. cit.*
37. *Ibid.*, p. 242.
38. *Ibid.*, p. 244.
39. For background, see Kenneth Jost, "Race in America," *CQ Researcher*, July 11, 2003, pp. 593-624.
40. Quoted in Greenhouse, *op. cit.*
41. "Controversial Bake Sale to Go On at CU, College Republicans Protesting Affirmative Action," 7 News, Feb. 10, 2004, www.thedenverchannel.com/news/2837956/detail.html.
42. Quoted in Kavita Kumar, "Affirmative action critic vows he'll try again," *St. Louis Post-Dispatch*, May 6, 2008, p. D1.
43. "Amendment 46: Formerly Proposed Initiative 2007-2008 #31," Colorado Secretary of State, undated, www.elections.colorado.gov/DDefault.aspx?tid=1036.
44. College data, undated, www.collegedata.com/cs/data/college/college_pg01_tmpl.jhtml?schoolId=111.
45. Adam Liptak, "Supreme Court Finds Bias Against White Firefighters," *The New York Times*, June 30, 2009.
46. Michael C. Dorf, "The Supreme Court Decides the New Haven Firefighter Case," July 1, 2009, *Findlaw*, http://writ.news.findlaw.com/dorf/20090701.html.
47. Edmund H. Mahony and Josh Kovner, "U.S. Supreme Court Rules in Favor of New England Firefighters." *Hartford Courant*, June 30, 2009.
48. Press release, Nov. 30, 2008, www.affirmativeaction.org/news.html.
49. Paul Basken, "Education Department Promises Push on Civil-Rights Enforcement," *The Chronicle of Higher Education*, March 8, 2010.
50. Libby Sander and Peter Schmidt, "Stepping Up the Pace at the Office of Civil Rights," *The Chronicle of Higher Education*, April 15, 2010.
51. See the joint brief at www.justice.gov/crt/briefs/fisher_appellee_brief.pdf.
52. Tamar Lewin, "Law School Admissions Lag Among Minorities," *The New York Times*, Jan. 6, 2010.
53. See SEAPHE.org.
54. Scott Jaschik, "Nebraska Bars Use of Race in Admissions," *Inside Higher Ed*, Nov. 5, 2008, www.insidehighered.com/news/2008/11/05/ affirm.
55. Colleen Slevin, "Colorado voters reject affirmative action ban," *Colorado Gazette*, Nov. 7, 2008.
56. Materials on the case can be found on SCOTUSBlog, www.scotusblog.com/case-files/cases/fisher-v-university-of-texas-at-austin/?wpmp_switcher=desktop.
57. See Fisher v. University of Texas, 631 F.3d 213 (5th Cir., 2011), www.ca5.uscourts.gov/opinions%5Cpub%5C09/09-50822-CV0.wpd.pdf (as revised Feb. 1, 2011). The denial of rehearing is found at www.ca5.uscourts.gov/opinions%5Cpub%5C09/09-50822-CV1.wpd.pdf. For coverage, see articles by Ralph K. M. Haurwit: "UT admission policy upheld," Austin American-Statesman, Jan. 19, 2011; "Court won't review UT admissions guidelines," ibid., June 22, 2011.
58. Quoted in Monica Rhor, "Top court to take up UT policy on race," The Houston Chronicle, Feb. 22, 2012, p. A1. See also Adam Liptak, "Justices Take Up Race as a Factor in College Entry," The New York Times, Feb. 22, 2012, p. A1.
59. The decision is Coalition to Defend Affirmative Action v. University of Michigan (6th Cir., July 1, 2011), www.ca6.uscourts.gov/opinions.pdf/11a0174p-06.pdf. See David Ashenfelter and Dawson

Bell, "Michigan ban on race in college admissions is illegal," Detroit Free Press, July 1, 2011; Tamar Lewin, "Michigan Rule on Admission to University Is Overturned," The New York Times, July 2, 2011, p. A10.

60. The decision is Coalition to Defend Affirmative Action v. Brown (9th Cir., April 2, 2012), www.ca9.uscourts.gov/datastore/opinions/2012/04/02/11-15100.pdf. See Carol J. Williams, "Racial policy ban is upheld," Los Angeles Times, p. AA4.

61. See "Arizona approves anti-affirmative action measure," The Associated Press, Nov. 2, 2010; Peter Schmidt, "New Hampshire Ends Affirmative-Action Preferences at Colleges," The Chronicle of Higher Education, Jan. 4, 2012.

62. See U.S. Departments of Education, Justice, "Guidance on the Voluntary Use of Race to Achieve Diversity and Avoid Racial Isolation in Elementary and Secondary Schools," www2.ed.gov/about/offices/list/ocr/docs/guidance-ese-201111.html; "Guidance on the Voluntary Use of Race to Achieve Diversity in Postsecondary Education," www.justice.gov/crt/about/edu/documents/guidancepost.pdf. The undated documents were released on Dec. 1, 2011.

63. The citation is 551 U.S. 701 (2007). For coverage of background and ruling, see Kenneth Jost, Supreme Court Yearbook 2006-2007.

64. See articles by Chris Kenning: "Court strikes down JCPS student-assignment plan," The Courier-Journal (Louisville), Oct. 1, 2011, p. A1; "Ky. Justices may favor JCPS," ibid., April 19, 2012, p. A1.

65. See Stephanie McCrummen, "In N.C., a new battle on school integration," The Washington Post, Jan. 12, 2011, p. A1.

66. See Julie Hubbard, "Metro Nashville schools rezoning lawsuit could echo far," The Tennessean (Nashville), April 30, 2012.

67. See Abbe Smith, "Firefighters get $2 million," New Haven Register, July 29, 2011, p. A1.

68. The decision is Briscoe v. New Haven, 10-1975-cv (2d Cir., Aug. 15, 2011), www.ca2.uscourts.gov/decisions/isysquery/2a558a1b-8e49-4693-80fe-73210ac25bd3/2/doc/10-1975_opn.pdf#xml=www.ca2.uscourts.gov/decisions/isysquery/2a558a1b-8e49-4693-80fe-73210ac25bd3/2/hilite/. For coverage, see Luther Turnelle, "Firefighter case is reinstated," New Haven Register, Aug. 16, 2011, p. A3. The Supreme Court declined to hear the city's appeal on June 11, 2012.

69. Press release, April 23, 2012, www.justice.gov/opa/pr/2012/April/12-crt-517.html. For coverage, see Steve Patterson, "U.S. sues city over firefighter tests," Florida Times-Union (Jacksonville), April 24, 2012, p. B3.

70. The case is Rothe Development Corp. v. Department of Defense (Fed. Cir., Nov. 4, 2008). For coverage, see Elise Castelli, "Court: DoD minority contracting program unconstitutional," Federal Times, Nov. 10, 2008, p. 6. See also Jody Feder and Kate M. Manuel, "Rothe Development Corporation v. Department of Defense: The Constitutionality of Federal Contracting Programs for Minority-Owned and Other Small Businesses," Congressional Research Service, March 16, 2009, www.fas.org/sgp/crs/misc/R40440.pdf.

BIBLIOGRAPHY

Books

Anderson, Terry H., *The Pursuit of Fairness: A History of Affirmative Action*, Oxford University Press, 2004.
A Texas A&M historian tells the complicated story of affirmative action and the struggles surrounding it.

Kahlenberg, Richard D., ed., *America's Untapped Resource: Low-Income Students in Higher Education*, The Century Foundation Press, 2004.
A liberal scholar compiles detailed studies that add up to a case for replacing race- and ethnic-based affirmative action with a system based on students' socioeconomic status.

Katznelson, Ira, *When Affirmative Action Was White: An Untold History of Racial Inequality in Twentieth-Century America*, Norton, 2005.
A Columbia University historian and political scientist argues that affirmative action — favoring whites — evolved as a way of excluding Southern blacks from federal social benefits.

Schmidt, Peter, *Color and Money: How Rich White Kids are Winning the War Over College Affirmative Action*, Palgrave Macmillan, 2007.
An editor at *The Chronicle of Higher Education* explores the realities of race, class and college admissions.

Sowell, Thomas, *Affirmative Action Around the World: An Empirical Study*, Yale University Press, 2004.
A prominent black conservative and critic of affirmative action dissects the doctrine and practice and its similarities to initiatives in the developing world, of which few Americans are aware.

Articles

Babington, Charles, "Might Obama's success undercut affirmative action," The Associated Press, June 28, 2008, www.usatoday.com/news/politics/2008-06-28-3426171631_x.htm.
In a piece that prompted a debate question to presidential candidate Barack Obama, a reporter examines a possibly paradoxical consequence of the 2008 presidential campaign.

Jacobs, Tom, "Affirmative Action: Shifting Attitudes, Surprising Results," *Miller-McCune*, June 20, 2008, www.miller-mccune.com/article/447.
A new magazine specializing in social issues surveys the long-running debate over university admissions. (*Miller-McCune* is published by SAGE Publications, parent company of CQ Press.)

Leonhardt, David, "The New Affirmative Action," *New York Times Magazine*, Sept. 30, 2007, p. 76.
A journalist specializing in economic and social policy explores UCLA's efforts to retool its admissions procedures.

Liptak, Adam, "Lawyers Debate Why Blacks Lag At Major Firms," *The New York Times*, Nov. 29, 2006, p. A1.
A law correspondent airs a tough debate over affirmative action's success, or lack of it, at big law firms.

Matthews, Adam, "The Fixer," *Good Magazine*, Aug. 14, 2008, www.goodmagazine.com/section/Features/the_fixer.
A new Web-based publication for the hip and socially conscious examines the career of black businessman and affirmative-action critic Ward Connerly.

Mehta, Seema, "UCLA accused of illegal admissions practices," *Los Angeles Times*, Aug. 30, 2008, www.latimes.com/news/local/la-me-ucla30-2008aug30,0,6489043.story.
Mehta examines the latest conflict surrounding the top-tier university's retailored admissions procedures.

Reports and Studies

Coleman, James E. Jr. and Mitu Gulati, "A Response to Professor Sander: Is It Really All About the Grades?" *North Carolina Law Review*, 2006, pp. 1823-1829.
Two lawyers, one of them a black who was a partner at a major firm, criticize Sander's conclusions, arguing he overemphasizes academic deficiencies.

Horn, Catherine L. and Stella M. Flores, "Percent Plans in College Admissions: A Comparative Analysis of Three States' Experiences," The Civil Rights Project, Harvard University, February 2003.
Educational policy experts with a pro-affirmative action perspective dig into the details of three states' alternatives to traditional affirmative action.

Prager, Devah, "The Mark of a Criminal Record," *American Journal of Sociology*, March 2003, pp. 937-975.
White people with criminal records have a better chance at entry-level jobs than black applicants with clean records, an academic's field research finds.

Sander, Richard H., "The Racial Paradox of the Corporate Law Firm," *North Carolina Law Review*, 2006, pp. 1755-1822.
A much-discussed article shows that a disproportionate number of black lawyers from top schools leave major law firms before becoming partners.

Swanson, Christopher B., "Who Graduates? Who Doesn't? A Statistical Portrait of Public High School Graduation, Class of 2001," The Urban Institute, 2004, www.urban.org/publications/410934.html.
A centrist think tank reveals in devastating detail the disparity in high schools between races and classes.

For More Information

American Association for Affirmative Action, 888 16th St., N.W., Suite 800, Washington, DC 20006; (202) 349-9855; www.affirmativeaction.org. Represents human resources professionals in the field.

American Civil Liberties Union, 125 Broad St., 18th Floor, New York, NY 10004; www.aclu.org/racialjustice/aa/index.html. The organization's Racial Justice Program organizes legal and voter support for affirmative action programs.

American Civil Rights Institute, P.O. Box 188350, Sacramento, CA 95818; (916) 444-2278; www.acri.org/index.html. Organizes ballot initiatives to prohibit affirmative action programs based on race and ethnicity preferences.

Diversity Web, Association of American Colleges and Universities, 1818 R St., N.W., Washington, DC 20009; www.diversityweb.org. Publishes news and studies concerning affirmative action and related issues.

www.jessicacorry.com. A Web site featuring writings by Jessica Peck Corry, director of the Colorado campaign for a racial preferences ban.

Project SEAPHE (The Scale and Effects of Admissions Preferences in Higher Education), UCLA School of Law, Box 951476, Los Angeles, CA 90095; (310) 267-4576; www.seaphe.org. Analyzes data on the effects of racial and other preferences.

U.S. Commission on Civil Rights, 624 Ninth St., N.W., Washington, DC 20425; (202) 376-7700; www.usccr.gov. Studies and reports on civil rights issues and implements civil rights laws.

7 Hate Groups

Peter Katel

Two police officers drove up to a brick house in the middle-class Pittsburgh neighborhood of Stanton Heights on April 4, responding to an emergency call from a woman about her 22-year-old son. "I want him gone," Margaret Poplawski told a 911 operator.[1]

She also said that he had weapons, but the operator failed to share that crucial information with the police, who apparently took no special precautions in responding. Seconds after officers Stephen J. Mayhle and Paul J. Sciullo walked into the house, Richard Poplawski opened fire, killing both men. He then shot and killed Eric Kelly, a policeman outside the house. After a four-hour standoff, Poplawski surrendered.[2] Hours after that, the Anti-Defamation League and a *Pittsburgh Post-Gazette* reporter traced a March 13 Web post by Poplawski to the neo-Nazi Web site Stormfront.

"The federal government, mainstream media and banking system in these United States are strongly under the influence of — if not completely controlled by — Zionist interest," the post said. "An economic collapse of the financial system is inevitable, bringing with it some degree of civil unrest if not outright balkanization of the continental U.S., civil/revolutionary/racial war. . . . This collapse is likely engineered by the elite Jewish powers that be in order to make for a power and asset grab."[3]

Obsessions with Jewish conspiracy, racial conflict and looming collapse of the political and social order have long festered in the extreme outposts of U.S. political culture. While extremists typically become active in times of social and economic stress, Timothy

Richard Poplawski, 22, faces murder charges in Pittsburgh after allegedly shooting and killing three police officers on April 4, 2009. Three weeks earlier, Poplawski, who tattooed on his chest what he reportedly described as an "Americanized" Nazi eagle, apparently posted an anti-Semitic message on Stormfront, a neo-Nazi Web site. The number of active hate groups in the nation has jumped to 926 groups — a 50 percent increase — since 2000.

From *CQ Researcher*,
May 8, 2009.

Hate Groups Active in All But Two States

Hate groups were active in all the states except Hawaii and Alaska in 2008, according to the Southern Poverty Law Center. Iowa, California, Texas and Mississippi had the largest concentrations of groups.

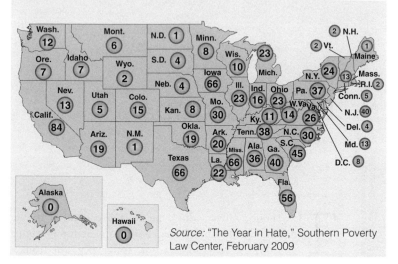

Source: "The Year in Hate," Southern Poverty Law Center, February 2009

McVeigh, the Oklahoma City bomber, struck in 1995 during a relatively tranquil, prosperous time.

Now, law enforcement officials warn, dire conditions throughout the country have created a perfect storm of provocations for right-wing extremists. In the midst of fighting two wars, the country is suffering an economic crisis in which more than 5 million people have lost their jobs, while the hypercharged debate over immigration — and the presence of about 12 million illegal immigrants — continues unresolved.[4]

"This is the formula — the formula for hate," says James Cavanaugh, special agent in charge of the Bureau of Alcohol, Tobacco, Firearms and Explosives (ATF) Nashville, Tenn., division and a veteran investigator of far-right extremists. "Everything's aligning for them for hate."

The Department of Homeland Security (DHS) drew a similar conclusion in early April, adding a concern over the apparent rekindling of extremist interest in recruiting disaffected military veterans.

"The consequences of a prolonged economic downturn . . . could create a fertile recruiting environment for right-wing extremists and even result in confrontations between such groups and government authorities," the DHS said.[5]

The election of Barack Obama as the nation's first African-American president also could prompt an extremist backlash. "Obama is going to be the spark that arouses the white movement," the Detroit-based National Socialist Movement* — considered a leading neo-Nazi organization — announced on its Web site.[6]

But the Obama effect will be negligible among hardcore, violent extremists, says an ex-FBI agent who worked undercover in right-wing terrorist cells in the early 1990s. "They're in an alternative universe," says Mike German, author of the 2007 book *Thinking Like a Terrorist*, and now a policy counselor to the American Civil Liberties Union on national-security issues. "When you believe the American government is the puppet of Israel, whether Obama is the face of the government instead of George W. Bush makes little difference."

Indeed, says Columbia University historian Robert O. Paxton, the Obama victory demonstrated that the country's worrisome conditions haven't sparked widespread rejection of the political system — the classic catalyst for major upsurges of extremism. "Sure, we have a black president, but if the Right were really at the door, we wouldn't have elected him," says Paxton, a leading scholar of European fascism.

Still, Paxton and others caution that the sociopolitical effects of the economic crisis may take a while to hit. The Montgomery, Ala.-based Southern Poverty Law Center (SPLC), which tracks the Ku Klux Klan and other "hate groups," reports activity by 926 such groups in 2008, a 50 percent increase over the number in 2000.[7] "That is a real and a significant rise," says Mark Potok, director of the center's Intelligence Project. Despite the increased activity, the center says there's nothing approaching a mass movement.

---

* "Nazi" is the German-language contraction of "National Socialist."

Moreover, drawing connections between extremist organizations and hate crimes can be complicated.

"Most hate crimes are not committed by members of organized hate groups," says Chip Berlet, senior analyst for Political Research Associates of Somerville, Mass., who has been writing about the far right for a quarter-century. "These groups help promote violence through their aggressive rhetoric. But you're more likely to be victim of hate crime from a neighbor."

For example, three young men from Staten Island, N.Y., charged with beating a 17-year-old Liberian immigrant into a coma on presidential election night last year were not accused of membership in anything more than a neighborhood gang. Their victim, who also lives on Staten Island, said his attackers, one of them Hispanic, yelled "Obama" as they set on him.[8]

Mental health problems also may play a role in such violence, not all of which is inspired by hate rhetoric. In the single deadliest attack on immigrants in memory, Jiverly Wong is charged with killing 13 people (and then himself) at an immigrants' service center in Binghamton, N.Y., one day before Poplawski's alleged killings in Pittsburgh. Eleven of Wong's victims were immigrants, like Wong, a native of Vietnam. Wong left a note in which he complained of his limited English-speaking ability and depicted himself as a victim of police persecution.[9]

But in other recent cases in which immigrants were targeted, the alleged shooters did invoke far-right views. Keith Luke, 22, who lived with his mother in the Boston suburb of Brockton, was charged in January with killing a young woman, shooting

Dozens of Extremist Events Planned This Summer

More than two dozen gatherings of white extremists will be held around the nation this summer, according to the Anti-Defamation League. Many are being held in traditional Ku Klux Klan (KKK) strongholds in the South and Midwest by groups such as the KKK, National Socialist Movement and Christian Identity organizations.

Upcoming Extremist Events in the United States
(Partial list, May-October)

Location	Event
Russelville, Ala.	Courthouse rally organized by Church of the National Knights of the Ku Klux Klan.
Odessa, Mo.	Paramilitary training organized by the Missouri Militia.
Phoenix, Ariz.	Gathering organized by neo-Nazi Nationalist Coalition Arizona with invitations to members of Stormfront, a hate Web site.
York County, Pa.	Open meeting of the neo-Nazi National Socialist Movement for current and interested members.
Marshall, Texas	KKK cookout on private property organized by the United White Knights.
Las Vegas, Nev.	Workshop organized by Paper Advantage, a sovereign citizen group advocating right-wing anarchy.
Champaign County, Ohio	Paramilitary training with the Unorganized Militia of Champaign County.
Burlington, N.C.	Conference organized by the neo-Confederate North Carolina Chapter of League of the South.
New Albany, Miss.	KKK rally at county courthouse followed by a gathering and cross-burning on private property.
Dawson Springs, Ky.	Annual Nordic Fest white power rally organized by the Imperial Klans of America.
Oceana and Muskegon counties, Mich.	Camping trip organized by the white-supremacist forum White Pride Michigan.
Schell City, Mo.	National youth conference organized by Church of Israel, whose followers practice Christian Identity, a racist and anti-Semitic religion.
Jackson, Miss.	Annual national conference of racist group Council of Conservative Citizens.
Sandpoint, Idaho	Weekend conference organized by America's Promise Ministries, practitioners of Christian Identity.
Pulaski, Tenn.	Weekend gathering commemorating the birthday of Nathan Bedford Forrest — the first KKK leader — including a march, cross-burning and fellowship.

Source: Anti-Defamation League

Members of the World Order of the Ku Klux Klan, one of scores of Klan groups in the United States, rally on Sept. 2, 2006, at Gettysburg National Military Park, site of a decisive Civil War battle.

and raping her sister and killing a 72-year-old man — all immigrants from Cape Verde. His planned next stop, police said, was a synagogue. Luke, whom one law enforcement source described as a "recluse," allegedly told police he was "fighting extinction" of white people.[10]

A similar motive was expressed by a 60-year-old Destin, Fla., man charged with killing two Chilean students and wounding three others, all visiting Florida as part of a cultural-exchange program. Shortly before the killings, Dannie Roy Baker had asked a neighbor, "Are you ready for the revolution?" And last summer, he had sent e-mails to Walton County Republican Party officials — who forwarded them to the sheriff's office. One said, in part, "The Washington D.C. Dictators have already confessed to rigging elections in our States for their recruiting dictators to overthrow us with foreign illegals here."[11]

Some immigrant advocates say such comments indicate that extremists are exploiting resentment of immigrants in the hope of stirring up more attacks.

"It is the perfect vehicle, particularly with the decline of the economy," says Eric Ward, national field director of the Chicago-based Center for New Community, which works with immigrants. "With American anxiety building, they hope that they can use immigrants as scapegoats to build their movement."

"Illegals are turning America into a third-world slum," says one of a series of leaflets distributed in the New Haven, Conn., area in early March by North-East White Pride (NEWP). "They come for welfare, or to take our jobs and bring with them drugs, crime and disease."

The NEWP Web site carries the cryptic slogan, "Support your local 1488." In neo-Nazi code, "88" represents "Heil Hitler," words that begin with the eighth letter in the alphabet. And "14" stands for an infamous, 14-word racist dictum: "We must secure the existence of our people and a future for white children." Its author was the late David Lane, a member of the violent neo-Nazi organization, The Order, who died in prison in 2007.[12]

The Order, whose crimes included the murder of a Jewish radio talk-show host in Denver in 1984, sprang from the far-right milieu, as did Oklahoma City bomber McVeigh. And a source of inspiration in both cases was a novel glorifying genocide of Jews and blacks, *The Turner Diaries*, authored by the late William Pierce, founder of the neo-Nazi National Alliance, based in West Virginia.[13]

Pierce's death from cancer in 2002 was one of a series of developments that left a high-level leadership vacuum in the extremist movement. One of those trying to fill it is Billy Roper, 37, chairman of White Revolution, a group based in Russellville, Ark. Roper predicts that racial-ethnic tensions will explode when nonstop immigration from Latin America forces the violent breakup of the United States.

"We're at a pre-revolutionary stage, where it's too late to seek recompense through the political process, and too early to start shooting," Roper says.

As police and scholars monitor extremist groups, here are some of the key questions they are asking:

Could the election of a black president and the nation's economic crisis spark a resurgence of far-right political activity or violence?

The precedent-shattering nature of Obama's presidency could provide enough of a spark for racist reaction, some extremism experts argue. Others question whether that's enough to propel significant numbers of people into outright rejection of the political system, even amid the nation's economic turbulence. They note that organized racist violence against African-Americans was already fading by the late 1960s, after civil rights had become the law of the land.

Nonetheless, at least some members of the far right are reacting. Shortly before the presidential election last year, federal agents charged an 18-year-old from Arkansas and a 20-year-old from Tennessee with plotting to kill Obama after first killing 88 black people, beheading 14 of them — apparent references to the "88" and "14" codes. The father of one of the young men said the alleged plans were no more than "a lot of talk." According to the SPLC, the 20-year-old, Daniel Cowart, had been a probationary member of a new and active skinhead organization, Supreme White Alliance, though the organization said he'd been expelled before the alleged murder plot was conceived.[14]

Michael Barkun, a professor of political science at Syracuse University, says older extremists may see Obama's election as a big favor to their movement. "They tend to think of it as a great recruiting tool," says Barkun, who specializes in political and religious extremism. "My sense is that from their point of view, they would see it as a continuation of what they regard as the marginalization of the white population: 'See, we were right all along.'"

But extremists may be disappointed, Barkun adds, given how the election itself showed the extent to which racism has weakened. Still, the economic crisis offers recruiting possibilities to extremists, because millions of people are suffering its effects. "I would be surprised if the economic crisis did not produce some very nasty side effects," he says, citing the pseudo-constitutional interpretations adopted by the "Posse Comitatus" movement that flourished in the 1980s. "Certainly some of the fringe legal doctrines on the far right lend themselves to exploitation here."*

Yet for a segment of U.S. society, Obama's election is already stoking the fires of rage, says another veteran observer of the far right. Michael Pitcavage, investigative research director for the Anti-Defamation League, says that immediately after the election, extremists with MySpace pages started including the slogan, "I have no president."

These are anecdotal signs, Pitcavage acknowledges. But he notes that at least one president in the recent past did prompt an extreme reaction on the far right. "The election of Bill Clinton, I would call one of the secondary causes of the resurgence of right-wing extremism in the 1990s," he says. Clinton's Vietnam War draft avoidance and his evasive acknowledgement of past drug use aroused enormous anger among extremists (as among mainstream conservatives), Pitcavage says — sentiments that expanded into conspiracist views after a violent confrontation between federal law enforcement officers and a heavily armed religious group in Waco, Texas.

But at least one right-wing writer on racial issues says that in his circles Obama's presidency has had little effect. "We have always had sophisticated readers whose views of the world are not going to be knocked askew by some unforeseen political event," says Jared Taylor, editor of *American Renaissance*, a magazine based in Oakton, Va., a Washington suburb. "Though I don't wish to detract at all from the symbolic importance of a non-white American president, it's very much part of a predictable sequence. Readers of *American Renaissance* don't necessarily approve of the idea of a black president, but it's not something that wakes them up to something they weren't aware of before." Taylor greeted Obama's election with an article headlined, "Transition to Black Rule?"[15]

Taylor's magazine opposes all anti-discrimination and affirmative-action laws but doesn't espouse violence. However, attendees at the magazine's annual conference in 2006 included well-known extremists, including

---

* Posse Comitatus means "power of the county," a phrase that adherents used to denote the supposed illegitimacy of the federal government. The Posse Comitatus Act of 1878 was passed to remove the U.S. Army from domestic law enforcement activities.

David Duke. When the former Louisiana Klan leader raised the issue of Jewish influence, a Jewish attendee walked out. Taylor later wrote that he would never exclude Jews, adding, "Some people in the [*American Renaissance*] community believe Jewish influence was decisive in destroying the traditional American consensus on race. Others disagree."[16]

As for the ailing economy, Taylor says it hasn't been helping his publication. "We haven't seen any sort of sudden leap in subscribers," he says. "If anything, the economic conditions are bad for us because we're a nonprofit organization. We depend on contributions; people have less to contribute."

Still, the sociopolitical consequences of the economic crisis transcend financial problems at individual outposts of right-wing opinion.

Cavanaugh, the longtime ATF official, is one of many who sees the global economic meltdown as an echo of the crisis in Germany's Weimar Republic in the 1920s and early '30s, which enabled Hitler's National Socialist Party to come to power.

"This is how they recruited," says Cavanaugh. "Nazism was founded on blaming the Jewish people for the economic crisis." In today's United States, Cavanaugh hypothesizes, extremists could try to make immigrants the group responsible for the crisis.

But Cavanaugh doubts that Obama's presidency, per se, appeals to extremists. Many of them view the conventional political system as the "Zionist Occupation Government," or ZOG. "The president has done more to unite the country — you can feel it," he says. "That doesn't help hate groups get stronger. They can rail against any president, and they have. Any president to them is the head of ZOG."

Are immigrants in danger from extremist violence?

Black Americans have been far and away the major targets of 20th-century extremist violence.

But organized racist violence, from cross-burning to bombings, lynching and assassinations of black community leaders or white civil rights supporters, has faded from the scene, despite episodic hate crimes that sometimes target Jews as well as blacks.

Obama's election demonstrated the extent to which the black-white divide in American life has narrowed. Indeed, when it comes to arousing political passion, race has been replaced by illegal immigrants, who number an estimated 12 million in the United States.[17]

"Black people are here, and no one is talking about deporting them," says Taylor of *American Renaissance*. "Immigration is a current and constant flow that is, in my view, only building up problems and conflict for the future, and that's a process that could be stopped. That is why it is much more a subject of political interest."

Bipartisan congressional legislation to provide a "path to citizenship" — restrictionists prefer the term "amnesty" — for illegal immigrants stalled during the George W. Bush administration.

Aside from mainstream political debate over the solution to illegal immigration, immigrant advocates say they're worried that violence against Latinos — or brown-skinned people thought to be immigrants — is on the rise. According to the most recent FBI statistics, there were 830 attacks of various kinds on Hispanics in 2007. By comparison, 1,087 attacks were made on homosexuals, who are also frequent targets of hate speech.[18] In 2000, there were 557 reported attacks on Hispanics compared to 1,075 attacks against homosexuals.[19]

But both conservatives and liberals take a dim view of those FBI statistics. Marcus Epstein, a conservative anti-immigration activist who draws a line between his views and those of extremists, criticizes the FBI categorization scheme for using the ethnic term "Hispanic" only for crime victims. Offenders, by contrast, are listed only by race, so "Hispanic" doesn't appear. The result, he argues, is that statistics are skewed so that any Hispanic hate-crime perpetrators are statistically invisible. (The FBI says that the agency "does not agree" that its categories "render the data invalid for statistical purposes.")

Epstein, executive director of The American Cause, a conservative organization founded by political commentator and immigration restrictionist Pat Buchanan, is particularly concerned about illegal immigrants with criminal records committing further crimes. He cites the case of Manuel Cazares, who turned himself in to police in Hannibal, Mo., in March, saying he'd killed an ex-girlfriend and a male friend of hers. Cazares, a Mexican citizen, was in the United States illegally, but police hadn't checked his status, although federal immigration authorities said his name wasn't in their database.[20] "Illegal immigrants kill American citizens — that greatly outweighs the number of crimes committed by right-wing white Americans against immigrants," Epstein says.

He cites a statistical analysis by Edwin S. Rubinstein, an economic consultant in Indianapolis and former senior fellow at the Hudson Institute, a conservative think tank. Writing on the VDare Web site, which opposes immigration except by white people, Rubinstein, while acknowledging that national data on crime and ethnicity are thin, extrapolated from California and national figures to estimate that in any given year illegal immigrants "could kill 2.6 persons per day across the U.S."[21]

The vast majority of violent crimes fall within city and state jurisdictions, not all of which collect data on ethnicity. Mark Hugo Lopez, associate director of the Pew Hispanic Center, and co-author of a recent report on Hispanics and federal crime, says, "The reason that we used federal statistics is that those are the cleanest data." The Pew study showed that 70 percent of Latino offenders were non-citizens, and that 3.1 percent of all Latino convicts were sentenced for crimes of violence, including murder.[22]

Others warn that hate crime statistics aren't reliable where immigrants are concerned. "One of the difficulties we have is getting certain communities to report hate crime," said Brian Levin, director of the Center for the Study of Hate and Extremism at California State University, San Bernardino. Illegal immigrants are especially reluctant, says Levin, in a widely shared observation.[23]

In any event, supercharged rhetoric from extremists has ratcheted up fear among immigrants and their advocates. Ward of the Center for New Community says that recent episodes of violence targeting immigrants reflect a general hostility toward immigrants that he's sensing on the street. For example, he says, following an organizational meeting in Wilmer, Minn., a town in the meat-processing factory belt of the upper Midwest, "A woman pulls up behind a car of our field people and starts screaming racial epithets."

Though of little significance by itself, Ward says it reflects an atmosphere that reminds him of "things I saw in the 1980s and '90s during the rise of the neo-Nazi movement." He adds, "These kinds of incidents, I would call an early warning of what will be the backlash."

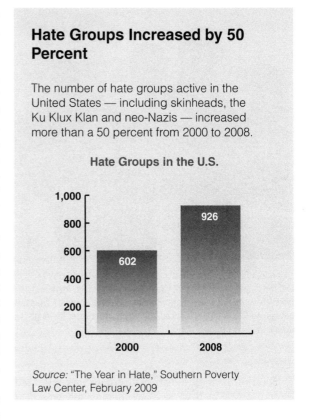

Hate Groups Increased by 50 Percent

The number of hate groups active in the United States — including skinheads, the Ku Klux Klan and neo-Nazis — increased more than a 50 percent from 2000 to 2008.

Hate Groups in the U.S.

- 2000: 602
- 2008: 926

Source: "The Year in Hate," Southern Poverty Law Center, February 2009

Immigration restrictionists argue that their political foes are whipping up passions in an effort to create the appearance that Latinos in general and immigrants in particular face growing danger.

"All hate crimes are abominable, and any decent person would oppose them no matter who the target is," says Ira Mehlman, national media director of the Federation for American Immigration Reform (FAIR), which advocates restricting immigration. "But they are hyping the statistics on hate crimes. Hate crimes against Hispanics are much fewer in actual number than attacks against gays or Jews, who represent much smaller percentages of the population."

Hard-core extremists still rank Jews as their No. 1 enemy, says Pitcavage at the Anti-Defamation League, which was formed in 1913 to combat anti-Semitism.

Oklahoma City bomber Timothy McVeigh, a neo-Nazi Army veteran, was executed in 2001 for killing 168 people, including 19 children, at the Murrah Federal Building. While extremists typically become active in times of social and economic stress, McVeigh struck in 1995 during a period of relative tranquility.

Some of the most horrific hate crimes are committed by "mission offenders," or mentally ill people who hear voices that command them to rid the world of a particular set of evildoers, Pitcavage says.[24] While they may target Jews — and those are often some of the most horrific crimes — "racial/ethnic targets" — including Latinos and immigrants in general — do run a risk from hate crime because they're "more visually identifiable and thus better targets of opportunity," he says.

Is right-wing and extremist speech encouraging hate crimes?

The killings of three Pittsburgh police officers intensified the ongoing debate over free speech and its consequences. Some liberal and left-wing commentators saw Richard Poplawski's horrific crime as an outgrowth, at least in part, of the far-right conspiracy culture that had influenced him, judging by his Web posts. In addition, they say, his rage had been stoked by conservative commentators. Still, the Pittsburgh reporter who helped trace those posts argues in the online magazine *Slate* that the writings reveal more inner torment than ideology.

Journalist Dennis B. Roddy wrote that Poplawski also posted to a non-racist conspiracist site — Infowars, which describes its politics as libertarian. There, the alleged cop-killer "seemed to find . . . a bridge from the near-mainstream to a level of paranoid obsession in search of an explanation for his life's failures. For that, one does not need an ideology, just an inclination."[25]

Nevertheless, Roddy acknowledges that Poplawski complained on Infowars that the site neglected race. Other commentators insisted that Poplawski's posts follow a clear pattern. "Poplawski's black-helicopter and anti-Semitic ravings put him at the outer edge of the right," wrote Gary Kamiya, executive editor of *Salon*, a liberal online magazine. "But his paranoid fear that Obama was going to take away his AK-47 is mainstream among conservatives . . . fomented by the NRA and echoed by right-wing commentators from Lou Dobbs to Limbaugh."[26]

Kamiya doesn't propose limiting free-speech rights, but he does argue that extreme anti-Obama and gun-rights rhetoric is bound to produce more episodes like the Pittsburgh shootings.

The U.S. Supreme Court has ruled that even hate-filled racist speechmaking is protected by the First Amendment. In 1969, the court overturned the terrorism-advocacy conviction of an Ohio Ku Klux Klan leader who'd given a speech including a call to "send the Jews back to Israel," and to "bury the niggers." The court ruled unanimously that the government may not "forbid or proscribe advocacy of the use of force or of law violation except where such advocacy is directed to inciting or producing imminent lawless action."[27]

Worries about the effects of vicious and hyperbolic speech haven't only come from the left. In 2005, Freedom House, a human-rights advocacy organization then headed by former CIA director James Woolsey, a neoconservative, issued a report accusing the government of Saudi Arabia of disseminating "hate propaganda" — targeting Christians, Jews and converts from Islam — in religious publications sent to mosques.[28]

In late March, an American writer of Arab descent wrote on a conservative Web site that American Muslims who get their news on satellite TV from the Middle East are, in effect, being brainwashed into a pro-jihadist outlook. "We must never underestimate the power of hate propaganda," Nonie Darwish wrote, "because, quite simply, it works. Believe it or not, if you grow up hearing 'holy' cursing day in and day out, it can feel and sound normal, justified and even good." Darwish didn't call for banning the transmissions.[29]

But the more explosive recent disputes over speech arise from the immigration conflict. At the center of the controversy are radio and cable TV commentators like Glenn Beck, of Fox News. In June 2007 (before he had joined Fox), Beck read on his radio program a fake commercial for "Mexinol" — a fuel produced from the bodies of illegal immigrants from Mexico.[30]

"We have a butt load of illegal aliens in our country," said the fake ad, which was ascribed to Evil Conservative Industries. "With Mexinol, your raw materials come to you in a seemingly never-ending stream." Beck tried to put some distance between himself and the ad's authors, though in a lighthearted tone. "I don't even know if that's conservative," he said, chuckling. "That would be . . . psychotic, perhaps?"[31]

Last year, Janet Murguía, president of the National Council of La Raza, a leading Hispanic organization, cited the segment in calling for cable channels "to clean up the rhetoric of their own commentators or take them out of their chairs." She argued that much of the commentary by the hosts and some of their guests spurred anti-immigrant violence. "When free speech transforms into hate speech, we've got to draw that line."[32]

Epstein of The American Cause argues that Murguía is trying to "muzzle" free speech. The painful reality of the nation's economic crisis, not anti-immigrant rhetoric — explains more about anti-Hispanic violence, he says.

"People should not hold an individual Hispanic responsible for the fact that wages are being depressed, and they can't get a job, or that schools are overcrowded, that there's an increase in crime in the community," he says. "But that's the reason these people are lashing out. In the few cases of [violence], they're responding to the problems that immigration causes."

Epstein argues that mainstream anti-immigration groups like FAIR provide a legitimate channel for citizens who favor limiting immigration to express their views. "If there was no one actually speaking for Americans, they're going to turn to more radical groups," he says. Epstein posts his writings on the VDare Web site but says he doesn't agree with all the views expressed on the site, some of them virulently racist.

A recent post by one contributor argued that hiring people of South Asian Indian ancestry guaranteed "corruption and ethnocentric discrimination"; another opined that hiring better public school teachers and firing less competent ones means "on net, firing blacks and hiring whites." And another contributor attacked "the cultural pollution of our 'entertainment industry,' which promotes diversity, multiculturalism and white demoralization."[33]

Cavanaugh of the ATF says he's aware that a constellation of legal organizations provide moral backing even for violent actions. In the civil rights days, such groups were known as the "white-collar Klan," he says. "They support people who will go out and do those things."

But, he says, free speech is free speech. "Is it illegal?" he asks rhetorically. "It's awful, but I can't do much about awful, and I shouldn't be able to."

BACKGROUND

Building Movements

Extreme-right political movements reached their peak in the 1930s in the United States and abroad. Adolf Hitler came to power in Germany in 1933. Benito Mussolini, originator of the term "fascism," who began his rule of Italy in 1922, soon forged an alliance with Hitler. Other far-right movements triumphed in Central Europe. The United States, of course, never succumbed to totalitarian rule. But the American extreme right did command a sizable sector of public opinion.[34]

As in Germany and elsewhere (though not to a major extent in Italy), hatred of Jews played a key role in the American right-wing mobilization, with communists and socialists close behind on the enemies list.

Henry Ford, founder of the Ford Motor Co., actively spread anti-Semitism in the 1920s, using a newspaper that he owned, the *Dearborn Independent*, to publish vast amounts of propaganda about a Jewish plot for world domination.[35]

After Ford withdrew from public anti-Semitic activity under pressure from Jewish organizations and the U.S. government, other leaders emerged. Gerald L. K. Smith, a minister and failed political candidate allied with hate-mongers, denounced President Franklin D. Roosevelt (FDR) and African-Americans as well as Jews. William

Dudley Pelley led the fascist Silver Legion — the "Silver Shirts" — which dedicated itself mainly to marches and other publicity-seeking events expressing hatred of Jews, blacks and all minorities.

The Rev. Charles Coughlin, a Roman Catholic priest, known as "Father Coughlin," soared to national prominence and influence through radio broadcasts from his church outside Detroit. At first a Roosevelt supporter, the "radio priest" by 1934 was raging against FDR and the Jews, on whom he blamed the Great Depression.

After the United States entered World War II, the Catholic Church and the federal government forced Coughlin off the air. Pelley was convicted in 1942 of sedition and intent to cause insurrection in the military and was sentenced to 15 years in prison.[36]

By war's end, American fascism as a mass movement had ended. But a core of committed activists kept the far right alive, spurred on by the Cold War against the Soviet Union and the first stirrings of the civil rights movement.[37]

As public opposition to communism grew, Smith preached that Jews and communists were one and the same and that the Holocaust never occurred.

The founding of the John Birch Society in 1958 marked the reemergence of conspiratorial, far-right views — minus the anti-Semitism — in respectable society. Birch Society doctrine viewed the United Nations as a communist organization. Founder Robert Welch, an executive in his brother's candy company, went further, calling President Dwight D. Eisenhower "a dedicated, conscious agent of the communist conspiracy."[38]

Welch's wild accusation stoked outrage in the political mainstream. President Harry S. Truman reportedly called the Birch Society "the Ku Klux Klan, without nightshirts."[39]

By the mid-1960s, the Klan — established in 1866 in Pulaski, Tenn. — had become the center of extremist resistance to the civil rights movement. Members and ex-members of the secret organization carried out some of the most notorious crimes of the era, including the 1963 bombing of the 16th Street Baptist Church in Birmingham, Ala., in which four young girls were killed; the assassination of civil rights leader Medgar Evers in Jackson, Miss., that same year; the murder of three civil rights workers in 1964 in Neshoba County, Miss.; and the killing of another civil rights worker in Alabama in 1965.[40]

Anti-civil rights violence ebbed after enactment of the Voting Rights Act in 1965. From then on, the extremist right became steadily more influenced by neo-Nazism. George Lincoln Rockwell, founder of the American Nazi Party, pioneered the white-nationalist trend. The former Navy pilot and World War II veteran was shot and killed by a dismissed follower in 1967.[41]

Rockwell had been a mentor to William Pierce, a former university physics professor who in 1974 founded the National Alliance, which became a major influence in the extremist right. Pierce became nationally notorious in the 1990s as author of *The Turner Diaries*, which laid out a scenario for white genocide of blacks, Jews and "race traitors" — a process led by a secret brotherhood known as The Order, which sets events in motion by blowing up FBI headquarters with a truck bomb.

The first open sign of a Klan-Nazi nexus was the 1979 killing in broad daylight of five Communist Workers Party members who were starting an anti-Klan march in Greensboro, N.C., in 1979.

Fighting and Killing

Less visibly, another trend was under way. An extreme anti-government and anti-Jewish movement founded in 1971 by William Potter Gale began growing, especially in the West and Midwest. Posse Comitatus ("Power of the County") held that the federal government was constitutionally illegitimate. For example, county justices of the peace held legal supremacy over the U.S. Supreme Court, according to Posse ideology, and federal currency was invalid.[42]

Posse alienation went far deeper. An anti-Semitic religious doctrine known as "Christian Identity" exerted deep influence on many Posse leaders and members, including Gale (despite his own definitively proved Jewish descent, which he denied). The doctrine — rejected by all mainstream Christian denominations — holds that white people are the genuine descendants of the Biblical Hebrews. That is, they're God's chosen people, and Jews and blacks are the devil's spawn. By 1976, the FBI estimated Posse membership at 12,000 to 50,000, not including sympathizers.

Posse Comitatus played a major role in raising the level of far-right extremism to a fever pitch in the last two decades of the 20th century. In the early 1980s, economic crisis gripped the Farm Belt, bringing a wave of foreclosures. The Posse launched a major recruiting drive, preaching that Jewish bankers were to blame for

CHRONOLOGY

1930s-1960s *Attempts to create U.S. versions of European fascism fail, but far-right activists build smaller organizations after World War II.*

1934 The Rev. Charles Coughlin ("Father Coughlin") gains a nationwide following for denouncing President Franklin D. Roosevelt and Jews.

1941-1942 Coughlin is forced off the air and another far-right leader, William Dudley Pelley, is sent to prison for sedition.

1952 Anti-Semite Gerald L.K. Smith fails to persuade the Republican Party to link communism and Jews.

1958 John Birch Society is founded.

1963 Ku Klux Klan members bomb a black church in Birmingham, Ala., killing four young girls.

1967 American neo-Nazi leader George Lincoln Rockwell is killed by an embittered ex-aide.

1969 U.S. Supreme Court rules that a Ku Klux Klan leader's denunciations of blacks and Jews are constitutionally protected speech.

1970s-1980s *Anti-government and anti-Jewish organizations turn to violence, most often against police officers, who are seen as agents of the "Zionist Occupation Government."*

1971 Anti-Semitic, Christian Identity activist William Potter Gale formulates the doctrine underlying the radically anti-government Posse Comitatus movement, which by 1976 has at least 12,000 members, according to the FBI.

1978 *The Turner Diaries,* a genocide fantasy by neo-Nazi William Pierce (pseudonym: Andrew Macdonald), is published.

1983 Posse Comitatus leader Gordon Kahl kills two federal marshals in North Dakota, later dies in a shootout with federal agents in Arkansas.

1984 The Order, a small extremist group inspired by *The Turner Diaries,* murders a Jewish talk-show host in Denver who had denounced racism.... The group's founder is killed later in a shootout in Washington state.

1988 A federal jury in Arkansas acquits 14 right-wing extremists, including five members of The Order, on sedition and other charges.

1990s *Extremist violence climaxes in armed confrontations with federal officers.*

1992 An attempt to arrest survivalist and Christian Identity proponent Randy Weaver in Ruby Ridge, Idaho, ends with the deaths of a marshal and Weaver's wife and young son.

1993 Extremist leaders gather in Estes Park, Colo., to plan cooperation with less-threatening groups.... Federal siege of the Branch Davidian religious-cult compound in Waco, Texas, leads to deaths of more than 80 people.... Extremists depict Ruby Ridge and Waco as examples of government ruthlessness.... Outrage at government helps build "patriot militia" movement.

1995 Timothy McVeigh, an extremist military veteran inspired by *The Turner Diaries,* detonates truck bomb outside Alfred P. Murrah Federal Building in Oklahoma City, killing 168 people.... Militia membership declines.

2000s *Extremist movement erodes further following 9/11 attacks and the removal of major figures by death and imprisonment, but economic crisis ignites fears of a resurgence.*

2001 McVeigh executed by lethal injection.

2004 Richard Butler, influential leader of Idaho-based "Aryan Nations," dies of natural causes.

2005 Up-and-coming extremist leader Matthew Hale, founder of World Church of the Creator, is sentenced to 40 years for conspiracy to commit murder.

2009 Homeland Security Department warns extremists could exploit economic crisis as a recruiting opportunity; critics blast department for focusing on ideology rather than criminal acts.

Concern About Extremism Rising in Europe

Czech Republic expels ex-Klan leader David Duke.

Memories of the horrific consequences of far-right extremism remain strong in Europe. Yet nearly 65 years after the Nazi Holocaust, the extreme right has been gaining ground in parts of the continent, prompting worries that ultranationalism is on the upswing.

"The possibilities for a rise of the far right in the light of the financial and economic crisis are there," Anton Pelinka, a professor of politics at Central European University in Budapest, Hungary, told *The Guardian*, a leading British newspaper.[1]

So far, the European far right is advancing further — at the polls and in the expansion of illegal neo-Nazi organizations — than in the United States. But the gains by European extremists give heart to their U.S. counterparts, who have long maintained ties to Europe, though some European governments do their best to disrupt the relationships. In April, the Czech Republic expelled ex-Ku Klux Klan leader David Duke, a neo-Nazi, who had been invited by an extremist Czech group to lecture in Prague and Brno.

And the British government announced in early May that it had barred — among others — Don Black, founder of the Stormfront Web site, from entering Britain.

Duke's aborted visit notwithstanding, transatlantic ties may have frayed somewhat following the 2002 death of William Pierce. The American neo-Nazi leader had been traveling regularly to Europe for meetings, says Mark Potok, Intelligence Project director at the Southern Poverty Law Center, in Birmingham, Ala. But even if Duke fails to take Pierce's place as emissary to the Old World, American far-right Web sites commonly post links to extremist Web sites and news from Europe.[2]

The news is plentiful. In Austria, the country's two far-right parties together won 29 percent of the vote in national parliamentary elections last year. One of the parties had been founded by Jörg Haider, who died in a car crash shortly after the vote. Haider made his brand of politics a major force by combining salesmanship, xenophobic opposition to immigration and appeals to the Nazi heritage of Adolf Hitler's country of birth.

Haider had been forced to quit as a provincial governor in 1991 (he was reelected in 1999) after praising Hitler's "orderly employment program." And in 1995 he praised Waffen SS veterans as "decent men of character who remained faithful to their ideals."[3]

Indicators of the growing strength of extremism extend into Germany and Britain as well as parts of the former Soviet bloc. In Russia, where ultranationalist groups, including neo-Nazis, are part of the political landscape, there were at least 85 systematic killings of migrant workers from Central Asia, as well as others seen as ethnically non-Slavic, in 2008, according to the Sova Center, a Moscow-based hate crime-monitoring group. The victims included a migrant worker from Tajikistan who was beheaded. Human-rights advocates who denounce these killings have been threatened with death themselves.[4]

Violence isn't limited to Russia. In late 2008, the police chief of Passau, a Bavarian town with a strong neo-Nazi presence, was stabbed following his 2008 order to open the grave of a former Nazi who had been buried with an illegal Swastika flag.[5]

The attack took place against a backdrop of increasing violence by German neo-Nazi organizations. A German newspaper reported that violent crimes originating in the extremist right increased by 15 percent during the first 10 months of 2008. And a government research institute reported that a greater segment of male teenagers — 5 percent — were

the falling grain prices and land values that brought many farmers to ruin.

One Posse tactic was to flood the federal court system with amateur lawsuits to cancel farmers' loan obligations, on the grounds that the loans were illegal. When authorities enforced foreclosure orders, trouble sometimes erupted.

In 1983, Gordon Kahl, a Christian Identity Posse activist who had served a prison term for tax evasion, killed two federal marshals following a meeting to recruit members in North Dakota. Kahl fled and was killed three months later in a gunfight with federal agents in Arkansas. Kahl became a martyr in extremist circles.

An almost identical episode took place the next year near Cairo, Neb., when a Posse sympathizer, Arthur Kirk, was killed in a shootout with state police officers serving foreclosure papers. Before the shooting

involved in neo-Nazi groups than in mainstream politics in 2007-2008. In formerly communist-ruled eastern Germany, nearly 10 percent of youths participated in far-right groups.[6]

Throughout Western Europe, the enormous growth of immigrant populations, especially from Muslim countries, has provided the biggest boost to right-wing parties — from traditional conservative groups to neo-Nazis — over the past two decades.

However, the European far right's growth isn't uniform. In France, Jean-Marie Le Pen, an apologist for Nazism who was one of the pioneers of the post-World War II extreme right, saw his National Front party win only 4.3 percent of the vote in parliamentary elections in 2007.[7] Analysts said that President Nicolas Sarkozy effectively co-opted Le Pen's anti-immigration politics, though without the ethnic and religious extremism. In 2002, Le Pen had finished second in the first round of the presidential race.[8]

Le Pen's counterparts across the English Channel are showing more success. The British National Party (BNP) is seen by some British politicians as likely to win the most votes in an election in June to choose European Parliament representatives. BNP leaders portray their party as defending the country against non-white immigrants. Pro-immigrant policies "have made white Britons second-class citizens," the party says.[9]

Meanwhile, the BNP is trying to play down its historic anti-Semitism. Party leader Nick Griffin wrote in 2007 that taking an "Islamophobic" stance "is going to produce on average much better media coverage than . . . banging on about 'Jewish power.'"[10]

That purely tactical shift notwithstanding, others in the European political world argue that old-school anti-Semitism is flourishing — on the left as well as the right — often disguised as opposition to Israeli policies.

"The extravagant rhetoric of the demagogic left and right is gaining ground, and the most obvious manifestation is the return of anti-Semitism as an organizing ideology," Dennis MacShane, a Labor Party member of Parliament, wrote in late 2008. "As jobs are lost and welfare becomes meaner and leaner, the politics of blaming the outsider can only grow."[11]

---

[1] Quoted in Kate Connolly, "Haider is our Lady Di," *The Guardian*, Oct. 18, 2008, p. A29. For background, see Sarah Glazer, "Anti-Semitism in Europe," *CQ Global Researcher*, June 2008, pp. 149-181.

[2] For example, see "Stormfront forum, international," www.stormfront.org/forum/forumdisplay.php?f=18; Kinism.net — Occidental Christianity, http://kinism.net/; The French Connection, http://iamthewitness.com/; League of American Patriots, http://leagueap.org/wordpress/?page_id=17.

[3] Quoted in Matt Schudel, "Jörg Haider; Politician Made Far-Right Party a Force in Austria," *The Washington Post*, Oct. 12, 2008, p. C8.

[4] Michael Schwirtz, "Migrant Worker Decapitated in Russia," *The New York Times*, Dec. 13, 2008; Luke Harding, "Putin's worst nightmare: Their mission is to cleanse Russia of its ethnic 'occupiers,'" *The Observer* magazine (U.K.), Feb. 8, 2009, p. 32; "Neo-Nazis threaten to murder journalists in Russia," Committee to Protect Journalists, Feb. 11, 2009, http://cpj.org/2009/02/neo-nazis-threaten-to-murder-journalists-in-russia.php.

[5] Nicholas Kulish, "Ancient City's Nazi Past Seeps Out After Stabbing," *The New York Times*, Feb. 12, 2009, p. A18; "Police Chief Long Reviled by NPD Leadership," *Spiegel Online International*, Dec. 19, 2008, www.spiegel.de/international/germany/0,1518,597645,00.html.

[6] *Ibid.*; and "German teens drawn to neo-Nazi groups — study," Reuters, March 17, 2009, http://in.reuters.com/article/worldNews/idINIndia-38554620090317.

[7] In 2008, Le Pen was fined 10,000 Euros for having called the Nazi occupation of France "not especially inhumane, even if there were a number of blunders." Quoted in "Le Pen fined over war comments," *The Irish Times* (Reuters), Feb. 9, 2008, p. A10.

[8] Adam Sage, "Hard-up National Front sells office to immigrants," *The Times* (London), Aug. 13, 2008, p. A37.

[9] "Immigration — time to say ENOUGH!" British National Party, undated, http://bnp.org.uk/policies-2/immigration. Also see Andrew Grice, "The BNP are now a bigger threat than ever," *The Independent* (London), April 10, 2009, p. A12.

[10] Quoted in Matthew Taylor, "BNP seeks to bury antisemitism and gain Jewish votes in Islamophobic campaign," *The Guardian* (London), April 10, 2008, p. A17.

[11] Denis MacShane, "Europe's Jewish Problem," *Newsweek*, International Edition, Dec. 15, 2008, p. 0.

---

started, Kirk denounced Jews, bankers and the Israeli intelligence agency, Mossad, to officers trying to get him to surrender.[43]

Ideology aside, some farmers who accepted help from the Posse were trying to survive financial crisis. Another group formed in the 1980s dedicated itself purely to violence. The Order (its name borrowed from *The Turner Diaries*) vowed to strike the "Zionist Occupation Government" in defense of "White America." Robert Mathews founded the small group with eight other men in the early 1980s. By 1983, The Order had begun committing armed robberies to raise money. In 1984, the group assassinated a Denver radio talk-show host, Alan Berg, who was Jewish, and had argued with racists on the air. Later that same year, the group robbed an armored car of $3.6 million.

Mathews died in a shootout with federal agents on Whidbey Island, near Seattle, in December 1984.

In 1985, 23 surviving members of the group went to trial or pleaded guilty to racketeering charges, with most receiving sentences of 40 to 100 years. David Lane later was sentenced to 150 years in a separate trial for participating in Berg's murder.[44]

Federal prosecutors in Fort Smith, Ark., failed, however to convict Lane and 13 other extremists of sedition in 1988. They'd been charged with plotting to overthrow the government and set up a separate white nation in the Pacific Northwest.[45]

That same year, in that very region, an upsurge of anti-minority violence by skinheads claimed the life of Ethiopian immigrant Mulugeta Seraw, who was bludgeoned to death with a baseball bat by the East Side White Pride gang. Three years later, Tom Metzger, an infamous San Diego extremist, was found responsible for the death, along with others, on the grounds that his White Aryan Resistance group had incited the group who killed Seraw. The verdict, in a civil suit brought by the SPLC, required Metzger and his codefendants to pay $12.5 million to Seraw's family.[46]

Explosion and Aftermath

The violence that marked the 1980s intensified in the '90s, sparked by the botched 1992 arrest of survivalist and Christian Identity adherent Randy Weaver for failing to appear in court on a gun-law charge. (He'd been given the wrong court date.) Weaver had holed up with his family in remote Ruby Ridge, in northern Idaho, which had become a center for the extreme right and was home to Christian Identity leader Richard Butler.[47]

When federal marshals attempted to arrest Weaver, who had not been involved in previous violence, a gunfight broke out in which Weaver's son and a marshal were killed; later, during a siege of the family's cabin, an FBI sniper killed Weaver's wife. Weaver surrendered and was sentenced to 18 months in prison.[48]

FBI handling of the case was widely considered a fiasco, and worse. But on the far right, a more ominous view prevailed: Ruby Ridge seemed to validate conspiracist fears of government violence against gun owners and opponents of the "New World Order" — far-right code for U.N.-controlled global government.

Months after Ruby Ridge, Christian Identity preacher Peter Peters organized a meeting of about 150 extremists at Estes Park, Colo. In a keynote speech, Louis Beam, a former leader of the Texas Klan and one of those acquitted in the Arkansas sedition case, outlined a strategy of "leaderless resistance" — formation of small cells of committed activists without central direction. A Vietnam veteran, Beam also spoke of the need for "camouflage" — the ability to blend in the public's eye the more committed groups of resistance "with mainstream 'kosher' associations that are generally seen as harmless."[49]

Similarly, others at the meeting advocated uniting with less extreme groups to form a broad anti-government movement.[50]

Meanwhile, a related development had just shocked the mainstream political establishment. David Duke, a former Klan leader who hadn't renounced his anti-black or anti-Jewish views, won the 1991 Republican primary for Louisiana governor. (He went on to lose the general election.)[51]

Following the Estes Park conclave, "militias" sprang up around the country, especially in the rural Midwest and West. Ideas animating the movement included survivalism, gun-rights defense and — among many members, but not all — far-right conspiracy theories. Among those who passed through militia circles was a U.S. Army veteran of the 1990-1991 Persian Gulf War, Timothy McVeigh.

But before McVeigh's name hit the headlines, a series of events near Waco, Texas, would seize national attention and electrify the far right. Members of the Branch Davidian religious cult, led by a fiery preacher named David Koresh, fired on ATF agents attempting to search for guns and ammunition believed to be stored at the Davidians' compound; four agents were killed. On April 19, 1993, after a 51-day siege, FBI agents moved on the compound with tanks. In the conflagration that resulted, Koresh and about 80 other Davidians died, including many children.

A widespread suspicion that FBI teargas canisters started the fire became a certainty on the far right. In those circles, Waco stood as evidence of government ruthlessness. Koresh, who had followed the Weaver case closely, probably wouldn't have been surprised. "Koresh spoke to me frequently on the phone about Ruby Ridge," says Special Agent Cavanaugh of the ATF, who negotiated with the Branch Davidian leader during the siege. Koresh and his top aide "were well-versed in everything that happened there and were spitting out 'New World Order' crackpot conspiracy theories."

In 2000, an outside counsel to the Justice Department concluded that the canisters hadn't started the fire but that Davidians themselves ignited it.[52]

But by then, April 19 had become notorious for another reason. On April 19, 1995, McVeigh detonated a bomb in a rented truck he parked in front of the Alfred P. Murrah Federal Building in Oklahoma City, killing 168 people, including 19 children. Arrested hours later after a traffic stop, McVeigh was later often described as a lone wolf. But, among other activities, he had sold *The Turner Diaries* at gun shows, which were popular with militia members and with extremists in general.

"McVeigh was not a lone extremist; instead, he was trained to make himself look like a lone extremist," wrote former FBI agent German. "It's a right-wing terrorism technique that comes complete with written instruction manuals."[53]

The bombing — for which McVeigh was executed in 2001 — made *Turner Diaries* author Pierce and his National Alliance notorious. But the bombing also saw a steep decline in militia membership, as those without a high level of commitment to extremist politics dropped away.

More blows followed. Pierce died of cancer in 2002. Two years later Butler died; earlier he had lost his Idaho compound after losing a civil lawsuit filed by the Southern Poverty Law Center.[54]

Then, in 2005, Matthew Hale, 33, considered an up-and-coming extremist leader as head of the World Church of the Creator, was sentenced to 40 years in federal prison for conspiring to kill a federal judge. Since his imprisonment, extremist-watchers say, no charismatic leader has emerged from the extremist world.

CURRENT SITUATION

Hate in April

Hitler was born in April, which marks the beginning of the public rally season for right-wing extremists, and for opponents who mount counterdemonstrations.[55]

This year promises to be a busy one for haters. In April alone, 32 conferences, celebrations, militia training sessions and other events were planned by neo-Nazi, Klan, Christian Identity and related organizations in 22 states, according to the Anti-Defamation League; dozens more events are scheduled into October.[56]

The list includes Hitler birthday commemorations in Illinois and North Carolina and a march by robed Klan members in Pulaski, Tenn., where Confederate veterans founded the Klan.

Counterdemonstrators showed for an NSM rally of about 70 members the day before at the Gateway Arch in St. Louis, Mo. No one was arrested, but the two groups yelled at each other and traded "Heil Hitler" salutes and raised-middle-finger retorts. A second group of counter-demonstrators organized by the ADL held a "rally for respect" at a nearby site.[57]

Commenting on the NSM rally, Lewis Reed, president of the St. Louis Board of Aldermen, said, "It's sad that there are still people today, in 2009, that only want to divide the races and breed hate."[58]

Yet neo-Nazi rallies, at least in major metropolitan areas, typically don't draw big crowds of extremists. In Skokie, Ill., a Chicago suburb with a large Jewish population — including Holocaust survivors — the opening of a state holocaust museum in April drew a neo-Nazi demonstration — of seven people. Twelve thousand people attended the opening ceremony, where former President Bill Clinton spoke.[59]

This year's rally season began with a snag. "East Coast White Unity" and "Volksfront" ("Peoples' Front" in German) had planned to meet in Boston over the April 11 weekend. But after the Boston Anti-Racist Coalition told the Veterans of Foreign Wars (VFW) about the nature of the "Patriot's Day" rally, the VFW withdrew permission to use their hall. Instead, the event was held at an American Legion Hall in Loudon, N.H.[60]

"These racist speakers, bands and their supporters will always have to walk on egg shells and face the very real prospect of their events being exposed to the general public, wherever and whenever they rear their ugly heads," the coalition said in a post on an anarchist Web site.[61]

But Roper of White Revolution replied, "Because a venue, or two, or three, has cancelled on us due to the efforts of anti-white, communist and Jewish activists, the event has not been cancelled and will go on," he said. "We plan for such eventualities in depth."[62]

For its part, One People's Project, an anti-supremacist organization, says it infiltrates neo-Nazi and Klan groups to find out about planned events in time to organize

"Fascism" Label Comes in Handy for Critics

But respected writers say it's a legitimate — if unlikely — concern.

Accompanying today's worries about an extremist resurgence are fears that the United States could, if economic conditions worsen, embrace fascism — the totalitarian ideology that modern hate groups champion.

But the concern focuses on the federal government itself, not fringe, neo-Nazi organizations. Indeed, some of President Barack Obama's foes are calling him a fascist, the same label some had applied to President George W. Bush.

The labeling would seem to show once again that "fascist" is one of the most loosely applied — and handy — terms in the political lexicon. Nevertheless, fascism isn't foreign to the United States, even though the word comes from 1920s Italy. Italian dictator Benito Mussolini coined "fascismo" to name the violence-glorifying, socialist-hating and ultranationalist movement he formed after World War I, appropriating a term then used for militant political groups of all stripes.[1]

Notwithstanding those Italian roots, Robert Paxton, one of the leading historians of the European far right, wrote that the first fascist group in history may have been the Ku Klux Klan. "By adopting a uniform . . . as well as by their techniques of intimidation and their conviction that violence was justified in the cause of their group's destiny," wrote Paxton, a Virginia native, "the first version of the Klan in the defeated American South was arguably a remarkable preview of the way fascist movements were to function in interwar Europe."[2]

But Paxton, an emeritus professor of social science at Columbia University, dismisses the attempt to label Obama fascist as a desperation move. "When there's a popular figure and you can't get a grip on opposing him, you call him a fascist," he says. "As opposed to Hitler and Mussolini in uniform, shrieking into microphones and juicing up the nationalism of crowds, Obama is a calm, reasonable person whose basic drives have all been toward bolstering democracy and the rule of law."

Obama's extreme critics insist otherwise. Obama heads a "Gestapo government," conservative blogger David Limbaugh (brother of radio commentator Rush Limbaugh) told a radio interviewer. And *The American Spectator*, a conservative magazine, likened Obama's economic policies to those of Mussolini.[3]

The author of the *Spectator* piece, senior editor Quinn Hillyer, added that he wouldn't go so far as to compare Obama's administration to that of Adolf Hitler, whose version of fascism turned out far deadlier than the Italian original. Still, he wrote, "The comparison of today's situation to that of Italian fascism is no mere scare tactic but a serious concern."[4]

In calling Obama a fascist, critics may simply be hoping for better results than they got when they tried pinning the "socialist" label on him during and after the 2008 presidential campaign. "We've so overused the word 'socialism' that it no longer has the negative connotation it had 20 years ago, or even 10 years ago," Sal Anuzis, former chairman of the Michigan Republican Party, told *The New York Times*. "Fascism — everybody still thinks that's a bad thing."[5]

To be sure, only a small minority accepts "fascist" as a compliment. But aiming it at a politician after first denouncing him as a leftist seems an odd tactic, given fascists' historic hatred of socialists.[6]

But that seemed to bother Obama's foes as little as the fact that they were borrowing from the vocabulary that some critics of the Bush administration used in 2001-2008.

The liberal group MoveOn.org, for instance, created an ad in 2004 that tried to connect Bush to Hitler, intoning: "A nation warped by lies. Lies fuel fear. Fear fuels aggression. Invasion. Occupation. What were war crimes in 1945 is foreign policy in 2003."[7]

Liberal author Naomi Wolf made a similar case in her book *The End of America*, published toward the end of the Bush administration.[8]

---

countermobilizations. "We can't keep on allowing groups like the Klan, Aryan Nations, National Alliance, National Vanguard and the National Socialist Movement to hold society at-large hostage," Daryle Lamont Jenkins of One People's Project said.[63]

On April 19, 2008, 30 to 40 members of the National Socialist Movement (NSM) rallied in Washington for an anti-immigration march from the National Mall to the U.S. Capitol. They were greeted by raucous counterdemonstrators, five of whom were arrested for allegedly assaulting police officers with pepper spray and a pole.[64]

White supremacist gatherings don't tend to be large affairs. Roper told a reporter by phone from the New Hampshire event that 200 people were participating,

"The Nazis rose to power in a living, if battered, democracy," Wolf wrote. "Dictators can rise in a weakened democracy even with a minority of popular support."[9]

Drawing in part from Paxton's most recent book on fascism, Wolf argued that erosions of civil liberties under the Bush administration paralleled events in Italy and Germany as Mussolini and Hitler moved toward totalitarian rule.

But these arguments leave out the widespread loss of faith in democracy, and the state of near-civil war that served as the backdrop to the rise of fascism in Italy and Germany, Paxton says.

By contrast, Americans opposed to Bush expressed their discontent within the system, by voting in Obama, Paxton notes. And the political climate even before that, when Wolf was writing, didn't begin to approach the Italian and German precedents. "In the collection of preconditions, you need something worse," he says. "A lost war, big-time national humiliation — we might get there, but we're not quite there yet — and a sense that our existing way of doing politics isn't working. And then power moving to the streets, with paramilitary organizations. I don't see any of that."

Paxton does agree that the detention and intelligence-gathering policies adopted after the Sept. 11, 2001, terrorist attacks could be compared with early moves by

Followers of the neo-Nazi NPD party stand defiantly near a "Berlin against Nazis" poster during a demonstration in Berlin on May 1, 2009. Anti-immigration neo-Nazis and skinheads often clash with anti-fascists on May Day in Germany.

Hitler upon winning election as chancellor in 1933. "You can draw some parallels — with care," he says. "The focus should be on steps away from the rule of law."

Still, Paxton discourages complacency. "In three years, if we're not out of this mess, we could see something that would call itself the patriotic party or the minutemen, a symbol that has a nice nationalistic resonance," he says. "It would sweep up all the discontented from the left and the right; it would be light on ideology. The immigration issue would be a very plausible gathering point for some sort of movement like this."

---

[1] Robert O. Paxton, *The Anatomy of Fascism* (2004), pp. 4-5.

[2] *Ibid.*, p. 49.

[3] Quinn Hillyer, "Il Duce, Redux?" *The American Spectator*, April 2, 2009, http://spectator.org/archives/2009/04/02/il-duce-redux. Limbaugh quoted in Carla Marinucci and Joe Garofoli, "Fascist? Socialist? Attacks on Obama take a shrill tone," *San Francisco Chronicle*, April 9, 2009, p. A1.

[4] Hillyer, *op. cit.*

[5] Quoted in John Harwood, "But Can Obama Make the Trains Run on Time?" *The New York Times*, April 20, 2009, www.nytimes.com/2009/04/20/us/politics/20caucus.html?scp=1&sq=fascism&st=cse.

[6] Paxton, *op. cit.*, pp. 60-67.

[7] Marinucci and Garofoli, *op. cit.*

[8] Naomi Wolf, *The End of America: Letters of Warning to a Young Patriot, A Citizen's Call to Action* (2007).

[9] *Ibid.*, pp. 39-40.

---

making it one of the bigger events of its type. But no independent confirmation was available.

In 2005, Roper organized a protest demonstration outside an event in Boston commemorating the 60th anniversary of the liberation of Nazi death camps. Police and counterprotesters far outnumbered Roper and his dozen or so demonstrators.[65]

However, on occasion, supremacists' crowds have been bigger, and violence has erupted. In 2002, about 60 supporters of the now-imprisoned Matthew Hale's World Church of the Creator gathered in York, Pa., where a former mayor and eight others had been charged in the 1969 death of a black woman during a racially charged riot. Several hundred counterprotesters fought with Hale's supporters in the city streets, as police tried to separate the groups. Twenty-five people were arrested.[66]

However, in April of that year, only about 30 to 40 neo-Nazis showed up in York for a Hitler's birthday celebration.[67]

Free Speech, Hate Speech

Some conservatives are attacking the Department of Homeland Security (DHS) examination of far-right extremism as a barely disguised attack on political foes of the Obama administration.

"One of the most embarrassingly shoddy pieces of propaganda I'd ever read out of DHS," thundered conservative blogger Michelle Malkin. Others in the conservative blogosphere shared her view that the report tried to tie conservatives to extremists.[68] Homeland Security Secretary Janet Napolitano later responded that the agency is on "the lookout for criminal and terrorist activity but we do not — nor will we ever — monitor ideology or political beliefs."[69]

The report noted that extremists are especially interested in recruiting veterans, an observation that triggered angry criticism from some veterans' organizations (see below). In essence the 14-page assessment holds that economic turmoil, the election of a black president and a growing number of veterans — whom right-wing extremists have a documented interest in recruiting — are creating a climate in which far-right extremism could flourish again. Specifically, the report said the DHS "assesses that right-wing extremist groups' frustration over a perceived lack of government action on illegal immigration has the potential to incite individuals or small groups toward violence." But any such violence would likely be "isolated" and "small-scale."[70]

Though critics later said the DHS failed to distinguish between extremists and mainstream political advocates, the report did try to draw that line. Debates on gun rights and other constitutional issues are often intense — but perfectly legal, the report said. "Violent extremists," it added, "may attempt to co-opt the debate and use the controversy as a radicalization tool."[71]

But Berlet of Political Research Associates argues that the report itself crosses into the potentially unconstitutional territory of monitoring ideological trends.

"The government should not be in the business of undermining radical ideas," he says. "As citizens we have a responsibility to challenge rhetoric that demonizes and scapegoats, but I don't think the First Amendment allows the government to be in that battle."

Despite attacks from the left as well as right, some commentators defended the report against its critics. "This DHS assessment was begun more than a year ago, before Barack Obama was even nominated," blogger Charles Johnson — a political independent who had been popular with conservative critics of Islam — wrote on his influential "Little Green Footballs" site. "It was not done at the behest of the Obama administration. . . . The DHS report is not intended to target anyone but the most extreme elements of the far right, and it's depressing to see so many bloggers jumping to totally unwarranted conclusions."[72]

Reaction to the document may have been especially intense because it followed closely on an uproar that greeted disclosure of a report on the "Modern Militia Movement" in Missouri. It was produced by a "fusion center," one of 70 around the country that were set up by law enforcement agencies after Sept. 11 to ensure that intelligence is shared between federal, state and local officers. The report mostly summarized information on extremist activities in the 1990s and outlined some ideas said to be circulating now on the far right.[73]

But the report lumped together extremists and mainstream political activists with no violent inclinations. "Militia members most commonly associate with third-party political groups," the report said, going on to name supporters of 2008 libertarian presidential candidate Bob Barr, Constitution Party candidate Chuck Baldwin and Rep. Ron Paul, R-Texas, who ran for the Republican Party presidential nomination.[74]

"This smacks of totalitarian regimes of days gone by," said Baldwin, one of many to react furiously to the document.[75]

Within weeks, the Missouri State Highway Patrol had apologized to the three politicians and replaced the head of the fusion center.[76]

Not all critics came from the right. "This is part of a national trend where intelligence reports are turning attention away from people who are actually doing bad things to people who are thinking thoughts that the government, for whatever reason, doesn't like," former FBI agent German told The Associated Press.[77]

The ACLU, where German is now a policy counselor, noted that the North Central Texas Fusion System had produced a report in February that tied former Rep. Cynthia McKinney and former U.S. Attorney General Ramsey Clark to "far left groups" that allegedly sympathize with the Iranian-backed Hezbollah militia of Lebanon and other armed movements in the Middle East.[78]

Fusion centers, German said, are an "equal opportunity infringer" on civil rights of citizens on the right and the left.[79]

Indeed, DHS says that it produced a report earlier this year on left-wing extremists. That report soon leaked out as well. The document forecast a rise in cyber-attacks aimed at businesses, especially those deemed to be violators of animal rights.[80]

Extremism-watchers, for their part, greeted the DHS report as an echo of their own conclusions. "This Homeland Security report reinforces our view that the current political and economic climate in the United States is creating the right conditions for a rise in extremist activity," said Potok of the SPLC.[81]

But one of the center's most ferocious left-wing critics, writer Alexander Cockburn, ridiculed that reasoning, accusing the center of "fingering militiamen in a potato field in Idaho" instead of "attacking the roots of Southern poverty, and the system that sustains that poverty as expressed in the endless prisons and death rows across the South, disproportionately crammed with blacks and Hispanics."[82]

Fights are also continuing over broadcasters' commentaries. In Boston, radio station WTKK-FM suspended right-wing radio talk-show host Jay Severin after he responded to the influenza outbreak with comments including: "So now, in addition to venereal disease and the other leading exports of Mexico — women with mustaches and VD — now we have swine flu." Mexicans, he said, are "the world's lowest of primitives."[83]

Franklin Soults, a spokesman for Massachusetts Immigrant and Refugee Advocacy Coalition, called Severin's language "dehumanizing."

Severin himself referred questions to his lawyer, George Tobia, who told the *Boston Globe* that he expected the broadcaster to be back on the air soon. "But I don't know when."[84]

Recruiting Veterans

Discharged from the U.S. Marine Corps after being arrested for allegedly taking part in armed robberies at two hotels in Jacksonville, N.C., a former lance corporal now faces prosecution for allegedly threatening President Obama's life.

Kody Brittingham, 20, who served in the 2nd Tank Battalion, 2nd Marine Division, was indicted in February for the alleged threat by a federal grand jury in Raleigh, N.C. An unnamed federal law enforcement official told the Jacksonville (N.C.) *Daily News* that the charge followed discovery of a journal in Brittingham's barracks at Camp Lejeune in which he laid out a plan to kill Obama, who at that point hadn't yet been inaugurated. Investigators reportedly also found white-supremacist literature among Brittingham's possessions.[85]

How plausible the alleged assassination plans were is not clear. But the arrest did reawaken concerns about white-supremacist and neo-Nazi recruitment of men with military training, especially those with combat experience (Brittingham, however, had never served overseas).

Those concerns aren't limited to extremism-watchers from advocacy organizations. An FBI report last year counted 203 individuals with "confirmed or claimed" military experience who had been spotted in extremist groups since the Sept. 11 attacks, which effectively marked the beginning of a period in which hundreds of thousands of military personnel began acquiring battlefield experience.[86]

Those 203 individuals represent a minuscule fraction of the country's 23.8 million veterans or 1.4 million active-duty personnel, the report acknowledged.[87]

The recent DHS assessment discussed extremist groups' interest in recruiting veterans, only to prompt outraged reaction from some veterans' organizations and some politicians. "To characterize men and women returning home after defending our country as potential terrorists is offensive and unacceptable," House Republican leader John Boehner of Ohio said in a press release. The Department of Homeland Security owes our veterans an apology."[88]

In discussing extremists' interest in veterans, the FBI said that neo-Nazis were not discouraged by the small number of vets who might be responsive to recruiting pitches.

"The prestige which the extremist movement bestows upon members with military experience grants them the potential for influence beyond their numbers," said the report, which is marked "unclassified/for official use only/ law enforcement sensitive." The report, now available

AT ISSUE

Is anti-immigration rhetoric provoking hate crimes against Latinos?

YES
Mark Potok
Director, Intelligence Project, Southern Poverty Law Center

Written for *CQ Researcher*, April 2009

Across the board, nativist organizations in America have angrily denounced those who suggest that demonizing rhetoric leads to hate violence. One of them even recently issued a press release criticizing the "outrageous behavior" of groups like the Southern Poverty Law Center that propose such a link and "provide no proof whatsoever."

Nativist organizations take the remarkable position that hate speech directed against Latino immigrants has no relationship at all to hate crime — not even the utterly false allegations that Latinos are secretly planning to hand the American Southwest over to Mexico, are far more criminal than others, are bringing dread diseases to the United States, and so on.

In addition to defying common sense, that head-in-the-sand approach completely ignores the statements that are typically made by hate criminals during their attacks.

Take the case of Marcelo Lucero, who was allegedly murdered by a gang of white teenagers in the Long Island town of Patchogue, N.Y., last November. Prosecutors say the suspects told detectives they regularly went "beaner jumping" — beating up Latinos — and that they used racial epithets during the attack. "Let's go find some Mexicans to [expletive] up," one said beforehand, according to *Newsday*.

Nativist groups use the fact that we don't know precisely where the teens' fury comes from to deny it was related to nativist demonization. But just because it's not possible to pinpoint the exact source of their racial anger — rhetoric from nativist groups, their parents, local anti-immigrant politicians, or pundits — does not mean it magically popped into the assailants' minds.

There is also hard evidence to back up the link between demonization and violence. According to FBI statistics, anti-Latino hate crimes went up 40 percent between 2003 and 2007 — the very same period that saw a remarkable proliferation of nativist rhetoric.

Experts agree that there is a link. "Racist rhetoric and dehumanizing images inspire violence perpetrated against innocent human beings," says Jack Levin, a nationally known hate crime expert at Northeastern University. "It's not just the most recent numbers. It's the trend over a number of years that lends credibility to the notion that we're seeing a very real and possibly dramatic rise in anti-Latino hate incidents."

Ignoring the role that demonization plays in such violence is a surefire way to generate more of it. Marcelo Lucero's murder is only the latest in a sad list of violent incidents inspired by ugly rhetoric that will certainly grow longer.

NO
Marcus Epstein
Executive Director, The American Cause

Written for *CQ Researcher*, April 2009

Last year, Barack Obama accused broadcasters Lou Dobbs and Rush Limbaugh of "feeding a kind of xenophobia." He added that their broadcasts were a "reason why hate crimes against Hispanic people doubled last year."

Obama's facts and logic are plain wrong. The FBI found only 745 anti-Latino hate crimes nationwide in 2007, down from 770 in 2006. In fact anti-Hispanic hate crimes per capita dropped 18 percent over the last decade.

Most of these hate crimes were for minor offenses, such as graffiti or name-calling, with only 145 aggravated assaults, two murders and no rapes in 2007. To put this in perspective, former Hudson Institute economist Ed Rubenstein estimates illegal aliens murder at least 949 people a year.

There is also no evidence that hate crimes are motivated by the immigration-control movement. Those who claim there's a connection cannot point to a single, significant commentator or politician who has advocated violence against Latinos. Nor can they find a single hate crime committed by their followers.

Although whites are the vast majority of listeners of conservative talk radio and television, they committed only 52 percent of hate crimes against Latinos — a percentage well below their proportion of 66 percent of the population. Moreover, Los Angeles County classified 42 percent of black-on-Hispanic hate crimes as "gang related." This is not to suggest that blacks cannot be racist, but that they are unlikely to be influenced by the purveyors of supposed anti-immigrant rhetoric.

The 2008 murder of José Osvaldo Sucuzhanay in Brooklyn by blacks who targeted him because they mistook him as gay was denounced as a significant anti-Hispanic, anti-immigrant hate crime by all New York politicians and by *The New York Times*. Even when they were at large, the race of the killers was rarely mentioned.

Groups like the Southern Poverty Law Center that perpetuate misconceptions about anti-Latino hate crimes make no secret of their goals. They want supporters of immigration control silenced because, in the words of La Raza president Janet Murguía, "We have to draw the line on freedom of speech, when freedom of speech becomes hate speech."

These organizations run relentless smear campaigns accusing virtually all opponents of illegal immigration — no matter how nuanced or tempered — of hate speech that must not be allowed on the airwaves, in print, or in front of Congress.

Before we abandon our core democratic principles of free speech and open debate in the name of stopping hate crimes, we should at least get our facts straight.

online, has circulated among journalists and nongovernmental specialists.[89]

Among a handful of specific cases, the FBI noted that two privates in the elite Army 82nd Airborne Division received six-year prison sentences for attempting to sell body armor and other equipment in 2007 to an undercover agent posing as a white-supremacist movement member. And in 2005, a former Army intelligence analyst who'd been convicted of a firearms violation founded a skinhead group that reportedly advocated training members in firearms, knife-fighting, close-quarters combat and "house sweeps."[90]

The FBI intelligence assessment followed an investigation by the SPLC. In 2006 the center published a detailed report that quoted neo-Nazi vets, a supremacist who had renounced the extremist cause, as well as a Defense Department investigator. Extremists "stretch across all branches of service, they are linking up across the branches once they're inside, and they are hard-core," investigator Scott Barfield told the SPLC. "We've got Aryan Nations graffiti in Baghdad."[91]

Worries about a neo-Nazi presence in the military had surfaced years before U.S. troops were deployed to Iraq and Afghanistan. The trigger was the random murder in 1995 of a black man and woman in Fayetteville, N.C., by two soldiers in the elite Army 82nd Airborne Division, whose home base is nearby Fort Bragg. In the uproar that followed, 22 members of the 82nd — including those arrested for the killing — were found by the Army to have extremist ties.[92]

But far-right efforts to penetrate the Armed Forces apparently continued. The SPLC published excerpts from a 1999 article in the *National Alliance* magazine by an Army Special Forces veteran who urged young supremacists to sign up. "Light infantry is your branch of choice," he wrote, "because the coming race war, and the ethnic cleansing to follow, will be very much an infantryman's war. It will be house-to-house, neighborhood-by-neighborhood, until your town or city is cleared and the alien races are driven into the countryside where they can be hunted down and 'cleansed.' "[93]

Supremacists who enlisted were told to stay undercover: "Do not — I repeat, do not — seek out other skinheads. Do not listen to skinhead 'music.' Do not keep 'racist' or 'White-supremacist tracts' where you live. During your service you will be subjected to a constant barrage of equal opportunity drivel. . . . Keep your mouth shut."[94]

Members of the National Socialist Movement demonstrate on the grounds of the U.S. Capitol on April 19, 2008. Fifteen years earlier, on another April 19, a fire during an FBI siege at the Branch Davidian compound outside Waco, Texas, killed David Koresh and about 80 followers, including many children.

OUTLOOK
Guns in Holsters

The possibility that far-right extremists will emerge from the margins is as uncertain as the course of today's economic crisis, veteran analysts say.

For their part, extremists including Roper of White Revolution harbor no doubt that the medium-term future will see the outbreak of major racial and ethnic violence accompanying the breakup of the United States. "A lot of people might think it's impossible, but if you had gone to those same people in 1980 and told them the Berlin Wall was going to fall and the Soviet Union was going to collapse without a single missile being launched, they would have thought that was impossible too," Roper says.

Others would argue that U.S. society and government have firmer foundations than the Soviet system, which came to power in 1917 and sustained itself first by mass terror and then by mass repression.

In any event, the consensus among monitors of the far right is that extremist intensity hasn't even reached the level of the 1990s — the point at which the extremist movement "goes from red-hot to white-hot," as Pitcavage of the ADL puts it.

A key indicator of the latter stage is the discovery of major conspiracies or actual large-scale attacks, such as the Oklahoma City bombing. "In the 1980s and mid-'90s, a variety of white-supremacist or anti-government extremist groups had huge plots — start a white revolution, break off part of the country, hit military targets," Pitcavage says. "What they shared was an elaborate large-scale conception, often far larger than actual capabilities. If we start seeing some more of these we will know that things are starting to go white-hot again."

The present crisis is too new to suddenly spawn a new wave of high-intensity extremism, Pitcavage adds. "Movements don't start overnight," he says. "It takes a while for people to experience these things and form a reaction to them."

But Barkun at Syracuse University says today's conditions are far more alarming than those of the "white-hot" years. War and global economic crisis alone open the possibility of a new extremism paradigm, he says.

"We're in an economic situation which is so dire and so long-lasting that it will have social and political effects," Barkun says. "Things may develop along entirely novel lines that don't necessarily arise out of pre-existing groups, or that can readily be placed along the right-wing continuum, where the extreme right and the extreme left come together."

He adds that he hasn't seen any evidence of this taking place. However, left-right extremes have met before, at least elsewhere. Mussolini's early fascist movement took in former socialists like him. The "socialist" in Germany's National Socialist (Nazi) Party did express some — short-lived — opposition to capitalism. Attempts by some European far-rightists to co-opt left-wing anarchists represent an attempt to revive that tradition.

Also up in the air, to Barkun and others, is whether America's tradition of racial conflict will reassert itself in a country whose demography has been transformed from the old, white majority-black minority pattern.

One effect of the growing Latino political presence likely will be an accommodation by the Republican Party, where most support for tougher immigration control has centered, says Potok of the Southern Poverty Law Center. The result would be that white, non-Hispanic voters alienated by demographic change fall away from the conventional political system. "When that happens, a lot of these people would just go home, but some percentage of them would go into that extremist world," he speculates. "For them, there's no way out of a multiracial system. So it's 'Let's go off and start our own country.'"

On the organizational side, Potok theorizes, the absence of major, controlling figures, such as Pierce of the National Alliance and Butler of Aryan Nations, may be a danger sign. "I understand that a lot of really scary people, like The Order, came out of the Alliance," he says, adding that some extremist leaders have a history of depicting a need for violence only at some indefinite point in the future. "Leaders ultimately have the effect of holding people back: 'We're going to kill the Jews, but keep your guns in your holsters.'"

NOTES

1. Quoted in Jonathan D. Silver, "911 Operator Failed to Warn About Weapons," *Pittsburgh Post-Gazette*, April 7, 2009, p. A1. Unless otherwise indicated, all details of this event are drawn from *Post-Gazette* articles published April 5-8, 2009.

2. Quoted in Michael A. Fucco, "Deadly Ambush Claims the Lives of 3 City Police Officers," *Pittsburgh Post-Gazette*, April 5, 2009, p. A1.

3. Quoted in Dennis B. Roddy, "On Web: Racism, Anti-Semitism, Warnings," *Pittsburgh Post-Gazette*, April 7, 2009, p. A1.

4. "The Employment Situation: March 2009," U.S. Bureau of Labor Statistics, April 3, 2009, www.bls.gov/news.release/empsit.nr0.htm; Jeffrey Passel and D'Vera Cohn, "Trends in Unauthorized Immigration," Pew Hispanic Center, Oct. 2, 2008, http://pewhispanic.org/reports/report.php?ReportID=94. *CQ Researcher* has published reports on immigration going back to the early 1920s. Three of the most recent are: Reed Karaim, "America's Border Fence," Sept. 19, 2008, pp. 745-768; Alan Greenblatt, "Immigration Debate," Feb. 1, 2008, pp. 97-120; and Peter Katel, "Real ID," May 4, 2007, pp. 385-408.

5. "Rightwing Extremism: Current Economic and Political Climate Fueling Resurgence in Radicalization and Recruitment," Homeland Security Department, April 7, 2009, http://images.logicsix.com/DHS_RWE.pdf.

6. "Why Obama is Good for Our Movement," National Socialist Movement, undated, www.nsm88.org/activities/why obama is good for our movement

.html. See also Alan Greenblatt, "Race in America," *CQ Researcher*, July 11, 2003, pp. 593-624.

7. David Holthouse, "The Year in Hate," Intelligence Report, Southern Poverty Law Center, spring 2009, www.splcenter.org/intel/intelreport/article.jsp?aid=1027. For background, see Kenneth Jost, "Hate Crimes," *CQ Researcher*, Jan. 8, 1993, pp. 1-24.

8. Tom Hays, "Feds charge 3 men in election bias attacks," The Associated Press, Jan. 7, 2009; Christine Hauser and Colin Moynihan, "Three Are Charged in Attacks on Election Night," *The New York Times*, Jan. 8, 2009, p. A25.

9. Manny Fernandez and Javier C. Hernandez, "Binghamton Victims Shared a Dream of Living Better Lives," *The New York Times*, April 5, 2009, www.nytimes.com/2009/04/06/nyregion/06victims.html?scp=7&sq=Jiverly Binghamton&st=cse; Al Baker and Liz Robbins, "Police Had Few Contacts With Killer," *The New York Times*, April 7, 2009.

10. Quoted in Jessica Fargen, "Sicko Kill Plot Emerges," *Boston Herald*, Jan. 23, 2009, p. 5; Milton J. Valencia, "Father of attacked Brockton sisters calls for justice," *Boston Herald*, Jan. 24, 2009, p. B3.

11. Quoted in Melissa Nelson, "FL man acted oddly before Chilean students' deaths," The Associated Press, March 13, 2009.

12. "Hate on Display: A Visual Database of Extremist Symbols, Logos and Tattoos," ADL, undated, www.adl.org/hate_symbols/numbers_14-88.asp. For a Web site filled with praise for Lane see www.freetheorder.org/dlrip.html.

13. Jeffrey Gettleman, "William L. Pierce, 68; Ex-Rocket Scientist Became White Supremacist," *Los Angeles Times*, July 24, 2002, p. B10.

14. Quoted in John Krupa, "Teen in plot lists drinking as his job," *Arkansas Democrat-Gazette*, Oct. 29, 2008; see also Holthouse, *op. cit.*

15. Jared Taylor, "Transition to Black Rule," *American Renaissance*, Nov. 14, 2008, www.amren.com/mtnews/archives/2008/11/transition_to_b.php.

16. Jared Taylor, "Jews and American Renaissance," *American Renaissance*, May 2006, www.amren.com/mtnews/archives/2006/04/jews_and_americ.php.

17. Passel and Cohn, *op. cit.*

18. "Hate Crime Statistics, Victims, 2007," FBI, www.fbi.gov/ucr/hc2007/table_07.htm.

19. *Ibid.*

20. Jim Salter, "Mo. town outraged over killings, illegal immigrant," The Associated Press, March 20, 2009; "Hannibal murder suspect is illegal alien," The Associated Press, March 4, 2009.

21. Edwin S. Rubinstein, "Illegals kill a dozen a day?" *VDare*, Jan. 12, 2007, www.vdare.com/rubenstein/070112_nd.htm.

22. Mark Hugo Lopez and Michael T. Light, "A Rising Share: Hispanics and Federal Crime," Pew Hispanic Center, Feb. 18, 2009, p. 4, http://pewhispanic.org/files/reports/104.pdf.

23. Quoted in Sarah Burge, "Hate Crimes Continue Their Rise in Riverside County," *Press-Enterprise* (Riverside, Calif.), July 20, 2006, p. B1. See also Denes Husty III, "Crime vs. Hispanics up," *The News-Press* (Fort Myers, Fla.) Feb. 11, 2007, p. A1, and Troy Graham, "Hate Crime Statistics Belie Truth," *Daily Press* (Newport News, Va.), Jan. 30, 2000, p. A1.

24. "A Local Prosecutor's Guide For Responding to Hate Crimes," American Prosecutors Research Institute, undated, www.ndaa.org/pdf/hate_crimes.pdf.

25. Dennis B. Roddy, "An Accused Cop Killer's Politics," *Slate*, April 10, 2009, www.slate.com/id/2215826/.

26. Gary Kamiya, "They're coming to take our guns away," *Salon.com*, April 7, 2009, www.salon.com/opinion/kamiya/2009/04/07/richard_poplowski.

27. Quoted in Adam Liptak, "The Nation: Prisons to Mosques; Hate Speech and the American Way," *The New York Times*, Jan. 11, 2004. The Supreme Court decision is *Brandenburg v. Ohio*, 395, U.S. 444 (1969).

28. Quoted in Katherin Clad, "Group cites Saudi 'hate' tracts," *The Washington Times*, Jan. 29, 2005, p. A1.

29. Nonie Darwish, "Muslim Hate," *FrontPageMagazine.com*, March 25, 2009, www.frontpagemag.com/Articles/Read.aspx?GUID=A629F1F3-BBBA-420-D-8C31-D340A577A083.

30. "Glen Beck joins Fox News," Reuters, Oct. 16, 2008, www.reuters.com/article/televisionNews/idUSTRE49G0NW20081017.

31. Eric Boehlert and Jamison Foser," On radio show, Beck read 'ad' for refinery that turns Mexicans into fuel," *County Fair blog*, Media Matters for America, June 29, 2007, (audio clip is posted), http://mediamatters.org/items/200706290010.

32. Ariel Alexovich, "A Call to End Hate Speech," *The New York Times, The Caucus blog*, Feb. 1, 2008, http://thecaucus.blogs.nytimes.com/2008/02/01/a-call-to-end-hate-speech/?scp=1&sq=murguia%20hate%20speech&st=Search; "President and CEO Janet Murguia's Remarks at the Wave of Hope press briefing," National Council of La Raza, Jan. 31, 2008, www.nclr.org/content/viewpoints/detail/50389/.

33. Steve Sailer, "What Obama hasn't figured out yet," *Vdare*, April 27, 2009, http://blog.vdare.com/archives/2009/04/27/what-obama-hasnt-figured-out-yet-better-teachers-means-___/; Patrick Cleburne, "More Indians means more . . .," *Vdare*, April 19, 2009, http://blog.vdare.com/archives/2009/04/19/more-indians-means-more-fill-in-blank/; Cooper Sterling, "Tom Tancredo at American University: Maybe It Is About Race," *Vdare*, March 14, 2009, www.vdare.com/sterling/090314_tancredo.htm.

34. Unless otherwise indicated this subsection draws on Robert O. Paxton, *The Anatomy of Fascism* (2004); William E. Leuchtenburg, *Franklin D. Roosevelt and the New Deal* (1963); and Chip Berlet and Matthew N. Lyons, *Right-Wing Populism in America: Too Close for Comfort* (2000); Daniel Levitas, *The Terrorist Next Door: The Militia Movement and the Radical Right* (2002).

35. See Binjamin Segel, *A Lie and a Libel: The History of the Protocols of the Elders of Zion* (1996). For an article in the *Dearborn Independent* that takes the Protocols as fact, see Henry Ford and the editors of the *Dearborn Independent*, " 'Jewish Protocols' Claim Partial Fulfillment," www.churchoftrueisrael.com/Ford/original/ij12.html.

36. Biographical sketch in "William Dudley Pelley Collection," University of North Carolina at Asheville, D. H. Ramsey Library, http://toto.lib.unca.edu/findingaids/mss/pelley/default_pelley_william_dudley.htm.

37. Unless otherwise indicated, this subsection draws on Levitas, *op. cit.*; and Berlet and Lyons, *op. cit.*

38. Quoted in *ibid.*, p. 180.

39. Quoted in Thomas M. Storke, "How Some Birchers Were Birched," *The New York Times*, Dec. 10, 1961.

40. See Shaila Dewan, "Revisiting '64 Civil Rights Deaths, This Time in a Murder Trial," *The New York Times*, June 12, 2005, p. A26; Manuel Roig-Franzia, "Reopened Civil Rights Cases Evoke Painful Past," *The New York Times*, Jan. 10, 2005, p. A1. For background on the KKK, see the following *Editorial Research Reports*, predecessor to *CQ Researcher*: K. Lee, "Ku Klux Klan," July 10, 1946; W.R. McIntyre, "Spread of Terrorism and Hatemongering," Dec. 3, 1958; H.B. Shaffer, "Secret Societies and Political Action," May 10, 1961; R.L. Worsnop, "Extremist Movements in Race and Politics," March 31, 1965; S. Stencel, "The South: Continuity and Change," March 7, 1980, and M.H. Cooper, "The Growing Danger of Hate Groups," May 12, 1989.

41. Fred P. Graham, "Rockwell, U.S. Nazi, Slain," *The New York Times*, Aug. 26, 1967.

42. Except where otherwise indicated, this subsection is drawn from Levitas, *op. cit.*, and James Ridgeway, *Blood in the Face: The Ku Klux Klan, Aryan Nations, Nazi Skinheads, and the Rise of a New White Culture* (1990).

43. Wayne King, "Right-Wing Extremists Seek to Recruit Farmers," *The New York Times*, Sept. 20, 1985, p. A13. See also "Arthur Kirk: Kirk & Radical Farm Groups," nebraskastudies.org, undated, www.nebraskastudies.org/1000/frameset_reset.html?www.nebraskastudies.org/1000/stories/1001_0112.html.

44. "Supremacists Sentenced," *The Washington Post*, Dec. 4, 1987; "Five White Supremacists Get Long Prison Terms," *Los Angeles Times*, Feb. 7, 1986, p. A41; "40-Year Sentences Given to 5 in White-Supremacist Group," *The New York Times* (The Associated Press), Feb. 8, 1986, p. A17.

45. "13 Supremacists Are Not Guilty of Conspiracies," *The New York Times*, April 8, 1988, p. A14.

46. Richard A. Serrano, "Metzger Must Pay $5 Million in Rights Death," *Los Angeles Times*, Oct. 23, 1990, p. A1.

47. Elaine Woo, "Richard Butler, 86; Supremacist Founded the Aryan Nations," *Los Angeles Times*, Sept. 9, 2004, p. B8.
48. David Johnston with Stephen Labaton, "F.B.I. Shaken by Inquiry Into Idaho Siege," *The New York Times*, Nov. 25, 1993, p. A1.
49. Louis Beam, "Leaderless Resistance," February 1992, www.louisbeam.com/leaderless.htm. See also "Militias," in Peter Knight, ed., *Conspiracy Theories in American History: An Encyclopedia* (2003), pp. 467-476.
50. Leonard Zeskind, "Armed and Dangerous," *Rolling Stone*, Nov. 2, 1995.
51. Megan K. Stack, "Duke Admits Bilking Backers," *Los Angeles Times*, Dec. 19, 200, p. A22.
52. Susan Schmidt, "Investigation Clears Agents at Waco," *The Washington Post*, July 22, 2000, p. A1. See also "Final Report to the Deputy Attorney General Concerning the 1993 Confrontation at the Mt. Carmel Complex," John C. Danforth, Special Counsel, Nov. 8, 2000, www.apologeticsindex.org/pdf/finalreport.pdf.
53. Mike German, *Thinking Like a Terrorist: Insights of a Former FBI Undercover Agent* (2007), p. 71.
54. Woo, *op. cit.*; "William Pierce, 69, Neo-Nazi Leader, Dies," *The New York Times*, July 24, 2002, p. A16.
55. "Hitler's birthday was April 20, 1889. Unwelcome distinction as Hitler's birthday burdens Austrian town," *The Globe and Mail* (Toronto), (Reuters), April 20, 1989.
56. "Schedule of Upcoming Extremist Events: 2009," regularly updated, www.adl.org/learn/Events_2001/events_2003_flashmap.asp.
57. Steve Giegerich, "Angry words fill air at neo-Nazi rally," *St. Louis Post-Dispatch*, April 19, 2009, p. A4.
58. Quoted in *ibid*.
59. Lisa Black, "Holocaust museum opens to 'fight capacity for evil,' " *Chicago Tribune*, April 20, 2009, p. A8.
60. Padraig Shea," Spurned by Hub hall, supremacist group holds rally in N.H.," *The Boston Globe*, April 12, 2009, p. B3; "White supremacists' event shifted to N.H.," UPI, April 12, 2009.
61. "We shut down the fascists!" Boston Anti-Racist Coalition, April 8, 2009, www.anarkismo.net/article/12633.
62. Billy Roper, "One If By Land, Two If By Sea," *White Revolution*, April 8, 2009, http://whiterevolution.com.
63. "Ku Klux Klan Coming to Your Town?" *The Tennessee Tribune* (Nashville), July 6, 2006, p. C8.
64. "Arrests, fights break out at neo-Nazi march," wtop.com, April 19, 2009, www.wtop.com/?sid=1389944&nid=25. Video available at Albert Xavier Barnes, "The Arrests, Counter-Demo," undated, www.truveo.com/The-Arrests-Counter-Demo-NSM-March-on-DC-19/id/3760920024.
65. Brooke Donald, "Two arrested outside Boston Holocaust gathering," The Associated Press, May 9, 2005.
66. R. Scott Rappold, "Mobs clash in York," *York Sunday News*, Jan. 13, 2002 , p. A1.
67. Marc Levy, "White supremacist rally sparsely attended," The Associated Press, April 22, 2002.
68. Michelle Malkin, "Confirmed: The Obama DHS hit job on conservatives is real," michellemalkin.com, April 14, 2009, http://michellemalkin.com/2009/04/14/confirme-the-obama-dhs-hit-job-on-conservatives-is-real/. See also Stephen Gordon, "Homeland Security document targets most conservatives and libertarians in the country," *The Liberty Papers* (blog), April 12, 2009, www.thelibertypapers.org/2009/04/12/homeland-security-document-targets-most-conservatives-and-libertarians-in-the-country.
69. Quoted in "Napolitano defends report on right-wing extremist groups," CNN, April 15, 2009, www.cnn.com/2009/POLITICS/04/15/extremism.report/.
70. "Rightwing Extremism. . . .," *op. cit.*, p. 5.
71. *Ibid.*, p. 6.
72. "About That DHS Report on Right-Wing Extremism," *Little Green Footballs*, April 14, 2009, http://littlegreenfootballs.com/article/33364_About_That_DHS_Report_on_Right-Wing_Extremism.

73. "The Modern Militia Movement," MIAC [Missouri Information Analysis Center] Strategic Report, Feb. 20, 2009, pp. 3-4, www.scribd.com/doc/13290698/The-Modern-Militia-MovementMissouri-MIAC-Strategic-Report-20Feb09-; David A. Lieb, "Analysis: Militia report unites ACLU, Republicans," The Associated Press, April 6, 2009.
74. "Modern Militia Movement," *op. cit.*
75. Chad Livengood, "Agency apologizes for militia report on candidates," *Springfield* (Mo.) *News-Leader*, p. A1.
76. Chris Blank, "Mo. Patrol names new leader for information center," The Associated Press, April 6, 2009.
77. Quoted in Lieb, *op. cit.*
78. Quoted in "Prevention Bulletin," North Central Texas Fusion System, Feb. 19, 2009, p. 4, www.privacylives.com/wp-content/uploads/2009/03/texasfusion_021909.pdf.
79. Quoted in Lieb, *op. cit.*
80. "Leftwing Extremists Likely to Increase Use of Cyber Attacks over the Coming Decade," Department of Homeland Security, Jan. 26, 2009, www.fas.org/irp/eprint/leftwing.pdf.
81. Quoted in "Homeland Security: Economic, Political Climate Fueling Extremism," Southern Poverty Law Center, April 15, 2009.
82. Quoted in *ibid.* Alexander Cockburn, "King of the Hate Business," *The Nation*, May 18, 2009, www.thenation.com/doc/20090518/cockburn.
83. Quoted in David Abel, "WTKK-FM suspends Severin for derogatory comments about Mexicans," *The Boston Globe*, April 30, 2009, www.boston.com/news/local/breaking_news/2009/04/_jay_severin.html.
84. Quoted in *ibid.*
85. Lindell Kay, "U.S. charges former Marine with making a threat against Obama," *Jacksonville Daily News*, Feb. 27, 2009, www2.journalnow.com/content/2009/feb/27/us-charges-former-marine-with-making-a-threat-agai.
86. "White Supremacist Recruitment of Military Personnel since 9/11," FBI, Counterterrorism Division, July 7, 2008, http://wikileaks.org/wiki/FBI:_White_Supremacist_Recruitment_of_Military_Personnel_2008.
87. *Ibid.*
88. "Boehner: Homeland Security Report Characterizing Veterans as Potential Terrorists is 'Offensive and Unacceptable,' " press release, April 15, 2009, http://republicanleader.house.gov/News/DocumentSingle.aspx?DocumentID=122567.
89. "White Supremacist Recruitment . . . ," *op. cit.* See also Jim Popkin, "White-power groups recruiting from military," "Deep Background — NBC News Investigates," July 16, 2008, http://deepbackground.msnbc.msn.com/archive/2008/07/16/1202484.aspx.
90. "White Supremacist Recruitment," *op. cit.*
91. David Holthouse, "A Few Bad Men," *Intelligence Report*, Southern Poverty Law Center, July 7, 2006, www.splcenter.org/intel/news/item.jsp?pid=79.
92. Art Pine, "Ft. Bragg Troops Restricted After Swastikas Are Painted," *Los Angeles Times*, July 17, 1996, p. A9; William Branigin and Dana Priest, "3 White Soldiers Held in Slaying of Black Couple," *The Washington Post*, Dec. 9, 1995, p. A1.
93. "Planning a Skinhead Infantry," sidebar to "A Few Bad Men," *op. cit.*, www.splcenter.org/intel/news/item.jsp?sid=21.
94. *Ibid.*

BIBLIOGRAPHY

Books

Berlet, Chip, and Matthew N. Lyons, *Right-Wing Populism in America: Too Close For Comfort*, Guilford Press, 2000.
Longtime analysts of the far right chronicle the long history of a movement that's larger than right-wing extremism.

German, Mike, *Thinking Like a Terrorist*, Potomac Books, 2007.
A former FBI agent recounts his undercover assignments in violent, far-right cells while arguing for government focus on law-breaking, not ideology.

Levitas, Daniel, *The Terrorist Next Door: The Militia Movement and the Radical Right*, St. Martin's Press, 2002.
The life of Posse Comitatus founder William Potter Gale provides the framework for an independent scholar's detailed history of domestic militias.

Paxton, Robert O., *The Anatomy of Fascism*, Alfred A. Knopf, 2004.
A leading scholar of the European extreme right distinguishes between its historic relics and the elements that survive.

Raspail, Jean, *The Camp of the Saints*, Charles Scribner's Sons, 1975.
Popular on the far right, this novel by a well-known French writer anticipates the fervent opposition to immigration from developing countries by depicting it as an invasion that will topple Western democratic societies.

Ridgeway, James, *Blood in the Face: Ku Klux Klan, Aryan Nations, Nazi Skinheads, and the Rise of a New White Culture*, Thunder's Mouth Press, 1990.
Journalist Ridgeway's prescient book includes documentary extremist material.

Articles

Blow, Charles M., "Pitchforks and Pistols," *The New York Times*, April 3, 2009, www.nytimes.com/2009/04/04/opinion/04blow.html.
A columnist argues that apocalyptic talk from conservative commentators preaching revolution and warning of gun-grabbing plans by the Obama administration may set off unstable minds.

Hedgecock, Roger, "Disagree with Obama? Gov't has eyes on you," WorldNetDaily, April 13, 2009, http://wnd.com/index.php?fa=PAGE.view&page Id=94799.
The conservative columnist who obtained the first leaked copy of the Department of Homeland Security's recent assessment of the far right attacks it as a justification for political surveillance of Obama administration critics.

Jenkins, Philip, "Home-grown terrorism," *Los Angeles Times*, March 10, 2008, p. A17.
During the presidential campaign, a prominent Penn State historian of religion forecast a new wave of right-wing extremism — and of repressive Democratic response.

Roddy, Dennis B., "An Accused Cop Killer's Politics," *Slate*, April 10, 2009, www.slate.com/id/2215826/.
A reporter who investigated the man charged in the recent Pittsburgh police killings finds his political ideas jumbled.

Serrano, Richard A., " '90s-style extremism withers," *Los Angeles Times*, March 11, 2008, p. A1.
Writing before the latest wave of concern about extremism, a veteran correspondent reported that the far right hadn't recovered from the blows it suffered early in the decade.

Shapiro, Walter, "Long Shadow," *The New Republic*, April 1, 2009, www.tnr.com/politics/story.html?id=9b2152b7-07fc-4503-9f33-4e2d222161d8.
A veteran political writer sees a likely surge in populist rage with violent undertones.

Reports and Studies

"The Modern Militia Movement," Missouri Information Analysis Center, Feb. 20, 2009, www.scribd.com/doc/13290698/The-Modern-Militia-Movement Missouri-MIAC-Strategic-Report-20Feb09.
The report, later repudiated by Missouri officials, triggered a nationwide controversy over government intrusion in political debate.

"Rightwing Extremism: Current Economic and Political Climate Fueling Resurgence in Radicalization and Recruitment," Department of Homeland Security, April 7, 2009, www.fas.org/irp/eprint/rightwing.pdf.
The controversial evaluation of the potential for a resurgence of the far right prompted a backlash against governmental monitoring of ideological trends.

"White Supremacist Recruitment of Military Personnel since 9/11," Federal Bureau of Investigation, July 7, 2008, http://wikileaks.org/wiki/FBI:_White_Supremacist_Recruitment_of_Military_Personnel_2008.
This recent and more focused FBI report on extremists' interest in recruiting veterans received little attention, except among specialists.

For More Information

The American Cause, 501 Church St., Suite 315, Vienna, VA 22180; (703) 255-2632. Educational organization founded in 1993 by conservative commentator Pat Buchanan that supports "conservative principles of national sovereignty, economic patriotism, limited government and individual freedom."

Anti-Defamation League, Law Enforcement Agency Research Network; http://adl.org/learn/default.asp. A monitoring and research program aimed mainly at keeping law enforcement agencies up to date on extremism.

Federal Bureau of Investigation, J. Edgar Hoover Building, 935 Pennsylvania Ave., N.W., Washington, DC 20535; (202) 324-3000; www.fbi.gov/hq/cid/civilrights/hate.htm. Provides statistics, information on the agency's anti-hate crime program and links to other sites.

Political Research Associates, 1310 Broadway, Suite 201, Somerville, MA 02144; (617) 666-5300; www.publiceye.org. A left-oriented think tank that investigates the far right.

Southern Poverty Law Center, 400 Washington Ave., Montgomery, AL 36104; (334) 956-8200; www.splcenter.org/. Specializes in suing extremist organizations; maintains a research arm that monitors the extreme right.

Stormfront, P.O. Box 6637, West Palm Beach, FL 33405; (561) 833-0030; www.stormfront.org/forum. A heavily trafficked far-right site.

White Aryan Resistance, Tom Metzger P.O. Box 401, Warasaw, IN 46581; www.resist.com. A Web site maintained by a longtime extremist leader.

8 Police Misconduct

Kenneth Jost

Natalie Gomez holds a picture of her brother, 22-year-old Alan Gomez, who was killed last year by Albuquerque, N.M., police. Ms. Gomez participated in a rally on June 14, 2011, protesting the police department's use of lethal force. The department's police union was found to have been giving officers involved in fatal shootings $500 to help them recover from stress. Critics have called the payments a bounty system for killing suspects.

From *CQ Researcher*,
April 6, 2012.

Wendell Allen was wearing only pajama bottoms when New Orleans police officers on a marijuana raid broke into his house in the city's middle-class Gentilly neighborhood on the evening of March 7. Armed with a search warrant, six officers, clad in plain clothes covered by jackets identifying them as police, announced their presence and, after receiving no response, barged in.

Allen, a 20-year-old former high school basketball star with a previous marijuana-related conviction, was in the stairwell, unarmed, when Officer Joshua Colclough fired a single gunshot that hit Allen in the chest. The bullet penetrated Allen's heart, aorta and lungs. He died "almost instantly," New Orleans Parish Coroner Frank Minyard said later.[1]

Allen's death, the second fatal shooting of an African-American youth by New Orleans police within a week, remains under what Superintendent Ronal Serpas promises will be "a complete and thorough" investigation. Colclough, in his fifth year with the force, gave a voluntary statement to investigators a week after the shooting. His attorney, Claude Kelly, says an "honest" investigation will show the shooting was justified.

Allen's family and leaders of the city's African-American community, however, have no doubt that the shooting was unwarranted. "There have been egregious wrongs done to the black community of New Orleans," W. C. Johnson, leader of the United New Orleans Front, declared as protesters massed outside police headquarters two days after the shooting. Helen Shorty, Allen's grandmother, called for Colclough to be booked for murder.[2]

Justice Department Targets Police Misconduct

U.S. Department of Justice investigators have examined the policies and practices of more than two dozen law enforcement agencies over the past decade and found a range of illegal or otherwise improper practices, ranging from harsh treatment of suspects and racial profiling to failure to probe allegations of sexual assault. Here are highlights from five recent Justice Department reports.

New Orleans

(March 17, 2011) Use of excessive force; unconstitutional stops, searches and arrests; biased policing; racial, ethnic and sexual-orientation discrimination; failure to provide effective policing services to persons with limited English proficiency; systemic failure to investigate sexual assaults and domestic violence.

Puerto Rico

(Sept. 7, 2011) Excessive force; unreasonable force, other misconduct designed to suppress exercise of First Amendment rights; unlawful searches and seizures; evidence of frequent failure to police sex crimes and incidents of domestic violence; evidence of discriminatory practices targeting individuals of Dominican descent; "staggering level" of crime and corruption.

Maricopa County, Ariz. (includes Phoenix)

(Dec. 15, 2011) Racial profiling of Latinos; unlawful stops, detentions and arrests of Latinos; unlawful retaliation against individuals who complain about or criticize the office's policies or practices; reasonable cause to believe the office operates its jails in a manner that punishes Latino inmates with limited English proficiency for failing to understand commands given in English and denying critical services provided to other inmates.

Seattle

(Dec. 16, 2011) Use of unnecessary or excessive force; lack of adequate training on use of force; failure of supervisors to provide oversight on use of force; serious concerns about possible discriminatory policing, particularly relating to pedestrian encounters.

East Haven, Conn.

(Dec. 19, 2011) Systematic discrimination against Latinos, including targeting Latinos for discriminatory traffic enforcement, treating Latino drivers more harshly than non-Latino drivers after a traffic stop and intentionally and woefully failing to design and implement internal systems of control that would identify, track and prevent such misconduct.

Source: U.S. Department of Justice, www.justice.gov/crt/about/spl/findsettle.php.

The shootings come as the long-troubled department is negotiating with the U.S. Department of Justice (DOJ) the terms of a possible agreement on wide-ranging reforms to be supervised by a federal court. The negotiations follow a scathing report by the Justice Department's civil rights division in March 2011 that accused the New Orleans police of routine constitutional violations, including use of excessive force, improper searches and racial and ethnic discrimination.[3]

The 158-page report is one of nine published so far by the civil rights division's so-called "special litigation section" under President Obama that have held police departments around the country up to highly critical scrutiny. In three reports published within five days in mid-December, Justice Department investigators upbraided Seattle police for use of excessive force and the Maricopa County, Ariz., sheriff's office and East Haven, Conn., police department for ethnic profiling of Latinos.

Racial profiling is also at the heart of the nationwide controversy over the Feb. 26 fatal shooting of a black Florida teenager by a white neighborhood watch volunteer. Trayvon Martin, 17, was shot as he was returning from a convenience store to the house of his father's girlfriend in Sanford, an Orlando suburb. George Zimmerman, whose mother is Hispanic, claims he shot the unarmed Martin in self-defense after following the youth because of what he regarded as suspicious behavior. The incident has touched off nationwide debate not only over racial profiling but also over Florida's so-called Stand Your Ground law, which allows someone to use deadly force when feeling threatened, with no duty to attempt to retreat.

The most recent reports by the Justice Department's police accountability unit exemplify its more aggressive stance after an eight-year period of dormancy under President George W. Bush. "They've been very assertive," says Samuel Walker, a professor of criminal justice, emeritus, at the University of Nebraska-Omaha and the nation's senior academic expert on police-accountability issues. In all, the unit is conducting 20 investigations of state or local law enforcement agencies.

Local police officials sometimes challenge the Justice Department's findings. "The department is not broken," a defiant Seattle Police Chief John Diaz declared as the DOJ's report was being released on Dec. 16. The city's mayor, Mike McGinn, backed him up.

Over time, however, local officials generally yield to federal authorities. In East Haven, Police Chief Leonard Gallo retired on Jan. 30 in the wake of DOJ criticism. In Seattle, McGinn rethought his initial skepticism about the report in the face of public criticism and directed Diaz to begin carrying out some of the Justice Department's proposed changes.

In Arizona, however, the outspoken Maricopa County Sheriff Joe Arpaio is refusing the Justice Department's insistence for court supervision of changes in police and jail policies. "None of us agreed to allow a federal monitor to come remove my authority as the elected sheriff of Maricopa County," Arpaio declared on April 3. The government now has the option of going to federal court on its own to force changes.[4]

Holding police departments accountable to the law has been an intractable problem since the era of urban police departments began in the 1830s.[5] The 20th century saw a succession of efforts to reduce or eliminate police misconduct, starting with a movement to professionalize policing and continuing through the mid-century criminal-law revolution under Chief Justice Earl Warren.

In the decades since, civilian review boards or other independent auditing mechanisms have advanced from

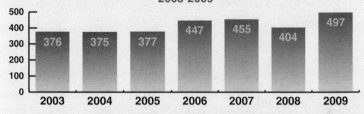

Killings of Arrestees by Police on Rise

From 2003 through 2009, law-enforcement officials committed 2,931 arrest-related killings, whether criminal or justifiable, of people in their custody. Some experts caution that the upward trend over the seven-year period may reflect improvements in data reporting.

Arrest-Related Killings by Law Enforcement Personnel, 2003-2009

Year	Killings
2003	376
2004	375
2005	377
2006	447
2007	455
2008	404
2009	497

Source: Andrea M. Burch, "Arrest-Related Deaths, 2003-2009 — Statistical Tables," Bureau of Justice Statistics, U.S. Department of Justice, November 2011, p. 4, bjs.ojp.usdoj.gov/content/pub/pdf/ard0309st.pdf

objects of fierce debate to structures viewed by police organizations themselves as "best practices." Congress in 1994 also gave the Justice Department a direct role in police reform by passing a law authorizing the federal government to sue state or local law enforcement agencies if it found a "pattern or practice" of violations of constitutional or federally protected rights.

The reforms have borne fruit in a general strengthening of policies and improved conduct by police officers in the nation's nearly 18,000 state or local law enforcement agencies nationwide. "We've seen a progressive improvement in the professionalism of law enforcement over the last 30 years," says Andrew Scott, a police consultant since his retirement as Boca Raton, Fla., police chief in 2006, after 30 years in law enforcement.

"Police departments have come a long way, both in terms of the officers and the leadership in policing," says Hubert Williams, president of the Police Foundation, a Washington-based research organization, and a former Newark, N.J., police chief.

Walker, a civil liberties-minded researcher on police practices and policies since the 1970s, agrees that police behavior has generally improved over the past few decades. But he says there is a continuing gap between the country's best and worst departments. "Some departments are taking up what I call the new accountability measures, moving forward, doing the right thing, and

An opponent of a controversial New York City Police Department "stop and frisk" policy marches in the Bronx borough on Jan. 27, 2012. The NYPD says the policy helps to prevent crime, but critics accuse the police of racial profiling and civil rights abuses. Out of 684,330 persons stopped by NYPD officers in 2011, the vast majority — 87 percent — were black or Hispanic.

news conference to release the report. Serpas said it contained few surprises and went on to pledge improvement. "I am convinced we will be a world-class police department," he said. A week later, Serpas said many of the reforms were already being put into effect.[6]

The Justice Department launched its investigation in May 2010 at the request of the city's newly inaugurated mayor, Mitch Landrieu. The investigation came on top of ongoing federal prosecutions of officers implicated in the attempted cover-up of the shooting of six unarmed black civilians on the Danziger Bridge six days after Hurricane Katrina devastated the city in September 2005.

By May 2010, four officers had already pleaded guilty to obstruction-type charges in connection with the shooting. In addition to one other guilty plea, five officers were convicted in August 2011 on federal civil rights charges after a seven-week trial. U.S. District Court Judge Kurt Engelhardt imposed sentences ranging from 38 to 65 years on four of the five defendants after an emotional sentencing hearing on April 4; a fifth defendant drew a six-year term. One other defendant is awaiting a retrial, set to begin in May, after a mistrial in January.[7]

As in previous investigations, Justice Department lawyers are negotiating with New Orleans officials on possible reforms. The changes would be included in a consent decree to be overseen by a federal court for a specified period. The department has followed the same procedure since the mid-1990s in such major cities as Pittsburgh, Cincinnati, Detroit and Los Angeles.

A one-day roundtable with police officials, experts and others convened by the Justice Department in June 2010 concluded the procedure has been effective in reforming police department practices. Experts generally agree. "Departments have come out of this much better than they went in," says David Harris, a professor at the University of Pittsburgh School of Law.

Some of the officials at the roundtable, however, complained that the process creates a "negative stigma" that takes time for a department to overcome.[8]

As assistant attorney general for civil rights, Perez has pushed the "pattern or practice" process more vigorously than any of his predecessors. In addition to New Orleans, Perez personally attended news conferences to announce the reports in Seattle and Maricopa County. "When police officers cross the line, they need to be held

reducing misconduct," Walker says. "And there are some that slip back."

The New Orleans department, by common agreement, ranks low on those measures. "The New Orleans Police Department has never been a model of good behavior so to speak," says Marjorie Esman, executive director of the American Civil Liberties Union of Louisiana (ACLU-La.).

Walker is even blunter: New Orleans is "everybody's candidate for the worst police department."

Far from fighting the Justice Department's findings, New Orleans superintendent Serpas joined the DOJ's civil rights chief Thomas Perez in the March 17, 2011,

accountable," Perez told *The Washington Post.* "Criminal prosecutions alone will not change the culture of a department."[9]

One of the supposed deterrents to police misconduct, however, is being weakened by the Supreme Court under Chief Justice John G. Roberts Jr., according to civil liberties advocates. The Roberts Court has issued three decisions in the past six years that somewhat narrow the exclusionary rule — the court-created doctrine that prohibits the use of evidence police find during illegal searches.

Meanwhile, the New York City Police Department, the nation's largest, is under a national spotlight after news reports, particularly by The Associated Press, detailing the department's secret infiltration and surveillance of Muslim and some liberal groups as part of counterterrorism investigations. The AP stories, dating from summer 2011 and continuing, show that the department investigated hundreds of mosques and Muslim student groups and infiltrated dozens. City officials are defending the practice, but some Muslim leaders are calling for the resignation of Police Commissioner Raymond Kelly.[10]

The Justice Department investigations, coupled with the recurrent local controversies over police behavior, focus increased national attention on such issues as use of force, racial profiling and police accountability. Here are some of the arguments being heard as those issues are debated:

Should police do more to control excessive force?

John Williams was carrying a board and an open wood-carving knife at an

---

Police Handle Tense Situations in Steps

Most law enforcement agencies have policies that guide their use of force. Such policies describe an escalating series of actions an officer may take to resolve a situation. Officers are instructed to respond with a level of force appropriate to the situation. An officer may move from one part of the continuum to another in a matter of seconds.

A typical use-of-force continuum:

Officer Presence — No force is used. Considered the best way to resolve a situation.
- The mere presence of a law-enforcement officer works to deter crime or defuse a situation.
- Officers' attitudes are professional and nonthreatening.

Verbalization — Force is not physical.
- Officers issue calm, nonthreatening commands, such as "Let me see your identification and registration."
- Officers may increase their volume and shorten commands in an attempt to gain compliance. Short commands might include "Stop" or "Don't move."

Empty-Hand Control — Officers use bodily force to gain control of a situation.
- *Soft technique.* Officers use grabs, holds and joint locks to restrain an individual.
- *Hard technique.* Officers use punches and kicks to restrain an individual.

Less-Lethal Methods — Officers use less-lethal technologies to gain control of a situation.
- *Blunt impact.* Officers may use a baton or projectile to immobilize a combative person.
- *Chemical.* Officers may use chemical sprays or projectiles embedded with chemicals to restrain an individual. Pepper spray is an example.
- *Conducted Energy Devices (CEDs).* Officers may use a device such as a Taser to immobilize an individual. Such devices discharge a high-voltage, low-amperage jolt of electricity at a distance.

Lethal Force — Officers use lethal weapons to gain control of a situation. These should be used if a suspect poses a serious threat to an officer or other individual.
- Officers use deadly weapons such as firearms to stop an individual's actions.

Source: www.nij.gov/nij/topics/law-enforcement/officer-safety/use-of-force/continuum.htm

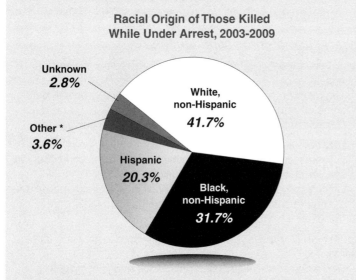

Half of Arrest-Related Killings Are of Minorities

More than half of the 2,958* people who were killed while under arrest from 2003 through 2009 were black or Hispanic. Whites comprised 42 percent of the total. All but 27 of the deaths were at the hands of law enforcement officers.

Racial Origin of Those Killed While Under Arrest, 2003-2009

- Unknown: 2.8%
- Other*: 3.6%
- White, non-Hispanic: 41.7%
- Hispanic: 20.3%
- Black, non-Hispanic: 31.7%

* Includes American Indians, Alaska Natives, Asians, Native Hawaiians, other Pacific Islanders and persons of two or more races.

Figures do not total 100 because of rounding.

Source: Andrea M. Burch, "Arrest-Related Deaths, 2003-2009 — Statistical Tables," Bureau of Justice Statistics, U.S. Department of Justice, November 2011, p. 6, bjs.ojp.usdoj.gov/content/pub/pdf/ard0309st.pdf

intersection near Seattle's Pioneer Square on Aug. 30, 2010, when Police Sgt. Ian Birk spotted him, got out of his patrol car and ordered him to drop the knife. When the hearing-impaired Williams failed to respond, Birk fired four shots from about nine feet away. Williams, a fixture at the nearby social service center for Native Americans, died at the scene.

Williams' death added to long simmering concerns about use of force by Seattle police forces. Led by the ACLU of Washington State, a coalition of 34 community groups asked the Justice Department to investigate. The department's devastating report, released on Dec. 16, found routine violations of constitutional rights when force was used, with a small number of officers responsible for a disproportionate number of instances and with scant internal review of the incidents. "Seattle cannot control its own officers," says Jennifer Shaw, deputy director of the ACLU affiliate.[11]

Statistics are hard to come by, but experts appear to agree that police use force less frequently today than in the past. "Overall, it is less frequent than it was in the 1960s," says the Police Foundation's Williams. A study by the International Association of Chiefs of Police (IACP), published in 2001, found that police used force 3.6 times per 10,000 service calls during the 1990s. Citing the IACP's and a more recent study, the National Institute of Justice, the Justice Department's research arm, concluded in 2011 that use of excessive force is "rare," even while conceding the difficulty of defining "excessive."[12]

As in Seattle, a small number of officers are typically found most likely to resort to force or to use excessive force in encounters with civilians. "The vast majority of officers do not engage in excessive use of force," says former chief Scott. "It is the small minority of officers who abuse their power."

The U.S. Supreme Court has given only limited guidance on use of force by police. The court ruled in 1985 that police can use deadly force when pursuing a fleeing suspect only if the suspect poses a significant threat of death or serious physical injury to the officer or others. In a broader ruling, the court held in 1989 that any use of force by an officer must be objectively reasonable. Factors to be considered include the severity of the crime, whether the suspect poses "an immediate safety threat" and whether the suspect is "actively resisting arrest" or attempting to escape. The court added that the "calculus of reasonableness" should take into account an officer's need to make "split-second judgments."[13]

"The legal standards are pretty loose," says Robert Kane, an associate professor at the University of Baltimore's School of Criminal Justice and co-author of a forthcoming book on police accountability issues. "There's a lot of gray in terms of trying to judge the appropriateness of force."

City governments are occasionally hit with five-, six- or even seven-figure damage awards in suits by victims of police beatings or shootings. As one dramatic example, Rodney King was awarded $3.8 million for the beating he suffered from Los Angeles police officers in 1991 after a high-speed car chase. Criminal prosecutions are more difficult. The King case ended in state court acquittals of four officers and a federal civil rights trial that ended with two convictions and two acquittals.

Internally, police departments appear to reject most citizen complaints of excessive force. In a recent study of eight local police departments, researchers at Michigan State University and Central Florida University found that six took no action on at least 90 percent of the complaints during the two-year period studied. Only three officers were suspended and one terminated because of use-of-force complaints during the period.[14]

The IACP's model policy on use of force largely restates the general guidelines from the Supreme Court, with added advisories against firing warning shots or shooting at a moving vehicle. Many departments provide more detailed guidance, including a so-called use of force continuum that correlates the level of force to be used with the suspect's level of resistance or threat to safety.

Walker says policies and training are the keys to reducing excessive force by police. "If you have a bad use-of-force incident, it's a mistake to focus on the officer because the underlying cause is some failure by the department: lack of proper training or lack of proper supervision," he says.

Should police do more to prevent racial and ethnic profiling?

Many studies over the past two decades have shown that African-American and Hispanic drivers are more likely to be stopped for traffic enforcement than white motorists. In a mammoth journalistic project, the *Hartford Courant* took the issue one step further earlier this year by analyzing what happened in Connecticut to drivers after they were stopped by local police.

The newspaper's analysis of more than 100,000 traffic stops found that blacks and Hispanics were far more likely to get a citation than whites stopped for the same offense. As one example, blacks were twice as likely and Hispanics four times as likely to be ticketed for improper taillights as whites stopped for the same reason. "This is beyond profiling," Glenn A. Cassis, executive director of the state's African-American Affairs Commission, told the newspaper. "This goes to actually a level of discrimination, and who gets the wink and who doesn't get the wink."[15]

The Justice Department's recent reports found similar evidence of racial or ethnic profiling in New Orleans, Maricopa County and East Haven. In New Orleans, investigators found that police shot 27 civilians during a 16-month period, all of them African-Americans. In Maricopa County, Latino drivers were four to nine times more likely to be subjected to traffic stops than similarly situated non-Latino drivers. In East Haven, Latinos make up about 10 percent of the population, but accounted for nearly 20 percent of traffic stops.[16]

The tensions between police departments, historically predominantly white, and African-American and Hispanic communities are of long standing. The U.S. Supreme Court's initial decision, in 1936, limiting police conduct during interrogations came in the case of three black tenant farmers who confessed to murder only after being tortured. Los Angeles police tacitly abetted white servicemen attacking Latinos in the "Zoot Suit" riots in 1943. The Kerner Commission report on urban riots of the 1960s listed the "deep hostility between police and ghetto communities as a primary cause of the disorders."

Racial profiling advanced to the top of the national agenda in the mid- and late-1990s — as seen in the popularizing of the grimly ironic phrase "driving while black." In litigation that documented the experiences of many African-Americans, ACLU affiliates in several states filed suits contesting the practice. Some states, including Connecticut, responded by passing laws requiring demographic statistics-gathering on traffic stops to try to spot signs of racial profiling.

Racial and ethnic profiling appears to be continuing despite increasing diversity on local police forces. The New Orleans police force is now majority black. In New York City, a majority of the police officers are black, Latino or Asian; whites comprise only 47 percent. Out of 684,330 persons stopped by NYPD officers in 2011, however, the vast majority — 87 percent — were either black or Hispanic.[17]

Harris, the Pittsburgh law professor and author of a book on racial profiling, says the practice "is a police issue, not a race issue." Profiling, he says, "is a product of the training, culture and customs within that department. Black officers are going to be trained like all others. They're going to want to fit in just like all officers."

Other experts say profiling results naturally from the demographics of crime. "This is a social issue," says the University of Baltimore's Kane. "We know that race and class are strongly tied up with crime, perceptions of crime and urban disorder. Crime and race are not randomly distributed across America."

"It is a problem, and it will continue to be a problem," says police consultant Scott. "But it may not be extending from a police officer's bigotry. If you have a particular segment of the community that is particularly involved in a particular crime, part of the profiling has to be the ethnicity of the offender."

Identifying impermissible profiling can also be difficult, Scott adds. "It may be insidiously nontransparent as to why an officer has stopped a particular individual," he says. In its report on East Haven, the Justice Department accused the force of "intentionally and woefully failing to design and implement internal systems of control that would identify, track, and prevent such misconduct." The report on Maricopa County faulted Sheriff Arpaio by name for using "unverified tips or complaints" that were "infected with bias against Latino persons."

Police Foundation president Williams says the responsibility for stopping the practice rests with police officials. "Are chiefs dealing with the problem?" he asks rhetorically. "I think they have policies that prohibit it, and from that perspective they're dealing with it. It's the enforcement of those policies that's the big question mark. In that area, there's more of a question mark."

Should police adopt stronger disciplinary measures for misconduct?

Jason Mucha has had a checkered career with the Milwaukee Police Department since being hired as an aide in 1996 while still a teenager. He was promoted to sergeant in 2005, but over the next few years was accused by 10 different suspects of either beating them or planting drugs or both. Although he was never disciplined, a state appeals court explicitly questioned Mucha's credibility as a witness, and the U.S. attorney's office dropped one case rather than put him on the stand.

The department's disciplinary procedure has now caught up with Mucha, however, after he and fellow squad members were accused of invasive body searches in drug investigations. Mucha and seven officers in his unit were stripped of police powers and reassigned to desk duties in March because of the accusations, according to the *Journal Sentinel*. Without confirming the report, Chief Edward Flynn told a news conference on March 22 that if the allegations were true, the searches would have violated state law.[18]

The *Journal Sentinel* has been on the department's case over discipline for years. A three-part series in October 2011 criticized the department for allowing "at least" 93 officers to remain on the force despite offenses such as drunken driving and domestic violence. A similar, nine-part series by the *Sarasota Herald Tribune* in December found that "thousands" of officers remain on the job in Florida police departments despite "arrests or evidence" implicating them in crimes punishable by prison sentences.[19]

Despite such newspaper investigations, some experts give police departments generally good marks for disciplining rogue cops. "Internal discipline is taken seriously by most if not all American police departments," the University of Baltimore's Kane says. "Police commanders and departments can often determine that a police officer is not good for the department and not good for the public."

Police Foundation president Williams gives a mixed review. "Some police departments are very good at discipline — a lot, not just a few," he says. "But I wouldn't want to say that all police departments are like that."

ACLU officials are more critical. "We have found problems with internal disciplinary procedures around the country," says Vanita Gupta, deputy legal director for the national ACLU. "To say that they are an adequate remedy for these violations is a real problem. It's just not how it plays out."

The disciplinary procedures that exist today are the culmination of decades of pressure from outside groups — in particular, groups such as the ACLU and other civil rights organizations — for more effective oversight of police practices in general and in specific cases. "Some form of citizen oversight exists in almost every city," according to the University of Nebraska's Walker.

In contrast to civilian review boards — perhaps the most common oversight mechanism — Walker says he prefers the appointment of an independent auditor for a department. "They have authority to review the operations of an agency and to make public reports," Walker explains. "That's the best solution for improving the department, not just finding guilt or innocence in a particular incident."

Roger Goldman, a professor at St. Louis University School of Law who has specialized in police accountability issues, notes that even when an officer has been removed from a force, he or she often looks for — and sometimes finds — a job with another law enforcement agency. To remedy the problem, Goldman favors a system of "decertifying" an officer for any police work after a finding of misconduct — akin to disbarment for lawyers, for example. "The problem can't be left up to local municipalities and police departments to handle," he says.

Police consultant Scott says police unions represent a big obstacle to strengthened discipline. "The unions can protect the incompetent, and the malicious, and allow them to get back on the streets," Scott says. "The unions have lost their way as to who they're supposed to represent in the bigger picture of law enforcement."

Other experts, however, stress the role of leadership at the top in improving discipline. "What you've got to have," says Williams, "is commitment at the highest levels of the department." The ACLU's Gupta agrees. "We know and police experts know how to implement best practices in this area," she says. "There are best practices out there, but there still remains a lot of work to be done."

BACKGROUND

Police Problems

Police misconduct has been a persistent problem since full-time police forces were first organized in the United States in the mid-19th century. Political patronage and financial corruption were dominant concerns in the 1800s; use of force and other coercive tactics and racial and ethnic discrimination became major issues in the 1900s. A reform movement to professionalize policing dates from the early 20th century. The Supreme Court began to exercise oversight by the 1930s and then brought about significant changes in police practices with decisions in the 1960s establishing new limits on interrogations and searches.[20]

The constables and night watches of the colonial and early post-independence years proved inadequate for law enforcement by the mid-19th century. The emergence of urban centers brought with it the breakdown of law and order due to interethnic clashes, economic discontent and conflict over political issues, including slavery. Philadelphia and Boston created police forces in the 1830s — not long after Sir Robert Peel in 1829 had created the first urban police force in London, England. New York City followed in 1845.

The 19th century officer was typically unarmed and untrained, inefficient and largely ineffective in preventing crime. He was likely chosen on the basis of political patronage and afforded no job security.* Corruption was "epidemic," according to a textbook by the University of Nebraska's Walker and Arizona State University professor of criminology Charles Katz, but reform efforts typically consisted merely of replacing supporters of one political faction with those of another. And "no attention" was given to the two issues that would dominate the 20th century: excessive force and racial discrimination.[21]

More serious reform efforts began in the early 20th century as part of Progressive Era movements to replace spoils-system, moneyed-interest politics with popular democracy and professional government services. Walker and Katz credit August Vollmer, chief of the Berkeley, Calif., police force from 1905 to 1932, as the father of the movement to define policing as a profession. He created college-level courses in police work and, along with other reformers, favored raising standards for hiring officers, eliminating political influence and placing control in the hands of qualified administrators.

But police reform "progressed very slowly," Walker and Katz write. And in 1931 Vollmer co-authored a critical report by the presidentially appointed National Commission on Law Observance and Enforcement, commonly called the Wickersham Commission. Among its findings: Physical brutality was "extensively practiced" by police departments around the country.

---

*Chicago is now believed to have hired the first female officer in 1891; Portland, Ore., followed in 1905, Los Angeles in 1910.

CHRONOLOGY

1960s *Supreme Court lays down rules for police searches, interrogation.*

1961 Supreme Court says states must adopt exclusionary rule to bar use of evidence found by police during unconstitutional searches (*Mapp v. Ohio*).

1966 Supreme Court requires police to advise suspects of rights before in-custody interrogation (*Miranda v. Arizona*).

1968 National Advisory Commission on Civil Disorders (Kerner Commission) report says distrust between police and "ghetto communities" was major cause of urban riots. . . . Law Enforcement Assistance Administration is established to provide federal grants to state, local law enforcement agencies; in 14-year lifetime, agency promotes accreditation standards, provides funds for officer training.

1990s *Justice Department gains power to investigate state, local law enforcement agencies.*

1991, 1992 Videotaped beating of Rodney King by Los Angeles police officers provokes debate over use of force, leads to riots in African-American neighborhoods after officers are prosecuted but acquitted.

1994 Congress authorizes Justice Department (DOJ) to investigate state, local law enforcement agencies for "pattern or practice" of violations of constitutional or statutory rights (42 U.S.C. § 14141).

Mid- to late '90s *Justice Department uses new law to get Pittsburgh and Steubenville, Ohio, police departments to agree to reforms; launches investigations in other cities, including Washington, D.C.*

1999, 2000 Los Angeles Police Department is rocked by disclosures of corruption, excessive force by antigang unit in predominantly Latino Rampart neighborhood; Justice Department, city agree in 2000 on reforms, court supervision.

2001-Present *Bush administration pulls back on police department investigations; Obama administration takes aggressive stance.*

2003 Detroit agrees to institute police reforms after investigation initiated in December 2000.

2005 Two African-American civilians killed, four others wounded by New Orleans police officers while crossing Danziger Bridge to flee post-Katrina flooding.

2006 Supreme Court allows use of evidence found in Detroit drug raid despite officers' failure to follow knock-and-announce rule (*Hudson v. Michigan*); first of Roberts Court rulings weakening enforcement of exclusionary rule.

2009 Eric Holder is named first African-American attorney general; chooses Thomas Perez to head Justice Department's civil rights division.

2010 Roundtable convened by Justice Department finds police investigations "effective" in promoting reform; some police officials complain of "negative stigma."

2011 Justice Department report sharply criticizes New Orleans Police Department for excessive force, discriminatory policing; police chief promises reforms (March 17). . . . Five New Orleans officers are convicted in federal civil rights trial in Danziger Bridge case (Aug. 5); five others had pleaded guilty earlier. . . . DOJ report lambasts Puerto Rico Police Department for excessive force, other issues (Sept. 7). . . . Three more DOJ reports fault police in Maricopa County (Phoenix), Ariz.; Seattle; East Haven, Conn. (Dec. 15, 16, 19).

2012 East Haven Police Chief Leonard Gallo retires (Jan. 30). . . . African-American teenager Trayvon Martin is shot and killed by neighborhood watch coordinator George Zimmerman in Sanford, Fla. (Feb. 26); death touches off debate over authorities' failure to arrest Zimmerman, Florida law easing rule on self defense. . . . Seattle mayor, police chief adopt plan to revise use-of-force policies, review racial profiling (March 29). . . . Puerto Rico Police Chief Emilio Díaz Cólon resigns to avoid hurting reforms (March 29). . . . Maricopa County Sheriff Joe Arpaio rejects Justice Department demand for court-supervised consent decree (April 3). . . . Justice Department weighs requests for formal investigations of police in Albuquerque, Omaha, elsewhere.

Supreme Court Eases Rules on Police Searches

Evidence gleaned illegally allowed in criminal trials.

Detroit police officers thought they were raiding a big crack-cocaine house when they converged, seven strong, on Booker Hudson's home on the afternoon of Aug. 27, 1998. Wary of being shot, Officer Jamal Good shouted, "Police. Search warrant," and then paused only a moment before barging in.

Good's nearly instantaneous entry violated a Supreme Court decision issued three years earlier, in *Wilson v. Arkansas*, that imposed a so-called knock-and-announce rule requiring police to wait a reasonable period after the initial knock before entering a private home.

When Hudson was tried on cocaine charges, he sought to exclude the evidence that police found in their search: five individually wrapped "rocks" of crack cocaine that he had in his pants pockets. Michigan courts refused, and so did the U.S. Supreme Court — in the first of three decisions under Chief Justice John G. Roberts Jr. that critics say have seriously weakened the so-called exclusionary rule against using evidence found during an illegal police search.

Writing for the majority in *Hudson v. Michigan* (2006), Justice Antonin Scalia said the costs of applying the exclusionary rule to knock-and-announce violations in terms of releasing criminals would outweigh any benefits in terms of protecting privacy or deterring improper police behavior. As one reason, Scalia pointed to what he called the "substantial" existing deterrents to police violations of search rules.

David Moran, then a Wayne State University law professor who represented Hudson before the Supreme Court, sharply disagreed. "It's a joke to say that the police will comply with the knock-and-announce rule without the exclusionary rule as a sanction," he said. [1]

The exclusionary rule, a distinctively U.S. legal doctrine, dates from a 1914 Supreme Court ruling applying it to federal court cases. The Supreme Court forced the same rule on state courts in 1961 in one of the first decisions under Chief Justice Earl Warren that expanded the rights of suspects and criminal defendants. The court trimmed but did not eliminate the rule under the next two chief justices, Warren E. Burger and William H. Rehnquist.

Supporters of the exclusionary rule, criminal defense attorneys and civil liberties advocates among others, echo Moran's view that the only effective deterrent to police misconduct in conducting searches is to exclude the evidence from trial. Critics say there are other deterrents, including police disciplinary procedures and civil damage suits.

As a White House lawyer under President Ronald Reagan, Roberts helped lay the basis for a series of attacks aimed at either amending or abolishing the exclusionary rule. Now, as chief justice, Roberts leads a five-vote conservative majority that critics say is transforming those broadsides into legal precedent. [2]

The *Hudson* case came in Roberts' first full term as chief justice. Three years later, Roberts wrote for the same 5-4 majority in a second decision cutting back on the exclusionary rule. The decision in *Herring v. United States* (2009) allowed the use of evidence that an Alabama man was carrying when he was arrested in 2004 on the basis of what was later found to be an outdated arrest warrant. Roberts said the exclusionary rule applies only to police conduct that is "sufficiently deliberate that exclusion can meaningfully deter it, and sufficiently culpable that such deterrence is worth the price paid by the justice system." [3]

In a third decision, the court in June 2011 held that the exclusionary rule does not require suppression of evidence obtained by police if they relied in good faith on an established court precedent, even if it was later overruled as violating the Fourth Amendment's protections against unreasonable searches and seizures (*Davis v. United States*). In January, however, the court gave defense lawyers and civil liberties advocates a significant victory by limiting the authority of police to attach a GPS tracking device to a vehicle for surveillance purposes. The unanimous ruling in *United States v. Jones* apparently requires police to get a search warrant unless they can show a reason for an exception. [4]

— *Kenneth Jost*

---

[1] Account taken from Kenneth Jost, *The Supreme Court Yearbook 2005-2006*.

[2] See Adam Liptak, "Justices Step Closer to Repeal of Evidence Ruling," *The New York Times*, Jan. 31, 2009, p. A1.

[3] See Kenneth Jost, *The Supreme Court Yearbook 2008-2009*.

[4] For coverage, see Adam Liptak, "Justices Reject GPS Tracking in a Drug Case," *The New York Times*, Jan. 24, 2012, p. A1.

The Supreme Court first entered the field in 1936 with a unanimous decision, *Brown v. Mississippi*, declaring the use of confessions obtained by torture-like interrogation to be a violation of the Due Process Clause. Over the next three decades, the court adopted a case-by-case approach that barred confessions if induced by either physical or psychological coercion.

By the 1960s, the court saw the need to adopt a stronger, preventive safeguard. The result was the controversial but now largely accepted decision, *Miranda v. Arizona* (1966), which required police to advise a suspect of his or her rights, including the right to remain silent, before any custodial interrogation — that is, any interrogation during which the suspect is not free to leave. Five years earlier, in *Mapp v. Ohio* (1961), the court had established another landmark limitation on police conduct by requiring states to enforce the exclusionary rule, which bars the use of evidence obtained by police during an unconstitutional search or arrest.[22]

The 1960s also saw agreement between Congress and the president to increase the federal role in professionalizing state and local police agencies. Since the 1930s, the FBI had been allowing local police officers to enroll in what was originally called the FBI Training School, now the FBI National Academy, in Quantico, Va. In 1968, Congress created, as part of the Omnibus Crime Control and Safe Streets Act, a new agency to support state and local law enforcement: the Law Enforcement Assistance Administration (LEAA).

In its 14 years of existence, LEAA funneled about $8 billion in grants to state and local police agencies. It was abolished in 1982, unpopular in Congress and among some experts, in part because of a penchant for funding expensive gadgetry. But it also is credited with helping establish standards for police and corrections agencies and with providing funds for training state and local police officers.

"LEAA was the catalyst that promoted the education of police officers by creating a significant amount of money for police officers to get educated," Police Foundation president Williams says today.[23]

Police Accountability

Despite widely acknowledged improvements in professionalism and accountability, major police departments around the country were beset by high-profile scandals during the final decades of the 20th century. Major controversies in New York City and Los Angeles resulted in the formation of blue-ribbon commissions that recommended significant changes, some eventually adopted. In Washington, Congress laid the foundation for increased police accountability with two legislative enactments: the 1994 provision authorizing Justice Department suits against rights-violating police departments and a 2000 provision requiring data collection on arrest-related deaths.

Financial corruption of the sort widespread in earlier eras continued as a recurrent issue. In the most dramatic episode, New York City police detective Frank Serpico blew the whistle on widespread bribery and extortion in the NYPD in a newspaper expose in 1970 and a year later as a witness before the blue-ribbon Knapp Commission.[24] The city's response to the commission's recommendations for internal reforms was criticized as timid. Two decades later, however, Mayor Rudy Giuliani established a standing independent commission to combat police corruption. Today, critics in New York continue to highlight allegations of misconduct, but the commission credits the department's Internal Affairs Bureau generally with "thorough and diligent investigations" of accusations.[25]

In the 1990s, the Los Angeles Police Department experienced two major scandals, each of which made national headlines. In the first, an onlooker captured on videotape the seemingly unjustified beating of an African-American suspect, Rodney King, by LAPD officers on the night of March 3, 1991, after a high-speed automobile chase. The blue-ribbon Christopher Commission created in the wake of the incident found that "a significant number" of officers repetitively used excessive force against suspects. The acquittals of the officers charged in the King beating in 1992 touched off riots in the city's largely African-American neighborhoods and helped force the resignation of Police Chief Daryl Gates. He was succeeded by Willie Williams, the LAPD's first African-American chief.

The King beating also led to the federal law authorizing the Justice Department to sue local police departments for rights violations. Members of Congress from California pushed the proposal unsuccessfully in 1991 and 1992; it was enacted in 1994 as a provision in the omnibus Violent Crime Control and Law Enforcement

Act, thanks in part to a push from then-Senate Judiciary Committee Chairman Joseph Biden. Despite its later importance, the provision attracted little attention. A detailed Justice Department fact sheet on the law failed to mention the provision.

By 1996, however, the department's civil rights division was beginning to use the new powers with investigations initiated in response to citizen complaints of police departments in Pittsburgh and Steubenville, Ohio. By the end of the decade, those cases had resulted in consent decrees requiring organizational changes. Nine other investigations were pending as the decade ended, including one in Washington, D.C., requested in 1999 by a new chief of police.

The department had already investigated the Los Angeles Police Department for three years when a new scandal erupted in 1999, featuring wide-ranging excessive force, corruption and obstruction of justice accusations against members of an antigang unit assigned to one of Los Angeles' predominantly Latino communities. The wide-ranging allegations of misconduct by Rampart Division officers included unprovoked shootings and beatings, planting of evidence, stealing and dealing in narcotics and covering up of the offenses. The scandal led to disciplinary actions against 58 officers, but an independent commission later criticized the department's response as inadequate.

The Justice Department intensified its investigation of the LAPD after the scandal. By mid-2000, government lawyers were threatening to sue the city in federal court unless it agreed to wide-ranging internal reforms. Mayor Richard Riordan resisted any agreement, but painstaking negotiations eventually resulted in the city's agreement to an enforceable consent decree that the city council approved by a vote of 11-2 on Nov. 2, 2000. Among other provisions, the agreement required creation of a new division to investigate all uses of force. The decree, formally entered in June 2001, was terminated in 2009.[26]

Meanwhile, Congress gave the federal government an additional tool for police accountability by passing the Death in Custody Reporting Act to collect data on deaths of inmates in prisons and jails and of suspects in police custody. The bill was approved by voice vote in the House of Representatives in June 2000 and by the Senate in September; President Bill Clinton signed it into law on Oct. 13. After setting up procedures, the Bureau of Justice Statistics began collecting reports on police-custody deaths in fiscal 2003.

Changing Priorities

The Justice Department's oversight of local law enforcement agencies lagged under President George W. Bush. Investigations and cases already initiated were continued, but reports on newly opened investigations took a deferential tone toward police policies. Obama's selection of civil rights-minded officials for key posts at the Justice Department signaled a likely change in priorities. Even before Perez's confirmation to head the civil rights division, the special litigation section's report on one local department took a sharper tone than those in the Bush years. By the end of 2011, the section's activist stance was evident with a record number of investigations open and stinging reports issued on five law enforcement bodies within four months.

As a presidential candidate in 2000, Bush said he believed police matters should be handled locally. Under Bush, the civil rights division became highly politicized, morale declined sharply and career lawyers left in droves. A later report by the Government Accountability Office found that the special litigation section suffered an attrition rate of 31 percent in 2005, 24 percent in 2006 and 18 percent in 2007.[27]

The special litigation section had achieved important victories early in the Bush years in investigations begun by the Clinton administration of police forces in Washington, D.C.; Detroit; and Prince George's County, Md. The investigation in Washington found "a pattern . . . of excessive force" by officers in the 1990s and applauded new efforts to reduce the problem. Police officials agreed to the appointment of a monitor to oversee the department for five years. In Detroit, a consent decree agreed to in June 2003 similarly provided for an outside monitor to check compliance with changes that included new steps to track officers named in excessive-force complaints. In Prince George's County in suburban Washington, D.C., the police agreed in January 2004 to curb excessive force by officers and restrict the use of police dogs, with compliance to be tracked by an outside monitor.[28]

In later years, however, reports on police departments appeared to steer clear of pointed criticism or threats of litigation. Instead, reports, such as one in August 2008 suggesting the Orange County (Fla.) Sheriff's Office

Florida Police Under Scrutiny in Trayvon Martin Case

Critics question handling of shooting by armed civilian.

The fatal shooting of an African-American teenager by a volunteer neighborhood watch coordinator in a gated suburban community in Florida has ignited a racially charged debate over the police department's handling of the case. The episode also puts a national spotlight on Florida's controversial Stand Your Ground law, which allows a civilian to use potentially lethal force in self-defense in public places without first trying to retreat to safety.[1]

Some six weeks after the Feb. 26 death of Trayvon Martin, a special state prosecutor is set to present evidence in the case on April 10 to a Seminole County grand jury. [*Update*: Special prosecutor Angela Corey announced on April 9 that the case would not be presented to the grand jury on April 10, but specified that the investigation was continuing.] The U.S. Justice Department is also reviewing the case. The moves have come, however, only after local and national protests over the authorities' decision that night not to file charges against George Zimmerman, a neighborhood watch volunteer since August 2011.

Martin, 17, was returning from a convenience store to the home of his father's girlfriend in the Retreat at Twin Lakes community in Sanford, Fla., shortly after 7 p.m. when he drew Zimmerman's suspicions. Martin was unarmed; he was carrying a bag of candy and a can of iced tea and wearing a gray hoodie to protect himself from the rain. Zimmerman, 28, a resident of white and Hispanic ancestry, was carrying a 9 mm handgun — despite earlier instructions from the Sanford police department's neighborhood watch liaison that volunteers should not be armed.

Zimmerman had volunteered for the neighborhood watch in August 2011 because of several burglaries in the gated community of some 260 homes. Suspicious of Martin, he placed a 911 call to the Sanford Police Department. Zimmerman said Martin was "just walking around" and appeared to be "up to no good." The police dispatcher advised Zimmerman not to follow Martin and to wait to meet a patrol officer. Later in the recorded four-minute call, Zimmerman is heard saying something listed on the police transcription as "unintelligible" and interpreted by others in the subsequent debate as a racial epithet.

An altercation of some sort ensued after Zimmerman — 5-foot-10, 170 pounds — got out of his vehicle and Martin — 6-foot-1, 150 pounds — realized he was being surveilled. An unidentified girlfriend of Martin's says Martin called her to complain about being followed. Zimmerman's father says his son told police that Martin challenged him, used a racial epithet, forced him to the ground and pummeled him with his fists.

Whatever the exact course of the dispute, Zimmerman fired a single shot that hit Martin in the chest. Martin died at the scene. The police officers who arrived handcuffed Zimmerman and took him to the police station, where he was questioned and released without having been tested for drugs or alcohol. A video appears to show a gash on the back of Zimmerman's head but no serious injury to his face despite Zimmerman's claim to have suffered a broken nose during the altercation. A funeral director who examined Martin's body said it showed no scrapes, bruises or other signs of a fight other than the single gunshot wound to his chest.

Martin's death drew no news coverage for almost two weeks until his father, Tracy Martin, held a news conference on March 8 to call for Zimmerman's arrest and demand the release of the tapes of Zimmerman's 911 call. The tapes, released over the next weekend, turned the episode from an overlooked local story into a round-the-clock nationwide controversy.

adopt new policies on the use of Tasers, generally included language specifying that the "technical assistance" being provided was viewed "as recommendations and not mandates."[29]

Obama's appointment of Eric Holder as the first African-American to serve as attorney general signaled a likely reinvigoration of the Justice Department's role in civil rights enforcement, including police-accountability

In the weeks since, Martin has been described as a typical teenage boy, with good manners and good attitude, but a record of three suspensions from his high school in north Miami-Dade County, where he lived with his mother. In February, he was staying with his father in Sanford after having been hit with a 10-day suspension because of marijuana residue found in his backpack.

Zimmerman is described as a former altar boy with unrealized ambitions of becoming a police officer, capable of kindness but also with a volatile temper. He was arrested in summer 2005 after pushing a Florida state alcohol agent during a raid at a college-area bar; the charge was dropped after Zimmerman agreed to a pretrial diversion program. A month later, he and his ex-fiancée obtained reciprocal domestic violence injunctions based on mutual accusations of physical violence.

From the outset, authorities in Sanford and Seminole County explained that Zimmerman had not been charged in the shooting in part because of a law Florida enacted in 2005 making it harder to prosecute individuals in the face of a claim of self-defense. The Stand Your Ground law extends the long-established "castle doctrine" — allowing the use of deadly force in self defense inside one's home — to any setting, private or public.

In its central provision, the 1,000-word statute provides that someone in a place where he or she has a right to be "has no duty to retreat and has the right to stand his or her ground and meet force with force, including deadly force if he or she reasonably believes it is necessary to do so to prevent death or great bodily harm to himself or herself or another or to prevent the commission of a forcible felony." The law specifically provides immunity from criminal or civil liability if the use of force is justified. [2]

Similar laws are on the books in about half the states. Coverage of the Florida episode has led to a national debate over the laws. Prosecutors in Florida said the law had made it harder to bring charges in homicides where the suspect claimed self-defense. Police organizations have criticized the laws, but gun-rights groups have defended them.

Only after a full month had passed since the shooting was it reported that Sanford Detective Chris Serino, the lead investigator in the case, had initially recommended

Protesters in downtown Los Angeles mark the one-month anniversary of the Feb. 26, 2012, killing of unarmed black teenager Trayvon Martin by a neighborhood watch volunteer in Florida.

charging Zimmerman with manslaughter only to be overruled by his chief and by state's attorney Norman Wolfinger, who has declined to comment on the report. Wolfinger was removed from the case after Gov. Rick Scott and Attorney General Pamela Bondi appointed Angela Corey, the state's attorney from the Jacksonville area, as special prosecutor.

— *Kenneth Jost*

---

[1] For a comprehensive overview, see Dan Barry, Serge F. Kovaleski, Campbell Robertson and Lizette Alvarez, "In the Eye of a Firestorm: In Florida, an Intersection of Tragedy, Race and Outrage," *The New York Times*, April 2, 2012, p. A1, www.nytimes.com/2012/04/02/us/trayvon-martin-shooting-prompts-a-review-of-ideals.html?_r=1&hp. The rapidly changing, heavily annotated Wikipedia entry on the case includes links to the 911 call made on the night of Trayvon Martin's shooting, to other police documents and to collections of news and commentary in *The New York Times* and *Wall Street Journal*, http://en.wikipedia.org/wiki/Shooting_of_Trayvon_Martin. Background details drawn from both accounts.

[2] See Title XLVI, Chap. 0776, www.flsenate.gov/Laws/Statutes/2011/Chapter0776/All.

---

investigations. As deputy attorney general in the Clinton administration, Holder had helped oversee police department investigations, including the filing of the suit against the Los Angeles Police Department in 2000. To head the civil rights division, Obama and Holder picked Perez, a former criminal prosecutor in the division from 1988 to 1995 who had gone on to hold political posts as deputy to the head of the division (1998-1999) and head of the

Office of Civil Rights in the Department of Health and Human Services (1999-2001). Perez drew Republican opposition because of his work with the immigrant rights group CASA de Maryland, but eventually won Senate confirmation on Oct. 6, 2009, by a vote of 72-22.[30]

Even before Perez took office, a slight change of tone was seen in the section's report on the Yonkers, N.Y., police department. The June 2009 report included the same "not a mandate" language used in earlier reports, but followed with a sentence "strongly" urging the department to adopt the recommendations listed. A report on the Inglewood, Calif., department issued in December "strongly" urged adoption of the recommended changes.

Stronger reports came in quick succession in 2011, beginning with the one on New Orleans in March. A report on Puerto Rico, issued on Sept. 7, found a pattern of "unreasonable force" along with "other misconduct" aimed at limiting free speech rights as well as "troubling evidence" of "discriminatory policing practices" targeting persons of Dominican descent. In releasing the report, Perez told reporters that the section had 17 investigations under way. The investigations are "really a cornerstone of our work," Perez said. Three months later, he elevated the issue further by personally attending December news conferences releasing the Seattle and Maricopa County reports.[31]

CURRENT SITUATION

Investigations Urged

With 20 investigations already under way, the Justice Department is being urged by citizen groups in several other cities to look into police departments with troubling records of fatal shootings and other uses of force against arrestees and suspects.

In the most recent request, the Omahans for Justice Alliance asked the Justice Department and U.S. Attorney Deborah Gilg on March 13 to investigate the Omaha Police Department. The 10-page letter cited an alleged pattern of excessive force, illegal arrests, disregard of state law and department polices and other misconduct.

"The kind of incidents that we've had are very, very serious and appear to get worse," University of Nebraska professor Walker, one of three co-signers of the letter, said at a news conference to announce the request. Supporting organizations include the ACLU of Nebraska, Nebraskans for Peace, Black Men United of Omaha, the NAACP's Omaha Branch and the Progressive Research Institute of Nebraska.[32]

In a prepared statement, Lt. Darci Tierney, a police spokeswoman, noted that the Justice Department had previously reviewed use-of-force incidents as part of "normal business practices." She voiced no objection to scrutiny of the additional incidents noted in the letter. "We strive to be a transparent agency, and if a citizen group feels the need for the Department of Justice to review these events, we welcome the review," Tierney said.[33]

Also in March, an Albuquerque citizens' group stepped up its calls for a federal investigation of the city's police department after two fatal shootings in mid-March brought the total to 18 over the past two years. Most of those killed have been young Hispanic men, according to Jewell Hall, executive director of the Martin Luther King Jr. Memorial Center. "I hope that they will do an investigation to get deep inside the Albuquerque Police Department," says Hall, a retired teacher.

The Albuquerque department drew national attention with the disclosure that the police union has had a practice for several years of giving officers involved in fatal shootings $500 to help them take time off to recover from stress related to the incidents. Critics said the payments appeared to be a bounty for killing a suspect. Police Chief Ray Schultz said he was unaware of the practice. With the controversy raging, two top officers of the Albuquerque Peace Officers Association resigned on March 27; their successors joined Schultz and Mayor Richard Berry on March 30 in announcing an end to the practice.[34]

Walker, who co-authored a study of the Albuquerque police department in 1997, says the number of deaths at the hands of police appeared to warrant a Justice Department investigation. "That's a lot of shootings," he told The Associated Press.[35]

The Justice Department has acknowledged the preliminary inquiry into the Albuquerque department but says it has made no decision on whether to open a formal investigation. The Justice Department had no response to the Omaha request in news coverage immediately afterward. Investigations are being sought in other cities, including Las Vegas, The Associated Press reported. Justice Department officials did not respond to a request from *CQ Researcher* for a complete list of current investigations.

AT ISSUE

Is the exclusionary rule needed to deter illegal police searches?

YES   Norman L Reimer
Executive Director, National Association of Criminal Defense Lawyers

Written for *CQ Researcher*, April 2012

While it is true that the Supreme Court has at times over the past decade treated the exclusionary rule with disdain, fortunately the court has not yet completely disavowed it. It is perhaps the only tool the courts have to circumscribe police behavior that violates the Fourth Amendment. Let me give you an example.

The Supreme Court in January decided a case — *U.S. v. Jones* — that is sure to be the first of many that will test the limits of government's ability to use modern technology to invade individual privacy. The court unanimously upheld the suppression of GPS tracking data, rejecting the government's sweeping claim that it can track a person's movements without spatial or temporal limitation, and without a warrant or any judicial oversight.

The idea that such surveillance could occur solely at the government's discretion prompted Chief Justice John G. Roberts Jr. to ask in astonishment whether, in the government's view, the FBI could put GPS monitors on the cars of every member of the court. The government's position was a resounding "yes." Fortunately for the future of privacy in a world in which technology now permits once unfathomable invasions of privacy, the court's decision was an equally resounding "no."

How massively was this taking place before the court's decision? During the oral argument, the deputy solicitor general acknowledged that the federal government alone has been using GPS devices "in the low thousands annually." Separate from that, state and local law enforcement authorities frequently employ GPS tracking devices — subjecting untold thousands to surveillance.

Was the court's invocation of the exclusionary rule, a venerable remedy that will soon celebrate its 100th anniversary in American jurisprudence, an effective tool to vindicate fundamental rights guaranteed by the Fourth Amendment? You bet it was. Within weeks, the FBI's general counsel, Andrew Weissmann, said the ruling in *U.S. v. Jones* caused a "sea change" in law enforcement. Following the oral argument and in anticipation of the ruling, the FBI scrambled to ensure that the government had warrants for 3,000 active GPS tracking devices.

After the decision, 250 of those tracking devices remained shut down. Many may eventually be reactivated where there is legal cause — as they should be. No doubt, states and localities are responding similarly to ensure compliance with the dictates of the Fourth Amendment. Thus, once again, the power of the exclusionary rule to rein in governmental abuse is vindicated.

NO   William J. Fitzpatrick
District Attorney, Onondaga County, N.Y.

Written for *CQ Researcher*, April 2012

As a prosecutor for 35 years, I have never met a cop who was deterred by a judicial opinion written five years after he or she made a split-second decision. The Supreme Court-crafted exclusionary rule has morphed from its intended restraint on police misconduct into a judicially sanctioned version of roulette.

Antoine Jones, a Washington, D.C., nightclub owner, was making money the old-fashioned way, entertaining his customers with hip-hop music and running the District's largest cocaine distribution ring. Rather than spend countless hours legally following Jones, police in 2005 decided to place a GPS tracking device on his wife's car, and even though not required, they actually got a search warrant to track the location of this vehicle.

This innovative tactic resulted in Jones' arrest and conviction as well as the seizure of five kilos of cocaine and $850,000 in ill-gotten drug proceeds.

Inexplicably, when the U.S. Attorney's office authorized the installation of the tracking device, the police did so one day beyond the sanctioned 10-day window.

In *United States v. Jones*, the Supreme Court ruled — for the first time — that the installation of a GPS device by the authorities on a suspect's car constituted a search under the Fourth Amendment. Thus the evidence obtained in the case was suppressed, despite the fact that, prior to the decision, the prevailing law was murky at best. Pardon me if I'm confused as to how this deters police misconduct. Would it not make more sense to punish the appropriate grammar school teachers who failed to properly train the future attorneys on how to read a calendar?

My colleagues have no problem with the GPS warrant requirement. What concerns us is the uncertainty and Draconian response to what may be charitably called a technical error. If we track EZ-Pass holders to locate an abducted child or trace a terrorist by using cell-tower records, do the criminals go free? While technology is changing rapidly, police who make life-and-death decisions do not have the luxury of waiting for the courts to delineate these constitutional boundaries before they take action.

Even the learned justices in *Jones* had little consensus on the grounds for the decision. Prosecutors merely want a rational approach to evidence suppression where concepts such as proportionality and good faith have some standing. You do not "deter" cops with a system that is, as Justice Lewis Powell said, "intolerably confusing." You only confuse cops and make the public less secure.

In both Omaha and Albuquerque, the groups pressing for federal investigations complained that civilians involved in police shootings or use-of-force incidents were predominantly people of color. The Omaha group also cited figures from a state commission showing that black drivers are stopped almost as often by the Omaha Police Department as white drivers are.

Both forces are predominantly white. In 2000, about 80 percent of the Omaha officers were white, and the Albuquerque department was 60 percent Anglo and 36 percent Hispanic, according to federal Bureau of Justice Statistics data.[36]

In Omaha, the citizens' group also is urging the city to re-establish the office of Public Safety Auditor. The office was created in 2001, but Mayor Mike Fahey fired Tristan Bonn from the post in October 2006, barely a week after she delivered a report sharply critical of the department. The city fought Bonn's lawsuit to regain the position and has failed to refill the position, according to the citizens' group.[37]

The current mayor, Jim Suttle, says there is no need for an auditor. "We have a lot of faith in our police chief," he told an Omaha television station in September 2011 in the midst of a controversy over the videotaped beating and kicking of a suspect in police custody.[38]

In Albuquerque, an officer involved in a November 2009 shooting was fired the next year after the department's internal affairs unit and the Independent Review Officer found the shooting unjustified. Schultz said he fired Brandon Carr because the officer lied to investigators about the events.

The city paid the victim's family $950,000 to settle a civil suit, but on March 30 the district attorney's office announced no criminal charges would be brought against Carr. Out of 29 police shootings since 2009, eight are awaiting grand jury action, but no criminal charges have been brought in the other 21, according to the *Albuquerque Journal*.[39]

Reforms Outlined

The Seattle Police Department is preparing to adopt a 20-point reform plan aimed at answering criticisms from citizens' groups and the Justice Department and perhaps avoiding federal court supervision for several years.

The plan, released by Mayor McGinn on March 29, includes steps to revamp use-of-force policies, strengthen the role of a newly established Force Review Board, collect data on possible racial profiling and improve diversity training. In one specific change, the plan responds to criticism of how police dealt with Occupy Seattle protesters in November by prohibiting the use of pepper spray except in self-defense or as "a last resort."

Seattle and Justice Department officials met behind closed doors the next day to discuss the plan. Seattle officials appeared to hope the department would back away from insisting that the city agree to a court order giving a federal judge supervisory authority over the plan's implementation for a specified number of years.[40]

Progress on a reform plan in Seattle came after negotiations between the Justice Department and New Orleans officials had stalled because of a bizarre incident involving the federal government's point person in the talks. Sal Perricone withdrew from the talks and then resigned from the U.S. Attorney's office in New Orleans in March after he acknowledged having used a pseudonym to post hundreds of online comments about law enforcement-related stories on the *Times-Picayune*'s website, nola.com.[41]

Two of the major groups involved in requesting the Justice Department investigation of the Seattle Police Department reacted approvingly to what McGinn called the 20/20 plan — 20 steps to be put into effect over 20 months. Estela Ortega, executive director of the Hispanic advocacy group El Centro de la Raza, appeared at the news conference with McGinn and Chief John Diaz and praised their willingness to work with community leaders on the plan.

In a brief statement, Kathleen Taylor, executive director of ACLU of Washington State, said the civil rights organization was "encouraged" by the plan. But she said a court-supervised consent decree "is critical to ensure that reforms are thoroughly implemented and are sustained for the long term."

The plan's use-of-force provisions call for developing "updated, clear policies" on the use of "lethal, less-lethal and non-lethal tools available to officers." Officers would be trained annually on the policies and on "de-escalation" of "low-level encounters." Sergeants and commanders are also to be given annual training on how to investigate and document use-of-force incidents.

Seattle's Force Review Board, established after the release of the Justice Department report in December, would be given a formal role. Some form of civilian review of the board's work would be instituted.

Issues of "biased policing" are to be addressed by streamlining race-data collection related to traffic stops and initiating the collection of race data for pedestrian encounters. The University of Washington's African-American Studies Department is to be engaged to review the department's practices as related to the issue.

In New Orleans, Perricone took himself out of the federal-local negotiations on March 16 after his role as pseudonymous online commentator came to light. Mayor Landrieu said Perricone's participation had "poisoned" the negotiations, but U.S. Attorney Jim Letten insisted the removal would not cause a delay.

ACLU official Esman says the ongoing talks are "very guarded," but she expects eventual agreement on a court-supervised consent decree. "Something will come of it," Esman says. "Whether it will be enough, whether it will work is anybody's guess."

Meanwhile, another of the police forces sharply criticized in Justice Department reports last year got new leadership in late March in a move that may ease the way for reforms. Puerto Rico Gov. Luis Fortuño named former FBI official Hector Pesquera as superintendent of the commonwealth's 17,000-person police department on March 29 following the resignation of Emilio Díaz Cólon from the post.

Díaz had been superintendent for only three months when the Justice Department report was released in September. He responded by denying any constitutional violations by the force. Over the next six months, Díaz was criticized for failing to offer an anticrime program. Fortuño quoted Díaz as saying he was resigning to avoid hurting prospective reforms.[42]

OUTLOOK

Police Under Pressure

Popular trends in law enforcement push police departments in opposite directions. Police departments use high-tech tools to surveil suspects, crack down on drugs and try to spot terrorists, even as officers are being urged to get out of their cars, walk the streets and engage the public in "community policing."[43]

Along with these competing visions of good policing come financial pressures as fiscally strapped local governments cut back on police departments' staffing, pay and services. In Detroit, police precincts are open only during daytime hours, and nonemergency reports have to be made through a central call center. To save $80 million in 2011, the Los Angeles City Council cut overtime pay for cops, but the department still had to find $41 million more in savings. And police departments around the country have been dealing with layoffs by taking reports on many property crimes over the phone instead of sending officers to investigate.[44]

The financial pressures lead police consultant Scott to worry about cutbacks in the training needed to ensure that officers live up to professional standards. "Law enforcement is not training its personnel the way it should," the former police chief says. "This is where I see many, many lawsuits that could be avoided if we as a public demanded to have better trained police officers."

Police accountability is being enhanced, however, by new technology, such as the video cameras now installed on many police cars to record officer-suspect encounters. "The way to encourage police reform and police accountability is [with] sunlight," says University of Baltimore professor Kane, "making these practices known to the public."

Technology at the same time increases the potential for police abuse of individual privacy and safety. Civil liberties groups complain that local police now are using cell phone tracking routinely and aggressively, often without much judicial oversight. Tasers, once seen as a non-lethal alternative to firearms for subduing suspects, are linked by the human rights group Amnesty International to hundreds of deaths of suspects — a risk that the manufacturer acknowledges but calls exaggerated.[45]

The high-power, high-tech weaponry provided to SWAT teams, especially for drug raids, is viewed disapprovingly, even by police-friendly experts. "In some cases, you've got this hypercoercion being used in situations that don't require this kind of force," Kane says. "It's almost like a toy that needs to be played with."

Even without high-power weaponry, the risk of unnecessary and excessive force, sometimes lethal, persists in police-civilian encounters. Review procedures in place, as in Albuquerque, often find officers' conduct justifiable, even as outside groups and victims' families disagree. But national police organizations appear to devote little attention to the subject. In assuming the presidency of the International Association of Chiefs of Police in November

2011, Quincy, Fla., Police Chief Walter McNeil said the group's highest priority would be "to continue a comprehensive violence-against-police-officers reduction strategy." McNeil did not address the issue of excessive force against civilians, nor has he mentioned the issue in his monthly column in the association's magazine despite the spate of critical Justice Department reports in December.[46]

Walker, the veteran of police accountability issues, worries that the post-9/11 emphasis on homeland security has been a setback for best police practices. "Your primary focus is not community policing, which tells you that the major things we have to do is work with people in the community," he says. And he worries about the impact of budget-imposed layoffs. "If the economy worsens," Walker says, "things could be very, very worse."

Still, Walker believes that excessive force and racial profiling are not intractable problems. "If these problems are persisting, it's just because [police leaders] are not paying attention," Walker says. "We have a much clearer picture of possible things we can do. It's just finding the will do to do them."

NOTES

1. Account drawn primarily from coverage by Brendan McCarthy in *The Times-Picayune* (New Orleans): "Raid details show focus on weed," March 10, 2012, p. A1; "Man killed by cops was not armed," March 9, 2012, p. A1. Some other information drawn from other *Times-Picayune* articles, most of them by McCarthy.

2. Johnson, Shorty quoted in McCarthy, *ibid.*, March 10.

3. The New Orleans report is available on the Justice Department's website: www.justice.gov/crt/about/spl/nopd.php. A complete list of Special Litigation Section cases and matters, including "Conduct of Law Enforcement Agencies Investigations" and "Conduct of Law Enforcement Agencies Complaints," is found here: www.justice.gov/crt/about/spl/findsettle.php.

4. Diaz quoted in Mike Carter, Steve Miletich, and Jennifer Sullivan, "City faces possibility of court intervention," *The Seattle Times*, Dec. 17, 2011, p. A1; Gallo's retirement reported in Denise Buffa and Josh Kovner, "Chief Steps Down," *Hartford Courant* (Conn.), Jan. 31, 2012, p. A1; Quoted in J. J. Hensley, "Negotiations between MCSO, DOJ fall apart," *The Arizona Republic* (Phoenix), April 4, 2012, p. A1.

5. For previous coverage, see these *CQ Researcher* reports: Kenneth Jost, "Policing the Police," March 17, 2000, pp. 209-240; Sarah Glazer, "Police Corruption," Nov. 24, 1995, pp. 1041-1064; Richard L. Worsnop, "Police Brutality," Sept. 6, 1991, pp. 633-656; and earlier reports in *CQ Researcher-plus Archives*.

6. See Brendan McCarthy and Laura Maggi, "NOPD deeply defective, report says," *The Times-Picayune*, March 18, 2011, p. A1; Brendan McCarthy, "Reforms in place, Serpas says," *ibid.*, March 24, 2011, p. B1. See also Laura Maggi, " 'Clear pattern' of excessive force cited," *ibid.*, March 18, 2011, p. A14.

7. See Brendan McCarthy, "Judge imposes stiff sentences on 5 NOPD officers convicted in Danziger shootings," nola.com, April 4, 2012, www.nola.com/crime/index.ssf/2012/04/judge_imposes_sentences_on_5_n.html. The defendants and their sentences are Robert Faulcon Jr., 65 years; Kenneth Bowen, 40 years; Robert Gisevius Jr., 40 years; Anthony Villavaso II, 38 years; Arthur "Archie" Kaufman, six years. For an overview of the case in advance of the trial, see Brendan McCarthy and Laura Maggi, "Federal prosecutors allege civil rights abuses," *The Times-Picayune*, June 19, 2011, A1; for a post-verdict account, see Katie Urbaszewski and Brendan McCarthy, "Danziger evidence outweighed chaos theory," *ibid.*, Aug. 23, 2011, p. A1.

8. "Taking Stock: Report from the 2010 Roundtable on the State and Local Law Enforcement Police Pattern or Practice Program (42 USC § 14141)," National Institute of Justice, September 2011, https://ncjrs.gov/pdffiles1/nij/234458.pdf.

9. Quoted in Jerry Markon, "Justice Dept. is policing the police," *The Washington Post*, Sept. 18, 2011, p. A3.

10. See "Highlights of AP's probe into NYPD intelligence operations," http://ap.org/media-center/nypd/investigation.

11. See "Investigation of the Seattle Police Department," U.S. Department of Justice, Civil Rights Division/U.S. Attorney's Office, Western District, Washington, Dec. 16, 2011, www.justice.gov/crt/about/spl/documents/spd_findletter_12-16-11.pdf. The letter requesting the investigation is on the ACLU's website: www.aclu-wa.org/re-request-investigate-pattern-or-practice-misconduct-seattle-police-department. For initial coverage of Williams' death, see Sara Jean Green and Steve Miletich, "Police have questions about shooting by cop," *The Seattle Times*, Sept. 1, 2010, p. A1.

12. "Police Use of Force in America," International Association of Chiefs of Police, 2001, www.theiacp.org/Portals/0/pdfs/Publications/2001useofforce.pdf; "Police Use of Force," National Institute of Justice, www.nij.gov/topics/law-enforcement/officer-safety/use-of-force/welcome.htm#note2 (modified January 2012).

13. The decisions are *Tennessee v. Garner*, 471 U.S. 1 (1985); *Graham v. Connor*, 490 U.S. 386 (1989).

14. William Terrill, Eugene A. Paoline III and Jason Ingram, "Final Technical Report Draft: Assessing Police Use of Force Policy and Outcomes," National Institute of Justice, February 2012, p. 159, www.ncjrs.gov/pdffiles1/nij/grants/237794.pdf.

15. Matthew Kauffman, "In Traffic Stops, Police Tougher on Blacks, Hispanics," *Hartford Courant* (Connecticut), Feb. 26, 2012, p. A1.

16. New Orleans data cited in Kenneth Jost, " 'Black on Black' Racial Profiling: Why?" *Jost on Justice* (blog), March 11, 2011; Justice Department findings on Maricopa County, www.justice.gov/crt/about/spl/mcso.php; East Haven; and www.justice.gov/crt/about/spl/documents/easthaven_findletter_12-19-11.pdf.

17. Figures from the New York Civil Liberties Union cited in Sean Gardiner, "Stop-and-Frisks Hit Record in 2011," *The Wall Street Journal*, Feb. 14, 2012, p. A21.

18. Gitta Laasby, "Flynn addresses inquiry into strip searches," *Journal Sentinel* (Milwaukee), March 23, 2012, p. B1. Background on Mucha drawn from past coverage by Gina Barton: "Gun Case Falls Apart With Cop's Testimony," *ibid.*, Aug. 8, 2010, p. A1; "Forceful Impact: Suspects have accused Sgt. Jason Mucha 10 times of beating them or planting drugs. He wasn't disciplined, but courts took notice," *ibid.*, Sept. 29, 2007, p. A1.

19. Anthony Cormier and Matthew Doig, "Unfit for Duty," *Herald-Tribune* (Sarasota, Fla.), December 2011 (nine parts), http://cops.htcreative.com/; Gina Barton, "At least 93 Milwaukee police officers have been disciplined for violating the law," *Journal Sentinel*, Oct. 23, 2011 (1st of 3 parts), www.jsonline.com/watchdog/watchdogreports/at-least-93-milwaukee-police-officers-have-been-disciplined-for-violating-law-132268408.html.

20. Background drawn in part from Samuel Walker and Charles M. Katz, *Police in America: An Introduction* (5th ed., 2005), chapter 2 (pp. 23-58). The sixth edition (2011) was not available for use before deadline.

21. *Ibid.*, pp. 33-34.

22. The major cases are *Brown v. Mississippi*, 297 U.S. 278 (1936); *Miranda v. Arizona*, 384 U.S. 436 (1966); *Mapp v. Ohio*, 367 U.S. 463 (1960). For background, see David G. Savage, Guide to the U.S. Supreme Court (5th ed., 2011), pp. 740-748 (confessions), 725-726 (exclusionary rule).

23. For an official assessment, see "LEAA/OJP Retrospective: 30 Years of Federal Support for State and Local Criminal Justice," U.S. Department of Justice, Office of Justice Programs, July 11, 1996, p. 3, www.ncjrs.gov/pdffiles1/nij/164509.pdf.

24. For background, see Glazer, *op. cit.*; Peter Maas, *Serpico* (1973), and the cinemazation of the same title, also 1973, with Al Pacino in the title role.

25. "14th Annual Report," City of New York Commission to Combat Police Corruption, February 2012, www.nyc.gov/html/ccpc/downloads/pdf/14th_annual_report.pdf.

26. See Tina Daunt and Jim Newton, "City OKs Police Reform Pact With U.S.," *Los Angeles Times*, Nov. 3, 2000.

27. See Ryan J. Reilly, "Report Delivers Hard Numbers on Bush Civil Rights Division," Main Justice, Dec. 7, 2009, www.mainjustice.com/2009/12/07/report-delivers-hard-numbers-on-bush-civil-rights-division/.

28. See David A. Fahrenthold, "U.S. Faults D.C. Police Use of Force in the '90s," *The Washington Post*, June 14, 2001, p. B1; "Findings Letter re Use of Force by the Washington Metropolitan Police Department," U.S. Department of Justice, June 13, 2001, www.justice.gov/crt/about/spl/documents/dcfindings.php; M.L. Erlick and Ben Schmitt, "U.S. Demand to Detroit: Stop Police Abuses Now," *Detroit Free-Press*, June 13, 2003; "Investigation of the Detroit Police Department" (technical assistance letters, 2002), U.S. Department of Justice, www.justice.gov/crt/about/spl/documents/dpd/detroit_cover.php; Jamie Stockwell and Ruben Castaneda, "Pr. George's Agrees to Curb Excessive Force by Police," *The Washington Post*, Jan. 23, 2004, p. A1; U.S. Department of Justice, "Investigation of the Prince George's County Police Department," Jan. 22, 2004, www.justice.gov/crt/about/spl/documents/pgpd/pgpd_cover.php.

29. "Investigation of the Orange County Sheriff's Office Use of Conducted Energy Devices," U.S. Department of Justice, Aug. 20, 2008, www.justice.gov/crt/about/spl/documents/orangecty_ta_ltr.pd.

30. Andrew Ramonas, "Senate Confirms Tom Perez," Main Justice, Oct. 6, 2009, www.mainjustice.com/2009/10/06/senate-confirms-tom-perez/. For a profile, see Jerry Zremski, "Former area man takes top civil rights post," *Buffalo News*, Nov. 14, 2009, p. A1.

31. Perez quoted in Markon, *op. cit.*

32. Quoted in Sarah Te Slaa, "Group Calls for Federal Investigation Into Police Department," KMTV (Omaha), March 13, 2012, www.kmtv.com/news/local/142578935.html. See also Roseann Moring, "Groups seek federal probe of Omaha police," *Omaha World-Herald*, March 14, 2012.

33. The statement is cited in full in "Police Respond to Complaint," WOWT, March 13, 2012, www.wowt.com/home/headlines/Police_Respond_to_Complaint_142541525.html?storySection=story.

34. See Jeff Proctor, "Cop Payments to Stop," *Albuquerque Journal*, March 30, 2012, p. A1; and earlier coverage by same reporter. For national coverage, see Manny Fernandez and Dan Frosch, "Payments to Albuquerque Officers Are Called a 'Bounty System,'" *The New York Times*, March 25, 2012, p. A20.

35. See Russell Contreras, "Albuquerque activists seek federal probe of police," The Associated Press, March 27, 2012. Some other background drawn from article.

36. See "Law Enforcement Management and Administrative Statistics, 2000," Bureau of Justice Statistics, April 2004, pp. 31, 32, http://bjs.ojp.usdoj.gov/content/pub/pdf/lema001a.pdf.

37. See Lynn Safranek, "Future of police auditor post under review," *Omaha World-Herald*, Oct. 31, 2006, p. 1B.

38. Liz Dorland, "Ernie Chambers Requests Federal Investigation Into Omaha Police Department," KMTV, Sept. 7, 2011, www.kmtv.com/news/local/129429963.html.

39. Jeff Proctor, "Fired Cop Cleared in Death of Vet," *Albuquerque Journal*, March 30, 2012, p. 41.

40. See "SPD 20/20: A Vision for the Future," City of Seattle, www.seattle.gov/mayor/media/PDF/SPD2020.pdf. For coverage, see Mike Carter, "Seattle mayor announces broad initiative to improve police force," *The Seattle Times*, March 29, 2012; Sara Jean Green, "Mayor's initiatives seem to address complaints of biased policing," *ibid*.

41. See Michelle Krupa and Gordon Russell, "Prosecutor bows out of NOPD talks," *The Times-Picayune*, March 17, 2012, p. A9.

42. "Former FBI director named Puerto Rico police chief," The Associated Press, March 29, 2012.

43. For background, see Richard L. Worsnop, "Community Policing," *CQ Researcher*, Feb. 5, 1993, pp. 97-120.

44. See Joe Rossiter, "Godbee: Virtual police precinct plan to go into effect Monday," *Detroit Free Press*, Jan. 31, 2012, p. A7; Kate Linthicum, "L.A. council cuts millions from budget," *Los Angeles Times*, May 19, 2011, p. AA1; Kevin Johnson, "Home burglarized? Fill out a form," *USA Today*, Aug. 25, 2010, p. 1A.

45. On use of cell phone tracking, see Eric Lichtblau, "Police Are Using Phone Tracking as Routine Tool," *The New York Times*, April 1, 2012, p. A1; on Tasers,

see CBS News, "Taser: An officer's weapon of choice," 60 Minutes (David Martin, correspondent; Mary Walsh, producer), Nov. 13, 2011, www.cbsnews.com/8301-18560_162-57323531/taser-an-officers-weapon-of-choice/.

46. See Walter A. McNeil, "The Year Ahead," *Police Chief*, November 2011, www.policechiefmagazine.org/magazine/index.cfm?fuseaction=display_arch&article_id=2519&issue_id=112011.

BIBLIOGRAPHY

Books

Delattre, Edwin J., *Characters and Cops: Ethics in Policing* (6th ed.), AEI Press, 2011.
A professor of philosophy, emeritus, at Boston University and an adjunct scholar at the American Enterprise Institute combines two decades of studying police behavior to examine a full range of ethics issues for law enforcement. Includes detailed notes, short bibliography.

Kane, Robert J., and Michael D. White, *Jammed Up: Bad Cops, Police Misconduct, and the New York City Police Department*, New York University Press, 2012 (forthcoming: Nov. 19).
The book examines the causes of — and responses to — alleged police misconduct based on unprecedented, complete access to the confidential files of more than 1,500 New York Police Department officers over a 20-year period. Includes detailed notes, bibliography. Kane is an associate professor at the University of Baltimore's School of Criminal Justice, White an associate professor at Arizona State University's School of Criminology and Criminal Justice. For an earlier article on their findings, see Robert J. Kane and Michael D. White, "Bad Cops: A study of career-ending misconduct among New York City police officers," *Criminology and Public Policy*, Vol. 8, No. 4 (November 2009), pp. 737-769. The issue includes three other policy essays on police misconduct.

Roberg, Roy, Kenneth Novak, and Gary Cordner, *Police & Society* (3d ed.), Roxbury Publishing, 2005.
The college textbook includes lengthy chapters on "Behavior and Misconduct," "Force and Coercion" and "Accountability and Ethics." Each chapter includes notes, suggested websites for further study. The book also comes with an interactive student study guide. The authors are professors, respectively, at San Jose State University, University of Missouri-Kansas City and Eastern Kentucky University.

Walker, Samuel, and Charles M. Katz, *Police in America: An Introduction* (6th ed.), McGraw-Hill, 2011.
The college textbook includes overviews of the history and current structure of U.S. law enforcement and individual chapters on police corruption and accountability, plus chapter notes, a glossary and an interactive student study guide. Walker is a professor of criminal justice, emeritus, at the University of Nebraska-Omaha and a longtime expert on police issues; Katz is an associate professor at Arizona State University's School of Criminology and Criminal Justice.

Walker, Samuel, *The New World of Police Accountability*, SAGE, 2005.
The book synthesizes major developments in police accountability over the previous decade. For an earlier account, see *Police Accountability: The Role of Citizen Oversight* (Thomson Learning, 2001). Walker maintains an informative website on police accountability issues, including a page covering developments in New Orleans (http://samuelwalker.net/). His other books include *Popular Justice: A History of American Criminal Justice* (2d ed.) (Oxford University Press, 1998); and *A Critical History of Police Reform: The Emergence of Professionalism* (Lexington, 1977).

Articles

Kocher, Charles, *et al.*, "Sustaining Police Operations at an Efficient and Effective Level under Difficult Economic Times," *Police Chief*, March 2012, www.policechiefmagazine.org/magazine/index.cfm?fuseaction=display&article_id=2621&issue_id=32012.
The article, co-authored by a retired deputy Camden, N.J., police chief, in the monthly magazine of the International Association of Chiefs of Police examines the need for adapting police department structures and operations in times of layoffs, cutbacks and consolidated services.

Reynolds, Dawn, "Coast to Coast — the Public and the Justice Department is Demanding More Accountability," National Association of Civilian Oversight of Law Enforcement, spring 2012,

www.nacole.org/sites/default/files/NACOLE_Review_Spring2012.pdf.
The article in the association's quarterly newsletter reviews the Justice Department's reports on Seattle; Maricopa County, Ariz., and East Haven, Conn.

Reports and Studies

"Taking Stock: Report from the 2010 Roundtable on the State and Local Law Enforcement Police Pattern or Practice Program (42 USC § 14141)," National Institute of Justice, September 2011, https://ncjrs.gov/pdffiles1/nij/234458.pdf.
The report includes a 10-page summary of the views expressed at a roundtable convened to assess the impact of the Justice Department's pattern or practice of police misconduct program. The report includes notes, a list of all participants and a list of settlements and investigations as of July 2010.

Weisburd, David, Rosann Greenspan, Edwin E. Hamilton, Kellie A. Bryant and Hubert Williams, "The Abuse of Police Authority: A National Study of Police Officers' Attitudes," Police Foundation, 2001, www.policefoundation.org/pdf/AOANarrative.pdf.
The first-ever national survey of police officers' attitudes found that most believe extreme abuse-of-authority cases are infrequent and that the public and the media are too concerned with such incidents.

For More Information

American Civil Liberties Union, 125 Broad St., New York, NY 10004; 212-549-2500; www.aclu.org. Has been active on racial profiling, use of force and other police-practices issues.

Fraternal Order of Police, Grand Lodge, 1410 Donelson Pike, A-17, Nashville, TN 37217; 615-399-0900; www.grandlodgefop.org. Largest membership organization representing rank-and-file law enforcement officers.

International Association of Chiefs of Police, 515 North Washington St., Alexandria, VA 22314; 703-836-6767; www.theiacp.org. Represents operating chief executives of international, federal, state and local law enforcement agencies of all sizes.

National Association of Civilian Oversight of Law Enforcement, 638 E. Vermont St., P.O. Box 1737, Indianapolis, IN 46206; 1-866-462-2653; www.nacole.org. Brings together individuals and agencies working to establish or improve oversight of police officers in the United States.

National Association of Criminal Defense Lawyers, 1025 Connecticut Ave., N.W., Suite 901, Washington, DC 20036; 202-872-8600; www.crimdefense.org. The largest organization exclusively representing criminal defense lawyers.

National District Attorneys Association, 44 Canal Center Plaza, Suite 110, Alexandria, VA 22314; 703-549-9222; www.ndaa.org. Represents criminal prosecutors in state, district, county and city attorneys' offices.

National Sheriffs' Association, 1450 Duke St., Alexandria, VA 22314; 1-800-424-7827; www.sheriffs.org. Represents and assists sheriffs' offices nationwide through education, training and information resources.

Police Foundation, 1201 Connecticut Ave., N.W., Washington, DC 20036-2636; 202-833-1460; www.policefoundation.org. Established by the Ford Foundation in 1970; sponsors research to support innovation and improvement in policing.

9 Hate Speech

Marcia Clemmitt and Charles S. Clark

The Rutgers University women's basketball team answers media questions about the derogatory remark made by popular shock jock Don Imus. The team later met with Imus and accepted his apology, but he was fired after public outrage led advertisers to abandon his program.

From *CQ Researcher*,
June 1, 2007 (updated October 14, 2010).

When radio host Don Imus offhandedly referred to the Rutgers University women's basketball team as "nappy-headed hos" on April 4, it was far from the first time that radio's original shock jock had used racist and sexist jokes on his program. Insults were long a stock in trade of "Imus in the Morning," the 10th-highest-rated radio talk show in the nation last April and also a staple on MSNBC's cable TV lineup, where ratings were rising.

To name just a few examples, in the early 1990s, Imus referred to then-*New York Times* White House correspondent Gwen Ifill, an African-American, as "the cleaning lady."[1] In December 2006, he used an anti-Semitic stereotype, calling the "Jewish management" of his employer, CBS Radio, "money-grubbing bastards."[2]

In 2001, *Chicago Tribune* columnist Clarence Page, then a regular guest on the program, asked Imus to promise to stop using phrases like "knuckle-dragging apes" to refer to black athletes and words like "thugs, pimps and muggers" to refer to non-criminal African-Americans. Imus agreed but quickly broke his pledge.[3]

The incident with the Rutgers team had a different outcome, however.

A liberal media-criticism group, Media Matters for America, noted the April 4 remark on its Web site. By April 6 the National Association of Black Journalists called for the 66-year-old Imus to be fired, and the Rev. Al Sharpton and other individuals and groups soon followed suit.

"Imus has a pathetic yet well-documented history of resorting to racist, sexist and homophobic commentary" and should resign

209

Beyond derailing Imus' nearly four-decade run as a radio host, the incident triggered a widespread debate about the public use of racist and sexist language, especially by shock jocks and some commentators, and in the lyrics of gangsta-rap music, which often refer to women as "bitches" and "hos," as Imus did.

Racist and sexist insults are common currency among radio shock talkers, who delight in "bringing private behavior out into public," giving the audience "the thrill of crossing that line," according to John Baugh, a professor of linguistics at Washington University in St. Louis. But when private language goes public, "a tremendous amount of bigotry can be exposed that's beneath the veneer" of polite society, Baugh says.

In the weeks since the Imus incident, radio networks have responded more firmly than usual to shock-jock forays into racist and sexist clowning, firing or suspending several hosts for comments not strikingly different from their usual fare.

Imus' former employer CBS Radio indefinitely suspended two New York shock jocks, JV and Elvis, for airing prank calls to Chinese restaurants that included terms like "shrimp flied lice." On May 15 XM Satellite Radio, a subscriber-only service not even carried over public airwaves, suspended shock jocks Gregg "Opie" Hughes and Anthony Cumia for 30 days for on-air comments surrounding a segment about a homeless man who declared he wanted to rape Secretary of State Condeleeza Rice and other women.

Some media analysts, noting that edgy content sells, predict the shock-jock crackdown is probably temporary.

Unlike some activists, the advertisers who abandoned "Imus in the Morning" "never intended to kill the show" and generally don't rule out sponsoring Imus again in the future, wrote Steve McClellan of *AdWeek* magazine. The program "helped sell marketers' products to more than

or be fired, said National Association of Hispanic Journalists President Rafael Olmeda in a statement.[4]

Imus' show has long been a popular stop for politicians such as Sens. John McCain, R-Ariz., and John Kerry, D-Mass., as well as powerful Washington journalists like "Meet the Press" host Tim Russert. Though some long-time guests like former *Boston Globe* columnist Tom Oliphant defended their friend and depicted his remark as a joke that misfired, advertisers including General Motors and American Express became concerned about the burgeoning public scrutiny and intensifying coverage of the flap in the press and pulled ads from the show. On April 11, MSNBC canceled "Imus in the Morning"; CBS followed suit the next day.[5]

Conservatives Are Top Talk Hosts

With at least 13.5 million weekly listeners, political commentator Rush Limbaugh drew the largest talk radio audience in fall 2006, followed by fellow conservatives Sean Hannity and Michael Savage. Don Imus, whose show was later canceled, was tied for 10th place.

Top Talk Radio Hosts, fall 2006

Host	Minimum Weekly Listeners
1. Rush Limbaugh	13.5 million
2. Sean Hannity	12.5 million
3. Michael Savage	8.25 million
4. Dr. Laura Schlessinger	8 million
5. Laura Ingraham	5 million
6. Glenn Beck	3.75 million
Neal Boortz	
Mike Gallagher	
7. Jim Bohannon	3.25 million
Clark Howard	
Mark Levin	
Bill O'Reilly	
8. Bill Bennett	3 million
Jerry Doyle	
Dave Ramsey	
Ed Schultz	
Doug Stephan	
9. Michael Medved	2.75 million
George Noory	

Host	Minimum Weekly Listeners
10. Dr. Joy Browne	2.25 million
Don Imus	
Kim Komando	
Jim Rome	
11. Bob Brinker	1.75 million
Tom Leykis	
12. Rusty Humphries	1.5 million
Lars Larson	
G. Gordon Liddy	
Mancow	
13. Alan Colmes	1.25 million
Al Franken	
Bill Handel	
Hugh Hewitt	
Lionel	
Stephanie Miller	
Randi Rhodes	
14. Dr. Dean Edell	1 million
Opie & Anthony	
Michael Reagan	

Source: *Talkers* magazine, 2007

2 million mostly affluent viewers and listeners each week," garnering $33 million in ads annually for MSNBC and another $11 million for WFAN, the New York radio station where it originated.[6]

But some conservative commentators warn that those liberal activist groups that pushed for Imus' firing are carrying on with their agendas in the hope of ending the dominance of conservative talk on radio and television. One possible way of doing this would be advocating for the restoration of the Federal Communications Commission's Fairness Doctrine, a rule requiring broadcasters who air programs on controversial subjects to give significant time to all sides of an issue. The agency repealed it in 1987.

"It wasn't exactly clear to me how [liberals] intended to bring back the Fairness Doctrine," Cliff Kincaid, chief writer and editor at the conservative media-criticism group Accuracy in Media, said at an April 13 forum at the conservative Washington-based think tank Free Congress Foundation. "But I think now with the Imus affair, we know." It's a "short leap from firing Imus to going after [conservative commentator] Rush Limbaugh."[7]

Some of the loudest criticisms that followed the Imus affair were aimed not at racist and sexist language used by whites like Imus and Limbaugh but by black musicians — mainly in gangsta-rap lyrics.

"Now that we've gotten Imus taken care of, can we finally address what's going on with the misogyny among rappers?" asked columnist Sue Hutchison in the April 13 *San Jose Mercury News*.[8]

"Hypocrisy abounds" around the Imus firing because the same terms Imus used "go on in rap music on hundreds of radio stations around the country" without any protest from the same African-Americans who protested Imus' language, said Dick Kernan, vice president of the Specs Howard School of Broadcasting in Southfield, Mich.[9]

Others argue that gangsta-rap lyrics and a radio broadcast aren't necessarily comparable forms of media.

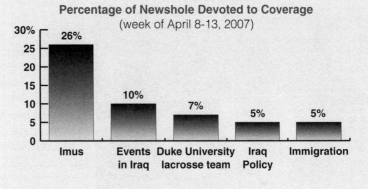

Imus Controversy Ignited Media Flood

In early April 2007, newspapers devoted more than a quarter of their "newshole" — the space devoted to news — to the controversy over Don Imus' racist remark about the Rutgers University women's basketball team. The next biggest topic was the Iraq War, which garnered just 10 percent of the newshole. Of all news stories so far in 2007 (not shown on graphic), only coverage of President Bush's troop "surge" in Iraq, in early January received more coverage (34 percent of the newshole). Total coverage of the Imus controversy received 26 percent of the coverage. Much of the Imus coverage revolved around the Rev. Al Sharpton, who skewered Imus on his talk show on April 9 and helped lead the campaign for Imus' firing.

Percentage of Newshole Devoted to Coverage
(week of April 8-13, 2007)

- Imus: 26%
- Events in Iraq: 10%
- Duke University lacrosse team: 7%
- Iraq Policy: 5%
- Immigration: 5%

Source: Project for Excellence in Journalism

Hip-hop "was a quick and easy scapegoat," says Tony N. Brown, a sociologist at Vanderbilt University. But the offensive lyrics generally aren't on display to the general public, he says. "To get these particular lyrics that people are talking about, you have to buy them," and radio bleeps or deletes them, he says.

Anger about sexist lyrics and use of other derogatory language like "nigger" in some rap music has been protested in African-American communities for years, although that fact hasn't been much noticed by the mainstream media, wrote journalist Richard Prince of the Maynard Institute for Journalism Education in Oakland, Calif. At soul singer James Brown's funeral last December, the Rev. Sharpton recalled that Brown had asked him, "What happened that we went from saying, 'I'm black and I'm proud' to calling us niggers and hos and bitches?"

"Sharpton has been out there talking about these lyrics for a long time," says Lee Thornton, a journalism

Civil rights activist and radio host the Rev. Al Sharpton became one of the first voices to call for the firing of Don Imus after he made a racial and gender slur against the Rutgers University women's basketball team. Some conservative commentators complained Sharpton hasn't made such high-profile protests against sexist lyrics by black rappers.

professor at the University of Maryland, College Park, and a former broadcaster.

To some analysts, aggressive language throughout the media is disturbing evidence that popular culture in the United States lacks civility.

"Mainstream media is becoming more like Imus" all the time, says Sheri Parks, associate professor of American studies at the university. "Ridicule and insults are the way we laugh now. We're moving closer and closer to that culture of meanness being completely mainstream."

As broadcasters, lawmakers and social critics debate the values and dangers of shock media to American culture, here are some of the questions being asked:

Have ethnic jokes and insults become too pervasive in society?

Ethnic putdowns and comedy making light of someone's gender have long been part of American culture. But social critics and other commentators argue that shock jocks, gangsta rappers and other personalities have taken things to the extreme by using slurs to target political opponents or other public figures, increasingly poisoning public discourse. The question is whether practitioners have gone over the line — and where exactly the line is?

Talk radio, at least, "is not getting dirtier, not getting cleaner" although the medium continues to expand, says Michael Harrison, founder and editor of *Talkers* magazine and a longtime observer of the phenomenon. "There's no trend toward nastiness."

In fact, ethnic humor and insults are ancient traditions and have long been a feature of American culture, says Leon Rappoport, professor emeritus of psychology at Kansas State University and author of a recent book on ethnic humor. "Dialect humor" stereotyping groups ranging from "operatic Italians to money-grubbing Jews" was a staple of the music halls and vaudeville stages of the early 20th century, for example, says Rappoport.

Later, when stage performers migrated to radio, joking based on ethnic stereotypes continued, says Rappoport. For example, radio comedian Fred Allen based much of his humor on a cast of invented characters representing stereotyped Irish, Jewish and Southern characters, among others.

Early radio and television talk-show host Joe Pyne regularly ridiculed his guests, sometimes with ethnic insults, through the 1960s, says Douglas Gomery, professor emeritus of journalism at the University of Maryland and resident scholar at the university's Library of American Broadcasting.

In 1968, when blacks rioted in several American inner cities, Pyne was suspended for a week after he pulled a gun out of his drawer while talking with an African-American guest.[10]

But some analysts argue that ethnic and gender slurs, along with other name-calling, have become disturbingly prevalent in media over the past few decades and foster hatred and intolerance.

Imus is "emblematic of our uncivil times," said Charles Haynes, a senior scholar at the First Amendment Center, an education organization in Arlington, Va. "In the Internet age, the impulse to offend apparently knows no bounds. People feel increasingly emboldened to say or write anything — however ugly, vulgar or downright hateful. . . . The anything-goes Web world has raised the bar for what counts as 'offensive speech' in America's public square," and "offensive speech sells," said Haynes.[11]

The open use of ethnic and gender slurs "has gotten worse" in recent years, says E. Faye Williams, a lawyer and businesswoman who chairs the National Congress of Black Women, a group that has long protested the stereotyping of African-American women, including in gangsta rap. Today's American media is rife with comedy, movies and music that negatively stereotype black women, in particular, she says.

Williams says the trend is especially troubling because programming with offensive material is sold to other countries. "It breaks my heart when I go to other countries and see that those negative stereotypes have been exported," Williams says.

Negative stereotypes of African-Americans are evident among Asian and Latin American immigrants to the United States. Many arrive "with anti-black stereotypes in their heads" that they picked up from American media viewed abroad, says Joe R. Feagin, a professor of sociology at Texas A&M University and author of numerous books documenting race-related experiences and attitudes.

In a recent study, for example, rural Taiwanese people who had never seen a black person "had anti-black attitudes" based on viewing American media, he says.

To some, the ethnic and racial putdowns are symptoms of a broader coarsening of American society. Name-calling and stereotyping go "way back in Western culture," says Deborah Tannen, professor of linguistics at Georgetown University and author of the 1999 book *The Argument Culture: Stopping America's War of Words*. But, she adds, "I've found lots and lots of evidence that it got worse in the 1990s," as name-calling and shouting replaced more civil debate in realms ranging from television shows to the courts. For example, several former U.S. senators have declared that they voluntarily left Congress in the 1990s because discourse there became vicious and harshly adversarial. Numerous lawyers say they left their profession for the same reason, Tannen says.

Former conservative journalist David Brock founded the liberal media-watchdog group Media Matters for America, credited with bringing shock jock radio host Don Imus' racially offensive remark to public attention by posting it on the group's Web site the same day he made the comment. The growing prominence of such Internet activism means fewer media gaffes now escape public scrutiny, analysts say.

There's no doubt "we have become a coarse society" over the past few decades, says Maryland's Thornton, whose network television jobs included a seven-year stint booking guests for the Rev. Jesse Jackson's "Both Sides" talk show on CNN.

"I cannot imagine dropping a person from the 1940s into our climate," says Thornton. "Decades ago, although there was racism underneath, people clothed themselves in a mannerly way. There were lines of public behavior. I don't think we know anymore in our culture what the lines are. That's why Imus was as surprised as anyone to find that he had crossed one," she says.

The insult culture "has gone to the point of no return, and we don't know how to rein it in," says Thornton. "The whole shock jock thing has contributed to the coarsening of dialogue," she says. Nevertheless, "The public appetite for this is overrated" by media outlets.

To some observers, using ethnic stereotypes as veiled or overt insults is an especially egregious form of argument and has gone too far in the media.

Who's Who of Shock Jocks

In the beginning was Imus.

Don Imus

Don Imus began his career as the first true "shock jock" in 1970 at a Cleveland radio station as a DJ. He quickly developed a popular repertoire of comic and raunchy bits such as asking female callers, "Are you naked?"

In the 1990s, the "Imus in the Morning" show gravitated toward news and political talk, with a growing list of influential guests including members of Congress and journalists from major news organizations such as NBC and *Newsweek*. The show mixed political talk with shock-jock banter. For example, Imus referred to *Washington Post* media reporter Howard Kurtz, a frequent guest, as a "boner-nosed . . . beanie-wearing Jewboy" and described New York Knicks basketball player Patrick Ewing as a "knuckle-dragging moron."

Imus was fired in April by both CBS Radio and MSNBC television, which had simulcast his radio program to rising ratings, after calling the Rutgers University women's basketball team "nappy-headed hos." Fired in the first months of a five-year, $40 million contract, Imus is suing CBS.

Radio's second iconic shock jock is **Howard Stern**, who got his first radio job in 1976 and transitioned into shock-jock stunts gradually a few years later. Stern's specialty is sex talk, though he's also done parodies like "Hill Street Jews." In 1985 NBC Radio briefly canceled Stern's show over a new segment called "Bestiality Dial-a-Date."

Howard Stern

His employer in the early 1990s, Infinity Broadcasting, racked up $1.7 million in Federal Communications Commission (FCC) indecency fines over Stern's show between 1990 and 1993. In 1992, for example, stations carrying Stern earned a $600,000 fine after Stern combined indecency with racial stereotypes when he said "the closest I came to making love to a black woman was I masturbated to a picture of Aunt Jemima on a pancake box."

Despite frequent suspensions, cancellations and station changes, Stern has been employed on radio consistently for more than three decades. Currently he hosts "The Howard

---

The liberal media-monitoring group Media Matters for America was chagrined when conservative radio talk-show host Limbaugh aimed racial stereotypes at both civil rights activist Sharpton and Democratic presidential candidate Sen. Barack Obama by playing a satirical song titled "Barack the Magic Negro," in which a singer impersonating Sharpton urges listeners not to vote for Obama because he's not a "real" black man like rapper Snoop Dogg.

However, others argue that racial stereotyping is no more harmful than strong, argumentative language.

Accuracy in Media's Kincaid says there's no essential difference between denigrating people through racial stereotypes or denigrating them for their individual actions, as liberal MSNBC host Keith Olbermann does in his nightly feature dubbing several individuals "the worst people in the world" for that day. In either case, it's a matter of "holding people up for public ridicule," says Kincaid.

Should the government do more to restrain hate speech?

The Federal Communications Commission (FCC) has the authority to limit sexually explicit speech and other public discourse it deems "indecent." Some observers believe the agency should adopt a similar approach toward "hate speech" involving demeaning racial or ethnic stereotypes. But such an expansion of regulatory power could collide with First Amendment concerns, particularly the libertarian belief that individuals, not the government, should be responsible for reining in inappropriate speech.

"The FCC needs to take a close look at its policies when it comes to the kind of language people use," says

Douglas Tracht

Stern Show" on Sirius Satellite Radio.

Shock talker **Doug "Greaseman" Tracht** has been an on-air personality since the early 1970s at several East Coast stations. He's most infamous for racist comments he made while working at Washington, D.C.-area stations, where he's spent most of his career.

In 1985, he was widely criticized for saying of the Martin Luther King Day holiday that "they should shoot four more of them and give us a whole week off." Between 1999 and 2002, Tracht was off the air entirely after he was fired over another racist comment. Tracht's broadcast features often-raunchy on-air skits and stories employing a large cast of fictional characters he developed over the years.

After two decades on broadcast radio, **Bubba the Love Sponge** was fired by Clear Channel Communications in 2004 after the FCC fined the company $755,000 based on complaints about Bubba's show, which has featured stunts like butchering a hog on air, shocking guests with electric collars and giving his co-workers a massive dose of laxatives to see who would be the last to move their bowels. Currently the program is carried on Sirius.

Jocks Gregg "Opie" Hughes and Anthony Cumia — **Opie and Anthony** — have migrated from broadcast radio to satellite and back again. Among other incidents, they were fired from a Boston station in 1998 for an April Fool's hoax claiming that then-Boston Mayor Thomas Merino had been killed in a car crash.

Gregg Hughes and Anthony Cumia

In May 2007, in an unusual twist, the two were fired by the unregulated subscription-radio service XM Satellite Radio but not by the CBS broadcast network, which also airs their show, after they joked about a homeless man raping Secretary of State Condoleeza Rice.

JV and Elvis — Jeff Vandergrift and Dan Lay — inhabited shock radio's "The Dog House with JV and Elvis" until their show was canceled by CBS in May 2007, in the wake of Imus' firing. Vandergrift and Lay aired a prank phone call in fake accents to a Chinese restaurant, requesting "shrimp flied lice," among other Asian-stereotyping jokes. The call — typical fare for the show — was made before Imus made his "nappy-headed hos" comment, but CBS didn't fire the two until after it fired Imus.

Bubba

Ohio State University sociologist K. Sue Jewell, author of the book *From Mammy to Miss America and Beyond: Cultural Images and the Shaping of U.S. Social Policy.* Jewell believes name-calling and stereotyping insults by high-profile media figures can strongly influence public opinion, particularly among young people, and "easily escalate to violence."

Williams of the National Congress of Black Women believes the FCC should remove shock jocks for offensive remarks on public airwaves, since they can find new homes on subscription satellite radio stations. She and other experts contend the FCC and Congress could easily justify expanding the agency's mandate, citing historical precedent.

"There are certain words that have historical baggage, and they probably shouldn't be used on the airwaves, which are owned by all of us. Given our national history of racial discrimination, I don't see why the FCC can't make that argument," says Leonard Baynes, a professor at New York's St. John's University School of Law. Baynes says the FCC should even consider levying similar restrictions on cable television content, noting cable operators currently are required to scramble indecent programming and take other steps to police content in order to get franchise licenses.

But some experts prefer the status quo be maintained, saying they fear government agencies will find it difficult to walk the center line and fight off the temptation to regulate speech that conflicts with an administration's political agenda.

"I support the FCC's ability to regulate obscenity — but I don't want to see their powers expanded" to sanction language that's racist or homophobic, for example, says Accuracy in Media's Kincaid. The answer to speech that offends people is more speech from the side that was offended, he says. "I want to see more speech, not less."

The best response "would be for people [like Imus] to bring onto their shows the people that disagree with them," says Kincaid, who co-hosted CNN's "Crossfire" talk program in the 1980s. Harking back to his on-air experience, Kincaid says, "I liked that show because of the two views" that were part of every program. But ensuring that opposing views are part of every discussion should be left to television and radio networks and hosts, not the government, he adds.

Even the FCC's current powers to regulate for "decency" can be misused to push a political agenda instead, said liberal writer and commentator Ted Rall, who contends the decision to pull shock jock Howard Stern's show from Clear Channel Communications' radio stations in 2004 had less to do with inappropriate remarks than with statements critical of the Bush administration.[12]

"If you don't think me going after Bush got me thrown off those stations, you got another think coming," said Stern. His days on broadcast radio were "numbered because I dared to speak out against the Bush administration and . . . the religious agenda of George W. Bush concerning stem cell research and gay marriage," he said. "What he is doing with the FCC is pushing this religious agenda."[13]

Some legal experts worry that legitimate free speech can be caught up in a dragnet of enforcement actions if the government more stringently polices the airwaves.

"Racist speech is — or should be — always over the line, and Imus' coarse and racist reference to the Rutgers team was all the worse because it seemed so casually uttered," said New York City-based First Amendment lawyer Floyd Abrams. Nevertheless, he said, "I am concerned about policing even errant speech to the point that we risk losing the enlivening and sometimes even acute commentary that accompanies it and of which even offensive speech is sometimes a part."[14]

Radio is by its nature a spontaneous medium, and that means inadvisable words will be uttered from time to time, says *Talkers* magazine's Harrison. "The spontaneity is what keeps people interested," he says. 'The more they regulate radio the more they'll kill it."

Harrison notes that radio has become such a niche medium that there's little reason to apply a new regulatory regime. Broadcast radio today is "just one little street down a much wider avenue" of largely unregulated media, making additional content regulation both unfair and pointless, he says.

Harrison says talk about new regulations smacks of hypocrisy when all types of objectionable discourse and pornography are conveyed on the Internet, which is unregulated.

L. Brent Bozell, founder of the conservative Media Research Center, adamantly opposes increased government regulation of argumentative speech. He argues, however, that a different kind of federal rule would help media consumers squelch such speech on their own, if they chose, at least on cable television. Under a "cable choice" set-up, cable subscribers could order and cancel channels individually, rather than being restricted to a cable company's prepackaged channel tiers.

A rule permitting such "cable choice" would "be a real market solution" to problems like Imus' racist speech, which was carried over MSNBC, says Bozell. "If the customer had the right" to stop paying for individual channels, "NBC and BET [Black Entertainment Television] would be very very careful about who they offended," and "if 2 percent of the people watched a certain network, the other 98 percent wouldn't have to pay for it," as happens today, he says.

Should Don Imus have been fired?

Few people defend the language Imus used to describe the Rutgers players. But while many commentators say his firing was justified, others find it hypocritical, in light of language found elsewhere in the media. And they wonder whether keeping him on the air might have helped spark a more enduring dialogue about racism and misogyny.

Firing Imus "was an appropriate response, and it should have happened sooner," says Ohio State's Jewell, adding that the public airwaves "should not be used to demean a culture."

"Blacks were more likely to want him to be fired," which illustrates the stark "racial divide" in America, says Baynes of St. John's Law School. In the dominant white culture, "there really isn't an appreciation and understanding of this minority point of view," which is the product of a longstanding historical linkage between use of racially demeaning language and racist actions, Baynes says.

"When someone uses that kind of language, it makes the hair on the back of your neck stand up because you don't know what that person would do in terms of firing you without cause or refusing to rent an apartment to you," Baynes says.

In contrast, he continues, "white people know the person who used the language as a friend, an aunt, an uncle, a grandpa, someone who may have loved them and been generous to them." In such a scenario, they are reluctant to speak out against racist language while acknowledging that someone who can be loving to friends and family also is capable of being hurtful.

Imus was fired largely because civil rights activists wielded economic power over advertisers to get him off the air — a positive but not extremely significant outcome, says Marc Lamont Hill, assistant professor of American studies at Temple University. The firing doesn't address any of the real racial problems afflicting African-Americans, such as poor schools or hiring and housing discrimination, says Hill. "I'd take a hundred Imuses if it meant that black people could have access to good health care," he says.

More important than Imus being fired was "the conversation on language that impugns people that's begun" in the wake of the incident, says Karl Frisch, media relations director at the liberal media-criticism organization Media Matters for America, one of the groups that first brought public attention to Imus' slur.

Some who are skeptical about the firing say that a better conversation on race might have ensued had Imus stayed on the job, however.

The firing was understandable but unfortunate, says Tom Taylor, editor of *Inside Radio* magazine. Earlier in Imus' career, after he beat personal problems with drugs and alcohol, "he did a great job of getting other guys alerted to that problem" through public-service work and his radio program. "To me, we've lost the opportunity" to see if "he could have done the same thing with racist language," Taylor says.

Radio is a niche medium where loyal but small audiences are in large part created and sustained by the particular talents of individual on-air personalities. Imus' niche was an unusual one, and his departure will be felt, Taylor says.

Angela Burt-Murray, editor-in-chief of *Essence* magazine, is one of several prominent black journalists — including Gwen Ifill of PBS and Al Roker of NBC — who called for CBS Radio to take a harder stance on Don Imus' April 4 remark about the Rutgers women's basketball team after he was suspended for two weeks. He was eventually fired by CBS on April 12.

The Imus audience "was never large" — 2 and a half to 3 million listeners, says Taylor. "But it was a very interesting audience," made up of "the type of American who watches the Sunday TV talk shows and would like to meet authors." The program "was sort of like an 18th-century Paris salon where you get this volatile mixture of guys" discussing a wide range of topics, he says. In particular, "publishers have been in tears" since the firing because Imus' show "was an almost irreplaceable stop on the book circuit."

Some critics believe firing Imus was hypocritical when one considers the offensive or questionable material that can be found on a daily basis in the media.

CHRONOLOGY

1960s-1970s *Supreme Court debates whether government bans on radio shock talk violate the Constitution. In sitcoms and standup comedy, insult humor replaces physical comedy, which is deemed too violent.*

1969 Supreme Court declares that the Federal Communications Commission's (FCC) Fairness Doctrine — requiring on-air controversial discussions to present all sides of the issue — is consistent with the First Amendment guarantee of free speech.

1968 Don Imus takes his first radio job in Cleveland.

1978 In a case involving comedian George Carlin's use of "seven dirty words," Supreme Court upholds FCC's right to bar broadcast of "indecent" material.

1980s *Raucous, risqué "morning zoo" programs become drive-time radio favorites.*

1984 Denver shock host Alan Berg is murdered by rightwing fanatics angered by his outspoken left-wing political and sex talk.

1987 FCC rescinds the Fairness Doctrine.

1990s *Talk radio burgeons after the Fairness Doctrine is scrapped. Political talk hosts pick up shock talk, especially ethnic and gender insults. A new form of hip-hop, gangsta rap, features sexist, violent lyrics.*

1993 St. Louis shock jocks Steve Shannon and D.C. Chymes are fired after telling a caller she is "acting like a nigger." They are soon hired by another local station.

1996 New York radio personality Bob Grant, who has a history of anti-black statements, is fired after a joke about Commerce Secretary Ron Brown, an African-American, who had just died in a plane crash.

1997 Imus is named one of *Time* magazine's 25 most influential Americans.

1999 Washington, D.C., shock jock Doug "Greaseman" Tracht is fired after saying, "Now you understand why they drag them behind trucks," referring to the Texas murder in which James Byrd, an African-American, was dragged behind a truck.

2000s *Shock talkers fired from broadcast radio find new homes on unregulated Internet and satellite radio.*

2003 Conservative radio host Rush Limbaugh is hired then quickly fired by ESPN after he says a biased liberal media pushed black Philadelphia Eagles quarterback Donovan McNabb to star status despite mediocre skills. . . . Rochester, N.Y., shock talker Bob Lonsberry is fired after comparing the city's African-American mayor to a monkey but is soon rehired by the same station.

2004 Rapper Nelly cancels a charity appearance at Spelman College, a historically black school for women in Atlanta, after students protest his sexist videos.

2005 Sportscaster Sid Rosenberg is banned from "Imus in the Morning" after saying singer Kylie Minogue, who has breast cancer, "won't look so good when she's got a bald head with one titty." He later returns to the show as a frequent guest. . . . New York radio host Miss Jones is briefly suspended for a song mocking tsunami victims as "Africans drowning, little Chinamen swept away. You could hear God laughing, 'Swim, you bitches, swim.'"

2006 Shock jock Howard Stern leaves the public airwaves for Sirius Satellite Radio.

2007 On April 4, Imus refers to Rutgers University female basketball players as "nappy-headed hos" and is fired a week later after advertisers pull their spots. Fired three months into a five-year $40 million contract with CBS Radio, Imus is suing the network. . . . CBS Radio fires New York shock jocks Jeff Vandergrift and Dan Lay — J.V. and Elvis — for a prank phone call to workers at a Chinese restaurant. . . . Some in the newly Democrat-controlled Congress mull regulating media violence and reviving the Fairness Doctrine.

> **December 2007** After calling members of the Rutgers University women's basketball team "nappy headed 'hos'" the previous April, disgraced talk show host Don Imus returns to the airwaves, albeit on local radio, on WABC in New York.
>
> ## 2008
>
> **Jan. 4** Golf Channel broadcaster Kelly Tilghman says young players who hope to defeat Tiger Woods should "lynch him in a back alley." She apologized and was suspended two weeks for her comment.
>
> **July 21** Conservative radio commentator Michael Savage calls autism's prevalence a "racket" by "poorer families who have found a new way to be parasites on the government" by seeking disability payments.
>
> ## 2009
>
> **Oct. 5** Imus returns to national audience on Fox Business Network. Earlier, he promises to "never say anything" that would make Rutgers team regret accepting his apology.
>
> ## 2010
>
> **March 22** Conservative commentator Ann Coulter tells a Muslim student at the University of Western Ontario in Canada to "take a camel" after Coulter was asked about her previous comment that Muslims shouldn't be allowed on airplanes.
>
> **Aug. 17** On-air therapist "Dr. Laura" Schlessinger announces she will end her syndicated radio show after apologizing for using the "N-word" multiple times on the air, claiming she was frustrated that blacks use the term but whites who do are considered racists.
>
> **Sept. 4** Boxer Floyd Mayweather Jr. unleashes a profanity-filled racist rant on the Internet against Filipino boxer Manny Pacquiao.

Kincaid of Accuracy in Media cites MSNBC's decision to air the profanity-laced video made by Seung-Hui Cho, the student who carried out the April 16 Virginia Tech University massacre.

The double standard isn't a particular surprise, however, since both MSNBC and CBS employed Imus because he was an edgy shock jock, then fired him for saying something shocking, says Kincaid. MSNBC, in particular, "helped to make him a star by putting their people on his show" as journalist-guests, he says.

"The policy ought to be that the media is in favor of free speech," says Kincaid. "So if you hire a commentator who's known for saying shocking things, then you accept that he will say shocking things.... People can apologize on the air and move on. That's freedom with responsibility."

"I thought CBS overreacted because I think that his intentions weren't derogatory," says Dennis Rome, a professor of criminal justice at the University of Wisconsin, Parkside.

Rome says while the language Imus used was objectionable, it continues to be widely used. He notes that gangsta rappers use words like "hos," saying it's a different thing for African-Americans to demean each other. "I don't agree," he says. "The real problem is that the language is being kept alive, no matter who's using it, and what we need to do is move on from it."

Rome adds, "Rush Limbaugh and others have said a lot worse" than the statement that lost Imus his job, and the damage potentially done by media personalities who use racial and gender stereotyping as part of political discourse "is far stronger, because they intend to be derogatory," Rome says. He predicts nothing will come of the Imus incident because he was quickly fired and the incident was swept under the rug.

"A better approach would have been, 'What do we do to balance this? What else can we put on the air to show more points of view?'" he says.

BACKGROUND

Historical Stereotypes

Imus sought to excuse his use of the phrase "nappy-headed hos" by saying he and his producers had picked up the words from hip-hop music, as well as from the Spike Lee film "School Daze." But historians and linguists say the words have a history stretching back to the days of slavery.[15]

Societal Conversation on Race Seems Unlikely

Racism experts say they are not surprised.

Soon after radio host Don Imus referred to the Rutgers University women's basketball team as "nappy-headed hos," groups like the National Association of Black Journalists and some media commentators began calling for a national "conversation on race." Such a dialogue was needed, some said, to confront the simmering differences that saw many African-Americans calling for the shock jock's firing while many whites saw the comments as no big deal.

But while some dialogue did soon begin about the sexism inherent in the gangsta-rap lyrics from which Imus said he picked up the term "ho," conversation about the radio host's casual use of a racist, sexist insult never really happened. Many racism experts say they're not surprised.

Racism "isn't on the docket as an issue," despite occasional flurries of attention when a celebrity like Imus crosses the line in public comments, says Marc Lamont Hill, an assistant professor of American studies at Temple University.

When whites who use words like "nappy-headed" say, " 'I said that, but I'm not a racist,' I do think that they're being serious," says Hill, who is black. "I believe that Imus could honestly say, 'I don't think I'm better than a black person.' " But "the broader context that makes the whole notion of 'nappy-headed' and 'ho' so painful is that he has the power to put a name on someone," Hill says.

"Being called a nigger isn't just an epithet. It's putting you in a certain position" because a white man has the power to do so, while African-Americans don't, says Hill. "I can call you a cracker, but I can't treat you like a cracker."

In the 1960s, during the civil rights era, "we had a way to talk about race" because discussion centered on laws that could quell overt oppression and segregation, says Shawn J. Parry-Giles, associate professor of communication at the University of Maryland, College Park. Today, with those laws on the books, "There is a sense among the majority group that we've done everything that we need to do." So when a potentially racist incident occurs, "we just individualize it," hoping that firing Imus, for example, ends the problem, Parry-Giles says.

The shock-radio era has "paralleled a societal era of ignoring race, on the grounds that our society should be color-blind," says Lee Anne Bell, director of the education program at Barnard College. "But if you can't talk about it, you can't confront it, and that makes colorblindness very insidious."

Overt racism among whites has drastically receded, but young, white men, especially, "still love to go for a beer with [white] friends and tell racist jokes," says Joe R. Feagin, a professor of sociology at Texas A&M University and co-author of a recent book on racist language and opinions among today's white college students.

And while Imus and the students Feagin surveyed generally excuse their private language, saying it doesn't make them racists, "it does mean something," Feagin says. When comedian and former "Seinfeld" actor Michael Richards railed at some African-American hecklers at a stand-up gig last year, he made "seven uses of the N-word," says Feagin. "That comes from something pretty deep."

If America ever does get serious about having a race conversation, scholars and educators on race and prejudice have some suggestions:

- Everyone must acknowledge, up front, that we routinely act to protect our own individual interests, and that those interests have race, gender and class implications, says Tony N. Brown, assistant professor of sociology at Vanderbilt University. "People say, 'I'm not racist or sexist in my language,' " Brown

Blacks' "nappy hair" was one of the physical characteristics seized upon by white slave owners to prove that "neither human physiology nor human nature was uniform" as a way of justifying their ownership of other humans, said Zine Magubane, assistant professor of sociology at Boston College.[16]

Slavery in America flourished at the same time many Europeans and American settlers were embracing the ideals of the Enlightenment, including human equality, as the inspiration for the French and American revolutions, Magubane said. To reconcile that apparent contradiction, some focused on physical differences between blacks and

says. "Nevertheless, "in my day-to-day actions, I do reinforce my own racial and gender and class interests, sometimes to the detriment of others' interests. I don't think positive things about the homeless," for example.

- Whites, the majority culture, "must be willing to admit there are things we don't know about racism, because people of color have to know when racism is operating just to get along in the world, but white people have our racism detectors set at a very low level," says Tim Wise, a lecturer on race and gender bias and founder of the Nashville-based Association for White Anti-Racist Education. Whites should "start with the assumption that when people of color say, 'Racism is operating,' they probably know what they're talking about, because they've spent a lifetime learning to distinguish between what's racism and what's just everyday insensitivity," Wise says.
- Everyone should hear as many first-person — preferably in-person — stories of Americans of all ethnicities as possible, says Feagin. "The more voices people read or encounter, the more they understand" others' points of view, he says.
- Conversation should "start with objective facts — that women earn 76 cents on the dollar compared to men, for comparable work; that black men are incarcerated at a very high rate," says Brown. "Then we can ask people to give their individual explanations for those facts," he says. "In those explanations, attitudes and beliefs would be revealed" and could then be examined and discussed, he says.
- Everyone should be willing to take responsibility for what they can control, not shift the discussion to what others are doing, says Wise. The nearly immediate shift of the Imus-spurred race discussion from his language to racism and misogyny expressed by hip-hop lyrics shows "how white Americans are so used to shifting the conversation away from things that are our responsibility," he says.

Comedian and former "Seinfeld" actor Michael Richards appears on the Rev. Jesse Jackson's radio show on Nov. 26, 2006, to make amends for a Nov. 17 racist outburst at a West Hollywood comedy club. When loud talk from a group of African-American audience members interrupted his act, Richards unleashed a racial tirade, calling the men "niggers" and alluding to lynching.

"Why can't we just stop and talk about ourselves for a minute, about our personal responsibility to challenge white people" over racist comments? asks Wise. "Our personal responsibility is to say, 'Cool. The next time something like Imus happens, we whites will deal with our people, just as we expect people of color to hold their group responsible for things like violent rap lyrics,' " he says. Black or white, "own the piece of the problem that's yours, and maybe we can jumpstart the conversation."

Few believe that a true cross-racial conversation on racial matters will begin in America any time soon, Imus or no Imus, however. Says Georgetown University professor of linguistics Deborah Tannen: "Things happen all the time that could spark that conversation, but they don't."

whites they said were signs blacks didn't have to be included on equal terms in a social contract.

For example, in his "Notes on the State of Virginia," Thomas Jefferson concluded that blacks couldn't be politically enfranchised members of the new American union because of their "physical and moral" differences from whites, such as not having long, flowing hair, Magubane wrote.[17]

Descriptions like "nappy headed" and "ho" to refer to African-American women are part of "a white, racial frame that we whites invented in the 1600s to explain how we as good Christians could enslave thousands of human

Many critics of Don Imus' firing contend that a double standard allows black rappers and hip-hop artists — like rapper Snoop Dogg — to use the same kind of offensive comments about women in their lyrics without being held accountable.

beings," says Feagin of Texas A&M. The stereotypes persist, including in some black music like gangsta rap, because "350 of our 400 years of history were years of extreme racial oppression. So in order to see ourselves as good people, we had to come up with" reasons for considering African-Americans lesser people and "hammer it into everybody's head, including black people," Feagin says.

While "ho" itself is a newer coinage, originating in the black community, words stereotyping African-American women as oversexed and as prostitutes — such as "wench" — were common from slavery days, largely to provide a rationale for the growth of a large mulatto class of mixed-race children, says Ohio State sociologist Jewell. "Where were all those mulatto children coming from?" — from "Jezebel — the bad black girl," she says. Words like "wench," "ho" and "Jezebel" convey the message that "these women of African descent are very hyper-sexed, worldly seductresses, and if you aren't careful, they will seduce you," she says.

Today, the stereotypes persist, although Americans generally think that the days of racism are over, says Feagin. "We passed civil rights laws in the 1960s, and now we think all the racial problems are over," he says. But if that had happened, it would mean "hundreds of years of history had been canceled, and that doesn't happen quickly."

In fact, the same racist language, including heavy use of "nigger," continues to be common among white people speaking in all-white groups, says Leslie Houts Picca, a sociologist at the University of Dayton. "We were really quite shocked at just how prevalent casual use of the N-word is," says Picca, who with coauthor Feagin recently published a book detailing race-related incidents that white college students revealed in diaries.

When asked about their objectionable speech, many white students said the words "had lost their racial connotations," says Picca. But in fact they "are centuries-old stereotypes, like lazy and criminal. They are not inventing them" but "bringing them down from history."

When used in public, as in Imus' comment, the words call up memories of a painful past for African-Americans, but not for whites, and this deepens the racial divide, says Feagin.

"Mulattos did not come from interracial marriage, and for every time a black man raped a white woman, there were a 1,000 cases the other way" in the days of slavery and legal segregation, a fact that haunts elderly African-American women, in particular, to this day, he says. "One of my grad students has been interviewing elderly African-Americans who lived under legal segregation," Feagin says. In one commonly remembered story, a white man enters a black home and rapes a teenage daughter, says Feagin. "That story has yet to be told" in history books and mainstream media, says Feagin. "Yet these elderly women and men tell these stories routinely. Some 80-year-old black women live today with their shades pulled down and no lights on. Their fathers told them to do that to protect themselves against white night riders," he says.

"That's why the black reaction and the white reaction to Imus are so different," says Feagin. "Blacks know that" racially charged language that seems innocuous to whites "can be extremely serious. If it's in a police officer's head, it can get you killed," he says.

Americans' typical reactions to visiting Africans further indicate that language like "nappy headed" and "ho" aren't so much a matter of racial stereotyping but stereotyping of African-Americans who are slave descendants, says Baugh, at Washington University. For example, Baugh says that when he hosted an African Fulbright scholar from Guinea, the man reported that the desk clerk at his American hotel was hostile until he explained that he was visiting from Africa. Then, the clerk's demeanor "changed immediately" to welcome, showing that the issue is not race but history, Baugh says.

Words that negatively stereotype are dangerous for anyone to use, including African-Americans, he says. "It is possible within one's own group to use a derogatory term [for that group] in a positive way," he says. "But when you breach that private world" — which is all too easy to do — "then trouble happens," he says.

For example, "the more you accept these words" for use in your own community, "the more you may be losing your right to claim discrimination" when the words are used against you, says St. John's Law School's Baynes. "If the word loses its currency" as a slur because it's so commonly used by black people, "when somebody uses the word and really means it, then what do you do?"

Shock Value

Risk, danger and excitement all are important components of popular entertainment. Add to that the spontaneity of live radio, and it's easy to see why hosts who "shock" have been a programming staple for decades — and why they sometimes cross the lines of acceptable speech. Nevertheless, media analysts point out that really shocking talk accounts for a small proportion of programming fare.

Shock of various kinds has "always been part of entertainment," so it's no wonder that radio talkers who say shocking things can draw big audiences, says Clarence W. Thomas, associate professor of mass communications at Virginia Commonwealth University. "A roller coaster, a slasher movie — they carry a shock, and they're beyond the norm of everyday life, and that's what makes them interesting and entertaining."

What puts the shock in shock radio is that "shock jocks pull ideas and images from private spaces and say them out loud," says Parks, at the University of Maryland. Racial and gender insults that most people utter only among friends and family, along with sex talk, are the main types of speech eligible for that treatment.

With radio increasingly segmented to appeal to niche audiences, programmers have determined that shock jocks most appeal to men and younger listeners, says the Library of American Broadcasting's Gomery. That, in turn, draws advertisers seeking to cater to demographically desirable niches. So some personalities regularly push the envelope, hoping to touch the hot-button interests of their core audience. Broadcast television networks, in contrast, have always strived to develop programs that appeal to the masses and offend no one, making them a bad fit for shock commentators, Gomery explains.

Shocking talk has existed on radio from its early days.

Father Charles E. Coughlin wielded enormous influence through his on-air commentaries in the 1930s and '40s. But he began to increasingly incense some listeners with anti-Semitic tirades and extreme criticism of President Franklin D. Roosevelt, communism and American involvement in World War II. Both the Roosevelt administration and the National Association of Broadcasters placed stricter limitations on who could get air time to speak about controversial issues. However, not until Coughlin's bishop ordered him to return to duty as a parish priest was his radio voice finally silenced.

In the 1940s through the '60s, radio host Joe Pyne pushed the envelope on insult speech, calling homeless people "stinky bums" and responding to guests with comments like "Why don't you take your teeth out, put them in backwards, and bite your throat?"

In the 1970s through the '90s, AM radio, in particular, shifted almost entirely away from music to talk formats, while FM became the medium of choice for music because of its better sound quality. The number of commercial news and talk stations swelled from 360 in 1990 to 802 by July 1993, according to Taylor of *Inside Radio*. Today, of the 10,600 commercial radio stations in the United States, about 1,360 are talk, while many of the 650 non-commercial public radio stations also embrace variants of the news and talk format.

Ethnic Humor's No Joke for Amateurs

It gets ugly when aggression overwhelms the humor.

Why did shock-radio host Don Imus call the Rutgers University women's basketball team "nappy-headed hos?" "I was trying to be funny," Imus explained on his April 9 broadcast, several days after the original comment had blown up into a full-fledged national brouhaha over whether racist and sexist jokes have become a blight on American media.

The debate goes on, in the wake of Imus' firing, with critics arguing that stereotyping jokes have explosive potential and should be used only with caution and, perhaps, not at all. But ethnic humor has a long and robust history, among jokers in public and in private, and few expect to see it abandoned any time soon.

In the 19th and early 20th century, ethnic humor was a staple of stage comedy, but its prevalence receded somewhat as radio brought comedy to the mass media, says Leon Rappoport, professor emeritus of psychology at Kansas State University and author of a recent book on ethnic humor.

The vaudeville stage abounded with "dialect humor," with stereotyped characters like "the operatic Italian" and "the money-grubbing Jew" that audiences easily recognized, Rappoport says. And in the early 20th century, when vaudevillians migrated to radio, the stereotyping humor continued. Fred Allen's radio skits, for example, based their humor on stereotyped characters such as a fast-talking Irishman, a Jewish housewife and numerous others.

Gradually, however, radio comedy "got cleaned up," with ethnic humor mainly expunged, Rappoport says. As a new mass medium, supported by advertisers, radio needed to entice many while offending few, and ethnic jokes — "which can be very aggressive" — risked turning off too many in the unseen listening audience. By the mid-20th century, ethnic humor had become much less prevalent, not only on radio but also on the stage, Rappoport says. By the early 1960s, however, ethnic jokes were being heard again in live comedy, by a new breed of edgy comics whose work was based on irony and social criticism, like Lenny Bruce.

Insult humor was briefly banished from public airwaves, but it returned beginning in the 1970s, says Sheri Parks, associate professor of American studies at the University of Maryland, College Park. Physical comedy and slapstick humor, often fairly violent, once abounded in American mass culture, from Charlie Chaplin to the Three Stooges. But when a 1972 U.S. surgeon general's report declared that violence in media leads to real-life violence, comics once again were forced to find non-physically violent ways to make people laugh, says Parks.

And since a key element in much humor is aggression, comics switched from physical to verbal violence — including stereotyping humor, Parks says. Over the past

Comedian George Carlin ran into legal troubles more than once over a routine discussing the "seven words you can never say on television," known as the "seven dirty words." In 1973, after a father complained to the FCC that his young son had heard the routine broadcast on a small New York radio station, the station fought the FCC's sanctions on the grounds that they restricted free speech. The legal case went all the way to the Supreme Court, which — in a 5 to 4 decision — upheld the FCC's right to bar broadcast of material the FCC considered "indecent" at times of day when children might hear it.[18]

The rise of talk radio has increased the likelihood of edgy content. This is particularly true during the 6 to 9 a.m. and 4 to 7 p.m. "drive-time" slots, when more males than females are stuck in their cars for long stretches of time, Gomery says. Because radio talk is spontaneous, unedited and generally unplanned, radio is a "hip, edgy, street-y kind of medium," says Harrison of *Talkers* magazine. Nevertheless, Harrison argues that once Imus and Howard Stern "brought radio into the latest chapter of street culture" back in the 1970s, "shock jock" stopped being a very relevant term. Today, "there are bad boys on the radio," he acknowledges. "But how could anything on radio be truly shocking when there's a wild assortment of perversions all over regular television?"

few decades "insult has become the dominant mode of comedy."

There may be a serious problem with raising generations of children exposed on a daily basis to insult humor on television, radio and movies, Parks says. Adults believe when children see comedians and sitcom characters insulting each other aggressively "they know that it's unusual behavior that they shouldn't engage in," she says. "But in fact children look to media for normative behaviors, and when they see or hear something, they just go ahead and do it, too."

Adults like Imus may have a similar problem, according to Arthur Asa Berger, professor of broadcast and electronic communication arts at San Francisco State University and author of books on humor and humor writing. "Humor is a very dangerous thing. There's a lot of aggression in it, and when the aggression overwhelms the humor, we don't excuse" the "hostile" joker, he says.

Some professional comedians employ stereotypes "in a mirthful way," using the context of the joke to convince an audience that "they don't actually mean what they're saying" in a stereotyping joke about a drunken Irishman, for example, says Berger.

Professional humorists are always aware of their role and develop a sense of how far they can go to get a laugh or make a point without crossing the line into speech that the audience will read as hateful rather than funny or insightful, says Berger. "Comedians work very hard to do that," he says. "But when people who aren't humorists start messing around with humor," most don't even realize what the pitfalls are, he says.

Lenny Bruce helped bring ethnic humor back to American comedy in the 1950s and 1960s.

When it comes to ethnic humor, most comedians agree that "anything goes as long as it's funny," says Rappoport. Nevertheless, "context and intent matter, and there has to be a grain of truth to it," he says. Comics like Richard Pryor, Robin Williams and Chris Rock have joked about ethnic groups, their own and other people's, and "the audience finds itself laughing even if they don't want to," Rappoport says.

But ethnic humor can also spell trouble, if the joker leans too heavily on the ethnic and not enough on the humor, he says. "The thing about the Imus statement is simply that it wasn't funny," says Rappoport. In the annals of humor, Imus is "a trivial footnote of somebody who went too far in the wrong context and then got what he deserved."

While shock talk is a persistent element in radio, it still doesn't account for much talking time, perhaps only 3 or 4 percent, says Gomery.

Stereotypes Spreading?

Though shock jocks may not be expanding their reach, shocking language, especially racial and gender stereotypes, has been increasingly used in other branches of the media in recent years, including comedy, gangsta-rap lyrics and on some radio shows featuring political talk.

Over the past few decades, for example, stereotyping insults have become a prominent mode of comedy, says Parks of the University of Maryland. Previously, a great deal of comedy in movies and on television was physical comedy, which was usually somewhat violent, she says.

The shift toward insult humor was mainly triggered by a 1972 surgeon general's report citing evidence that violence in media leads to violence in real life, says Parks. When the FCC responded by discouraging violent content, comedians shifted to other forms of humor, mainly opting for insults based on ethnic or racial stereotypes.

The shocking language that's garnered the most attention in the wake of Imus' comment has been racial and, especially, gender stereotypes in gangsta-rap lyrics. As with

Journalist Gwen Ifill — moderator of PBS' "Washington Week" — declined to appear on Don Imus' radio show in 1993 when she was a New York Times Washington correspondent. In apparent retaliation, Imus said the Times was "wonderful" because "it lets the cleaning lady cover the White House."

insult humor, the use of stereotyping in African-American music has greatly expanded in recent years.

"In R&B and soul music, African-American women were respected, and even when hip-hop got started, it didn't focus on misogynistic lyrics," says Ohio State University's Jewell.

Gradually, however, the top-selling, highest-profile hip-hop shifted toward lyrics that celebrate the "bling" and flash of a "gangsta" lifestyle and heavily feature misogynistic language like "bitch" and "ho."

Hip-hop "started as a radical critique of society" and especially of racism, says Feagin of Texas A&M. "When it became clear to the music industry that music with a beat could sell across racial lines," social criticism in lyrics "wasn't sold aggressively. White people — who buy 70 percent of rap records — don't want to hear about it."

Consequently, the most commercially successful hip-hop has been lowest-common-denominator music portraying women, especially African-American women, as wholly sexualized rather than romantic objects, says Jewell. The proliferation of the sexualized stereotypes — and frequent references to women as "hos" and "bitches" — "has some far-reaching consequences" for black women, because they're widely "perceived as having low morals" as well as being powerless, she says.

This has seeped into talk radio and television, says Parry-Giles at the University of Maryland. The racially diverse College Park campus is just outside Washington, where the intersection of media, politics and race is the focus of several academic programs. Stereotyping insults are "pervasive across the right and the left" on talk radio, she says, noting that progressive talk host Stephanie Miller repeatedly uses Asian stereotypes when she discusses North Korea on her program, Parry-Giles says.

Several conservative talk-radio hosts are especially notorious for race and gender stereotypes and insults. Michael Savage, whose San Francisco-based show is nationally syndicated by the independent Talk Radio Network, has frequently labeled countries with non-white populations as "turd world nations" and referred to the May 2000 "Million Mom March" on Washington for gun control as the "Million Dyke March," according to the liberal media-criticism group Fairness & Accuracy In Reporting.[19]

CURRENT SITUATION
New Crackdown

There are comparatively few rules governing broadcast content, and the ones that exist mostly focus on indecent sexual content. While radio stations have occasionally fired or suspended shock jocks for insulting and stereotyping ethnic and racial comments, sex-related antics have triggered much of the disciplinary action, and most fired jocks have been rehired fairly quickly by their old station or a new one.

Today, however, some liberal media critics such as Media Matters for America are focusing public attention on racist and misogynistic comments and insults. While some commentators applaud, others worry that a crackdown on insult speech could prompt an overreaction by advertisers and regulators.

Advertisers quickly pulled out of sponsorships of Imus' program in the wake of the Rutgers University flap, placing economic pressure on MSNBC and then

AT ISSUE

Is ethnic and racial humor dangerous?

YES
Arthur Asa Berger
Professor of Broadcast and Electronic Communication Arts, San Francisco State University

Written for *CQ Researcher*, May 2007

Ethnic humor divides as it derides. Societies generally contain many ethnic, racial and religious groups, each of which has distinctive cultural traits, beliefs and values. While ethnic humor may seem to be trivial, it corrodes our sense of community and makes it more difficult for us to live together harmoniously. It focuses on our differences and insults, attacks and humiliates its victims. It is based on stereotyping, which suggests that all members of various ethnic or other groups are the same as far as certain traits deemed "undesirable" by those who use ethnic humor are concerned. This humor can lead to feelings of inferiority and even self-hatred by members of groups attacked by it, while it coarsens and desensitizes those who use it.

Humor is an enigmatic matter that has fascinated our greatest philosophers and thinkers from Aristotle's time to the present. Scholars disagree about why we laugh, but two of the dominant theories about humor — Aristotle's view that it is based upon feelings of superiority and Freud's notion that it involves masked hostility and aggression — apply to ethnic humor.

There is an ethnocentric bias reflected in ethnic humor, a feeling held by those who use this humor that they are superior and that their cultural beliefs and values are the only correct ones. While ethnic humor is widespread — it's found in most countries — it varies considerably from mild teasing to terribly insulting and even vicious humor. Every society seems to find some minority "out-group" to ridicule. But sometimes ethnic humor — about Jews and African-Americans, for example — can easily become anti-Semitic and racist.

People who ridicule Jewish-American "princesses" or "dumb Poles" and other ethnic groups think they are just being funny when they tell friends insulting riddles. We might ask "funny to whom?" Such humor isn't amusing to members of the groups that are ridiculed. Those who use ethnic humor feel that they can make fun of ethnic groups with impunity, but in multicultured societies, fortunately, that is no longer the case. The excuse given by people who use ethnic humor, "I was just trying to be funny," isn't acceptable anymore.

Humor can be liberating and has many benefits, but when it is used to ridicule and insult people, it is harmful to members of the ethnic groups that are victimized by this humor and to society at large. Ethnic humor isn't just a laughing matter.

NO
Leon Rappoport
Professor Emeritus of Psychology, Kansas State University

Written for *CQ Researcher*, May 2007

It is hard to think of any serious harm associated with ethnic humor if you have ever fallen down laughing at a routine by Whoopi Goldberg, Robin Williams or Chris Rock, or heard Jackie Mason's lines about the differences between Jews and gentiles. Yet controversies over humor based on ethnic, racial or gender stereotypes go all the way back to the plays of Aristophanes (circa 430 B.C.), and subsequent writers and performers, from Shakespeare through Richard Pryor and Mel Brooks, have been catching flak about it ever since.

Modern social-science studies aimed at settling the harm question have not produced any smoking-gun evidence. The cautious conclusion of a 2004 review of experimental research was that exposure to disparagement humor did not reinforce negative images of the targeted group. Relevant field studies have shown that people feel no significant malice when laughing at jokes based on ethnic stereotypes, and common-sense observations support this: Where are all the suffering victims of the Polish jokes, dumb-blonde jokes, Jewish-American mother and princess jokes that have come and gone over recent years, not to mention the Lutherans, Catholics and Unitarians regularly worked over in Garrison Keillor's monologues on "A Prairie Home Companion"?

The prominent ethnic-humor scholar Christie Davies (author of three important books on the subject) maintains that laughter at such jokes has little to do with social attitudes but reflects the powerful surge of pleasure we tend to feel from "playing with aggression." And this includes members of the group being ridiculed, who often are most amused by clever takes on the stereotypes they know best. This was clearly true among the hundreds of diverse college students who took the class on ethnic humor I taught for several years. They would frequently be particularly carried away with laughter when seeing videos of comedians playing with ironic clichés about their own ethnic, racial or gender group. Like most Americans today, these students grew up in our humor-saturated TV culture and are thus well prepared to maintain a healthy sense of critical distance while enjoying satire, parody and ridicule — remember Boris and Natasha on "Bullwinkle"? — in the context of ethnic humor.

Part of what holds our increasingly multiethnic society together is our rich stock of ironic humor. The fact that we can play with our differences, even at the risk of occasionally offending each other, deserves recognition as a matter of pride rather than prejudice.

CBS Radio to fire the veteran host. New York shock jocks JV and Elvis were also recently fired after a racist prank call to a Chinese restaurant, and another New York radio personality, comedian Donnell "Ashy" Rawlings, was fired for anti-Semitic comments.[20]

"The striking thing to me is that this was one of the less offensive quotes from Imus," says Robert Entman, professor of media and public affairs at George Washington University and author of books on media and race and media and political discourse. "He's said many anti-Semitic things and things demeaning to black people that he should have gotten into trouble for decades ago."

This time was different, in part because the target of Imus' remarks was a group of admirable student athletes — as opposed to well-known public figures — which made the "nappy-headed hos" comment seem particularly inappropriate. The Internet also gave interest groups a 24-hour medium to air their complaints and criticisms.

"Imus lost his job because of the Internet," says Kelly McBride, ethics group leader at the Poynter Institute in St. Petersburg, Fla., a nonpartisan media-education organization. "The Internet provides a new venue where enough people can learn about events, complain to each other and lobby advertisers. Some people describe it as an Internet lynch mob, and I think that can be a danger. But I also think that it's democracy at its finest."

Among those leading the Internet criticism of Imus' comment was Media Matters for America, a group founded in 2004 by conservative-turned-liberal writer and journalism activist David Brock to combat what Brock calls media misinformation that advances a conservative agenda, including race- and gender-related insults and stereotyping.

Also fueling efforts to get Imus' employers to take action were changing demographics that have given women and African-Americans and other ethnic minorities more clout in the workplace and the economy, some analysts say.

NBC weatherman Al Roker, PBS journalist Gwen Ifill and former NAACP President Bruce Gordon, now on the Board of Directors of CBS, were among the African-Americans who called for the networks to cancel Imus after his April comments, and their comments apparently carried weight with the networks and advertisers.

"The more you have diverse voices out there, the less likely incidents like this are to happen," says St. John's Law School's Baynes. "Otherwise, people say, 'Well, it's just words.'"

In addition, "women and African-Americans are major buyers today, both groups much richer than they used to be," and advertisers "want to attract them," as they may not have in the past, says the Library of American Broadcasting's Gomery. "That's a big part of this story."

As for Imus, two days after the controversial remark, he offered an apology: "My characterization [of the team] was thoughtless and stupid. . . . And we're sorry," he said on his April 6 program. Three days later, he added: "Here's what I have learned: that you can't make fun of everybody, because some people don't deserve it. And because the climate on this program has been what it has been for 30 years doesn't mean that it has to be that way for the next five years or whatever, because that has to change . . . and I understand that."[21]

Fairness Revisited?

Much of the media scrutiny of racist and sexist language immediately turned to hip-hop lyrics. However, some conservatives worry that the activists who helped oust Imus also will seek to silence conservative political talk show hosts by pressing the federal government to revive the Fairness Doctrine. Following Imus' remarks, the main public and media debate quickly turned to criticism of hip-hop and to whether the Rev. Sharpton, the Rev. Jackson and other black leaders who strenuously called for Imus' firing had spoken out against gangsta rappers.

Imus firing "is so hypocritical because big media groups like CBS — which owns BET and MTV — traffic in bad language and racist language like the N-word" every time they show a gangsta-rap video, says the Media Research Center's Bozell. "I think the criticism of Imus is reverse racism." In music, he adds, "it's supposedly OK because black people say it."

The quick backlash against hip-hop happened "because it was a quick and easy scapegoat," says Brown of Vanderbilt. He says the radio comments and gangsta-rap lyrics aren't comparable because gangsta rap is seldom broadcast uncut. "To get these particular lyrics that people are talking about, you have to buy them," he says. In general, "they aren't even played on radio."

Meanwhile, some conservatives argue that Imus' firing was the first shot in a war aimed at getting conservative voices such as Bill O'Reilly, Limbaugh and Neal Boortz off radio and television.

Although Imus wasn't a conservative, he has been a vocal opponent of Sen. Hillary Rodham Clinton, D-N.Y., and that made him a target of the same groups who want to silence conservatives, says Kincaid of Accuracy in Media.

Some Imus opponents have called for FCC regulation of stereotyping, derogatory remarks over the airwaves, Kincaid notes. He fears any group that feels it was denigrated over the public airwaves will be able to seek redress at the FCC, a move he believes could impinge on free speech.

Others believe the FCC should do more to ensure that more views get aired. "Why not bring back the Fairness Doctrine?" asks Baynes of St. John's Law School. The FCC rule was largely scrapped in 1987 because the commission feared it might violate broadcasters' free-speech rights.

The rule may be difficult to police, given the range of views on some subjects, Baynes acknowledges. "But the question is, 'Do you think now is better?' I think it's worse." Baynes says the doctrine should also be applied to cable systems, which now have to comply with some federal regulations, including ones requiring them to scramble sexually explicit content.

Some Democrats in Congress would like to revive the rule. Rep. Dennis Kucinich, D-Ohio, chairmain of the House Oversight and Government Reform subcommittee, plans hearings on the Fairness Doctrine.[22] House Energy and Commerce Chairman John D. Dingell of Michigan told a conference of advertisers in May that he, too, wants to explore reviving the doctrine.[23]

But "the Fairness Doctrine is an absolute abomination," according to Bozell. "In simple words, it says, 'There ought to be liberal voices on talk radio to offset conservative voices,'" he says.

"But there's already National Public Radio, and if there were a market for more then there would be more liberal voices," Bozell, adds. When the doctrine was in place, many radio stations simply stopped airing discussion of public issues altogether because it was too difficult to find representatives for all opposing views — clearly not an outcome that anyone is looking for, he says.

OUTLOOK

Business as Usual?

Will Imus' firing mark an end to ethnic and gender insults and stereotyping in American media? Few think that's likely. The main reason: Edginess attracts viewers.

Case in point: When outspoken TV personality Rosie O'Donnell joined the talk show "The View," the ratings went up, says Accuracy in Media editor Kincaid. "Imus' ratings also had been going up before the Rutgers incident," he adds.

"Every couple of years some controversy erupts over race, and generally everybody goes back to their normal activities soon afterward," says George Washington University's media and public affairs professor Entman. Racial tension in America, which did come to the surface briefly following Imus' remark, is "a low-grade infection whose symptoms are always present but are tolerable to the majority," he says.

Advertisers would probably welcome Imus back to radio after the controversy dies down, but it's not clear whether a suitable radio venue exists, industry experts say.

For example, General Motors, a big sponsor that quickly pulled ads from the Imus show when controversy began building, would not rule out advertising on an Imus program in the future. Since Imus has apologized for his remarks and vowed to change his tone in the future, the automaker is "open to revisiting at some point down the road" a stint as an Imus advertiser, should his show return, a company spokesperson told *AdWeek* magazine.[24]

But "media options for Imus appear to be limited," said Mike Kinosian, a columnist for the industry publication *Inside Radio*.[25]

"There are only a handful of major radio networks, and it is hard to imagine one would step forward and take him," and "it would be problematic for him [to be] on a small, low-level, unfunded network," said Cary Pahigian, president and general manager in the Portland, Maine, office of Michigan-based Saga Communications, which owns and operates radio and television stations. Satellite radio also is likely out, for the time being at least, since the two big satellite networks — XM and Sirius — hope to merge, and with FCC scrutiny heavy on them at present, "this isn't something they would want to tackle," Pahigian said.[26]

As for gangsta rap, a newly formed coalition opposing sexist lyrics will increase the pressure for performers and record companies to halt the use of sexist language like "ho" and "bitch," says Williams, of the National Congress of Black Women (NCBW), which has been urging music companies to drop such language for years. This spring, however, other groups including the National Organization for Women and the National Council of Women's

Organizations have joined with NCBW to fight the sexist language. "With all of us working together, it's only a matter of time," she says.

When it comes to radio, even more targeted niche programs will develop as audio migrates from the airwaves to satellite and the Internet, analysts predict.

That inevitable shift means that radio "will find room for Imus and his language again," predicts the Media Research Center's Bozell.

Other changes also are in store for radio as audiences inevitably grow restless with the brand of talk radio that's dominated for a decade and a half, says Harrison of *Talkers* magazine. "We've been at the peak of a trend of political talk" that is mainly right-wing, he says. Now "people are tired of it," and public boredom spells the end of phenomena of popular culture. Progressive and liberal talk could burgeon in that climate, he predicts.

More than an opening for progressives, though, Americans currently have an appetite for non-partisan political talk, Harrison says. The talker who likely will flourish next "can be liberal, can be conservative," he says. "They'll express ideas," but not fervently back either political party, he predicts.

As for damping down the culture of insult and argument, "that's basically up to everyone," says Georgetown's Tannen. Many people do object to stereotyping insults, for example, uttered privately or in public. But "it's up to us to say something when we hear that talk," she says.

UPDATE

On-air therapist Dr. Laura Schlessinger is not a shock jock, but she sometimes acts like one on the radio. On Aug. 17, 2010, the widely syndicated "Dr. Laura" stunned her 9 million weekly listeners with news that she was giving up radio to "regain my First Amendment rights." It's a stance taken to heart by many broadcasting personalities and the fans who thrive on the often edgy cacophony of voices that make up much of national talk radio today.

Schlessinger, famous for dispensing "tough love" advice for solving personal problems, had recently bombarded an African-American caller with the N-word, claiming she was frustrated that blacks often use the racial epithet but whites who use it are considered racist. "I articulated the N-word all the way out — more than one time," Schlessinger said in a later interview with CNN's Larry King. "And that was wrong. I'll say it again — that was wrong. . . . I realized I had made a horrible mistake, and was so upset I could not finish the show."[27]

Former Alaska governor and Republican vice presidential candidate Sarah Palin took to Twitter to urge Schlessinger not to "retreat" but to "reload," declaring that the talk diva would be "even more powerful & effective w/out the shackles."

Use of N-word Criticized

But Schlessinger's departure was celebrated on the left, by mental health specialist Michael Bader, for example, who wrote on his *Psychology Today* blog: "The evidence is overwhelming that Pretend-Dr. Laura is a homophobe, misogynist, routinely blames the victim, and is relentlessly cruel in both tone and content to people who call her show for help.* The final straw — her use of the N-word on a recent broadcast — was a natural extension of her personality and politics."[28]

Renowned linguist Deborah Tannen of Georgetown University says Schlessinger was "right to resign, but her major offense was not her use of the word but her entire stance toward the caller and the group the caller is a part of." Tannen says what matters is not the N-word itself but the way it is used; hearing it from a white comedian is very different from hearing it on the Black Entertainment Network.

The National Association of Black Journalists framed the issue more concretely. NABJ President Kathy Times called for a national forum on "talk show hate." Despite Schlessinger's apology and planned resignation, "there are deeper issues that must be addressed by the company that syndicates her show — Premiere Radio Networks," Times said. "Why wait until the next on-air personality slips up? Is it time for the N-word and other racial epithets to be added to the list of seven dirty words (made famous by comedian George Carlin)? The use of those words hits broadcasters where it hurts them most — on the bottom line with fines and lost advertising revenue."[29]

Few in the talk radio industry, however, seem worried about a listener backlash. "In year 2010, nothing that Howard Stern, Don Imus or Laura Schlessinger can say is shocking," says Michael Harrison, editor and publisher of *Talkers* magazine, which recently celebrated its

---

* Schlessinger is neither a medical doctor nor a psychologist but holds a Ph.D. in physiology.

20th anniversary. "Shock jock is an outdated term from 25 [or] 30 years ago, while today you've got Internet porn and all that language you hear in the school yard."

"Tolerance is different nowadays," he adds. "You no longer have a general public, just competing factions in the public. So when something controversial is said to a certain [political] faction, it is now taken out and amplified to others who otherwise wouldn't have heard it. So it becomes shocking to them."

New Breed

Another new wrinkle in talk radio is the way controversial personalities today "are a different breed from the Howard Stern, Don Imus and shock jock variety of years past," says Richard Prince, who writes the "Journal-isms" blog for the Oakland, Calif.–based Maynard Institute for Journalism Education. "In the Obama era, the controversy has taken a political turn. It is the Glenn Beck and Rush Limbaugh comments that get attention these days, and they assume a larger importance because they are taken to represent those of a segment of the electorate." Prince notes that unlike Limbaugh and Beck, Imus was never considered the head of a political party.

On-air personalities who fall into disfavor can stage comebacks. The best example is the cranky Imus, whose April 2007 reference to the Rutgers University women's basketball team as "nappy-headed 'hos'" forced him off the air. Imus returned to the radio airwaves on WABC in New York that December and to a national audience on the Fox Business Network in the fall of 2009. He still attracts such diverse and relatively high-brow guests as Frank Rich, a liberal columnist for *The New York Times*, conservative commentator Laura Ingraham and comedian Harry Shearer. The black journalists' association issued a statement promising to monitor his performance. "Don Imus has a right to work, and I hope he will use his new platform responsibly," said Times, the NABJ president.[30]

Banned in England

Controversy is like mother's milk for many shock jocks. There is no better example than the acerbic conservative talk-show host and author Michael Savage, ranked fourth in *Talkers Magazine*'s top 100 show hosts, with 9 million weekly listeners. Savage, who defines his rightist politics as focused on borders, language and culture, has been the subject of multiple boycotts of sponsors and defamation lawsuits. He has infuriated the Council on American-Islamic Relations by insulting Islam and calling for the deportation of American Muslims. He has upset numerous parents of autistic children by accusing them of using the disease as a "racket" for milking the government for disability payments. And he has been physically banned from the United Kingdom for allegedly advocating hate and violence against ethnic minorities.[31]

On-air commentators like Glenn Beck, above, and Rush Limbaugh, who focus on political matters, often get the most attention and generate the most controversy. Unlike shock jocks like Don Imus, the conservative Limbaugh and Beck are seen as the virtual heads of a political party.

Fairness Doctrine

For decades, critics of controversial broadcasters have called for a restoration of the Fairness Doctrine, which, before it was abolished in 1987, required owners of radio and TV stations both to broadcast controversial issues of public importance and to present them in a fair and balanced manner. Currently, however, legislation dealing with the Fairness Doctrine has been offered only by conservative lawmakers seeking to enact a law *preventing* the Federal Communications Commission from restoring it.

The doctrine is unlikely to be restored because "most in the broadcasting field think it infringes on First Amendment rights," says Harrison. "That's enough of a reason, but another is that the doctrine is also out of date. It came from a period when broadcasting licenses were scarce resources, but today information is available from so many sources that we can't keep track of them. Proposals to regulate politically," he adds, "seem out of touch, and it would be another nail in the coffin of terrestrial radio."

That leaves critics of shock jocks with the tool of moral suasion. "The most effective thing government can do to discourage on-air racism is to speak out against it," says Prince. "And that should be echoed by private citizens. Government can play a role in making such attitudes unacceptable. But media owners hold the ultimate sanction: If they make it known that those who engage in that kind of behavior will be fired, that sends the most powerful message of all."

As Tannen wrote in her bestseller *The Argument Culture: Stopping America's War of Words*, the broadcast world has come to believe there is entertainment value in watching fights. "That's what shock jocks do to get you to tune in," she says. "It's very harmful to our culture."

NOTES

1. Gwen Ifill, "Trash Talk Radio," *The New York Times*, April 10, 2007.
2. "Imus Has Long Record of Incendiary Remarks," National Association of Black Journalists Web site, April 18, 2007; www.nabj.org.
3. Richard Prince, "NABJ Says It Still Wants Radio Host Out by Monday," *Journal-isms* column, Maynard Institute for Journalism Education, April 6, 2007.
4. "NAHJ Condemns Radio Host Don Imus for Racial Remarks," press release, National Association of Hispanic Journalists, April 9, 2007.
5. "Rallying Around Their Racist Friend," media advisory, Fairness & Accuracy in Media, April 11, 2007; www.fair.org.
6. Steve McClellan, "They Bailed for Now, But Advertisers Forgive," *AdWeek*, April 16, 2007; www.adweek.com.
7. Quoted in Alex Koppelman, "Is Rush Limbaugh Next?" *Salon.com*, April 16, 2007; www.salon.com.
8. Quoted in Richard Prince, "After Imus, Sights Set on Rap Music," *Journal-isms*, Maynard Institute for Journalism Education, April 14, 2007.
9. Quoted in Adam Graham, "Imus Storm Hits Hip-Hop World," *Detroit News*, April 14, 2007; www.detnews.com.
10. Billy Ingram, "Legendary Broadcaster Joe Pyne," *TVParty.com*; www.tvparty.com/empyne.html.
11. Charles Haynes, "Imus, Coulter, and the Marketplace for Offensive Speech," *Commentary*, First Amendment Center, April 15, 2007; www.firstamentmentcenter.org.
12. Ted Rall, "First They Came for the Shock Jocks," TedRall.com and Common Dreams News Center, March 11, 2004; www.commondreams.org.
13. Quoted in *ibid*.
14. Quoted in Dipayan Gupta and Thomas Rogers, "Safe Speech," *Salon.com*, May 1, 2007; www.salon.com.
15. For background, see John Michael Kittross and Christopher H. Sterling, *Stay Tuned: A History of American Broadcasting* (2002); William Triplett, "Broadcast Indecency," *CQ Researcher*, April 16, 2004, pp. 321-344; Alan Greenblatt, "Race in America," *CQ Researcher*, July 11, 2003, pp. 593-624; Kenneth Jost, "Talk Show Democracy," *CQ Researcher*, April 29, 1994, pp. 361-384; and M. Costello, "Blacks in the News Media," *CQ Researcher*, Aug. 16, 1972; "First Amendment and Mass Media," *CQ Researcher*, Jan. 21, 1970, both available at *CQ Researcher Plus Archive*; www.cqpress.com.
16. Zine Magubane, "Why 'Nappy' Is Offensive, *The Boston Globe*, April 12, 2007.
17. *Ibid*.
18. The case is *Federal Communications Commission v. Pacifica Foundation*, 438 U.S. 726, 98 S. Ct. 3026 (1978). The seven words are: shit, piss, fuck, cunt, cocksucker, motherfucker and tits.
19. "GE, Microsoft Bring Bigotry to Life," Fairness & Accuracy in Reporting, Feb. 12, 2003; www.fair.org.
20. Gil Kaufman, "Is Shock Radio Dead? More Potty-Mouthed DJs Join Don Imus in Doghouse," *MTV News*, May 15, 2007; www.mtv.com.
21. Imus' April 6 apology is quoted in "Cleaning up the I-Mess," transcript, "Paula Zahn Now," *CNN.com*, April 13, 2007, http://transcripts.cnn.com/TRANSCRIPTS/0704/13/pzn.01.html; "Imus Puts Remarks Into Context," transcript, "Imus in the Morning," *MSNBC.com*, April 9, 2007, www.msnbc.msn.com/id/18022596.

22. Nate Anderson, "Dennis Kucinich: Bring Back the Fairness Doctrine," *Ars Technica* blog, Jan. 17, 2007; http://arstechnica.com.
23. Ira Teinowitz, "Dingell Backs Return of Fairness Doctrine," *TV Week.com*, May 2, 2007; www.tvweek.com/news.cms?newsId=11988.
24. Quoted in McClellan, *op. cit.*
25. Mike Kinosian, "Minus Imus," *Inside Radio*, April 19, 2007; www.insideradio.com.
26. Quoted in *ibid.*
27. Rachel Weiner, "Sarah Palin Defends Dr. Laura," *The Washington Post,* Aug. 19, 2010.
28. Michael Bader, "Why We Love Dr. Laura," "What Is He Thinking?" blog, *Psychology Today*, Aug. 23, 2010.
29. National Association of Black Journalists press release, Aug. 19, 2010.
30. National Association of Black Journalists press release, Oct. 6, 2009.
31. See http://news.bbc.co.uk/2/hi/uk_news/8033319.stm. For a profile of Savage, see Kelefa Sanneh, "Party of One," *The New Yorker*, Aug. 3, 2009.

BIBLIOGRAPHY

Books

Kittross, John Michael, and Christopher H. Sterling, *Stay Tuned: A History of American Broadcasting*, **Lawrence Erlbaum Associates, 2002.**
The editor of *Media Ethics* magazine and a George Washington University professor of media and public affairs chronicle the growth and development of electronic media and broadcasting in the United States, including the development of shock radio and broadcast-content regulation.

Picca, Leslie Houts, and Joe R. Feagin, *Two-Faced Racism: Whites in the Backstage and Frontstage*, **Routledge, 2007.**
An assistant professor and a professor of sociology from the University of Dayton and Texas A&M University examine the racial attitudes of white college students who chronicled their race-related experiences and thoughts in detailed diaries. They argue that racism has receded from public life in America but that many people still actively engage in racist talk among close friends and family.

Rappoport, Leon, *Punchlines: The Case for Racial, Ethnic, and Gender Humor*, **Praeger, 2005.**
A professor emeritus of psychology at Kansas State University details the history of stereotyping humor and argues that it can serve important social functions, including as a tool to combat prejudice.

Articles

"What Happens When Shock Jocks Go Too Far?" POV: The Fire Next Time, Public Broadcasting Service Web site, www.pbs.org/pov/pov2005/thefirenexttime/special_case studies.html, 2005.
This Web article by producers of a PBS documentary on how talk radio divided a Montana community relates stories of shock jocks who transgressed community standards for acceptable speech and faced controversy.

Kinosian, Mike, "Don's Gone: Post Imess," *Inside Radio*, **April 26, 2007, www.insideradio.com.**
A columnist for a radio trade publication chronicles Don Imus' career and interviews industry insiders about what his firing may mean to broadcasters.

Koppelman, Alex, "Is Rush Limbaugh Next?" *Salon*, **April 16, 2007, www.salon.com.**
Panelists at an April meeting of the conservative Free Congress Foundation predicted that congressional Democrats will try to revive the Fairness Doctrine requiring broadcasters to air all sides of controversial issues. They discussed strategies to stop revival of the doctrine, which media analysts argued would endanger conservative political commentators like Rush Limbaugh.

Llorente, Elizabeth, "Hispanics Steamed by Shock Radio Stunt," *The Record* **[Bergen, N.J.], March 22, 2007.**
Hispanic community leaders in New Jersey protested when shock radio hosts Craig Carton and Ray Rossi, known as "The Jersey Guys," launched a show segment called "La Cuca Gotcha," during which they urged listeners to report suspected illegal immigrants either to the station or to immigration authorities. Critics called for a boycott of the show's advertising, saying that the hosts encouraged racial profiling and vigilante activity.

McBride, Sara, and Brian Steinberg, "Finding a Replacement for Imus Won't Be Easy," *The Wall Street Journal*, **April 16, 2007, p. B1.**

Controversial radio hosts bring in big audiences and ad revenues, but talented shock talkers who can entertain a national audience aren't plentiful, so stations hire, fire and rehire the same people over and over. Increasing the difficulty for broadcast radio are satellite channels that have lured some top talent to the unregulated medium.

McClellan, Steve, "They Bailed for Now, But Advertisers Forgive," *AdWeek,* **April 16, 2007, www.adweek.com.**
A journalist who covers the advertising industry argues that advertisers who pulled out of Imus' show didn't want the program canceled.

Steinberg, Jacques, "Talk Radio Tries for Humor and a Political Advantage," *The New York Times,* **April 20, 2007.**
Shock jocks joked about Virginia Tech mass shooter Seung-Hui Cho while conservative radio hosts speculated about how his Korean background may have played into his becoming a murderer.

Walker, Jesse, "Tuning Out Free Speech," *The American Conservative,* **April 23, 2007, www.adconmag.com.**
The editor of libertarian *Reason* magazine argues that the history of the Federal Communications Commission's Fairness Doctrine shows that the doctrine stifled speech on the public airwaves.

Reports and Studies

Post-Conference Report: Rethinking the Discourse on Race: A Symposium on How the Lack of Racial Diversity in the Media Affects Social Justice and Policy, **The Ronald H. Brown Center for Civil Rights and Economic Development, St. John's University School of Law, October 2006.**
Conferees at a 2006 forum provide updates on ethnic diversity in media organizations and how the media shape Americans' views of race.

For More Information

Accuracy in Media, 4455 Connecticut Ave., N.W., Suite 330, Washington, DC 20008; (202) 364-4401; www.aim.org/index. A conservative media-criticism group that tracks and disseminates information about liberal bias it observes in the media.

Ban the N-Word, http://banthenword.com. An activist group that disseminates information about racist language and stereotypes in media, including detailed reviews of movies and new music releases.

Fairness and Accuracy in Reporting, 112 W. 27th St., New York, NY 10001; (212) 633-6700; www.fair.org/index.php. A liberal media-criticism group that disseminates information about and advocates for diverse opinions in media, especially inclusion of minority viewpoints.

Inside Radio, www.insideradio.com. An insider publication for the radio industry that posts up-to-date news and commentary on radio-related events.

Maynard Institute for Journalism Education, 1211 Preservation Park Way, Oakland, CA 94612; (510) 891-9202; www.mije.org. A nonprofit education center for minority journalists that chronicles race-related issues in media such as the Imus controversy on its extensive Web site.

Media Matters for America, 1625 Massachusetts Ave., NW, Suite 600, Washington, DC 20036; (202) 756-4100; http://mediamatters.org/index. A liberal media-criticism group that tracks factual errors and misleading statements in the media, focusing on misinformation that may advance a conservative political agenda, and urges journalists to issue corrections of the errors.

Media Research Center, 325 S. Patrick St., Alexandria, VA 22314; (703) 683-9733. A conservative media-criticism group that tracks and posts commentary on examples of liberal media bias and on events that threaten conservative media.

Talkers Magazine, 650 Belmont Ave., Springfield, MA 01108; (413) 739-8255; www.talkers.com. A publication covering talk radio that posts news and commentary about the industry on its Web site.

TimWise.org, www.timwise.org. An anti-racism educator who posts essays and reports on historical and current racial dilemmas in America.

10 Racial Diversity in Public Schools

Kenneth Jost and Charles S. Clark

White enrollment at Seattle's Ballard High School is above previous guidelines five years after a racial-diversity plan was suspended because of a legal challenge. The Supreme Court's June 28 decision invalidating racial-balance plans in Seattle and Louisville, Ky., bars school districts from using race for student-placement decisions but may permit some race-conscious policies to promote diversity.

From *CQ Researcher*,
September 14, 2007 (updated August 12, 2010).

Hannah MacNeal's parents were glad to learn of an opening at the popular magnet elementary school near their upscale neighborhood in eastern Louisville, Ky. When they applied in mid-August for Hannah to enroll as a fourth-grader at Greathouse/Shryock Elementary, however, school system officials said she could not be admitted.

The reason: Hannah is white.

Only six weeks earlier, the U.S. Supreme Court had ruled that Jefferson County Public Schools (JCPS) — which includes Louisville — was violating the Constitution by assigning students to schools on the basis of their race.

Hannah's stepmother, Dana MacNeal, was surprised and upset when she learned Hannah would have been admitted to the school if she had been black. And she was all the more upset when JCPS Student Placement Director Pat Todd insisted on Aug. 14 that the Supreme Court ruling allowed the school system to continue maintaining separate attendance zones for black and white students for Greathouse/Shryock and two of the system's other three magnet elementary schools.

The school system's lawyers were surprised as well to learn of the policy. After the MacNeals decided to fight the decision keeping Hannah in her regular elementary school, officials agreed to enroll her at Greathouse/Shryock and scrap the racially separate boundary zones beginning in 2008.[1]

"Of course, they backed off from the position, knowing they were wrong," says Louisville attorney Ted Gordon, who represented the MacNeals in the latest round in his long-running battle to overturn Jefferson County's school racial-diversity policies. "They have to follow the law."

School Racial-Balance Plans in Louisville and Seattle

The Supreme Court's June 28, 2007, ruling on the school racial-diversity plans in Seattle and Jefferson County (Louisville) bars the use of racial classifications in individual pupil assignments but appears to permit some "race-neutral" policies aimed at racial diversity.

Jefferson County (Louisville) (98,000 students; 35 percent African-American)

History: County was racially segregated before *Brown v. Board of Education* ruling; court-ordered desegregation plan in 1975 called for crosstown busing between predominantly African-American West End and mainly white neighborhoods in eastern suburbs; court order dissolved in 2000; school board adopts pupil-assignment plan with use of racial classifications to promote diversity; assignment plan still in effect after Supreme Court decision, pending new plan expected for 2009-2010 academic year.

Details: Plan classifies students as "black" or "white" (including Asians, Hispanics and others); guidelines call for each elementary, middle or high school to have between 15 percent and 50 percent African-American enrollment; residence-based system assigns students to school within residential "cluster"; most West End neighborhoods assigned to schools outside area; student applications for transfer from assigned school evaluated on basis of several factors, including effect on racial makeup; under Supreme Court decision, individual transfer requests will no longer be denied on basis of race.

Seattle (45,000 students: 58 percent "non-white")

History: No history of mandatory segregation, but racially identifiable neighborhoods: predominantly black south of downtown, predominantly white to the north; racial-balance plan with crosstown busing voluntarily adopted in 1978; school choice introduced in 1990s, with race as one "tiebreaker" to distribute students among oversubscribed schools; school board suspended the plan in 2002 because of legal challenge; Supreme Court ruling held plan invalid.

Details: Ninth-graders permitted to apply to up to three of district's 10 high schools; tiebreakers used for applications to oversubscribed schools; sibling preference was most important factor, race second; race used if school's enrollment deviated by specified percentage from overall racial demographics: 40 percent white, 60 percent non-white.

The Supreme Court's fractured ruling struck down pupil-assignment policies adopted in 2000 limiting African-American enrollment at any individual school in Jefferson County to between 15 percent and 50 percent of the student body. The ruling also rejected the Seattle school system's use of race as a "tiebreaker" for assigning students to high schools; the plan had been suspended in 2002 because of the litigation.[2]

In response to the MacNeals' case, Todd's office drew up new boundary zones for the four magnet elementary schools that were approved by the school board on Sept. 10. For the longer term, officials are trying to find ways to maintain a measure of racial balance in the 98,000-student school system under the Supreme Court decision, which bars the use of racial classifications in individual pupil assignments but appears to permit some "race-neutral" policies aimed at racial diversity.

"We are going to do our best to achieve it," says JCPS Superintendent Sheldon Berman. "We are deeply committed to retaining the qualities of an integrated environment."

The court's June 28 decision dealt a blow to hundreds of school systems around the country that have adopted voluntary race-mixing plans after court-ordered desegregation plans lapsed in recent years.

Five of the justices — led by Chief Justice John G. Roberts Jr. — said using racial classifications in pupil assignments violated the Equal Protection Clause of the 14th Amendment. That is the same provision the court cited a half-century earlier in the famous *Brown v. Board of Education* (1954) ruling that found racial segregation in public schools unconstitutional.[3]

In a strong dissent, the court's four liberal justices — led by Stephen G. Breyer — said the ruling contradicted previous decisions upholding race-based pupil assignments and would hamper local school boards' efforts to prevent "resegregation" in individual schools. But one of the justices in the majority — Anthony M. Kennedy — joined the liberal minority in endorsing racial diversity as a legitimate goal. Kennedy listed several "race-neutral" policies, such as drawing attendance zones or building new schools to include students from different racial neighborhoods, that schools could adopt to pursue the goal.

The ruling drew sharp criticism from traditional civil rights advocates. "It's preposterous to think the 14th Amendment was designed to permit individual white parents to strike down a plan to help minority students have better access to schools and to prevent school districts from having integrated schools that are supported by a majority of the community," says Gary Orfield, a longtime civil rights advocate and director of the Civil Rights Project at UCLA's Graduate School of Education and Information Sciences.

Ted Shaw, president of the NAACP Legal Defense Fund, said the ruling blocks school boards from using "one of the few tools that are available" to create racially diverse schools. "The court has taken a significant step away from the promise of *Brown*," says Shaw. "And this comes on top of the reality that many school districts are highly segregated by race already."

Conservative critics of race-based school policies, however, applauded the ruling. "I don't think school districts should be drawing attendance zones or building schools for the purpose of achieving a politically correct racial mix," says Roger Clegg, president of the Center for Equal Opportunity, which joined in a friend-of-the-court brief supporting the white families that challenged the Seattle and Louisville school policies.

"A lot of parents out there don't like it when their students are treated differently because of race or ethnicity," Clegg adds. "After these decisions, the odds favor those parents and those organizations that oppose school boards that practice racial or ethnic discrimination."

School officials in Louisville and Seattle and around the country are generally promising to continue race-mixing policies within the limits of the court's decision. "School boards are going to have to do the hard work to find more tailored ways of approaching diversity in their schools," says Francisco Negrón, general counsel of the National School Boards Association.

The evidence in Louisville and nationally suggests, however, that the goal will be hard to achieve. In

Racial Classifications Barred But Diversity Backed

The Supreme Court's June 28 decision in Parents Involved in Community Schools v. Seattle School District No. 1 invalidating pupil-assignment plans in Seattle and Louisville bars school systems from assigning individual students to schools based on their race. In a partial concurrence, however, Justice Anthony M. Kennedy joined with the four dissenters in finding racial diversity to be a legitimate government interest and in permitting some race-conscious policies to achieve that goal.

Roberts (plurality opinion)

Scalia   Thomas   Alito

"Racial balancing is not transformed from 'patently unconstitutional' to a compelling state interest simply by relabeling it 'racial diversity.'"

Kennedy (concurring in part)

". . . [A] district may consider it a compelling interest to achieve a diverse student body. Race may be one component of that diversity. . . . What the government is not permitted to do . . . is to classify every student on the basis of race and to assign each of them to schools based on that classification."

Breyer (dissenting)

Stevens   Souter   Ginsburg

"The plurality . . . undermines [*Brown v. Board of Education's*] promise of integrated primary and secondary education that local communities have sought to make a reality. This cannot be justified in the name of the Equal Protection Clause."

Credits: AFP/Getty Images/Paul J. Richards (Alito, Kennedy, Roberts, Souter, Scalia, Thomas); Getty Images/Mark Wilson (Ginsburg, Stevens); AFP/Getty Images/ Brendan Smialowski (Breyer)

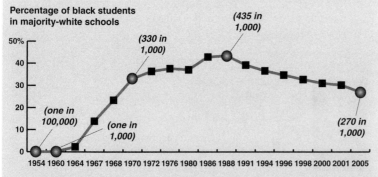

Southern Schools Least Segregated, But Slipping

Schools in the South were the least segregated in the nation in the 1970s and '80s, a distinction they maintained in the 2005 school year. But Southern schools have been resegregating steadily since 1988.

Change in Black Segregation in Southern Schools, 1954-2005

Source: Gary Orfield and Chungmei Lee, "Historic Reversals, Accelerating Resegregation, and the Need for New Integration Strategies," Civil Rights Project, UCLA, August 2007

Louisville, nine schools are now outside the district's 15/50 guidelines, with several having more than 55 percent African-American enrollment, according to Todd. "If the board wants to continue to maintain diversity, we've already had some significant slippage at some selected schools," he says.[4]

Nationally, a new report by the UCLA Civil Rights Project concludes that African-American and Latino students are increasingly isolated from white students in public schools. Overall, nearly three-fourths of African-American students and slightly over three-fourths of Latino students attend predominantly minority schools. Both figures have been increasing since 1980, the report says.[5]

Critics of race-based pupil assignments are unfazed by the trends. "We're past guidelines, we're past quotas and we need to move on," says Gordon of the Louisville statistics. He calls instead for an array of reforms focused on schools with high concentrations of low-income students.

"All other things being equal, I like racially diverse schools," says Abigail Thernstrom, a senior fellow at the conservative Manhattan Institute and a former member of the Massachusetts Board of Education. "But I do not think it works from any angle to have government entities — whether they are federal courts or local school boards — try to engineer diversity."

Supporters of racial-balance plans argue that diversity in the classroom helps boost academic achievement for minority students without adversely affecting achievement for white students. Opponents dispute those claims.

The debate over diversity also highlights a secondary dispute over the widespread practice of "tracking" — the offering of separate courses for students based on ability or previous achievement. Supporters say the practice matches curriculum to students' needs and abilities, but critics say it results in consigning already disadvantaged students — including a disproportionate number of African-Americans — to poor-quality education.

Meanwhile, some experts and advocates are calling for shifting the focus away from race and instead trying to promote socioeconomic integration — mixing low-income and middle- and upper-class students. Richard Kahlenberg, a senior fellow with the left-of-center Century Foundation who is most closely associated with the movement, says policies aimed at preventing high concentrations of low-income students will produce academic gains along with likely gains in racial and ethnic diversity.

"Providing all students with the chance to attend mixed-income schools can raise overall levels of achievement," Kahlenberg writes in a report released on the day of the Supreme Court decision.[6]

As the debate over diversity in public-school classrooms continues, here are the major questions being considered.

Should school systems promote racial diversity in individual schools?

School officials in Lynn, Mass., a former mill town 10 miles northeast of Boston, take pride in a pupil-assignment system that has helped maintain racial balance in most schools even as the town's Hispanic population has steadily increased over the past decade. "We work very hard to promote integration and cultural diversity so that our children are able to get along with each other," says Jan Birchenough, the administrator in charge of compliance with the state's racial-balance law.

White Students Are Racially Isolated

Segregation remained high in 2005-06 for all racial groups except Asians. White students remained the most racially isolated, although they attended schools with slightly more minority students than in the past. The average white student attended schools in which 77 percent of their peers were white. Meanwhile, more than half of black and Latino students' peers were black or Latino, and fewer than one-third of their classmates were white.

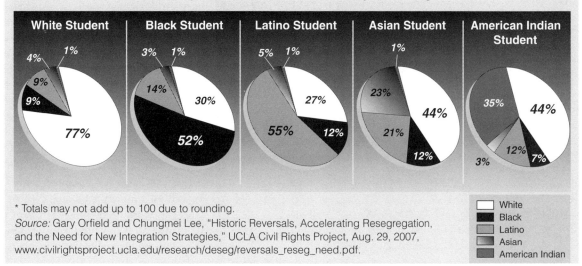

Racial Composition of Schools Attended by the Average . . .

* Totals may not add up to 100 due to rounding.
Source: Gary Orfield and Chungmei Lee, "Historic Reversals, Accelerating Resegregation, and the Need for New Integration Strategies," UCLA Civil Rights Project, Aug. 29, 2007, www.civilrightsproject.ucla.edu/research/deseg/reversals_reseg_need.pdf.

But attorney Chester Darling says Lynn's policy of denying any transfer requests that would increase racial imbalance at an individual school "falls squarely within" the kinds of plans prohibited by the Supreme Court decision in the Louisville and Seattle cases. "It can't be race-neutral if you use the word race," says Darling, who is asking a federal judge in Boston to reopen a previously unsuccessful suit filed by parents challenging the policy.[7]

Critics of race-based assignment plans hope the Supreme Court decision will persuade or force school districts like Lynn's to drop any use of racial classifications in pupil placement. "Most school districts will look at the decision's bottom line, will consider that the Louisville and Seattle plans were not sloppily done, and yet at the end of the day were declared unconstitutional," says Clegg of the Center for Equal Opportunity. "This cost the school boards a lot of time and money, and they're going to have to pay the other side's lawyer."

But school board officials say the court's fractured ruling leaves room for local systems to consider race in trying to create racial and ethnic mixing in individual schools.

"Race is still not out of the question," says Negrón of the school boards' association. "A plurality of the court said certain things that are not the law of the land. What the majority has done is invalidate these particular programs, but certainly left the door wide open to the use of race — which continues to be a compelling government interest."

Apart from the legal issue, supporters and opponents of racial-diversity plans also disagree on their educational and other effects. "There's a consensus in the academic world that there are clear educational benefits, and the benefits aren't just for minority students," says UCLA Professor Orfield.

Conversely, "racial isolation leads to reduced achievement," says Negrón.

Critics of racial-diversity policies, however, say those benefits are unproven and the logic of the claimed cause-effect relationship unconvincing. "There is very little empirical evidence," says Thernstrom, the Manhattan Institute fellow.

"I don't think how well you learn or what you learn depends on the color of the skin of the person sitting

Non-Racial Approaches to Integration

Some 40 school districts around the country are seeking to diversify enrollment in individual schools through socioeconomic integration — typically, by setting guidelines for the percentage of students eligible for free or reduced-price lunch. Here are some of the districts taking such approaches, as drawn from a report by the Century Foundation's Richard Kahlenberg, a strong advocate of the policies.

School District *Enrollment: Percentage of whites (W), African-Americans (B), Hispanics (H), Asian-Americans (A)*

Berkeley, Calif. *(9,000: 31% W, 29% B, 17% H, 8% A)*
Socioeconomic and racial diversity guidelines were adopted in 2004 to replace a voluntary racial-integration plan; plan being phased-in one grade at a time; in 2005-06, eight of 11 elementary schools were within 15% of the districtwide average of 40% of students receiving subsidized lunches; most parents (71%) still receive first choice of schools.

Brandywine, Del. *(11,000: 54% W, 39% B, 3% H, 4% A)*
The district — comprising parts of Wilmington and surrounding suburbs — was granted an exception in 2001 by state Board of Education to law mandating neighborhood schools; plan limits subsidized-lunch enrollment to between 16% and 73%; plan credited with maintaining racial diversity; some evidence of academic gains in higher grades.

Cambridge, Mass. *(6,000: 37% B, 35% W, 15% H, 11% A)*
Plan adopted in 2001 to replace race-conscious "controlled choice" system says individual schools should be within 15 percentage points of districtwide percentage of free/reduced lunch students; race remains a potential factor in assignments; racial diversity maintained, socioeconomic diversity increased; limited evidence finds academic gains for low-income students, no negative effect on middle-income students.

Charlotte-Mecklenburg, N.C. *(129,000: 42% B, 36% W, 14% H, 4% A)*
School board dropped racial-desegregation effort, adopted public school choice plan after school system was declared "unitary" in 2001, or no longer a dual system based on race; plan gives some priority to low-income students in schools with concentrated poverty, but transfers to higher-performing schools are permitted only if seats are available; plan seen as unsuccessful in creating racial or socioeconomic integration.

La Crosse, Wis. *(7,000: 20% minority)*
Was first district to adopt socioeconomic integration policy in 1991-92 in response to influx of Hmong refugees; plan used redrawn attendance zones and busing to spread low-income students among elementary schools and two high schools; plan largely survived political battle in 1992-93 that included recall of several school board members; plan touted as success, but enrollments at most elementary schools have been and still are outside guidelines.

next to you," says Clegg. "Students in overwhelmingly white schoolrooms in Idaho and in overwhelmingly African-American classrooms in Washington, D.C., can each learn."

Critics cite as one concrete disadvantage the time spent on buses when students are transported out of their neighborhoods for the sake of racial balance.

"There's no educational benefit there, and it's a waste of their very precious time," says Thernstrom. The travel burdens also hamper student participation in extracurricular activities and parental involvement, the critics say.

In traditional desegregation plans, those burdens typically fell for the most part on African-American students, who were transported out of their neighborhoods to schools in predominantly white areas. Busing was "usually a one-way street" for African-Americans, says James Anderson, head of the department of educational-policy studies at the University of Illinois, Champaign-Urbana.

In recent years, however, school-choice policies in some communities have meant increased busing for whites as well as minority students. Negrón cites the example of Pinellas County (Clearwater), Fla., which has a universal-choice program allowing students to enroll in any school in the county and providing transportation if requested. "It is a cost," Negrón says. "But school districts are finding that it depends on the facts and circumstances."

Civil rights advocates counter that racial isolation imposes much more serious costs for minority students. "The consequences of segregation of African-American students in public schools — and it is increasingly true for Latino students — have been concentration of poverty, deprivation of resources and a host of other problems that do impact on the quality of education," says the Legal Defense Fund's Shaw.

Like many of the critics, Thernstrom stops short of absolute opposition to any race-conscious school policies. "I don't mind" redrawing attendance zones for racial mixing, she says, "but I don't think we should be starry-eyed about what it's going to achieve."

Michael Rosman, president of the Center for Individual Rights, says schools should try to prevent "racial isolation" in individual schools "if it is shown to have deleterious educational effects."

But Illinois Professor Anderson says school boards should take affirmative steps to "take advantage" of diversity. "We could build wonderful, intellectually rich environments where kids really do have an exchange of ideas and an exchange of cultures and come out of that with a cosmopolitan sense of culture that is unique," he says. "How can you be global," he adds, "yet at the same time so parochial?"

Should school systems seek to promote socioeconomic integration in individual schools?

The consolidated school system in Wake County, N.C. — encompassing the rapidly growing Research Triangle Park area (near Raleigh and Durham) — made nationwide news in 2000 by dropping the use of racial guidelines in favor of socioeconomic-integration policies. The "Healthy School" assignment guidelines call for limiting individual schools to no more than 40 percent enrollment of students receiving free or reduced-price lunches or 25 percent enrollment of students performing below grade level.

Seven years later, the policies are a bragging point for the school system and exhibit No. 1 for advocates of socioeconomic integration. "Classrooms that are balanced from a diversity point of view are important to maintaining academic performance," says Michael Evans, the school system's communications director, citing the district's declining achievement gap for African-American, Hispanic and low-income students.

Some Wake County parents are not sold, however. Dave Duncan, the one-time president of the now largely inactive advocacy group Assignment by Choice, discounts the claimed academic gains by pointing to the relatively small percentage of students assigned under

School District *Enrollment: Percentage of whites (W), African-Americans (B), Hispanics (H), Asian-Americans (A)*

Manatee County, Fla. (*42,000: 60% W, 20% H, 15% B, 4% other*)
District south of Tampa Bay has had limited success with a plan adopted in 2002 admitting students to schools based on maintaining socioeconomic balance: Only 10 elementary schools were within guidelines in 2005-06; among 14 schools with above-average low-income enrollment, only four showed adequate academic gains.

McKinney, Tex. (*20,000: 64% W, 21% H, 11% B, 3% other*)
Dallas suburb adopted socioeconomic-balance policy in 1995 by redrawing attendance zones; low-income students perform better on statewide tests than low-income students statewide; some opposition to longer bus rides, but plan said to have broad support.

Minneapolis, Minn. (*36,000: 41% B, 28% W, 16% H, 10% A*)
Desegregation suit settled in state court in 2000 with agreement to adopt four-year experiment to encourage socioeconomic integration; plan provides transportation for low-income students to suburban schools; also requires wealthier magnet schools in Minneapolis to set aside seats for low-income students; 2,000 low-income students attended suburban schools over four-year period; legislature voted to extend program after end of experiment.

Omaha, Neb. (*47,000: 44% W, 32% B, 21% H*)
School board adopted plan aimed at socioeconomic integration after system was declared unitary in 1999; low-income students given preference in weighted lottery for admission to magnet schools; 2006 proposal to expand plan to recently annexed neighborhoods prompted backlash in state legislature, but education groups won passage of 2007 bill to establish goal of socioeconomic diversity throughout metropolitan area.

Rochester, N.Y. (*33,000: 64% B, 22% H, 13% W*)
Managed-choice plan adopted in city in 2002 includes socioeconomic-fairness guidelines; vast majority of elementary school students (83%) are economically disadvantaged; plan seen as likely to have limited effect unless interdistrict choice program is established between city and suburbs.

San Francisco (*55,000: 32% Asian, 22% H, 13% B, 9% W*)
Student-assignment plan adopted in 2001 replaced racial-desegregation scheme with plan aimed at socioeconomic diversity; seven-part definition includes SES (socioeconomic status), academic achievement, language, other factors; plan seen as fairly successful in balancing schools by SES, less so in producing racial diversity; district is consistently top-performing urban district in state.

Wake County (Raleigh), N.C. (*136,000: 54% W, 27% B, 10% H, 5% A*)
Guidelines adopted in 2000 replacing racial guidelines limit schools to 40% free/reduced lunch, 25% reading below grade level; policies credited with maintaining racial diversity; role in academic gains questioned; school-zone changes due to growth draw criticism from some families.

Sources: Richard D. Kahlenberg, Century Foundation, "Rescuing *Brown v. Board of Education:* Profiles of Twelve School Districts Pursuing Socioeconomic School Integration," Century Foundation, June 28, 2007, www.tcf.org; news accounts.

the guidelines and the comparable academic gains statewide. The school system "used the diversity issue as a smoke screen when there is criticism or opposition to the way they do the student-assignment process," Duncan says.

As the most prominent advocate of socioeconomic integration, the Century Foundation's Kahlenberg acknowledges varied results in districts with such policies. But he strongly argues that the policy of mixing students by socioeconomic background offers educational benefits in its own right and practical advantages for districts trying to promote racial diversity without running afoul of the Supreme Court's new limits on race-based assignments.

"There's a wide body of research that the single, best thing you can do for low-income kids is to give them the opportunity to attend a middle-class school," says Kahlenberg. Despite some well-publicized exceptions, schools with "concentrated levels of poverty" tend to have more student-discipline problems, lower caliber teachers and principals and less parental involvement than predominantly middle- or upper-class schools, he explains. Socioeconomic integration, he says, results in higher academic achievement for low-income students and no adverse effect on others as long as there is "a strong core of students with middle-class background."

Kahlenberg says socioeconomic integration is also likely to produce some racial and ethnic mixing since the poverty rate among African-Americans and Latinos is higher than among whites. In educational terms, however, he says socioeconomic diversity is more valuable than racial diversity because the academic gains of mixing by class and income appear to be well established, while the claimed gains of race mixing are in dispute.

Traditional civil rights advocates like the Legal Defense Fund's Shaw do not quarrel with socioeconomic integration but insist that it is "not an adequate substitute for racial integration."

Orfield agrees that socioeconomic integration is "a good idea" but quickly adds, "You can't achieve racial integration very well by using social and economic integration."

"If you talk to districts that have relied solely on that, it doesn't reach all of the students that they need to reach," says Negrón at the school boards association.

For their part, conservatives raise fewer objections to mixing students by socioeconomic background than by race, but they worry the practice may merely be a pretext for racial classifications. "It has fewer constitutional problems," says Thernstrom. "It is less politically controversial."

"It's better than race-based student assignments," says Clegg at the Center for Equal Opportunity. "But if you're using socioeconomic status simply as a proxy for race, many of the same policy and legal problems remain."

Thernstrom is unconvinced, however, of the claimed academic benefits. "There are no proven results from it," she says. She scoffs at what she calls "the notion that if you sit next to somebody, differences [in values] are going to somehow melt away."

In any event, Clegg says he opposes either racial or socioeconomic mixing if it requires assigning students to schools distant from their homes. "Neighborhood schools are the preferable means of assignment," he says, "because you're not having to pay for busing and you're not having to put children on long bus rides, which keep them from engaging in extracurricular activities."

Kahlenberg disagrees. "I haven't heard anyone make a convincing case that from an educational perspective the best way to assign students is the place where their parents can afford to live," he says. "That's the way we do it, but there's no argument that's the best way to educate kids in our society."

From opposite perspectives, however, both Orfield and Thernstrom agree that socioeconomic integration engenders some of the same kinds of opposition that racial integration does. "You do have a lot of middle-class flight as a result," Thernstrom says. "It's not really more popular than racial integration," Orfield says.

Despite the resistance, Kahlenberg believes the policy would fulfill a fundamental goal of public education in the United States. "Most people believe at least in theory that education is the way for kids of any background to do well," he says. "As long as we have economically segregated schools, that promise is broken."

Is the focus on diversity interfering with efforts to improve education in all schools?

As he wrapped up his legal challenge to the Louisville pupil-assignment plan before the Supreme Court, attorney Gordon depicted the case as a choice between "diversity" and "educational outcome."

"For me," Gordon told the justices during the Dec. 4 arguments, "I would use all these millions of dollars. I would reduce teacher-student ratio. I would give incentive pay to the better teachers. I would [build] more magnet schools, more traditional schools."

"We presuppose that we're going to have bad schools and good schools in this country," he continued. "I don't think we can no [sic] longer accept that."

Gordon describes himself as a civil rights liberal, but his argument parallels the views of conservatives like

Clegg. "School districts should be worrying less about the racial and ethnic mix than about improving the education that's offered at all schools," Clegg says.

"If you're just focusing on racial diversity, as it's called, for its own sake without trying to assess whether you're improving the educational outcomes," says Rosman, "then you're detracting from the overall goal of achieving educational excellence. In some instances, that's happened."

"The solution is to reduce the gap, the racial gap, the ethnic gap, the socioeconomic gap," says Thernstrom. "Then kids will be looked at as just kids without any kind of assumptions made about, you know, are they like me?"

Traditional civil rights groups and advocates insist that diversity and educational reform complement rather than conflict with each other. In any event, they say, the push for diversity is neither so strong nor so extensive as the critics contend.

"We haven't had any federal policy of promoting diversity since 1981," says Orfield, referring to the first year of Ronald Reagan's presidency. "We haven't had any new lawsuits to integrate schools for a long time. Ever since 1980, most desegregation plans have had voluntary choice and magnet schools, and almost all of them are part and parcel of educational reform plans."

John Trasviña, president and general counsel of the Mexican American Legal Defense and Educational Fund (MALDEF), calls the claimed conflict between diversity and educational quality "a diversion." Referring to educational reform, he says, "We aren't doing that either. It's always easy to say let's address some other issue. When it comes to do that, it's not done."

Diversity advocates dispute critics' suggestion that racial or economic integration has been pursued solely for its own sake with no attention to improving educational quality. "I don't think anybody ever thought that school integration by itself was a sufficient policy," Orfield says.

"The whole reason for economic integration is to promote academic achievement and raise the quality of schooling," says Kahlenberg. "No one has figured out how to make separate schools for rich and poor work well, certainly not for poor kids."

Orfield and Kahlenberg also dismiss concerns that the transportation costs entailed in some diversity plans take scarce dollars from other, more promising school-improvement initiatives. "We've spent billions and billions of dollars on low-income schools, which hasn't produced a lot of results," Kahlenberg says.

Orfield is even blunter about recent efforts to reduce the racial gap. "It's been a failure," he says. Desegregation and anti-poverty programs of the 1960s and '70s did narrow the racial-achievement gap, Orfield writes in the recent UCLA Civil Rights Project report. But he says "most studies" find that President Bush's No Child Left Behind law — which specifically calls for narrowing the achievement gap between white and minority pupils — has had "no impact" on the disparities so far.[8]

From opposite perspectives, Thernstrom and Trasviña lay out demanding agendas for schools to try to close the racial gap. "I want more learning going on," says Thernstrom. "You need really good schools. The day should be longer, the teachers should be better, the principals should have more authority.

"Our kids aren't learning enough in school," she continues. "That will level the playing field."

"We clearly need to improve the quality of our schools," says Trasviña. He calls for steps to reduce the dropout rate and to channel more students into so-called STEM courses (science, technology, engineering and math). But diversity helps, not hurts reform efforts, he says.

"While it is true that simply putting children of different backgrounds in seats in the same classroom does not necessarily improve the classroom experience by itself, [diversity] adds to it," Trasviña says. "And it adds to the political will to make sure that people understand that these are our schools."

BACKGROUND

The "Common School"

The idea of free, universal public education has been espoused in the United States since the Revolutionary Era and still holds a central place in American thought as a tool for personal development and social cohesion. But the ideal of equal educational opportunity for all has never obtained in practice. Even as education became more nearly universal in the 20th century, African-Americans and other racial and ethnic minorities faced blatant discrimination that was only partly alleviated by landmark court rulings outlawing legally mandated segregation.[9]

George Washington and Thomas Jefferson were among the nation's early leaders to call in general terms for mass

CHRONOLOGY

Before 1950 *Free, universal public education is enshrined as American ideal and advances in practice, but African-Americans, Hispanics and Asian-Americans are consigned to separate and unequal schools in much of the country.*

1950s-1960s *Racial segregation in public schools is ruled unconstitutional, but desegregation is slow.*

1954, 1955 Supreme Court's unanimous decision in *Brown v. Board of Education* (1954) outlaws mandatory racial segregation in public schools; a year later court says school districts must dismantle dual systems "with all deliberate speed" (*Brown II*). "Massive resistance" in South stalls integration.

1964, 1965 Civil Rights Act of 1964 authorizes Justice Department to file school-desegregation suits; Title I of Elementary and Secondary Education Act provides targeted aid to school districts for low-income students.

1968 Supreme Court tells school districts to develop plans to dismantle dual systems "now."

1970s-1980s *Busing upheld as desegregation tool but draws strong protests in North and West as well as South; Supreme Court, Justice Department withdraw from desegregation cases.*

1971 Supreme Court unanimously upholds federal courts' power to order crosstown busing to desegregate schools.

1973 Supreme Court rejects federal constitutional right to equal school funding; one month later, New Jersey supreme court is first to sustain funding-equity suit under state constitution.

1974 U.S. Supreme Court, 5-4, bars court-ordered desegregation between inner cities and suburbs; decision is first in series of closely divided rulings that limit desegregation remedies.

1983 U.S. Department of Education report "A Nation at Risk" paints critical picture of rising mediocrity in U.S. schools, shifts agenda away from equity issues.

1990s *Racial isolation increases for African-Americans, Latinos; "reverse discrimination" suits by white students backed in some federal courts, fail in others.*

1991 LaCrosse, Wis., becomes first school district to aim to balance enrollment by students' income status: "socioeconomic integration."

1995 Supreme Court signals federal courts to wrap up desegregation cases; lower courts respond by generally granting "unitary" status to school systems seeking to be freed from desegregation orders.

1998, 1999 Federal appeals courts in Boston, Richmond, Va., bar racial preferences in public school admission.

2000-Present *Socioeconomic integration advances; Latinos become largest ethnic minority; Supreme Court ruling bars racial classifications in pupil assignments.*

2000 Wake County (Raleigh), N.C., becomes largest school district to try socioeconomic integration.

2001 President George W. Bush wins congressional approval of No Child Left Behind Act, requiring school districts to meet achievement benchmarks, including closing racial gap.

2001-2005 White families challenge racial-diversity plans in Seattle and Louisville, Ky; federal courts back school districts, ruling plans are "narrowly tailored" to achieve "compelling" interest in diversity.

2005, 2006 Bush nominates John G. Roberts Jr. and Samuel A. Alito Jr. to Supreme Court; both win Senate confirmation, strengthening conservative majority on court.

2007 Supreme Court ruling in Louisville and Seattle cases limits use of race in pupil assignments, but five justices say race-neutral measures can be used to promote compelling interest in diversity; school boards vow to try to maintain racial diversity; advocates push socioeconomic integration on legal, political grounds.

2008

Feb. 23 — Federal judge lifts 1974 desegregation order for Mark Twain Intermediate School in Brooklyn, N.Y., effectively eliminating racial quotas.

Nov. 4 — Nebraska votes to ban affirmative action; Colorado rejects a proposed ban.

2009

June 11 — California Supreme Court rejects challenge to the Berkeley Unified School District's policy of considering the racial composition of students' neighborhoods in deciding where pupils will enroll.

2010

March 8 — Education Secretary Arne Duncan speaks on the state of minorities in education in Selma, Ala.

March 26 — Department of Justice signs consent agreement with Monroe School District in Louisiana to level offerings of advanced-placement and gifted-and-talented courses with predominantly white and predominantly black schools.

March 29 — Delaware and Tennessee named first winners of Department of Education's Race to the Top competition, designed to spur reforms in state and local K-12 education.

June 20 — Boston College launches $20 million program to improve urban education and better prepare low-income students from the area for college.

July 20 — Nineteen arrested in protest of Wake County (Raleigh, N.C.) School Board's decision to dismantle a decade-old policy of busing students to achieve diversity.

---

public education, but the educational "system" of the early 19th century consisted of private academies, rural district schools and a handful of "charity" schools in cities. Horace Mann, the so-called father of American public education, used his appointment as Massachusetts' first commissioner of education in 1837 to advocate the "common school" — publicly supported and open to all. As University of Wisconsin educational historian William Reese explains, Mann saw education as a way to restore social harmony at a time of social tensions between rich and poor and between native-born and immigrants. Others saw the same connection. His fellow New Englander Alpheus Packard wrote in the 1840s of the "sons of wealth and poverty" gaining mutual respect by sitting side by side in a public school.[10]

Abolitionist Mann's vision had no practical meaning, however, for African-American slaves before the Civil War and only limited significance for their descendants for decades after slavery was abolished. Both before and after the Civil War, the vast majority of African-Americans "lived in states that were openly and explicitly opposed to their education," according to the University of Illinois' Anderson.

After emancipation slaves who had learned to read and write became teachers in rudimentary schools, aided by Northern missionaries and philanthropists and some sympathetic white Southerners. With the end of Reconstruction, however, Southern leaders "pushed back the gains that had been made," Anderson says. In a racially segregated system in the early 20th century, per capita spending for black pupils in the South amounted to one-fourth to one-half of the amount spent on whites.[11]

Education was becoming nearly universal for white Americans, even as racial segregation became entrenched for African-Americans and, in many places, for Mexican- and Asian-Americans.[12] Elementary school attendance was nearly universal by the 1920s. High schools — once viewed as fairly selective institutions — began doubling in enrollment each decade after 1890 thanks to a declining market for child labor and the growing enforcement of new compulsory education laws. Secondary school enrollment increased from 50 percent of 14-17-year-olds in 1920 to nearly 95 percent of that age group by the mid-1970s. Meanwhile, the average school year was also

"Tracking" Leads to Racial Separation in Classes

But grouping students by ability has wide support.

Ballard High School sits on a spacious campus in an overwhelmingly white suburban neighborhood in the eastern end of Jefferson County, Ky. As part of Jefferson County Public Schools' racial balance policies, however, Ballard's attendance zone includes neighborhoods on the opposite side of the county in Louisville's predominantly African-American West End section.

By drawing students from the West End, the school achieved around 25 percent black enrollment in the 2006-07 academic year. But despite the measure of racial balance in overall enrollment, Ballard students say blacks and whites are less than fully integrated inside. "Kids naturally separate," remarks Ben Gravel, a white 12th-grader, as he arrives at school on Aug. 13 for the opening of a new school year.

At Ballard — and in schools around the country — the racial separation is especially pronounced in the classroom itself. African-American students are disproportionately enrolled in less challenging, "low-track" classes and underrepresented in higher-track classes, such as advanced placement (AP) courses and international baccalaureate (IB) programs. In 2006, for example, African-Americans comprised about 13 percent of graduating high school seniors but only 6 percent of the total number of students who took advanced placement exams administered by the College Board.[1]

The widespread practice of tracking — or "ability grouping" as supporters prefer to call it — has been a contentious issue within education circles for more than two decades. "Detracking" advocates have had occasional success in pushing reforms, but the practice has persisted — in part because of strong resistance from parents of students enrolled in higher-track courses.[2]

Supporters say the practice matches curricular offerings to students' abilities and achievement level. "It doesn't make sense to the average person that you would put a non-reader in the same English classroom as some kid who's reading Proust," says Tom Loveless, director of the Brown Center on Educational Policy at the Brookings Institution in Washington.

Critics say the practice simply keeps already-disadvantaged students on a path to lower academic achievement. "If you have classes that are structured to give kids less of a challenge, those kids tend to fall farther behind," says Kevin Welner, an associate professor at the University of Colorado's School of Education in Boulder.

Civil rights advocates say the enrollment patterns reflect what they call "segregation by tracking." In her critique of the practice, Jeannie Oakes, director of urban schooling at UCLA's Graduate School of Education and Information Studies, cited research evidence indicating that African-American and Latino students were more likely to be assigned to low-track courses than white students even when they had comparable abilities or test scores.[3]

---

increasing — from 144 days in 1900 to 178 days in 1950. And per capita investment in education rose during the same period from 1.2 percent of national income to 2 percent.

The Supreme Court's 1954 decision in *Brown* outlawing racial segregation in public schools capped a half-century-long campaign by the NAACP to gain a measure of equal educational opportunity for African-Americans.[13] The legal campaign — directed by the future Supreme Court justice, Thurgood Marshall — was waged at a deliberate pace even as many black students and families were agitating for better schools at the local level. The eventual decision seemed far from inevitable beforehand.

Only after 1950 did the NAACP decide to ask the court to abolish segregation rather than try to equalize the separate school systems. And the justices were closely divided after the first round of arguments in 1952; they joined in the unanimous ruling in 1954 only after a second round of arguments and shrewd management of the case by the new chief justice, Earl Warren.*

---

*California, home to the nation's largest concentration of Asian-Americans and the secondlargest concentration of Mexican-Americans after Texas, had abolished racial segregation in schools by law in 1947.

"I wouldn't use the phrase 'segregation by tracking.' A lot of it is self-tracking," counters Abigail Thernstrom, a senior fellow at the conservative Manhattan Institute and co-author of a book on the educational gap between white and minority students. "Is it terrible that we have so few Latino and black students who are prepared to take the most educationally rigorous courses?" she adds. "Of course, it's terrible."

Welner acknowledges minority students often choose low-track courses, but faults school systems instead of the students. Minority parents and students often lack the information needed to understand the different course offerings, he says. And students "sometimes don't want to be the only minority in the high-track class," he says.

Loveless acknowledges the critics' complaints about low-track classes, but says the solution is to reform not to abolish them. "Let's fix the low-track classes," he says. Despite the critics' doubts, he says many private, charter and parochial schools have developed low-track curricula that more effectively challenge students than those often found in public schools.

"If we know how to create a high-track class, why would we then create a separate set of classes that don't have those opportunities?" Welner asks. "Why would we let students opt for a lesser education?"

Loveless says under a random-assignment system, high-achieving students "would lose quite a bit," middle-range students "would lose a bit" and lowest-achieving students "would probably benefit a little bit" — mainly by reducing the concentration of students with behavioral issues in low-track classes.

Welner disagrees that high-achieving students are necessarily harmed by reforms. "Good detracking doesn't take anything away from these kids," he says. "The high achievers are not only holding their own but are doing better after the reform."

Despite the recurrent clashes at the local level, Loveless predicts that tracking will continue to be a widespread practice. "Polls are very clear," he says. "Parents, teachers and students favor ability grouping. Those are three important constituency groups."

Sixth-graders study science as part of the international baccalaureate curriculum at Harbour Pointe Middle School in Mukilteo, Wash.

---

[1] College Board, "Advanced Placement: Report to the Nation 2006," p. 11 (www.collegeboard.com). For background, see Marcia Clemmitt, "AP and IB Programs," *CQ Researcher*, March 3, 2006, pp. 193-216.

[2] For opposing views, see Tom Loveless, *The Tracking Wars: State Reform Meets School Policy* (1999); Jeannie Oakes, *Keeping Track: How Schools Structure Inequality* (2d ed.), 2005.

[3] *Ibid.*, pp. 230-231.

The high court's "remedial" decision one year later in *Brown II* directed school districts to desegregate "with all deliberate speed." Many Southern politicians lent support to a campaign of "massive resistance" to the ruling by diehard segregationists. A decade after *Brown*, fewer than 5 percent of black students in the South were attending majority-white schools; more than three-fourths were attending schools with 90 percent minority enrollment.[14] In 1968, an evidently impatient Supreme Court declared that school districts had to develop plans to dismantle dual systems that promised "realistically" to work — and to work "now." Three years later, a new chief justice, Warren E. Burger, led a unanimous court in upholding the authority of local federal courts to order school districts to use cross-neighborhood busing as part of a desegregation plan.[15]

"Elusive" Equality

The campaign to desegregate schools stimulated broader efforts in the late 20th century to equalize educational opportunity at national, state and local levels. Initially, desegregation advanced in the South and to a lesser extent in other regions. But integration eventually stalled in the face of white opposition to busing, ambivalence among blacks and Supreme Court decisions easing pressure on

More Blacks and Latinos Attend Poorest Schools

The vast majority (79 percent) of white students attend schools where less than half the student body is poor, compared with 37 percent of black students and 36 percent of Hispanics. For schools where at least 91 percent of the students are poor, whites made up just 1 percent of the student body compared with 13 and 15 percent, respectively, for blacks and Hispanics.

Distribution of Students in Public Schools by Percentage Who Are Poor, 2005-2006

Percent Poor	Percentage of each race				
	White	Black	Latino	Asian	American Indian
0-10%	20	5	7	23	17
11-20%	17	5	5	14	6
21-30%	16	7	7	12	8
31-40%	14	9	8	11	9
41-50%	12	11	9	9	11
51-60%	9	11	10	8	11
61-70%	6	12	11	6	11
71-80%	3	13	12	6	10
81-90%	2	14	14	6	8
91-100%	1	13	15	4	9

* Totals may not add up to 100 due to rounding.

Source: Gary Orfield and Chungmei Lee, "Historic Reversals, Accelerating Resegregation, and the Need for New Integration Strategies," Civil Rights Project, UCLA, August 2007

Total number of students (in millions)

White	28
Black	8
Latino	10
Asian	2
American Indian	1

suburban districts. Three years later, the court essentially freed school districts from any obligation to prevent resegregation after adopting a racially neutral assignment plan. The decisions coincided with widespread opposition to busing for racial balance among white families in many communities, most dramatically in Boston in the 1970s, where police escorts were needed for buses taking pupils from predominantly black Roxbury to predominantly white South Boston.

African-American students and families, meanwhile, had mixed reactions to desegregation generally and busing in particular, according to Professor Anderson. In many districts, desegregation meant the closing or transformation of historically black schools that had provided a good education for many students. In the South, desegregation also often meant the loss of black principals and teachers. And busing was a "one-way street" for African-Americans: most plans entailed the transportation of black students away from their neighborhoods to a mixed reception at best in predominantly white communities.

From the start, the NAACP and other civil rights groups had viewed desegregation not only as a goal in its own right but also — and perhaps

local school districts to take affirmative steps to mix white and black students. School funding reform efforts produced some results, but as the 21st century began educational equality remained — in Professor Reese's word — "elusive."[16]

The Supreme Court's unanimity in school race cases broke down in the 1970s, and a continuing succession of closely divided decisions reduced districts' obligations to develop effective integration plans. In one of the most important rulings, the justices in 1974 divided 5-4 in a case from Detroit to bar court-ordered desegregation between predominantly black inner cities and predominantly white

more importantly — as an instrument to equalize educational opportunities for black and white pupils. In the heady days of the civil rights era, Congress had put educational equality on the national agenda in 1965 by passing a law as part of President Lyndon B. Johnson's "war on poverty" to provide federal aid targeted to poor children.[17] By the end of the century, however, Title I of the Elementary and Secondary Education Act was seen as having produced mixed results at best — in part because allocation formulas shaped by the realities of congressional politics directed much of the money to relatively well-to-do suburban districts.

Do Racial Policies Affect Academic Achievement?

Most studies find beneficial effects from integration.

When the Supreme Court outlawed racial segregation in schools in 1954, it relied heavily on research by the African-American psychologist Kenneth Clark purporting to show that attending all-black schools hurt black students' self-esteem. Over time, the court's reliance on Clark's study drew many critics, who questioned both the research and its prominent use in a legal ruling.

A half-century later, as they considered challenges to racial-diversity plans in Seattle and Louisville, Ky., the justices were deluged with sometimes conflicting research studies on the effects of racial policies on educational achievement. Among 64 friend-of-the-court briefs, nearly half — 27 — cited social science research. Most found beneficial effects from racial integration, but a minority questioned those claims.

The National Academy of Education, a select group of education scholars, created a seven-member committee to evaluate the various studies cited in the various briefs. Here are the committee's major conclusions from the research, released on June 29 — one day after the court found the school districts' plans unconstitutional:

Academic achievement. White students are not hurt by desegregation efforts or adjustments in racial composition of schools. African-American student achievement is enhanced by less segregated schooling, although the magnitude of the influence is quite variable. The positive effects for African-American students tend to be larger in the earlier grades.

Near-term intergroup relations. Racially diverse schools and classrooms will not guarantee improved intergroup relations, but are likely to be constructive. The research identifies conditions that need to be present in order for diversity to have a positive effect and suggests steps schools can take to realize the potential for improvement.

Long-term effects of school desegregation. Experience in desegregated schools increases the likelihood over time of greater tolerance and better intergroup relations among adults of different racial groups.

The critical-mass question. Racial diversity can avoid or mitigate harms caused by racial isolation, such as tokenism and stereotyping, particularly when accompanied by an otherwise beneficial school environment. Some briefs suggest a minimum African-American enrollment of 15 percent to 30 percent to avoid these harms, but the research does not support specifying any particular percentage.

Race-neutral alternatives. No race-neutral policy is as effective as race-conscious policies for achieving racial diversity. Socioeconomic integration is likely to marginally reduce racial isolation and may have other benefits. School choice generally and magnet schools in particular have some potential to reduce racial isolation, but could also increase segregation.

Source: Robert L. Linn and Kevin G. Welner (eds.), "Race-Conscious Policies for Assigning Students to Schools: Social Science Research and the Supreme Court Cases," National Academy of Education, June 29, 2007 (www.naeducation.org/Meredith_Report.pdf).

Meanwhile, advocates of educational equity had turned to the courts to try to reduce funding disparities between school districts — with mixed results.[18] The Supreme Court ruled in 1973 that funding disparities between districts did not violate the federal Constitution. One month later, however, the New Jersey Supreme Court became the first state tribunal to find differential school funding to run afoul of a state constitutional provision. Over the next three decades, school funding suits resulted in court rulings in at least 19 states finding constitutional violations and ordering reforms. But funding disparities persisted. In a wide-ranging survey in 1998, *Education Week* gave 16 states a grade of C- or below on educational equity between school districts.[19]

At the same time, school policymakers were focusing on clamorous calls to improve educational quality stimulated by the publication in 1983 of a report by the Reagan administration's Department of Education sharply criticizing what was depicted as rising mediocrity in U.S. schools. The debate generated by "A Nation at Risk" brought forth all manner of proposals for imposing educational standards, revising curricula or introducing competition within public school systems or between public and private schools. The debate diverted policymakers' attention to some extent from diversity issues and led many white parents to worry more about their own children's education than about educational equity or diversity.[20]

Minnijean Brown, 15, one of the Little Rock Nine, arrives at Central High School on Sept. 25, 1957, guarded by soldiers sent by President Dwight. D. Eisenhower. Brown and eight other African-American students desegregated the Arkansas school three years after the Supreme Court's landmark *Brown v. Board of Education* ruling.

By the end of the 1990s, federal courts were all but out of the desegregation business, and racial isolation — "resegregation" to civil rights advocates — was on the rise. In a trio of cases in 1991, 1993 and 1995, the Supreme Court gave federal courts unmistakable signals to withdraw from superintending desegregation plans. School districts that sought to be declared "unitary" — or no longer dual in nature — and freed from desegregation decrees, like Jefferson County, invariably succeeded. By 2001, at least two-thirds of black students and at least half of Latino students nationwide were enrolled in predominantly minority schools. And after narrowing in the 1980s, the educational-testing gaps between white and black students began to widen again in the 1990s. In 2000, the typical black student scored below about 75 percent of white students on most standardized tests.[21]

"Diversity" Challenged

Even as courts reduced the pressure on school districts to desegregate, hundreds of school systems adopted voluntary measures aimed at mixing students of different racial and ethnic backgrounds. Some plans that made explicit use of race in pupil assignments drew legal challenges from white families as "reverse discrimination." Meanwhile, several dozen school systems were adopting — and achieving some success with — diversity plans tied to socioeconomic status instead of race. Support for socioeconomic integration appeared to increase after the Supreme Court's June 28 decision in the Seattle and Louisville cases restricting the use of race in pupil assignments but permitting race-neutral policies to achieve diversity in the classroom.

School boards that voluntarily sought to achieve racial and ethnic mixing claimed that the policies generally improved education for all students while benefiting disadvantaged minorities and promoting broad political support for the schools. Many plans — like those in Seattle and Louisville — explicitly considered race in some pupil assignments, and several drew legal challenges. In November 1998 the federal appeals court in Boston struck down the use of racial preferences for blacks and Hispanics for admission to the prestigious Boston Latin School. Then in fall 1999, the federal appeals court in Richmond, Va., ruled in favor of white families challenging race-based policies in two districts in the Washington, D.C., suburbs. The rulings struck down a weighted lottery that advantaged blacks and Hispanics in Arlington County, Va., and a transfer policy in Montgomery County, Md., that limited students from changing schools in order to maintain racial balance.[22]

The idea of socioeconomic integration first gained national attention when the midsized town of La Crosse, Wis., redrew attendance zones in the early 1990s to shift students from an overcrowded, predominantly affluent high school to the town's second high school in the blue-collar section with a growing Hmong population. In Kahlenberg's account, the plan survived concerted political opposition, produced measurable educational progress and now enjoys widespread support. Cambridge, Mass., substituted socioeconomic integration policies for racial busing in 1999 after the federal appeals court ruling in the Boston Latin case. Wake County, N.C., similarly dropped its racial balancing plan in 2000 in favor of an assignment plan tied to free or reduced-lunch status to comply with the rulings by the Richmond-based appeals court in the Arlington and Montgomery County cases. By 2003, Kahlenberg claimed some 500,000 students nationwide were enrolled in school systems that used economic status as a factor in pupil assignments.[23]

In the main, however, school districts that had adopted racial balancing plans stuck with them despite legal challenges. Seattle adopted its "open choice" plan in 1998 — some two decades after it had become the largest school district in the nation to voluntarily adopt a racial busing plan. The ad hoc group Parents Involved in Community Schools filed its suit challenging the use of race as a "tiebreaker" in pupil assignments in July 2000. That same year, Jefferson County Public Schools adopted its controlled choice plan after a federal judge freed the system from a desegregation decree dating to 1975. Parent Crystal Meredith challenged the race-based assignments in April 2003. Federal district judges upheld the plans — in April 2001 in the Seattle case and in June 2004 in the Jefferson County case. The 4th U.S. Circuit Court of Appeals in Cincinnati then upheld the Jefferson County plan in July 2005. The Seattle case followed a more complicated appellate route. The school district suspended the plan after an initial setback in 2002, but eventually the 9th U.S. Circuit Court of Appeals in San Francisco upheld the plan in October 2005.

The Supreme Court's decision to hear the two cases immediately raised fears among civil rights advocates that the conservative majority fortified by President George W. Bush's appointments of Chief Justice Roberts and Justice Samuel A. Alito Jr. would strike down the plans. Questions by Roberts and Alito during arguments on Dec. 4, 2006, left little doubt about their positions. The high-drama announcement of the decision on June 28 lasted nearly 45 minutes with Roberts, Kennedy and Breyer each delivering lengthy summaries of his opinion from the bench.

"The way to stop discrimination on the basis of race," Roberts declared as he neared his conclusion, "is to stop discriminating on the basis of race."

Breyer was equally forceful in his dissent. "This is a decision that the court and this nation will come to regret," he said.

Almost immediately, however, Kennedy's pivotal concurrence began to draw the closest scrutiny as advocates and observers tried to discern what alternatives remained for school boards to use in engineering racial diversity. The National School Boards Association urged local boards to continue seeking diversity through "careful race-conscious policies." Administrators in Seattle and Louisville said they planned to do just that.

But Clegg of the Center for Equal Opportunity said school systems would be better off to drop racial classifications. "At the end of the day, these two plans didn't pass muster," he said. "And the impact will be to persuade other school districts that this is not a good idea."[24]

CURRENT SITUATION

"Resegregation" Seen

The Louisville and Seattle school systems are in the opening weeks of a new academic year, with few immediate effects from the Supreme Court decision invalidating their previous pupil-assignment plans. Officials in both districts are working on new pupil-assignment plans to put into effect starting in fall 2009, with racial diversity still a goal but race- or ethnic-based placements no longer permitted.

Both school systems, however, are reporting what civil rights advocates call "resegregation" — higher percentages of African-American students in predominantly minority schools. Critics of racial-diversity policies object to the term, arguing that segregation refers only to legally enforced separation of the races. Whatever term is used, a new report documents a national trend of "steadily increasing separation" in public schools between whites and the country's two largest minority groups: Latinos and African-Americans.

The report by the UCLA Civil Rights Project shows, for example, that the percentage of black students in majority-white schools rose from virtually zero in 1954 to a peak of 43.5 percent in 1988 before beginning a steady decline. In 2005 — the most recent year available — 27 percent of black students attended majority-white schools.

Meanwhile, the proportion of African-Americans attending majority-minority schools has been slowly increasing over the past two decades — reversing gains in integration in the 1960s and '70s — while the percentage of Latino students in majority-minority schools has grown steadily since the 1960s. In 2005, 73 percent of black students were in majority-minority schools, and more than one-third — 38 percent — were in "intensely segregated" schools with 90 to 100 percent minority enrollment. For Latinos, 78 percent of students were in majority-minority schools.

By contrast, Asian-Americans are described in the report as "the most integrated" ethnic group in public schools. In 2005, the average Asian student attended a school with 44 percent white enrollment — compared to 30 percent white enrollment for the average black student and 27 percent white enrollment for the average Latino. The report attributed the higher integration for Asians to greater residential integration and relatively small numbers outside the West.

Seattle was already experiencing increasing racial isolation after suspending its previous placement plan, which included race as one "tiebreaker" in pupil assignments. "There has been a decline in racial diversity since suspension of the plan," says Seattle Public Schools spokeswoman Patti Spencer.

AT ISSUE

Is racial diversity in the classroom essential to a good education?

YES
Janet W. Schofield
Professor of Psychology, University of Pittsburgh

Written for *CQ Researcher*, September 2007

Education in a democratic society serves three basic purposes. It provides students with workforce skills, prepares them to function as thoughtful and informed citizens in a cohesive country and enriches their lives by awakening them to new knowledge, perspectives and possibilities. Racial diversity in schools and classrooms enhances the attainment of each of these goals.

The ability to work effectively with individuals from diverse backgrounds is a fundamental workplace skill, as the well-known report "What Work Requires of Schools," issued by President George H.W. Bush's administration, points out. Yet, many students never develop this skill because our country's neighborhoods, social institutions and religious organizations are often highly segregated. Racially diverse schools provide a milieu essential to the development of this crucial skill.

Racially diverse schools also have a vital role to play in developing fair-minded citizens and in promoting social cohesion. Research demonstrates that in-school contact with individuals from different backgrounds typically reduces prejudice, a fundamentally important outcome in our increasingly diverse society. In addition, students who attend diverse schools are more likely than others to choose diverse work and residential settings as adults, thus promoting social cohesion.

Racially diverse schools also enrich students' understanding and expand their perspectives by placing them in contact with others whose views and life experiences may be very different. Just as visiting a foreign country is a much richer and more powerful experience than reading about it, interacting with students from different backgrounds brings their perspectives and experiences alive in a way not otherwise possible.

Even individuals who discount the arguments above must acknowledge that heavily segregated minority schools disadvantage the very students most in need of an excellent educational environment. Such schools typically have relatively impoverished curricular offerings, great difficulty recruiting experienced teachers and high teacher-turnover rates, all of which may help to explain why research suggests that attending such schools typically undermines students' achievement relative to similar peers in more diverse schools.

Racial diversity in and of itself does not guarantee a good education, but as a recent report by the National Academy of Education suggests, it creates preconditions conducive to it. In our increasingly diverse democracy, the educational cost of segregated schools is too high for majority and minority students alike.

NO
Abigail Thernstrom
Senior Fellow, Manhattan Institute
Co-author, No Excuses: Closing the Racial Gap in Learning

Written for *CQ Researcher*, September 2007

Racially diverse classrooms are desirable — of course. But are they essential to a good education? Absolutely not. If they were, big-city school districts would be stuck providing lousy educations for America's most disadvantaged children into the indefinite future. A large majority of students in 26 out of the 27 central-city districts with a public school population of at least 60,000 are non-white. The white proportion in these districts averages 16 percent. Thus, big-city schools will not be racially "diverse" unless we start flying white kids from Utah into, say, Detroit.

Or rather, they will not be racially "diverse" according to the Seattle school board's definition in the racial balancing plan the Supreme Court condemned last term. Seattle had divided students into only two racial groups: white and non-white. If schools were half-Asian, half-white, that was fine; if they were 30 percent white with the rest Asian, they weren't sufficiently "diverse," and educational quality would be somehow lacking.

What racial stereotyping! Do all non-white students express the same non-white views — with all white students having a "white" outlook? In fact, why is racial diversity the only kind that counts for those concerned about the group clustering in certain schools? What about a social class or religious mix?

And on the subject of racial stereotyping, do we really want to embrace the ugly assumption that black kids are incapable of learning unless they're hanging around some white magic? Good inner-city schools across the country are teaching the children who walk through the door. In excellent schools, if every one of the students is black — reflecting the demography of the neighborhood — the expectations for educational excellence do not change. And happily, there are no compelling studies showing enormous positive gains for black students when they attend schools with large numbers of whites.

Good education is not confined to academic learning. But there is no evidence that schools engaging in coercive racial mixing build a lifelong desire to "socialize with people of different races," as Seattle assumed. Visit a school lunchroom! Racial and ethnic clustering will be very much in evidence.

Those who insist school districts should turn themselves inside out to engineer racial diversity haven't a clue as to the limits of social policy. And they demean the capacity of non-Asian minority kids to learn, whatever the color of the kid in the seat next to them.

In Louisville, nine schools now have African-American enrollment above the previous guideline limit of 50 percent — most of them in predominantly black neighborhoods in Louisville's West End or the heavily black areas in southwestern Jefferson County. Black enrollment in some schools in the predominantly white East End has declined, though not below the minimum figure of 15 percent in the previous guidelines.

The 15/50 guidelines remain "a goal," according to Student Placement Director Todd. "We're trying to prevent as much slippage as possible."

In Seattle, outgoing Superintendent Raj Manhas told reporters after the Supreme Court ruling that the school district would look at "all options available to us" to try to preserve racial diversity in the schools.[25] The new superintendent, Maria Goodloe-Johnson, is an African-American who was sharply critical of racial policies in her previous position as superintendent in Charleston, S.C. Since taking office in Seattle in July, however, Goodloe-Johnson has not addressed racial balance, according to Spencer.[26]

Opponents of the race-based policies say school districts should refocus their efforts. "Where school districts should focus is on education standards, not creating a specific racial mix of students," says Sharon Browne, a staff attorney with the Pacific Legal Foundation, the conservative public interest law firm that supported the legal challenges in Louisville and Seattle.

"The guidelines are gone," says attorney Gordon in Louisville. "They're past tense."

In Seattle, Kathleen Brose, the longtime school activist who founded Parents Involved in Community Schools to challenge the use of race for high school placements, says diversity is "important," but parental choice is more important. "The school district has been so focused on race," she adds, "that, frankly, I think they forgot about academics."

Legal Options Eyed

School boards around the country are re-examining their legal options for promoting diversity. At the same time, they are bracing for new legal challenges to their diversity plans that, so far, have not materialized.

The National School Boards Association plans to provide local boards with advisories on what policies can be used under the Supreme Court's decision to promote racial balance. But General Counsel Negrón expects few changes as a result of the ruling.

"School districts are not going to be changing their policies drastically to the extent that they will be abandoning their choices of diversity or integration as their goal, if that's what they've chosen to do," Negrón says. "School districts are going to comply with the law as they understand it. And there's a lot of room in Justice Kennedy's concurrence for school districts to be creative and innovative."

Barring any consideration of race, Negrón adds, "was just not what the decision stood for."

Pacific Legal Foundation attorney Browne, however, worries that school districts are not complying with the ruling. "We are very disappointed that there are school districts who are ignoring the decision by the U.S. Supreme Court and continuing to use race [in pupil assignments]," she says.

Browne says school districts should have begun developing contingency plans for assigning students on a non-racial basis after the oral arguments in the Seattle and Louisville cases in December indicated the court would find both plans unconstitutional.

The Louisville and Seattle cases themselves are still pending in lower federal courts, with winning lawyers in both cases asking the courts to order the school boards to pay attorneys' fees.

In Seattle, the firm of Davis Wright Tremaine is seeking $1.8 million in attorneys' fees despite having previously said that it was handling the parents' case pro bono — for free. "Congress specifically and explicitly wrote into the law that if the government is found to have violated citizens' civil rights, then the prevailing party should seek fee recovery," explained Mark Usellis, a spokesman for the firm. The school system reported spending $434,000 in legal fees on the case.[27]

Louisville solo practitioner Gordon is asking to be paid $200 per hour for the "hundreds of hours" he devoted to the case plus a bonus for the national impact of the case. Without specifying a figure, he also wants to be reimbursed for spending his own money on expenses and court costs. Meanwhile, plaintiff Crystal Meredith is asking for $125,000 in damages, which she attributes to lost wages, invasion of privacy and emotional distress.[28]

Gordon says he received several complaints from parents whose applications for transfers for their children had been denied on the basis of limited capacity at the school they had chosen. Gordon says he suspected school officials were actually denying the transfers on racial grounds, but the MacNeals' case was the only "smoking gun" he found.

The Pacific Legal Foundation is following up on "many inquiries" received from parents since the Supreme Court ruling, according to Browne, but no new cases have been filed. She declined to say where the complaints originated. The foundation has suits pending in California courts against the Los Angeles and Berkeley school districts over race-based policies.

If any new legal challenges are filed, Negrón expects federal courts will defer to local school boards' decisions, for the most part. The [Supreme Court] didn't tell us exactly what to do," he explains. "School districts will be trying their best to come up with something that meets the requirements of the law and at the same time meets their educational interest in regard to diversity."

OUTLOOK

"Minimal Impact"?

In striking down the Seattle and Jefferson County racial-balance plans, Chief Justice Roberts cited figures from the two school districts showing that the policies actually affected relatively few students — only 52 pupils in Seattle and no more than 3 percent of the pupil assignments in Jefferson County. The "minimal impact," he wrote, "casts doubt on the necessity of using racial classifications."

Writing for the dissenters, however, Justice Breyer cast the stakes in broader terms by citing the growing percentage of black students in majority non-white schools nationwide. The Louisville and Seattle school boards, Breyer said, were asking to be able to continue using tools "to rid their schools of racial segregation." The plurality opinion, he concluded, was "wrong" to deny the school boards' "modest request."

Two months after the ruling, civil rights advocates are continuing to voice grave concerns that the decision will hasten what they call the resegregation of public schools nationwide. "We're going to have a further increase in segregation of American schools," says UCLA's Orfield. "School districts are going to have to jump through a whole series of hoops if they want to have some modest degree of integration."

Legal Defense Fund President Shaw fears new challenges not only to pupil-assignment plans but also to mentoring and scholarship programs specifically targeting racial minorities. "Our adversaries are not going to go away," says Shaw. "They're going to continue to attack race-conscious efforts to address racial inequality."

Opponents of racial-balance plans either discount the fears of increased racial isolation or minimize the harms of the trend if it materializes.

"I don't think there will be dramatic consequences from these decisions," says Rosman of the Center for Individual Rights. School systems with an interest in racial diversity "will find a way to do that legally," he says. "For schools that use race explicitly, it will still be a contentious matter."

"There's going to be less and less focus on achieving politically correct racial and ethnic balance and more focus on improving education," says the Center for Equal Opportunity's Clegg. "That's where the law's headed, and that's where policy's headed. We ought to be worrying less about integration anyhow."

For his part, the Century Foundation's Kahlenberg stresses that the number of school districts with race-conscious policies — guesstimated at around 1,000 — is a small fraction of the nationwide total of 15,000 school systems. Many of the districts that have been seeking racial balance will likely shift to socioeconomic integration, he says, "because that's a clearly legal way to raise academic achievement for kids and create some racial integration indirectly."

In Louisville, the county school board did vote on Sept. 10 to broaden its diversity criteria to include socioeconomic status. "Race will still be a factor," Superintendent Berman said, "but it will not be the only factor."[29] Meanwhile, Student Placement Director Todd says Jefferson County's use of non-contiguous school-attendance zones to mix students from different racially identifiable neighborhoods is likely to be continued.

In his concurring opinion, Justice Kennedy suggested "strategic site selection" as another permissible policy to promote racial diversity — placing new schools so they draw students from different racial neighborhoods. The suggestion may prove impractical in many school districts. Jefferson County opened one new school this fall — in the rapidly growing and predominantly white eastern end, far removed from the African-American neighborhoods in the West End. As Breyer noted in his opinion, many urban school systems are unlikely to be building new schools because they are losing not gaining enrollment.

Changing demographics and changing social attitudes are inevitably bringing about changes in the schools. Within a decade or so, demographers expect white students will no longer comprise a majority of public school enrollment. And, as Abigail Thernstrom notes, young people have different attitudes toward race than their parents or grandparents.

"In terms of racial attitudes, we're on a fast track," Thernstrom says. "Young kids are dating across racial and ethnic lines. America is changing in very terrific ways and has been for some time. I expect that change to continue."

But University of Wisconsin educational historian Reese cautions against expecting racial issues to disappear. "It's like a never-never land to imagine that racial issues can somehow disappear," he says. "It's a nice thing to say that we should live in a kind of perfect world, but we don't. I can't imagine that it will disappear. It couldn't have disappeared in the past, and it won't disappear in the future."

UPDATE

"Hey, hey, ho, ho, resegregation has got to go." So echoed the 1960s-style chant of protesters at a July 20, 2010, meeting of the school board in North Carolina's Wake County (Raleigh). Police arrested 19 for disrupting discussion of a new neighborhood school-busing plan that dismantles existing school assignments intended to achieve racial diversity. A rally earlier in the day in Raleigh drew 1,000 people. They heard speakers invoke memories of separate water fountains for blacks and whites and compare the Wake controversy to the early 1950s school-desegregation battle that culminated in the Supreme Court's landmark ruling in *Brown v. Board of Education*.[30]

Such fear of public school "resegregation" has haunted some American communities ever since the Supreme Court's June 28, 2007, decision in *Parents Involved in Community Schools v. Seattle School District No. 1* invalidating race-conscious pupil-assignment plans in Seattle and metropolitan Louisville, Ky. And despite active national school-reform efforts by the nation's first African-American president, many families and policy advocates who wish to preserve racial diversity in schools express disappointment in the Obama administration's priorities in this area.

"Obama is emphasizing charter schools, which are racially isolating, and firing teachers at high-poverty schools," says Richard Kahlenberg, a senior fellow at the Century Foundation and longtime student of the racial make-up of schools. "As far as I can tell, he's been silent on the Wake County situation."

Scholars at the University of California at Los Angeles Civil Rights Project also scolded the Obama team for failing to deliver on promised guidance on how voluntary integration of schools should proceed in the wake of the 2007 high-court ruling. The complex, 5-2 decision "confused many educators, and it was somewhat unclear what did remain legal," they wrote in a recent report reviewing the response to the ruling.[31] "In 2008, the Bush administration sent a letter to school districts misguidedly interpreting the *Parents Involved* decision in a way that suggested only race-neutral means of pursuing integration would be legal. This was an inaccurate description of [Justice Anthony] Kennedy's controlling opinion and suggested that school authorities should abandon all efforts to intentionally pursue integration."

The UCLA researchers were also responsible for recent research stating that the increasingly popular movement to create more parental choices in charter schools continues "to stratify students by race, class, and possibly language, and [charter schools] are more racially isolated than traditional public schools in virtually every state and large metropolitan area in the country." Nationally, 70 percent of black charter students attend schools where at least 90 percent of students are minorities, double the figure for traditional public schools, the researchers found.[32]

Others, however, found clarity in the Supreme Court ruling. "Any fair reading of the decision is that any kind of race consciousness by school boards in assignment of students is legally very dangerous," says Roger Clegg, president and general counsel of the Center for Equal Opportunity, a Falls Church, Va., think tank opposed to racial preferences. "And it wouldn't be politically wise for Obama to mount any kind of counter-crusade."

Clegg discourages the term "resegregate," which he says calls to mind the period in history when schools

U.S. Secretary of Education Arne Duncan listens to students, teachers and former students describe their educational experience as he visits Robert E. Lee High School in Montgomery, Ala., during brief stops at schools in Montgomery and Selma, Ala., in March.

were deliberately segregated by law. "We're talking [now] about racial imbalances due to student choice and residential living patterns," he says. "Reasonable people can disagree about the best way to achieve balance. But those who believe that competition and choice are essential have the better argument. The overwhelming majority of parents and students of all racial groups would prefer to have better schools and more choices rather than some politically correct racial and ethnic mix."

Education Secretary Arne Duncan in March 2010 made a much-publicized visit to Selma, Ala., to speak on the state of minorities in education at the Edmund Pettus Bridge, site of a dramatic confrontation between billy club-wielding police and civil rights marchers in 1965. Duncan promised to reinvigorate his department's Office of Civil Rights, reduce resource disparities among schools and confront continuing barriers to achieving the Rev. Martin Luther King Jr.'s vision of a colorblind society.

Yet Duncan also suggested that modern times call for a more individualistic approach. "The civil rights struggle has grown more complex since the days of Selma," he said. "Freedom, it turns out, is not only the right to sit in the front of the bus, or cast a ballot. It's not even just the opportunity to purchase a home without fear of discrimination, as essential as that is. . . . No, freedom is also the ability to think on your own and to pursue your own path as far as your gifts can take you — and only education can give you that freedom, can open those doors."[33]

Specifically, Duncan's department has pursued school integration with two competitive-grant programs. One provides technical assistance to districts preparing pupil-placement policies that don't run afoul of the Supreme Court ruling, one of which is being used by Kentucky's Jefferson County (Louisville), a party to the *Parents Involved* suit. Another is new funding for the Magnet Schools Assistance Program (MSAP), a long-standing effort that encourages creation of attractive voluntary programs that draw students from many neighborhoods. The department's description mentions reducing racial isolation as a priority.

The overall trend since the *Parents Involved* ruling, says Kahlenberg, is to assign school zones with an eye on minimizing concentrations of children of low socioeconomic status. "There's no legal problem with it, and it accomplishes a fair amount of racial integration," he says. Back in 2000, only two or three school districts were using such methods, he adds, while in the year the Supreme Court ruled there were 40, and now there are more than 70. "A lot of school districts after the ruling could have walked away and said, 'Our hands are tied,'" Kahlenberg says. "Instead, some said, 'we value racial integration, so let's come up with a legally permissible way to integrate.'" Research confirms that low-income children achieve more when they're in school with middle-class children, he says.

The main arena for diversity issues, of course, is in school districts around the country. In Seattle, where the Supreme Court case originated, a new school boundary set to take effect this fall is based on neighborhood proximity and does not mention race as a factor in a decision-making process that included public hearings. A Seattle secondary school, Cleveland High, is set to open as a citywide magnet school focusing on math, science, engineering and technology, though, as in many districts reeling from the recession, funding is shaky.

And in Jefferson County (the second party to the suit), school officials are considering the percentage of minority students in the greater Louisville area as well as the education and income of adults in the area when weighing admissions, said Pat Todd, director of student assignment for Jefferson County schools. "This gives us more racial, ethnic and economic diversity," she said.[34]

Louisville school officials are using an analytical tool called "opportunity mapping," which was developed at Ohio State University's Kirwan Institute for the Study of Race and Ethnicity.[35]

In Chicago, a city with neighborhoods long divided along racial lines whose school system was previously run by Secretary Duncan, a recent plan to use students' social and economic profiles instead of race to increase classroom diversity is raising fears that it will set back the modest progress toward integration achieved in recent decades. Amanda Orellano, whose daughter is the third generation in her family to attend a prominent Chicago magnet school that is moving away from a race-based enrollment policy, said, "Somebody's going to feel that they're the only one here that's this way or that way, and feel isolated."[36]

The Justice Department, as it has since the birth of the civil rights movement in the 1950s, continues to monitor racial discrimination in more than 200 mostly Southern school districts on their compliance with decades-old court desegregation orders. Recently, the department sued the school board in Walthall, Miss., for a policy that permitted white students to transfer out of a predominantly black high school to a majority-white school. In April, a federal judge ruled that the policy created "racially identifiable" schools in violation of a 1970 desegregation order.[37]

In some cases, the department focuses not just on school demographics or attendance zones but on equal availability of quality academic programs and clean, modern physical plants. In March 2010, Justice announced it had signed a consent agreement with the Monroe City School District in Louisiana to equalize the offering of advanced placement and gifted-and-talented courses between the predominantly black and white high schools. Subject to court approval, the settlement was based on agreement that the unequal offerings under the existing system violated the equal protection provisions of the 1964 Civil Rights Act.

The new focus on pursuing diversity using socioeconomic status has not prevented one of the oldest civil rights organizations, the NAACP Legal Defense Fund, from continuing to emphasize race-based disparities even in what some had hoped would be President Obama's "post-racial America." In its recommendations for the still-in-progress reauthorization of the No Child Left Behind law, the group proposed that parents receive progress reports from the Education Department's Office of Civil Rights and that schools designate a point-of-contact to receive parental complaints about racial discrimination.

"Some have articulated a belief that our nation is unable to garner the resources to provide a high-quality education for all students, and therefore we should just save those we can," the group wrote. "But as civil rights advocates, our objective is not to support prescriptions that only have the capacity to change a few schools for a few students.... Securing equal access to high-quality education is the civil rights battle of this generation."[38]

NOTES

1. For coverage, see Chris Kenning, "Separate attendance zones voided," *The* [Louisville] *Courier-Journal*, Aug. 29, 2007, p. 1A.

2. The decision is *Parents Involved in Community Schools v. Seattle School District No. 1*, 552 U.S. ___ (2007); the companion case was *Meredith v. Jefferson County Public Schools*. For a detailed chronicle of the cases, see Kenneth Jost, "Court Limits Use of Race in Pupil Assignments," in *The Supreme Court Yearbook 2006-2007*, http://library.cqpress.com/scyb/.

3. For background, see Kenneth Jost, "School Desegregation," *CQ Researcher*, April 23, 2004, pp. 345-372.

4. See Chris Kenning, "JCPS sees change in racial makeup," *The* [Louisville] *Courier-Journal*, Sept. 2, 2007, p. 1A.

5. Gary Orfield and Chungmei Lee, "Historic Reversals, Accelerating Resegregation, and the Need for New Integration Strategies," UCLA Civil Rights Project (formerly based at Harvard University), August 2007, pp. 29, 35.

6. Richard D. Kahlenberg, "Rescuing *Brown v. Board of Education*: Profiles of Twelve School Districts Pursuing Socioeconomic School Integration," June 28, 2007, p. 3.

7. For coverage, see Peter Schworm, "AG Urges Court to Uphold Lynn Plan," *The Boston Globe*, July 18, 2005, p. B4.

8. Orfield and Lee, *op. cit.*, pp. 7-8. For background, see Barbara Mantel, "No Child Left Behind," *CQ Researcher*, May 27, 2005, pp. 469-492.

9. Background drawn in part from William J. Reese, *America's Public Schools: From the Common School to "No Child Left Behind"* (2005); R. Freeman Butts, *Public Education in the United States: From Revolution to Reform* (1978).

10. Reese, *op. cit.*, pp. 10-11, 25-26.

11. For background, see James Anderson, *The Education of Blacks in the South, 1860-1935* (1988). See also Heather Andrea Williams, *Self-Taught: African American Education in Slavery and Freedom* (2003).

12. For background, see "School Desegregation," *op. cit.*, p. 350 (Latinos), pp. 356-357 (Asian-Americans), and sources cited therein.

13. Some background drawn from James T. Patterson, Brown v. Board of Education: *A Civil Rights Milestone and Its Troubled Legacy* (2001).

14. For data, see *ibid.*, pp. 228-230.

15. The decisions are *Green v. County School Board of New Kent County*, 391 U.S. 430 (1968), and *Swann v. Charlotte-Mecklenburg County Board of Education*, 402 U.S. 1 (1971).

16. Reese, *op. cit.*, p. 246. For background on later school desegregation cases, see Patterson, *op. cit.*

17. For background, see H. B. Shaffer, "Status of the War on Poverty," in *Editorial Research Reports*, Jan. 25, 1967, available at *CQ Researcher Plus Archive*, http://library.cqpress.com.

18. Background drawn from Kathy Koch, "Reforming School Funding," *CQ Researcher*, Dec. 10, 1999, pp. 1041-1064.

19. The decisions are *San Antonio Independent School District v. Rodriguez*, 411 U.S. 1 (1973), and *Robinson v. Cahill*, 62 A.2d 273 (N.J. 1973).

20. For background, see Charles S. Clark, "Attack on Public Schools," *CQ Researcher*, July 26, 1996, pp. 649-672.

21. See Patterson, *op. cit.*, p. 214 n.19, p. 234.

22. The decisions are *Wessmann v. Gittens*, 160 F.3d 790 (1st Cir. 1998); *Tuttle v. Arlington County School Board*, 195 F.3d 698 (4th Cir. 1999), *Eisenberg v. Montgomery County Public Schools*, 197 F.3d 123 (4th Cir. 1999). For coverage, see Beth Daley, "Court Strikes Down Latin School Race Admission Policy," *The Boston Globe*, Nov. 20, 1998, p. A1; Jay Mathews, "School Lottery Loses on Appeal," *The Washington Post*, Sept. 26, 1999, p. C1 (Arlington County); Brigid Schulte, "School Diversity Policy Is Overruled," *ibid.*, Oct. 7, 1999, p. A1 (Montgomery County).

23. See Richard D. Kahlenberg, *All Together Now* (2003 ed.)., p. xiii.

24. Quoted in Andrew Wolfson, "Desegregation Decision: Some Find 'Sunshine' Amid Rain," *The [Louisville] Courier-Journal*, June 29, 2007, p. 6K.

25. Quoted in Jessica Blanchard and Christine Frey, "District Vows to Seek Out Diversity Answers," *Seattle Post-Intelligencer*, June 29, 2007, p. A1.

26. See Emily Heffter, "First Day of School for Chief," *Seattle Times*, July 10, 2007, p. B1.

27. See Emily Heffter, "Law firm wants school district to pay $1.8M," *Seattle Times*, Sept. 6, 2007, p. B5.

28. Chris Kenning and Andrew Wolfson, "Lawyer in schools case seeks fees, bonus," *The [Louisville] Courier-Journal*, July 29, 2007, p. 1A.

29. Quoted in Antoinette Konz, "Schools adopt guidelines for assignment plan," *The [Louisville] Courier-Journal*, Sept. 11, 2007.

30. Mike Baker, "Racial Tensions Roil NC School Board; 19 arrests," The Associated Press, July 20, 2010.

31. Adai Tefera, Genevieve Siegel-Hawley and Erica Frankenberg, "School Integration Efforts Three Years After 'Parents Involved,'" The Civil Rights Project/Proyecto Derechos Civiles, University of California, Los Angeles, June 28, 2010.

32. Howard Blume, "Charter Schools' Growth Promoting Segregation, Studies Say," *Los Angeles Times*, Feb. 4, 2010.

33. Sam Dillon, "Officials Step Up Enforcement of Rights Laws in Education," *The New York Times*, March 7, 2010, p. A11.

34. Tefera, *et al.*, UCLA Civil Rights Project, *op. cit.*

35. See Susan Eaton and Steven Rivkin, "Is Desegregation Dead?" *Education Next*, fall 2010. See also

http://kirwaninstitute.org/research/gismapping/opportunity-mapping/.

36. Crystal Yednak and Darnell Little, "City Schools' New Criteria for Diversity Raise Fears," *Chicago News Cooperative*, Dec. 20, 2009.

37. Stephanie McCrummen, "Ruling on Racial Isolation in Miss. Schools Reflects Troubling Broader Trend," *The Washington Post*, April 20, 2010.

38. "Framework for Providing All Students an Opportunity to Learn through Reauthorization of the Elementary and Secondary Education Act," NAACP Legal Defense Fund, July 26, 2010, www.naacpldf.org.

BIBLIOGRAPHY

Books

Frankenberg, Erika, and Gary Orfield (eds.), *Lessons in Integration: Realizing the Promise of Racial Diversity in American Schools*, **University of Virginia Press, 2007.**

Twelve essays by 19 contributors examine the educational and social effects of desegregation and the disadvantages to students in segregated schools. Orfield is co-director of the Civil Rights Project, UCLA Graduate School of Education and Information Studies (formerly, the Harvard Civil Rights Project); Frankenberg is a study director for the project. Includes notes, 46-page bibliography.

Loveless, Tom, *The Tracking Wars: State Reform Meets School Policy*, **Brookings Institution Press, 1999.**

The director of the Brown Center on Educational Policy at Brookings depicts tracking as a traditional educational practice and detracking as "a gamble" that may hurt rather than help students in low-achievement schools. Includes detailed notes.

Oakes, Jeannie, *Keeping Track: How Schools Structure Inequality* **(2d ed.), Yale University Press, 2005.**

The director of urban schooling at UCLA's Graduate School of Education and Information Studies updates the landmark critique of tracking that launched a detracking reform movement after its publication in 1985. Includes detailed notes.

Patterson, James T., *Brown v. Board of Education: A Civil Rights Milestone and Its Troubled Legacy*, **Oxford University Press, 2001.**

An emeritus professor of history at Brown University gives a compact account of the landmark school desegregation case and a legacy described as "conspicuous achievement" along with "marked failures."

Reese, William J., *America's Public Schools: From the Common School to "No Child Left Behind,"* **Johns Hopkins University Press, 2005.**

A professor of educational-policy studies at the University of Wisconsin-Madison provides an accessible overview of the history of U.S. public education from Horace Mann's advocacy of the "common school" through 20th-century developments.

Thernstrom, Abigail, and Stephan Thernstrom, *No Excuses: Closing the Racial Gap in Learning*, **Simon & Schuster, 2003.**

The authors decry the persistent achievement gap between white and black students but discount the importance of racial isolation in schools as a cause. Includes extensive statistical information, notes. Both authors are senior fellows with the Manhattan Institute; Abigail Thernstrom is vice chair of the U.S. Civil Rights Commission, Stephan Thernstrom a professor of history at Harvard.

Articles

Simmons, Dan, "A Class Action: Leaders Tried to Rein In Effects of Poverty in Public Schools; Voters Were in No Mood for Busing," *La Crosse* (Wis.) *Tribune*, Jan. 21, 2007, p. 1.

The story and an accompanying sidebar ("Balance by Choice") examine the history and current status of the La Crosse school district's 15-year experiment with socioeconomic integration.

Reports and Studies

Kahlenberg, Richard D., "Rescuing *Brown v. Board of Education:* Profiles of Twelve School Districts Pursuing Socioeconomic School Integration," Century Foundation, June 28, 2007, www.tcf.org.

The 42-page report describes the mixed results of socioeconomic integration in 12 school systems, with lengthy treatment of three: La Crosse, Wis.; Cambridge, Mass.; and Wake County (Raleigh), N.C. For a book-length treatment, see Kahlenberg, *All Together Now: Creating Middle-Class Schools through Public School Choice* (Brookings Institution Press, 2001).

Linn, Robert L., and Kevin G. Welner (eds.), "Race-Conscious Policies for Assigning Students to Schools: Social Science Research and the Supreme Court Cases," National Academy of Education, June 29, 2007, www.naeducation.org/Meredith_Report.pdf.
The 58-page report details social-science research on the effects of racial diversity in schools and finds "general support" for the conclusion that the overall academic and social effects of increased racial diversity are "likely to be positive."

Orfield, Gary, and Chungmei Lee, "Historic Reversals, Accelerating Resegregation, and the Need for New Integration Strategies," UCLA Civil Rights Project, Aug. 29, 2007, www.civilrightsproject.ucla.edu.
The 50-page report finds "accelerating isolation" of African-American and Latino students in public schools and recommends a variety of measures to counter the trend, including an attack on housing segregation, socioeconomic integration of schools and congressional initiatives "to require and/or to support racial progress."

On the Web

The *Courier-Journal* has an extensive compilation of articles, photographs and information on the course of school desegregation in Louisville and Jefferson County (www.courier-journal.com/desegregation). Current coverage can be found on the Web sites of Seattle's two newspapers, the *Seattle Times* (http://seattletimes.nwsource.com/html/education/) and the *Seattle Post-Intelligencer* (http://seattlepi.nwsource.com/).

For More Information

American Educational Research Association, 1430 K St., N.W., Suite 1200, Washington, DC 20005; (202) 238-3200; www.aera.net. National research society encouraging scholarly research in efforts to improve education.

Center for Individual Rights, 1233 20th St., N.W., Suite 300, Washington, DC 20036; (202) 833-8400; www.cir-usa.org. Nonprofit public-interest law firm opposed to racial preferences.

Center for Equal Opportunity, 7700 Leesburg Pike, Suite 231, Falls Church, VA 22043; (703) 442-0066; www.ceousa.org. Think tank devoted to equal opportunity and racial harmony.

Century Foundation, 41 E. 70th St., New York, NY 10021; (212) 535-4441; www.tcf.org. Public-policy institution promoting methods for socioeconomic integration in education.

Mexican American Legal Defense and Educational Fund, 634 S. Spring St., Los Angeles, CA 90014; (213) 629-2512; www.maldef.org. Protects and promotes the civil rights of Latinos living in the United States.

NAACP Legal Defense and Educational Fund, 99 Hudson St., Suite 1600, New York, NY 10013; (212) 965-2200; http://naacpldf.org. Serves as legal counsel on issues of race, with emphasis on education, voter protection, economic justice and criminal justice.

National School Boards Association, 1680 Duke St., Alexandria, VA 22314; (703) 838-6722; www.nsba.org. Seeks to foster excellence and equity in public education by working with school board leadership.

Here is contact information for the school districts involved in the Supreme Court decision, Parents Involved in Community Schools v. Seattle School District No. 1:

Jefferson County Public Schools, VanHoose Education Center, 3332 Newburg Rd., P.O. Box 34020, Louisville, KY 40232-4020; (502) 485-3011; www.jefferson.k12.ky.us.

Seattle School District No. 1, 2445 Third Ave. South, Seattle, WA 98134; (206) 252-0000; www.seattleschools.org.

11

Bilingual Education vs. English Immersion

Kenneth Jost

Miriam Flores remembers that her daughter Miriam was doing well in her first two years in school in the border town of Nogales, Ariz.

"She knew how to read and write in Spanish," Flores says of her daughter, now a college student. "She would even correct the teacher on accents and spelling."

In the third grade, however, Miriam began having difficulties. Her grades went down, and she began having nightmares.

Miriam's mother has a simple explanation for the change. In the early 1990s, Nogales provided bilingual education — teaching English learners in both their native language and English — but only through the first two grades. "It was the language," Flores says.

Miriam's new teacher did not speak Spanish, taught only in English and seemed uninterested in Miriam's language difficulties, Flores says. "Miriam is a very quiet child, and I thought it was strange that the teacher would say that she talked a lot," Flores recalls today. "Then Miriam told me, 'I ask the other kids what the teacher is saying.' She didn't understand."[1]

Flores' frustrations with her daughter's schooling led her to join with other Spanish-speaking Nogales families in 1992 in filing a federal suit aimed at improving educational opportunities for non-English-speaking students in the overwhelmingly Hispanic town. The class action suit claimed the school district was failing to comply with a federal law — the Equal Educational Opportunities Act of 1974 — which requires each state to take "appropriate action" to ensure that English-language learners (ELLs) enjoy "equal participation in its instructional programs."

Protesters at Arizona's capitol in Phoenix oppose Proposition 203 on Nov. 6, 2000. The next day voters decisively approved the ballot measure ending bilingual education in the state in favor of so-called sheltered English immersion. Similar measures in California and Massachusetts at about the same time reflected a popular backlash against bilingual education since the 1980s.

From *CQ Researcher*, December 11, 2009.

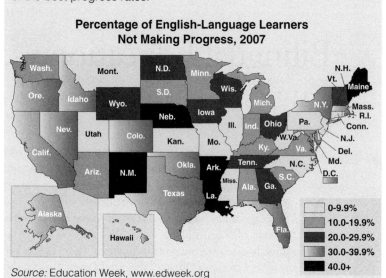

English Learners Doing Poorly in Big States

More than 30 percent of the English-language learners are not making progress in 18 states, including those with big Hispanic populations, such as California, Florida, New York and Texas. Smaller states such as Connecticut, Delaware and Rhode Island have some of the best progress rates.

Percentage of English-Language Learners Not Making Progress, 2007

Source: Education Week, www.edweek.org

Seventeen years later, the case is still in federal court. The plaintiffs won a pivotal decision in 2001 requiring Arizona to boost funding for English-language learning in Nogales and the rest of the state. In a narrowly divided decision in June, however, the Supreme Court gave state officials an opportunity to set aside the lower court ruling.

Writing for the 5-4 majority, Justice Samuel A. Alito Jr. said the federal district judge had failed to adequately consider changed circumstances since 2001. Among other changes, Alito cited the state's decision to drop bilingual education in favor of so-called "sheltered English immersion" as the officially prescribed method of instruction for students with limited English proficiency.[2]

Arizona's voters had decisively rejected bilingual education in a 2000 ballot measure. Along with similar measures passed in California in 1998 and Massachusetts in 2002, Arizona's Proposition 203 embodied a popular backlash against bilingual education that had grown since the 1980s. Critics of bilingual teaching viewed it as a politically correct relic of the 1960s and '70s that had proven academically ineffective and politically divisive.

The debate between English-only instruction and bilingual education has been fierce for decades. "People get very hot under the collar," says Christine Rossell, a professor of political science at Boston University and critic of bilingual education.

Those who support a bilingual approach, says Arizona Superintendent of Instruction Thomas Horne, "aren't interested in teaching the kids English," but want to maintain "a separatist nationalism that they can take advantage of." Horne, a Republican, intervened with the state's GOP legislative leaders to try to undo the federal court injunction.

"When I tell people that the best way to learn English is to be taught in Spanish, they think I'm joking," says Rossell.

Supporters insist that bilingual education is the best way to ensure long-term educational achievement for English-language learners. "We have gone backwards on educating non-English speakers," says José Ruiz-Escalante, a professor of bilingual education at the University of Texas-Pan American in Edinburg and president of the National Association for Bilingual Education. English-only proponents, he says, are "in such a hurry for students to speak English that we're not paying attention to their cognitive development."

"The important thing that students need to learn is how to think," Ruiz-Escalante continues. "It doesn't matter whether you learn to think in Spanish or in English. Kids will learn to speak English, but they will be limited" in their academic learning.[3]

Out of nearly 50 million pupils in U.S. public elementary and secondary schools, about 5.1 million — more than one-tenth — are classified as having limited English proficiency. The number is growing because of increased immigration, both legal and illegal. The vast majority of English-language learners — nearly

80 percent — speak Spanish as their first language. But schools are also coping with rising numbers of students who speak a variety of other languages, almost all of which have far less similarity to English than Spanish has.

"It's a growing challenge," says Patte Barth, director of the Center for Public Education at the National School Boards Association (NSBA). "We have many more children coming into our schools for whom their first language is not English. At the same time, the need to educate every child to a high level is much more important than it was even 20 years ago."

The imperative for results stems in part from enactment early in 2002 of the No Child Left Behind Act, the centerpiece of President George W. Bush's educational-accountability initiative. The act mandated annual testing of students in grades 3-8 and required that schools demonstrate "adequate yearly progress," including closing the achievement gap for English-language learners, at the risk of financial penalties for noncompliance.[4]

The act also withdrew the federal preference for bilingual education over English-only instruction. Even so, Latino advocacy groups that have long complained of inadequate attention to Spanish-speaking students applaud the law's emphasis on accountability. The act "changed the debate from what kind of education and curriculum to one of how do you best educate these kids," says Raul Gonzalez, director of legislative affairs for NCLR, formerly the National Council of La Raza. "That's where we think the debate should be."

The federal government has no official count on the number of English learners in each instructional method,

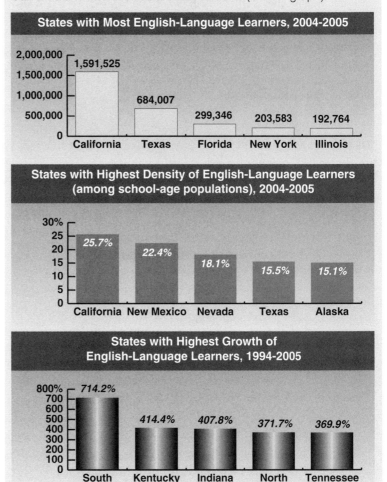

but the most recent survey by researchers indicates that the majority — about 60 percent — are in all-English curricula. Of that number, 12 percent receive no special services at all to aid English proficiency.

A Bilingual/Immersion Glossary

The dizzying number of terms and acronyms in the teaching-English field reflects the intensity and complexity of the debate over which method works best. Here are some of the key terms:

Annual Measurable Achievement Objective (AMAO) — These are the criteria for the reports mandated by the No Child Left Behind Act (NCLB) on the progress of limited English proficiency (LEP) students in English-language acquisition and academic achievement.

Adequate Yearly Progress (AYP) — The accountability system mandated by NCLB requires each state to ensure all schools and districts meet set standards.

Bilingual Education — Teaching non-English-speaking people in both their native language and in English.

Dual Language — Programs that help students develop full literacy skills in English and another language.

Early Exit Transitional — Programs that help students develop English skills as quickly as possible, without delaying learning of academic core content. Instruction begins in native language and then moves rapidly to English, with students transitioning to mainstream classrooms as soon as possible.

Elementary and Secondary Education Act (ESEA) — Funds primary and secondary education, and forbids establishment of a national curriculum. Originally enacted in 1965, the act was reauthorized as the No Child Left Behind Act.

English Language Development (ELD) — Programs in which students leave mainstream classrooms to spend part of their day receiving ESL instruction focusing on grammar, vocabulary and communication skills, not academic content. Typically there is no support for students' native languages. Also known as ESL Pull-Out.

English Language Proficiency (ELP) Standards — Assist teachers in evaluating LEP students' progress in their acquisition of English and facilitate the alignment of curriculum between ESL services and general education programs.

English as a Second Language (ESL) — Refers to non-English speakers and programs designed to teach them English.

ESL Push-In — These are programs for ESL students who attend mainstream classrooms and receive instruction in English with native-language support as needed from ESL teachers.

Heritage Language Programs — These target non-English-speaking students or those who have weak literary skills in their native language, frequently American Indians. Also known as Indigenous Language Programs.

The remaining English learners — about 40 percent — receive some form of bilingual instruction using their native language and English. The length of time in the bilingual programs varies from as little as one year to several. And, as Stanford University education professor Claude Goldenberg notes, there is no way to know the amount of support the students receive or the quality of the instruction.[5]

In Arizona, state policy calls for English-language learners to receive four hours a day of intensive English instruction apart from their mainstream, English-only classes. Since the so-called "pullout" policy was implemented in 2008, the rate of reclassifying students from English-language learners to English-proficient has increased, Horne says. "Students need to learn English quickly to compete," he says.

Tim Hogan, executive director of the Arizona Center for Law in the Public Interest and the lead attorney in the *Flores* case, says it is "too early to tell" whether the four-hour pullout approach will be more effective than past policies that he describes as ineffective. But Hogan alleges that the policy segregates Spanish speakers from other students and risks delaying graduation by taking class time away from academic subjects.

Hogan stresses, however, that the lawsuit is aimed at ensuring adequate funding for English-language instruction, not at imposing a specific educational method. "We proved that the state funding [for English-language instruction] was totally arbitrary," he says.

Horne counters that the Supreme Court decision leaves funding decisions up to the state. "The district court judges are being told not to micromanage the finances of the state education system," he says.

Voluminous, statistics-heavy studies are cited by opposing advocacy groups as evidence to support their respective positions on the bilingual versus English-only debate. But Barth says language politics, not research, often determines school districts' choice of instructional method. "A lot of it is political," she says. "A lot of decisions about language instruction aren't really informed by the research about what works for children."

Whatever approach is used, many researchers say English-language learners' needs are not being met. In their new book, *Educating English Learners for a Transformed World*, former George Mason University professors Virginia Collier and Wayne Thomas — who strongly advocate bilingual education — cite statistics showing a big achievement gap at the high-school level between native English speakers and students who entered school as English learners. Native English speakers have average scores on standardized tests around the 50th percentile, Collier and Thomas say, while English learners average around the 10th to 12th percentile.[6]

Despite decades of attention and debate on the issue, "not much has happened," says Kenji Hakuta, a professor at Stanford University's School of Education in Palo Alto, Calif. "The problems of English-language learners persist whether it's English-only or bilingual education."

As educators look for ways to best teach students with limited English skills, here are some of the major questions being debated:

Immersion — Learning a language by spending all or part of the time speaking solely in the target language.

Late Exit Transitional — Instruction designed to help students develop some skills and proficiency in their native language, as well as strong skills and proficiency in English. Instruction in lower grades is in the native language, and in English in upper grades. Also known as Developmental Bilingual or Maintenance Education.

Limited English Proficiency (LEP) — Denotes individuals who cannot communicate effectively in English, such as those not born in the United States or whose native language is not English.

Local Education Agency (LEA) — A board of education or other public authority that has administrative control of, or performs a service for, publicly funded schools.

National Assessment of Educational Process (NAEP) — The continuing assessment of American students in targeted grades and various subject areas — known as the "Nation's Report Card" — is carried out by the U.S. Department of Education's National Center for Education Statistics.

National Clearinghouse for English Language Acquisition and Language Instruction Educational Programs (NCELA) — Supports the U.S. Department of Education's Office of English Language Acquisition in its mission to implement NCLB as it applies to English-language learners.

No Child Left Behind Act of 2001 (NCLB) — The most recent reauthorization of the ESEA calls for standards-based education reform and requires assessments of all students in certain grades before states can receive federal funding for schools.

Office of English Language Acquisition, Language Enhancement, and Academic Achievement for Limited English Proficient Students (OELA) — A U.S. Department of Education office that helps ensure English-language learners and immigrant students attain English proficiency and achieve academically.

Sheltered English Immersion — Classes specifically for ESL students aimed at improving their English-speaking, reading and writing skills. Prepares students for entry into mainstream classrooms.

Structured English Immersion (SEI) — Classes for LEP students only where the goal is fluency in English. All instruction is in English, adjusted to the proficiency of students so the subject matter is comprehensible.

Two-Way Immersion — Programs designed to develop proficiency in both native language and English through instruction in both languages. Also known as Two-Way Bilingual.

Source: "The Biennial Report to Congress on the Implementation of the Title III State Formula Grant Program," U.S. Department of Education, School Years 2004-2006, June 2008, www.ed.gov/about/offices/list/oela/title3biennial0406.pdf.

Is bilingual education effective for English-language learners?

Todd Butler teaches social studies and language arts to fourth-grade English learners in Mansfield, Texas, a rapidly growing exurb south of Fort Worth. Butler, an Anglo who began studying Spanish in fourth grade himself, uses only Spanish for social studies but alternates day by day between English and Spanish for language arts.

Butler, recipient of the National Association for Bilingual Education's teacher of the year award in 2009, is firmly convinced of the merits of bilingual education, especially in the so-called dual-language model now used in Mansfield and advancing in other school districts. By contrast, the older model — known as "transitional bilingual education" — focuses on using bilingual education only for a limited period.

"We don't do kids any favor by shoving them into English as fast as we can," says Butler, a teacher with more than a quarter-century of experience. "The research shows very clearly that the longer we can give them support in their language, the better they're going to do not just in elementary school but in secondary school as well."

The strongest supporting evidence comes from long-term research by George Mason scholars Collier and Thomas. The veteran researchers examined achievement levels through high school among English learners in 35 school districts who were taught using different instructional models. "Our research shows what works in the long term is different from what works in the short term," Thomas explains.

There is little difference in achievement levels between English learners in the elementary grades, the researchers found, regardless of whether the students were taught in dual-language, transitional-bilingual or English-as-a-Second-Language (ESL) models. By high school, however, the dual-language students come closer to narrowing the gap between them and the English-proficient students than those using the ESL approach. Students from transitional bilingual programs are in-between.

Students in English-only programs "look as though they're doing really well in early grades," Thomas explains, "but they've experienced a cognitive slowdown as they're learning English." As the two authors conclude in their book: "The more children develop their first language..., the more successful they will be in academic achievement in English by the end of their school years."[7]

The national school boards group agrees on the advantages of "first-language" instruction for English learners. "ELL students with formal schooling in their first language tend to acquire English proficiency faster than their peers without it," the NSBA's Center for Public Education concluded after reviewing the research. The center added that it takes four to seven years to become proficient in "academic English — the language needed to succeed in the classroom."[8]

Opponents of bilingual education say it fails because it does not completely close the gap between English learners and English-proficient students. "There is very little research to say that these programs are having good results," says Rosalie Pedalino Porter, a longtime critic of bilingual education who was ESL coordinator in Newton, Mass., in the 1980s. "It never proved itself effective, and all sorts of excuses are still being made." Porter now serves on the board of the pro-English advocacy group Center for Equal Opportunity.

To critics, bilingual education simply delays students' mastery of the new language: English. "If you don't pull them out [for English instruction], they're not going to learn English fast enough," says Arizona education chief Horne.

Supporters of bilingual education counter that the short-term perspective is ultimately detrimental for English learners. "Most districts are still in a hurry for them to learn English," says NABE president Ruiz-Escalante. They end up "learning English at the expense of an education."

"Schools are in a difficult position," says James Crawford, a bilingual-education advocate and author of a textbook on English learners now in its fifth edition. "Short-term pressures have determined how children are being taught." Crawford first developed an expertise in bilingual education as a writer and editor for *Education Week;* he also served as NABE's executive director until 2006.[9]

Some experts say the lines in the perennial and heated debate are beginning to blur. "The argument of bilingual education versus English immersion sounds like a fairly old way of characterizing the problem," says Stanford professor Hakuta.

Is "English immersion" effective for English learners?

As chief executive officer of the United Neighborhood Organization, Juan Rangel superintends a network of eight charter schools serving predominantly Hispanic communities in Chicago. UNO schools follow a philosophy of strong discipline, high expectations and English immersion — or teaching only using English — instead of bilingual education.

According to a study by the pro-English Lexington Institute, English learners from UNO schools score higher than their counterparts from other Chicago schools, who are subject to statewide bilingual-education requirements.[10] But Rangel says English immersion also promotes assimilation for Hispanic students. "What it means is having our families and children have an understanding of belonging," Rangel told *Education Week* reporter Mary Ann Zehr. "They have a role in developing this country."[11]

Rangel says bilingual education has not worked as intended. Some parents interviewed agreed. Guadalupe Garcia, an immigrant from Mexico with a fourth-grade education, told Zehr that the bilingual education one of her daughters received in a regular Chicago school was "pura español" — pure Spanish. Another of her daughters entered a UNO school in second grade speaking no English but could speak English well within a year and a half.

Advocates of English immersion emphasize assimilation as one of their reasons for favoring it over bilingual instruction. "I believe in the beauty of bilingualism," says Porter, of the pro-English advocacy group Center for Equal Opportunity, "but I have a very, very strong commitment to children like me who don't speak English at all." Porter was born in Italy and spoke no English when she immigrated with her family at age 6.

But the advocates of English immersion also claim that studies in two states that changed from bilingual to English instruction — Arizona and California — show that the change improved academic performance. Justice

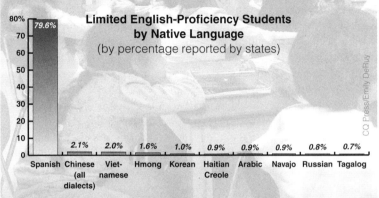

Most Student Native Speakers Are Hispanic

More than three-quarters of U.S. students with limited English proficiency (LEP) are native Spanish speakers. About 7 percent of LEPs are native speakers of Asian languages.

Limited English-Proficiency Students by Native Language (by percentage reported by states)

Spanish 79.6%, Chinese (all dialects) 2.1%, Vietnamese 2.0%, Hmong 1.6%, Korean 1.0%, Haitian Creole 0.9%, Arabic 0.9%, Navajo 0.9%, Russian 0.8%, Tagalog 0.7%

Source: "The Biennial Report to Congress on The Implementation of the Title III State Formula Grant Program: School Years 2004-06," U.S. Department of Education, June 2008

Alito pointed to both studies in the Supreme Court's decision in the *Flores* case as evidence of "documented, academic support for the view that SEI [structured English immersion] is significantly more effective than bilingual education."[12] Critics, however, say both studies are flawed.

In one of the studies, Kelly Torrance, identified as an adjunct scholar with the Lexington Institute, a pro-English think tank based in Washington, D.C., cited statistics from California showing that the number of English learners who scored in the top two categories of proficiency on the state's English-language development test increased from 25 percent in 2001 to 47 percent in 2005. "This striking improvement is big news," wrote Torrance.[13]

Bilingual-education advocates dismiss the studies. Stephen Krashen, a linguistics professor at the University of Southern California in Los Angeles, says the state introduced the English test in 2001 and that improved scores are typical for the first few years after introduction of a new test. He points to several other studies by university academics that conclude dropping bilingual education did not accelerate English learners' development.[14]

The Arizona Department of Education similarly concluded in a report prepared in July 2004 that English learners in the state had benefited from the switch from bilingual education to English immersion following voters' decisive rejection of bilingual education in the 2000 ballot measure, Proposition 203. "Students in English immersion outperformed students in bilingual in all areas," Superintendent Horne says in describing the report.[15]

Jeff MacSwan, a professor of linguistics at Arizona State University in Tempe, says the state's report "has been completely discredited." In letters to the editor at the time and in comments since, MacSwan notes that the comparisons found in the study failed to control for other potential causes of the differences, including poverty, length of time in the United States or initial language proficiency. "That's a huge thing," he says.

In a more recent study he coauthored, MacSwan says it is impossible to determine whether English learners are doing better or worse since passage of Proposition 203, but that they continue to suffer "a persistent and dramatic achievement gap" in comparison to English-proficient students.[16]

Porter insists that English learners need only a little concentrated language instruction to become proficient. "They need two to three hours a day of intensive language instruction," she says. "These children within a year of this intensive instruction can make the transition from their native language to English."

Some supporters of bilingual education stop short of flatly dismissing English-only approaches. "You could find an elementary program that was English-only, and they did well," says Barth with the school boards' group. "But on average, that's an outlier."

"Any well-implemented program can work," says Stanford's Hakuta. "The issue is giving kids access to academic content that sparks their curiosity. The fundamental piece is that education isn't pouring knowledge into empty vessels. You have to get kids interested and excited in the content of what you're teaching."

Should funding for English-language learning be increased?

Twice in the past decade, federal district judges in Arizona have found that the state was not spending enough money to help English-language learners become proficient in English. State officials welcomed the first of the rulings, by Judge Alfred Marquez, in January 2000 as a useful spur to increase funding for English instruction.

In 2006, however, the state's Republican-controlled legislature approved only part of the funding increase proposed by then-Gov. Janet Napolitano, a Democrat, to satisfy the federal court. The new plan increased the special funding for English-language learners to $432 per student from the previous $358. Judge Raner Collins, who had taken over the *Flores* case after Marquez's retirement, found the new spending levels still inadequate.

In its ruling in June, the Supreme Court said that both Collins and the 9th U.S. Circuit Court of Appeals placed too much emphasis on funding levels in refusing the plea by the state's legislative leaders and Superintendent of Instruction Horne to reopen the case. Dissenting justices countered that the adequacy of the state's resources devoted to English-language instruction "has always been the basic contested issue" in the case.

Today, plaintiffs' attorney Hogan acknowledges that the Supreme Court's decision shifts the focus of the case away from funding and toward the effectiveness of the state's prescribed model of structured English immersion with English learners taken out of their mainstream English-only classes for four-hour "pull-out" sessions for intensive English instruction.

Nationwide, the question of funding for English-language instruction continues to be a point of discussion, but the lines are not as sharply drawn as they are on the instructional model used. "It's not about resources; it's about the quality of the program," says NABE president Ruiz-Escalante. "Whatever resources are available need to be devoted to appropriate programs that meet the educational needs of the students. Money alone is not the solution."

"The amount of money spent on a program is not a guarantee that a good education is produced," says English-immersion advocate Porter. "Certainly, there's a floor level. But to equate the amount of dollars with wonderful educational outcomes simply cannot be done. The real proof is not the amount of money but the evidence of student success."

Some bilingual-education advocates, in fact, minimize the need for additional resources for English-language learners. In their book, Collier and Thomas contend that bilingual (dual-language) instruction — that is, using a bilingual teacher to teach English learners in the same grade-level, mainstream curriculum as other students — is "the most cost-effective" educational model. The only additional cost, they say, is for materials. By contrast, they call ESL pullout "the least cost-effective model," because extra resource teachers are needed.

For her part, Barth, with the school boards' Center for Public Education, also says educational costs for English learners are not necessarily higher than for English-proficient students. But she does point to some needed additional resources that "could use funding," such as "more ESL teachers" and "broader access to good pre-K programs."

"We also know that students who come into school without English tend to be in communities that are poorer, and they tend to go to schools that have fewer resources," Barth says. But she adds, "That's not the same as saying it costs more to educate an ESL child."

In Arizona, Superintendent Horne says the state is meeting federal requirements for teaching English learners. "The law requires appropriate action to teach kids English," he says. "We're clearly doing that. I think we're one of the leaders in the nation."

Gonzalez of NCLR (La Raza), however, says Arizona is misusing funds provided under Title III of the No Child Left Behind Act, the language-acquisition section. "The federal law says you cannot use Title III to supplant your state funds or your Title I funds," Gonzalez says, referring to the major federal aid program for disadvantaged school districts. "Title III is complementary. Arizona was supplanting funds and using Title III funds for those purposes."

Veronica Rivera, a legislative staff attorney with the Mexican American Legal Defense and Education Fund (MALDEF) in Washington, says funding is partly to blame for "inadequate" programs for Spanish-speaking students in some states and school districts. But she also points to a need for consistent standards for bilingual teachers. "Some states and local education agencies require some type of bilingual certification," Rivera says. "Most of them do, but not all of them."

Whatever federal funding is provided, Gonzalez says No Child Left Behind helps English learners by holding school districts accountable for measurable results.

"Everyone knew that these kids weren't doing well in school for decades, but there was no accountability," he says. "No one suffered except the kids."

Julie Maxwell-Jolly, director of the Center for Applied Policy in Education at the University of California-Davis, agrees. "We have seen from No Child Left Behind that [English learners] are not achieving," she says. "That's been good. It's really shined a light."

BACKGROUND

American Languages

The American melting pot has always included many languages in addition to English — the dominant tongue since colonial times. Through much of the 19th century, non-English speakers commonly received some instruction in their native languages, whether in public or private schools. From the late 19th century on, however, opposition to rising immigration — along with anti-German sentiment during and after World War I — drove native-language instruction out of most public schools. The rise of bilingual education beginning in the 1960s was premised on a need to use native languages in some form for non-English speakers, but a backlash developed among critics who viewed the policy as failing either to educate or to assimilate youngsters with limited English proficiency.[17]

The European colonists encountered Native Americans who spoke a variety of mostly unwritten languages. Besides the British colonists, the early Americans included many Dutch and a lesser number of French, Germans and Swedes, who brought their native languages with them. African slaves, with limited if any formal schooling, learned English through their work, but not necessarily standard English. New waves of non-English speakers were added through the 19th and early 20th centuries with the conquests of the Mexican-American War (Spanish), the import of Chinese labor (Mandarin and Cantonese) and the immigration from southern and eastern Europe (Italian, Greek, Portuguese, Russian and Polish among many other European languages, along with Hebrew and Yiddish).

At first, the use of non-English languages was "supported, tolerated or sanctioned" by public and parochial schools, according to historian Guadalupe San Miguel Jr.,

CHRONOLOGY

1960s-1970s *Civil rights era sparks moves to improve language instruction for non-English-speaking students.*

1967 Bilingual Education Act is passed by Congress and signed by President Lyndon B. Johnson; law provides financial aid to school districts to help students with limited English.

1970 Regulations issued by Department of Health, Education and Welfare (HEW) instruct federally financed school districts to "rectify" language deficiencies of non-English-speaking students.

1971 Massachusetts law requires "transitional bilingual education" in all public schools.

1974 Supreme Court in *Lau v. Nichols* requires public school systems to provide non-English-speaking students with "basic English skills" needed to profit from attendance.... Congress codifies requirement later in year in Equal Educational Opportunities Act.

1975 HEW's Office of Civil Rights issues *Lau* regulations requiring use of non-English languages for language-minority students.

1978 Study by private research institute questions the benefits of bilingual education.

1980s-1990s *Opposition to bilingual education forms, grows.*

1980 Carter administration proposes regulations requiring bilingual education.

1981 Reagan administration cancels proposed bilingual-education regulation; begins reducing federal aid to English-language instruction.... Study by Education Department questions benefits of bilingual education.... Federal appeals court, in Texas case, says English-language instruction must be based on "sound educational theory," adequately resourced and proven to be effective (*Castañeda v. Pickard*).

1982 Federal appeals court lifts statewide injunction requiring Texas to improve English-language instruction after state legislature passes bilingual-education law.

1983 U.S. English organization founded to lobby for official English laws; many states pass such laws in 1980s, '90s.

1990 Veteran teacher Rosalie Pedalino Porter's book *Forked Tongue* sharply attacks bilingual education.

1991 Report prepared for U.S. Department of Education finds English-immersion and bilingual education both effective methods but says non-English-speaking students benefit from longer instruction in native language.

1992 Spanish-speaking families in Nogales, Ariz., file federal court suit saying school district fails to provide adequate language instruction.

1998 California voters approve Proposition 227 requiring English immersion for non-English-speaking students, with provision for parents to request waiver.

2000-Present *Support for bilingual education recedes further; plaintiffs in Arizona, Texas cases suffer setbacks.*

2000 Arizona held in contempt of court by federal judge for not providing adequate funding for language instruction.... State's voters approve Proposition 203, prescribing English-only for language instruction.

2002 President George W. Bush signs No Child Left Behind Act, repealing Bilingual Education Act but holding school districts accountable for non-English-speaking students to meet proficiency standards; English-language acquisition aid is revamped, reducing assistance to districts with large numbers of language-minority students.... Massachusetts voters approve English-only instruction.

2006 Arizona legislature approves modest increase in state aid for language instruction; federal judge deems funding inadequate, reaffirms statewide injunction; state education chief intervenes to undo injunction.

2008-2009 Federal judge in Texas says state not satisfying federal standards for English learners in secondary schools; federal appeals court issues stay in February 2009.... Supreme Court in June 2009 orders judge in Arizona case to reconsider effort to undo injunction; new hearing set for Dec. 14.

a professor at the University of Houston. Language-policy decisions were made at the state and local level. By mid-century, however, the federal government began discouraging the use of languages other than English in newly acquired territories. States followed. California prescribed English in schools in 1855, five years after statehood. As immigration increased, many other states passed similar laws in the late 19th century. World War I fueled anti-German sentiment that led to English-only laws in the Midwest in states with large German populations.

By the 1920s, most states had English-only laws for public school instruction. Teachers and administrators supported the policies, sometimes even with corporal punishment. President Lyndon B. Johnson's biographer Robert Caro writes that as a teacher in southwest Texas, Johnson sometimes spanked Mexican-American students if he heard them using Spanish on the playground. Three decades later, however, Johnson's fellow Texan and Democrat, Sen. Ralph Yarbrough, came to see the English-only policy as "the cruelest form of discrimination" against the state's large Mexican-American population and others with limited English proficiency. With Johnson in the White House, Yarbrough authored the Bilingual Education Act to encourage and provide financial assistance for programs to recognize the special needs of limited-English-speaking children. The act, attached as Title VII to the omnibus Elementary and Secondary Education Act, cleared Congress in December 1967; Johnson signed it into law the next month.

The new law authorized up to $85 million in federal aid for bilingual education, but only $7.5 million was appropriated the first year. The law did not specify any instructional method for English-language learners. In 1970, regulations issued by the old Department of Health, Education and Welfare (HEW) directed school districts receiving federal aid to "rectify" language deficiencies among non-English speakers but again did not specify a curriculum or instructional method. Meanwhile, however, states were beginning to enact their own initiatives. Massachusetts enacted a law in 1971 establishing what it called "transitional bilingual education." Texas followed suit two years later. Some other states passed laws authorizing but not mandating bilingual education.

The Supreme Court took on the issue in a case from San Francisco brought by Chinese-American students under Title VI of the Civil Rights Act of 1964, which prohibits discrimination in federally assisted services by state or local governments. The plaintiffs in *Lau v. Nichols* claimed that out of 2,856 Chinese-speaking students in the school system, only 1,000 received any supplemental instruction in English. Unanimously, the high court agreed that the school district was violating the Civil Rights Act.

"It seems obvious," Justice William O. Douglas wrote in the main opinion, "that the Chinese-speaking minority receive fewer benefits than the English-speaking majority from respondents' school system." Once again, the decision did not instruct local school systems on how to carry out the federal requirement. In a concurring opinion, Justice Harry A. Blackmun suggested that a school district with fewer non-English speakers might not be subject to the same requirement.[18]

Language Debates

With federal support, bilingualism advanced in the 1970s in schools as well as in society at large. With the election of Republican President Ronald Reagan, however, the federal government set itself against bilingual education and in support of "English-only" instruction. Opposition to bilingual education grew in the 1990s. Supporters of bilingual education succeeded in getting Congress to reauthorize the federal law, but California in 1998 became the first of three states to approve voter initiatives to limit the use of languages other than English in public schools.

Congress responded to the Supreme Court's decision later in 1974 with a law, the Equal Educational Opportunities Act, which codified the requirement that school districts take affirmative steps to deal with the needs of language-minority children. The next year, Congress recognized language minorities in a different context by amending the Voting Rights Act to require bilingual registration and voting materials in electoral districts with at least 5 percent language-minority population. For schools, HEW's Office of Civil Rights in 1975 issued the so-called *Lau* guidelines, which — for the first time — specifically required the use of non-English languages and cultures for language-minority students. The guidelines, however, stressed the goal of helping language-minority children gain proficiency in English.

The growing bilingual-education movement was challenged by several studies — including a major report

Native Americans Fight Language Extinction

"It is about losing history and identity."

Leaders from three Cherokee nations came together in October to mark the opening of the Eastern Band of Cherokee Indians' Kituwah Academy, a language-immersion school for kindergarteners to fifth-graders in Cherokee, N.C.

"It is a wonderful initiative for the Cherokee," says Ellen L. Lutz, executive director for Cultural Survival, a nonprofit advocacy group in Cambridge, Mass., which promotes the rights of indigenous communities. "Young, self-confident Cherokee kids will not forget who they are because of the education they receive at this school."

In 1838 members of the Ketoowah and Cherokee nations in Oklahoma were relocated from their homes by military force in direct violation of an 1832 Supreme Court ruling affirming their right to remain on their traditional territory. Some evaded relocation while others returned to tribal lands in North Carolina. In recent years, profits from several enterprises have encouraged the tribes to take on the multigenerational challenge of preserving their own language. The Cherokee Nation of Oklahoma opened its own immersion school in 2003, and its curriculum serves as the basis for the Eastern Band's.

Many such Indian schools have opened throughout the nation, but some Indian communities have opted for informal language instruction outside the classroom. The Hualapai Tribe in Arizona, for example, holds summer camps for younger generations.

Of the nation's 175 surviving Native American dialects, only 20 are expected to remain in 2050, according to the Indigenous Language Institute (ILI), a nonprofit advocacy group in Santa Fe, N.M. Fifty currently surviving languages have five or fewer speakers — all older than 70 — and face imminent extinction, according to Cultural Survival.

"This is a linguistic emergency," says Ineé Yang Slaughter, executive director of ILI. "It is about losing history and identity."

More than a century ago, during attempts to assimilate Native Americans into mainstream society, the federal government targeted Native American languages in a campaign termed by some linguists as "linguistic genocide."

In an 1887 report, Commissioner of Indian Affairs J.D.C. Atkins wrote, "In the difference of language today lies two-thirds of our trouble.... Schools should be established, which children should be required to attend; their barbarous dialects should be blotted out and the English language substituted."[1]

During the same period, boarding schools established by the Bureau of Indian Affairs tried to stamp out native languages. Under English-only rules students were punished and humiliated for speaking their native language.

The coercive assimilation policy met with limited success in eradicating Indian languages, but over time the policies took a toll on the identity of many Indians, alienating them from their cultural roots. Moreover, the policies left a

published in 1978 under the auspices of the American Institutes for Research — that showed no achievement gains from the use of native-language instruction for non-English speakers. Despite the controversies, the Department of Education — carved out of HEW under President Jimmy Carter — proposed regulations in August 1980 that tightened the requirement for bilingual education. The proposed guidelines, viewed by some as an appeal by Carter for Hispanic votes in the November election, called for bilingual education in any school with at least 25 limited-English-proficiency students in two consecutive grades.

The Reagan administration instituted what historian San Miguel calls a period of "retrenchment and redefinition" for bilingual education. On Feb. 2, 1981 — just two weeks after Reagan took office — Education Secretary Terrel Bell withdrew the proposed bilingual-education regulations from the Carter administration. Reagan himself told reporters he was opposed to bilingual education. He called it "absolutely wrong" to have a bilingual-education program "that is now openly, admittedly dedicated to preserving their native language and never getting them adequate in English."[19] Reagan's views helped encourage a growing English-only movement, legacy of opposition toward bilingual and immersion education among Indians who remembered the pain they suffered in school and wanted to shield their children from similar experiences.

"The boarding schools turned to indoctrination. Native languages were burned out of their mouths," says Lutz. "Over time, the experience led grandparents to refuse to speak the native tongues to younger generations."

The eventual economic and social mobility of Native Americans aided in the beginning of several grassroots movements in the 1970s to bring back mother tongues.

"The next generation would say, 'It's my language. It's my people. America took it from me. I want it back,'" explains Lutz.

Prodded by language activists, Congress passed the Native American Languages Acts in 1990 and 1992 to facilitate efforts to preserve Native American languages. Among other things, the laws concluded that academic performance was directly tied to a respect for the first language of students.

While the U.S. Department of Education and the National Science Foundation already provided federal help for cultural preservation, the acts made tribes eligible for funding to carry out language conservation and renewal.

Eastern Band Cherokee Indians attend the opening of Kituwah Academy, in Cherokee, N.C., in October. Housed in the renovated Boundary Tree Lodge, a historic visitors' lodge, the school teaches academic subjects and the Cherokee language (Kituwah).

Despite the recent surge in teaching Native Americans their native languages, several challenges still remain. Indian-language speakers often lack the academic credentials to teach, while outside teachers are not well-versed in the cultural and linguistic nuances of Native Americans.

"The key is teaching the language to communicate as opposed to more traditional textbook education," says Slaughter. "Classroom teaching isn't always the best way to teach students to actually use the language in their communities."

But perhaps the biggest problem is the need to compete with other more pressing priorities such as health care, economic development, housing and general academic learning.

"These other issues are critical," Slaughter says. "But this is not just a language issue, it is an issue of cultural identity being lost. Once a language is gone, it is gone forever. We know that learning our languages strengthens us both as individuals and as a nation."

— *Darrell Dela Rosa*

---

[1] James Crawford, "Loose Ends in a Tattered Fabric," American Immigration Lawyers Association, www.ailadownloads.org/advo/Crawford-LanguageRights.pdf.

which succeeded over the course of the decade in enacting official-English measures in more than a dozen states.

For schools, the administration began cutting funding for bilingual education; from a high of $158 million in fiscal 1979, federal support fell to $133 million by 1984. A study by two Education Department researchers published in 1981 again questioned the effects of bilingual education. The department's inspector general published a harsh audit of bilingual programs in seven school districts in Texas, which required them to refund federal grants because of failing to meet stated goals. Enforcement actions by the department's Office of Civil Rights to require bilingual programs, however, declined sharply.

The decline began and continued in the face of an influential ruling in 1981 by the federal appeals court for Texas that reinforced the federal requirement for bilingual instruction under the Equal Educational Opportunities Act. The ruling in *Castañeda v. Pickard* specified that bilingual-education programs must be "based on sound educational theory"; "implemented effectively with resources for personnel, instructional materials, and space"; and proven effective in overcoming language barriers and handicaps.[20]

As Reagan's Republican successor, President George H. W. Bush proved to be sympathetic to bilingual education. In a critical step, Bush allowed the publication in 1991 of an in-depth study of bilingual education commissioned under Reagan but withheld from publication. The Ramirez report — so-called after its principal investigator, J. David Ramirez — was summarized in a press release as affirming the effectiveness of the three most common language-instruction programs: immersion, early-exit bilingual or late-exit bilingual. As bilingual-education advocate Crawford notes, however, on closer examination the study supports longer bilingual instruction. The study found that students in late-exit programs had accelerated progress over time and that, regardless of instructional method, students generally needed five years or longer to achieve proficiency in English.[21]

The opposition to bilingual education continued to grow in the 1990s. After a decade of teaching English-language learners in bilingual Massachusetts, Porter harshly criticized the policy in her book, *Forked Tongue*, in 1990. Like other critics, Porter depicted bilingual instruction as ineffective educationally and politically and culturally divisive. Despite the criticism, the federal bilingual-education law was reenacted in 1994 under a Democratic-controlled Congress and a Democratic president, Bill Clinton.

Four years later, however, bilingual-education opponents won a major state-level victory with California's adoption of Proposition 227, a voter initiative that made so-called sheltered English-immersion the standard instructional method throughout the state for English-language learners. The initiative was bankrolled by Ron Unz, a millionaire businessman-turned-politician and political activist. Passed in 1998 with about 61 percent of the vote, the initiative requires sheltered English immersion for limited English proficiency (LEP) students during a transition not expected to last more than one year with transfer to mainstream classrooms after attaining "a good working knowledge" of English. Parents can waive the English-only rule if they show that native-language instruction would benefit their child. Two states followed California with stricter English-only initiatives: Arizona in 2000, Massachusetts in 2002.

Language Tests

Bilingual education had fallen so out of favor by the start of the 21st century that President George W. Bush and Congress combined to repeal the federal Bilingual Education Act and expunge the term from federal law. Bush successfully pushed for a new federal law, the No Child Left Behind Act, which required standardized testing of all schools with penalties for those found to be "underperforming." Supporters said the law would hold schools accountable for teaching English learners, but bilingual-education advocates feared misleading results from testing English learners only in English. Meanwhile, the Arizona bilingual education suit moved up to an eventual Supreme Court decision that tilted in favor of English immersion and appeared to limit federal courts' authority to order extra funding for English-language learners.

Bush made the education reform bill his major social policy initiative, securing bipartisan support by appealing to Republicans with test-based standards to hold schools accountable and to Democrats with increased funding to help schools meet the standards. Largely unnoticed in the main debates, the act's Title III replaced the Bilingual Education Act with the English Acquisition Act. As Crawford explains in his historical account, the act increased the authorized funding for English-language instruction but allocated the moneys according to a population-based formula instead of through competitive grants. As a result, funding was no longer concentrated on proven programs, but spread widely. Average grants the first year amounted to only $150 per student, far less than the average grant under the old law.[22]

The act — passed by Congress in December 2001 and signed by Bush on Jan. 8, 2002 — pointedly makes no recommendation as to a particular method of instruction for English learners. As part of the change, the Office of Bilingual Education was renamed the Office of English Language Acquisition, Language Enhancement, and Academic Achievement for Limited English Proficient Students — OELA for short. As the Department of Education explained, the act required state and local education agencies to establish English-proficiency standards; provide quality language instruction based on scientific research; and place highly qualified teachers in English-language classes. All English-language learners were to be tested annually "so that their parents will know how they are progressing."[23]

Nearly five years later, guidebooks issued by the Education Department late in 2006 designed to provide scientifically based recommendations on teaching methods continued to give school districts no guidance on the bilingual versus English-only debate. "We intentionally avoided that," Russell Gersten, a bilingual-education critic who headed the panel of experts that reviewed the guidebooks, told *Education Week*. David Francis, a University of Houston professor and bilingual-education supporter who led the writing of the guidebooks, concurred with the decision. But bilingual-education supporter Krashen at the University of Southern California complained that the guidebooks were "omitting something that is important."[24]

The debate that policy makers tried to duck continued among researchers. A study of California schools published in March 2006 examining the impact of Proposition 227 concluded that no single instructional method for English learners was significantly better than another.

Unz, the English-only activist who had funded the initiative, criticized the study, insisting his analysis showed that the switch from bilingual to predominantly English-only had raised achievement levels. In any event, the study confirmed the drop in bilingual instruction from about 60 percent of English learners to only 8 percent. It also showed that only 40 percent of English learners were reclassified as proficient after 10 years of public schooling.[25]

Two years later, two University of California research centers found no gains in English proficiency in California or the two other states with similar measures, Arizona and Massachusetts. "There's no visual evidence that these three states are doing better than the national average or other states" in educating English learners, Russell Rumberger, director of the Linguistic Minority Research Institute at UC-Santa Barbara, told *Education Week*. The institute partnered with UCLA's Civil Rights Project on the study, which found a greater achievement gap for English learners in the three states than in two states, New Mexico and Texas, which continued to use native-language instruction for English learners. Gersten minimized the findings. He told the publication Proposition 227 had helped English learners by raising expectations and giving them the same curriculum as other students.[26]

Meanwhile, the Arizona suit had reached a critical stage with Judge Raner Collins' ruling in December 2005 that the state was in civil contempt for failing

First lady Michelle Obama attends a Cinco de Mayo celebration at the Latin American Montessori Bilingual (LAMB) Public Charter School in Washington, on May 4, 2009. Bilingual-education advocates are hoping for support from the Obama administration, which backs "transitional bilingual education" and promises to help English learners by "holding schools accountable for making sure these students complete school."

to "appropriately and constitutionally" fund English-language instruction. Collins' decision four months later to reject the legislature's funding increase and impose civil fines was set aside in August 2006 by the 9th U.S. Circuit Court of Appeals, which ordered a full hearing. After an eight-day hearing in January 2007, Collins reaffirmed his ruling, which the 9th Circuit upheld a year later.

On appeal by Superintendent Horne and the Republican legislative leaders, however, the Supreme Court in June 2009 ordered Collins to reconsider the motion to modify the injunction issued nine years earlier. For the majority, Justice Alito pointed to four changed circumstances warranting reconsideration, starting with the state's switch to English immersion. Research on English-language learning instruction, Alito wrote, "indicates there is documented, academic support for the view that SEI [sheltered English immersion] is significantly more effective than bilingual education." The other three factors cited were the federal No Child Left Behind Act; "structural and management reforms" in Nogales itself and the state's increased education funding.

Writing for the four dissenters, Justice Stephen G. Breyer said he would have upheld Judge Collins' order. The high court ruling, Breyer wrote, "will make it more difficult for federal courts to enforce ... those federal standards."

CURRENT SITUATION
Lagging Indications

English-language learners (ELLs) are lagging behind other students on math and reading achievement tests, and one-fourth are failing to make progress toward language proficiency, according to state data collected by the federal Department of Education.

Opposing camps in the bilingual versus English-immersion debate predictably blame the achievement and language-proficiency gaps on school districts' failure to adopt their differing prescriptions on the best instructional model to use for English learners. Some experts with less partisan views, however, point to other factors, including the concentration of English learners in high-poverty, lower-resourced schools. English learners score far below the national average for fourth-graders in both reading and math on the National Assessment of Educational Progress (NAEP), often called the nation's report card. The gap widens in test scores for eighth-graders, according to a recent analysis by the Pew Hispanic Center.[27]

The center's analysis of the 2005 NAEP showed, for example, that nearly three-fourths of fourth-grade English learners (73 percent) scored below "basic" on reading — double the national average of 36 percent. For eighth-graders, the national average of below-basic scores fell to 27 percent, but the percentage of English learners scoring below basic remained almost unchanged at 71 percent.

A similar pattern was seen on math scores. Among English learners, 46 percent of fourth-graders scored below basic, compared to the national average of 20 percent. For eighth-graders, the gap widened markedly: 71 percent of English learners below basic compared to a national average of 31 percent.

On all four tests, only small fractions of English learners were rated as proficient or advanced, scores attained by roughly one-third of the students nationwide. The center's analysis, by senior researcher Richard Fry, found that English learners' scores were far below the average of white students and measurably below the averages for blacks and Hispanics.

Language-proficiency testing required of the states by the No Child Left Behind Act shows more directly the achievement gap for English learners. The federal law requires all public school students, including English learners, to meet reading and math proficiency standards by 2014. In tests administered in 2006 and 2007, however, only one-sixth of English learners nationwide were listed as having attained proficiency. One-fourth of the English learners were shown as not making progress.[28]

Both Fry and Barth at the school boards' Center for Public Education point to some precautions in interpreting the statistics. They both note, for example, that — in contrast to ethnic and racial groupings — students classified as English learners at one point can be reclassified as language-proficient later and no longer be included in the group.

Barth also stresses that English-language learners "are not a monolithic group." The vast majority are Spanish speakers, she says, but the others represent more than 400 different languages. Family backgrounds vary greatly as well: Some come from homes with well-educated parents, while others have parents with limited education and literacy. As a result, Barth says, "the range of performance between the high- and low-performing ELL students is greater than the gap between ELLs and their English-speaking peers."

Despite those precautions, bilingual-education advocates decry what they see as the lagging achievement scores for English learners. "Most U.S. schools are dramatically under-educating" English learners, Collier and Thomas write.[29] Both they and journalist-author Crawford blame in part the popularity of English-immersion programs. English-only programs "continue to spread," and enrollment in bilingual programs declines, Crawford says, despite what he calls "increasing" evidence that bilingual programs are more effective.

From the opposite perspective, author Porter of the Center for Equal Opportunity says English-immersion programs are best-suited to the English learners who present the biggest challenges for schools: students from immigrant families typically poor and often headed by parents with limited education. "These children have to be given a priority education," Porter says. "What is important? First, give them English-language skills."

The Pew Center's Fry suggests, however, that English-learners' gaps may be related to the characteristics of the schools that most attend. In a second, recent report, Fry found that in the states with the largest concentration of English learners, the ELL students were concentrated in

AT ISSUE

Is bilingual education best for English-language learners?

YES — James Crawford
President, Institute for Language and Education Policy; coauthor, English Learners in American Classrooms: 101 Questions, 101 Answers

Written for *CQ Researcher*, November 2009

Bilingual education, perhaps the least understood program in our public schools, also turns out to be among the most beneficial. Its effectiveness — both in teaching English and in fostering academic learning in English — has been validated in study after study.

Yet U.S. media rarely report such findings. All too often, bilingualism is portrayed as a political controversy rather than a set of pedagogical challenges, a conflict over immigration instead of an effort to turn language "problems" into classroom resources.

In education, of course, there is no one-size-fits-all. What works for one student or group of students will not necessarily work for others. All things being equal, however, a large and consistent body of research shows that bilingual education is a superior way to teach English-language learners. Building on — rather than discarding — students' native-language skills creates a stronger foundation for success in English and academics.

This is a counterintuitive finding for many Americans, so it needs some explaining. Why does bilingual education work? Three reasons:

- When students receive some lessons in their native language, the teacher does not need to "dumb down" instruction in simplified English. So they have access to the same challenging curriculum as their English-speaking peers, rather than falling behind.
- The more these students progress in academic subjects, the more contextual knowledge they acquire to make sense of lessons in English. And the more "comprehensible input" they receive in English, the faster they acquire the language.
- Reading provides a foundation for all learning. It is much more efficiently mastered in a language that children understand. As they acquire English, these literacy skills are easily transferred to the new language. Once you can read, you can read!

Finally, let's consider the alternative: all-English "immersion." Independent studies have shown that after several years of such programs in California and Arizona, there has been no benefit for children learning English. In fact, the "achievement gap" between these students and fluent English speakers seems to be increasing.

Unfortunately, so is the gap between research and policy. Bilingual education has fallen out of favor politically for reasons that have nothing to do with its academic effectiveness. If we seriously hope to integrate immigrants as productive members of our society, that will have to change.

NO — Rosalie Pedalino Porter
Board member, Center for Equal Opportunity

Written for *CQ Researcher*, December 2009

Bilingual education is the least effective method for teaching English-language learners. To meet the stated goals of federal and state laws of the past 40 years — that students would learn the English language rapidly and master school subjects taught in English — the experimental, theoretical model called bilingual education is a demonstrable, documented failure.

As a Spanish-English bilingual teacher in Massachusetts — the first state to mandate bilingual education — I saw firsthand the model's inadequacies. Our students were taught all subjects in Spanish most of the school day and provided brief English lessons. They were segregated by language and ethnicity in substantially separate classrooms for three to six years. The costs to school districts for this separate program are not as damaging as "the negative effect on English-language learner achievement," as documented in the 2009 study by the Texas Public Policy Foundation.

Reliable research was never the strong point in reporting on bilingual education in its first two decades. Valid studies of student achievement both in learning English and school subjects began to be published in the 1980s. Reliable studies must include two similar groups of students (socioeconomic status, level of English fluency), one enrolled in a bilingual program, one enrolled in an English-immersion program. At the end of two, three or four years, an objective assessment of which group of students showed measurable success in English language and academic learning can be determined.

From Dade County, Fla., in 1988, El Paso, Texas, in 1992, New York City in 1995, and numerous reports from California and Arizona over the past 10 years, English-immersion students outscored their counterparts in bilingual programs both in rapid acquisition of English language and literacy and on state tests of reading and math. The evidence for the superiority of English immersion surely influenced public opinion in the initiative referenda that legally threw out bilingual teaching by citizen vote in California (1998), Arizona (2000) and Massachusetts (2002). Of the 10 states that originally mandated native-language instruction bilingual programs, only four remain: Illinois, New Jersey, New York and Texas.

The debate is effectively over. A high accolade comes from the U. S. Supreme Court's recent ruling in the *Flores* case, which found "documented academic support for the view that structured English immersion is significantly more effective than bilingual education."

central city schools with higher average enrollment and higher student-to-teacher ratios than other public schools in the state. The schools with concentrated ELL populations also had a "substantially greater proportion" of students who qualified for free or reduced-price school lunches.[30]

Significantly, Fry found that the English learners' achievement gap was narrower in schools that had "at least a minimum threshold number of white students." Barth similarly sees what she calls "linguistically isolated" schools as a substantial cause of the achievement gap.

"We sometimes give the least to the kids and the schools that have the least to begin with," Barth says. "Those schools have greater challenges and aren't being given much to work with in terms of resources."

Fighting in Court

Civil rights lawyers in two states with substantial Latino populations are waging legal battles begun decades ago to improve English-language instruction for Spanish-speaking students.

Lower federal court judges issued broad rulings in both cases telling state officials in Arizona to increase spending on English learners and in Texas to improve services and monitoring for English learners in secondary schools. But plaintiffs in both cases suffered setbacks earlier this year.

The 5th U.S. Circuit Court of Appeals issued a stay of the lower court judge's January 2008 order in the Texas case in February pending its own review of the decision. A three-judge panel is currently deliberating on the case following oral arguments on June 2.[31]

The Supreme Court's June 26 decision in the Arizona case (*Horne v. Flores*) sent that 17-year-old lawsuit back to federal district court in Phoenix. The ruling requires Judge Collins to reconsider the effort by Superintendent of Instruction Horne either to modify or dissolve the injunction requiring more funding first issued by Judge Marquez in 2000 and reaffirmed by Collins in 2006.

Today, plaintiffs' lawyers in both cases say the state education systems are failing the public schools' English learners, who number more than 600,000 in Texas and nearly 170,000 in Arizona.

Roger Rice, an attorney who has worked on the Texas case since the early 1970s, blames poor performance and

Lourdes Carmona teaches Spanish pronunciation to first-graders at Birdwell Elementary School in Tyler, Texas. She was recruited from Spain, along with her husband, to teach Spanish-speaking youngsters in their native language.

high dropout rates for English learners in secondary schools in part on lack of monitoring by state officials. "The Texas language program, particularly at the secondary level, is failing," says Rice, founder of the Massachusetts-based advocacy group META (Multicultural Education Training and Advocacy). "And Texas has not evaluated the program to know why it's failing and has not made the changes to make it succeed."

In Arizona, plaintiffs' attorney Hogan says the state's model of four-hour pullouts for language instruction for English learners segregates them unnecessarily and unlawfully. "This is classic segregation," Hogan says. "Kids in these classes are regarded by others as dumb, as second-class citizens."

State officials are defending their programs in both cases. Lawyers for the Texas Education Agency told the appeals court in June that a computerized tracking system adequately monitors performance of English learners. They also urged the appeals court to dismiss the entire case, originally filed by the Justice Department as a desegregation suit in 1970 and expanded by Latino advocacy groups in 1975 to specifically address English-learners' rights under the federal Equal Educational Opportunities Act.

Lawyers representing Horne and state legislative leaders told Supreme Court justices that the mandate for increased funding originally issued in 2000 had been superseded by the voter-approved decision to shift from bilingual to English immersion and by the passage of the federal No Child Left Behind Act. Since the ruling, Horne has continued to defend the new system. "Kids who come to this country need to learn English quickly," he says.

The Texas case lay dormant for a quarter-century after the 5th Circuit appeals court in 1982 reversed a ruling by U.S. District Judge Wayne Justice two years earlier that the state was not providing equal opportunities to English learners as the federal law required. The appeals court noted that the Texas legislature had passed a bilingual-education law and held that the state was entitled to time to bring schools into compliance.

With assistance from MALDEF, Rice moved to reopen the Texas case in 2006 after education officials decided to drop active monitoring of classes and materials for English learners. Justice initially ruled in 2007 that state officials were complying with the ruling, but he reversed himself in 2008 in an 88-page decision sharply critical of poor performance and high dropout rates for English learners in secondary schools.

In the Arizona case, Collins ruled in 2007 that the changes in educational policy and the additional funding approved by the legislature in 2006 did not solve what he termed the "resource" problem. The 9th U.S. Circuit Court of Appeals upheld his decision to leave the injunction in place, but the Supreme Court's conservative majority said Collins had given inadequate consideration to the various changes.

Significantly for the plaintiffs in Arizona and in other cases, however, the justices rejected the state's argument that compliance with the No Child Left Behind Act was sufficient to establish compliance with the earlier law requiring equal opportunities for English learners. The act's funding and its reporting and assessment schemes could be relevant, Alito explained, but not necessarily determinative under the 1974 act.

Appeals court judges closed the hearing in the Texas case in June by cautioning lawyers not to expect a quick ruling. In Arizona, opposing lawyers submitted new filings to Collins earlier in the fall; Collins is to hold a hearing on Dec. 14 to determine whether to limit further proceedings to Nogales schools or to apply any ruling statewide.

OUTLOOK
Getting Results?

Two well-regarded school districts in the Washington, D.C., suburbs take different approaches to teaching English learners. Administrators in Montgomery County, Md., and Arlington, Va., both say they practice "immersion" as the best way to teach English to Latino students who enter their school systems more familiar with Spanish than with the nation's dominant tongue. But immersion has different meanings for the two systems.[32]

In Montgomery County, Spanish-speaking students at Sargent Shriver Elementary School — about half the student body — are immersed in English. ESL teachers "plug in" to mainstream classrooms to help English learners along or "pull out" students for individualized or group tutoring. Karen Woodson, the school district's head of ESL programs, says flexibility is important but stresses that the system strongly opposes use of native-language instruction to help students acquire English-language proficiency.

Across the Potomac River in Arlington, some Latino students are immersed in two languages: Spanish and English. At Francis Scott Key Elementary School ("Escuela Key"), each class is divided between Spanish and English speakers, and instruction is equally divided between the two languages. Principal Marjorie Myers says she favors dual-language immersion as the best long-term strategy for English learners even at the expense of short-term gains on language-proficiency tests.

In its influential *Castañeda* decision on the rights of English learners almost three decades ago, the federal appeals court in New Orleans said that courts ruling on such cases should examine three factors: whether a school system was using a program based on "sound educational theory," whether adequate resources were being provided and whether the program was proving to be effective.

In the intervening decades, many school systems picked one educational theory — bilingual education — or another — English immersion. The issue of adequate resources is muddy, with bilingual-education advocates claiming their approach is both better and cheaper. But the question of results appears less ambiguous. English learners lag in academic performance and in graduation rates, and the gaps do not appear to be narrowing.

With the number of English learners in public schools rapidly increasing — projected to be one-fourth of the school population by 2025 — the need to close that gap will only increase.[33] "It's going to be a long-term persistent problem," says Stanford professor Hakuta. "The number of English learners has increased to the point where it's no longer an issue like special education, a small subset. In many districts, it's a majority of the students."

Since the 1980s, teaching English learners has been an intensely political issue. English-immersion advocate Porter notes that former Boston University president John Silber, a critic of bilingualism and multiculturalism, once called English-language learning a "third-rail" issue — dangerous for politicians to touch.

In recent years, however, the politicization of the issue appears to be ebbing somewhat. "The black and white distinctions that existed before 1998 are no longer there," says Don Soifer, education analyst with the pro-English Lexington Institute.

In California, for example, the state's English-only initiative — Proposition 227 — remains on the books but has not stopped the Ventura County Unified School District from creating dual-language immersion programs at eight elementary- and middle-school campuses. "I think parents throughout the state recognize the value of having their kids be bilingual and biliterate," says associate superintendent Roger Rice.[34]

Bilingual-education advocates are hoping for support for their view from the Obama administration. The administration's stated agenda supports "transitional bilingual education" and promises to help English learners by "holding schools accountable for making sure these students complete school." The administration's education initiatives since January have given no emphasis to the issue, however, and the Education Department's Office of English Language Acquisition is operating with an interim director.

For educators, the next big event in Washington is the anticipated fight in Congress over reauthorizing the No Child Left Behind Act. Experts and advocates on both sides of the language-instruction issue applaud the act's goal — and 2014 deadline — of requiring language proficiency for English learners. But the National Education Association, the powerful teachers' union, wants more testing to be done in students' native language. Testing English learners in English "may be setting these students up for more failure," the NEA says in a policy brief.[35]

Despite the political controversies, some experts are predicting progress for English learners. "What we have now is good methodology about what works," says Barth with the school boards' Center for Public Education. "As we're collecting more data, we're seeing gains among English-language learners, and we're finding out more and more about what propels those gains. The more that information gets out, the politics will quiet down."

NOTES

1. Flores was interviewed in Spanish by *CQ Researcher* staff writer Peter Katel. See also Eddi Trevizo and Pat Kossan, "Mom at Head of Suit Still Worried About English Learners," *The Arizona Republic*, June 26, 2009, p. 15.

2. The decision is *Horne v. Flores*, 557 U.S. — (June 25, 2009). For coverage, see Pat Kossan, "A Win for State on English Learners," *The Arizona Republic*, June 26, 2009, p. 1.

3. For previous coverage, see these *CQ Researcher* reports: Craig Donegan, "Debate Over Bilingualism," Jan. 19, 1996, pp. 49-72; and Richard L. Worsnop, "Bilingual Education," Aug. 13, 1993, pp. 697-720; and these in *Editorial Research Reports*: Sarah Glazer, "Bilingual Education: Does It Work?," March 11, 1988; pp. 125-140, and Sandra Stencel, "Bilingual Education," Aug. 19, 1977, pp. 617-636.

4. For background, see Barbara Mantel, "No Child Left Behind," *CQ Researcher*, May 27, 2005, pp. 469-492.

5. Claude Goldenberg, "Teaching English Language Learners: What the Research Does — and Does Not — Show," *American Educator*, summer 2008, www.aft.org/pubs-reports/american_educator/issues/summer08/goldenberg.pdf. Goldenberg cited A. M. Zehler, *et al.*, "Descriptive Study of Services to LEP0 Students and LEP Students with Disabilities, Vol. 1, Research Report," Development Associates, Inc., 2003.

6. Virginia P. Collier and Wayne P. Thomas, *Educating English Learners for a Transformed World* (2009), pp. 3-4. The authors, professors emeriti at George Mason University, in Fairfax, Va., identify themselves as educational consultants on their Web site, www.thomasandcollier.com.
7. *Ibid.*, p. 48. Statistical chart appears at p. 55.
8. "What research shows about English language learners: At a glance," Center for Public Education undated, www.centerforpubliceducation.org/site/apps/nlnet/content3.aspx?c=lvIXIiN0JwE&b=5127871&content_id={DE9F2763-8DA4-4C2A-B3D1-9AEF8B3AEDA1}&notoc=1.
9. James Crawford, *Educating English Learners: Language Diversity in the Classroom* (5th ed.), 2004.
10. Collin Hitt, "Charter Schools and Changing Neighborhoods: Hispanic Students and English Learners in Chicago," Lexington Institute/Illinois Policy Institute, Sept. 29, 2009, www.lexingtoninstitute.org/library/resources/documents/Education/FinalProof9.29.09.pdf.
11. See Mary Ann Zehr, "Nurturing 'School Minds': Through order and English immersion, a network of charter schools strives to turn Latino students into informed citizens and leaders inside and outside the community," *Education Week*, Oct. 7, 2009, p. 24.
12. *Horne v. Flores, op. cit.*, p. 24 of slip opinion and footnote 10.
13. Kelly Torrance, "Immersion Not Submersion: Converting English Learner Programs from Bilingual Education to Structured English Immersion in California and Elsewhere," October 2005; and "Immersion Not Submersion: Volume II: Lessons from Three California School Districts' Switch from Bilingual Education to Structured Immersion," March 2006, www.lexingtoninstitute.org/library/resources/documents/Education/immersion-not-submersion-converting-english.pdf.
14. Stephen Krashen, "Proposition 227 and Skyrocketing Test Scores in California: An Urban Legend," *Educational Leadership*, December 2004/January 2005, www.sdkrashen.com/articles/prop227/index.html.
15. See Arizona Department of Education, "The Effects of Bilingual Education Programs and Structured English Immersion Programs on Student Achievement: A Large-Scale Comparison," July 2004, http://epsl.asu.edu/epru/articles/EPRU-0408-66-OWI.pdf. The report is identified as a draft, but no later version was prepared.
16. Kate Mahoney, Jeff MacSwan, Tom Haladyna and David Garcia, "*Castañeda*'s Third Prong: Evaluating the Achievement of Arizona's English Learners Under Restrictive Language Policy," in Patricia Gandara and Megan Hopkins, *Forbidden Language: English Learners and Restrictive Language Policies* (forthcoming January 2010).
17. Background drawn from Guadalupe San Miguel Jr., *Contested Policy: The Rise and Fall of Federal Bilingual Education in the United States, 1960-2001* (2004). See also James Crawford, *Educating English Learners: Language Diversity in the Classroom* (5th ed.,), 2004; Rosalie Pedalino Porter, *Forked Tongue: The Politics of Bilingual Education* (2d ed.), 1996.
18. The decision is *Lau v. Nichols*, 414 U.S. 563 (1974). San Miguel writes erroneously at one point that the court decided the case on constitutional grounds.
19. Quoted in Crawford, *op. cit.*, p. 120.
20. The citation is 648 F.2d 989 (5th Cir. 1981). Despite the favorable legal standard, the defendant Raymondville Independent School District, in south Texas near the Mexican border, ultimately won a ruling that it was providing adequate bilingual education to the Mexican-American students in the system. See Richard R. Valencia, *Chicano Students and the Courts: The Mexican American Struggle for Educational Equality* (2008), pp. 187-191.
21. Crawford, *op. cit.*, pp. 148-152 in 4th ed.
22. Crawford, *op. cit.*, pp. 356-357.
23. Quoted in *ibid.*, p. 355.
24. All three quoted in Mary Ann Zehr, "Guides Avoid Bilingual versus English-Only Issue," *Education Week*, Nov. 8, 2006, p. 20.
25. Linda Jacobson, "Prop. 227 Seen as Focusing on 'Wrong Issue,'" *Education Week*, March 1, 2006, p. 18.
26. Mary Ann Zehr, "NAEP Scores in States That Cut Bilingual Ed Fuel Concerns on ELLs," *Education

Week. May 14, 2008, p. 14. NAEP — commonly called the nation's report card — stands for National Assessment of Educational Progress.

27. Richard Fry, "How Far Behind in Math and Reading are English Language Learners?," Pew Hispanic Center, June 6, 2007, http://pewhispanic.org/files/reports/76.pdf. The report does not include national averages, which were supplied from the National Assessment of Educational Progress Web site: http://nationsreportcard.gov/reading_math_2005/.

28. Data from edweek.org, the Web site of *Education Week* and *Teachers Magazine.* See "English Language Learners" page on www.edcounts.org/createtable/viewtable.php.

29. Collier and Thomas, *op. cit.*, p. 3.

30. Richard Fry, "The Role of Schools in the English Language Learner Achievement Gap," Pew Hispanic Center, June 26, 2008, http://pewhispanic.org/reports/report.php?ReportID=89.

31. The case is *United States v. Texas*, 08-40858. The Latino advocacy groups GI Forum and League of United Latin American Citizens (LULAC) intervened in 1975 in what was originally a school desegregation case to raise English-language learning issues under the Equal Educational Opportunities Act of 1974.

32. Reporting by editorial intern Emily DeRuy, University of California, San Diego.

33. See Goldenberg, *op. cit.*, p. 10.

34. Quoted in Cheri Carlson, "Three more schools add bilingual immersion programs," *Ventura County Star*, July 15, 2009.

35. "English Language Learners Face Unique Challenges," National Education Association, fall 2008, www.nea.org/assets/docs/mf_PB05_ELL.pdf.

BIBLIOGRAPHY
Books

Collier, Virginia P., and Wayne P. Thomas, *Educating English Learners for a Transformed World,* **Fuente Press, 2009.**
Two former George Mason University professors specializing in research for "at-risk" students examine different methods for teaching English-language learners and repeat their research findings that English learners benefit from additional time in native-language instruction. The book closes with 11 recommendations for educators to follow in designing programs for English learners. Includes nine-page list of references.

Crawford, James, *Educating English Learners: Language Diversity in the Classroom* **(5th ed.), Bilingual Education Services, 2004.**
The longtime advocate for bilingual education provides a comprehensive history of language-education policies against the backdrop of growing language diversity due to increased immigration. Crawford, a former education reporter, served as executive director of the National Association for Bilingual Education and now writes and advocates on bilingual education as head of the Institute for Language Education and Policy. Includes chapter notes, 24-page compilation of sources and suggested readings.

Gandara, Patricia, and Megan Hopkins (eds.), *Forbidden Language: English Learners and Restrictive Language Policies,* **Teachers College Press, 2010.**
The book examines the most up-to-date research on the impact of "restrictive language policies" adopted in three states by ballot measures: Arizona, California and Massachusetts. Gandara is professor of education at the University of California-Los Angeles; Hopkins is a doctoral student at UCLA's Graduate School of Education and Information Studies.

Porter, Rosalie Pedalino, *Forked Tongue: The Politics of Bilingual Education* **(2d ed.), Transaction, 1996.**
A prominent critic of bilingual education argues in favor of early and intensive instruction in English with no separation of language-minority children from fellow students. Porter served as director of language-instruction programs in Newton, Mass., in the 1980s and later as director of the READ Institute (Research in English Acquisition and Development), which has now been folded into the Center for Equal Opportunity. Includes chapter notes, four-page list of references. Porter is author most recently of the autobiographical *American Immigrant: My Life in Three Languages* (iUniverse, 2009).

San Miguel, Guadalupe Jr., *Contested Policy: The Rise and Fall of Federal Bilingual Education in the United States, 1960-2001,* **University of North Texas Press, 2004.**

The compact history traces the history of federal policy on education for English-language learners from the genesis of the Bilingual Education Act in the 1960s through its repeal with the No Child Left Behind Act in 2001. San Miguel is a professor of history at the University of Houston. Includes chapter notes, 45-page bibliographical essay organized by time period.

Schmid, Ronald Sr., *Language Policy and Identity in the United States,* **Temple University Press, 2000.**

A professor of political science at California State University-Long Beach examines the debate over bilingual education in the United States in the broader context of language policy with comparisons to policies in other multilingual countries. Includes chapter notes, 18-page list of references.

Valencia, Richard R., *Chicano Students and the Courts,* **New York University Press, 2008.**

A 46-page chapter sketches the history of bilingual education for Mexican-Americans since the Mexican-American War, discusses major bilingual-education suits in the 1970s and '80s and briefly treats the passage of state "English-only" initiatives and the repeal of the federal Bilingual Education Act. Valencia is a professor with the Center for Mexican American Studies at the University of Texas in Austin.

Articles

Goldenberg, Claude, "Teaching English Language Learners: What the Research Does — and Does Not — Show," American Educator, summer 2008, www.aft.org/pubs-reports/american_educator/issues/summer08/goldenberg.pdf.

A professor of education at Stanford University delineates three conclusions from the research on English learners, including the key finding that teaching students in their first language promotes higher levels of reading achievement in English. Adapted from "Improving Achievement for English Language Learners, in Susan B. Neuman (ed.), *Educating the Other America: Top Experts Tackle Poverty, Literacy, and Achievement in Our Schools* (Paul H. Brooke Publishing Co., 2008).

Reports and Studies

Rossell, Christine H., "Dismantling Bilingual Education, Implementing English Immersion: The California Initiative," Public Policy Institute of California, 2002, www.eric.ed.gov/ERICWebPortal/custom/portlets/recordDetails/detailmini.jsp?_nfpb=true&_&ERICExtSearch_SearchValue_0=ED467043&ERICExtSearch_SearchType_0=no&accno=ED467043.

The detailed report by the Boston University political scientist concludes that Proposition 227, the California initiative that restricted bilingual education in public schools, may have benefited English learners but cautions that English learners continued to suffer achievement gaps because of immigration status and family backgrounds.

For More Information

American Unity Legal Defense Fund, P.O. Box 420, Warrenton, VA 20187; www.americanunity.org. An educational organization that promotes conservative immigration reform in the legal arena.

Asian American Justice Center, 1140 Connecticut Ave., N.W., Suite 1200, Washington, DC 20036; (202) 296-2300; www.advancingequality.org. Works to advance human and civil rights for Asian Americans by providing them the tools and support needed to participate in the democratic process.

Asian American Legal Defense and Education Fund, 99 Hudson St., 12 th Floor, New York NY 10013; (212) 966-5932; www.aaldef.org. Promotes the civil rights of Asian Americans through litigation, advocacy, education and community organizing.

Center for Equal Opportunity, 7700 Leesburg Pike, Suite 231, Falls Church, VA 22043; (703) 442-0066; www.ceousa.org. Promotes color-blind public policies and seeks to block the expansion and use of racial preferences in employment, education and voting by promoting the assimilation of immigrants and opposing teaching in students' native languages.

Congressional Hispanic Caucus Institute, 911 2nd St., N.E., Washington, DC 20002; (202) 543-1771; www.chci.org. Helps increase opportunities for Hispanics to participate in the American policy-making process by offering educational and leadership-development programs.

English First, 666 Fu Zhou Rd., Shanghai, China 200001; +86 21 6133 6262; www.englishfirst.com. The world's largest private education company, specializing in language training, educational tours and cultural exchange.

Institute for Language and Education Policy, P.O. Box 19025, Portland, OR 97280; www.elladvocates.org. Promoting research-based policies in serving English and heritage language learners to ensure that policies for serving children reflect the latest research about language and education.

Mexican American Legal Defense and Education Fund, 1016 16th St., N.W., Suite 100, Washington, DC 20036; (202) 293-2828; www.maldef.org. Promotes equality and justice through advocacy, litigation, public policy and education in the areas of employment, immigrants' rights, political access, voting rights and language rights.

National Association for Bilingual Education, 8701 Georgia Ave., N.W., Suite 611, Silver Spring, MD 20910; (240) 450-3700; www.nabe.org. Represents both English-language learners and bilingual education professionals through affiliate organizations in 23 states.

National Clearinghouse for English Language Acquisition, 2011 I St., N.W., Suite 300, Washington, DC 20006; (202) 321-6223; www.ncela.gwu.edu. Supports the U.S. Department of Education's Office of English Language Acquisition.

NCLR (National Council of La Raza), 1126 16th St., N.W., Washington, DC 20036; (202) 785-1670; www.nclr.org. The largest national Hispanic civil rights and advocacy organization in the U.S. works to improve opportunities for Hispanic Americans through applied research, policy analysis and advocacy.

National Education Association, 1201 16th St., N.W., Washington, DC 20036; (202) 833-4000; www.nea.org. An organization of 3.2 million members aimed at promoting the right of every child to quality public education, as well as advocating for education professionals.

National School Boards Association, 1680 Duke Street, Alexandria, VA 22314; (703) 838-6722; www.nsba.org. Seeks excellence and equity in public education through school board leadership in all communities.

Office of English Language Acquisition, Language Enhancement, and Academic Achievement for Limited English Proficient Students, 400 Maryland Ave., S.W., Washington, DC 20202; (202) 401-1423; www.ed.gov/about/offices/list/oela/index.html. Provides national leadership to help English-language learners and immigrant students attain English proficiency.

12

Fixing Urban Schools

Marcia Clemmitt and Charles S. Clark

Philadelphia police officers guard West Philadelphia High School on March 12, 2007, where a teacher was attacked by three students three days earlier. Experts suggest that a "behavior gap" between black and white students parallels the academic achievement gap between high- and low-performing students.

"I didn't go to school much in elementary, and they saw me as a bad girl" who skipped class, says Jeanette, a Houston high-school student who dropped out several times but is struggling to get a diploma. After her parents divorced when she was in grade school, she fell into a pattern typical of urban students, repeatedly "switching schools," sometimes living with her mother, sometimes her father and sometimes with an aunt who "didn't make us go to school" at all.[1]

In middle school, Jeanette began taking drugs but later got involved in sports, which motivated her to try, sometimes successfully, to keep up her grades and stay off drugs. Some teachers have tried hard to help her, but like many troubled urban kids, she pulls back. "If I need help . . . I don't say anything. . . . They have to ask me." Still, Jeanette is determined to avoid the fate of her parents, who dropped out of school when they had her. At the time, her mother was only 13. "I don't want to live like them. I want to have a better life," she says.

Jeanette typifies the daunting challenge that urban schools face in promoting academic achievement among children whose lives have been disordered and impoverished.

Most middle-class families with children have moved to the suburbs, leaving urban schools today overwhelmingly populated by low-income, African-American and Hispanic students. "Nationally, about 50 percent of all black and Latino students attend schools in which 75 percent or more of the students are low-income, as measured by eligibility for free and reduced-price lunch," according to the Center for Civil Rights at the University

From *CQ Researcher*,
April 27, 2007 (updated June 5, 2012).

Minority Districts Often Get Less Funding

In 28 states, school districts with high-minority enrollments received less per-pupil funding (shown as a negative number, top map) than districts with low-minority levels. For example, in Illinois, the highest-minority districts received an average of $1,223 less per student than the lowest-minority districts. In 21 states, the highest-minority districts received more per pupil (shown as a positive number, bottom map), than the districts with the lowest-minority enrollments. For example, in Georgia, the highest-poverty districts received $566 per student more than the lowest-poverty districts.

Minority Funding Gaps by State, 2004

Note: Hawaii is not shown because data are not available.
Source: Funding Gaps 2006, The Education Trust, 2006

of North Carolina. Only 5 percent of white students attend such high-poverty schools.[2]

These schools, mostly urban, aren't making the grade, even in the context of lagging achievement in American schools overall.

Although states show significant variations, nationwide "71 percent of eighth-graders are not reading at grade level," and the percentage shoots up to between 80 and 90 percent for students of color, says former Gov. Bob Wise, D-W.Va., now president of the Alliance for Excellent Education, a broad-based coalition that advocates for academically stronger high schools.

Furthermore, of the approximately 15,000 U.S. high schools, 2,000 — mostly in cities — account for half of the nation's school dropouts, says Wise.

When President George W. Bush joined Massachusetts Sen. Edward M. Kennedy and other congressional Democrats to enact the No Child Left Behind Act (NCLB) in 2002, a key aim was requiring states to report achievement scores for all student groups. That ensured that lagging scores of low-income and minority students wouldn't be masked by having only state or district overall average scores reported.[3]

This year, Congress is expected to provide funding to keep the law in operation, but there's considerable disagreement about where federal education law should go next, and lawmakers may wait until next year to consider revisions.

NCLB's test-score reporting requirements "make it more possible to look at whether schools are doing well just for more affluent students or for poor students" as well, and that's valuable, says Jeffrey Henig, professor of political science and education at Columbia University's Teachers College.

But some supporters, including President Bush, say the NCLB has done more than just improve data-gathering, arguing that the law itself has pushed achievement upward. "Fourth-graders are reading better. They've made more progress in five years than in the previous 28 years combined," he said on March 2.[4]

Many education analysts disagree with that rosy assessment. The small improvement in fourth-grade reading and mathematics scores is part of a long-term trend, which began years before NCLB was even enacted, said Harvard University Professor of Education Daniel M. Koretz. "There's not any evidence that shows anything has changed" since NCLB, he said.[5]

And for urban schools, the post-NCLB picture is especially grim.

Of the non-achieving schools in New York state, for example, 90 percent are in cities and 80 percent in the state's five biggest cities, says David Hursh, an associate professor of teaching and curriculum at the University of Rochester's Margaret Warner Graduate School of Education.

The gap between average reading scores of black and white fourth-graders narrowed by only one point on the 500-point National Assessment of Educational Progress test (NAEP) between 2002 and 2005, and the narrowing appears to be part of a long-term trend, since it narrowed by three points between 1998 and 2005. Between 2002 and 2005, the reading-score gap between white and black eighth-graders actually widened, from 25 points to 28 points.[6]

The continuing severe achievement gap, newly highlighted by NCLB's data-reporting requirements, leaves lawmakers and educators scratching their heads about what to do next.

Some analysts say lagging achievement in urban schools demonstrates that poor families in poor communities require much more intense interventions than middle-class students, including better teachers and longer school days as well as improved health care, nutrition and parenting education.

A public school enrolling mainly middle-class white students has a one-in-four chance of producing good test scores, across years and in different subject matter, according to Douglas N. Harris, assistant professor of education policy at the University of Wisconsin, Madison. A school with a predominantly low-income minority population has a 1-in-300 chance of doing so.[7]

Experts blame the poor outcome on the fact that urban schools, like all schools, are staffed and organized to provide substantial extra help to only 15 percent of students and curriculum enrichment to another 15, while "the students in the middle are supposed to take care of themselves," says Robert Balfanz, associate research scientist at the Johns Hopkins University Center on the Social Organization of Schools and associate director of the Talent Development High School program, a reform initiative in 33 schools nationwide. The formula for extra help fits most suburban schools, "but in urban schools 50 to 60 percent, and sometimes up to

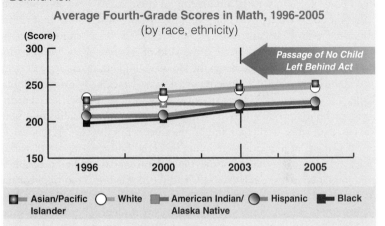

All Racial/Ethnic Groups Improved on Test

Fourth-graders in all racial and ethnic groups began modestly improving in math on the National Assessment for Educational Progress several years before passage of the No Child Left Behind Act.

Average Fourth-Grade Scores in Math, 1996-2005 (by race, ethnicity)

* Some data for 1996 and 2000 not available

Source: U.S. Department of Education, National Center for Education Statistics

80 percent, of the kids are 'high-needs,' defined as English-as-a-second-language students, special-education students or students below grade level or with severe attendance problems.

"We're not set up to respond when that many kids need one-on-one tutoring, monitoring of their attendance on a daily basis, [or] people calling up to say, 'Glad you came today,' " Balfanz says.

One of the biggest problems is the kind of "student mobility" experienced by Jeanette, the Houston dropout.

"Homelessness is much underreported," says James F. Lytle, a professor at the University of Pennsylvania and former school superintendent in Trenton, N.J. "Statistics are based on who's in shelters and on the streets. But 20 to 30 percent of our kids were living in 'serial households' on a day-to-day basis," or moving about from parents to grandparents to relatives to friends — not living in the same house all the time.

Inner-city schools have a 40 to 50 percent student-mobility rate, which means up to half the students change schools at least once a year because of parents losing or changing jobs, evictions and other factors, says Columbia University's Henig. That disrupts students' ability to keep up with work and build relationships with the adults in a school.

In addition, city students miss school for a wide range of reasons, including high asthma rates; lack of school buses, forcing kids to get to school on their own, often through unsafe neighborhoods; and family responsibilities, like caring for younger siblings.

"Imagine the teacher's dilemma in a classroom where the population is different every day," says Balfanz.

But some conservative analysts argue that a large proportion of high-needs students is still no reason for schools to fail.

"Schools frequently cite social problems like poverty . . . and bad parenting as excuses for their own poor performance," said Jay P. Greene, a senior fellow at the Manhattan Institute, a conservative think tank. "This argument that schools are helpless in the face of social problems is not supported by hard evidence. . . . The truth is that certain schools do a strikingly better job than others," including public, private and charter schools.[8]

Some educators say one solution for low-quality urban schools is establishing publicly funded "charter" schools and awarding vouchers for private-school tuition.[9] When choice is expanded, "urban public schools that once had a captive clientele must improve the education they provide or else students . . . will go elsewhere," said Greene.[10]

But others argue that lessons from successful urban schools, including charters, demonstrate that raising low-income students' achievement requires resources and staff commitment that may be tough for the nation to muster.

"Teachers in high-poverty urban schools are as much as 50 percent more likely to . . . leave than those in low-poverty schools," in part because of the intensity of the work, according to researchers at the University of California, Santa Cruz.[11]

A second-grade teacher fluent in Spanish who reported working 10 hours a day, six days a week said she'd probably stop teaching when she had children: "It's too time-consuming and energy-draining," she said.[12]

"None of the teachers in our sample could conceive of being a successful urban teacher without an extraordinary — perhaps unsustainable — commitment to the work," the researchers commented.[13]

Not just schools but communities must help in the effort to improve students' performance.

"There ought to be a parade through the heart of town" every time a student achieves an academic goal, says Hugh B. Price, a fellow at the Brookings Institution, a liberal think tank. "We need to wrap and cloak kids in this message of achievement." That's how the military successfully trains soldiers, Price says. "They will praise anything that's good."

Schools and communities also have a role in helping parents better equip their children for school, says Mayor Douglas H. Palmer of Trenton, N.J., president of the National Conference of Democratic Mayors. "You don't have to be rich to talk to your child, help her build vocabulary and learn to reason and negotiate," as psychologists recommend, he says. "We can help parents with these skills."

As educators and lawmakers debate the next steps to improving urban schools, here are some of the questions being asked:

Has the No Child Left Behind law helped urban students?

NCLB was intended to improve overall academic achievement and raise achievement for minority and low-income students, in particular, mainly by requiring more student testing, getting schools to report test data separately for student groups including minorities and the poor and requiring schools to employ better-qualified teachers.

The law, scheduled for reauthorization this year, gets praise for focusing attention on the so-called achievement gap between minority and low-income students and their middle-class counterparts. But critics say the legislation doesn't do enough to assure that low-performing urban schools get the excellent teachers they need.

Student achievement also has improved slightly under the law, some advocates point out. "Is NCLB really paying off? The answer is yes," U.S. Chamber of Commerce Senior Vice President Arthur J. Rothkopf told a joint House-Senate committee hearing on March 13. While current testing data is still "abysmal," it nevertheless "represents improvement from where this nation was" before the law.

The law has benefited urban schools by raising reading scores for African-American and Hispanic fourth- and eighth-graders and math scores for African-American and Hispanic fourth-graders to "all-time highs." Achievement gaps in reading and math between white fourth-graders and African-American and Hispanic fourth-graders also have diminished since NCLB, he noted.[14]

NCLB's data-reporting requirements have "lifted the carpet" to reveal two previously unrecognized facts about American education — "the continuing underperformance of the whole system and the achievement gap" for low-income and minority students, says Daniel A. Domenech, senior vice president and top urban-education adviser for publisher McGraw-Hill Education and former superintendent of Virginia's vast Fairfax County Public Schools.[15]

And while some critics complain that NCLB gave the federal government too much say over education — traditionally a state and local matter — "there needs to be a strong federal role for these kids" in low-income urban schools "because they have been left behind," says Gary Ratner, a public-interest lawyer who is founding executive director of the advocacy group Citizens for Effective Schools. "States and localities have not stepped up."

Now NCLB "has got the country's attention," and when Congress reauthorizes the law, "the federal role can be redirected to focus on Title I schools" — those serving a large proportion of disadvantaged students — "and do more of the things that professional educators support," Ratner says.

NCLB's requirement that every school "have very qualified teachers is good," says Gary Orfield, a professor of social policy at the Harvard Graduate School of Education and director of The Civil Rights Project.

But critics argue that NCLB doesn't put muscle behind the high-quality teacher requirement and sets unrealistic goals and timetables for school progress.

NCLB actually "incentivizes teachers to leave failing schools," the last thing lawmakers intended, says Jennifer King-Rice, an economist who is associate professor of education policy at the University of Maryland, College Park. "Teachers say, 'I can't produce the AYP [average yearly progress] results'" the law calls for in low-performing schools with few resources and, frustrated, go elsewhere, she says. Nevertheless, it's still unclear whether and how the government can enforce the qualified-teacher rule.

The law provides no additional funding to help schools meet the teacher-quality goal, said Richard J. Murnane, professor of education and society at the Harvard Graduate School of Education. "Teaching in these schools is extremely difficult work," and "very few school districts provide extra pay or other inducements to attract talented teachers to these schools.[16]

"As a result, all too often these schools are left with the teachers other schools don't want," he continued. "And the teachers who do have options exercise seniority rights to leave . . . as soon as they can."[17]

The achievement targets set by NCLB are panned by many. The main goal schools must meet is moving kids over a standardized-testing threshold from "basic" or "below basic" understanding of reading and math to a "proficient" level or above. But focusing on that narrow goal as the key measure by which schools are judged created bad incentives to game the system, many analysts say.

Rather than concentrating on raising overall achievement or trying to give the most help to students who score lowest, many schools concentrate "on students who are on the bubble" — those who need to raise their scores by only a few points to move into the "proficient" range — and "forget the others," says Patrick McQuillan, an associate professor of education at Boston College's Lynch

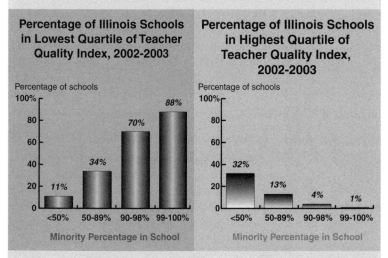

Minority Enrollment and Teacher Quality

In Illinois, 88 percent of the schools that were virtually 100 percent minority ranked in the lowest quartile of the state's Teacher Quality Index (graph at left). By comparison, only 1 percent of the all-minority schools ranked in the highest quartile (right). High-quality teachers have more experience, better educations and stronger academic skills. Similar patterns are found in most other states.

Source: "Teaching Inequality: How Poor and Minority Students Are Shortchanged on Teacher Quality," The Education Trust, June 2006

School of Education. Schools that succeed at pushing the scores of "bubble" students up by a few points are deemed successful, according to current NCLB standards, even if they leave the neediest students even farther behind, he says.

The law's pronouncement that 100 percent of U.S. students will test at the "proficient" level is simply unrealistic, some critics say.

"We've never fully funded education in the United States," and achievement continues to lag far below the "proficient" level, especially for low-income students, says Domenech. So "let's not kid around and say that by 2014" all students will be academically proficient, he says. "That's like saying, 'I'm going to push you out the window, and I know you can fly.' "

Furthermore, NCLB's focus on a handful of standardized tests as the sole measures of children's progress puts teachers in an ethical bind that "definitely lowers their morale," says Marshalita Sims Peterson, an associate professor of education at Atlanta's Spelman College, an historically black school for women.

Teachers in training are taught that students are individuals with a wide variety of learning styles, and that no single assessment can define a student, says Peterson. The NCLB's excessive focus on a single measurement of achievement "leaves the teacher in an awful position" she says. "You need to keep the job, but when you are actually completing that form" stating the single score "for a third-grader, you're asking, 'Is that all there is to this child?' "

Should governments make schools more racially and economically diverse?

Today, most African-American and Latino students attend urban schools with a high concentration of low-income students and very few white classmates.

Some advocates argue that the country has backtracked to an era of separate but unequal schools and say government programs aimed at creating more racially and socioeconomically diverse schools are good tools for narrowing the achievement gap. Opponents of government interference with children's attendance at neighborhood schools argue that with residential neighborhoods increasingly segregated by race and income, school integration is unrealistic, and that governments should focus instead on improving achievement in urban schools.[18]

"The effort to get the right racial balance is misguided" and represents a kind of "liberal racism — a belief that black children need to be in school with white children to learn," says Stephan Thernstrom, a history professor at Harvard University and a fellow at the conservative Manhattan Institute.

If integration "can be managed naturally, that's fine, but there is no clear correlation that can be drawn from data" showing it's important for closing the achievement gap, Thernstrom says. He rejects as incomplete and flawed studies that suggest integration does make a big difference. Furthermore, "if you need a white majority to learn," learning will soon be impossible in America, since Hispanic, Asian and African-American populations are growing faster than the current white majority, he notes.

Racial concentration is not the same as segregation and doesn't stand in the way of achievement, said his wife, Manhattan Institute Senior Fellow Abigail Thernstrom. School districts are powerless to change housing demographics, making it highly unlikely that racial concentration of students ever could be ended, she said.[19]

Some school districts are attempting to integrate lower-income and higher-income students, rather than integrating schools based on race. But Abigail Thernstrom argued that giving children a longer commute to schools outside their neighborhoods, for any reason, simply wastes time better spent in the classroom. "Busing doesn't raise the level of achievement," she told C-SPAN. "Now they're going to start busing on the basis of social class. And I have a very simple view of that. Stop moving the kids around and teach them."[20]

Meanwhile, some charter schools — such as the Knowledge Is Power Program (KIPP), begun in Houston — are making great strides in reducing the urban achievement gap, and for the most part those schools are not racially integrated, wrote *New York Times Magazine* features editor Paul Tough last year.

Most of the 70 schools that make up the three charter networks he observed have "only one or two white children enrolled, or none at all," he noted. Leaders of the networks, all of them white, actually intend to educate their students separately from middle-class students, according to Tough. However, unlike those who've argued that schools can be "separate but equal," the successful high-intensity charter schools aim for "separate but better." Their founders argue that

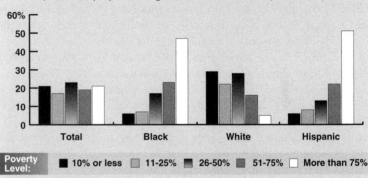

Blacks, Hispanics Attend High-Poverty Schools

Black and Hispanic students are more likely to be concentrated in high-poverty schools than white students. Forty-seven percent of black and 51 percent of Hispanic fourth-graders were in the highest-poverty schools in 2003 vs. 5 percent of white fourth-graders. By contrast, only 6 percent of black and Hispanic fourth-graders were in the lowest-poverty schools compared with 29 percent of whites.

Percentage of Fourth-Graders in High-Poverty Schools
(Based on proportion eligible for free or reduced-price lunch)

Poverty Level: ■ 10% or less ▨ 11-25% ▨ 26-50% ▨ 51-75% □ More than 75%

Source: "The Condition of Education 2004 in Brief" National Center for Education, June 2004

"students who enter middle school significantly behind grade level don't need the same good education that most American middle-class students receive; they need a better education," he said.[21]

But many advocates argue that data show a proven way to improve education for thousands of low-income students rather than for the handful that attend the highly successful charter schools is integration of minority and poor students with middle-class children.

School desegregation by race "has clear academic benefits," wrote R. Scott Baker, an associate professor of education at Wake Forest University. Data from Charlotte, N.C., show that the longer both black and white students spent in desegregated elementary schools, the higher their standardized test scores in middle and high school. Research also suggests that "where school desegregation plans are fully and completely implemented," local housing also becomes more integrated.[22]

In the 1960s and '70s some federal courts mandated programs to help urban minority families move to middle-class white suburbs. Long-term data from those cases show that children who moved did better than those who stayed behind, according to Howell S. Baum, a professor of urban studies and planning at the University of Maryland. In St. Louis, 50 percent of the black students who moved to the suburbs graduated from high school, compared to 26 percent of those who remained in the high-minority, low-income urban schools.[23]

Many policy analysts agree that segregating low-income children in some public schools "perpetuates failure," wrote the Century Foundation's Task Force on the Common School. Nevertheless, there is an "equally durable political consensus that nothing much can be done about it." The panel argued that this must change: "Eliminating the harmful effects of concentrated school poverty is the single most important step that can be taken for improving education in the United States."[24]

"Dozens of studies" dating back to the 1960s "find that low-income children have . . . larger achievement gains over time when they attend middle-class schools," said the panel.[25]

"The tragedy right now is that places that were once forced to [integrate their schools] now aren't allowed to," says Orfield of The Civil Rights Project. "That will be seen as a cosmic blunder" for white Americans as well, he said. "We're not preparing ourselves for the multiracial society and world" of the 21st century.

Are teachers prepared to teach successfully in urban classrooms?

Urban schools have high teacher turnover, low test scores and many reported discipline problems. Furthermore, most of America's teaching force still consists of white, middle-class women, while urban schoolchildren are low-income minorities, creating a culture gap that may be hard to bridge.

Consequently, some analysts argue that today's teachers aren't prepared to teach successfully in urban classrooms for a variety of reasons, from discipline to second-language issues. Others, however, point to sterling examples of teachers and schools that do succeed and argue that the real problem is teachers not following good examples.

Fifth-grade teacher Rafe Esquith, at the Hobart Elementary School in central Los Angeles, routinely coaches his urban Korean and Central American-immigrant students to top standardized-test scores. Furthermore, his classes produce Shakespearean plays so impressive they've been invited to perform with Britain's Royal Shakespeare Company, said Abigail Thernstrom.[26]

But despite Esquith's success, "nobody copies him," even in his own school, said Thernstrom. "I went to the fifth-grade [classroom] next door [to Esquith's] one day," and "it was perfectly clear nothing was going on." When Thernstrom suggested the teacher might copy Esquith's methods — which include beginning class as early as 6 a.m. and working with students at his home on weekends — he remarked that "it's an enormous amount of work."[27]

Today, around the country, "we do have shining examples" of schools that succeed at urban education, says Timothy Knowles, executive director of the University of Chicago's Center for Urban School Improvement and a former deputy school superintendent in Boston.

Ratner, of Citizens for Effective Schools, agrees. "I spent time in an elementary school in Chicago a few years ago where all the teachers were teaching reading," even at the upper grades, equipping students with the vocabulary and comprehension skills needed for future academic work, he says. "They had a good principal, and they were showing that it can be done."

But while successful urban schools and classrooms are out there, many education analysts say the know-how and resources needed to spread that success to millions of students are sorely lacking.

Some individual schools are closing the achievement gap for needy students, but "very few, if any" entire school districts have had equivalent success, says Knowles.

Charter schools also haven't seen their successes spread as widely as many hoped.

Out of Ohio's "300-plus charter schools," for example, "some . . . are indeed excellent, but too many are appalling," wrote analysts Terry Ryan and Quentin Suffran of the conservative Thomas B. Fordham Foundation in a recent report.[28]

There are reasons for that, said Mark Simon, director of the Center for Teacher Leadership at Johns Hopkins University, in Baltimore. "Teaching lower-class kids well is tougher than teaching middle-class kids." Furthermore, "it is surprising how little we know about teaching practices that cause students to succeed, particularly in high-poverty schools."[29]

"You have poverty in many districts, but in urban schools you have a concentration of it" that makes teaching successfully there much harder than in middle-class suburbs, says Timothy Shanahan, professor of urban education at the University of Illinois at Chicago and president of the International Reading Association. Schools are traditionally set up to deal with 15 to 20 percent of a student body having very high needs, says Shanahan. But urban schools usually have 50 percent or more of their students needing special attention of some kind, "and that's a huge burden on the teachers," he says.

"Literally, we have 5-year-olds who come into the Chicago school system not knowing their own names," he says. "I know local neighborhoods with gang problems, where the kids are up all night. Their mothers are hiding them under the bed to protect them from shootings in the street. Then teachers can't keep them awake in class."

The nation's rapidly growing Hispanic population is heavily concentrated in urban schools. That new phenomenon presents another tough obstacle for the urban teaching force, because "older teachers know nothing about working with non-native English speakers," says McQuillan of Boston College.

Not just language but race complicates urban-school teaching. As many as 81 percent of all teacher-education students are white women.[30]

"Those most often entering teaching continue to be white, monolingual, middle-class women," wrote Jocelyn A. Glazier, assistant professor of education at the University of North Carolina at Chapel Hill.[31]

Many teachers, especially white women, shy away from making tough demands on African-American students, according to a survey of urban community leaders by Wanda J. Blanchett, associate professor of urban special education at the University of Wisconsin, Milwaukee. "Especially with African-American males, you hear the teachers say, 'Oh, he is such a nice kid.' But . . . this irks me when teachers baby their students to death instead of pushing. . . . I get that a lot when you have white teachers who have never worked with black students from the urban environment."[32]

Many entering education students at Indiana University-Purdue University, in Indianapolis, balked at the school's fieldwork and student-teaching venues, which were in urban schools, wrote Professor Christine H. Leland and Professor Emeritus Jerome C. Harste. "They saw our program's urban focus as an obstacle to their career goals" of teaching in schools like the suburban ones most had attended.[33]

Some viewed urban students as an alien race they didn't want to learn to know. "Students rarely felt the need to interrogate their underlying assumption that poor people deserve the problems they have" or "spent any time talking or thinking about issues such as poverty or racism," Leland and Harste wrote. After student teaching, however, some students changed their plans and applied to become urban teachers.[34]

Race is a taboo subject in America, which some analysts say compounds urban teachers' difficulties. Many teacher-preparation programs center on an effort not to see or at least not to acknowledge race differences, according to Glazier. But "by claiming not to notice [race], the teacher is saying that she is dismissing one of the most salient features of a child's identity."[35]

"Many teachers believe that if they recognize a student's race or discuss issues of ethnicity in their classroom, they might be labeled as insensitive and racist," wrote Central Michigan University graduate student in education Dreyon Wynn and Associate Dean Dianne L. H. Mark. But white teachers' deliberate color-blindness ignores students "unique culture, beliefs, perceptions, [and] values," blocking both learning and helpful student-teacher relationships, Mark and Wynn argue.[36]

BACKGROUND

Educating the Poor

American education has long struggled with providing equal education for the poor, racial minorities and non-English-speaking immigrants. Until recently, however, even people who never made it through high school could usually find a good job. A new, global, technical economy may be changing that.

In the earliest years in the United States, schooling wasn't widespread. A farm-based economy made extensive education unnecessary for most people. In 1805, more than 90 percent of Americans had completed a fifth-grade education or less, and education for richer people was often conducted by private tutors.[37]

CHRONOLOGY

1950s-1960s *Concerns grow over student achievement and racially segregated schools.*

1954 Supreme Court rules in *Brown v. Board of Education* that separate schools are inherently unequal.

1965 Title I of the new Elementary and Secondary Education Act (ESEA) targets the largest pool of federal education assistance to help schools serving disadvantaged students.

1966 Sociologist James S. Coleman's "Equality of Educational Opportunity" report concludes that disadvantaged African-American students do better in integrated classrooms.

1969 National Assessment of Educational Progress (NAEP) tests launched but report statewide average scores only, allowing states to mask lagging achievement among poor and minority students.

1970s-1980s *Latinos are becoming most segregated minority in U.S. schools. "Magnet schools" are established. School integration efforts gradually end.*

1973 Supreme Court rules in *San Antonio Independent School District v. Rodriguez* the Constitution does not guarantee equal education for all children.... In *Keyes v. School District No. 1*, the court bans city policies that segregate Denver schools.

1990s-2000s *Steady gains in African-American students' test scores over the past two decades begin to taper off by decade's end.... Poverty concentrates in cities.... Governors lead efforts to raise education standards.*

1990 New Jersey Supreme Court rules in *Abbott v. Burke* the state must provide more funding for poor schools than for richer ones.

1991 Minnesota enacts first charter-school law.

1994 In reauthorizing ESEA, Congress requires states receiving Title I funding for disadvantaged students to hold them to the same academic standards as all students.

1995 Knowledge Is Power Program charter schools launched in Houston and New York City.... Boston creates Pilot School program to research ideas for urban-school improvement.

1999 Florida establishes first statewide school-voucher program.

2000 Countywide, income-based school integration launched in Raleigh, N.C.

2002 Cambridge, Mass., schools begin integration based on income.

2002 No Child Left Behind Act (NCLB) requires states to report student test scores "disaggregated" by race, income and gender to avoid masking the failing scores of some groups.... U.S. Supreme Court rules in favor of Ohio's school-voucher program, which allows public funding for tuition at Cleveland parochial schools.... State takes over Philadelphia's bankrupt school system, allows private companies to run some schools.

2005 Hoping to halt isolation of the lowest-income students in inner-city schools, Omaha, Neb., tries but fails to annex neighboring suburban districts.

2006 Department of Education admits that few students in failing city schools receive the free tutoring NCLB promised and that no states have met the 2006 deadline for having qualified teachers in all classrooms.... Government Accountability Office finds that nearly one-third of public schools, most in low-income and minority communities, need major repairs.

2007 Gov. Deval L. Patrick, D-Mass., puts up $6.5 million to help schools lengthen their hours.... Democratic Mayor Adrian Fenty, of Washington, D.C., is the latest of several mayors to take control of schools.... New York City Schools Chancellor Joel Klein says he will fire principals of schools with lagging test scores.... Teachers' unions slam report calling for all high-school seniors to be proficient in reading and math by 2014.... Houston school district calls for state to replace NCLB-related standardized periodic testing on math and reading with traditional end-of-course subject-matter exams.

2007

June 2007 — U.S. Supreme Court invalidates school-attendance-zone plans used in Seattle and Louisville to achieve greater racial diversity. The 5-4 ruling in *Parents Involved in Community Schools v. Seattle Dist. No. 1* said the Seattle School District's plan to use race as a consideration in student assignments was unconstitutional.

2008

Nov. 26, 2008 — Washington, D.C., School Chancellor Michelle Rhee appears on the cover of Time.

2009-2010 *Educational reforms have been made by 28 states under the administration's $4 billion state grant education initiative, Race to the Top. The number of reforms is triple that of the previous two years.*

2009 — Education Secretary Arne Duncan rescinds pending scholarships under the D.C. Opportunity Scholarship Program, and Congress declines to reauthorize.

2010 — Obama administration unveils its blueprint to overhaul No Child Left Behind Act. . . . In the District of Columbia in June, school officials and the teachers' union finalize a contract that, in addition to granting a retroactive pay increase, requires all teachers in the system to be evaluated in part on whether their students' test scores improve, and offers sizable pay increases to teachers who opt for and succeed in a special new pay-for-performance arrangement. . . . Civil Rights Project at UCLA reviews school integration efforts and calls on the Obama administration to issue guidance on how race can be considered in public education. . . . Washington, D.C., School Chancellor Rhee dismisses 241 teachers.

2011 Thirty-seven states provide less funding to local schools than in the 2010-2011 school year.

January — Newly elected Republican governors and legislators in states including Wisconsin, Ohio, Indiana, Idaho, New Jersey and Florida propose bills to lower costs and improve education by ending teacher tenure, limiting teachers' collective bargaining rights, instituting merit pay and firing teachers based on student-achievement test results.

March — *USA Today* reports possible evidence of cheating on standardized tests at Washington, D.C., schools.

May — Georgia Bureau of Investigation reports that 178 teachers and principals in Atlanta conspired to change student-achievement test scores.

November — U.S. Department of Education data show that many districts don't provide high-poverty schools with resources equal to those provided to schools in wealthier neighborhoods.

2012

March — For the fourth consecutive year, many teachers in the Los Angeles and San Francisco school districts receive warnings that their jobs are at risk.

May — A committee of the Illinois legislature supports requiring school districts to provide more funding for charter schools; Chicago Teachers Union campaigns against the proposal. . . . Schools nationwide perform poorly on a science-achievement test, but black and Hispanic students slightly narrow the gap between their scores and those of white students. . . . Federal Communications Commission announces it will inform phone companies that they must follow a 15-year-old rule requiring them to give schools bargain prices so more can afford good Internet access.

2013

January 1 — Urban schools could face major cuts in federal Title I funds if Congress doesn't resolve a budget stalemate.

Dropouts' Problems Often Begin Early

Clear warning signs appear, such as skipping class

With the baby-boom generation on the verge of retirement, sustaining the American workforce and economy depends on having a cadre of new young workers to replace them, says former Gov. Bob Wise, D-W.Va., now president of the Alliance for Excellent Education. But with jobs in the fastest-growing economic sectors now requiring at least a high-school diploma and, often, two years or more of post-high-school training, coming up with an adequately trained new workforce won't be easy, Wise says.

The annual graduation rate has risen from a little over 50 percent per year in the late 1960s to 73.9 percent in 2003. If it's to rise higher, however, the improvement must come among poor and minority students, mostly in urban schools, who are far less likely than others to earn diplomas.[1]

For example, while about two-thirds of all students who enter ninth grade graduate four years later, on-time graduation rates for minority and low-income students, especially males, are much lower. In 2001, for example, only about 50 percent of African-American students and 51 percent of Latino students graduated on time, compared to 75 percent of white students and 77 percent of Asian and Pacific Islanders.[2]

Students with family incomes in the lowest 20 percent dropped out of school at six times the average rate of wealthier students.[3]

In about a sixth of American high schools, the freshman class routinely shrinks by 40 percent or more by the time students reach senior year. For the most part, those schools serve low-income and minority students. Nearly half of African-American students, 40 percent of Latino students and 11 percent of white students attend high schools where graduation is not the norm. A high school with a majority of students who are racial or ethnic minorities is five times more likely to promote only 50 percent or fewer freshmen to senior status within four years than a school with a white majority.[4]

Meanwhile, the earning power of dropouts has been dropping for three decades. For example, the earnings of male dropouts fell by 35 percent between 1971 and 2002, measured in 2002 dollars. Three-quarters of state prison inmates and 59 percent of federal inmates are dropouts. In 2001, only 55 percent of young adult dropouts were employed. Even the death rate is 2.5 times higher for people without a high-school education than for people with 13 years or more of schooling.[5]

But if the consequences are known, the cures may be harder to pinpoint.

Many educators say dropping out starts early. "Disengagement doesn't start in the ninth grade. It starts in fifth," says James F. Lytle, a University of Pennsylvania professor and former superintendent of the Trenton, N.J., public schools. For on-track students in middle-class schools, "middle school has the most interesting, exciting stuff in class" — science experiments, readings about interesting people in history and studies "of how the world works" — he says.

But once students are judged to be reading behind grade level, as happens with many urban fifth-graders, middle schools turn to "dumbed-down remedial work" that's below students' real intellectual level and leaves them bored and dispirited, Lytle says. It doesn't have to be that way, he says. "But I wish that educational courseware was farther down the road" of providing ways to combine skills teaching with subject matter that is at students' actual age level.

State legislatures were just beginning to debate whether to establish free tax-funded schools for all children.[38] Nevertheless, even in those early days, some religious and other charitable groups considered it a moral duty to educate the poor. In New York City, for example, the Association of Women Friends for the Relief of the Poor opened a charity school in 1801. By 1823 the group was providing free elementary education for 750 children, with some public assistance. Similar charity schools sprang up in most other major cities.

But as all states began establishing public education systems — between the late 18th and the mid-19th century — questions over equality in education arose, first for black students and later for immigrants. "When public schools opened in Boston in the late 18th century, black children were neither barred nor segregated,"

"Kids disengage early," says Lalitha Vasudevan, an assistant professor at Columbia University's Teachers College who works in an education program for young African-American males who've been diverted from jail and are mostly dropouts. "Often, early on, they've had teachers say things to them that they interpret as, 'You don't really care that I'm here,' " she says.

Dropping out "is not a decision that is made on a single morning," says a report from the Bill & Melinda Gates Foundation. In an extensive survey of dropouts, researchers found that "there are clear warning signs for at least one-to-three years" before students drop out, such as frequently missing school, skipping class, being held back a grade or frequently transferring among schools.[6]

Some key factors cited by the dropouts in the Gates study: Schools don't respond actively when students skip class and don't provide an orderly and safe environment. "In middle school, you have to go to your next class or they are going to get you," said a young male dropout from Philadelphia. "In high school, if you don't go to class, there isn't anybody who is going to get you. You just do your own thing."[7]

Lytle says cities could also establish post-dropout academies, like the Dropout Recovery High School he started in Trenton, which helped increase that city's graduation numbers.

"Rather than defining the whole problem as stopping dropouts, we can also reach out to those who already have," he says. "There are a slew of people around" who are out of school and would like to go back, from teenage mothers caring for their children to 60-year-olds, he says. "They need a school that is built around their lives. I simply don't understand why urban districts haven't been more imaginative" about this.

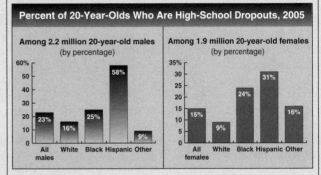

Majority of Dropouts Are Hispanic, Black

More than 50 percent of 20-year-old male high-school dropouts are Hispanic or African-American (graph at left). By comparison, 55 percent of the females are black or Hispanic (graph at right).

Percent of 20-Year-Olds Who Are High-School Dropouts, 2005

Among 2.2 million 20-year-old males (by percentage): All males 23%, White 16%, Black 25%, Hispanic 58%, Other 9%

Among 1.9 million 20-year-old females (by percentage): All females 15%, White 9%, Black 24%, Hispanic 31%, Other 16%

Source: "The Costs and Benefits of an Excellent Education for All of America's Children," Teachers College, Columbia University, January 2007

[1] Nancy Martin and Samuel Halperin, *Whatever It Takes: How Twelve Communities are Reconnecting Out-of-School Youth,* American Youth Policy Forum, www.aypf.org/publications/WhateverItTakes/WITfull.pdf.

[2] *Ibid.*

[3] *Ibid.*

[4] Robert Balfanz and Nettie Legters, "Locating the Dropout Crisis," Center for Social Organization of Schools, Johns Hopkins University, June 2004.

[5] Martin and Halperin, *op. cit.*

[6] John M. Bridgeland, John J. DiIulio, Jr. and Karen Burke Morison, *The Silent Epidemic: Perspectives of High School Dropouts,* Bill & Melinda Gates Foundation, March 2006.

[7] Quoted in *ibid.*

wrote Derrick Bell, a visiting professor at the New York University School of Law. "But by 1790, racial insults and mistreatment had driven out all but three or four black children."[39]

Later, some black families joined with white liberals to form black-only schools in Massachusetts and in other states. But complaints about poor conditions and poor teaching in those schools led others to sue for integrated education.

Even in the early 19th century, some courts were bothered by race-based inequities in education, said Bell. A federal court struck down a Kentucky law directing that school taxes collected from white people would maintain white schools, and taxes from blacks would operate black schools. "Given the great disparities in taxable resources" this would result in an inferior education for black children, the court said.[40]

The "Behavior Gap" Between Black and White Students

Many educators blame a system that's middle-class and white-centered

Data from around the country indicate that black students, especially males, are cited much more often for disciplinary infractions than whites. The resulting "behavior gap" parallels the much-talked-about academic achievement gap.

Many analysts blame the phenomenon in part on a "culture clash" between black students, many poor, and an education system that's white-centered and middle-class. But there's little agreement about exactly what the gap means and what to do about it.

"You find the gap in all schools," including wealthy ones, says Clara G. Muschkin, a researcher at the Duke University Center for Child and Family Policy. Nevertheless, some evidence suggests there may also be a behavior gap between richer and poorer students, which accounts for just under a third of the black-white gap, Muschkin says.

In North Carolina schools, the racial gap "is persistent at all the grades" but is widest in seventh grade, says Muschkin. About 30 percent of black seventh-graders and 14 percent of whites have at least one disciplinary infraction reported during the school year.

African-American male students have the highest rates of suspensions and expulsions in most metropolitan areas around the country, according to Denise L. Collier, a doctoral candidate in education at California State University, Los Angeles. In New York, for example, where African-American males are 18 percent of the student population, they account for 39 percent of school suspensions and 50 percent of expulsions. In Los Angeles, black males make up 6 percent of the population but account for 18 percent of suspensions and 15 percent of expulsions.[1]

Some educators say that many urban African-American students don't learn at home the kinds of communication behaviors that are the norm for the middle class, and that this lack of background accounts for much of the gap.

"Americans of a certain background learn . . . early on and employ . . . instinctively" techniques like sitting up straight, asking questions and tracking a speaker with their eyes in order to take in information, said David Levin, a founder of the Knowledge Is Power Program (KIPP) charter schools, which serve mainly black and Hispanic students in several cities.[2]

When students in one Levin class were asked to "give us the normal school look," they responded by staring off into space and slouching, recounted *New York Times Magazine* editor Paul Tough in an article last year on successful urban charter schools. "Middle-class Americans know intuitively that 'good behavior' is mostly a game with established rules; the KIPP students seemed to be experiencing the pleasure of being let in on a joke," Tough observed.[3]

Behavior like a proper in-school work ethic has to be taught "in the same way we have to teach adding fractions with unlike denominators," said Dacia Toll, founder of the Amistad Academy charter school in New Haven, Conn. "But once children have got the work ethic and the commitment to others and to education down, it's actually pretty easy to teach them."

The academic gap that puts many black students in remedial instruction as they move through school may worsen the problem, says Robert Balfanz, associate research scientist at the Johns Hopkins University Center on the Social Organization of Schools. "In traditional remedial

Around the 1820s, waves of non-English immigration began, raising new controversies over educating poor children of sometimes-despised ethnicities.

Before 1820, most U.S. immigrants were English, and a few were Dutch. But between 1820 and 1840 Irish immigrants became the first in a long parade of newcomers judged inferior by the predominantly English population. A rising tide of immigration in the late 19th and early 20th centuries included many non-English-speakers — Italians, Germans, Chinese, Russians, Poles and many others — who posed new challenges for schools and were looked down on by many citizens.

instruction, I assume you know nothing, so I teach the times table" and basic reading skills like letter sounds, he says. "But the majority of kids behind can actually read at a basic level. What they're missing is comprehension skill, vocabulary. So they get bored and frustrated."

Middle-class education majors student-teaching in urban schools found that using books about topics their students personally had encountered — including homelessness, racism and poverty — decreased discipline problems, even though the teachers initially resisted the books as inappropriate for children, according to Professor Christine H. Leland and Professor Emeritus Jerome C. Harste of Indiana University-Purdue University, Indianapolis. Once the student teachers broached the tough subject matter, they began reporting "fewer discipline problems . . . the children listened carefully and engaged in thoughtful discussions when they perceived that the issues being discussed were worth their attention."[4]

Many African-American student discipline problems involve "defiance" issues such as acting threatening or making excessive noise rather than activities like drug use or leaving the classroom without permission, according to University of Virginia Assistant Professor Anne Gregory.[5]

Seventy-five percent of African-American disciplinary referrals were for "defiance" behaviors in a study Gregory cites, many more than for other ethnic groups. That may suggest that teachers judge African-American students' behavior more "subjectively" than that of other students, Gregory says. Based on their past feelings of being restricted and excluded, some African-American students may be more likely to act out when they perceive that teachers are being unfair, Gregory suggests.

"If I was this little Caucasian boy or this preppy girl, she wouldn't talk with me that way. I am like the opposite. I am this little thug . . . I mean, she don't know," one student in Gregory's study said of a teacher perceived to be unfair.[6]

Avoiding excessive discipline battles in urban schools requires a seemingly contradictory set of characteristics that not everyone can muster, said Franita Ware, a professor of education at Spelman College, a historically black school for women in Atlanta. Teachers who succeed tend to be "warm demanders," those whom "students believed . . . did not lower their standards" but also "were willing to help them."[7]

"Sometimes I mean-talk them in varying degrees of severity," one teacher told Ware. But "sometimes you have to go back and say, 'What was really going on with you when I yelled at you? I'm just so sorry.' "[8]

Often the adult is the provocateur in the behavior situation, even if they don't realize it, such as when a student finds the nurse's office door locked at 3:02 and starts pounding on it, says James F. Lytle, a professor at the University of Pennsylvania and former school superintendent in Trenton, N.J.

"A lot of it is just the way you talk to people — respect," Lytle says. "Many are so accustomed to being denigrated. The kids have so little that the protection of one's ego is very important."

---

[1] Denise L. Collier, "Sally Can Skip But Jerome Can't Stomp: Perceptions, Practice, and School Punishment (Preliminary Results)," paper presented at the American Educational Research Association annual meeting, San Francisco, Calif., April 2006.

[2] Quoted in Paul Tough, "What It Takes To Make a Student," *New York Times Magazine*, Nov. 26, 2006, p. 51.

[3] *Ibid.*

[4] Christine H. Leland and Jerome C. Harste, "Doing What We Want to Become: Preparing New Urban Teachers," *Urban Education*, January 2005, p. 67.

[5] Anne Gregory, "Justice and Care: Teacher Practices To Narrow the Racial Discipline Gap," paper presented at the American Educational Research Association annual conference, San Francisco, Calif., April 2006.

[6] Quoted in *ibid*.

[7] Franita Ware, "Warm Demander Pedagogy: Culturally Responsive Teaching that Supports A Culture of Achievement for African-American Students," *Urban Education*, July 2006, p. 427.

[8] Quoted in *ibid*.

The new immigrants generally clustered in cities, the economic engines of the time, and overcrowded city schools were charged with integrating them into American life. Critics charged that the urban schools used rigid instruction and harsh discipline to control classrooms bursting with 60 or more children, many of whom spoke no English.

Two Tracks

In the economy of the early 20th century, however, there remained little need for most students to learn more than basic reading and writing, so the failure of poor urban schools to produce many graduates wasn't seen as a problem.

In current debates over U.S. education, "people aren't looking at education historically" and therefore expect American schools to do things they were never designed to do, says Ratner of Citizens for Effective Schools.

"We consciously decided to have a two-track system," he says. In the early 20th century, education experts generally agreed that "in the industrial age there are lots of immigrants and poor people, and most are going to work on the assembly line, so how about if we create an academic track and a general/vocational track" mostly for the poor?

The school system that we have "was never set up to educate all students to the levels of proficiency now being asked for," Ratner says.

"I graduated exactly 40 years ago, and then about half the kids — 52 percent — were graduating," says Wise of the Alliance for Excellent Education. "And the non-graduates could still get good jobs."

But today "the fastest-growing sectors of the economy require two years of post high-school training," says Daniel J. Cardinali, president of Communities In Schools, a dropout-prevention group that helps school districts bring services like tutoring and health care to needy students.

Calls in the 1990s for higher academic standards by groups like The Business Roundtable brought widespread attention to the problems of low student achievement, especially in low-income schools.

Today few question the premise that all students should attain higher levels of literacy, mathematical problem-solving and critical thinking. Many who work in schools argue that simply setting higher standards isn't nearly enough, however, especially for urban schools where most students already are behind grade level.

As standards rise, for example, "ninth-graders are increasingly placed in introductory algebra classes . . . despite skill gaps in fundamental arithmetic," wrote Balfanz and Ruth Curran Neild, research scientists at the Johns Hopkins University Center on the Social Organization of Schools.

But few resources exist to help kids catch up, "nor are there many curriculum materials that specifically target the spotty skills of urban ninth-graders," the Johns Hopkins researchers said. And when students reading behind grade level enter middle and high school, their "secondary-certified English teachers" — educated to teach high-school-level literature and composition — "are generally unprepared" to diagnose reading problems or to teach the comprehension strategies and background vocabulary they need. Science and history teachers are even less prepared to help, Balfanz and Neild said.[41]

Retooling the school system to support higher standards may seem daunting, but "a quick walk through history" shows that it wouldn't be the first time the United States has made heroic efforts on education, says Wise. For example, "after World War II, you had soldiers coming home in need of better skills, and you had the GI Bill" to help them continue their educations.

Then "in the civil rights era we said, 'We believe that every child should be able to enter school,' and that happened," Wise says. "Now we're saying that every child should graduate."

For a time, the civil rights era seemed to be accelerating growing academic parity in learning, at least between black and white students. Following World War II, standardized test scores for black students began moving closer to white students' scores. The years from the 1960s to the '80s saw fully half of the black-white academic achievement gap eliminated, says The Civil Rights Project's Orfield.

In the late '80s, however, the progress of African-American students in closing the gap stalled, and between 1988 and 1994, average test scores for black students actually began falling.[42]

Minority Schools

U.S. schools briefly became more integrated after the civil rights battles of the 1950s and '60s, but shifting housing patterns have caused the concentration of poor, minority and non-English-speaking students in urban schools to rise for the past 25 years.

"One thing that's not fully understood is that, through a long historical process, we've concentrated our most needy students in a small subset of schools and districts" in rural and, mostly, urban areas, vastly increasing the burden those schools face in raising academic achievement, says Balfanz.

In its landmark 1954 *Brown v. Board of Education* ruling, the Supreme Court declared it illegal to intentionally segregate schools by race.[43] In 1964, Congress passed the Civil Rights Act, outlawing discrimination in any institution that received federal funds, including schools.[44] As a result, more schools accommodated lower-income students along with middle-class students, white students and students from other ethnic groups.

The civil rights era lasted a scant 20 years, however, and housing patterns and new waves of immigration soon led to concentrations of poor and minority students in many urban school districts again.

As early as 1974, the Supreme Court effectively set limits on how far racial integration of students could go. The court ruled in *Milliken v. Bradley* that the remedy to racial segregation in Detroit could not include moving children to schools in the surrounding suburbs.[45]

Then, in the 1980s, federal efforts to desegregate schools effectively ended. During the presidency of Ronald Reagan (1981-1988), the U.S. Justice Department backed off forcing states to comply with desegregation mandates. Two Supreme Court decisions in the early 1990s effectively declared the goal of black-white school integration had been addressed, as the court ruled that school districts could be excused from court-ordered busing if they had made good-faith efforts to integrate, even if they had not fully complied with court orders.[46]

At the same time, however, Hispanic students were becoming a new minority that concentrated in schools with bigger academic challenges than others, such as teaching English-language learners.

The segregation of Latino students soared during the civil rights era. In 1973, in *Keyes v. School District No. 1*, the Supreme Court outlawed policies in Denver that had the effect of segregating Hispanic and African-American children into separate schools. In ensuing years, however, this somewhat complex ruling was only spottily enforced, according to civil rights advocates.[47]

Today Latinos "are America's most segregated minority group," said Orfield. The average Latino student goes to a school that is less than 30 percent white, has a majority of poor children and an "increasing concentration" of students who don't speak English.[48]

Poor in School

Until around the 1970s, children of all races and classes attended urban schools, and their average achievement levels didn't draw the same alarmed attention as today. Urban sprawl and white flight from cities over the past three decades have not only increased the number of urban schools with high minority populations but also

Edwin Bradley listens to his fifth-grade daughter Antoinette read at the South Street School library in Newark, N.J. One of the poorest in the state, the school district has been encouraged under a new program to support parental involvement in an attempt to improve student performance.

increased the concentration of urban poverty as well, increasing the burden on urban schools.

"Sprawl is a product of suburban pulls and urban pushes," said the University of Maryland's Baum. "Families move to the suburbs for good housing, open space. They leave cities to avoid bad schools, threats to safety . . . contact with other races and poor public services."[49]

Furthermore, minority children are more concentrated in urban areas than the general population, largely because white families with children move to suburbs while childless whites are more likely to remain in the city, said Baum. Nationally, in nearly all school districts with more than 25,000 students, interracial contact has declined since 1986.[50]

Even more than ethnic minorities, poor people have concentrated in cities, says Balfanz. Over the past 20 years, even in periods when overall poverty has dropped, "the cities have gotten poorer and the concentration of poverty there deeper."

Between 1960 and 1987, the national poverty rate for people in central cities rose from 13.4 percent to 15.7 percent. At the same time, the poverty rate for rural residents fell by one-half and for suburban residents by one-third. By 1991, 43 percent of people with incomes below the federal poverty line lived in central cities.[51]

AT ISSUE

Would raising teacher pay help struggling schools?

YES
Patty Myers
Technology Coordinator,
Great Falls (Montana) Public Schools

From testimony on behalf of the National Education Association before U.S. Senate Committee on Finance, March 20, 2007

Ensuring a highly qualified teacher in every classroom is critical to closing achievement gaps and maximizing student learning. No single factor will make a bigger difference in helping students reach high academic standards....

Unfortunately, difficulty in attracting quality teachers and high turnover rates severely hamper the ability to maintain a high-quality learning environment. Approximately one-third of the nation's new teachers leave the profession during their first three years, and almost one-half leave during their first five years. And turnover in low-income schools is almost one-third higher than the rate in all schools.

The teaching profession has an average national starting salary of $30,377. Meanwhile, computer programmers start at an average of $43,635, public accounting professionals at $44,668 and registered nurses at $45,570.

Annual pay for teachers has fallen sharply over the past 60 years in relation to the annual pay of other workers with college degrees. The average earnings of workers with at least four years of college are now over 50 percent higher than the average earnings of a teacher. Congress should reward states that set a reasonable minimum starting salary for teachers and a living wage for support professionals working in school districts. NEA recommends that all teachers in America enter the classroom earning at least $40,000 annually.

NEA also supports advancing teacher quality at the highest-poverty schools by providing $10,000 federal salary supplements to National Board Certified Teachers. Congress also should fund grants to help teachers in high-poverty schools pay the fees and access professional supports to become certified.

Often schools with the greatest needs and, consequently, the most challenging working conditions have the most difficulty retaining talented teachers.... Many hard-to-staff schools are high-poverty inner-city school or rural schools that, as a consequence of their location in economically depressed or isolated districts, offer comparatively low salaries and lack [the] amenities with which other districts attract teachers.

NEA strongly supports federal legislation with financial incentives for teaching in high-poverty schools, such as the Teacher Tax Credit Act introduced in the 109th Congress. The bill would provide a non-refundable tax credit to educators who work at schools that are fully eligible for federal Title I funds for disadvantaged students and would help hard-to-staff schools retain the quality teachers they need to succeed.

NO
Jay P. Greene
Senior Fellow, Manhattan Institute

Posted on the Web, 2006

The common assertion that teachers are severely underpaid is so omnipresent that many Americans simply accept it as gospel. But the facts tell a different story.

The average teacher's salary does seem modest at first glance: about $44,600 in 2002 for all teachers. But when we compare it to what workers of similar skill levels in similar professions are paid, we find that teachers are not shortchanged.

People often fail to account for the relatively low number of hours that teachers work. Teachers work only about nine months per year. During the summer they can either work at other jobs or use the time off however else they wish. Either way, it's as much a form of compensation as a paycheck.

The most recent data indicate that teachers average 7.3 working hours per day, and that they work 180 days per year, or about 1,314 hours. Americans in normal 9-to-5 professions who take two weeks of vacation and another 10 paid holidays put in 1,928 hours. This means the average teacher's base salary is equivalent to a full-time salary of $65,440.

In 2002, elementary-school teachers averaged $30.75 per hour and high-school teachers $31.01 — about the same as architects, civil engineers and computer-systems analysts. Even demanding, education-intensive professions like dentistry and nuclear engineering didn't make much more per hour.

Some argue that it's unfair to calculate teacher pay on an hourly basis because teachers perform a large amount of work at home — grading papers on the weekend, for instance. But people in other professions also do off-site work.

Many assume that teachers spend almost all of the school day teaching. But in reality, the average subject-matter teacher taught fewer than 3.9 hours per day in 2000. This leaves plenty of time for grading and planning lessons.

It is well documented that the people drawn into teaching these days tend to be those who have performed least well in college. If teachers are paid about as well as employees in many other good professions, why aren't more high performers taking it up?

One suspects that high-performing graduates tend to stay away because the rigid seniority-based structure doesn't allow them to rise faster and earn more money through better performance or by voluntarily putting in longer hours. In any case, it's clear that the primary obstacle to attracting better teachers isn't simply raising pay.

"The nation's student population is two-thirds middle class (not eligible for federally subsidized lunches), yet one-quarter of American schools have a majority of students from low-income households," according to The Century Foundation.[52]

Among the burdens urban schools bear are poverty-related learning deficiencies children bring to school with them, regulations and economic barriers that limit urban-school resources, and a historical role as job providers in inner cities.

A large body of research shows that many low-income parents interact with their children in ways that hinder them in school, wrote Tough last year in *The New York Times Magazine*. For example, professional parents speak to their young children about two-and-a-half more times in an hour than poor parents do and encourage them verbally about six times more often than they discourage them; low-income parents discourage their children about three times as often as they encourage them, he said.

Unlike poor parents, middle-class parents also encourage their children to question, challenge and negotiate. In short, "in countless ways, the manner in which [poor children] are raised puts them at a disadvantage" in a school culture, Tough noted.[53]

For a variety of reasons, urban schools also have a much harder time keeping good teachers. "Many thousands — perhaps millions — of urban students don't have permanent, highly qualified teachers, ones with the skill to communicate important stuff to kids," says Kitty Kelly-Epstein, a professor of education at the Fielding Graduate University in Santa Barbara, Calif. In California, at least, state rules force some urban school districts to rely on temporary teachers because not enough applicants have required certifications, she says. "There never has been a time when low-income schools were fully staffed," she says.

With joblessness high in cities, especially for minority applicants, it's also "not uncommon" for school districts to be the major job source in the area, according to Johns Hopkins University Associate Professor of Education Elaine M. Stotko and colleagues. In a tradition that dates back to patronage systems in the early 20th century, urban politicians often interfere with schools' hiring the best managerial and teaching candidates by pressuring them to hand out jobs "as political favors."[54]

The Supreme Court is due to rule by the end of June in two race-based integration cases. With a new conservative majority, the court is widely expected to rule in favor of the white parents who are seeking to end race-based school integration in Seattle and Louisville, Ky. Decisions against the school districts could end many similar programs around the country, many of which were court-ordered in the past.[55]

But some school districts still worry that schools with high concentrations of minority and poor students harm achievement. Over the past several years, a few districts, including Raleigh, N.C., and Cambridge, Mass., have experimented with integrating students by socioeconomic status. In 2000, for example, the school board in Wake County, N.C., which includes Raleigh and its suburbs, replaced its racial integration system with the goal that no school should have 40 percent of students eligible for free or reduced-price lunch.[56]

Raleigh's effort was simpler politically than most, because the school district contains both the area's low-poverty and high-poverty schools. If the higher-income suburbs had been outside the district, political push-back would have made the program a tougher sell.

Some early Raleigh results look promising. On the state's 2005 High School End of Course exams, 63.8 percent of the low-income students passed, as did 64.3 percent of its African-American seniors, compared to pass rates in the high-40 and low 50-percent range for the state's other urban districts.[57]

CURRENT SITUATION

Congress Divided

The No Child Left Behind Act (NCLB), enacted in 2002, is intended to push American schools to raise achievement for all students, including low-income and minority children. As such, it represents one more step down a road that Congress embarked on in its 1994 reauthorization of the Elementary and Secondary Education Act — exerting federal influence to ensure that all students meet higher academic standards.

With NCLB up for reauthorization, Congress is struggling to figure out its next steps, with little apparent agreement on the horizon. With the press of other business, and strong disagreements in Congress about the education law, it's not clear that it will be reauthorized this year. The new congressional Democratic majority has already begun to hold hearings, however.

The Knowledge Is Power Program (KIPP) charter school in the Bronx, N.Y., boasts the highest test scores in the area. Although most KIPP schools are not racially integrated, they are reducing achievement gaps between black and white students.

U.S. businesses have become increasingly involved in education policy, and many business leaders are urging Congress to continue and strengthen federal efforts to raise academic standards and provide incentives for states and localities to extensively retool their school systems to improve student achievement.

"Unless we transform the American high school, we will limit economic opportunities for millions of Americans," declared Microsoft Chairman Bill Gates at a Senate Health, Education, Labor and Pensions Committee hearing on March 7.[58]

Meanwhile, a group of conservative congressional Republicans has introduced legislation that would replace most of the NCLB achievement and reporting requirements that determine funding with block-grant funding that states could get whether they met NCLB standards or not. The measure would restore states and localities to their traditional role as prime overseers of schools, said Rep. Peter Hoekstra, R-Mich., who sponsored the legislation. "President Bush and I just see education fundamentally differently," he said. "The president believes in empowering bureaucrats in Washington, and I don't."[59]

But many congressional Democrats argue that a strengthened federal hand in education is warranted, partly because NCLB data now clearly reveal that the state-run systems of old have left so many poor and minority children disastrously behind.

Rep. George Miller, D-Calif., and Sen. Kennedy, key supporters of NCLB and chairs of the House and Senate committees that govern it, have both held pre-authorization hearings this year. Both say they're committed to increasing resources for struggling schools in a new bill, especially by supporting the hiring and training of more and better teachers.

"We know the law has flaws, but we also know that with common-sense changes and adequate resources, we can improve it by building on what we've learned," said Kennedy in a statement.

Retooling NCLB?

Education analysts have no shortage of changes to suggest.

President Bush is looking at "tinkering" with NCLB in a reauthorization, but Democrats are "interested in something broader," says Cardinali of Communities in Schools. "The [current] law is too fixated on academics," he says. After 30 years of experience helping students get additional services they need like tutoring and health care, "we've learned that student services are a critical component," he says.

"The brutal truth is that there is only one institution in America where you can get to kids in a thoughtful way — the school," he says. "Let's make that the center" where parents and children can get needs met that are critical for learning readiness. "Are we trying to make public education something it's not? No. It's a holistic view" of what it takes to educate a child.

One gap the University of Chicago's Knowles would like to see rectified: In NCLB's reporting requirements "the unit of analysis is the kid, the school and the district, and there's a stunning absence there if we really believe that instruction is at the heart of learning." Research indicates, he says, that individual classroom teachers may be the strongest in-school influence on student achievement.

However, "Democrats' strong ties to labor" helped keep teacher accountability out of the bill, he says.

In addition, "higher ed has been given pretty much a free pass," Knowles says. A future bill should focus attention on which education schools are producing the best-quality teachers.

Low-achieving schools shouldn't be punished, but given the tools to do better, says Knowles. Supports like teacher development and well-integrated extra services like social workers, closely targeted on high-need schools, are a "precondition" for improvement, he says.

Another key: additional flexibility for leaders of low-achieving schools to hire and fire and set policy and schedules. Principals say, "Yeah, you give me the hiring and firing of teachers and I'll give you the better results," and they're correct, says Knowles.

Reporting data for accountability isn't the problem. It's the very narrowly focused reporting requirement, many analysts say.

"Replace the overreliance on standardized testing with multiple measures," such as attendance figures and accurate dropout rates, says the University of Rochester's Hursh.

The federal government should also support strong, unbiased research on what improves instruction, especially in the middle- and high-school years, which are federally funded at a tiny fraction of the level of elementary schools and colleges, says Wise of the Alliance for Excellent Education. "No state or local district has the money for this," he says.

OUTLOOK
Agreeing to Disagree

There's growing agreement that schools should be educating all students to a higher standard. However, there's still disagreement about how much and what kind of help schools would need to do it.

An ideal outcome would be for institutions that are the most lasting presence in cities, such as business groups like the Chamber of Commerce, local hospitals and colleges to take ownership of urban education to drive change, says Balfanz of Johns Hopkins. A movement in that direction may be beginning, he says. "For awhile, there were mainly rhetorical reports," but today groups like the Chamber of Commerce are producing more potentially useful policy work, he says.

"The climate is shifting" toward the conclusion that everyone needs a diploma, says Balfanz. "You can't even find an employer who says, 'I'll hire people who aren't high-school graduates.'" So when students drop out, "it just feeds the next generation of poverty," he says.

There's currently an opportunity to revise NCLB in a way that helps low-achieving schools, says the University of Chicago's Knowles. Nevertheless, "people have already formed hard opinions," and debate could turn solely partisan, he says.

Lawmakers must aim for a delicate balance on federal initiatives, says Columbia's Henig. Federal interventions must aim at "making local processes work," since local on-the-ground actions are ultimately what make or break schools, he says.

The University of Pennsylvania's Lytle fears that privatization may be on the verge of overwhelming education, with potentially disastrous consequences for low-income families.

"I think the K-12 education business is in the process of deconstructing," he says. "The middle class is looking outside the schools" to private tutoring companies and Internet learning for academics. "More and more, for them, schools are amounting to expensive child care." Some states are aggressively pioneering "virtual" online charter schools and charters granted to home-schoolers, he says.

"The cost side and the efficacy side of education are on a collision course, and I think Congress will end up endorsing fairly radical experimentation" with vouchers, for example, Lytle says. "They'll say, 'There's no evidence that reducing class size or other expensive measures helps, so let's let American ingenuity work. Where does that leave urban kids? Out of luck," Lytle says. "You've got to be pretty sophisticated to make market forces work for you."

But "there's been progress in the last decade with whole-school reform," says Balfanz. "The big question now is how we [change] whole school districts. "It's a big job but within human capacity," he says.

2010 UPDATE

An array of forces has slowed long-sought progress in narrowing the minority-student achievement gap among urban schools. Those forces include mixed results in nationwide test scores, three years of delay in reauthorizing the federal No Child Left Behind Act and a pivotal 2007 Supreme Court ruling on school desegregation that, combined with a severe recession, has steered the education debate toward favoring economic considerations over racial equity.

"As a nation we decided long ago against separate but equal, but the reality is we're moving fast to becoming a majority-minority population," former West Virginia Gov. Bob Wise, president of the Alliance for Excellent

Davis Guggenbeim, director of "Waiting Superma," a documentary about the public school in Amercia, and Michelle Rhee, D.C. Public Schools Chancellor, attend the Silverdocs Festival in Silver Spring, Md.

Education, said in a recent interview. "So we need to focus on each child having a quality school no matter where they live." Because the modern economy now requires success by poor children as well as by those bound for higher-paying jobs, Wise said, education reform must link both economic performance and social justice.

The economic pressure on schools continues. A recent study by labor economist Anthony Carnevale of Georgetown University found that two-thirds of the 47 million new jobs he expects the U.S. economy to create between 2008 and 2018 will require workers who have at least some college education.[60] That is a sea change from a half-century ago when nearly two-thirds of jobs were filled by those with only a high school diploma.

The latest student test scores from the nation's urban K-12 schools show some noteworthy but unspectacular improvements. According to a new experimental index of urban student performance in the reading portion of the National Assessment of Educational Progress (NAEP), average reading scores for students in large-city school districts in grades four and eight rose by several points on the proficiency scale between 2003 and 2009, a change that narrowed the achievement gap to 10 points when compared with the national sampling.[61]

Lagging in Math

In math, according to a March analysis of NAEP scores and state tests by the Council of the Great City Schools, 79 percent of districts increased the percentage of fourth-graders who scored at or above proficient between 2006 and 2009, with a fourth of the districts raising scores by more than 10 percent.[62] Yet "despite significant gains in performance and faster rates of improvement than their states," the assessment said, "the majority of urban school districts continue to score below state averages on fourth- and eighth-grade mathematics assessments."

The decades-old assumption that school districts should actively pursue racial integration was challenged by a June 2007 U.S. Supreme Court ruling that invalidated school-attendance-zone plans used in Seattle and metropolitan Louisville to achieve greater diversity. In a 5-4 ruling in *Parents Involved in Community Schools v. Seattle Dist. No. 1*, the majority, in an opinion written by Chief Justice John G. Roberts Jr., said, "The way to stop discrimination on the basis of race is to stop discriminating on the basis of race."[63] Roberts deplored what he saw as an "ends justify the means" approach to achieving integration. "[R]acial classifications," he argued, "are simply too pernicious to permit any but the most exact connection between justification and classification."

The dissent by the court's liberal justices argued that Roberts' opinion undermined the promise of integrated schools the court set down in its 1954 landmark decision in *Brown v. Board of Education*, a change that Justice John Paul Stevens called "a cruel irony." Justice Anthony Kennedy, in a concurring opinion, left open the possibility of a more modest consideration of race in drawing school boundaries.

The court's ruling was hardly the last word, however. In a June 2010 review of school integration efforts since the Supreme Court decision, the Civil Rights Project at UCLA said the "divided decision confused many educators and it was somewhat unclear what did remain legal."[64] It noted that "economic pressure is forcing school districts to make deep cuts in services, which is another potential constraint for integration efforts," and it called on the Obama administration to issue new guidance on how race can be considered.

One of the nation's most troubled urban districts, the District of Columbia, in spring 2010 became the scene for ratification of a highly innovative teachers' contract.

For nearly three years, national attention had focused on the controversial tenure of D.C. Public Schools Chancellor Michelle Rhee. Her efforts at reforming the system's bureaucracy and sweeping away incompetent teachers — she appeared on the Nov. 26, 2008, cover of *Time* holding a broom — had put her at odds with the local branch of the American Federation of Teachers. Her reputation for tough management has attracted private foundation money to help the D.C. schools, and her future in the job became an issue in the current mayoral race.

Further roiling the waters was Rhee's firing of 241 teachers this summer, including 165 who received poor appraisals under a new evaluation system based in part on students' standardized test scores.[65]

Paying for Success

But in June 2010, school officials and the teachers' union finalized a contract that, in addition to granting a retroactive pay increase, requires all teachers in the system to be evaluated in part on whether their students' test scores improve, and it offers sizable pay increases to teachers who opt for and succeed in a special new pay-for-performance arrangement.[66]

D.C.'s special constitutional status that gives Congress a major say in its education policies continued to play a role in the district's efforts to improve results. Since 2004, Congress has funded the D.C. Opportunity Scholarship Program, a unique, federally funded voucher option favored by many conservatives that has given some 3,700 students $7,500 per year to attend any accredited private school that will accept them.[67]

But the Democratic takeover of Congress and the election of President Obama brought a change in priorities. Education Secretary Arne Duncan in 2009 rescinded the pending scholarships, and Congress declined to reauthorize them. An Education Department report found that the voucher program had not demonstrated much impact on test scores, though graduation rates for students in the program topped those of other students in D.C. Public Schools.[68]

Virtually every tool in the school reform grab bag — from charter schools to new teacher-accountability rules to dropout-prevention efforts — will be affected by the long-delayed reauthorization of the Elementary and Secondary Education Act (ESEA), known since 2002 as No Child Left Behind. The law has long been the center of disputes over reliance on student test scores. Its deadlines for improving student proficiency are seen by many as unrealistic, and critics have considered its funding levels inadequate. The bill has run into a new set of obstacles in the Obama era.

A Call for Flexibility

In a March 15, 2010, "blueprint" to overhaul No Child Left Behind, the Obama team argued that the law had "created incentives for states to lower their standards; emphasized punishing failure over rewarding success; focused on absolute scores, rather than recognizing growth and progress; and prescribed a pass-fail, one-size-fits-all series of interventions for schools that miss their goals." It called for greater flexibility in methodology to turn around some 5,000 schools labeled as underperforming.

But the reauthorization, though the subject of a dozen or more hearings this year in the House and Senate, has continued to divide Congress. One reason is the attention devoted to Obama's competitive $4 billion state grant education initiative, called Race to the Top. It is viewed by some as highly successful in providing incentives to states to enact reforms. Though only Delaware and Tennessee have won grants so far, 28 states have made reforms in 2009 and 2010, or triple the number during the previous two years, according to *Education Week*.[69] Yet in a surprise twist, the ravages to state and local budgets wrought by the current recession prompted the House to pass an emergency jobs bill that would shift funds from Race to the Top to preserve current teacher salaries.

In another division among education reformers, the teachers' unions want to make the rewrite of the law less "punitive" toward teachers and more cognizant of family income disparities. "Today, students' success in school depends in large part on the zip code where they live," National Education Association president Dennis Van Roekel told Congress. "Students who struggle the most in impoverished communities too often don't attend safe schools with reliable heat and air conditioning; too often do not have safe passage to and from school; and far too often do not have access to great teachers on a regular and consistent basis."[70]

Former Gov. Wise worries that if the reauthorization is not completed this year, the nation must continue with the existing No Child Left Behind, which he sees as inflexible and short on help for high schools. The law "focused on where the problems are, and a light has been shined on the fact that students of color or low economic status are not making it," Wise says. "But the law does not have adequate remedies. It's like a compact disc in an iPod world."

2012 UPDATE

As state and local governments continue to grapple with crippling funding shortages — and draconian cuts in federal spending loom — lawmakers and school districts look for economical ways to boost student achievement. Some argue for competition-based strategies such as closing schools and firing teachers based on test scores and allowing privately run charter schools to vie for public funding. Critics of such market-oriented reforms, however, argue that such measures won't solve the problems facing high-poverty urban schools.

Many states have cut their contribution to local school districts since the economic crisis began four years ago.

In the 2011-2012 school year, 37 states were providing less funding per student to local schools than they did in 2010-2011, according to the Center on Budget and Policy Priorities (CBPP), a liberal, nonprofit research group. Thirty states provide less local-school funding than they did four years ago, and 17 have cut per-student funding by more than 10 percent since the recession began in 2008. Four states — South Carolina, Arizona, California and Hawaii — cut per-student funding by more than 20 percent, according to the CBPP.[71]

Next year, the U.S. Department of Education (DOE) could suffer a 7.8 percent cut in its funding — most of which supports state and local education initiatives — unless Congress resolves a budget stalemate that began in 2011. Last fall, with congressional Republicans and Democrats unable to agree on a combination of spending cuts and tax increases to reduce the federal deficit, Congress agreed to allow the hefty DOE cut and other budget reductions to take effect on Jan. 1, 2013, if the legislative standoff continues. With House Republicans, in particular, continuing to declare that tax increases are off the table for deficit reduction, a deal to avoid the mandatory cuts — including at least a $3.5 billion reduction in education funding — seems out of reach for now.[72]

More than a third of those cuts — about $1.3 billion — would come directly from federal funds for schools in low-income areas — known as Title I schools. Most Title I schools, which have large numbers of economically disadvantaged students and others at high risk of dropping out, are in urban areas.[73]

Funding Cuts

A DOE study concluded last year that Title I funds are being used to compensate for cuts in state and local education funding for high-poverty schools instead of merely supplementing those funds. As a result, the DOE concluded, poor school districts are spending substantially less per student than wealthier districts.[74]

For example, DOE found that in districts with both Title I and non-Title I schools, more than 40 percent of Title I schools spent less money per student on staffing than non-Title-I schools did.[75]

The "findings confirm an unfortunate reality in our nation's education system," said Education Secretary Arne Duncan. "Many schools serving low-income children aren't getting their fair share of funding," and "in far too many places Title I dollars are filling budget gaps rather than being extra."[76]

As a result of the financial crisis and related government budget struggles, severe financial troubles have plagued many urban schools.

In Ypsilanti, Mich., for example, schools face a debt expected to reach $9.4 million by the end of this school year, despite previous spending cuts. Reductions in school support staff, for example, have already gone "beyond a point where work can be completed effectively," according to a deficit-elimination plan prepared by district officials.[77]

While many states promised to restore the education funding once the financial crisis waned, some have decided instead to use the money for tax cuts.

Lawmakers in Kansas, for instance, slashed school funding by nearly $700 per student since 2008, resulting in — among other things — large-scale layoffs and school closures in Wichita and other urban schools. "We couldn't take another year like the last three," Wichita

Public Schools Superintendent John Allison said recently.[78]

So when he heard that the state would have a $300 million surplus this year, he said, "We thought, 'Finally, things are going to start getting back to normal.' " Instead, lawmakers last month used the surplus to reduce the top tax rate from 6.45 percent to 4.9 percent — the largest tax cut in state history. Critics said that by 2018 the tax cut would convert this year's surplus into long-term budget deficits totaling $2.5 billion. Education spending was increased by only $58 per student for next year.[79]

In some districts, staff and resource cuts are accompanied by a continuing atmosphere of worry and uncertainty that has eroded morale. In the San Francisco and Los Angeles school districts, for example, state law requires teachers who are at risk of being laid off within the next year to receive advance warning in March. By 2012, as budget woes continue, some teachers had received a warning for four years running.

Uncertainty saps energy needed to operate schools properly, teachers and administrators say. "I've seen teachers who have cried," said Phyllis Bradford, senior director of human resources for the Los Angeles Unified School District. "Others have moved out of state. . . . It's a very depressing time."[80]

Alternatives Sought

Looking for budget savings and an alternative to what they view as failing urban public schools, some lawmakers have embraced proposals to boost charter schools and other alternatives, such as vouchers to help families place their children in private schools, including religious schools. A wave of Republican governors and state legislators who swept into office in 2010 have been the principal, but not sole, backers of such plans.

In 2011, for example, newly elected Wisconsin Gov. Scott Walker, a Republican, shepherded a substantial expansion of Wisconsin's school-voucher program through the legislature. The program began as a low-income-only program for Milwaukee but was subsequently expanded to include Racine, the state's fifth-largest city. Among other changes, the expanded voucher program eliminated an enrollment cap; raised the income cap for eligible families to 300 percent of the federal poverty level while allowing families to continue receiving voucher support if their income rises after a student enrolls; and allows Milwaukee students to use vouchers at schools in the surrounding county.[81]

In Pennsylvania, newly elected Republican Gov. Tom Corbett tried but failed last year to form a statewide voucher program. Pennsylvania school-choice proponents, who have advocated for vouchers for the last two decades, expressed frustration after the state's Republican-controlled House of Representatives failed to approve Corbett's plan. "It's beyond disappointing," said Dawn Chavous, executive director of Students First PA, a non-partisan group pushing to provide more alternatives to traditional schools. "We're going to keep fighting. I'm not going to go anywhere."[82]

In Philadelphia, school-system leaders announced this year that looming "severe, long-term deficits" estimated at $1.1 billion by 2017, plus slow progress in improving learning, make it imperative to close many neighborhood schools, restructure school-district administration and promote charter schools over the next five years.[83]

"In spite of progress" in academics," we are not improving nearly fast enough" compared to cities such as San Diego and Boston, school district leaders said in a report.[84] And while "efforts to reduce violence are paying off" — with violent incidents dropping from 3.7 per 100 students in 2007-08 to 2.6 in 2001-2011 — violence "continues to plague our schools."[85] One key to improving the schools while balancing the budget, the leaders said: "Promote equal access to quality choices for parents by expanding high-performing district and charter programs."[86]

But many local activists dub the proposal a stealth maneuver to privatize public schools and diminish the district's power under the guise of saving it. "No one would debate that there are financial problems in the district," said the Rev. Mark Kelly Tyler, pastor of Mother Bethel AME Church, in South Philadelphia. "But is it so bad that the only answer is to shutter 64 schools and remove the remaining 20 percent to charter schools?"[87]

In Illinois, a legislative committee backed a plan in May 2012 to require school districts to direct more money to charter schools. The measure, which has not yet been voted on by the full legislature, is intended to provide "equal funding for our charter schools, equal funding with the public schools," which is "an issue of fairness," said Rep. Daniel Burke, D-Chicago, the measure's sponsor.[88]

The Chicago Teachers Union has strongly opposed the legislation, however, arguing that traditional public schools, "funded almost entirely by taxes," may actually have fewer available resources than the many charter schools that "receive private money from corporate privatization proponents."[89]

Meanwhile, researchers continue to examine whether promoting measures such as charter schools and vouchers makes budgetary sense or improves learning. Findings are mixed. For example, statewide achievement scores in Illinois, released in December 2011, showed that one chain of nine charter schools in Chicago beat the district average, but scores at other charter chains fell well below district averages.[90]

By contrast, in one of the largest studies of its kind, the Center for Research on Education Outcomes (CREDO) at Stanford University found in 2009 that Chicago and Denver charter-school students outpaced their public-school counterparts on the National Assessment of Student Progress (NAEP), which is often called the "nation's report card." In Arizona, Ohio and Texas, charter-school students lagged public-school students' achievement, while in Washington, D.C., public- and charter-school students showed similar achievement levels, the study found.[91]

Groups such as the conservative Thomas B. Fordham Institute, an education-policy think tank in Washington, support charter schools partly because, theoretically, they are more likely to operate like businesses, facing bankruptcy and quick closure if they fail in their educational mission. However, a 2010 Fordham analysis found that 72 percent of the charter schools — and 80 percent of traditional public schools — that were low-achieving in 2004-2004 were still operating, and still performing poorly, five years later.[92]

Critics of urban public schools often charge that public school systems siphon money that could be used for student learning and that charter schools can reverse that pattern. However, Michigan State University Professor of Educational Administration David Arsen and University of Utah Assistant Professor of Educational Leadership and Policy Yongmei Ni, found that, at least in Michigan, charter schools spend twice as much per student on administration as traditional public schools and 20 percent less on instruction.[93]

Cheating Scandals

In the current wave of school reform plans that began about a decade ago — including the federal No Child Left Behind Act (NCLB), signed into law in 2002 — many seek to hold schools and, increasingly, individual teachers accountable for low student achievement by imposing sanctions if test scores or other measures don't improve.

Under NCLB, sanctions include expanded opportunities for parents to move their children to higher-performing schools. And if students' standardized-test scores continue to lag, schools could experience mass staff firings and reorganization.

How well such methods work is a matter of increasing debate, however, especially in the wake of several administrative scandals in which schools in several cities were suspected of altering students' test scores, presumably to avoid sanctions.

Throughout the 2000s, the Atlanta school system had gained nationwide attention for repeatedly raising test scores. But in 2008 and 2009, the *Atlanta Journal-Constitution* reported that, based on the paper's statistical analysis, many of the increases were so unlikely that they raised suspicions that the district had manipulated test results.

In July 2011, the Georgia Bureau of Investigation accused 178 Atlanta teachers and principals of engaging in a "conspiracy" to change students' test answers. In what has been called the biggest school-cheating scandal in U.S. history, 82 of the people named in the Bureau report confessed to the scheme, in which teachers and administrators erased students' wrong test answers and replaced them with correct responses.[94]

The Georgia Bureau of Investigation found that administrators rather than teachers were apparently the driving force behind most of the cheating. Several teachers who tried to blow the whistle on the scandal found themselves the subject of intimidation and, in one case, even an ethics investigation led by school administrators.[95]

Opponents of basing high-stakes decisions about schools and teachers primarily on standardized-test scores argue that the practice itself invites cheating. "When test scores are all that matter, some educators feel pressured to get the scores they need by hook or by crook," said Robert Shaeffer, a spokesman for National Center for Fair & Open Testing, which opposes heavy reliance on standardized tests for school decision making. "The higher the stakes, the greater the incentive to manipulate, to cheat."[96]

While Atlanta remains the most heavily substantiated case of widespread cheating, various analyses in the past two years have suggested that other districts also have cheated on the tests.

A March 2011 *USA Today* investigation, for example, concluded that patterns of erased-then-replaced test answers at some Washington, D.C., schools suggested that teachers and administrators may have changed students' answers to produce higher scores. At some D.C. schools that had been touted as nationwide models for learning improvement, students' tests had astonishingly high numbers of erasures in which wrong answers were changed to right answers — far more than would be likely to occur by chance, according to the paper.[97] Questions about the D.C. tests remain unresolved.

Investigations, mainly by newspapers, have turned up possible evidence of cheating in Baltimore, Dallas, Detroit, Houston and Los Angeles, as well as some non-urban districts.[98]

Adding Values

Meanwhile, efforts are expanding to hold individual teachers accountable for students' academic improvement, such as by offering merit pay based in whole or in part on standardized test scores.

In April 2011, for example, the Los Angeles Unified School District publicly released school-by-school results of its new so-called value-added measure of school and teacher performance and announced that it would soon take the more controversial step of telling individual teachers how they'd performed on the new measurement system. The value-added system compares progress of an individual student in a given year to the student's progress in previous school years, as measured by standardized tests. Teachers are then scored on how well their current students perform, compared to how those same students performed in

Thousands of teachers, school workers, students and parents participate in a "state of Emergency" rally in downtown Los Angeles on May 13, 2011, to protest proposed education budget cuts.

past years. By comparing each student only to his or her own past achievements, the method takes into account such factors as poverty or learning disabilities, which an individual teacher can't control, supporters of value-added rankings say.[99]

Many other analysts, as well as teachers' unions, argue that the test-based value-added measures are too narrow to use as a basis for evaluating teacher pay and promotions. In Los Angeles and New York City, for example, tense negotiations continue between the school districts and teachers and their unions over whether the measures should be used as a primary evaluation tool.[100]

Test Results

Recent test scores on student achievement show mixed results, both for the nation as a whole and for low-income and minority students, who make up a large part of the urban-school population.

On the most recent NAEP, only 32 percent of eighth-graders scored at a "proficient" level in science and only 2 percent at an "advanced" level, for example. However, a longstanding science achievement gap between white eighth-graders and black and Hispanic eighth-graders has slightly narrowed recently, as black and Hispanic students have raised their scores at a slightly faster rate than white students. Between 2009 and 2011, white students raised their average science score on the biannual test by 1 point, compared to three points for black students and five for Hispanics.[101]

Meanwhile, NAEP has undertaken an experimental, voluntary program that gathers detailed data from a group of urban districts as part of a project to determine whether NAEP can be used for district-to-district comparisons. In the experimental program, math scores in participating districts — all of them urban — improved somewhat in 2011 compared with 2009, but reading scores did not. Urban districts continue to lag far behind rural and suburban districts in NAEP scores, however, and most of the math-score increase in urban areas came from higher-income students. Still, most of the urban districts have improved in both math and reading since the early 2000s.[102]

"We've been able to close the gap between [large cities] and the nation by between 25 percent and 36 percent" since 2003, said Michael Casserly, executive director of the Council of the Great City Schools, a coalition of the city's largest urban school districts. "It says to us that many urban school districts in aggregate appear to be moving in the right direction."[103]

But progress is far too slow, said other analysts. "There's nobody who's performing at advanced levels," said Mark Schneider, a vice president of the American Institutes for Research, a Washington-based social-science research group that has been involved in NAEP and other federal education programs. "This is just really, really, really depressing."[104]

One surprise in the findings was Atlanta's results. While Atlanta cheated on the state tests, its performance on the national test — untainted by cheating — was well above average. On NAEP, Atlanta schools made significant continuing gains throughout the past decade, including in 2011, demonstrating that — despite the scandal —"what you saw by way of reform in the school district was real," said Casserly.[105]

NOTES

1. Quoted in Judy Radigan, "Reframing Dropouts: The Complexity of Urban Life Intersects with Current School Policy," paper presented at the Texas Dropout Conference, Houston, Oct. 6, 2006.

2. "The Socioeconomic Composition of the Public Schools: A Crucial Consideration in Student Assignment Policy," University of North Carolina Center for Civil Rights, Jan. 7, 2005, www.law.unc.edu/PDFs/charlottereport.pdf.

3. For background, see Barbara Mantel, "No Child Left Behind," *CQ Researcher*, May 7, 2005, pp. 469-492.

4. Quoted in David J. Hoff and Kathleen Kennedy Manzo, "Bush Claims About NCLB Questioned," *Education Week*, March 9, 2007, www.edweek.org.

5. Quoted in *ibid*.

6. "The Nation's Report Card: Reading 2005," U.S. Department of Education Institute of Education Sciences, www.nationsreportcard.gov.

7. Douglas N. Harris, "Ending the Blame Game on Educational Inequity: A Study of 'High-Flying' Schools and NCLB," Education Policy Studies Laboratory, Arizona State University, March 2006.

8. Jay P. Greene, "Education Myths," The American Enterprise Online, American Enterprise Institute, August 2006.

9. For background, see Charles S. Clark, "Charter Schools," *CQ Researcher*, Dec. 20, 2002, pp. 1033-1056; Kenneth Jost, "School Vouchers Showdown," *CQ Researcher*, Feb. 15, 2002, pp. 121-144.

10. Greene, *op. cit.*

11. Brad Olsen and Lauren Anderson, "Courses of Action: A Qualitative Investigation Into Urban Teacher Retention and Career Development," *Urban Education*, January 2007, p. 5.

12. Quoted in *ibid.*, p. 14.

13. *Ibid.*

14. Arthur J. Rothkopf, "Elementary and Secondary Education Act Reauthorization: Improving NCLB To Close the Achievement Gap," testimony before the Senate Committee on Health, Education, Labor, and Pensions and the House Committee on Education and Labor, March 13, 2007.

15. For background, see Kenneth Jost, "Testing in Schools," *CQ Researcher*, April 20, 2001, pp. 321-344.

16. Richard J. Murnane, "Improving the Education of Children Living in Poverty," unpublished paper, Jan. 25, 2007.

17. *Ibid.*
18. For background, see Kenneth Jost, "School Desegregation," *CQ Researcher*, April 23, 2004, pp. 345-372.
19. Quoted in "Center on Race and Social Problems Commemorates *Brown v. Board of Education*," University of Pittsburgh School of Social Work, May 7, 2004.
20. Quoted in Brian Lamb, "No Excuses: Closing the Racial Gap in Learning," transcript, "Booknotes," C-SPAN, Feb. 1, 2004.
21. Paul Tough, "What It Takes To Make a Student," *The New York Times Magazine*, Nov. 26, 2006, p. 70.
22. R. Scott Baker, "School Resegregation: Must the South Turn Back?" *Journal of Southern History*, November 2006, p. 993.
23. Howell S. Baum, "Smart Growth and School Reform: What If We Talked About Race and Took Community Seriously?" *Journal of the American Planning Association*, winter 2004, p. 14.
24. "Divided We Fail: Coming Together Through Public School Choice," Task Force on the Common School, The Century Foundation Press, 2002, p. 3.
25. *Ibid.*, p. 13.
26. Quoted in Lamb, *op. cit.*
27. *Ibid.*
28. Terry Ryan and Quentin Suffren, "Charter School Lessons from Ohio," *The Education Gadfly*, Thomas B. Fordham Foundation, March 15, 2007, www.edexcellence.net.
29. Mark Simon, "What Teachers Know," *Poverty & Race*, September/October 2004, www.prrac.org.
30. Dreyon Wynn and Dianne L. H. Mark, "Book Review: Educating Teachers for Diversity: Seeing With a Cultural Eye," *Urban Education*, May 2005, p. 350.
31. Jocelyn A. Glazier, "Moving Closer to Speaking the Unspeakable: White Teachers Talking About Race," *Teacher Education Quarterly*, winter 2003.
32. Wanda J. Blanchett, "Urban School Failure and Disproportionality in a Post-*Brown* Era," *Remedial and Special Education*, April 2005, p. 70.
33. Christine H. Leland and Jerome C. Harste, "Doing What We Want to Become: Preparing New Urban Teachers," *Urban Education*, January 2005, p. 60.
34. *Ibid.*, p. 62.
35. Glazier, *op. cit.*
36. Wynn and Mark, *op. cit.*
37. For background, see Wayne J. Urban and Jennings L. Wagoner, *American Education: A History* (2003); Stanley William Rothstein, *Schooling the Poor: A Social Inquiry Into the American Educational Experience* (1994).
38. For background, see Kathy Koch, "Reforming School Funding," *CQ Researcher*, Dec. 10, 1999, pp. 1041-1064.
39. Derrick Bell, *Silent Covenants:* Brown v. Board of Education *and the Unfulfilled Hopes for Racial Reform* (2004), p. 88.
40. *Ibid.*, p. 91.
41. Ruth Curran Neild and Robert Balfanz, "An Extreme Degree of Difficulty: The Educational Demographics of Urban Neighborhood High Schools," *Journal of Education for Students Placed at Risk*, spring 2006, p. 135.
42. V. W. Ipka, "At Risk Children in Resegregated Schools; An Analysis of the Achievement Gap," *Journal of Instructional Psychology*, December 2003, p. 294.
43. The case is *Brown v. Board of Education of Topeka*, 347 U.S. 483 (1954).
44. For background, see Jost, "School Desegregation," *op. cit.*; Gary Orfield and John T. Yun, "Resegregation in American Schools," The Civil Rights Project, Harvard University, June 1999, www.civilrightsproject.harvard.edu/research/deseg/reseg_schools99.php.
45. The case is *Milliken v. Bradley*, 418 U.S. 717 (1974).
46. Ipka, *op. cit.* The cases are *Board of Education of Oklahoma City v. Dowell*, 498 U.S. 237 (1991) and *Freeman v. Pitts*, 498 U.S. 1081 (1992).
47. Gary Orfield and Chungmei Lee, "Racial Transformation and the Changing Nature of Segregation," The Civil Rights Project, Harvard University, January 2006, www.civilrightsproject.harvard.edu; *Keyes v. School District No. 1*, Denver, Colorado, 413 U.S. 189 (1973).

48. Gary Orfield and Susan E. Eaton, "Back to Segregation," *The Nation*, March 3, 2003, p. 5.

49. Baum, *op. cit.*

50. *Ibid.*

51. Neild and Balfanz, *op. cit.*, p. 126.

52. "Divided We Fail," *op. cit.*, p. 17.

53. Tough, *op. cit.*

54. Elaine M. Stotko, Rochelle Ingram and Mary Ellen Beaty-O'Ferrall, "Promising Strategies for Attracting and Retaining Successful Urban Teachers," *Urban Education*, January 2007, p. 36.

55. Patrick Mattimore, "Will Court Put Integration on Hold?" *San Francisco Examiner*, Dec. 8, 2006, www.exaaminer.com. The cases — argued on Dec. 4, 2006 — are *Meredith v. Jefferson County Board of Education*, 05-915; and *Parents Involved in Community Schools v. Seattle School District No. 1*, 05-908.

56. Richard Kahlenberg, "Helping Children Move from Bad Schools to Good Ones," The Century Foundation, 2006, www.tcf.org/list.asp?type=PB&pubid=565.

57. *Ibid.*

58. Quoted in Michael Sandler, "Minding Their Business," *CQ Weekly*, April 2, 2007, p. 952.

59. Quoted in Jonathan Weisman and Amit R. Paley, "Dozens in GOP Turn Against Bush's Prized 'No Child' Act," *The Washington Post*, March 15, 2007, p. A1.

60. Written testimony of Anthony P. Carnevale, director, Georgetown University Center on Education and the Workforce, U.S. Senate Committee on Health, Education, Labor and Pensions, Feb. 24, 2010, http://help.senate.gov/imo/media/doc/Carnevale.pdf.

61. Council of the Great City Schools, press release, May 20, 2010, www.cgcs.org/pressrelease/TUDA_Reading2010.pdf.

62. "Beating the Odds: Analysis of Student Performance on State Assessments and NAEP," Council of the Great City Schools, March 2010.

63. Linda Greenhouse, "Justices Limit the Use of Race in School Plans for Integration," *The New York Times*, June 28, 2007, p. A1.

64. Civil Rights Project, University of California at Los Angeles, www.civilrightsproject.ucla.edu/research/deseg/school-integration-three-years-after-parents-involved.pdf.

65. Bill Turque, "Rhee dismisses 241 D.C. teachers; union vows to contest firing," *The Washington Post*, July 24, 2010, p. A1, www.washingtonpost.com/wp-dyn/content/article/2010/07/23/AR2010072303093.html.

66. Bill Turque, "D.C. Teachers' Contract Passes Its Final Hurdle; Council Unanimously Approves Pact that Bases Pay on Results," *The Washington Post*, June 30, 2010.

67. "Opportunity Denied," editorial, *The Washington Post*, June 23, 2010.

68. "Evaluation of the DC Opportunity Scholarship Program: Final Report," U.S. Department of Education, June 2010, http://ies.ed.gov/ncee/pubs/20104018/pdf/20104018.pdf.

69. Chad Adelman, "How Race to the Top Could Inform ESEA Reauthorization," *Education Week*, June 28, 2010.

70. Testimony before Senate Health, Education, Labor and Pensions Committee, March 9, 2010.

71. Phil Oliff and Michael Leachman, "New School Year Brings Steep Cuts in Funding for Schools," Center on Budget and Policy Priorities, Oct. 7, 2011, www.cbpp.org/files/9-1-11sfp.pdf.

72. Jamie Baxter, "We Must Avoid Sequestration: Savage Cuts in Education Funding Would Cripple Our Schools," *Post-Gazette.com* (Pittsburgh), May 3, 2012, www.post-gazette.com/stories/opinion/perspectives/we-must-avoid-sequestration-savage-cuts-in-education-funding-would-cripple-our-schools-634125.

73. *Ibid.*

74. Ruth Heuer and Stephanie Stullich, "Comparability of State and Local Expenditures Among Schools Within Districts: A Report from the Study of School-level Expenditures," U.S. Department of Education, 2011, www2.ed.gov/rschstat/eval/title-i/school-level-expenditures/school-level-expenditures.pdf; "The Potential Impact of Revising Title I Comparability Requirement to Focus on

75. School-level Expenditures," U.S. Department of Education, November 2011, www2.ed.gov/rschstat/eval/title-i/comparability-requirement/comparability-policy-brief.pdf.
75. "The Potential Impact of Revising Title I Comparability," *ibid.*, p. 3.
76. Quoted in Alyson Klein, "Poor Schools Shortchanges on Funding, Ed Dept. Says," *Education Week blogs*, Nov. 30, 2011, http://blogs.edweek.org/edweek/campaign-k-12/2011/11/for_years_advocates_for_poor.html.
77. "Narrative Section, Deficit Elimination Plan," School District of Ypsilanti, December 2011, www.ypsd.org/downloads/financial/2011-2012_deficit_elimination_plan_20111214_111811_7.pdf.
78. Mike Alberti, "States to residents, localities: forget promises to restore funding," Remapping Debate, www.remappingdebate.org/article/states-residents-localities-forget-promises-restore-funding.
79. *Ibid.*
80. Quoted in Christina Hoag, "California's Fourth Year of Teacher Layoffs Spurs Concerns," The Associated Press/ABC News, May 5, 2012, http://abcnews.go.com/US/wireStory/califs-4th-year-teacher-layoffs-spur-concerns-16285889#.T616a1JzaUk.
81. "2011-2013 Legislative Session," "Accurate Information About School Choice," SchoolChoiceWI.org, www.schoolchoicewi.org/stgov/detail.cfm?id=10; Patrick Marley and Jason Stein, "Senate OK'd Budget Goes to Walker," *Journal Sentinel online* (Milwaukee), June 16, 2011, www.jsonline.com/news/statepolitics/124004679.html, and Amy Hetzner and Erin Richards, "Budget Cuts $834 Million from Schools," *Journal Sentinel online* (Milwaukee), March 1, 2011, www.jsonline.com/news/statepolitics/117192683.html.
82. Quoted in Jan Murphy and Charles Thompson, "State House Rejects School-voucher Proposal," PennLive.com/*The Patriot-News* (Harrisburg), Dec. 14, 2011.
83. "A Blueprint for Transforming Philadelphia's Public Schools" (Draft), School District of Philadelphia, http://thenotebook.org/sites/default/files/BlueprintPublicPresentation_4_22_12.pdf.
84. *Ibid.*, p. 4.
85. *Ibid.*, p. 5.
86. *Ibid.*
87. Quoted in Julianne Hing, "The Remaking of Philadelphia Public Schools: Privatization or Bust," *Color Lines*, May 11, 2012, http://colorlines.com/archives/2012/05/the_remaking_of_philadelphia_public_schools_privatization_or_bust.html.
88. Jim Broadway, "Bill to Give More Cash to Charters Moves Forward," State School News Service/Catalyst Chicago, May 9, 2012, www.catalyst-chicago.org/notebook/2012/05/09/20105/bill-give-more-cash-charters-moves-forward.
89. Quoted in *ibid.*
90. Rosalyn Rossi and Art Golab, "Chicago Charter Schools Produce Wildly Uneven Results on State Tests," *Chicago Sun-Times*, Jan. 1, 2012, www.suntimes.com/news/education/9145306-418/story.html.
91. "Multiple Choice: Charter School Performance in 16 States," Center for Research on Education Outcomes, 2009, http://credo.stanford.edu/reports/MULTIPLE_CHOICE_CREDO.pdf.
92. David A. Stuit, "Are Bad Schools Immortal?" Thomas B. Fordham Institute, December 2010, www.edexcellencemedia.net/publications/2010/20101214_AreBadSchoolImmortal/Fordham_Immortal.pdf.
93. Emily Pfund, "Study Finds Michigan Charter Schools Spend Twice as Much as Public Schools," *Central Michigan Life*, Central Michigan University, April 26, 2012, www.cm-life.com/2012/04/26/study-focuses-on-michigan-charter-schools-finds-charter-schools-spend-twice-as-much-as-public-schools.
94. Patrik Jonsson, "America's Biggest Teacher and Principal Cheating Scandal Unfolds in Atlanta," *The Christian Science Monitor*, July 5, 2011, www.csmonitor.com/USA/Education/2011/0705/America-s-biggest-teacher-and-principal-cheating-scandal-unfolds-in-Atlanta; and "School Cheating Investigation: Atlanta Journal-Constitution Flags Improbable Test Scores in Analysis," Associated Press/*Huffington Post*, March 25, 2012, www.huffingtonpost.com/2012/03/24/schools-cheating-investig_n_1377767.html.
95. Jonsson, *ibid.*

96. Quoted in *ibid.*

97. Jack Gillum and Marisol Bello, "When Standardized Test Scores Soared in DC, Were the Gains Real?" *USA Today*, March 30, 2011, www.usatoday.com/news/education/2011-03-28-1Aschooltesting28_CV_N.htm.

98. "School Cheating Investigation: Atlanta Journal Constitution Flags Improbable Test Scores in Analysis," *op. cit.*

99. Jason Song and Jason Felch, "L.A. Unified Releases School Ratings Using 'Value-added' Method," *Los Angeles Times*, April 12, 2011, http://articles.latimes.com/2011/apr/12/local/la-me-0413-value-add-20110414; for background, see Marcia Clemmitt, "School Reform," *CQ Researcher*, April 29, 2011, pp. 385-408.

100. Fernanda Santos and Anna M. Phillips, "With Release of Teacher Data, Setback for Union Turns Into Rallying Cry," *The New York Times*, Feb. 26, 2012, www.nytimes.com/2012/02/27/nyregion/teacher-ratings-produce-a-rallying-cry-for-the-union.html.

101. Sarah D. Sparks, "Most 8th Graders Fall Short on NAEP Science Test," *Education Week*, May 10, 2012, www.edweek.org/ew/articles/2012/05/10/31naep_ep.h31.html?tkn=VPXFO3wzO2s%2Bbex2WwFqNNnCfYtzrpCNzSmA&cmp=ENL-EU-NEWS1,k, and "The Nation's Report Card: Science 2011," National Center for Education Statistics, May 2012, http://nces.ed.gov/nationsreportcard/pubs/main2011/2012465.asp.

102. Christina Samuels, "Urban NAEP Scores Show Math Scores Up, Reading Mostly Flat," *Education Week blogs*, Dec. 7, 2011, http://blogs.edweek.org/edweek/District_Dossier/2011/12/urban_naep_scores_show_math_up.html; and Joy Resmovits, "City-level National Tests Show Slight Math Growth, No Change in Reading," *Huffington Post*, Dec. 7, 2011, www.huffingtonpost.com/2011/12/07/urban-schools-test_n_1132775.html.

103. Quoted in Resmovits, *ibid.*

104. Quoted in *ibid.*

105. Quoted in *ibid.*

BIBLIOGRAPHY

Books

Kozol, Jonathan, *The Shame of the Nation: The Restoration of Apartheid Schooling in America*, Three Rivers Press, 2006.
A longtime education writer and activist reports on his five-year journey to closely observe 60 schools in 11 states. He describes almost entirely resegregated urban schools with dilapidated buildings, dirty classrooms and a dearth of up-to-date textbooks.

Rothstein, Richard, *Class and Schools: Using Social, Economic, and Education Reform to Close the Black-White Achievement Gap*, Economic Policy Institute, 2004.
A research associate at a think tank concerned with low- and middle-income workers and families argues that raising the achievement of urban students requires public policies that address students' multiple social and economic needs.

Thernstrom, Abigail, and Stephan Thernstrom, *No Excuses: Closing the Racial Gap in Learning*, Simon & Schuster, 2004.
A husband and wife who are senior fellows at the conservative Manhattan Institute for Public Policy Research argue that charter schools and the No Child Left Behind Act's focus on holding schools accountable for poor student achievement can close the achievement gap for urban students.

Articles

Boo, Katherine, "Expectations," *The New Yorker*, Jan. 15, 2007, p. 44.
A reform-minded superintendent closes Denver's lowest-achieving high school, hoping its students will accept the offer to enroll in any other city school, including some with mainly online classes. Mostly Latinos from the city's poorest families, the displaced students struggle with losing their old school, which has provided many with a sense of community, and with new choices that confront them, as well as the ever-present choice of dropping out.

Moore, Martha T., "More Mayors Are Moving To Take Over School System," *USA Today*, March 21, 2007, p. A1.

Albuquerque's mayor is among those who believe they could run schools better than their local school boards.

Saulny, Susan, "Few Students Seek Free Tutoring or Transfers From Failing Schools," *The New York Times*, **April 6, 2006, p. 20.**
The No Child Left Behind Act promises free tutoring for many students in low-achieving schools, but few of those students' families know about the option or have been able to enroll their children in good-quality tutoring programs.

Tough, Paul, "What It Takes To Make a Student," *The New York Times Magazine*, **Nov. 26, 2006, p. 44.**
A handful of charter schools are making strides against the achievement gap. But largely because low-income and minority students arrive at school with smaller vocabularies and far less knowledge about how to communicate with adults and behave in a learning situation, the work requires extra-long school hours and intense teacher commitment.

Reports and Studies

Beating the Odds: An Analysis of Student Performance and Achievement Gaps on State Assessments: Results from the 2005-2006 School Year, Council of the Great City Schools, **April 2007.**
A group representing 67 of the country's largest urban school districts examines in detail the recent performance of urban students on state tests.

Divided We Fail: Coming Together Through Public School Choice, Task Force on the Common School, The Century Foundation, **2002.**
Basing its discussion on the idea that race- and class-segregated schools have proven a failure, a nonpartisan think tank explores the possibility of encouraging cross-district integration of low-income and middle-income students by methods like establishing high-quality magnet schools in cities.

Engaging Schools: Fostering High School Students' Motivation to Learn, Committee on Increasing High School Students' Engagement and Motivation to Learn, National Research Council, **2003.**
A national expert panel examines methods for re-engaging urban high-school students who have lost their motivation to learn, a problem they say is widespread but solvable.

Bridgeland, John M., John J. DiIulio, Jr., and Karen Burke Morison, *The Silent Epidemic: Perspectives of High School Dropouts*, *Bill & Melinda Gates Foundation*, **March 2006.**
Nearly half of high-school dropouts say they left school partly because they were bored. A third of the students left because they needed to work, and more than a fifth said they left to care for a family member.

Levin, Henry, Clive Belfield, Peter Muennig and Cecilia Rouse, "The Costs and Benefits of an Excellent Education for All of America's Children," *Teachers College, Columbia University*, **January 2007;** www.cbcse.org/media/download_gallery/Leeds_Report_Final_Jan2007.pdf.
A team of economists concludes that measures to cut the number of school dropouts would pay for themselves with higher tax revenues and lower government spending.

For More Information

Achieve, Inc., 1775 I St., N.W., Suite 410, Washington, DC 20006; (202) 419-1540; www.achieve.org. An independent bipartisan group formed by governors and business leaders to promote higher academic standards.

Alliance for Excellent Education, 1201 Connecticut Ave., N.W., Suite 901, Washington, DC 20036; (202) 828-0828; www.all4ed.org. A nonprofit research and advocacy group seeking policies to help at-risk high-school students.

The Center for Education Reform, 1001 Connecticut Ave., N.W., Suite 204, Washington, DC 20036; (202) 822-9000; www.edreform.com. A nonprofit advocacy group that promotes school choice in cities.

The Century Foundation, 41 E. 70th St., New York, NY 10021; (212) 535-4441; www.tcf.org. Supports research on income inequality and urban policy.

Citizens for Effective Schools, 8209 Hamilton Spring Ct., Bethesda, MD 20817; (301) 469-8000; www.citizenseffectiveschools.org. An advocacy group that seeks policy changes to minimize the achievement gap for low-income and minority students.

Council of the Great City Schools, 1301 Pennsylvania Ave., N.W., Suite 702, Washington, DC 20004; (202) 393-2427; www.cgcs.org. A coalition of 67 urban school systems dedicated to improving urban schools.

Education Next, Hoover Institution, Stanford University; www.educationnext.org. A quarterly journal on education reform published by a conservative think tank.

The Education Trust, 1250 H St., N.W., Suite 700, Washington, DC 20005; (202) 293-1217; www2.edtrust.org. Dedicated to closing the achievement gap in learning and college preparation for low-income and minority students.

National Center for Education Statistics, 1990 K St., N.W., Washington, DC 20006; (202) 502-7300; http://nces.ed.gov. A Department of Education agency that provides statistics and analysis on U.S. schools, student attendance and achievement.